HARRAP'S
FIVE LANGUAGE DICTIONARY

English-French-German-Italian-Spanish

HARRAP

FIVE-LANGUAGE DICTIONARY

Compilers: Monika Eberhard, Ursula Guidi, Beatrix Haag,
Nicola Petersen, Marcus Rathbone, Hildegard Schulte-Umberg,
Montserrat Vancells
Designer: Inga Koch

First published in Great Britain 1991
by HARRAP BOOKS Ltd
Chelsea House, 26 Market Square, Bromley, Kent BR1 1NA

© 1991 Compact Verlag München

ISBN 0 245-60346-8

ISBN 0-13-387986-0 (United States)

Printed in Germany

FOREWORD

The steady growth of international communication – particularly within today's unified Europe – means that knowledge of foreign languages is becoming an increasingly important requirement in all areas of life. This new dictionary meets the demand for a practical, up-to-date reference source by providing the user with access to a general vocabulary of 20,000 headwords and 80,000 translations in five major European languages: English, French, German, Italian and Spanish.

The multilingual integration of all the headwords within a single alphabetical sequence makes it quick and easy to look up a particular word and its translations in any of the five languages.

Convenient and comprehensive, this international dictionary will prove an invaluable reference for all day-to-day communication needs.

ABBREVIATIONS

D= GERMAN
E= ENGLISH
F= FRENCH
I= ITALIAN
ES= SPANISH
f= feminine
m= masculine
n= neuter

	D	E	F	I	Es
a (Es)	nach	after/to	après/selon	a/in/verso/dopo	—
a¹ (I)	an	at/on/by	à/près de	—	junto a
a² (I)	nach	after/to	après/selon	—	a/hacia/después
à (F)	an	at/on/by	—	a/in/su	junto a
ab (D)	—	from	à partir de/dès	da	a partir de/de
abajo¹ (Es)	herunter	down	en bas	giù	—
abajo² (Es)	nieder	inferior	bas(se)	in basso	—
abajo³ (Es)	unten	downstairs	dessous	sotto/giù	—
abandonner¹ (F)	aufgeben	give up	—	rinunciare	renunciar
abandonner² (F)	verlassen	leave	—	lasciare	dejar
abarrotado (Es)	überfüllt	crowded	bondé(e)	pieno(a) zeppo(a)	—
a bassa voce (I)	leise	quietly	à voix basse	—	sin ruido
abbassare (I)	senken	lower	baisser	—	bajar
abbastanza¹ (I)	genug	enough	assez	—	bastante
abbastanza² (I)	ziemlich	quite	assez	—	bastante
abbestellen (D)	—	cancel	décommander	annullare	anular el pedido de
abbezahlen (D)	—	pay off	payer à tempérament	pagare a rate	pagar a plazos
abbiegen (D)	—	turn off	tourner	svoltare	torcer
abbigliamento (I)	Kleidung f	clothing	habits m pl	—	vestuario m
abblasen (D)	—	call off	annuler	disdire	anular
abbozzo (I)	Entwurf m	outline	esquisse f	—	proyecto m
abbracciare (I)	umarmen	embrace	embrasser	—	abrazar
abbreviation (E)	Abkürzung f	—	abréviation f	abbreviazione f	abreviatura f
abbreviazione (I)	Abkürzung f	abbreviation	abréviation f	—	abreviatura f
abbrustolire (I)	rösten	roast	griller	—	tostar
Abend (D)	—	evening	soir m	sera f	noche f
Abendessen (D)	—	supper	dîner m	cena f	cena f
abends (D)	—	in the evening	le soir	di sera	por la tarde
Abenteuer (D)	—	adventure	aventure f	avventura f	aventura f
aber (D)	—	but	mais	ma	pero
abergläubisch (D)	—	superstitious	superstitieux (-euse)	superstizioso(a)	supersticioso(a)
abertura (Es)	Eröffnung f	opening	ouverture f	apertura f	—
abfahren (D)	—	depart	partir (de)	partire	salir
Abfahrt (D)	—	departure	départ m	partenza f	salida f
Abfall (D)	—	rubbish	déchets m pl	immondizia f	basura f
Abfalleimer (D)	—	bin	poubelle f	pattumiera f	cubo de la basura m
Abflug (D)	—	take-off	décollage m	decollo m	despegue m
abhängen (D)	—	depend	dépendre	dipendere	depender
abholen (D)	—	pick up	aller chercher	andare a prendere	recoger
abierto¹ (Es)	geöffnet	open	ouvert(e)	aperto(a)	—
abierto² (Es)	offen	open	ouvert(e)	aperto(a)	—
abile¹ (I)	clever	clever	futé(e)	—	listo(a)
abile² (I)	geschickt	skilful	habile	—	mañoso(a)
ability (E)	Fähigkeit f	—	capacité f	capacità f	capacidad f
abitante¹ (I)	Bewohner m	inhabitant	habitant m	—	habitante m
abitante² (I)	Einwohner m	inhabitant	habitant m	—	habitante m

	D	E	F	I	Es
abitare (I)	wohnen	live	habiter	—	vivir
abituale (I)	gewöhnlich	usual	habituel(le)	—	habitual
abituare (I)	gewöhnen, sich	get used to	habituer, se	—	acostumbrarse
abitudine (I)	Gewohnheit *f*	habit	habitude *f*	—	costumbre *f*
Abitur (D)	—	German school leaving examinations	baccalauréat *m*	maturità *f*	bachillerato *m*
Abkürzung (D)	—	abbreviation	abréviation *f*	abbreviazione *f*	abreviatura *f*
abladen (D)	—	unload	décharger	scaricare	descargar
able (E)	imstande	—	capable	capace	en condiciones
ablehnen (D)	—	reject	refuser	rifiutare	rehusar
ablenken (D)	—	distract	distraire	distrarre	desviar
Abmachung (D)	—	agreement	accord *m*	accordo *m*	acuerdo *m*
abnehmen¹ (D)	—	lose weight	maigrir	dimagrire	adelgazar
abnehmen² (D)	—	take away	décrocher	staccare	descolgar
abnutzen (D)	—	wear out	user	consumare	desgastar
abogado (Es)	Rechtsanwalt *m*	lawyer	avocat *m*	avvocato *m*	—
abominable (E)	abscheulich	—	affreux(-euse)	disgustoso(a)	horrible
about¹ (E)	etwa	—	environ	pressappoco	unos
about² (E)	ungefähr	—	environ	pressappoco	aproximadamente
above¹ (E)	darüber	—	au dessus	sopra	por encima
above² (E)	oben	—	en haut	sopra	arriba
abraten (D)	—	warn	déconseiller	sconsigliare	desaconsejar
abrazar (Es)	umarmen	embrace	embrasser	abbracciare	—
abrebotellas (Es)	Flaschenöffner *m*	bottle opener	ouvre-bouteilles *m*	apribottiglie *m*	—
Abreise (D)	—	departure	départ *m*	partenza *f*	salida *f*
abreisen (D)	—	leave	partir	partire	salir
abréviation (F)	Abkürzung *f*	abbreviation	—	abbreviazione *f*	abreviatura *f*
abreviatura (Es)	Abkürzung *f*	abbreviation	abréviation *f*	abbreviazione *f*	—
abricot (F)	Aprikose *f*	apricot	—	albicocca *f*	albaricoque *m*
abrigo (Es)	Mantel *m*	coat	manteau *m*	cappotto *m*	—
abril (Es)	April *m*	April	avril *m*	aprile *m*	—
abrir (Es)	öffnen	open	ouvrir	aprire	—
abroad (E)	Ausland *n*	—	étranger *m*	estero *m*	extranjero *m*
abrupt (D)	—	abrupt	subit(e)	improvviso(a)	súbito(a)
abrupt (E)	abrupt	—	subit(e)	improvviso(a)	súbito(a)
abrüsten (D)	—	disarm	désarmer	disarmare	desarmar
Absage (D)	—	refusal	refus *m*	risposta negativa *f*	negativa *f*
abschalten (D)	—	switch off	éteindre	spegnere	desconectar
abscheulich (D)	—	abominable	affreux(-euse)	disgustoso(a)	horrible
Abschied (D)	—	parting	adieux *m pl*	addio *m*	despedida *f*
abschleppen (D)	—	take in tow	remorquer	rimorchiare	remolcar
Abschleppwagen (D)	—	breakdown service	dépanneuse *f*	carro soccorso *m*	coche-grúa *m*
absence (E)	Abwesenheit *f*	—	absence *f*	assenza *f*	ausencia *f*
absence (F)	Abwesenheit *f*	absence	—	assenza *f*	ausencia *f*
Absender (D)	—	sender	expéditeur *m*	mittente *m*	remitente *m*
absent (E)	abwesend	—	absent(e)	assente	ausente
absent (F)	abwesend	absent	—	assente	ausente
Absicht (D)	—	intention	intension *f*	intenzione *f*	intención *f*

	D	E	F	I	Es
absichtlich (D)	—	intentionally	exprès	apposta	adrede
absolument (F)	unbedingt	absolutely	—	assolutamente	absolutamente
absolutamente (Es)	unbedingt	absolutely	absolument	assolutamente	—
absolutely (E)	unbedingt	—	absolument	assolutamente	absolutamente
abspülen (D)	—	wash up	faire la vaisselle	sciacquare	lavar
abstammen (D)	—	be descended	descendre	discendere	descender
Abstand (D)	—	distance	distance f	distanza f	distancia f
absteigen (D)	—	dismount	descendre	scendere	descender
abstellen (D)	—	turn off	arrêter	spegnere	desconectar
Absturz (D)	—	crash	chute f	caduta f	caída f
abstürzen (D)	—	crash	faire une chute	precipitare	caer a tierra
absurdo[1] (Es)	Unsinn m	nonsense	bêtises f pl	nonsenso m	—
absurdo[2] (Es)	unsinnig	nonsensical	insensé(e)	insensato(a)	—
Abteil (D)	—	compartment	compartiment m	scompartimento m	compartimiento m
Abteilung (D)	—	department	département m	reparto m	departamento m
abuela (Es)	Großmutter f	grandmother	grand-mère f	nonna f	—
abuelo (Es)	Großvater m	grandfather	grand-père m	nonno m	—
abuelos (Es)	Großeltern pl	grandparents	grands-parents m pl	nonni m pl	—
a buon mercato (I)	billig	cheap	bon marché(e)	—	barato(a)
aburrido (Es)	langweilig	boring	ennuyeux(-euse)	noioso(a)	—
aburrirse (Es)	langweilen, sich	get bored	ennuyer, se	annoiarsi	—
abus (F)	Mißbrauch m	abuse	—	abuso m	abuso m
abusar (Es)	mißbrauchen	abuse	abuser de	abusare	—
abusare (I)	mißbrauchen	abuse	abuser de	—	abusar
abuse[1] (E)	mißbrauchen	—	abuser de	abusare	abusar
abuse[2] (E)	Mißbrauch m	—	abus m	abuso m	abuso m
abuser de (F)	mißbrauchen	abuse	—	abusare	abusar
abuso (Es)	Mißbrauch m	abuse	abus m	abuso m	—
abuso (I)	Mißbrauch m	abuse	abus m	—	abuso m
abwärts (D)	—	downwards	en bas	in giù	hacia abajo
abwaschen (D)	—	wash off	laver	lavar via	lavar
abwechseln (D)	—	take turns	alterner	alternarsi	alternar
abwesend (D)	—	absent	absent(e)	assente	ausente
Abwesenheit (D)	—	absence	absence f	assenza f	ausencia f
abziehen (D)	—	subtract	soustraire	sottrarre	restar
acabar[1] (Es)	erledigen	take care of	régler	sbrigare	—
acabar[2] (Es)	enden	end	finir	finire	—
acampar (Es)	zelten	camp	camper	campeggiare	—
à carreaux (F)	kariert	checked	—	a quadretti	a cuadros
a casa (Es)	nach Hause	home	à la maison	a casa	—
a casa[1] (I)	daheim	at home	à la maison	—	en casa
a casa[2] (I)	nach Hause	home	à la maison	—	a casa
a causa de (Es)	wegen	because of	à cause de	a causa di	—
a causa di (I)	wegen	because of	à cause de	—	a causa de
à cause de (F)	wegen	because of	—	a causa di	a causa de
accadere[1] (I)	geschehen	happen	arriver	—	ocurrir
accadere[2] (I)	vorkommen	occur	exister	—	suceder

	D	E	F	I	Es
accanto a (I)	neben	beside/next to	près de	—	al lado de
accelerare (I)	beschleunigen	accelerate	accélérer	—	acelerar
accelerate (E)	beschleunigen	—	accélérer	accelerare	acelerar
accélérer (F)	beschleunigen	accelerate	—	accelerare	acelerar
accendere[1] (I)	anmachen	put on	allumer	—	encender
accendere[2] (I)	anzünden	light	allumer	—	encender
accendere[3] (I)	anstellen	turn on	mettre en marche	—	poner
accendere[4] (I)	einschalten	switch on	allumer	—	conectar
accendersi (I)	zünden	ignite	allumer, se	—	encender
accendino (I)	Feuerzeug n	lighter	briquet m	—	mechero m
accent (E)	Akzent m	—	accent m	accento m	acento m
accent (F)	Akzent m	accent	—	accento m	acento m
accento (I)	Akzent m	accent	accent m	—	acento m
accept (E)	annehmen	—	accepter	accettare	aceptar
acceptance (E)	Annahme f	—	réception f	accettazione f	aceptación f
accepter (F)	annehmen	accept	—	accettare	aceptar
accès[1] (F)	Zutritt m	admission	—	accesso m	acceso m
accès[2] (F)	Zugang m	access	—	entrata f	entrada f
acceso (Es)	Zutritt m	admission	accès m	accesso m	—
access (E)	Zugang m	—	accès m	entrata f	entrada f
accesso (I)	Zutritt m	admission	accès m	—	acceso m
accettare[1] (I)	annehmen	accept	accepter	—	aceptar
accettare[2] (I)	übernehmen	take over	reprendre	—	tomar posesión de
accetazione (I)	Annahme f	acceptance	réception f	—	aceptación f
accettazione bagagli (I)	Gepäckannahme f	luggage desk	enregistrement des bagages m	—	recepción de equipajes f
acchiappare[1] (I)	erwischen	catch	attraper	—	atrapar
acchiappare[2] (I)	fangen	catch	attraper	—	coger
acciaio (I)	Stahl m	steel	acier m	—	acero m
accident (E)	Unfall m	—	accident m	incidente m	accidente m
accident (F)	Unfall m	accident	—	incidente m	accidente m
accident de voiture (F)	Autounfall m	car accident	—	incidente stradale m	accidente de automóvil m
accidente (Es)	Unfall m	accident	accident m	incidente m	—
accidente de automóvil (Es)	Autounfall m	car accident	accident de voiture m	incidente stradale m	—
acción (Es)	Tat f	deed	action f	azione f	—
acclimater, se (F)	einleben, sich	settle into	—	ambientarsi	familiarizarse
accoglienza (I)	Aufnahme f	reception	accueil m	—	acogida f
accogliere (I)	aufnehmen	receive	accueillir	—	recibir
accommodation (E)	Unterkunft f	—	logement m	alloggio m	hospedaje m
accompagnare[1] (I)	begleiten	accompany	accompagner	—	acompañar
accompagnare[2] (I)	mitgehen	go along with	accompagner	—	acompañar
accompagner[1] (F)	begleiten	accompany	—	accompagnare	acompañar
accompagner[2] (F)	mitgehen	go along with	—	accompagnare	acompañar
accompany (E)	begleiten	—	accompagner	accompagnare	acompañar
acconsentire (I)	zustimmen	agree	être d'accord	—	consentir
acconto (I)	Anzahlung f	deposit	acompte m	—	primer pago m
accord[1] (F)	Abmachung f	agreement	—	accordo m	acuerdo m

	D	E	F	I	Es
accord² (F)	Verständigung f	agreement	—	accordo m	acuerdo m
accordarsi (I)	einigen, sich	agree	mettre d'accord, se	—	ponerse de acuerdo
accorder (F)	gewähren	grant	—	concedere	conceder
accordo¹ (I)	Abmachung f	agreement	accord m	—	acuerdo m
accordo² (I)	Verständigung f	agreement	accord m	—	acuerdo m
accorgersi di (I)	merken	notice	remarquer	—	notar
account (E)	Konto n	—	compte m	conto m	cuenta f
accrocher (F)	aufhängen	hang up	—	appendere	colgar
accueil (F)	Aufnahme f	reception	—	accoglienza f	acogida f
accueillir (F)	aufnehmen	receive	—	accogliere	recibir
accuracy (E)	Genauigkeit f	—	exactitude f	precisione f	exactitud f
accurato (I)	sorgfältig	careful	soigneux(-euse)	—	cuidadoso(a)
aceite (Es)	Öl n	oil	huile f	olio m	—
aceituna (Es)	Olive f	olive	olive f	oliva f	—
acelerar (Es)	beschleunigen	accelerate	accélérer	accelerare	—
acento (Es)	Akzent m	accent	accent m	accento m	—
aceptación (Es)	Annahme f	acceptance	réception f	accettazione f	—
aceptar¹ (Es)	annehmen	accept	accepter	accettare	—
aceptar² (Es)	übernehmen	take over	reprendre	accettare	—
acera (Es)	Gehweg m	pavement	trottoir m	marciapiede m	—
acercarse (Es)	nähern, sich	approach	approcher, se	avvicinarsi	—
acero (Es)	Stahl m	steel	acier m	acciaio m	—
acertar (Es)	gelingen	succeed	réussir	riuscire	—
aceto (I)	Essig m	vinegar	vinaigre m	—	vinagre m
achat¹ (F)	Einkauf m	shopping	—	spesa f	compra f
achat² (F)	Kauf m	purchase	—	acquisto m	compra f
acheter (F)	kaufen	buy	—	comprare	comprar
acheteur (F)	Käufer m	buyer	—	acquirente m	comprador m
acht (D)	—	eight	huit	otto	ocho
achtgeben (D)	—	take care	faire attention	badare	atender
Achtung! (D)	—	attention!	attention!	attenzione!	¡atención!
achtzehn (D)	—	eighteen	dix-huit	diciotto	dieciocho
achtzig (D)	—	eighty	quatre-vingts	ottanta	ochenta
acid (E)	Säure f	—	acide m	acido m	ácido m
acide (F)	Säure f	acid	—	acido m	ácido m
ácido (Es)	Säure f	acid	acide m	acido m	—
acido¹ (I)	sauer	sour	aigre	—	agrio(a)
acido² (I)	Säure f	acid	acide m	acido m	—
acier (F)	Stahl m	steel	—	acciaio m	acero m
Acker (D)	—	field	champ m	campo m	campo m
aclimatarse (Es)	anpassen, sich	adapt	adapter, se	adattarsi	—
acogida (Es)	Aufnahme f	reception	accueil m	accoglienza f	—
acompañar¹ (Es)	begleiten	accompany	accompagner	accompagnare	—
acompañar² (Es)	mitgehen	go along with	accompagner	accompagnare	—
acompte (F)	Anzahlung f	deposit	—	acconto m	primer pago m
à condition que (F)	vorausgesetzt	provided	—	presumendo	supuesto
aconsejar (Es)	raten	advise	conseiller	consigliare	—
acostumbrarse (Es)	gewöhnen, sich	get used to	habituer, se	abituare	—

	D	E	F	I	Es
acqua (I)	Wasser *n*	water	eau *f*	—	agua *f*
acquaintance (E)	Bekannter *m*	—	ami *m*	conoscente *m*	conocido *m*
acqua minerale (I)	Mineralwasser *n*	mineral water	eau minérale *f*	—	agua mineral *f*
acqua potabile (I)	Trinkwasser *n*	drinking water	eau potable *f*	—	agua potable *f*
acquavite (I)	Schnaps *m*	spirits	eau-de-vie *f*	—	aguardiente *m*
acque (I)	Gewässer *n*	waters	eaux *f pl*	—	aguas *f pl*
acquérir (F)	erwerben	acquire	—	acquistare	adquirir
acquire[1] (E)	besorgen	—	procurer	procurare	conseguir
acquire[2] (E)	erwerben	—	acquérir	acquistare	adquirir
acquirente (I)	Käufer *m*	buyer	acheteur *m*	—	comprador *m*
acquistabile (I)	erhältlich	available	en vente	—	que puede adquirirse
acquistare (I)	erwerben	acquire	acquérir	—	adquirir
acquisto (I)	Kauf *m*	purchase	achat *m*	—	compra *f*
across[1] (E)	hinüber	—	de l'autre côté	di là	hacia el otro lado
across[2] (E)	quer	—	en travers	di trasverso	al través
act[1] (E)	darstellen	—	représenter	rappresentare	representar
act[2] (E)	handeln	—	agir	agire	obrar
act[3] (E)	verfahren	—	procéder	procedere	proceder
acteur (F)	Schauspieler *m*	actor	—	attore *m*	actor *m*
actif[1] (F)	aktiv	active	—	attivo(a)	activo(a)
actif[2] (F)	tätig	active	—	attivo(a)	activo(a)
action (F)	Tat *f*	deed	—	azione *f*	acción *f*
actitud (Es)	Einstellung *f*	attitude	attitude *f*	atteggiamento *m*	—
active[1] (E)	aktiv	—	actif(-ive)	attivo(a)	activo(a)
active[2] (E)	tätig	—	actif(-ive)	attivo(a)	activo(a)
actividad (Es)	Tätigkeit *f*	activity	activité *f*	attività *f*	—
activité (F)	Tätigkeit *f*	activity	—	attività *f*	actividad *f*
activity (E)	Tätigkeit *f*	—	activité *f*	attività *f*	actividad *f*
activo[1] (Es)	aktiv	active	actif(-ive)	attivo(a)	—
activo[2] (Es)	fleißig	diligent	travailleur(-euse)	diligente	—
activo[3] (Es)	lebendig	alive	vivant(e)	vivo(a)	—
activo[4] (Es)	tätig	active	actif(-ive)	attivo(a)	—
actor (E)	Schauspieler *m*	—	acteur *m*	attore *m*	actor *m*
actor (Es)	Schauspieler *m*	actor	acteur *m*	attore *m*	—
actually (E)	eigentlich	—	en fait	in fondo	en realidad
actualmente (Es)	nun	now	maintenant	adesso	—
a cuadros (Es)	kariert	checked	à carreaux	a quadretti	—
acuerdo[1] (Es)	Abmachung *f*	agreement	accord *m*	accordo *m*	—
acuerdo[2] (Es)	Verständigung *f*	agreement	information *f*	accordo *m*	—
adapt (E)	anpassen, sich	—	adapter, se	adattarsi	aclimatarse
adapter, se (F)	anpassen, sich	adapt	—	adattarsi	aclimatarse
adattarsi (I)	anpassen, sich	adapt	adapter, se	—	aclimatarse
adatto[1] (I)	geeignet	suitable	approprié(e)	—	indicado(a)
adatto[2] (I)	passend	suitable	assorti(e)	—	apropiado(a)
adatto[3] (I)	zweckmäßig	suitable	approprié(e)	—	adecuado(a)
add[1] (E)	anbauen	—	ajouter	ampliare	ampliar
add[2] (E)	hinzufügen	—	ajouter	aggiungere	añadir

	D	E	F	I	Es
addestramento (I)	Ausbildung *f*	education	formation *f*	—	formación *f*
addestrare (I)	ausbilden	educate	former	—	instruir
addieren (D)	—	add up	additionner	sommare	sumar
addio (I)	Abschied *m*	parting	adieux *m pl*	—	despedida *f*
additionner (F)	addieren	add up	—	sommare	sumar
addormentarsi (I)	einschlafen	fall asleep	endormir, se	—	adormecerse
addossare (I)	aufbürden	burden	charger	—	cargar
address¹ (E)	adressieren	—	adresser	indirizzare	poner las señas en
address² (E)	Anschrift *f* / Adresse *f*	—	adresse *f*	indirizzo *m*	dirección *f*
add up (E)	addieren	—	additionner	sommare	sumar
adecuado (Es)	zweckmäßig	suitable	approprié(e)	adatto(a)	—
adelantar (Es)	überholen	overtake	doubler	sorpassare	—
¡adelante! (Es)	los!	off!	allons-y!	avanti!	—
adelante¹ (Es)	vorwärts	forward(s)	en avant	avanti	—
adelante² (Es)	weiter	further	plus éloigné(e)	più ampio(a)	—
adelgazar (Es)	abnehmen	lose weight	maigrir	dimagrire	—
además (Es)	außerdem	besides	en outre	inoltre	—
adentro (Es)	herein	in	vers l'intérieur	dentro	—
Ader (D)	—	vein	veine *f*	vena *f*	vena *f*
adesso¹ (I)	jetzt	now	maintenant	—	ahora
adesso² (I)	nun	now	maintenant	—	actualmente
ad est (I)	östlich	eastern	d'est	—	al este
a destra (I)	rechts	right	à droite	—	a la derecha
adhesivo (Es)	Klebstoff *m*	glue	colle *f*	colla *f*	—
adicional (Es)	zusätzlich	in addition	supplémentaire	supplementare	—
adieux (F)	Abschied m	parting	—	addio m	despedida f
¡adiós!¹ (Es)	wiedersehen!	good-bye!	au revoir!	arrivederci!	—
¡adiós!² (Es)	wiederhören!	good-bye!	au revoir!	a risentirci!	—
adivinanza (Es)	Rätsel *n*	riddle	devinette *f*	enigma *m*	—
adivinar (Es)	raten	guess	deviner	indovinare	—
adjust (E)	einstellen	—	régler	regolare	ajustar
Adler (D)	—	eagle	aigle *m*	aquila *f*	águila *f*
admettre (F)	zulassen	permit	—	permettere	permitir
administración (Es)	Verwaltung *f*	administration	administration *f*	amministrazione *f*	—
administration (E)	Verwaltung *f*	—	administration *f*	amministrazione *f*	administración *f*
administration (F)	Verwaltung *f*	administration	—	amministrazione *f*	administración *f*
admirar (Es)	bewundern	admire	admirer	ammirare	—
admire (E)	bewundern	—	admirer	ammirare	admirar
admirer (F)	bewundern	admire	—	ammirare	admirar
admission (E)	Zutritt *m*	—	accès *m*	accesso *m*	acceso *m*
a dónde (Es)	wohin	where to	où	dove	—
adoquinado (Es)	Pflaster *n*	pavement	pavé *m*	lastricato *m*	—
adorar (Es)	anbeten	worship	adorer	adorare	—
adorare (I)	anbeten	worship	adorer	—	adorar
adorer (F)	anbeten	worship	—	adorare	adorar
adormecerse (Es)	einschlafen	fall asleep	endormir, se	addormentarsi	—
ad ovest (I)	westlich	western	de l'ouest	—	occidental

	D	E	F	I	Es
adquirir (Es)	erwerben	acquire	acquérir	acquistare	—
adrede (Es)	absichtlich	intentionally	exprès	apposta	—
Adresse (D)	—	address	adresse *f*	indirizzo *m*	dirección *f*
adresse (F)	Anschrift *f* / Adresse *f*	address	—	indirizzo *m*	dirección *f*
adresser (F)	adressieren	address	—	indirizzare	poner las señas en
adressieren (D)	—	address	adresser	indirizzare	poner las señas en
à droite (F)	rechts	right	—	a destra	a la derecha
aduana (Es)	Zoll *m*	customs	douane *f*	dogana *f*	—
adult (E)	Erwachsener *m*	—	adulte *m*	adulto *m*	adulto *m*
adulte[1] (F)	erwachsen	grown up	—	adulto(a)	adulto(a)
adulte[2] (F)	Erwachsener *m*	adult	—	adulto *m*	adulto *m*
adulto[1] (Es)	erwachsen	grown up	adulte	adulto(a)	—
adulto[2] (Es)	Erwachsener *m*	adult	adulte *m*	adulto *m*	—
adulto[1] (I)	erwachsen	grown up	adulte	—	adulto(a)
adulto[2] (I)	Erwachsener *m*	adult	adulte *m*	—	adulto *m*
advance booking (E)	Vorverkauf *m*	—	location *f*	vendita anticipata *f*	venta anticipada *f*
advantage (E)	Vorteil *m*	—	avantage *m*	vantaggio *m*	ventaja *f*
adventure (E)	Abenteuer *n*	—	aventure *f*	avventura *f*	aventura *f*
adversaire (F)	Gegner *m*	opponent	—	avversario *m*	adversario *m*
adversario (Es)	Gegner *m*	opponent	adversaire *m*	avversario *m*	—
advertir (Es)	warnen	warn	prévenir de	ammonire	—
advertise (E)	werben	—	faire de la publicité	fare propaganda	hacer propaganda
advertisement[1] (E)	Annonce *f*	—	annonce *f*	annuncio *m*	anuncio *m*
advertisement[2] (E)	Inserat *n*	—	annonce *f*	inserzione *f*	anuncio *m*
advertisement[3] (E)	Reklame *f*	—	publicité *f*	réclame *f*	anuncio *m*
advertising (E)	Werbung *f*	—	publicité *f*	pubblicità *f*	publicidad *f*
advice (E)	Rat *m*	—	conseil *m*	consiglio *m*	consejo *m*
advise (E)	raten	—	conseiller	consigliare	aconsejar
aereo (I)	Flugzeug *n*	aeroplane	avion *m*	—	avión *m*
aérer (F)	lüften	air	—	arieggiare	ventilar
aeroplane (E)	Flugzeug *n*	—	avion *m*	aereo *m*	avión *m*
aéroport (F)	Flughafen *m*	airport	—	aeroporto *m*	aeropuerto *m*
aeroporto (I)	Flughafen *m*	airport	aéroport *m*	—	aeropuerto *m*
aeropuerto (Es)	Flughafen *m*	airport	aéroport *m*	aeroporto *m*	—
a este lado (Es)	herüber	over	par ici	da questa parte	—
afectuoso (Es)	herzlich	cordial	cordial(e)	cordiale	—
afeitar (Es)	rasieren	shave	raser	fare la barba	—
affair (E)	Angelegenheit *f*	—	affaire *f*	affare *m*	asunto *m*
affaire (F)	Angelegenheit *f*	affair	—	affare *m*	asunto *m*
affamato (I)	hungrig	hungry	affamé(e)	—	hambriento(a)
affamé (F)	hungrig	hungry	—	affamato(a)	hambriento(a)
affare (I)	Angelegenheit *f*	affair	affaire *f*	—	asunto *m*
affascinante[1] (I)	charmant	charming	charmant(e)	—	encantador(a)
affascinante[2] (I)	entzückend	delightful	ravissant(e)	—	encantador(a)
affascinato (I)	entzückt	delighted	ravi(e)	—	encantado(a)
affaticare (I)	anstrengen	make an effort	faire des efforts	—	cansar
Affe (D)	—	ape	singe *m*	scimmia *f*	mono *m*

	D	E	F	I	Es
affermare (I)	behaupten	assert	affirmer	—	afirmar
affermer (F)	verpachten	lease out	—	affittare	arrendar
afferrare[1] (I)	ergreifen	seize	saisir	—	coger
afferrare[2] (I)	greifen	seize	saisir	—	coger
affettato (I)	Aufschnitt *m*	cold meat	charcuterie *f*	—	loncha *f*
affiche (F)	Plakat *n*	poster	—	affisso *m*	cartel *m*
affidabile (I)	zuverlässig	reliable	sûr(e)	—	de confianza
affilare (I)	schärfen	sharpen	aiguiser	—	afilar
affirmer (F)	behaupten	assert	—	affermare	afirmar
affisso (I)	Plakat *n*	poster	affiche *f*	—	cartel *m*
affittare[1] (I)	mieten	rent	louer	—	alquilar
affittare[2] (I)	verpachten	lease out	affermer	—	arrendar
affittare[3] (I)	vermieten	rent	louer	—	alquilar
affitto (I)	Miete *f*	rent	loyer *m*	—	alquiler *m*
affondare[1] (I)	sinken	sink	couler	—	hundirse
affondare[2] (I)	versinken	sink	enfoncer, se	—	hundirse
affrancare (I)	frankieren	stamp	affranchir	—	franquear
affrancatura (I)	Porto *n*	postage	port *m*	—	franqueo *m*
affranchir (F)	frankieren	stamp	—	affrancare	franquear
affrettarsi (I)	beeilen, sich	hurry up	dépêcher, se	—	darse prisa
affreux (F)	abscheulich	abominable	—	disgustoso(a)	horrible
afilar (Es)	schärfen	sharpen	aiguiser	affilare	—
afirmación (Es)	Aussage *f*	statement	déclaration *f*	dichiarazione *f*	—
afirmar (Es)	bejahen	agree with	répondre par l'affirmative à	approvare	—
aflojar (Es)	nachlassen	slacken	apaiser, se	allentare	—
à fond (F)	gründlich	thorough	—	a fondo	a fondo
a fondo (Es)	gründlich	thorough	à fond	a fondo	—
a fondo (I)	gründlich	thorough	à fond	—	a fondo
afortunado (Es)	erfolgreich	successful	avec succès	pieno(a) di successi	—
afoso (I)	schwül	sultry	lourd(e)	—	sofocante
Africa (E)	Afrika	—	Afrique *f*	Africa *f*	Africa *f*
Africa (Es)	Afrika	Africa	Afrique *f*	Africa *f*	—
Africa (I)	Afrika	Africa	Afrique *f*	—	Africa *f*
Afrika (D)	—	Africa	Afrique *f*	Africa *f*	Africa *f*
Afrique (F)	Afrika	Africa	—	Africa *f*	Africa *f*
after[1] (E)	nachdem	—	après que	dopo	después que
after[2] (E)	nach	—	après/selon	a/in/verso/dopo	a/hacia/después
afternoon (E)	Nachmittag *m*	—	après-midi *m*	pomeriggio *m*	tarde *f*
afterwards[1] (E)	danach	—	après	poi/dopo	después
afterwards[2] (E)	darauf	—	dessus/ensuite	dopo/su	encima
afterwards[3] (E)	nachher	—	ensuite	dopo	después
afuera[1] (Es)	außen	outside	au dehors	fuori	—
afuera[2] (Es)	draußen	outside	dehors	fuori	—
again[1] (E)	nochmals	—	encore une fois	di nuovo	otra vez
again[2] (E)	wieder	—	de nouveau	di nuovo	de nuevo
against (E)	gegen	—	contre	contro	contra
against it (E)	dagegen	—	contre cela	contro	contra

	D	E	F	I	Es
à gauche (F)	links	left	—	a sinistra	a la izquierda
age (E)	Alter *n*	—	âge *m*	età *f*	edad *f*
âge (F)	Alter *n*	age	—	età *f*	edad *f*
agence de voyages (F)	Reisebüro *n*	travel agency	—	agenzia turistica *f*	agencia de viajes *f*
agent de police (F)	Polizist *m*	policeman	—	poliziotto *m*	policía *m*
agenzia turistica (I)	Reisebüro *n*	travel agency	agence de voyages *f*	—	agencia de viajes *f*
aggiungere (I)	hinzufügen	add	ajouter	—	añadir
agglomerato (I)	Siedlung *f*	settlement	cité *f*	—	colonia *f*
aggressione (I)	Überfall *m*	raid	attaque *f*	—	asalto *m*
agir (F)	handeln	act	—	agire	obrar
agire (I)	handeln	act	agir	—	obrar
agitar[1] (Es)	schütteln	shake	secouer	agitare	—
agitar[2] (Es)	aufregen	excite	énerver	agitare	—
agitare[1] (I)	aufregen	excite	énerver	—	agitar
agitare[2] (I)	schütteln	shake	secouer	—	agitar
agité (F)	aufgeregt	excited	—	eccitato(a)	excitado(a)
aglio (I)	Knoblauch *m*	garlic	ail *m*	—	ajo *m*
agneau (F)	Lamm *n*	lamb	—	agnello *m*	cordero *m*
agnello (I)	Lamm *n*	lamb	agneau *m*	—	cordero *m*
ago (I)	Nadel *f*	needle	aiguille *f*	—	aguja *f*
agosto (Es)	August *m*	August	août *m*	agosto *m*	—
agosto (I)	August *m*	August	août *m*	—	agosto *m*
agotado (Es)	erschöpft	exhausted	épuisé(e)	esausto(a)	—
agradable[1] (Es)	angenehm	pleasant	agréable	gradevole	—
agradable[2] (Es)	mild	mild	doux(douce)	mite	—
agradable[3] (Es)	nett	nice	joli(e)	carino(a)	—
agradecer (Es)	danken	thank	remercier	ringraziare	—
agradecer algo (Es)	bedanken	say thank you	remercier	ringraziare	—
agradecido (Es)	dankbar	grateful	reconnaissant(e)	grato(a)	—
agradecimiento (Es)	Dank *m*	thanks	remerciement *m*	ringraziamento *m*	—
agrandar (Es)	vergrößern	enlarge	agrandir	ingrandire	—
agrandir (F)	vergrößern	enlarge	—	ingrandire	agrandar
agréable[1] (F)	angenehm	pleasant	—	gradevole	agradable
agréable[2] (F)	gemütlich	comfortable	—	comodo(a)	cómodo(a)
agree[1] (E)	ausmachen	—	convenir	stabilire	convenir
agree[2] (E)	einigen, sich	—	mettre d'accord, se	accordarsi	ponerse de acuerdo
agree[3] (E)	übereinstimmen	—	être d'accord	concordare	estar de acuerdo
agree[4] (E)	zustimmen	—	être d'accord	acconsentire	consentir
agreed (E)	einverstanden	—	d'accord	d'accordo	de acuerdo
agreement[1] (E)	Abmachung *f*	—	accord *m*	accordo *m*	acuerdo *m*
agreement[2] (E)	Verständigung *f*	—	accord *m*	accordo *m*	acuerdo *m*
agree upon (E)	vereinbaren	—	convenir de	fissare	convenir
agree with (E)	bejahen	—	répondre par l'affirmative à	approvare	afirmar
agricoltore (I)	Landwirt *m*	farmer	agriculteur *m*	—	agricultor *m*
agriculteur (F)	Landwirt *m*	farmer	—	agricoltore *m*	agricultor *m*
agricultor (Es)	Landwirt *m*	farmer	agriculteur *m*	agricoltore *m*	—

	D	E	F	I	Es
agrio (Es)	sauer	sour	aigre	acido(a)	—
agua (Es)	Wasser n	water	eau f	acqua f	—
agua mineral (Es)	Mineralwasser n	mineral water	eau minérale f	acqua minerale f	—
aguantar (Es)	aushalten	bear	supporter	sopportare	—
agua potable (Es)	Trinkwasser n	drinking water	eau potable f	acqua potabile f	—
aguardiente (Es)	Schnaps m	spirits	eau-de-vie f	acquavite f	—
aguas (Es)	Gewässer n	waters	eaux f pl	acque f pl	—
águila (Es)	Adler m	eagle	aigle m	aquila f	—
aguja (Es)	Nadel f	needle	aiguille f	ago m	—
agujero (Es)	Loch n	hole	trou m	buco m	—
ahead (E)	voraus	—	en avant	avanti	delante
ähneln (D)	—	resemble	ressembler	assomigliare	parecer
ahnen (D)	—	suspect	douter, se	supporre	suponer
ähnlich (D)	—	similar	semblable	simile	parecido(a)
Ahnung (D)	—	presentiment	pressentiment m	presentimento m	presentimiento m
ahogarse (Es)	ertrinken	drown	noyer, se	annegare	—
ahora (Es)	jetzt	now	maintenant	adesso	—
ahora mismo (Es)	soeben	just now	à l'instant même	poco fa	—
ahorrar (Es)	sparen	save	économiser	risparmiare	—
aide (F)	Hilfe f	help	—	aiuto m	ayuda f
aider (F)	helfen	help	—	aiutare	ayudar
aider qn (F)	behilflich sein	help s.b.	—	aiutare	ayudar a alguien
aigle (F)	Adler m	eagle	—	aquila f	águila f
aigre (F)	sauer	sour	—	acido(a)	agrio(a)
aiguille (F)	Nadel f	needle	—	ago m	aguja f
aiguiser (F)	schärfen	sharpen	—	affilare	afilar
ail (F)	Knoblauch m	garlic	—	aglio m	ajo m
aile (F)	Flügel m	wing	—	ala f	ala f
ailleurs (F)	woanders	elsewhere	—	altrove	en otra parte
aimable[1] (F)	freundlich	friendly	—	gentile	amistoso(a)
aimable[2] (F)	liebenswürdig	kind	—	gentile	gentil
aimer[1] (F)	lieben	love	—	amare	amar
aimer[2] (F)	mögen	like	—	piacere	querer
aîné (F)	ältere(r,s)	elder	—	maggiore	mayor
ainsi (F)	so	like this	—	cosí	así
air[1] (E)	lüften	—	aérer	arieggiare	ventilar
air[2] (E)	Luft f	—	air m	aria f	aire m
air (F)	Luft f	air	—	aria f	aire m
aire (Es)	Luft f	air	air m	aria f	—
air mail (E)	Luftpost f	—	poste aérienne f	posta aerea f	correo aéreo m
airport (E)	Flughafen m	—	aéroport m	aeroporto m	aeropuerto m
aiutare[1] (I)	behilflich sein	help s.b.	aider qn	—	ayudar a alguien
aiutare[2] (I)	helfen	help	aider	—	ayudar
aiuto (I)	Hilfe f	help	aide f	—	ayuda f
ajo (Es)	Knoblauch m	garlic	ail m	aglio m	—
ajouter[1] (F)	anbauen	add	—	ampliare	ampliar
ajouter[2] (F)	hinzufügen	add	—	aggiungere	añadir
ajustar (Es)	einstellen	adjust	régler	regolare	—

	D	E	F	I	Es
Aktenmappe (D)	—	file	porte-documents *m*	cartella *f*	cartera *f*
aktiv (D)	—	active	actif(-ive)	attivo(a)	activo(a)
Akzent (D)	—	accent	accent *m*	accento *m*	acento *m*
ala (Es)	Flügel *m*	wing	aile *f*	ala *f*	—
ala (I)	Flügel *m*	wing	aile *f*	—	ala *f*
a la derecha (Es)	rechts	right	à droite	a destra	—
a la izquierda (Es)	links	left	à gauche	a sinistra	—
à la maison¹ (F)	daheim	at home	—	a casa	en casa
à la maison² (F)	nach Hause	home	—	a casa	a casa
alambre (Es)	Draht *m*	wire	fil de fer *m*	filo metallico *m*	—
alargar¹ (Es)	strecken	stretch	allonger	stendere	—
alargar² (Es)	verlängern	extend	prolonger	allungare	—
alarm clock (E)	Wecker *m*	—	réveil *m*	sveglia *f*	despertador *m*
a la sombra (Es)	schattig	shady	ombragé(e)	ombroso(a)	—
a la vez (Es)	gleichzeitig	simultaneous	en même temps	contemporaneo(a)	—
albaricoque (Es)	Aprikose *f*	apricot	abricot *m*	albicocca *f*	—
albergo (I)	Hotel *n*	hotel	hôtel *m*	—	hotel *m*
albern (D)	—	foolish	sot(te)	sciocco(a)	tonto(a)
albero (I)	Baum *m*	tree	arbre *m*	—	árbol *m*
albicocca (I)	Aprikose *f*	apricot	abricot *m*	—	albaricoque *m*
alcalde (Es)	Bürgermeister *m*	mayor	maire *m*	sindaco *m*	—
alcanzar¹ (Es)	erreichen	reach	atteindre	raggiungere	—
alcanzar² (Es)	reichen	pass	passer	passare	—
alcanzar³ (Es)	treffen	hit	toucher	colpire	—
alcohol (E)	Alkohol *m*	—	alcool *m*	alcol *m*	alcohol *m*
alcohol (Es)	Alkohol *m*	alcohol	alcool *m*	alcol *m*	—
alcol (I)	Alkohol *m*	alcohol	alcool *m*	—	alcohol *m*
alcool (F)	Alkohol *m*	alcohol	—	alcol *m*	alcohol *m*
alcuni¹ (I)	einige	some	quelques	—	algunos(as)
alcuni² (I)	etliche	several	quelques	—	algunos(as)
al di là (I)	jenseits	beyond	de l'autre côté	—	al otro lado
al di sotto di (I)	unter	under	sous	—	debajo de
alegrarse (Es)	freuen, sich	be glad	être heureux(-euse)	rallegrarsi	—
alegre (Es)	munter	lively	éveillé(e)	vivace	—
alegría (Es)	Freude *f*	joy	joie *f*	gioia *f*	—
alemán¹ (Es)	deutsch	German	allemand(e)	tedesco(a)	—
alemán² (Es)	Deutscher *m*	German	Allemand *m*	tedesco	—
Alemania (Es)	Deutschland	Germany	Allemagne *f*	Germania *f*	—
alergia (Es)	Allergie *f*	allergy	allergie *f*	allergia *f*	—
al este (Es)	östlich	eastern	d'est	ad est	—
à l'extérieur (F)	auswärts	out(wards)	—	fuori	fuera
alfabeto (Es)	Alphabet *n*	alphabet	alphabet *m*	alfabeto *m*	—
alfabeto (I)	Alphabet *n*	alphabet	alphabet *m*	—	alfabeto *m*
alfombra (Es)	Teppich *m*	carpet	tapis *m*	tappeto *m*	—
algo¹ (Es)	etwas	something	quelque chose	qualcosa	—
algo² (Es)	irgend etwas	something	n'importe quoi	qualsiasi cosa	—
algodón¹ (Es)	Baumwolle *f*	cotton	coton *m*	cotone *m*	—

	D	E	F	I	Es
algodón² (Es)	Watte f	cotton wool	ouate f	ovatta f	—
alguien (Es)	jemand	somebody	quelqu'un	qualcuno	—
alguno (Es)	irgend jemand	somebody	n'importe qui	qualcuno	—
algunos¹ (Es)	etliche	several	quelques	alcuni(e)	—
algunos² (Es)	einige	some	quelques	alcuni(e)	—
aliment (F)	Speise f	food	—	cibo m	comida f
alimentación¹ (Es)	Ernährung f	nourishment	nourriture f	alimentazione f	—
alimentación² (Es)	Verpflegung f	catering	nourriture f	vitto m	—
alimentar (Es)	ernähren	feed	nourrir	nutrire	—
alimentari¹ (I)	Eßwaren pl	foodstuffs	produits alimentaires m pl	—	comestibles m pl
alimentari² (I)	Lebensmittel pl	food	alimentation f	—	alimentos m pl
alimentation (F)	Lebensmittel pl	food	—	alimentari m pl	alimentos m pl
alimentazione¹ (I)	Ernährung f	nourishment	nourriture f	—	alimentación f
alimentazione² (I)	Essen n	food	repas m	—	comida f
alimentazione³ (I)	Nahrung f	food	nourriture f	—	nutrición f
alimento (Es)	Kost f	food	nourriture f	cibo m	—
alimentos (Es)	Lebensmittel pl	food	alimentation f	alimentari m pl	—
à l'instant même (F)	soeben	just now	—	poco fa	ahora mismo
à l'intérieur (F)	drinnen, innen	inside	—	dentro	dentro
à l'intérieur de (F)	innerhalb	within	—	entro	dentro de
a little (E)	bißchen	—	un peu	un po	un poquito
alive (E)	lebendig	—	vivant(e)	vivo(a)	vivo(a)
aliviarse (Es)	erholen, sich	recover	reposer, se	rimettersi	—
Alkohol (D)	—	alcohol	alcool m	alcol m	alcohol m
all (E)	alle	—	tous(toutes)	tutti(e)	todos(as)
al lado de (Es)	neben	beside	près de	accanto a	—
alle (D)	—	all	tous(toutes)	tutti(e)	todos(as)
allée (F)	Auffahrt f	drive	—	salita d'ingresso f	entrada f
allegro (I)	lustig	funny	marrant(e)	—	divertido(a)
allein (D)	—	alone	seul(e)	solo(a)	solo(a)
Allemagne (F)	Deutschland	Germany	—	Germania f	Alemania f
allemand (F)	deutsch	German	—	tedesco(a)	alemán(-ana)
Allemand (F)	Deutscher m	German	—	tedesco m	alemán m
allentare (I)	nachlassen	slacken	apaiser, se	—	aflojar
aller (F)	gehen	go	—	andare	andar
aller bien (F)	passen	suit	—	stare bene	venir bien
aller chercher¹ (F)	abholen	pick up	—	andare a prendere	recoger
aller chercher² (F)	holen	fetch	—	andare a prendere	traer
allergia (I)	Allergie f	allergy	allergie f	—	alergia f
Allergie (D)	—	allergy	allergie f	allergia f	alergia f
allergie (F)	Allergie f	allergy	—	allergia f	alergia f
allergy (E)	Allergie f	—	allergie f	allergia f	alergia f
aller plus loin (F)	weitergehen	go on	—	proseguire	proseguir
aller, s'en (F)	weggehen	go away	—	andare via	marcharse
alles (D)	—	everything	tout	tutto	todo
allevare (I)	züchten	breed	élever		criar
allgemein (D)	—	general	général(e)	generale	general

	D	E	F	I	Es
allí¹ (Es)	dort	there	là/y	là	—
allí² (Es)	da	there	là/ici	qui/là	—
allmählich (D)	—	gradual	graduel(le)	graduale	gradual
allô! (F)	hallo!	hello!	—	pronto!	¡diga!
alloggio (I)	Unterkunft *f*	accommodation	logement *m*	—	hospedaje *m*
all one colour (E)	einfarbig	—	uni(e)	monocolore	de un solo color
allonger (F)	strecken	stretch	—	stendere	alargar
allons-y! (F)	los!	off!	—	avanti!	¡adelante!
allontanare (I)	entfernen	remove	éloigner	—	quitar
allora (I)	damals	at that time	à cette époque	—	entonces
allow¹ (E)	erlauben	—	permettre	permettere	permitir
allow² (E)	gestatten	—	permettre	permettere	permitir
Alltag (D)	—	everyday life	vie quotidienne *f*	vita quotidiana *f*	vida cotidiana *f*
all the same (E)	egal	—	égal(e)	uguale	igual
allumer¹ (F)	anzünden	light	—	accendere	encender
allumer² (F)	anmachen	put on	—	accendere	encender
allumer³ (F)	einschalten	switch on	—	accendere	conectar
allumer, se (F)	zünden	ignite	—	accendersi	encender
allumette (F)	Streichholz *n*	match	—	fiammifero *m*	cerilla *f*
allungare (I)	verlängern	extend	prolonger	—	alargar
almacén (Es)	Lager *n*	store	magasin *m*	magazzino *m*	—
al massimo (I)	höchstens	at the most	tout au plus	—	a lo sumo
almendra (Es)	Mandel *f*	almond	amande *f*	mandorla *f*	—
almeno¹ (I)	mindestens	at least	au moins	—	por lo menos
almeno² (I)	wenigstens	at least	au moins	—	por lo menos
almohada (Es)	Kopfkissen *n*	pillow	oreiller *m*	guanciale *m*	—
almond (E)	Mandel *f*	—	amande *f*	mandorla *f*	almendra *f*
Almosen (D)	—	alms	aumône *f*	elemosina *f*	limosna *f*
alms (E)	Almosen *n*	—	aumône *f*	elemosina *f*	limosna *f*
a lo largo de (Es)	entlang	along	le long de	lungo	—
alone (E)	allein	—	seul(e)	solo(a)	solo(a)
along (E)	entlang	—	le long de	lungo	a lo largo de
a long time ago (E)	längst	—	depuis bien longtemps	da molto	hace mucho
alors (F)	damals	at that time	—	allora	entonces
a lo sumo (Es)	höchstens	at the most	tout au plus	al massimo	—
a lot of (E)	viel	—	beaucoup de	molto(a)	mucho(a)
al otro lado¹ (Es)	drüben	over there	de l'autre côté	dall'altra parte	—
al otro lado² (Es)	jenseits	beyond	de l'autre côté	al di là	—
Alphabet (D)	—	alphabet	alphabet *m*	alfabeto *m*	alfabeto *m*
alphabet (E)	Alphabet *n*	—	alphabet *m*	alfabeto *m*	alfabeto *m*
alphabet (F)	Alphabet *n*	alphabet	—	alfabeto *m*	alfabeto *m*
alpinista (Es)	Bergsteiger *m*	mountaineer	alpiniste *m*	alpinista *m*	—
alpinista (I)	Bergsteiger *m*	mountaineer	alpiniste *m*	—	alpinista m
alpiniste (F)	Bergsteiger *m*	mountaineer	—	alpinista *m*	alpinista *m*
alquilar¹ (Es)	mieten	rent	louer	affittare	—
alquilar² (Es)	vermieten	rent	louer	affittare	—
alquiler (Es)	Miete *f*	rent	loyer *m*	affitto *m*	—

	D	E	F	I	Es
already (E)	bereits/schon	—	déjà	già	ya
alrededor (Es)	herum	around	autour	intorno	—
alrededor de (Es)	um	at/around	autour de/à	intorno a/a	—
alrededores (Es)	Umgebung f	surroundings	environs m pl	dintorni m pl	—
als (D)	—	when	quand	quando	cuando
also (D)	—	therefore	donc	dunque/quindi	así
also (E)	auch	—	aussi	anche/pure	también
al sur (Es)	südlich	southern	au sud	a sud	—
alt (D)	—	old	vieux, vieil, vieille	vecchio(a)	viejo(a)
alt! (I)	halt!	stop!	stop!	—	¡alto!
alta marea (I)	Flut f	high tide	marée haute f	—	marea alta f
alta montagna (I)	Hochgebirge n	high mountain-chain	haute montage f	—	montañas elevadas f pl
alta stagione (I)	Hochsaison f	high season	pleine saison f	—	temporada alta f
altavoz (Es)	Lautsprecher m	loudspeaker	haut-parleur m	altoparlante m	—
Alter (D)	—	age	âge m	età f	edad f
alteration (E)	Umbuchung f	—	transfert m	riporto m	cambio m
ältere (D)	—	elder	aîné(e)	maggiore	mayor
alternar (Es)	abwechseln	take turns	alterner	alternarsi	—
alternarsi (I)	abwechseln	take turns	alterner	—	alternar
alterner (F)	abwechseln	take turns	—	alternarsi	alternar
altertümlich (D)	—	dated	antique	antico(a)	antiguo(a)
altezza (I)	Höhe f	height	hauteur f	—	altura f
although (E)	obwohl/obgleich	—	bien que	benché	aunque
altmodisch (D)	—	old-fashioned	démodé(e)	fuori moda	pasado(a) de moda
alto (Es)	hoch	up/high	haut(e)	alto(a)	—
¡alto! (Es)	halt!	stop!	stop!	alt!	—
alto (I)	hoch	up/high	haut(e)	—	alto(a)
altogether (E)	insgesamt	—	dans l'ensemble	complessivamente	en suma
altoparlante (I)	Lautsprecher m	loudspeaker	haut-parleur m	—	altavoz m
al través (Es)	quer	across	en travers	di trasverso	—
altrettanto (I)	ebenfalls	as well	aussi	—	también
altrimenti (I)	sonst	otherwise	autrement	—	por lo demás
altro (I)	andere(r,s)	other	autre	—	otra(o)
altrove (I)	woanders	elsewhere	ailleurs	—	en otra parte
altura (Es)	Höhe f	height	hauteur f	altezza f	—
alumno (Es)	Schüler m	pupil	élève m	scolaro m	—
always¹ (E)	immer	—	toujours	sempre	siempre
always² (E)	stets	—	toujours	sempre	siempre
alzare¹ (I)	erheben	raise	lever	—	elevar
alzare² (I)	heben	lift	soulever	—	levantar
alzarsi (I)	aufstehen	get up	lever, se	—	levantarse
amable (Es)	lieb	sweet	gentil(le)	caro(a)	—
ama de casa (Es)	Hausfrau f	housewife	femme de maison f	casalinga f	—
amande (F)	Mandel f	almond	—	mandorla f	almendra f
amanecer (Es)	dämmern	dawn	poindre	spuntare	—
amapola (Es)	Mohn m	poppy	coquelicot m	papavero m	—
amar (Es)	lieben	love	aimer	amare	—

	D	E	F	I	Es
amare (I)	lieben	love	aimer	—	amar
amargo[1] (Es)	bitter	bitter	amer(-ère)	amaro(a)	—
amargo[2] (Es)	herb	bitter	âcre	amaro(a)	—
amarillo (Es)	gelb	yellow	jaune	giallo(a)	—
amaro[1] (I)	bitter	bitter	amer(-ère)	—	amargo(a)
amaro[2] (I)	herb	bitter	âpre	—	amargo(a)
ambasciata (I)	Botschaft f	embassy	ambassade f	—	embajada f
ambassade (F)	Botschaft f	embassy	—	ambasciata f	embajada f
ambientarsi (I)	einleben, sich	settle into	acclimater, se	—	familiarizarse
ambiente (I)	Umwelt f	environment	environnement m	—	medioambiente m
ambos (Es)	beide	both	tous/toutes les deux	entrambi	—
ambulance (E)	Krankenwagen m	—	ambulance f	ambulanza f	ambulancia f
ambulance (F)	Krankenwagen m	ambulance	—	ambulanza f	ambulancia f
ambulancia (Es)	Krankenwagen m	ambulance	ambulance f	ambulanza f	—
ambulanza (I)	Krankenwagen m	ambulance	ambulance f	—	ambulancia f
amélioration (F)	Besserung f	improvement	—	miglioramento m	restablecimiento m
améliorer (F)	verbessern	improve	—	migliorare	mejorar
a memoria (Es)	Andenken n	souvenir	souvenir m	ricordo m	—
a memoria (I)	auswendig	by heart	par cœur	—	de memoria
aménager (F)	einrichten	fit out	—	arredare	equipar
amenazar[1] (Es)	drohen	threaten s.b.	menacer	minacciare	—
amenazar[2] (Es)	androhen	threaten	menacer	minacciare	—
amenazar[3] (Es)	bedrohen	threaten	menacer	minacciare	—
a menudo (Es)	oft	often	souvent	spesso	—
amer (F)	bitter	bitter	—	amaro(a)	amargo(a)
America (E)	Amerika n	—	Amérique f	America f	América f
América (Es)	Amerika n	America	Amérique f	America f	—
America (I)	Amerika n	America	Amérique f	—	América f
America del Nord (I)	Nordamerika n	North America	Amérique du Nord f	—	América del Norte f
América del Norte (Es)	Nordamerika n	North America	Amérique du Nord f	America del Nord f	—
américain (F)	amerikanisch	American	—	americano(a)	americano(a)
American (E)	amerikanisch	—	américain(e)	americano(a)	americano(a)
americano (I)	amerikanisch	American	américain(e)	—	americano(a)
americano (Es)	amerikanisch	American	américain(e)	americano	—
Amerika (D)	—	America	Amérique f	America f	América f
amerikanisch (D)	—	American	américain(e)	americano(a)	americano(a)
Amérique (F)	Amerika n	America	—	America f	América f
Amérique du Nord (F)	Nordamerika n	North America	—	America del Nord f	América del Norte f
ameublement (F)	Einrichtung f	furnishing	—	arredamento m	mobiliario m
a mezzogiorno (I)	mittags	at midday	à midi	—	mediodía
ami[1] (F)	Freund m	friend	—	amico m	amigo m
ami[3] (F)	Bekannter m	acquaintance	—	conoscente m	conocido m
amicizia (I)	Freundschaft f	friendship	amitié f	—	amistad f
amico[1] (I)	befreundet	friendly	ami(e)	—	amigo(a)
amico[2] (I)	Freund m	friend	ami m	—	amigo m
ami de (F)	befreundet	friendly	—	amico(a)	amigo(a) de
à midi (F)	mittags	at midday	—	a mezzogiorno	mediodía

	D	E	F	I	Es
amigo (Es)	Freund *m*	friend	ami *m*	amico *m*	—
amigo de (Es)	befreundet	friendly	ami(e) de	amico(a)	—
amistad (Es)	Freundschaft *f*	friendship	amitié *f*	amicizia *f*	—
amistoso (Es)	freundlich	friendly	aimable	gentile	—
amitié (F)	Freundschaft *f*	friendship	—	amicizia *f*	amistad *f*
ammalarsi (I)	erkranken	get ill	tomber malade	—	enfermar
amministrazione (I)	Verwaltung *f*	administration	administration *f*	—	administración *f*
ammirare (I)	bewundern	admire	admirer	—	admirar
ammobiliare (I)	möblieren	furnish	meubler	—	amueblar
ammobiliato (I)	möbliert	furnished	meublé(e)	—	amueblado(a)
ammonire¹ (I)	mahnen	warn	exhorter	—	notificar
ammonire² (I)	warnen	warn	prévenir de	—	advertir
amor (Es)	Liebe *f*	love	amour *m*	amore *m*	—
amore (I)	Liebe *f*	love	amour *m*	—	amor *m*
amount (E)	Betrag *m*	—	montant *m*	somma *f*	importe *m*
amour (F)	Liebe *f*	love	—	amore *m*	amor *m*
amoureux (F)	verliebt	in love	—	innamorato(a)	enamorado(a)
Ampel (D)	—	traffic lights	feux *m pl*	semaforo *m*	semáforo *m*
ampliar (Es)	anbauen	add	ajouter	ampliare	—
ampliare (I)	anbauen	add	ajouter	—	ampliar
amplio¹ (Es)	breit	broad	large	largo(a)	—
amplio² (I)	weit	far	éloigné(e)	—	ancho(a)
ampoule (F)	Glühbirne *f*	light bulb	—	lampadina *f*	lámpara *f*
Amt (D)	—	office	bureau *m*	ufficio *m*	oficio *m*
amtlich (D)	—	official	officiel(le)	ufficiale	oficial
amueblado (Es)	möbliert	furnished	meublé(e)	ammobiliato(a)	—
amueblar (Es)	möblieren	furnish	meubler	ammobiliare	—
amuser, se (F)	amüsieren, sich	enjoy o.s.	—	divertirsi	divertirse
amüsieren, sich (D)	—	enjoy o.s.	amuser, se	divertirsi	divertirse
an (D)	—	at/on/by	à/près de	a/in/su	junto a
añadir (Es)	hinzufügen	add	ajouter	aggiungere	—
Ananas (D)	—	pineapple	ananas *m*	ananas *m*	piña *f*
ananas (F)	Ananas *f*	pineapple	—	ananas *m*	piña *f*
ananas (I)	Ananas *f*	pineapple	ananas *m*	—	piña *f*
anatra (I)	Ente *f*	duck	canard *m*	—	pato *m*
anbauen¹ (D)	—	add	ajouter	ampliare	ampliar
anbauen² (D)	—	cultivate	cultiver	coltivare	cultivar
anbeten (D)	—	worship	adorer	adorare	adorar
anbieten (D)	—	offer	offrir	offrire	ofrecer
anbringen (D)	—	fasten	fixer	fissare	colocar
anche (I)	auch	also/too	aussi	—	también
ancho (Es)	weit	far	éloigné(e)	largo(a)	—
ancora (I)	noch	still	encore	—	aún/todavía
and (E)	und	—	et	e	y
andar¹ (Es)	gehen	go	aller	andare	—
andar² (Es)	geben	give	donner	dare	—
andare¹ (I)	fahren	drive	conduire	—	conducir
andare² (I)	gehen	go	aller	—	andar

	D	E	F	I	Es
andare a prendere[1] (I)	abholen	pick up	aller chercher	—	recoger
andare a prendere[2] (I)	holen	fetch	aller chercher	—	traer
andare a trovare (I)	besuchen	visit	rendre visite à	—	visitar
andare avanti (I)	vorangehen	go ahead	marcher devant	—	pasar adelante
andare a vela (I)	segeln	sail	faire de la voile	—	navegar a vela
andare in fretta (I)	eilen	hurry	dépêcher, se	—	darse prisa
andare insieme (I)	mitgehen	go along with	accompagner	—	acompañar
andare via (I)	weggehen	go away	s'en aller	—	marcharse
Andenken (D)	—	souvenir	souvenir *m*	ricordo *m*	recuerdo *m*
andere (D)	—	other	autre	altro(a)	otra(o)
andererseits (D)	—	on the other hand	d'autre part	d'altra parte	por otra parte
ändern (D)	—	change	changer	cambiare	cambiar
anders (D)	—	different	différent(e)	differente	diferente
anderthalb (D)	—	one and a half	un(e) et demi(e)	uno(a) e mezzo	uno(a) y medio(a)
androhen (D)	—	threaten	menacer	minacciare	amenazar
âne (F)	Esel *m*	donkey	—	asino *m*	burro *m*
anello (I)	Ring *m*	ring	bague *f*	—	sortija *f*
Anfang (D)	—	beginning	commencement *m*	inizio *m*	inicio *m*
anfangen (D)	—	start	commencer	cominciare	empezar
Anfänger (D)	—	beginner	débutant(e)	principiante *m*	principiante *m*
anfitrión (Es)	Gastgeber *m*	host	hôte *m*	ospite *m*	—
anfordern (D)	—	request	demander	esigere	pedir
Angabe (D)	—	information	information *f*	indicazione *f*	información *f*
ange (F)	Engel *m*	angel	—	angelo *m*	ángel *m*
angeblich (D)	—	pretended	prétendu(e)	presunto(a)	supuesto(a)
angeboren (D)	—	inborn	inné(e)	innato(a)	innato(a)
Angebot (D)	—	offer	offre *f*	offerta *f*	oferta *f*
angel (E)	Engel *m*	—	ange *m*	angelo *m*	ángel *m*
ángel (Es)	Engel *m*	angel	ange *m*	angelo *m*	—
Angelegenheit (D)	—	affair	affaire *f*	affare *m*	asunto *m*
angeln (D)	—	fish	pêcher	pescare	pescar con caña
angelo (I)	Engel *m*	angel	ange *m*	—	ángel *m*
angenehm (D)	—	pleasant	agréable	gradevole	agradable
anger (E)	Wut *f*	—	colère *f*	rabbia *f*	rabia *f*
Angestellter (D)	—	employee	employé *m*	impiegato *m*	empleado *m*
anglais (F)	englisch	English	—	inglese	inglés(-esa)
Anglais (F)	Engländer *m*	Englishman	—	inglese *m*	inglés *m*
Angleterre (F)	England *n*	England	—	Inghilterra *f*	Inglaterra *f*
angolo (I)	Ecke *f*	corner	coin *m*	—	esquina *f*
angreifen (D)	—	attack	attaquer	attaccare	atacar
angry (E)	ärgerlich	—	fâché(e)	arrabbiato(a)	enfadado(a)
Angst (D)	—	fear	peur *f*	paura *f*	miedo *m*
ängstlich (D)	—	fearful	peureux(-euse)	pauroso(a)	miedoso(a)
anhaben (D)	—	have on	porter	indossare	llevar
anhalten (D)	—	stop	arrêter	fermare	parar
Anhalter (D)	—	hitch-hiker	auto-stoppeur *m*	autostoppista *m*	autoestopista *m*
animado (Es)	belebt	lively	animé(e)	animato(a)	—

	D	E	F	I	Es
animal (E)	Tier *n*	—	animal *m*	animale *m*	animal *m*
animal (Es)	Tier *n*	animal	animal *m*	animale *m*	—
animal (F)	Tier *n*	animal	—	animale *m*	animal *m*
animale (I)	Tier *n*	animal	animal *m*	—	animal *m*
animato (I)	belebt	lively	animé(e)	—	animado(a)
animé (F)	belebt	lively	—	animato(a)	animado(a)
ánimo (Es)	Gemüt *n*	disposition	disposition *f*	animo *m*	—
animo (I)	Gemüt *n*	disposition	disposition *f*	—	ánimo *m*
ankle (E)	Knöchel *m*	—	cheville *f*	caviglia *f*	tobillo *m*
ankommen (D)	—	arrive	arriver	arrivare	llegar
Ankunft (D)	—	arrival	arrivée *f*	arrivo *m*	llegada *f*
Anlage (D)	—	plant	construction *f*	impianto *m*	establecimiento *m*
Anlaß (D)	—	occasion	occasion *f*	occasione *f*	ocasión *f*
anmachen (D)	—	put on	allumer	accendere	encender
anmelden (D)	—	announce	annoncer	annunciare	anunciar
annaffiare (I)	gießen	water	arroser	—	regar
Annahme[1] (D)	—	acceptance	réception *f*	accettazione *f*	aceptación *f*
Annahme[2] (D)	—	assumption	supposition *f*	supposizione *f*	suposición *f*
année (F)	Jahr *n*	year	—	anno *m*	año *m*
annegare (I)	ertrinken	drown	noyer, se	—	ahogarse
annehmen[1] (D)	—	accept	accepter	accettare	aceptar
annehmen[2] (D)	—	suppose	supposer	supporre	suponer
anniversaire (F)	Geburtstag *m*	birthday	—	compleanno *m*	cumpleaños *m*
anno (I)	Jahr *n*	year	année *f*	—	año *m*
annoiarsi (I)	langweilen, sich	get bored	ennuyer, se	—	aburrirse
Annonce (D)	—	advertisement	annonce *f*	annuncio *m*	anuncio *m*
annonce[1] (F)	Anzeige *f*	announcement	—	annuncio *m*	anuncio *m*
annonce[2] (F)	Annonce *f*	advertisement	—	annuncio *m*	anuncio *m*
annonce[3] (F)	Inserat *n*	advertisement	—	inserzione *f*	anuncio *m*
annonce[4] (F)	Meldung *f*	report	—	annuncio *m*	aviso *m*
annoncer[1] (F)	ansagen	announce	—	annunciare	anunciar
annoncer[2] (F)	anmelden	announce	—	annunciare	anunciar
annoncer[3] (F)	melden	report	—	annunciare	declarar
annotare (I)	notieren	note down	noter	—	anotar
announce[1] (E)	ansagen	—	annoncer	annunciare	anunciar
announce[2] (E)	anmelden	—	annoncer	annunciare	anunciar
announcement (E)	Anzeige *f*	—	annonce *f*	annuncio *m*	anuncio *m*
annoy[1] (E)	ärgern	—	fâcher	arrabbiare	enfadar
annoy[2] (E)	belästigen	—	importuner	importunare	molestar
annuaire du téléphone (F)	Telefonbuch *n*	phone book	—	elenco telefonico *m*	guía telefónica *f*
annual (E)	jährlich	—	annuel(le)	annuale	anual
annuale (I)	jährlich	annual	annuel(le)	—	anual
annuel (F)	jährlich	annual	—	annuale	anual
annuire (I)	nicken	nod	faire un signe de la tête	—	inclinar la cabeza
annul (E)	annullieren	—	annuler	annullare	anular
annuler (F)	annullieren	annul	—	annullare	anular
annullare[1] (I)	annullieren	annul	annuler		anular

	D	E	F	I	Es
annullare² (I)	abbestellen	cancel	décommander	—	anular el pedido de
annullieren (D)	—	annul	annuler	annullare	anular
annunciare¹ (I)	ansagen	announce	annoncer	—	anunciar
annunciare² (I)	anmelden	announce	annoncer	—	anunciar
annunciare³ (I)	melden	report	annoncer	—	declarar
annuncio¹ (I)	Anzeige f	announcement	annonce f	—	anuncio m
annuncio² (I)	Annonce f	advertisement	annonce f	—	anuncio m
annuncio³ (I)	Meldung f	report	annonce f	—	aviso m
año (Es)	Jahr n	year	année f	anno m	—
Año Nuevo (Es)	Neujahr n	New Year	nouvel an m	Capodanno m	—
a nord (I)	nördlich	northerly	du nord	—	del norte
anotar (Es)	notieren	note down	noter	annotare	—
anpassen, sich (D)	—	adapt	adapter, se	adattarsi	aclimatarse
anprobieren (D)	—	try on	essayer	provare	probar
anrechnen (D)	—	charge	compter	mettere in conto	poner en cuenta
Anruf (D)	—	call	coup de téléphone m	chiamata f	llamada f
anrufen (D)	—	ring up	téléphoner	telefonare	llamar por teléfono
ansagen (D)	—	announce	annoncer	annunciare	anunciar
anschauen (D)	—	look at	regarder	guardare	mirar
anscheinend (D)	—	seemingly	apparemment	apparentemente	aparentemente
Anschluß (D)	—	connection	correspondance f	coincidenza f	conexión f
Anschrift (D)	—	address	adresse f	indirizzo m	dirección f
ansehen (D)	—	look at	regarder	guardare	mirar
Ansicht (D)	—	opinion	avis m	opinione f	opinión f
Ansichtskarte (D)	—	postcard	carte postale f	cartolina f	tarjeta postal f
anständig (D)	—	decent	convenable	decente	decente
anstatt (D)	—	instead of	au lieu de	invece di	en vez de
anstellen (D)	—	turn on	mettre en marche	accendere	poner
anstoßen (D)	—	bump	heurter	urtare	empujar
anstrengen (D)	—	make an effort	faire des efforts	affaticare	cansar
anstrengend (D)	—	tiring	fatigant(e)	faticoso(a)	fatigoso(a)
Anstrengung (D)	—	strain	effort m	fatica f	esfuerzo m
answer¹ (E)	antworten	—	répondre	rispondere	responder
answer² (E)	Antwort f	—	réponse f	risposta f	respuesta f
answer³ (E)	beantworten	—	répondre à	rispondere a	responder a
anteayer (Es)	vorgestern	day before yesterday	avant-hier	l'altro ieri	—
anterior (Es)	vorhergehend	preceding	précédent	precedente	—
antes¹ (Es)	eher	sooner	plus tôt	prima	—
antes² (Es)	früher	earlier	autrefois	prima	—
antes³ (Es)	vorher	before	avant	prima	—
antes⁴ (Es)	zuvor	before	auparavant	prima	—
antes que¹ (Es)	bevor	before	avant que	prima che	—
antes que² (Es)	ehe	before	avant que	prima che	—
antico (I)	altertümlich	dated	antique	—	antiguo(a)
antigüedades (Es)	Antiquitäten pl	antiques	antiquités f pl	oggetti antichi m	—
antiguo (Es)	altertümlich	dated	antique	antico(a)	—
antipasto (I)	Vorspeise f	appetizer	hors-d'œuvre m	—	primer plato m

	D	E	F	I	Es
antique (F)	altertümlich	dated	—	antico(a)	antiguo(a)
antiques (E)	Antiquitäten *pl*	—	antiquités *f pl*	oggetti antichi *m*	antigüedades *f pl*
Antiquitäten (D)	—	antiques	antiquités *f pl*	oggetti antichi *m*	antigüedades *f pl*
antiquités (F)	Antiquitäten *pl*	antiques	—	oggetti antichi *m*	antigüedades *f pl*
Antrag (D)	—	application	demande *f*	domanda *f*	solicitud *f*
Antwort (D)	—	answer	réponse *f*	risposta *f*	respuesta *f*
antworten (D)	—›	answer	répondre	rispondere	responder
anual (Es)	jährlich	annual	annuel(le)	annuale	—
anular¹ (Es)	abblasen	call off	souffler	disdire	—
anular² (Es)	annullieren	annul	annuler	annullare	—
anular³ (Es)	tilgen	erase	effacer	estinguere	—
anular el pedido de (Es)	abbestellen	cancel	décommander	annullare	—
anunciar¹ (Es)	anmelden	announce	annoncer	annunciare	—
anunciar² (Es)	ansagen	announce	annoncer	annunciare	—
anuncio¹ (Es)	Annonce *f*	advertisement	annonce *f*	annuncio *m*	—
anuncio² (Es)	Anzeige *f*	announcement	annonce *f*	annuncio *m*	—
anuncio³ (Es)	Inserat *n*	advertisement	annonce *f*	inserzione *f*	—
anuncio⁴ (Es)	Reklame *f*	advertisement	publicité *f*	réclame *f*	—
anwenden (D)	—	apply	employer	impiegare	usar
Anwesen (D)	—	premises	domaine *m*	podere *m*	posesión *f*
anwesend (D)	—	present	présent(e)	presente	presente
any (E)	beliebig	—	n'importe quel	qualsiasi	a voluntad
Anzahl (D)	—	number	nombre *m*	numero *m*	número *m*
Anzahlung (D)	—	deposit	acompte *m*	acconto *m*	primer pago *m*
Anzeige¹ (D)	—	announcement	annonce *f*	annuncio *m*	anuncio *m*
Anzeige² (D)	—	denunciation	dénonciation *f*	denuncia *f*	denuncia *f*
anziehen (D)	—	put on	mettre	indossare	ponerse
Anzug (D)	—	suit	costume *m*	vestito *m*	traje *m*
anzünden (D)	—	light	allumer	accendere	encender
août (F)	August *m*	August	—	agosto *m*	agosto *m*
apagar¹ (Es)	ausmachen	switch off	éteindre	spegnere	—
apagar² (Es)	auslöschen	extinguish	éteindre	estinguere	—
apagar³ (Es)	löschen	extinguish	éteindre	spegnere	—
apaiser, se (F)	nachlassen	slacken	—	allentare	aflojar
aparato (Es)	Apparat *m*	apparatus	appareil *m*	apparecchio *m*	—
aparcar (Es)	parken	park	garer	parcheggiare	—
aparecer (Es)	erscheinen	appear	apparaître	apparire	—
aparente (Es)	anscheinend	seemingly	apparemment	apparentemente	—
apart (E)	auseinander	—	séparé(e)	separato(a)	lejos/distante
à part (F)	extra	extra	—	a parte	separado(a)
a parte (I)	extra	extra	à part	—	separado(a)
a partir de (Es)	ab	off	à partir de/dès	da	—
à partir de (F)	ab	off	—	da	a partir de/de
ape (E)	Affe *m*	—	singe *m*	scimmia *f*	mono *m*
à peine (F)	kaum	hardly	—	appena	apenas
apellido (Es)	Nachname *m*	surname	nom de famille *m*	cognome *m*	—
apenas (Es)	kaum	hardly	à peine	appena	—

	D	E	F	I	Es
aperto¹ (I)	geöffnet	open	ouvert(e)	—	abierto(a)
aperto² (I)	offen	open	ouvert(e)	—	abierto(a)
apertura (I)	Eröffnung f	opening	ouverture f	—	abertura f
a pesar de (Es)	trotz	despite	malgré	nonostante	—
apestar (Es)	stinken	stink	puer	puzzare	—
apetito (Es)	Appetit m	appetite	appétit m	appetito m	—
Apfel (D)	—	apple	pomme f	mela f	manzana f
Apfelsine (D)	—	orange	orange f	arancia f	naranja f
aplastar (Es)	zerdrücken	squash	écraser	sgualcire	—
aplaudir (Es)	klatschen	applaud	applaudir	battere le mani	—
aplauso (Es)	Beifall m	applause	applaudissements m pl	applauso m	—
aplazar (Es)	verschieben	postpone	remettre	rimandare	—
apologize (E)	entschuldigen, sich	—	excuser, se	scusarsi	disculparse
apology (E)	Entschuldigung f	—	excuse f	scusa f	disculpa f
apostar (Es)	wetten	bet	parier	scommettere	—
Apotheke (D)	—	chemist's	pharmacie f	farmacia f	farmacia f
apoyar (Es)	unterstützen	support	soutenir	assistere	—
apoyo (Es)	Unterstützung f	support	soutien m	sostegno m	—
apparaître (F)	erscheinen	appear	—	apparire	aparecer
Apparat (D)	—	apparatus	appareil m	apparecchio m	aparato m
apparatus (E)	Apparat m	—	appareil m	apparecchio m	aparato m
apparecchio¹ (I)	Apparat m	apparatus	appareil m	—	aparato m
apparecchio² (I)	Gerät n	appliance	appareil m	—	utensilio m
appareil¹ (F)	Apparat m	apparatus	—	apparecchio m	aparato m
appareil² (F)	Gerät n	appliance	—	apparecchio m	utensilio m
appareil photo (F)	Fotoapparat m	camera	—	macchina fotografica f	máquina fotográfica f
apparemment (F)	anscheinend	seemingly	—	apparentemente	aparentemente
apparence (F)	Aussehen n	appearance	—	aspetto m	aspecto m
apparentemente (I)	anscheinend	seemingly	apparemment	—	aparentemente
apparire (I)	erscheinen	appear	apparaître	—	aparecer
appartamento (I)	Wohnung f	flat	appartement m	—	piso m
appartement (F)	Wohnung f	flat	—	appartamento m	piso m
appartenere (I)	gehören	belong	appartenir	—	pertenecer
appartenir (F)	gehören	belong	—	appartenere	pertenecer
appassire (I)	welken	wither	faner, se	—	marchitarse
appear (E)	erscheinen	—	apparaître	apparire	aparecer
appearance (E)	Aussehen n	—	apparence f	aspetto m	aspecto m
appeler¹ (F)	nennen	call	—	chiamare	nombrar
appeler² (F)	rufen	shout	—	chiamare	llamar
appeler, se (F)	heißen	be called	—	chiamarsi	llamarse
appena¹ (I)	kaum	hardly	à peine	—	apenas
appena² (I)	sobald	as soon as	dès que	—	tan pronto como
appendere (I)	aufhängen	hang up	accrocher	—	colgar
Appetit (D)	—	appetite	appétit m	appetito m	apetito m
appétit (F)	Appetit m	appetite	—	appetito m	apetito m
appetite (E)	Appetit m	—	appétit m	appetito m	apetito m
appetito (I)	Appetit m	appetite	appétit m	—	apetito m

	D	E	F	I	Es
appetizer (E)	Vorspeise f	—	hors-d'œuvre m	antipasto m	primer plato m
applaud (E)	klatschen	—	applaudir	battere le mani	aplaudir
applaudir (F)	klatschen	applaud	—	battere le mani	aplaudir
applaudissements (F)	Beifall m	applause	—	applauso m	aplauso m
applause (E)	Beifall m	—	applaudissements m pl	applauso m	aplauso m
applauso (I)	Beifall m	applause	applaudissements m pl	—	aplauso m
apple (E)	Apfel m	—	pomme f	mela f	manzana f
appliance (E)	Gerät n	—	appareil m	apparecchio m	utensilio m
application¹ (E)	Antrag m	—	demande f	domanda f	solicitud f
application² (E)	Bewerbung f	—	candidature f	domanda d'impiego f	aspiración f
apply¹ (E)	anwenden	—	employer	impiegare	usar
apply² (E)	bewerben, sich	—	poser sa candidature	concorrere	presentarse
apporter (F)	mitbringen	bring (along)	—	portare con sé	traer
apposta (I)	absichtlich	intentionally	exprès	—	adrede
apprendista (I)	Lehrling m	apprentice	apprenti m	—	aprendiz m
apprendre¹ (F)	erfahren	learn	—	venire a sapere	enterarse
apprendre² (F)	lernen	learn	—	imparare	aprender
apprenti (F)	Lehrling m	apprentice	—	apprendista m	aprendiz m
apprentice (E)	Lehrling m	—	apprenti m	apprendista m	aprendiz m
approach¹ (E)	entgegenkommen	—	venir à la rencontre	venire incontro	venir al encuentro
approach² (E)	nähern, sich	—	approcher, se	avvicinarsi	acercarse
approcher, se (F)	nähern, sich	approach	—	avvicinarsi	acercarse
approprié¹ (F)	geeignet	suitable	—	adatto(a)	indicado(a)
approprié² (F)	zweckmäßig	suitable	—	adatto(a)	adecuado(a)
approuver (F)	billigen	approve of	—	approvare	aprobar
approvare¹ (I)	bejahen	agree with	répondre par l'affirmative à	—	afirmar
approvare² (I)	billigen	approve of	approuver	—	aprobar
approvare³ (I)	genehmigen	approve	autoriser	—	permitir
approve (E)	genehmigen	—	autoriser	approvare	permitir
approve of (E)	billigen	—	approuver	approvare	aprobar
approvvigionare (I)	versorgen	provide	fournir	—	proveer
appuntamento (I)	Verabredung f	date	rendez-vous m	—	cita f
appuntito (I)	spitz	pointed	pointu(e)	—	puntiagudo(a)
âpre (F)	herb	bitter	—	amaro(a)	amargo(a)
aprender (Es)	lernen	learn	apprendre	imparare	—
aprendiz (Es)	Lehrling m	apprentice	apprenti m	apprendista m	—
après¹ (F)	danach	afterwards	—	poi/dopo	después
après² (F)	nach	after/to	—	a/in/verso/dopo	a/hacia/después
après-demain (F)	übermorgen	day after tomorrow	—	dopodomani	pasado mañana
après-midi (F)	Nachmittag m	afternoon	—	pomeriggio m	tarde f
après que (F)	nachdem	after	—	dopo	después que
apretar (Es)	drücken	press	presser	premere	—
apribottiglie (I)	Flaschenöffner m	bottle opener	ouvre-bouteilles m	—	abrebotellas m
apricot (E)	Aprikose f	—	abricot m	albicocca f	albaricoque m

	D	E	F	I	Es
Aprikose (D)	—	apricot	abricot *m*	albicocca *f*	albaricoque *m*
April (D)	—	April	avril *m*	aprile *m*	abril *m*
April (E)	April *m*	—	avril *m*	aprile *m*	abril *m*
aprile (I)	April *m*	April	avril *m*	—	abril *m*
aprire (I)	öffnen	open	ouvrir	—	abrir
aprobar (Es)	billigen	approve of	approuver	approvare	—
apropiado (Es)	passend	suitable	assorti(e)	adatto(a)	—
aproximadamente (Es)	ungefähr	about	environ	pressappoco	—
apuesta (Es)	Wette *f*	bet	pari *m*	scommessa *f*	—
a quadretti (I)	kariert	checked	à carreaux	—	a cuadros
a quarter (E)	Viertel *n*	—	quart *m*	quarto *m*	cuarto *m*
aquel (Es)	jene(r,s)	that	ce, cette	quello(a)	—
aquí¹ (Es)	her	here	ici	qua/qui/da	—
aquí² (Es)	hier	here	ici	qui	—
aquila (I)	Adler *m*	eagle	aigle *m*	—	águila *f*
araignée (F)	Spinne *f*	spider	—	ragno *m*	araña *f*
araña (Es)	Spinne *f*	spider	araignée *f*	ragno *m*	—
arancia¹ (I)	Apfelsine *f*	orange	orange *f*	—	naranja *f*
arancia² (I)	Orange *f*	orange	orange *f*	—	naranja *f*
Arbeit (D)	—	work	travail *m*	lavoro *m*	trabajo *m*
arbeiten (D)	—	work	travailler	lavorare	trabajar
Arbeiter (D)	—	worker	ouvrier *m*	operaio *m*	trabajador *m*
arbeitslos (D)	—	unemployed	en chômage	disoccupato(a)	desempleado(a)
Arbeitslosigkeit (D)	—	unemployment	chômage *m*	disoccupazione *f*	desempleo *m*
arbitre (F)	Schiedsrichter *m*	referee	—	arbitro *m*	árbitro *m*
arbitrio (Es)	Zoll *m*	duty	droits de douane *m pl*	dazio *m*	—
árbitro (Es)	Schiedsrichter *m*	referee	arbitre *m*	arbitro *m*	—
arbitro (I)	Schiedsrichter *m*	referee	arbitre *m*	—	árbitro *m*
árbol (Es)	Baum *m*	tree	arbre *m*	albero *m*	—
arbre (F)	Baum *m*	tree	—	albero *m*	árbol *m*
arbusto (Es)	Strauch *m*	bush	buisson *m*	cespuglio *m*	—
arder (Es)	brennen	burn	brûler	bruciare	—
area (E)	Fläche *f*	—	surface *f*	area *f*	área *f*
area (I)	Fläche *f*	area	surface *f*	—	área *f*
arena (Es)	Sand *m*	sand	sable *m*	sabbia *f*	—
argent¹ (F)	Geld *n*	money	—	denaro *m*	dinero *m*
argent² (F)	Silber *n*	silver	—	argento *m*	plata *f*
argent de poche (F)	Taschengeld *n*	pocket money	—	denaro per le piccole spese *m*	dinero de bolsillo *m*
argento (I)	Silber *n*	silver	argent *m*	—	plata *f*
ärgerlich (D)	—	angry	fâché(e)	arrabbiato(a)	enfadado(a)
ärgern (D)	—	annoy	fâcher	arrabbiare	enfadar
argomento (I)	Argument *n*	argument	argument *m*	—	argumento *m*
Argument (D)	—	argument	argument *m*	argomento *m*	argumento *m*
argument¹ (E)	Argument *n*	—	argument *m*	argomento *m*	argumento *m*
argument² (E)	Streit *m*	—	dispute *f*	lite *f*	disputa *f*
argument (F)	Argument *n*	argument	—	argomento *m*	argumento *m*

	D	E	F	I	Es
argumento (Es)	Argument n	argument	argument m	argomento m	—
aria (I)	Luft f	air	air m	—	aire m
árido (Es)	dürr	skinny	maigre	secco(a)	—
arieggiare (I)	lüften	air	aérer	—	ventilar
arise (E)	entstehen	—	naître	nascere	surgir
a risentirci! (I)	wiederhören!	good-bye!	au revoir!	—	¡adiós!
arm (D)	—	poor	pauvre	povero(a)	pobre
Arm (D)	—	arm	bras m	braccio m	brazo m
arm (E)	Arm m	—	bras m	braccio m	brazo m
arma (Es)	Waffe f	weapon	arme f	arma f	—
arma (I)	Waffe f	weapon	arme f	—	arma m
armadio[1] (I)	Kleiderschrank m	wardrobe	garde-robe f	—	armario ropero m
armadio[2] (I)	Schrank m	cupboard	armoire f	—	armario m
armario (Es)	Schrank m	cupboard	armoire f	armadio m	—
armario ropero (Es)	Kleiderschrank m	wardrobe	garde-robe f	armadio m	—
Armband (D)	—	bracelet	bracelet m	bracciale m	pulsera f
armchair (E)	Sessel m	—	fauteuil m	poltrona f	sillón m
arme (F)	Waffe f	weapon	—	arma f	arma m
Ärmel (D)	—	sleeve	manche f	manica f	manga f
Ärmelkanal (D)	—	Channel	Manche f	Manica f	Canal de la Mancha m
armoire (F)	Schrank m	cupboard	—	armadio m	armario m
aroma (Es)	Duft m	scent	odeur f	profumo m	—
aromatico (I)	würzig	spicy	épicé(e)	—	aromático(a)
aromático (Es)	würzig	spicy	épicé(e)	aromatico(a)	—
around (E)	herum	—	autour	intorno	alrededor
arrabbiare (I)	ärgern	annoy	fâcher	—	enfadar
arrabbiato[1] (I)	ärgerlich	angry	fâché(e)	—	enfadado(a)
arrabbiato[2] (I)	wütend	furious	furieux(-euse)	—	furioso(a)
arrampicarsi (I)	klettern	climb	grimper	—	escalar
arrange (E)	arrangieren	—	arranger	arrangiare	organizar
arranger (F)	arrangieren	arrange	—	arrangiare	organizar
arrange to meet (E)	verabreden	—	prendre rendez-vous	darsi appuntamento	concertar una cita
arrangiare (I)	arrangieren	arrange	arranger	—	organizar
arrangieren (D)	—	arrange	arranger	arrangiare	organizar
arredamento (I)	Einrichtung f	furnishing	ameublement m	—	mobiliario m
arredare (I)	einrichten	fit out	aménager	—	equipar
arreglar (Es)	aufräumen	clear away	ranger	mettere in ordine	—
arrendar (Es)	verpachten	lease out	affermer	affittare	—
arrepentirse (Es)	bereuen	regret	regretter	pentirsi	—
arrest (E)	verhaften	—	arrêter	arrestare	detener
arrestare (I)	verhaften	arrest	arrêter	—	detener
arrêt (F)	Haltestelle f	stop	—	fermata f	parada f
arrêter[1] (F)	aufhören	stop	—	cessare	terminar
arrêter[2] (F)	anhalten	stop	—	fermare	parar
arrêter[3] (F)	ausschalten	switch off	—	spegnere	desconectar
arrêter[4] (F)	abstellen	turn off	—	spegnere	desconectar
arrêter[5] (F)	verhaften	arrest	—	arrestare	detener

	D	E	F	I	Es
arriba (Es)	oben	above	en haut	sopra	—
arrière-grands-parents (F)	Urgroßeltern *pl*	great-grandparents	—	bisnonni *m pl*	bisabuelos *m pl*
arriesgar (Es)	riskieren	risk	risquer	rischiare	—
arrival (E)	Ankunft *f*	—	arrivée *f*	arrivo *m*	llegada *f*
arrivare¹ (I)	ankommen	arrive	arriver	—	llegar
arrivare² (I)	eintreffen	arrive	arriver	—	llegar
arrivare a (I)	gelangen	attain	arriver à	—	conseguir
arrive¹ (E)	ankommen	—	arriver	arrivare	llegar
arrive² (E)	eintreffen	—	arriver	arrivare	llegar
arrivederci! (I)	wiedersehen!	good-bye!	au revoir!	—	¡adiós!
arrivée (F)	Ankunft *f*	arrival	—	arrivo *m*	llegada *f*
arriver¹ (F)	ankommen	arrive	—	arrivare	llegar
arriver² (F)	eintreffen	arrive	—	arrivare	llegar
arriver³ (F)	geschehen	happen	—	accadere	ocurrir
arriver⁴ (F)	passieren	happen	—	succedere	pasar
arriver à (F)	gelangen	attain	—	arrivare a	conseguir
arrivo (I)	Ankunft *f*	arrival	arrivée *f*	—	llegada *f*
arroser (F)	gießen	water	—	annaffiare	regar
arrostire (I)	braten	roast	rôtir	—	asar
arrostito (I)	gebraten	fried	rôti(e)	—	asado(a)
arrosto (I)	Braten *m*	roast	rôti *m*	—	asado *m*
arrow (E)	Pfeil *m*	—	flèche *f*	freccia *f*	flecha *f*
arroz (Es)	Reis *m*	rice	riz *m*	riso *m*	—
arrugginire (I)	rosten	rust	rouiller	—	oxidarse
arrugginito (I)	rostig	rusty	rouillé(e)	—	oxidado(a)
arruinar (Es)	verderben	ruin	détruire	rovinare	—
Art¹ (D)	—	way	manière *f*	modo *m*	manera *f*
Art² (D)	—	species	espèce *f*	specie *f*	especie *f*
art (E)	Kunst *f*	—	art *m*	arte *f*	arte *m*
art (F)	Kunst *f*	art	—	arte *f*	arte *m*
arte (Es)	Kunst *f*	art	art *m*	arte *f*	—
arte (I)	Kunst *f*	art	art *m*	—	arte *m*
artesanía (Es)	Handwerk *n*	craft	métier *m*	artigianato *m*	—
artesano (Es)	Handwerker *m*	craftsman	artisan *m*	artigiano *m*	—
article (E)	Artikel *m*	—	article *m*	articolo *m*	artículo *m*
article (F)	Artikel *m*	article	—	articolo *m*	artículo *m*
articolo (I)	Artikel *m*	article	article *m*	—	artículo *m*
artículo (Es)	Artikel *m*	article	article *m*	articolo *m*	—
artificial (E)	künstlich	—	artificiel(le)	artificiale	artificial
artificial (Es)	künstlich	artificial	artificiel(le)	artificiale	—
artificiale (I)	künstlich	artificial	artificiel(le)	—	artificial
artificiel (F)	künstlich	artificial	—	artificiale	artificial
artigianato (I)	Handwerk *n*	craft	métier *m*	—	artesanía *f*
artigiano (I)	Handwerker *m*	craftsman	artisan *m*	—	artesano *m*
Artikel (D)	—	article	article *m*	articolo *m*	artículo *m*
artisan (F)	Handwerker *m*	craftsman	—	artigiano *m*	artesano *m*
artist (E)	Künstler *m*	—	artiste *m*	artista *m*	artista *m*

	D	E	F	I	Es
artista (Es)	Künstler *m*	artist	artiste *m*	artista *m*	—
artista (I)	Künstler *m*	artist	artiste *m/f*	—	artista *m/f*
artiste (F)	Künstler *m*	artist	—	artista *m*	artista *m/f*
Arznei (D)	—	medicine	médicament *m*	medicina *f*	medicina *f*
Arzt (D)	—	doctor	médecin *m*	medico *m*	médico *m*
a saber (Es)	nämlich	namely	à savoir	cioè	—
asado¹ (Es)	Braten *m*	roast	rôti *m*	arrosto *m*	—
asado² (Es)	gebraten	fried	rôti(e)	arrostito(a)	—
asaltar (Es)	überfallen	raid	attaquer	assalire	—
asalto (Es)	Überfall *m*	raid	attaque *f*	aggressione *f*	—
asar (Es)	braten	roast	rôtir	arrostire	—
as a result of (E)	infolge	—	par suite de	in seguito a	por
à savoir (F)	nämlich	namely	—	cioè	a saber
ascend (E)	aufsteigen	—	monter	salire	subir
ascenseur (F)	Fahrstuhl *m*/Lift *m*	elevator	—	ascensore *m*	ascensor *m*
ascensor (Es)	Fahrstuhl *m*/Lift *m*	elevator	ascenseur *m*	ascensore *m*	—
ascensore (I)	Fahrstuhl *m*/Lift *m*	elevator	ascenseur *m*	—	ascensor *m*
Asche (D)	—	ash	cendre *f*	cenere *f*	ceniza *f*
Aschenbecher (D)	—	ashtray	cendrier *m*	portacenere *m*	cenicero *m*
asciugamano (I)	Handtuch *n*	towel	serviette *f*	—	toalla *f*
asciugare (I)	trocknen	dry	sécher	—	secar
asciutto (I)	trocken	dry	sec(sèche)	—	seco(a)
ascoltare (I)	zuhören	listen	écouter	—	escuchar
ascoltatore (I)	Hörer *m*	listener	auditeur *m*	—	oyente *m*
asegurar (Es)	versichern	assure	assurer	assicurare	—
aseo (Es)	Pflege *f*	care	soins *m pl*	cura *f*	—
asesinato (Es)	Mord *m*	murder	meurtre *m*	assassinio *m*	—
as far as (E)	soweit	—	autant que	fin dove	hasta tanto
ash (E)	Asche *f*	—	cendre *f*	cenere *f*	ceniza *f*
ashtray (E)	Aschenbecher *m*	—	cendrier *m*	portacenere *m*	cenicero *m*
así¹ (Es)	also	therefore	donc	dunque/quindi	—
así² (Es)	so	like this	ainsi	così	—
asidero (Es)	Griff *m*	handle	poignée *f*	maniglia *f*	—
asiento¹ (Es)	Sitzplatz *m*	seat	place assise *f*	posto a sedere *m*	—
asiento² (Es)	Sitz *m*	seat	siège *m*	sede *f*	—
asilo (infantile) (I)	Kindergarten *m*	nursery school	jardin d'enfants *m*	—	jardin de infancia *m*
a sinistra (I)	links	left	à gauche	—	a la izquierda
asino (I)	Esel *m*	donkey	âne *m*	—	burro *m*
asistir a (Es)	beistehen	stand by s.b.	assister	assistere	—
as is well known (E)	bekanntlich	—	comme on sait	com'è noto	como es sabido
ask¹ (E)	auffordern	—	inviter	invitare	invitar
ask² (E)	fragen	—	demander	domandare	preguntar
as long (E)	solange	—	tant que	finché	en tanto que
asociación (Es)	Verein *m*	club	association *f*	associazione *f*	—
asombrar (Es)	wundern	wonder	étonner, se	stupire	—
asombrarse (Es)	staunen	be astonished	étonner, se	stupirsi	—
aspecto¹ (Es)	Aussehen *n*	appearance	apparence *f*	aspetto *m*	—

	D	E	F	I	Es
aspecto² (Es)	Miene f	expression	mine f	aspetto m	—
asperger (F)	spritzen	squirt	—	spruzzare	salpicar
aspettare¹ (I)	erwarten	expect	attendre	—	esperar
aspettare² (I)	warten	wait	attendre	—	esperar
aspetto¹ (I)	Aussehen n	appearance	apparence f	—	aspecto m
aspetto² (I)	Miene f	expression	mine f	—	expresión f
aspiración (Es)	Bewerbung f	application	candidature f	domanda d'impiego f	—
aspirador (Es)	Staubsauger m	vacuum-cleaner	aspirateur m	aspirapolvere m	—
aspirapolvere (I)	Staubsauger m	vacuum-cleaner	aspirateur m	—	aspirador m
aspirateur (F)	Staubsauger m	vacuum-cleaner	—	aspirapolvere m	aspirador m
assaggiare (I)	versuchen	try	essayer	—	probar
assalire (I)	überfallen	raid	attaquer	—	asaltar
assassinio (I)	Mord m	murder	meurtre m	—	asesinato m
assegno (I)	Scheck m	cheque	chèque m	—	cheque m
assegno turistico (I)	Reisescheck m	traveller's cheque	chèque de voyage m	—	cheque de viaje m
assente (I)	abwesend	absent	absent(e)	—	ausente
assenza (I)	Abwesenheit f	absence	absence f	—	ausencia f
asseoir, se (F)	hinsetzen	sit down	—	sedersi	sentarse
assert (E)	behaupten	—	affirmer	affermare	afirmar
assetato (I)	durstig	thirsty	assoiffé(e)	—	sediento(a)
assez¹ (F)	genug	enough	—	abbastanza	bastante
assez² (F)	ziemlich	quite	—	abbastanza	bastante
assicurare (I)	versichern	assure	assurer	—	asegurar
assicurazione (I)	Versicherung f	insurance	assurance f	—	seguro m
assiette (F)	Teller m	plate	—	piatto m	plato m
assigner (F)	vorladen	summon	—	citare in giudizio	citar
assister (F)	beistehen	stand by s.b.	—	assistere	asistir a
assistere¹ (I)	beistehen	stand by s.b.	assister	—	asistir a
assistere² (I)	unterstützen	support	soutenir	—	apoyar
association (F)	Verein m	club	—	associazione f	asociación f
associazione (I)	Verein m	club	association f	—	asociación f
assoiffé (F)	durstig	thirsty	—	assetato(a)	sediento(a)
assolutamente (I)	unbedingt	absolutely	absolument	—	absolutamente
assomigliare (I)	ähneln	resemble	ressembler	—	parecer
as soon as (E)	sobald	—	dès que	appena	tan pronto como
assorti (F)	passend	suitable	—	adatto(a)	apropiado(a)
assortire (I)	sortieren	sort	trier	—	clasificar
assume (E)	voraussetzen	—	supposer	presupporre	suponer
assumere (I)	einstellen	employ	recruter	—	emplear
assumption (E)	Annahme f	—	supposition f	supposizione f	suposición f
assurance (F)	Versicherung f	insurance	—	assicurazione f	seguro m
assurdo (I)	sinnlos	senseless	insensé(e)	—	inútil
assure (E)	versichern	—	assurer	assicurare	asegurar
assurer (F)	versichern	assure	—	assicurare	asegurar
Ast (D)	—	branch	branche f	ramo m	rama f
asta (I)	Stange f	pole	barre f	—	barra f
astiquer (F)	polieren	polish	—	lucidare	pulir

	D	E	F	I	Es
astucieux (F)	schlau	clever	—	astuto(a)	astuto(a)
astuto (I)	schlau	clever	astucieux(-euse)	—	astuto(a)
astuto (Es)	schlau	clever	astucieux(-euse)	astuto(a)	—
a sud (I)	südlich	southern	du sud	—	al sur
asunto (Es)	Angelegenheit f	affair	affaire f	affare m	—
asustar (Es)	erschrecken	frighten	effrayer	spaventare	—
as well as (E)	sowohl	—	aussi bien	tanto...quanto	tanto...
at¹ (E)	um	—	autour de/à	intorno a/a	alrededor de/a las
at² (E)	bei	—	chez/près de	da/presso	cerca de/junto a
at³ (E)	an	—	à/près de	a/in/su	junto a
atacar (Es)	angreifen	attack	attaquer	attaccare	—
at all¹ (E)	irgend	—	d'une façon ou d'une autre	in qualche modo	cualquiera
at all² (E)	überhaupt	—	en général	in genere	en general
atar (Es)	binden	bind	attacher	legare	—
ataúd (Es)	Sarg m	coffin	cercueil m	bara f	—
atelier (F)	Werkstatt f	workshop	—	officina f	taller m
atelier de réparation d'autos (F)	Autowerkstatt f	repair shop	—	autofficina f	taller de reparaciones m
Atem (D)	—	breath	respiration f	fiato m	respiro m
à temps (F)	rechtzeitig	in time	—	in tempo	a tiempo
¡atención! (Es)	Achtung!	attention!	attention!	attenzione!	—
atender¹ (Es)	sorgen	worry about	occuper de, se	prendersi cura di	—
atender² (Es)	achtgeben	take care	faire attention	badare	—
atento (Es)	aufmerksam	attentive	attentif(-ive)	attento(a)	—
aterrizaje (Es)	Landung f	landing	atterrissage m	atterraggio m	—
aterrizar (Es)	landen	land	atterrir	atterrare	—
atestiguar (Es)	bescheinigen	certify	attester	attestare	—
at first (E)	zuerst	—	d'abord	dapprima	primero
a third (E)	Drittel n	—	tiers m	terzo m	tercio m
at home (E)	daheim	—	à la maison	a casa	en casa
a tiempo (Es)	rechtzeitig	in time	à temps	in tempo	—
at last (E)	endlich	—	enfin	finalmente	finalmente
at least¹ (E)	mindestens	—	au moins	almeno	por lo menos
at least² (E)	wenigstens	—	au moins	almeno	por lo menos
at least³ (E)	zumindest	—	au moins	per lo meno	por lo menos
atmen (D)	—	breathe	respirer	respirare	respirar
at midday (E)	mittags	—	à midi	a mezzogiorno	a mediodía
at nighttime (E)	nachts	—	la nuit	di notte	por la noche
atormentar (Es)	quälen	torture	torturer	tormentare	—
atraer (Es)	locken	attract	attirer	attirare	—
atrapar (Es)	erwischen	catch	attraper	acchiappare	—
atrás (Es)	zurück	back	de retour	indietro	—
à travers (F)	hindurch	through	—	attraverso	a través de
atravesar (Es)	überqueren	cross	traverser	attraversare	—
a través de (Es)	hindurch	through	à travers	attraverso	—
atreverse (Es)	wagen	dare	oser	osare	—
atrevido (Es)	frech	cheeky	insolent(e)	sfacciato(a)	—
atributo (Es)	Eigenschaft f	quality	qualité f	qualità f	—

atropellar

	D	E	F	I	Es
atropellar (Es)	überfahren	run over	écraser	investire	—
attaccare (I)	angreifen	attack	attaquer	—	atacar
attacher (F)	binden	bind	—	legare	atar
attack (E)	angreifen	—	attaquer	attaccare	atacar
attain (E)	gelangen	—	arriver à	arrivare a	conseguir
attaque (F)	Überfall *m*	raid	—	aggressione *f*	asalto *m*
attaquer[1] (F)	angreifen	attack	—	attaccare	atacar
attaquer[2] (F)	überfallen	raid	—	assalire	asaltar
atteggiamento (I)	Einstellung *f*	attitude	attitude *f*	—	actitud *f*
atteindre (F)	erreichen	reach	—	raggiungere	alcanzar
attendant (E)	Wärter *m*	—	gardien *m*	custode *m*	guarda *m*
attendre[1] (F)	erwarten	expect	—	aspettare	esperar
attendre[2] (F)	warten	wait	—	aspettare	esperar
attentif (F)	aufmerksam	attentive	—	attento(a)	atento(a)
attention! (E)	Achtung!	—	attention!	attenzione!	¡atención!
attention! (F)	Achtung!	attention!	—	attenzione!	¡atención!
attentive (E)	aufmerksam	—	attentif(-ive)	attento(a)	atento(a)
attento (I)	aufmerksam	attentive	attentif(-ive)	—	atento(a)
attenzione! (I)	Achtung!	attention!	attention!	—	¡atención!
atterraggio (I)	Landung *f*	landing	atterrissage *m*	—	aterrizaje *m*
atterrare (I)	landen	land	atterrir	—	aterrizar
atterrir (F)	landen	land	—	atterrare	aterrizar
atterrissage (F)	Landung *f*	landing	—	atterraggio *m*	aterrizaje *m*
Attest (D)	—	certificate	certificat *m*	certificato *m*	certificado *m*
attestare (I)	bescheinigen	certify	attester	—	atestiguar
attestation (F)	Bescheinigung *f*	certificate	—	certificato *m*	certificado *m*
attester (F)	bescheinigen	certify	—	attestare	atestiguar
at that time (E)	damals	—	à cette époque	allora	entonces
at the front (E)	vorn(e)	—	devant	davanti	delante
at the most (E)	höchstens	—	tout au plus	al massimo	a lo sumo
attimo (I)	Augenblick *m*	moment	instant *m*	—	momento *m*
attirare (I)	locken	attract	attirer	—	atraer
attirer (F)	locken	attract	—	attirare	atraer
attitude (E)	Einstellung *f*	—	attitude *f*	atteggiamento *m*	actitud *f*
attitude (F)	Einstellung *f*	attitude	—	atteggiamento *m*	actitud *f*
attività (I)	Tätigkeit *f*	activity	activité *f*	—	actividad *f*
attivo[1] (I)	aktiv	active	actif(-ive)	—	activo(a)
attivo[2] (I)	tätig	active	actif(-ive)	—	activo(a)
attore (I)	Schauspieler *m*	actor	acteur *m*	—	actor *m*
attract (E)	locken	—	attirer	attirare	atraer
attraper[1] (F)	erwischen	catch	—.	acchiappare	atrapar
attraper[2] (F)	fangen	catch	—	acchiappare	coger
attraversare (I)	überqueren	cross	traverser	—	atravesar
attraverso (I)	hindurch	through	à travers	—	a través de
atún (Es)	Thunfisch *m*	tuna	thon *m*	tonno *m*	—
auberge[1] (F)	Gasthaus *n*	inn	—	osteria *f*	posada *f*
auberge[2] (F)	Wirtshaus *n*	inn	—	osteria *f*	restaurante *m*
au cas où (F)	falls	in case	—	qualora	en caso de que

	D	E	F	I	Es
auch (D)	—	also/too	aussi	anche/pure	también
aucun (F)	keine(r,s)	none	—	nessuno(a)	ninguno(a)
au dehors (F)	außen	outside	—	fuori	afuera
au-dehors (F)	hervor	forth	—	fuori	delante
audience (E)	Publikum *n*	—	spectateurs *m pl*	pubblico *m*	público *m*
auditeur (F)	Hörer *m*	listener	—	ascoltatore *m*	oyente *m*
auf (D)	—	on/on top/onto	sur	su/sopra	sobre/en/hacia
aufbewahren (D)	—	keep	garder	conservare	guardar
aufbürden (D)	—	burden	charger	addossare	cargar
Aufenthalt (D)	—	stay	séjour *m*	soggiorno *m*	estancia *f*
Auffahrt[1] (D)	—	drive	allée *f*	salita d'ingresso *f*	entrada *f*
Auffahrt[2] (D)	—	slip road	bretelle d'accès *f*	entrata *f*	vía de acceso *f*
auffallen (D)	—	be noticeable	faire remarquer, se	dare nell'occhio	llamar la atención por algo
auffordern (D)	—	ask	inviter	invitare	exigir
Aufführung (D)	—	performance	représentation *f*	recita *f*	representación *f*
Aufgabe (D)	—	task	tâche *f*	incarico *m*	tarea *f*
Aufgang (D)	—	staircase	montée *f*	scala *f*	subida *f*
aufgeben (D)	—	give up	abandonner	rinunciare	renunciar
aufgeregt (D)	—	excited	agité(e)	eccitato(a)	excitado(a)
aufhängen (D)	—	hang up	accrocher	appendere	colgar
aufhören (D)	—	stop	arrêter	cessare	terminar
aufladen (D)	—	load	charger	caricare	cargar
auflösen (D)	—	dissolve	dénouer	sciogliere	deshacer
aufmerksam (D)	—	attentive	attentif(-ive)	attento(a)	atento(a)
Aufnahme[1] (D)	—	reception	accueil *m*	accoglienza *f*	acogida *f*
Aufnahme[2] (D)	—	photograph	photographie *f*	fotografia *f*	fotografía *f*
aufnehmen[1] (D)	—	receive	accueillir	accogliere	recibir
aufnehmen[2] (D)	—	photograph	photographier	fotografare	fotografiar
aufpassen (D)	—	pay attention	faire attention	fare attenzione	prestar atención
aufräumen (D)	—	clear away	ranger	mettere in ordine	arreglar
aufrecht (D)	—	upright	droit(e)	diritto(a)	derecho(a)
aufregen (D)	—	excite	énerver	agitare	agitar
aufregend (D)	—	exciting	énervant(e)	eccitante	emocionante
aufrichtig (D)	—	honest	sincère	onesto(a)	sincero(a)
Aufschnitt (D)	—	cold meat	charcuterie *f*	affettato *m*	fiambre *m*
Aufseher (D)	—	guard	gardien *m*	custode *m*	vigilante *m*
Aufstand (D)	—	rebellion	soulèvement *m*	insurrezione *f*	revuelta *f*
aufstehen (D)	—	get up	lever, se	alzarsi	levantarse
aufsteigen (D)	—	ascend	monter	salire	subir
aufwachen (D)	—	wake up	réveiller, se	svegliarsi	despertarse
aufwachsen (D)	—	grow up	grandir	crescere	criarse
aufwärts (D)	—	upwards	vers le haut	in su	hacia arriba
aufwecken (D)	—	wake up	réveiller	svegliare	despertar
Aufzug (D)	—	elevator	ascenseur *m*	ascensore *m*	ascensor *m*
Auge (D)	—	eye	œil *m* (yeux *pl*)	occhio *m*	ojo *m*
Augenarzt (D)	—	eye specialist	oculiste *m*	oculista *m*	oculista *m*
Augenblick (D)	—	moment	instant *m*	attimo *m*	momento *m*

	D	E	F	I	Es
augenblicklich (D)	—	instantaneous	instantané(e)	instantaneo(a)	instantáneo(a)
augmenter[1] (F)	erhöhen	raise	—	innalzare	elevar
augmenter[2] (F)	vermehren	increase	—	aumentare	aumentar
augmenter[3] (F)	zunehmen	increase	—	aumentare	aumentar
auguri (I)	Glückwunsch *m*	congratulations	félicitations *f pl*	—	felicitaciones *f pl*
August (D)	—	August	août *m*	agosto *m*	agosto *m*
August (E)	August *m*	—	août *m*	agosto *m*	agosto *m*
aujourd'hui (F)	heute	today	—	oggi	hoy
au lieu de[1] (F)	anstatt	instead of	—	invece di	en vez de
au lieu de[2] (F)	statt	instead	—	invece di	en vez de
aumentar[1] (Es)	vermehren	increase	augmenter	aumentare	—
aumentar[2] (Es)	zunehmen	increase	augmenter	aumentare	—
aumentare[1] (I)	vermehren	increase	augmenter	—	aumentar
aumentare[2] (I)	zunehmen	increase	augmenter	—	aumentar
au milieu (F)	mitten	in the middle	—	in mezzo	en medio
au milieu de (F)	inmitten	in the middle of	—	in mezzo a	en medio de
au moins[1] (F)	mindestens	at least	—	almeno	por lo menos
au moins[2] (F)	wenigstens	at least	—	almeno	por lo menos
au moins[3] (F)	zumindest	at least	—	per lo meno	por lo menos
aumône (F)	Almosen *n*	alms	—	elemosina *f*	limosna *f*
aún (Es)	noch	still	encore	ancora	—
aunque (Es)	obwohl/ obgleich	although	bien que	benché	—
aunt (E)	Tante *f*	—	tante *f*	zia *f*	tía *f*
auparavant (F)	zuvor	before	—	prima	antes
au revoir![1] (F)	wiederhören!	good-bye!	—	a risentirci!	¡adiós!
au revoir![2] (F)	wiedersehen!	good-bye!	—	arrivederci!	¡adiós!
auricular (Es)	Hörer *m*	receiver	récepteur *m*	ricevitore *m*	—
aus (D)	—	off/from/ out of	de/par/hors de	da/di	de/por
ausbilden (D)	—	educate	former	addestrare	instruir
Ausbildung (D)	—	education	formation *f*	addestramento *m*	formación *f*
Ausdruck (D)	—	expression	expression *f*	espressione *f*	término *m*
ausdrücklich (D)	—	explicit	exprès(-esse)	espresso(a)	explícito(a)
auseinander (D)	—	apart	séparer	separato(a)	lejos/distante
ausencia (Es)	Abwesenheit *f*	absence	absence *f*	assenza *f*	—
ausente (Es)	abwesend	absent	absent(e)	assente	—
Ausflug (D)	—	outing	excursion *f*	gita *f*	excursión *f*
Ausfuhr (D)	—	export	exportation *f*	esportazione *f*	exportación *f*
ausführen (D)	—	export	exporter	esportare	exportar
ausführlich (D)	—	detailed	détaillé(e)	dettagliato(a)	detallado(a)
ausfüllen (D)	—	fill in	remplir	riempire	llenar
Ausgang (D)	—	exit	sortie *f*	uscita *f*	salida *f*
ausgebucht (D)	—	fully booked	complet(-ète)	esaurito(a)	completo(a)
ausgehen (D)	—	go out	sortir	uscire	salir
ausgenommen (D)	—	except	exepté	eccetto	excepto
ausgeschlossen (D)	—	impossible	hors de question	escluso(a)	imposible
ausgezeichnet (D)	—	excellent	excellent(e)	eccellente	excelente
aushalten (D)	—	bear	supporter	sopportare	aguantar

	D	E	F	I	Es
auskennen, sich (D)	—	know one's way about	connaître, s'y	conoscere	conocer a fondo
Auskunft (D)	—	information	renseignement *m*	informazione *f*	información *f*
auslachen (D)	—	laugh at	rire de qn	deridere	reírse de
ausladen (D)	—	unload	décharger	scaricare	descargar
Ausland (D)	—	abroad	étranger *m*	estero *m*	extranjero *m*
Ausländer (D)	—	foreigner	étranger *m*	straniero *m*	extranjero *m*
ausländisch (D)	—	foreign	étranger(-ère)	straniero(a)	extranjero(a)
ausleihen (D)	—	lend	prêter	dare in prestito	prestar
auslöschen (D)	—	extinguish	éteindre	estinguere	apagar
ausmachen[1] (D)	—	agree	convenir	stabilire	convenir
ausmachen[2] (D)	—	switch off	éteindre	spegnere	apagar
Ausnahme (D)	—	exception	exception *f*	eccezione *f*	excepción *f*
auspacken (D)	—	unpack	défaire	disfare	deshacer
Ausreise (D)	—	departure	départ *m*	partenza *f*	salida *f*
ausrichten (D)	—	pass on a message	transmettre	riferire	comunicar
ausrufen (D)	—	exclaim	crier	esclamare	exclamar
ausruhen (D)	—	rest	reposer, se	riposare	descansar
Aussage (D)	—	statement	déclaration *f*	dichiarazione *f*	afirmación *f*
ausschalten (D)	—	switch off	arrêter	spegnere	desconectar
aussehen (D)	—	look	avoir l'air	avere l'aspetto	parecer
Aussehen (D)	—	appearance	apparence *f*	aspetto *m*	aspecto *m*
außen (D)	—	outside	au dehors	fuori	afuera
außer (D)	—	except	hors de	eccetto	salvo
außerdem (D)	—	besides	en outre	inoltre	además
außergewöhnlich (D)	—	exceptional	exceptionnel(le)	straordinario(a)	excepcional
außerhalb (D)	—	out of	hors de	fuori di	fuera de
äußerlich (D)	—	external	externe	esterno(a)	superficial
außerordentlich (D)	—	extraordinary	extraordinaire	straordinario(a)	extraordinario(a)
aussi[1] (F)	auch	also/too	—	anche/pure	también
aussi[2] (F)	ebenfalls	likewise	—	altrettanto	también
aussi bien (F)	sowohl	as well as	—	tanto...quanto	tanto...
Aussicht (D)	—	view	vue *f*	vista *f*	vista *f*
Aussprache[1] (D)	—	discussion	discussion *f*	discussione *f*	discusión *f*
Aussprache[2] (D)	—	pronunciation	prononciation *f*	pronuncia *f*	pronunciación *f*
aussprechen (D)	—	pronounce	prononcer	pronunciare	pronunciar
aussteigen (D)	—	get off	descendre	scendere	bajar
ausstellen (D)	—	exhibit	exposer	esporre	exponer
Ausstellung (D)	—	exhibition	exposition *f*	esposizione *f*	exposición *f*
aussuchen (D)	—	select	choisir	scegliere	escoger
Austausch (D)	—	exchange	échange *m*	scambio *m*	cambio *m*
austauschen (D)	—	exchange	échanger	scambiare	cambiar
austeilen (D)	—	distribute	distribuer	distribuire	distribuir
Auster (D)	—	oyster	huître *f*	ostrica *f*	ostra *f*
Austria (E)	Österreich *n*	—	Autriche *f*	Austria *f*	Austria *f*
Austria (Es)	Österreich *n*	Austria	Autriche *f*	Austria *f*	—
Austria (I)	Österreich *n*	Austria	Autriche *f*	—	Austria *f*
austríaco[1] (Es)	österreichisch	Austrian	autrichien(ne)	austriaco(a)	—

	D	E	F	I	Es
austríaco² (Es)	Österreicher *m*	Austrian	Autrichien *m*	austriaco *m*	—
austriaco¹ (I)	österreichisch	Austrian	autrichien(ne)	—	austríaco(a)
austriaco² (I)	Österreicher *m*	Austrian	Autrichien *m*	—	austríaco *m*
Austrian¹ (E)	österreichisch	—	autrichien(ne)	austriaco(a)	austríaco(a)
Austrian² (E)	Österreicher *m*	—	Autrichien *m*	austriaco *m*	austríaco *m*
ausüben (D)	—	practise	exercer	esercitare	ejercer
Ausverkauf (D)	—	sale	soldes *m pl*	saldi *m pl*	liquidación *f*
ausverkauft (D)	—	sold out	épuisé(e)	esaurito(a)	vendido(a)
Auswahl (D)	—	choice	choix *m*	scelta *f*	elección *f*
auswählen (D)	—	choose	choisir	scegliere	eligir
auswandern (D)	—	emigrate	émigrer	emigrare	emigrar
auswärts (D)	—	out(wards)	à l'extérieur	fuori	fuera
Ausweis (D)	—	passport	pièce d'identité *f*	documento d'identità *m*	documento de identidad *m*
auswendig (D)	—	by heart	par cœur	a memoria	de memoria
ausziehen¹ (D)	—	take off	enlever	levare	quitarse
ausziehen² (D)	—	move out	déménager	sloggiare	mudarse
autant que (F)	soweit	as far as	—	fin dove	hasta tanto
auteur (F)	Autor *m*	author	—	autore *m*	autor(a) *m(f)*
author (E)	Autor *m*	—	auteur *m*	autore *m*	autor(a) *m(f)*
authorities (E)	Behörde *f*	—	autorités *f pl*	autorità *f pl*	autoridades *f pl*
authority (E)	Vollmacht *f*	—	procuration *f*	delega *f*	poder *m*
authorization (E)	Genehmigung *f*	—	autorisation *f*	permesso *m*	permiso *m*
autista¹ (I)	Chauffeur *m*	chauffeur	chauffeur *m*	—	chófer *m*
autista² (I)	Fahrer *m*	driver	conducteur *m*	—	conductor *m*
Auto (D)	—	car	voiture *f*	automobile *f* / macchina *f*	coche *m*
Autobahn (D)	—	motorway	autoroute *f*	autostrada *f*	autopista *f*
autobús¹ (Es)	Bus *m*	bus	bus *m*	autobus *m*	—
autobús² (Es)	Omnibus *m*	omnibus	autobus *m*	autobus *m*	—
autobus (F)	Omnibus *m*	omnibus	—	autobus *m*	autobús *m*
autobus¹ (I)	Bus *m*	bus	bus *m*	—	autobús *m*
autobus² (I)	Omnibus *m*	omnibus	autobus *m*	—	autobús *m*
autoestopista (Es)	Anhalter *m*	hitch-hiker	auto-stoppeur *m*	autostoppista *m*	—
autofficina (I)	Autowerkstatt *f*	repair shop	atelier de réparation d'autos *m*	—	taller de reparaciones *m*
Automat (D)	—	vending machine	distributeur automatique *m*	distributore automatico *m*	distribuidor automático *m*
automatical (E)	automatisch	—	automatique	automatico(a)	automático(a)
automatico (I)	automatisch	automatic	automatique	—	automático(a)
automático (Es)	automatisch	automatic	automatique	automatico(a)	—
automatique (F)	automatisch	automatic	—	automatico(a)	automático(a)
automatisch (D)	—	automatic	automatique	automatico(a)	automático(a)
automne (F)	Herbst *m*	autumn	—	autunno *m*	otoño *m*
automobile (I)	Auto *n*	car	voiture *f*	—	coche *m*
autopista (Es)	Autobahn *f*	motorway	autoroute *f*	autostrada *f*	—
Autor (D)	—	author	auteur *m*	autore *m*	autor(a) *m(f)*
autor (Es)	Autor *m*	author	auteur *m*	autore *m*	—
autore (I)	Autor *m*	author	auteur *m*	—	autor(a) *m(f)*

	D	E	F	I	Es
autoridades (Es)	Behörde *f*	authorities	autorités *f pl*	autorità *f pl*	—
autorisation (F)	Genehmigung *f*	authorization	—	permesso *m*	permiso *m*
autoriser (F)	genehmigen	approve	—	approvare	permitir
autorità (I)	Behörde *f*	authorities	autorités *f pl*	—	autoridades *f pl*
autorités (F)	Behörde *f*	authorities	—	autorità *f pl*	autoridades *f pl*
autoroute (F)	Autobahn *f*	motorway	—	autostrada *f*	autopista *f*
autoservicio (Es)	Selbstbedienung *f*	self service	libre-service *m*	self-service *m*	—
auto-stoppeur (F)	Anhalter *m*	hitch-hiker	—	autostoppista *m*	autoestopista m
autostoppista (I)	Anhalter *m*	hitch-hiker	auto-stoppeur *m*	—	autoestopista *m*
autostrada (I)	Autobahn *f*	motorway	autoroute *f*	—	autopista *f*
Autounfall (D)	—	car accident	accident de voiture *m*	incidente stradale *m*	accidente de automóvil *m*
autour (F)	herum	around	—	intorno	alrededor
autour de (F)	um	at/around	—	intorno a/a	alrededor de/a las
Autowerkstatt (D)	—	repair shop	atelier de réparation d'autos *m*	autofficina *f*	taller de reparaciones *m*
autre (F)	andere(r,s)	other	—	altro(a)	otra(o)
autrefois (F)	früher	earlier	—	prima	antes
autrement (F)	sonst	otherwise	—	altrimenti	por lo demás
Autriche (F)	Österreich *n*	Austria	—	Austria *f*	Austria *f*
autrichien (F)	österreichisch	Austrian	—	austriaco(a)	austríaco(a)
Autrichien (F)	Österreicher *m*	Austrian	—	austriaco	austríaco *m*
autumn (E)	Herbst *m*	—	automne *m*	autunno *m*	otoño *m*
autunno (I)	Herbst *m*	autumn	automne *m*	—	otoño *m*
available[1] (E)	erhältlich	—	en vente	acquistabile	que puede adquirirse
available[2] (E)	vorhanden	—	présent(e)	disponibile	presente
avaler (F)	schlucken	swallow	—	inghiottire	tragar
avancer (F)	vorgehen	proceed	—	procedere	proceder
avant (F)	vorher	before	—	prima	antes
avantage (F)	Vorteil *m*	advantage	—	vantaggio *m*	ventaja *f*
avant-dernier (F)	vorletzte(r,s)	one before last	—	penultimo(a)	penúltimo(a)
avant-hier (F)	vorgestern	day before yesterday	—	l'altro ieri	anteayer
avanti[1] (I)	voraus	ahead	en avant	—	delante
avanti[2] (I)	vorwärts	forward(s)	en avant	—	adelante
avanti! (I)	los!	off!	allons-y!	—	¡adelante!
avant que[1] (F)	bevor	before	—	prima che	antes que
avant que[2] (F)	ehe	before	—	prima che	antes que
avanzare (I)	übrigbleiben	be left	rester	—	quedar
avare (F)	geizig	mean	—	avaro(a)	avaro(a)
avaro (I)	geizig	mean	avare	—	avaro(a)
avaro (Es)	geizig	mean	avare	avaro(a)	—
avec (F)	mit	with	—	con	con
avec cela (F)	damit	with it	—	con questo	con ello
a veces (Es)	manchmal	sometimes	quelquefois	talvolta	—
avec plaisir (F)	gern	willingly	—	volentieri	con gusto
avec succès (F)	erfolgreich	successful	—	pieno(a) di successi	afortunado(a)
avenir (F)	Zukunft *f*	future	—	futuro *m*	futuro *m*

	D	E	F	I	Es
aventura (Es)	Abenteuer n	adventure	aventure f	avventura f	—
aventure (F)	Abenteuer n	adventure	—	avventura f	aventura f
average (E)	durchschnittlich	—	moyen(ne)	medio(a)	medio(a)
aver bisogno di¹ (I)	benötigen/ brauchen	need	avoir besoin de	—	necesitar
aver bisogno di² (I)	bedürfen	need	nécessiter	—	necesitar
avere (I)	haben	have	avoir	—	tener
avere freddo (I)	frieren	be cold	avoir froid	—	tener frío
avere intenzione di (I)	vorhaben	intend	avoir l'intention de	—	tener la intención de
avere l'aspetto (I)	aussehen	look	avoir l'air	—	parecer
avere (I) (l')intenzione di (I)	beabsichtigen	intend	avoir l'intention de	—	proyectar
avere luogo (I)	stattfinden	take place	avoir lieu	—	tener lugar
avería (Es)	Panne f	breakdown	panne f	panna f	—
aves (Es)	Geflügel n	poultry	volaille f	pollame m	—
aveugle (F)	blind	blind	—	cieco(a)	ciego(a)
avión (Es)	Flugzeug n	aeroplane	avion m	aereo m	—
avion (F)	Flugzeug n	aeroplane	—	aereo m	avión m
avis (F)	Ansicht f	opinion	—	opinione f	opinión f
avisar (Es)	benachrichtigen	inform	informer	informare	—
aviso (Es)	Meldung f	report	annonce f	annuncio m	—
avispa (Es)	Wespe f	wasp	guêpe f	vespa f	—
avocat (F)	Rechtsanwalt m	lawyer	—	avvocato m	abogado m
avoid (E)	meiden/vermeiden	—	éviter	evitare	evitar
avoir (F)	haben	have	—	avere	tener
avoir besoin de (F)	benötigen/ brauchen	need	—	aver bisogno di	necesitar
avoir confiance (F)	vertrauen	trust	—	fidarsi	confiar
avoir froid (F)	frieren	be cold	—	avere freddo	tener frío
avoir honte (F)	schämen	be ashamed	—	vergognarsi	tener vergüenza
avoir l'air (F)	aussehen	look	—	avere l'aspetto	parecer
avoir le droit (F)	dürfen	be allowed	—	potere	poder
avoir lieu (F)	stattfinden	take place	—	avere luogo	tener lugar
avoir l'intention de¹ (F)	beabsichtigen	intend	—	avere (l')intenzione di	proyectar
avoir l'intention de² (F)	vorhaben	intend	—	avere intenzione di	tener la intención de
avoir un rhume (F)	erkältet sein	have a cold	—	essere raffreddato(a)	estar acatarrado(a)
avoisinant (F)	benachbart	neighbouring	—	vicino	vecino
à voix basse (F)	leise	quietly	—	a bassa voce	sin ruido
a voluntad (Es)	beliebig	any	n'importe quel	qualsiasi	—
avouer (F)	gestehen	confess	—	confessare	confesar
avril (F)	April m	April	—	aprile m	abril m
avveduto (I)	besonnen	sensible	réfléchi(e)	—	sensato(a)
avvenimento (I)	Ereignis n	event	événement m	—	suceso m
avventura (I)	Abenteuer n	adventure	aventure f	—	aventura f
avversario (I)	Gegner m	opponent	adversaire m	—	adversario m
avvicinarsi (I)	nähern, sich	approach	approcher, se	—	acercarse
avvocato (I)	Rechtsanwalt m	lawyer	avocat m	—	abogado m

	D	E	F	I	Es
avvolgere[1] (I)	einwickeln	wrap up	envelopper	—	envolver
avvolgere[2] (I)	wickeln	wind	enrouler	—	envolver
awake (E)	wach	—	réveillé(e)	sveglio(a)	despierto(a)
away[1] (E)	fort	—	parti	via	lejos
away[2] (E)	weg	—	pas là	via	fuera
ayer (Es)	gestern	yesterday	hier	ieri	—
ayuda (Es)	Hilfe f	help	aide f	aiuto m	—
ayudar (Es)	helfen	help	aider	aiutare	—
ayudar a alguien (Es)	behilflich sein	help s.b.	aider qn	aiutare	—
ayunar (Es)	fasten	fast	jeûner	digiunare	—
ayuntamiento (Es)	Rathaus n	town hall	mairie f	municipio m	—
azafata (Es)	Stewardeß m	stewardess	hôtesse de l'air f	hostess f	—
azione (I)	Tat f	deed	action f	—	acción f
azúcar (Es)	Zucker m	sugar	sucre m	zucchero m	—
azul (Es)	blau	blue	bleu(e)	blu	—
Baby (D)	—	baby	bébé m	bebè m	bebé m
baby (E)	Baby n	—	bébé m	bebè m	bebé m
bac (F)	Fähre f	ferry	—	traghetto m	transbordador m
baccalauréat (F)	Abitur n	German school leaving examinations	—	maturità f	bachillerato m
bachelor (E)	Junggeselle m	—	célibataire m	scapolo m	soltero m
bachillerato (Es)	Abitur n	German school leaving examinations	baccalauréat m	maturità f	—
baciare (I)	küssen	kiss	embrasser	—	besar
bacio (I)	Kuß m	kiss	baiser m	—	beso m
back[1] (E)	Rücken m	—	dos m	schiena f	espalda m
back[2] (E)	zurück	—	de retour	indietro	atrás
backen (D)	—	bake	faire cuire	cuocere (al forno)	cocer (al horno)
Bäckerei (D)	—	bakery	boulangerie f	panetteria f	panadería f
backwards (E)	rückwärts	—	en arrière	in dietro	marcha atrás
bacon (E)	Speck m	—	lard m	lardo m	tocino m
Bad (D)	—	bath	bain m	bagno m	baño m
bad[1] (E)	schlecht	—	mauvais(e)	cattivo(a)	malo(a)
bad[2] (E)	übel	—	mauvais(e)	cattivo(a)	malo(a)
badare (I)	achtgeben	take care	faire attention	—	atender
Badeanzug (D)	—	swimsuit	maillot de bain m	costume da bagno m	traje de baño m
Badehose (D)	—	swimming trunks	maillot slip de bain m	costume da bagno m	bañador m
Bademeister (D)	—	baths attendant	maître baigneur m	bagnino m	bañero m
baden (D)	—	bathe	baigner, se	fare il bagno	bañarse
Badewanne (D)	—	bath tub	baignoire f	vasca da bagno f	bañera f
Badezimmer (D)	—	bathroom	salle de bains f	stanza da bagno f	cuarto de baño m
bad luck (E)	Pech n	—	malchance f	sfortuna f	mala suerte f
baffi (I)	Schnurrbart m	moustache	moustache f	—	bigote m
bag (E)	Tüte f	—	sac m	sacchetto m	bolsa f
bagage à main (F)	Handgepäck n	hand-luggage		bagaglio a mano m	equipaje de mano m
bagages (F)	Gepäck n	luggage	—	bagaglio m	equipaje m

	D	E	F	I	Es
bagaglio (I)	Gepäck n	luggage	bagages m pl	—	equipaje m
bagaglio a mano (I)	Handgepäck n	hand-luggage	bagage à main m	—	equipaje de mano m
bagnato (I)	naß	wet	mouillé(e)	—	húmedo(a)
bagnino (I)	Bademeister m	baths attendant	maître baigneur m	—	bañero m
bagno (I)	Bad n	bath	bain m	—	baño m
bague (F)	Ring m	ring	—	anello m	sortija f
Bahnhof (D)	—	station	gare f	stazione f	estación f
Bahre (D)	—	stretcher	brancard m	barella f	camilla f
baigner, se (F)	baden	bathe	—	fare il bagno	bañarse
baignoire (F)	Badewanne f	bath tub	—	vasca da bagno f	bañera f
bailar (Es)	tanzen	dance	danser	ballare	—
baille (Es)	Tanz m	dance	danse f	ballo m	—
bain (F)	Bad n	bath	—	bagno m	baño m
baiser (F)	Kuß m	kiss	—	bacio m	beso m
baisser[1] (F)	herabsetzen	lower	—	diminuire	rebajar
baisser[2] (F)	senken	lower	—	abbassare	bajar
bajar[1] (Es)	aussteigen	get off	descendre	scendere	—
bajar[2] (Es)	hinuntergehen	descend	descendre	scendere	—
bajar[3] (Es)	senken	lower	baisser	abbassare	—
bajo (Es)	niedrig	low	bas(se)	basso(a)	—
bake (E)	backen	—	faire cuire	cuocere (al forno)	cocer (al horno)
bakery (E)	Bäckerei f	—	boulangerie f	panetteria f	panadería f
balai (F)	Besen m	broom	—	scopa f	escoba f
balance (F)	Waage f	scales	—	bilancia f	balanza f
balancer, se (F)	schaukeln	swing	—	dondolare	columpiarse
balanza (Es)	Waage f	scales	balance f	bilancia f	—
balayer[1] (F)	fegen	sweep	—	scopare	barrer
balayer[2] (F)	kehren	sweep	—	scopare	barrer
balbettare (I)	stottern	stutter	bégayer	—	tartamudear
balcón (Es)	Balkon m	balcony	balcon m	balcone m	—
balcon (F)	Balkon m	balcony	—	balcone m	balcón m
balcone (I)	Balkon m	balcony	balcon m	—	balcón m
balcony (E)	Balkon m	—	balcon m	balcone m	balcón m
bald (D)	—	soon	bientôt	presto	pronto
bald (E)	kahl	—	chauve	calvo(a)	calvo(a)
Balkon (D)	—	balcony	balcon m	balcone m	balcón m
Ball (D)	—	ball	balle f	palla f	pelota f
ball (E)	Ball m	—	balle f	palla f	pelota f
ballare (I)	tanzen	dance	danser	—	bailar
balle (F)	Ball m	ball	—	palla f	pelota f
ballo (I)	Tanz m	dance	danse f	—	baile f
bambino (I)	Kind n	child	enfant m	—	niño m
bambola (I)	Puppe f	doll	poupée f	—	muñeca f
bañador (Es)	Badehose f	swimming trunks	maillot slip de bain m	costume da bagno m	—
banana (E)	Banane f	—	banane f	banana f	plátano m
banana (I)	Banane f	banana	banane f	—	plátano m

	D	E	F	I	Es
Banane (D)	—	banana	banane *f*	banana *f*	plátano *m*
banane (F)	Banane *f*	banana	—	banana *f*	plátano *m*
bañarse (Es)	baden	bathe	baigner, se	fare il bagno	—
banca (I)	Bank *f*	bank	banque *f*	—	banco *m*
banco (Es)	Bank *f*	bank	banque *f*	banca *f*	—
banco di vendita (I)	Ladentisch *m*	counter	comptoir *m*	—	mostrador *m*
banconota (I)	Schein *m*	note	billet *m*	—	billete *m*
Band (D)	—	ribbon	bandeau *m*	nastro *m*	cinta *f*
band[1] (E)	Kapelle *f*	—	orchestre *m*	banda *f*	banda *f*
band[2] (E)	Schar *f*	—	bande *f*	schiera *f*	grupo *m*
banda (Es)	Kapelle *f*	band	orchestre *m*	banda *f*	—
banda (I)	Kapelle *f*	band	orchestre *m*	—	banda *f*
bandage (E)	Binde *m*	—	bandage *m*	fascia *f*	faja *f*
bandage (F)	Binde *m*	bandage	—	fascia *f*	faja *f*
bande (F)	Schar *f*	band	—	schiera *f*	grupo *m*
bandeau (F)	Band *n*	ribbon	—	nastro *m*	cinta *f*
bandeja (Es)	Tablett *n*	tray	plateau *m*	vassoio *m*	—
bande magnétique (F)	Tonband *n*	tape	—	nastro magnetico *m*	cinta magnetofónica *f*
bandera[1] (Es)	Fahne *f*	flag	drapeau *m*	bandiera *f*	—
bandera[2] (Es)	Flagge *f*	flag	pavillon *m*	bandiera *f*	—
bandiera[1] (I)	Flagge *f*	flag	pavillon *m*	—	bandera *f*
bandiera[2] (I)	Fahne *f*	flag	drapeau *m*	—	bandera *f*
bañera (Es)	Badewanne *f*	bath tub	baignoire *f*	vasca da bagno *f*	—
bañero (Es)	Bademeister *m*	baths attendant	maître baigneur *m*	bagnino *m*	—
Bank (D)	—	bank	banque *f*	banca *f*	banco *m*
bank (E)	Bank *f*	—	banque *f*	banca *f*	banco *m*
baño (Es)	Bad *n*	bath	bain *m*	bagno *m*	—
banque (F)	Bank *f*	bank	—	banca *f*	banco *m*
baptême (F)	Taufe *f*	baptism	—	battesimo *m*	bautizo *m*
baptism (E)	Taufe *f*	—	baptême *m*	battesimo *m*	bautizo *m*
Bär (D)	—	bear	ours *m*	orso *m*	oso *m*
bara (I)	Sarg *m*	coffin	cercueil *m*	—	ataúd *m*
barato (Es)	billig	cheap	bon marché(e)	a buon mercato	—
barba (Es)	Bart *m*	beard	barbe *f*	barba *f*	—
barba (I)	Bart *m*	beard	barbe *f*	—	barba *f*
barbe (F)	Bart *m*	beard	—	barba *f*	barba *f*
barbilla (Es)	Kinn *n*	chin	menton *m*	mento *m*	—
barca (I)	Boot	boat	bateau *m*	—	bote *m*
barcaza (Es)	Kahn *m*	barge	barque *f*	chiatta *f*	—
barco (Es)	Schiff *n*	ship	navire *m*	nave *f*	—
barcollare[1] (I)	taumeln	reel	tituber	—	vacilar
barcollare[2] (I)	wanken	stagger	chanceler	—	vacilar
barella (I)	Bahre *f*	stretcher	brancard *m*	—	camilla *f*
barge (E)	Kahn *m*	—	barque *f*	chiatta *f*	barcaza *f*
Bargeld (D)	—	cash	espèces *f pl*	contanti *m pl*	dinero al contado *m*
barque (F)	Kahn *m*	barge	—	chiatta *f*	barcaza *f*

	D	E	F	I	Es
barre (F)	Stange *f*	pole	—	asta *f*	vara *f*
barrel (E)	Tonne *f*	—	tonneau *m*	botte *f*	barril *m*
barrer[1] (Es)	fegen	sweep	balayer	scopare	—
barrer[2] (Es)	kehren	sweep	balayer	scopare	—
barrera (Es)	Schranke *f*	barrier	barrière *f*	sbarra *f*	—
barrier (E)	Schranke *f*	—	barrière *f*	sbarra *f*	barrera *f*
barrière (F)	Schranke *f*	barrier	—	sbarra *f*	barrera *f*
barril (Es)	Tonne *f*	barrel	tonneau *m*	botte *f*	—
barro (Es)	Schlamm *m*	mud	boue *f*	fango *m*	—
Bart (D)	—	beard	barbe *f*	barba *f*	barba *f*
barzelletta (I)	Witz *m*	joke	plaisanterie *f*	—	chiste *m*
bas[1] (F)	Strumpf *m*	stocking	—	calza *f*	media *f*
bas[2] (F)	niedrig	low	—	basso(a)	bajo(a)
bas[3] (F)	nieder	inferior	—	in basso	abajo
base (E)	Grundfläche *f*	—	base *f*	base *f*	base *f*
base[1] (Es)	Basis *f*	basis	base *f*	base *f*	—
base[2] (Es)	Grundfläche *f*	base	base *f*	base *f*	—
base[1] (F)	Basis *f*	basis	—	base *f*	base *f*
base[2] (F)	Grundfläche *f*	base	—	base *f*	base *f*
base[1] (I)	Basis *f*	basis	base *f*	—	base *f*
base[2] (I)	Grundfläche *f*	base	base *f*	—	base *f*
basilare (I)	grundsätzlich	fundamental	par principe	—	por principio
Basis (D)	—	basis	base *f*	base *f*	base *f*
basis (E)	Basis *f*	—	base *f*	base *f*	base *f*
basket (E)	Korb *m*	—	panier *m*	cesto *m*	cesta *f*
bassa marea (I)	Ebbe *f*	low tide	marée basse *f*	—	marea baja *f*
bassa stagione (I)	Vorsaison *f*	low season	basse saison *f*	—	pretemporada *f*
basse saison (F)	Vorsaison *f*	low season	—	bassa stagione *f*	pretemporada *f*
basso (I)	niedrig	low	bas(se)	—	bajo(a)
bastante[1] (Es)	genug	enough	assez	abbastanza	—
bastante[2] (Es)	ziemlich	quite	assez	abbastanza	—
bastar (Es)	genügen	suffice	suffire	bastare	—
bastare (I)	genügen	suffice	suffire	—	bastar
bastón (Es)	Stock *m*	stick	bâton *m*	bastone *m*	—
bastone (I)	Stock *m*	stick	bâton *m*	—	bastón *m*
basura (Es)	Abfall *m*	rubbish	déchets *m pl*	immondizia *f*	—
bateau (F)	Boot	boat	—	barca *f*	bote *m*
batería (Es)	Batterie *f*	battery	batterie *f*	batteria *f*	—
bath (E)	Bad *n*	—	bain *m*	bagno *m*	baño *m*
bathe (E)	baden	—	baigner, se	fare il bagno	bañarse
bathroom (E)	Badezimmer *n*	—	salle de bains *f*	stanza da bagno *f*	cuarto de baño *m*
baths attendant (E)	Bademeister *m*	—	maître baigneur *m*	bagnino *m*	bañero *m*
bath tub (E)	Badewanne *f*	—	baignoire *f*	vasca da bagno *f*	bañera *f*
bâtiment (F)	Gebäude *n*	building	—	edificio *m*	edificio *m*
bâton (F)	Stock *m*	stick	—	bastone *m*	bastón *m*
battere[1] (I)	pochen	knock	frapper	—	golpear
battere[2] (I)	schlagen	hit	battre	—	golpear

	D	E	F	I	Es
battere a macchina (I)	tippen	type	taper (à la machine)	—	escribir a máquina
battere le mani (I)	klatschen	applaud	applaudir	—	aplaudir
batteria (I)	Batterie f	battery	batterie f	—	batería f
Batterie (D)	—	battery	batterie f	batteria f	batería f
batterie (F)	Batterie f	battery	—	batteria f	batería f
battery (E)	Batterie f	—	batterie f	batteria f	batería f
battesimo (I)	Taufe f	baptism	baptême m	—	bautizo m
battre (F)	schlagen	hit	—	battere	golpear
battre, se (F)	kämpfen	fight	—	combattere	luchar
Bau (D)	—	construction	construction f	costruzione f	construcción f
Bauch (D)	—	stomach	ventre m	pancia f	vientre m
bauen (D)	—	build	construire	costruire	construir
Bauer (D)	—	farmer	paysan m	contadino m	campesino m
Bauernhof (D)	—	farmhouse	ferme f	fattoria f	granja f
Baum (D)	—	tree	arbre m	albero m	árbol m
Baumwolle (D)	—	cotton	coton m	cotone m	algodón m
bautizo (Es)	Taufe f	baptism	baptême m	battesimo m	—
bavarder (F)	schwatzen	chatter	—	chiacchierare	charlar
be (E)	sein	—	être	essere/stare	ser/estar
beabsichtigen (D)	—	intend	avoir l'intention de	avere (l')intenzione di	proyectar
beach (E)	Strand m	—	plage f	spiaggia f	playa f
beachten (D)	—	take notice of	considérer	osservare	prestar atención a
be allowed (E)	dürfen	—	avoir le droit	potere	poder
Beamter (D)	—	civil servant	fonctionnaire m	impiegato statale m	funcionario m
bean (E)	Bohne f	—	haricot m	fagiolo m	judía f
beantworten (D)	—	answer	répondre à	rispondere a	responder a
bear[1] (E)	aushalten	—	supporter	sopportare	aguantar
bear[2] (E)	Bär m	—	ours m	orso m	oso m
bear[3] (E)	ertragen	—	supporter	sopportare	soportar
beard (E)	Bart m	—	barbe f	barba f	barba f
be ashamed (E)	schämen	—	avoir honte	vergognarsi	tener vergüenza
be astonished (E)	staunen	—	étonner, se	stupirsi	asombrarse
beau (F)	schön	beautiful	—	bello(a)	hermoso(a)
beaucoup de[1] (F)	viele	many/a lot of	—	molti(e)	muchos(as)
beaucoup de[2] (F)	viel	a lot of	—	molto(a)	mucho(a)
beau-frère (F)	Schwager m	brother-in-law	—	cognato m	cuñado m
beauftragen (D)	—	instruct	charger de	incaricare	encargar
beauté (F)	Schönheit f	beauty	—	bellezza f	belleza f
beautiful (E)	schön	—	beau, bel, belle	bello(a)	hermoso(a)
beauty (E)	Schönheit f	—	beauté f	bellezza f	belleza f
beaux-parents (F)	Schwiegereltern pl	parents-in-law	—	suoceri m pl	suegros m pl
bebé (Es)	Baby n	baby	bébé m	bebè m	—
bébé (F)	Baby n	baby	—	bebè m	bebé m
bebè (I)	Baby n	baby	bébé m	—	bebé m
beber (Es)	trinken	drink	boire	bere	—
bebida (Es)	Getränk n	drink	boisson f	bevanda f	—

	D	E	F	I	Es
be called (E)	heißen	—	appeler, se	chiamarsi	llamarse
because (E)	weil	—	parce que	perché	porque
because of (E)	wegen	—	à cause de	a causa di	a causa de
be cold (E)	frieren	—	avoir froid	avere freddo	tener frío
become (E)	werden	—	devenir	diventare	llegar
bed (E)	Bett *n*	—	lit *m*	letto *m*	cama *f*
bedanken (D)	—	say thank you	remercier	ringraziare	agradecer algo
bedauern (D)	—	regret	regretter	deplorare	lamentar
Bedauern (D)	—	regret	regret *m*	dispiacere *m*	compasión *f*
bedecken (D)	—	cover	couvrir	coprire	cubrir
bedeckt (D)	—	covered	couvert(e)	coperto(a)	cubierto(a)
be defeated (E)	unterliegen	—	être vaincu(e) par qn	soccombere	sucumbir
be descended (E)	abstammen	—	descendre	discendere	descender
bedeuten (D)	—	mean	signifier	significare	significar
bedeutend (D)	—	significant	important(e)	importante	importante
Bedeutung (D)	—	meaning	signification *f*	significato *m*	significado *m*
bedienen (D)	—	serve	servir	servire	servir
Bedienung (D)	—	service	service *m*	servizio *m*	servicio *m*
Bedingung (D)	—	condition	condition *f*	condizione *f*	condición *f*
bedrohen (D)	—	threaten	menacer	minacciare	amenazar
bedroom (E)	Schlafzimmer *n*	—	chambre à coucher *f*	camera da letto *f*	dormitorio *m*
bedürfen (D)	—	need	nécessiter	aver bisogno di	necesitar
Bedürfnis (D)	—	need	besoin *m*	bisogno *m*	necesidad *f*
beef (E)	Rindfleisch *n*	—	viande de bœuf *f*	carne di manzo *f*	carne de vaca *f*
beeilen, sich (D)	—	hurry up	dépêcher, se	affrettarsi	darse prisa
beeinflussen (D)	—	influence	influencer	influenzare	influir
beenden (D)	—	stop	terminer	terminare	terminar
beer (E)	Bier *n*	—	bière *f*	birra *f*	cerveza *f*
beerben (D)	—	inherit from	hériter	ereditare	heredar
Beerdigung (D)	—	funeral	enterrement *m*	funerale *m*	entierro *m*
beetle (E)	Käfer *m*	—	coléoptère *m*	coleottero *m*	escarabajo *m*
Befehl (D)	—	order	ordre *m*	ordine *m*	mando *m*
befestigen (D)	—	fasten	fixer	fissare	sujetar
befinden, sich (D)	—	feel	trouver, se	trovarsi	encontrarse
before[1] (E)	bevor	—	avant que	prima che	antes que
before[2] (E)	ehe	—	avant que	prima che	antes que
before[3] (E)	vor	—	devant/avant	davanti a	delante de
before[4] (E)	vorher	—	avant	prima	antes
before[5] (E)	zuvor	—	auparavant	prima	antes
before noon (E)	Vormittag *m*	—	matinée *f*	mattina *f*	mañana *f*
befreundet (D)	—	friendly	ami(e)	amico(a)	amigo(a)
befriedigen (D)	—	satisfy	satisfaire	soddisfare	satisfacer
befürchten (D)	—	fear	craindre	temere	temer
begabt (D)	—	gifted	doué(e)	dotato(a)	dotado(a)
bégayer (F)	stottern	stutter	—	balbettare	tartamudear
begegnen (D)	—	meet	rencontrer	incontrare	encontrar

	D	E	F	I	Es
begeistern (D)	—	inspire	enthousiasmer	entusiasmare	entusiasmar
begeistert (D)	—	enthusiastic	enthousiaste	entusiasta	entusiasta
begin (E)	beginnen	—	commencer	cominciare	empezar
Beginn (D)	—	beginning	commencement *m*	inizio *m*	principio *m*
beginnen (D)	—	begin	commencer	cominciare	empezar
beginner (E)	Anfänger *m*	—	débutant	principiante *m*	principante *m*
beginning¹ (E)	Anfang *m*	—	commencement *m*	inizio *m*	inicio *m*
beginning² (E)	Beginn *m*	—	commencement *m*	inizio *m*	principio *m*
be glad (E)	freuen, sich	—	être heureux (-euse)	rallegrarsi	alegrarse
begleiten (D)	—	accompany	accompagner	accompagnare	acompañar
begreifen (D)	—	comprehend	comprendre	comprendere	comprender
begrenzen (D)	—	limit	limiter	limitare	limitar
begrüßen (D)	—	greet	saluer	salutare	saludar
behalten (D)	—	keep	garder	tenere	retener
Behälter (D)	—	container	récipient *m*	recipiente *m*	recipiente *m*
behandeln (D)	—	treat	traiter	trattare	tratar
Behandlung (D)	—	treatment	traitement *m*	trattamento *m*	tratamiento *m*
behaupten (D)	—	assert	affirmer	affermare	afirmar
behave (E)	benehmen, sich	—	comporter, se	comportarsi	comportarse
behaviour (E)	Benehmen *n*	—	conduite *f*	comportamento *m*	comportamiento *m*
behilflich sein (D)	—	help s.b.	aider qn	aiutare	ayudar a alguien
behind (E)	hinten	—	derrière	dietro	detrás
behind it (E)	dahinter	—	derrière	dietro	detrás
Behörde (D)	—	authorities	autorités *f pl*	autorità *f pl*	autoridad *f*
bei (D)	—	at/near	chez/près de	da/presso	cerca de/ junto a
beide (D)	—	both	tous/toutes les deux	entrambi(e)	ambos(as)
Beifahrer (D)	—	passenger	passager *m*	passeggero *m*	pasajero *m*
Beifall (D)	—	applause	applaudissements *m pl*	applauso *m*	aplauso *m*
Beilage (D)	—	supplement	supplément *m*	supplemento *m*	suplemento *m*
Beileid (D)	—	condolence	condoléances *f pl*	condoglianza *f*	pésame *m*
Bein (D)	—	leg	jambe *f*	gamba *f*	pierna *f*
beinahe (D)	—	nearly	presque	circa/quasi	casi
being (E)	Wesen *n*	—	être *m*	essere *m*	ser *m*
Beispiel (D)	—	example	exemple *m*	esempio *m*	ejemplo *m*
beißen (D)	—	bite	mordre	mordere	morder
beistehen (D)	—	stand by s.b.	assister	assistere	asistir a
Beitrag (D)	—	contribution	contribution *f*	contributo *m*	cuota *f*
bejahen (D)	—	agree with	répondre par l'affirmative à	approvare	afirmar
bekannt (D)	—	well known	connu(e)	conosciuto(a)	conocido(a)
Bekannter (D)	—	aquaintance	ami *m*	conoscente *m*	conocido *m*
bekanntlich (D)	—	as is well known	comme on sait	com'è noto	notoriamente
Bekenntnis (D)	—	confession	confession *f*	confessione *f*	confesión *f*
beklagen (D)	—	deplore	plaindre de, se	lamentare	quejarse
bekommen (D)	—	get	recevoir	ricevere	recibir
belästigen (D)	—	annoy	importuner	importunare	molestar

	D	E	F	I	Es
be late (E)	verspäten	—	être en retard	ritardare	llevar retraso
belebt (D)	—	lively	animé(e)	animato(a)	animado(a)
be left (E)	übrigbleiben	—	rester	avanzare	quedar
beleidigen (D)	—	insult	offenser	offendere	ofender
Beleidigung (D)	—	insult	offense f	offesa f	ofensa f
beleuchten (D)	—	illuminate	éclairer	illuminare	iluminar
Beleuchtung (D)	—	lighting	éclairage m	illuminazione f	iluminación f
belga (Es)	Belgier m	Belgian	Belge m	belga m	—
belga (I)	Belgier m	Belgian	Belge m	—	belga m
Belge (F)	Belgier m	Belgian	—	belga m	belga m
Belgian (E)	Belgier m	—	Belge m	belga m	belga m
Bélgica (Es)	Belgien n	Belgium	Belgique f	Belgio f	—
Belgien (D)	—	Belgium	Belgique f	Belgio f	Bélgica f
Belgier (D)	—	Belgian	Belge m	belga m	belga m
Belgio (I)	Belgien n	Belgium	Belgique f	—	Bélgica f
Belgique (F)	Belgien n	Belgium	—	Belgio f	Bélgica f
Belgium (E)	Belgien n	—	Belgique f	Belgio f	Bélgica f
Belieben (D)	—	will	plaisir m	piacere m	placer m
beliebig (D)	—	any	n'importe quel	qualsiasi	a voluntad
beliebt (D)	—	popular	populaire	popolare	estimado(a)
believe (E)	glauben	—	croire	credere	creer
bell¹ (E)	Glocke f	—	cloche f	campana f	campana f
bell² (E)	Klingel f	—	sonnette f	campanello m	timbre m
belle-mère (F)	Schwieger-mutter f	mother-in-law	—	suocera f	suegra f
belle-sœur (F)	Schwägerin f	sister-in-law	—	cognata f	cuñada f
belleza (Es)	Schönheit f	beauty	beauté f	bellezza f	—
bellezza (I)	Schönheit f	beauty	beauté f	—	belleza f
bello (I)	schön	beautiful	beau, bel, belle	—	hermoso(a)
belohnen (D)	—	reward	récompenser	premiare	recompensar
Belohnung (D)	—	reward	récompense f	ricompensa f	recompensa f
belong (E)	gehören	—	appartenir	appartenere	pertenecer
belt¹ (E)	Gurt m	—	ceinture f	cinghia f	cinturón m
belt² (E)	Gürtel m	—	ceinture f	cintura f	cinturón m
bemerken (D)	—	notice	remarquer	notare	darse cuenta
be mistaken (E)	irren	—	tromper, se	sbagliare	equivocarse
bemitleiden (D)	—	pity	plaindre	compatire	compadecerse de
bemühen, sich (D)	—	make an effort	efforcer, se	sforzarsi	esforzarse
Bemühung (D)	—	effort	effort m	sforzo m	esfuerzo m
benachbart (D)	—	neighbouring	avoisinant(e)	vicino(a)	vecino(a)
benachrichtigen (D)	—	inform	informer	informare	avisar
benachteiligen (D)	—	disadvantage	désavantager	svantaggiare	perjudicar
benché (I)	obwohl/obgleich	although	bien que	—	aunque
bend¹ (E)	biegen	—	plier	piegare	doblar
bend² (E)	Kurve f	—	virage m	curva f	curva f
bene (I)	wohl	well	bien	—	bien
Benehmen (D)	—	behaviour	conduite f	comportamento m	comportamiento m
benehmen, sich (D)	—	behave	comporter, se	comportarsi	comportarse

	D	E	F	I	Es
beneiden (D)	—	envy	envier	invidiare	envidiar
benessere (I)	Wohl n	welfare	bien m	—	bienestar m
beni (I)	Güter f	goods	marchandises f pl	—	bienes f pl
be noticeable (E)	auffallen	—	faire remarquer, se	dare nell'occhio	llamar la atención
benötigen (D)	—	need	avoir besoin de	aver bisogno di	necesitar
benutzen (D)	—	use	utiliser	usare	usar
benvenuto (I)	willkommen	welcome	bienvenu(e)	—	bienvenido(a)
Benzin (D)	—	petrol	essence f	benzina f	gasolina f
benzina (I)	Benzin n	petrol	essence f	—	gasolina f
beobachten (D)	—	observe	observer	osservare	observar
be of use (E)	taugen	—	convenir pour	essere portato(a)	valer
be on strike (E)	streiken	—	faire grève	scioperare	hacer huelga
bequeath (E)	vererben	—	léguer	lasciare in eredità	transmitir hereditariamente
bequem (D)	—	comfortable	confortable	comodo(a)	cómodo(a)
Bequemlichkeit (D)	—	convenience	confort m	comodità f	comodidad f
bere (I)	trinken	drink	boire	—	beber
berechnen (D)	—	charge	calculer	calcolare	calcular
bereit (D)	—	ready	prêt(e)	pronto(a)	dispuesto(a)
bereits (D)	—	already	déjà	già	ya
bereuen (D)	—	regret	regretter	pentirsi	arrepentirse
Berg (D)	—	mountain	mont m	monte m	montaña f
bergab (D)	—	downhill	en descendant	in discesa	cuesta abajo
bergauf (D)	—	uphill	en montant	in salita	cuesta arriba
Bergsteiger (D)	—	mountaineer	alpiniste m	alpinista m	alpinista m
Bericht (D)	—	report	rapport m	relazione f	relación f
berichten (D)	—	report	faire un rapport	riferire	informar
berretto (I)	Mütze f	cap	casquette f	—	gorra f
Beruf (D)	—	profession	profession f	professione f	profesión f
beruhigen (D)	—	calm	calmer, se	calmare	calmar
berühmt (D)	—	famous	célèbre	famoso(a)	famoso(a)
berühren (D)	—	touch	toucher	toccare	tocar
besar (Es)	küssen	kiss	embrasser	baciare	—
beschädigen (D)	—	damage	endommager	danneggiare	deteriorar
Beschädigung (D)	—	damage	endommagement m	danno m	deterioro m
beschaffen (D)	—	get	procurer	procurare	proporcionar
beschäftigen (D)	—	occupy/employ	occuper	occupare	ocupar
beschäftigt (D)	—	busy	occupé(e)	occupato(a)	ocupado(a)
bescheiden (D)	—	modest	modeste	modesto(a)	modesto(a)
bescheinigen (D)	—	certify	attester	attestare	atestiguar
Bescheinigung (D)	—	certificate	attestation f	certificato m	certificado m
beschleunigen (D)	—	accelerate	accélérer	accelerare	acelerar
beschließen (D)	—	decide	décider	decidere	decidir
beschreiben (D)	—	describe	décrire	descrivere	describir
beschützen (D)	—	protect	protéger	proteggere	proteger
Beschwerde (D)	—	complaint	plainte f	reclamo m	reclamación f
beschweren, sich (D)	—	complain	plaindre, se	lamentarsi	quejarse

	D	E	F	I	Es
Besen (D)	—	broom	balai *m*	scopa *f*	escoba *f*
besetzt (D)	—	engaged	occupé(e)	occupato(a)	ocupado(a)
besichtigen (D)	—	have a look at	visiter	visitare	visitar
beside (E)	neben	—	près de	accanto a	al lado de
besides (E)	außerdem	—	en outre	inoltre	además
be silent (E)	schweigen	—	taire, se	tacere	callar
Besitz (D)	—	possession	propriété *f*	proprietà *f*	posesión *f*
besitzen (D)	—	possess	posséder	possedere	poseer
Besitzer (D)	—	owner	propriétaire *m*	proprietario *m*	proprietario *m*
beso (Es)	Kuß *m*	kiss	baiser *m*	bacio *m*	—
besoin (F)	Bedürfnis *n*	need	—	bisogno *m*	necesidad *f*
besondere (D)	—	special	spécial(e)	straordinario(a)	extraordinario(a)
besonders (D)	—	especially	surtout	particolarmente	sobre todo
besonnen (D)	—	sensible	réfléchi(e)	avveduto(a)	sensato(a)
besorgen (D)	—	acquire	procurer	procurare	conseguir
besprechen (D)	—	discuss	discuter	discutere	discutir
besser (D)	—	better	meilleur(e)	meglio	mejor
Besserung (D)	—	improvement	amélioration *f*	miglioramento *m*	restablecimiento *m*
best (E)	beste(r,s)	—	meilleur(e)	migliore	óptimo(a)
bestätigen (D)	—	confirm	confirmer	confermare	confirmar
beste (D)	—	best	meilleur(e)	migliore	óptimo(a)
bestellen (D)	—	order	commander	ordinare	pedir
bestimmt (D)	—	definitely	certainement	certamente	ciertamente
Besuch (D)	—	visit	visite *f*	visita *f*	visita *f*
besuchen (D)	—	visit	rendre visite à	andare a trovare	visitar
Besucher (D)	—	visitor	visiteur *m*	visitatore *m*	visitante *m*
bet[1] (E)	wetten	—	parier	scommettere	apostar
bet[2] (E)	Wette *f*	—	pari *m*	scommessa *f*	apuesta *f*
bête[1] (F)	dumm	stupid	—	stupido(a)	tonto(a)
bête[2] (F)	doof	daft	—	scemo(a)	estúpido(a)
beten (D)	—	pray	prier	pregare	rezar
bêtises (F)	Unsinn *m*	nonsense	—	nonsenso *m*	absurdo *m*
beträchtlich (D)	—	considerable	considérable	considerevole	notable
Betrag (D)	—	amount	montant *m*	somma *f*	importe *m*
betray (E)	verraten	—	trahir	tradire	traicionar
betreffen (D)	—	concern	concerner	riguardare	concernir
betreten (D)	—	enter	entrer dans	entrare	entrar
betrinken, sich (D)	—	get drunk	enivrer, se	ubriacarsi	emborracharse
Betrug (D)	—	fraud	tromperie *f*	inganno *m*	engaño *m*
betrügen (D)	—	cheat	tromper	ingannare	engañar
betrunken (D)	—	drunk	soûl(e)	ubriaco(a)	borracho(a)
Bett (D)	—	bed	lit *m*	letto *m*	cama *f*
better (E)	besser	—	meilleur(e)	meglio	mejor
betún (Es)	Schuhcreme *f*	shoe polish	cirage *m*	lucido per scarpe *m*	—
between (E)	zwischen	—	entre	tra/fra	entre
beunruhigen (D)	—	disturb	inquiéter	preoccupare	inquietar
beurre (F)	Butter *f*	butter	—	burro *m*	mantequilla *f*

	D	E	F	I	Es
beurteilen (D)	—	judge	juger	giudicare	juzgar
bevanda (I)	Getränk n	drink	boisson f	—	bebida f
Bevölkerung (D)	—	population	population f	popolazione f	población f
bevor (D)	—	before	avant que	prima che (di)	antes que
bevorzugen (D)	—	prefer	préférer	perferire	preferir
bewachen (D)	—	guard	garder	sorvegliare	vigilar
bewegen (D)	—	move	bouger	muovere	mover
Bewegung (D)	—	movement	mouvement m	movimento m	movimiento m
bewegungslos (D)	—	motionless	immobile	immobile	inmóvil
Beweis (D)	—	proof	preuve f	prova f	prueba f
beweisen (D)	—	prove	prouver	provare	probar
bewerben, sich (D)	—	apply	poser sa candidature	concorrere	presentarse
Bewerbung (D)	—	application	candidature f	domanda d'impiego f	solicitud f
Bewohner (D)	—	inhabitant	habitant m	abitante m	habitante m
bewölkt (D)	—	cloudy	couvert(e)	nuvoloso(a)	nublado(a)
be worth (E)	gelten	—	valoir	valere	valer
be worth while (E)	lohnen	—	en valoir la peine	valere la pena	valer la pena
bewundern (D)	—	admire	admirer	ammirare	admirar
bewußt (D)	—	deliberate	délibéré(e)	intenzionale	intencionado
beyond (E)	jenseits	—	de l'autre côté	al di là	al otro lado
bezahlen (D)	—	pay	payer	pagare	pagar
Bezahlung (D)	—	payment	paiement m	pagamento m	pago m
beziehen (D)	—	cover	recouvrir	ricoprire	tapizar
Beziehung[1] (D)	—	relation	rapport m	relazione f	relación f
Beziehung[2] (D)	—	relationship	relation f	rapporto m	relaciones f pl
biancheria (I)	Wäsche f	washing	linge m	—	ropa f
biancheria intima (I)	Unterwäsche f	underwear	sous-vêtements m pl	—	ropa interior f
bianco (I)	weiß	white	blanc(he)	—	blanco(a)
bibbia (I)	Bibel f	Bible	Bible f	—	Biblia f
Bibel (D)	—	Bible	Bible f	bibbia f	Biblia f
Bible (E)	Bibel f	—	Bible f	bibbia f	Biblia f
Bible (F)	Bibel f	Bible	—	bibbia f	Biblia f
Biblia (Es)	Bibel f	Bible	Bible f	bibbia f	—
bicchiere (I)	Glas n	glass	verre m	—	vaso m
bicicleta (Es)	Fahrrad n	bicycle	bicyclette f	bicicletta f	—
bicicletta (I)	Fahrrad n	bicycle	bicyclette f	—	bicicleta f
bicycle (E)	Fahrrad n	—	bicyclette f	bicicletta f	bicicleta f
bicyclette (F)	Fahrrad n	bicycle	—	bicicletta f	bicicleta f
biegen (D)	—	bend	plier	piegare	doblar
bien (Es)	wohl	well	bien	bene/forse	—
bien[1] (F)	wohl	well	—	bene/forse	bien
bien[2] (F)	Wohl n	welfare	—	benessere m	bienestar m
bienes (Es)	Güter f	goods	marchandises f pl	beni m pl	—
bienestar (Es)	Wohl n	welfare	bien m	benessere m	—
bien que (F)	obwohl/obgleich	although	—	benché	aunque
bientôt (F)	bald	soon	—	presto	pronto

	D	E	F	I	Es
bienvenido (Es)	willkommen	welcome	bienvenu(e)	benvenuto(a)	—
bienvenu (F)	willkommen	welcome	—	benvenuto(a)	bienvenido(a)
Bier (D)	—	beer	bière *f*	birra *f*	cerveza *f*
bière (F)	Bier *n*	beer	—	birra *f*	cerveza *f*
bieten (D)	—	offer	offrir	offrire	ofrecer
big (E)	groß	—	grand(e)	grande	grande
bigliettaio (I)	Schaffner *m*	conductor	contrôleur *m*	—	revisor *m*
biglietto (I)	Fahrkarte *f*	ticket	billet *m*	—	billete *m*
biglietto non vincente (I)	Niete *f*	blank	mauvais numéro *m*	—	número sin premio *m*
bigote (Es)	Schnurrbart *m*	moustache	moustache *f*	baffi *m pl*	—
bijoutier (F)	Juwelier *m*	jeweller	—	gioielliere *m*	joyero *m*
bijoux (F)	Schmuck *m*	jewellery	—	gioielli *m pl*	joyas *f pl*
bilancia (I)	Waage *f*	scales	balance *f*	—	balanza *f*
Bild (D)	—	picture	image *f*	immagine *f*	cuadro *m*
bilden (D)	—	form	former	formare	formar
Bildhauer (D)	—	sculptor	sculpteur *m*	scultore *m*	escultor *m*
Bildung[1] (D)	—	formation	formation *f*	formazione *f*	formación *f*
Bildung[2] (D)	—	education	éducation *f*	istruzione *f*	educación *f*
bilingual (E)	zweisprachig	—	bilingue	bilingue	bilingüe
bilingue (F)	zweisprachig	bilingual	—	bilingue	bilingüe
bilingue (I)	zweisprachig	bilingual	bilingue	—	bilingüe
bilingüe (Es)	zweisprachig	bilingual	bilingue	bilingue	—
bilis (Es)	Galle *f*	gall	fiel *m*	cistifellea *f*	—
bill (E)	Rechnung *f*	—	facture *f*	fattura *f*	factura *f*
billet[1] (F)	Fahrkarte *f*	ticket	—	biglietto *m*	billete *m*
billet[2] (F)	Schein *m*	note	—	banconota *f*	billete *m*
billete[1] (Es)	Fahrkarte *f*	ticket	billet *m*	biglietto *m*	—
billete[2] (Es)	Fahrschein *m*	ticket	ticket *m*	biglietto *m*	—
billete[3] (Es)	Schein *m*	note	billet *m*	banconota *f*	—
billig (D)	—	cheap	bon marché(e)	a buon mercato	barato(a)
billigen (D)	—	approve of	approuver	approvare	aprobar
billion (E)	Milliarde *f*	—	milliard *m*	miliardo *m*	mil millones *m*
bin (E)	Abfalleimer *m*	—	poubelle *f*	pattumiera *f*	cubo de la basura *m*
binario (I)	Gleis *n*	track	voie *f*	—	vía *f*
bind (E)	binden	—	attacher	legare	atar
Binde (D)	—	bandage	bandage *m*	fascia *f*	faja *f*
binden (D)	—	bind	attacher	legare	atar
binoculars (E)	Fernglas *n*	—	jumelles *f pl*	cannocchiale *m*	gemelos *m pl*
biondo (I)	blond	blond	blond(e)	—	rubio(a)
bird (E)	Vogel *m*	—	oiseau *m*	uccello *m*	pájaro *m*
Birne (D)	—	pear	poire *f*	pera *f*	pera *f*
biro (E)	Kugelschreiber *m*	—	stylo à bille *m*	biro *f*	bolígrafo *m*
biro (I)	Kugelschreiber *m*	biro	stylo à bille *m*	—	bolígrafo *m*
birra (I)	Bier *n*	beer	bière *f*	—	cerveza *f*
birth (E)	Geburt *f*	—	naissance *f*	nascita *f*	nacimiento *m*
birthday (E)	Geburtstag *m*	—	anniversaire *m*	compleanno *m*	cumpleaños *m*

	D	E	F	I	Es
bis (D)	—	until	jusqu'à	fino a	hasta
bisabuelos (Es)	Urgroßeltern *pl*	great-grandparents	arrière-grands-parents *m pl*	bisnonni *m pl*	—
bisbigliare (I)	flüstern	whisper	chuchoter	—	cuchichear
biscotte (F)	Zwieback *m*	rusk	—	fette biscottate *f pl*	bizcocho *m*
biscotti (I)	Gebäck *n*	pastry	pâtisserie *f*	—	pastas *f pl*
biscotto (I)	Keks *m*	biscuit	biscuit *m*	—	galleta *f*
biscuit (E)	Keks *m*	—	biscuit *m*	biscotto *m*	galleta *f*
biscuit (F)	Keks *m*	biscuit	—	biscotto *m*	galleta *f*
bisher (D)	—	so far	jusqu'à présent	finora	hasta ahora
bisnonni (I)	Urgroßeltern *pl*	great-grandparents	arrière-grands-parents *m pl*	—	bisabuelos *m pl*
bisogno (I)	Bedürfnis *n*	need	besoin *m*	—	necesidad *f*
bißchen (D)	—	a little	un peu	un po'	un poquito
bistro (F)	Kneipe *f*	pub	—	osteria *f*	tasca *f*
bite (E)	beißen	—	mordre	mordere	morder
bitte (D)	—	please	s'il vous plaît	prego	por favor
Bitte (D)	—	request	demande *f*	domanda *f*	ruego *m*
bitten (D)	—	request	demander	pregare	rogar
bitter (D)	—	bitter	amer(-ère)	amaro(a)	amargo(a)
bitter[1] (E)	bitter	—	amer(-ère)	amaro(a)	amargo(a)
bitter[2] (E)	herb	—	âpre	amaro(a)	amargo(a)
bizarre (F)	seltsam	strange	—	strano(a)	extraño(a)
bizcocho (Es)	Zwieback *m*	rusk	biscotte *f*	fette biscottate *f pl*	—
black (E)	schwarz	—	noir(e)	nero(a)	negro(a)
blackberry (E)	Brombeere *f*	—	mûre *f*	mora *f*	zarzamora *f*
blackmail (E)	Erpressung *f*	—	chantage *m*	ricatto *m*	chantaje *m*
bladder (E)	Blase *f*	—	vessie *f*	vescica *f*	vejiga *f*
blade (E)	Klinge *f*	—	lame *f*	lama *f*	cuchilla *f*
blame (E)	vorwerfen	—	reprocher	rimproverare	echar en cara
blanc (F)	weiß	white	—	bianco(a)	blanco(a)
blanchisserie (F)	Wäscherei *f*	laundry	—	lavanderia *f*	lavandería *f*
blanco (Es)	weiß	white	blanc(he)	bianco(a)	—
blank (E)	Niete *f*	—	mauvais numéro *m*	biglietto non vincente *m*	número sin premio *m*
blanket (E)	Decke *f*	—	couverture *f*	coperta *f*	techo *m*
Blase[1] (D)	—	bladder	vessie *f*	vescica *f*	vejiga *f*
Blase[2] (D)	—	bubble	bulle *f*	bolla *f*	burbuja *f*
blasen (D)	—	blow	souffler	soffiare	soplar
blaß (D)	—	pale	pâle	pallido(a)	pálido(a)
Blatt (D)	—	leaf	feuille *f*	foglia *f*	hoja *f*
blau (D)	—	blue	bleu(e)	blu	azul
blé (F)	Weizen *m*	wheat	—	frumento *m*	trigo *m*
Blech (D)	—	sheet metal	tôle *f*	latta *f*	chapa *f*
bleed (E)	bluten	—	saigner	sanguinare	sangrar
bleiben (D)	—	stay	rester	rimanere	quedarse
Bleistift (D)	—	pencil	crayon *m*	matita *f*	lápiz *m*
blesser[1] (F)	verletzen	injure	—	ferire	herir

	D	E	F	I	Es
blesser² (F)	verwunden	wound	—	ferire	herir
blessure¹ (F)	Verletzung *f*	injury	—	ferita *f*	herida *f*
blessure² (F)	Wunde *f*	wound	—	ferita *f*	herida *f*
bleu (F)	blau	blue	—	blu	azul
Blick (D)	—	look	regard *m*	sguardo *m*	vista *f*
blicken (D)	—	look	regarder	guardare	mirar
blind (D)	—	blind	aveugle	cieco(a)	ciego(a)
blind (E)	blind	—	aveugle	cieco(a)	ciego(a)
blinken (D)	—	flash	clignoter	lampeggiare	emitir reflejos
Blitz (D)	—	lightning	éclair *m*	lampo *m*	rayo *m*
blond (D)	—	blond	blond(e)	biondo(a)	rubio(a)
blond (E)	blond	—	blond(e)	biondo(a)	rubio(a)
blond (F)	blond	blond	—	biondo(a)	rubio(a)
blood (E)	Blut *n*	—	sang *m*	sangue *m*	sangre *f*
bloom (E)	blühen	—	fleurir	fiorire	florecer
bloß (D)	—	only	seulement	soltanto	sólo
blouse (E)	Bluse *f*	—	chemisier *m*	camicetta *f*	blusa *f*
blow¹ (E)	blasen	—	souffler	soffiare	soplar
blow² (E)	Stoß *m*	—	coup *m*	spinta *f*	empujón *m*
blow³ (E)	Schlag *m*	—	coup *m*	colpo *m*	golpe *m*
blu (I)	blau	blue	bleu(e)	—	azul
blue (E)	blau	—	bleu(e)	blu	azul
blühen (D)	—	bloom	fleurir	fiorire	florecer
Blume (D)	—	flower	fleur *f*	fiore *m*	flor *f*
Blumenkohl (D)	—	cauliflower	chou-fleur *m*	cavolfiore *m*	coliflor *f*
blusa (Es)	Bluse *f*	blouse	chemisier *m*	camicetta *f*	—
Bluse (D)	—	blouse	chemisier *m*	camicetta *f*	blusa *f*
Blut (D)	—	blood	sang *m*	sangue *m*	sangre *f*
bluten (D)	—	bleed	saigner	sanguinare	sangrar
boarding house (E)	Pension *f*	—	pension *f*	pensione *f*	pensión *f*
boarding school (E)	Internat *n*	—	internat *m*	collegio *m*	internado *m*
boat (E)	Boot *n*	—	bateau *m*	barca *f*	bote *m*
boca (Es)	Mund *m*	mouth	bouche *f*	bocca *f*	—
bocca (I)	Mund *m*	mouth	bouche *f*	—	boca *f*
bocciolo (I)	Knospe *f*	bud	bourgeon *f*	—	yema *f*
boceto (Es)	Skizze *f*	sketch	esquisse *f*	schizzo *m*	—
bocina (Es)	Hupe *f*	horn	claxon *m*	clacson *m*	—
boda¹ (Es)	Hochzeit *f*	wedding	mariage *m*	nozze *f pl*	—
boda² (Es)	Heirat *f*	marriage	mariage *m*	matrimonio *m*	—
Boden (D)	—	floor	terre *f*	terra *f*	suelo *m*
body¹ (E)	Körper *m*	—	corps *m*	corpo *m*	cuerpo *m*
body² (E)	Karosserie *f*	—	carrosserie *f*	carrozzeria *f*	carrocería *f*
bœuf¹ (F)	Ochse *m*	ox	—	bue *m*	buey *m*
bœuf² (F)	Rind *n*	cow	—	manzo *m*	buey *m*
Bohne (D)	—	bean	haricot *m*	fagiolo *m*	judía *f*
boire (F)	trinken	drink	—	bere	beber
bois (F)	Holz *n*	wood	—	legno *m*	madera *f*

	D	E	F	I	Es
boisson (F)	Getränk *n*	drink	—	bevanda *f*	bebida *f*
boîte[1] (F)	Dose *f*	tin	—	scatola *f*	lata *f*
boîte[2] (F)	Schachtel *f*	box	—	scatola *f*	caja *f*
boîte aux lettres (F)	Briefkasten *m*	letterbox	—	cassetta postale *f*	buzón *m*
boîte de nuit (F)	Nachtlokal *n*	(night) club	—	night *m*	local nocturno *m*
bolígrafo (Es)	Kugelschreiber *m*	biro	stylo à bille *m*	biro *f*	—
bolla (I)	Blase *f*	bubble	bulle *f*	—	burbuja *f*
bollettino meteorologico (I)	Wetterbericht *m*	weather report	bulletin météorologique *m*	—	informe metereológico *m*
bolsa (Es)	Tüte *f*	bag	sac *m*	sacchetto *m*	—
bolsa de compra (Es)	Einkaufstasche *f*	shopping bag	sac à provision *m*	borsa della spesa *f*	—
bolso[1] (Es)	Handtasche *f*	handbag	sac à main *m*	borsetta *f*	—
bolso[2] (Es)	Tasche *f*	handbag	sac *m*	borsa *f*	—
bolt (E)	Riegel *m*	—	verrou *m*	catenaccio *m*	cerrojo *m*
bomba (Es)	Pumpe *f*	pump	pompe *f*	pompa *f*	—
bon[1] (F)	Gutschein *m*	voucher	—	buono *m*	vale *m*
bon[2] (F)	gut	good/well	—	buono(a)/bene	bueno(a)/bien
Bonbon (D)	—	sweet	bonbon *m*	caramella *f*	caramelo *m*
bonbon (F)	Bonbon *n*	sweet	—	caramella *f*	caramelo *m*
bondé (F)	überfüllt	crowded	—	pieno(a) zeppo(a)	abarrotado(a)
bone (E)	Knochen *m*	—	os *m*	osso *m*	hueso *m*
bonito (Es)	hübsch	pretty	joli(e)	carino(a)	—
bon marché[1] (F)	billig	cheap	—	a buon mercato	barato(a)
bon marché[2] (F)	preiswert	inexpensive	—	conveniente	económico(a)
book[1] (E)	buchen	—	retenir	prenotare	reservar
book[2] (E)	Buch *n*	—	livre *m*	libro *m*	libro *m*
book[3] (E)	vormerken	—	prendre note de	prendere nota di	tomar nota
book[4] (E)	vorbestellen	—	réserver	prenotare	hacer reservar
book-keeping (E)	Buchhaltung *f*	—	comptabilité *f*	contabilità *f*	contabilidad *f*
bookshop (E)	Buchhandlung *f*	—	librairie *f*	libreria *f*	librería *f*
Boot (D)	—	boat	bateau *m*	barca *f*	bote *m*
boot[1] (E)	Kofferraum *m*	—	coffre *m*	portabagagli *m*	maletero *m*
boot[2] (E)	Stiefel *m*	—	botte *f*	stivale *m*	bota *f*
bord[1] (F)	Rand *m*	brim	—	margine *m*	borde *m*
bord[2] (F)	Ufer *n*	shore/bank	—	riva *f*	orilla *f*
borde (Es)	Rand *m*	brim	bord *m*	margine *m*	—
borgen (D)	—	lend	prêter	prestare	prestar
boring (E)	langweilig	—	ennuyeux(-euse)	noioso(a)	aburrido(a)
born (E)	geboren	—	né(e)	nato(a)	nacido(a)
borracho (Es)	betrunken	drunk	soûl(e)	ubriaco(a)	—
borsa (I)	Tasche *f*	handbag	sac *m*	—	bolso *m*
borsa della spesa (I)	Einkaufstasche *f*	shopping bag	sac à provision *m*	—	bolsa de compra *f*
borsetta (I)	Handtasche *f*	handbag	sac à main *m*	—	bolso *m*
bosco (I)	Wald *m*	forest	forêt *f*	—	bosque *m*
böse (D)	—	wicked	méchant(e)	cattivo(a)	malo(a)
bosque[1] (Es)	Forst *m*	forest	forêt *f*	foresta *f*	—
bosque[2] (Es)	Wald *m*	forest	forêt *f*	bosco *m*	—

	D	E	F	I	Es
boss (E)	Chef m	—	patron m	capo m	jefe m
bota (Es)	Stiefel m	boot	botte f	stivale m	—
bote (Es)	Boot n	boat	bateau m	barca f	—
botella (Es)	Flasche f	bottle	bouteille f	bottiglia f	—
bote neumático (Es)	Schlauchboot n	(rubber) dinghy	canot pneumatique m	canotto pneumatico m	—
both (E)	beide	—	tous/ toutes les deux	entrambi(e)	ambos(as)
botón (Es)	Knopf m	button	bouton m	bottone m	—
Botschaft[1] (D)	—	message	message m	messaggio m	mensaje m
Botschaft[2] (D)	—	embassy	ambassade f	ambasciata f	embajada f
botte (F)	Stiefel m	boot	—	stivale m	bota f
botte (I)	Tonne f	barrel	tonneau m	—	barril m
bottiglia (I)	Flasche f	bottle	bouteille f	—	botella f
bottle (E)	Flasche f	—	bouteille f	bottiglia f	botella f
bottle opener (E)	Flaschenöffner m	—	ouvre-bouteilles m	apribottiglie m	abrebotellas m
bottone (I)	Knopf m	button	bouton m	—	botón m
bouche (F)	Mund m	mouth	—	bocca f	boca f
boucher (F)	Metzger m	butcher	—	macellaio m	carnicero m
boucherie (F)	Metzgerei f	butcher's	—	macelleria f	carnicería f
boucle (F)	Locke f	curl	—	riccio m	rizo m
bouclier (F)	Schild n	shield	—	scudo m	escudo m
boue (F)	Schlamm m	mud	—	fango m	barro m
bouée de sauvetage (F)	Rettungsring m	lifebelt	—	salvagente m	salvavidas m
bouffer (F)	fressen	eat	—	mangiare	devorar
bouger (F)	bewegen	move	—	muovere	mover
bougie (F)	Kerze f	candle	—	candela f	vela f
bouillon (F)	Brühe f	broth	—	brodo m	caldo m
boulangerie (F)	Bäckerei f	bakery	—	panetteria f	panadería f
bouquet (F)	Strauß m	bunch	—	mazzo m	ramo m
bourgeois (E)	spießig	—	bourgeois(e)	da piccolo(a) borghese	pequeño(a) burgués(-esa)
bourgeois (F)	spießig	bourgeois	—	da piccolo(a) borghese	pequeño(a) burgués(-esa)
bourgeon (F)	Knospe f	bud	—	bocciolo m	yema f
bouteille (F)	Flasche f	bottle	—	bottiglia f	botella f
bouton (F)	Knopf m	button	—	bottone m	botón m
bowl (E)	Schüssel m	—	jatte f	scodella f	fuente f
box[1] (E)	Kiste f	—	caisse f	cassetta f	caja f
box[2] (E)	Loge f	—	loge f	palco m	palco m
box[3] (E)	Schachtel f	—	boîte f	scatola f	caja f
boy (E)	Junge m	—	garçon m	ragazzo m	chico m
bracciale (I)	Armband n	bracelet	bracelet m	—	pulsera f
braccio (I)	Arm m	arm	bras m	—	brazo m
bracelet (E)	Armband n	—	bracelet m	bracciale m	pulsera f
bracelet (F)	Armband n	bracelet	—	bracciale m	pulsera f
brain (E)	Hirn n	—	cerveau m	cervello m	cerebro m
brake[1] (E)	bremsen	—	freiner	frenare	frenar
brake[2] (E)	Bremse f	—	frein m	freno m	freno m

	D	E	F	I	Es
brancard (F)	Bahre *f*	stretcher	—	barella *f*	camilla *f*
branch[1] (E)	Ast *m*	—	branche *f*	ramo *m*	rama *f*
branch[2] (E)	Filiale *f*	—	succursale *f*	filiale *f*	sucursal *f*
branch[3] (E)	Zweig *m*	—	branche *f*	ramo *m*	rama *f*
branche[1] (F)	Ast *m*	branch	—	ramo *m*	rama *f*
branche[2] (F)	Zweig *m*	branch	—	ramo *m*	rama *f*
Brand (D)	—	fire	incendie *m*	incendio *m*	incendio *m*
brand (E)	Marke *f*	—	marque *f*	marca *f*	marca *f*
bras (F)	Arm *m*	arm	—	braccio *m*	brazo *m*
braten (D)	—	roast	rôtir	arrostire	asar
Braten (D)	—	roast	rôti *m*	arrosto *m*	asado *m*
brauchen (D)	—	need	avoir besoin de	aver bisogno di	necesitar
braun (D)	—	brown	marron	marrone	marrón
Braut (D)	—	bride	mariée *f*	sposa *f*	novia *f*
brav (D)	—	good	gentil(le)	bravo(a)	bueno(a)
brave (E)	tapfer	—	courageux(-euse)	coraggioso(a)	valiente
bravo (I)	brav	good	gentil(le)	—	bueno(a)
brazo (Es)	Arm *m*	arm	bras *m*	braccio *m*	—
bread (E)	Brot *n*	—	pain *m*	pane *m*	pan *m*
break[1] (E)	brechen	—	casser	rompere	romper
break[2] (E)	Pause *f*	—	pause *f*	pausa *f*	pausa *f*
breakdown (E)	Panne *f*	—	panne *f*	panne *f*	avería *f*
breakdown van (E)	Abschlepp-wagen *m*	—	dépanneuse *f*	carro attrezzi *m*	camión grúa *m*
breakfast (E)	Frühstück *n*	—	petit-déjeuner *m*	colazione *f*	desayuno *m*
break in (E)	einbrechen	—	cambrioler	fare irruzione	irumpir
breast (E)	Brust *f*	—	poitrine *f*	petto *m*	pecho *m*
breath (E)	Atem *m*	—	respiration *f*	fiato *m*	respiro *m*
breathe (E)	atmen	—	respirer	respirare	respirar
brechen (D)	—	break	casser	rompere	romper
breed (E)	züchten	—	élever	allevare	criar
breit (D)	—	broad	large	largo(a)	amplio(a)
Breite (D)	—	width	largeur *f*	larghezza *f*	extensión *f*
Bremse (D)	—	brake	frein *m*	freno *m*	freno *m*
bremsen (D)	—	brake	freiner	frenare	frenar
brennen (D)	—	burn	brûler	bruciare	arder
bretelle d'accès (F)	Auffahrt *f*	slip road	—	entrata *f*	vía de acceso *f*
brick (E)	Ziegel *m*	—	brique *f*	mattone *m*	ladrillo *m*
bride (E)	Braut *f*	—	mariée *f*	sposa *f*	novia *f*
bridge (E)	Brücke *f*	—	pont *m*	ponte *m*	puente *m*
Brief (D)	—	letter	lettre *f*	lettera *f*	carta *f*
Briefkasten (D)	—	letterbox	boîte aux lettres *f*	cassetta delle lettere *f*	buzón *m*
Briefmarke (D)	—	stamp	timbre *m*	francobollo *m*	sello *m*
bright (E)	hell	—	clair(e)	chiaro(a)	claro(a)
brillar (Es)	glänzen	shine	briller	splendere	—
Brille (D)	—	glasses	lunettes *f pl*	occhiali *m pl*	gafas *f pl*
briller (F)	glänzen	shine	—	splendere	brillar
brim (E)	Rand *m*	—	bord *m*	margine *m*	borde *m*

bring (along)

	D	E	F	I	Es
bring (along) (E)	mitbringen	—	apporter	portare con sé	traer
bring back (E)	zurückbringen	—	rapporter	riportare	devolver
bringen (D)	—	fetch	porter	portare	llevar
brique (F)	Ziegel *m*	brick	—	mattone *m*	ladrillo *m*
briquet (F)	Feuerzeug *n*	lighter	—	accendino *m*	mechero *m*
broad (E)	breit	—	large	largo(a)	amplio(a)
broadcast (E)	senden	—	transmettre	trasmettere	transmitir
broadcasting (E)	Rundfunk *m*	—	radio *f*	radio *f*	radiodifusión *f*
brocca (I)	Krug *m*	jug	cruche *f*	—	jarro(a) *m(f)*
brochure (E)	Prospekt *n*	—	prospectus *m*	dépliant *m*	prospecto *m*
brodo (I)	Brühe *f*	broth	bouillon *m*	—	caldo *m*
broken (E)	kaputt	—	cassé(e)	rotto(a)	roto(a)
broken piece (E)	Scherbe *f*	—	tesson *m*	coccio *m*	pedazo *m*
broma¹ (Es)	Spaß *m*	fun	plaisir *m*	scherzo *m*	—
broma² (Es)	Scherz *m*	joke	plaisanterie *f*	scherzo *m*	—
Brombeere (D)	—	blackberry	mûre *f*	mora *f*	zarzamora *f*
bromear (Es)	spaßen	joke	plaisanter	scherzare	—
broom (E)	Besen *m*	—	balai *m*	scopa *f*	escoba *f*
brosse (F)	Bürste *f*	brush	—	spazzola *f*	cepillo *m*
brosse à dents (F)	Zahnbürste *f*	toothbrush	—	spazzola da denti *m*	cepillo de dientes *m*
Brot (D)	—	bread	pain *m*	pane *m*	pan *m*
Brötchen (D)	—	roll	petit pain *m*	panino *m*	panecillo *m*
broth (E)	Brühe *f*	—	bouillon *m*	brodo *m*	caldo *m*
brother (E)	Bruder *m*	—	frère *m*	fratello *m*	hermano *m*
brother-in-law (E)	Schwager *m*	—	beau-frère *m*	cognato *m*	cuñado *m*
brothers and sisters (E)	Geschwister *pl*	—	frère(s) et sœur(s) *pl*	fratelli *m pl*	hermanos *m pl*
brouillard (F)	Nebel *m*	fog	—	nebbia *f*	niebla *f*
brown (E)	braun	—	marron	marrone	marrón
bruciare¹ (I)	brennen	burn	brûler	—	arder
bruciare² (I)	verbrennen	burn	brûler	—	quemar
Brücke (D)	—	bridge	pont *m*	ponte *m*	puente *m*
Bruder (D)	—	brother	frère *m*	fratello *m*	hermano *m*
Brühe (D)	—	broth	bouillon *m*	brodo *m*	caldo *m*
bruire (F)	rauschen	rush	—	mormorare	susurrar
bruit¹ (F)	Geräusch *n*	sound	—	rumore *m*	ruido *m*
bruit² (F)	Krach *m*	noise	—	chiasso *m*	ruido *m*
bruit³ (F)	Lärm *m*	noise	—	rumore *m*	ruido *m*
bruja (Es)	Hexe *f*	witch	sorcière *f*	strega *f*	—
brûler¹ (F)	brennen	burn	—	bruciare	arder
brûler² (F)	verbrennen	burn	—	bruciare	quemar
Brunnen (D)	—	fountain	fontaine *f*	fontana *f*	fuente *f*
brush¹ (E)	Bürste *f*	—	brosse *f*	spazzola *f*	cepillo *m*
brush² (E)	Pinsel *m*	—	pinceau *m*	pennello *m*	pincel *m*
Brust (D)	—	breast	poitrine *f*	petto *m*	pecho *m*
brutto (I)	häßlich	ugly	laid(e)	—	feo(a)
bubble (E)	Blase *f*	—	bulle *f*	bolla *f*	burbuja *f*

	D	E	F	I	Es
buccia (I)	Schale *f*	peel	peau *f*	—	piel *f*
bucear (Es)	tauchen	dive	plonger	immergere	—
Buch (D)	—	book	livre *m*	libro *m*	libro *m*
buchen (D)	—	book	retenir	prenotare	reservar
Buchhaltung (D)	—	book-keeping	comptabilité *f*	contabilità *f*	contabilidad *f*
Buchhandlung (D)	—	bookshop	librairie *f*	libreria *f*	librería *f*
Buchstabe (D)	—	letter	lettre *f*	lettera *f*	letra *f*
buchstabieren (D)	—	spell	épeler	sillabare	deletrear
bucket (E)	Eimer *m*	—	seau *m*	secchio *m*	cubo *m*
buco (I)	Loch *n*	hole	trou *m*	—	agujero *m*
buco della chiave (I)	Schlüsselloch *n*	keyhole	trou de la serrure *m*	—	ojo de la cerradura *m*
bud (E)	Knospe *f*	—	bourgeon *m*	bocciolo *m*	yema *f*
budino (I)	Pudding *m*	pudding	flan *m*	—	flan *m*
bue (I)	Ochse *m*	ox	bœuf *m*	—	buey *m*
bueno¹ (Es)	brav	good	gentil(le)	bravo(a)	—
bueno² (Es)	gut	good/well	bon(ne)/bien	buono(a)/bene	—
buey¹ (Es)	Ochse *m*	ox	bœuf *m*	bue *m*	—
buey² (Es)	Rind *n*	cow	bœuf *m*	manzo *m*	—
Bügeleisen (D)	—	iron	fer à repasser *m*	ferro da stiro *m*	plancha *f*
bügeln (D)	—	iron	repasser	stirare	planchar
Bühne (D)	—	stage	scène *f*	palcoscenico *m*	escenario *m*
build (E)	bauen	—	construire	costruire	construir
building (E)	Gebäude *n*	—	bâtiment *m*	edificio *m*	edificio *m*
buio¹ (I)	finster	dark	sombre	—	oscuro(a)
buio² (I)	Finsternis *f*	darkness	obscurité *f*	—	oscuridad *f*
buisson (F)	Strauch *m*	bush	—	cespuglio *m*	arbusto *m*
bull (E)	Stier *m*	—	taureau *m*	toro *m*	toro *m*
bulle (F)	Blase *f*	bubble	—	bolla *f*	burbuja *f*
bulletin (F)	Zeugnis *n*	report	—	pagella *f*	informe *m*
bulletin météorologique (F)	Wetterbericht *m*	weather report	—	bollettino metereologico *m*	informe metereológico *m*
bummeln (D)	—	stroll	flâner	girellare	callejear
bump (E)	anstoßen	—	heurter	urtare	empujar
bunch (E)	Strauß *m*	—	bouquet *m*	mazzo *m*	ramo *m*
Bundeskanzler (D)	—	Federal Chancellor	chancelier fédéral *m*	cancelliere federale *m*	canciller federal *m*
Bundesstraße (D)	—	Federal Highway/ main road	route nationale *f*	strada statale *f*	carretera nacional *f*
bunt (D)	—	coloured	coloré(e)	variopinto(a)	de colores
buono¹ (I)	gut	good	bon(ne)	—	bueno(a)
buono² (I)	Gutschein *m*	voucher	bon *m*	—	vale *m*
burbuja (Es)	Blase *f*	bubble	bulle *f*	bolla *f*	—
burden (E)	aufbürden	—	charger	addossare	cargar
bureau¹ (F)	Amt *n*	office	—	ufficio *m*	oficio *m*
bureau² (F)	Büro *n*	office	—	ufficio *m*	oficina *f*
bureau de change (E)	Wechselstube *f*	—	bureau de change *m*	ufficio di cambio *m*	casa de cambio *f*
bureau de change (F)	Wechselstube *f*	bureau de change	—	ufficio di cambio *m*	casa de cambio *f*
bureau de poste (F)	Postamt *n*	post office	—	ufficio postale *m*	oficina de correos *f*

	D	E	F	I	Es
bureau des objets trouvés (F)	Fundbüro n	lost property office	—	ufficio oggetti smarriti m	oficina de objetos perdidos f
Burg (D)	—	fortress	château fort m	rocca f	fortaleza f
bürgerlich (D)	—	civil	civil(e)	civile	civil
Bürgermeister (D)	—	mayor	maire m	sindaco m	alcalde m
burn[1] (E)	brennen	—	brûler	bruciare	arder
burn[2] (E)	verbrennen	—	brûler	bruciare	quemar
Büro (D)	—	office	bureau m	ufficio m	oficina f
burro (Es)	Esel m	donkey	âne m	asino m	—
burro (I)	Butter f	butter	beurre m	—	mantequilla f
Bursche (D)	—	fellow	garçon m	ragazzo m	chico m
burst (E)	platzen	—	éclater	scoppiare	reventar
Bürste (D)	—	brush	brosse f	spazzola f	cepillo m
Bus (D)	—	bus	bus m	autobus m	autobús m
bus (E)	Bus m	—	bus m	autobus m	autobús m
bus (F)	Bus m	bus	—	autobus m	autobús m
buscar (Es)	suchen	look for	chercher	cercare	—
bush (E)	Strauch m	—	buisson m	cespuglio m	arbusto m
business hours (E)	Öffnungzeiten pl	—	heures d'ouverture f pl	orario d'ufficio m	horario de oficina m
businessman (E)	Kaufmann m	—	commerçant m	commerciante m	comerciante m
bussare (I)	klopfen	knock	frapper	—	golpear
busta (I)	Umschlag m	envelope	enveloppe f	—	sobre m
busy (E)	beschäftigt	—	occupé(e)	occupato(a)	ocupado(a)
but[1] (E)	aber	—	mais	ma	pero
but[2] (E)	sondern	—	mais	ma/bensì	sino
but[1] (F)	Zweck m	purpose	—	scopo m	finalidad f
but[2] (F)	Ziel n	goal	—	meta f	intención f
butcher (E)	Metzger m	—	boucher m	macellaio m	carnicero m
butcher's (E)	Metzgerei f	—	boucherie f	macelleria f	carnicería f
Butter (D)	—	butter	beurre m	burro m	mantequilla f
butter (E)	Butter f	—	beurre m	burro m	mantequilla f
butterfly (E)	Schmetterling m	—	papillon m	farfalla f	mariposa f
button (E)	Knopf m	—	bouton m	bottone m	botón m
buy (E)	kaufen	—	acheter	comprare	comprar
buyer (E)	Käufer m	—	acheteur m	acquirente m	comprador m
buzón (Es)	Briefkasten m	letterbox	boîte aux lettres f	cassetta delle lettere f	—
by chance (E)	zufällig	—	par hasard	per caso	por casualidad
bye! (E)	tschüs!	—	salut!	ciao!	¡hasta luego!
by heart (E)	auswendig	—	par cœur	a memoria	de memoria
by the way (E)	übrigens	—	d'ailleurs	del resto	por lo demás
cabalgar (Es)	reiten	ride	monter	cavalcare	—
caballo (Es)	Pferd n	horse	cheval m	cavallo m	—
cabaña (Es)	Hütte f	hut	cabane f	capanna f	—
cabane (F)	Hütte f	hut	—	capanna f	cabaña f
cabbage (E)	Kohl m	—	chou m	cavolo m	col f
cabeza (Es)	Kopf m	head	tête f	testa f	—
cabin (E)	Kabine f	—	cabine f	cabina f	cabina f

	D	E	F	I	Es
cabina (Es)	Kabine f	cabin	cabine f	cabina f	—
cabina (I)	Kabine f	cabin	cabine f	—	cabina f
cabina de teléfono (Es)	Telefonzelle f	phone box	cabine téléphonique f	cabina telefonica f	—
cabina telefonica (I)	Telefonzelle f	phone box	cabine téléphonique f	—	cabina de teléfono f
cabine (F)	Kabine f	cabin	—	cabina f	cabina f
cabine téléphonique (F)	Telefonzelle f	phone box	—	cabina telefonica f	cabina de teléfono f
cabinets (F)	Klosett n	lavatory	—	gabinetto m	retrete m
cable (E)	Kabel n	—	câble m	cavo m	cable m
cable (Es)	Kabel n	cable	câble m	cavo m	—
câble (F)	Kabel n	cable	—	cavo m	cable m
cabra (Es)	Ziege f	goat	chèvre f	capra f	—
caccia (I)	Jagd f	hunt	chasse f	—	caza f
cacciare (I)	jagen	hunt	chasser	—	cazar
cacciavite (I)	Schrauben- zieher m	screwdriver	tournevis m	—	destornillador m
cacher (F)	verstecken	hide	—	nascondere	ocultar
cada (Es)	jede(r,s)	each/every	chaque	ogni/ognuno	—
cada hora (Es)	stündlich	hourly	toutes les heures	ogni ora	—
cadáver (Es)	Leiche f	corpse	cadavre m	cadavere m	—
cadavere (I)	Leiche f	corpse	cadavre m	—	cadáver m
cada vez (Es)	jedesmal	each time	chaque fois	ogni volta	—
cadavre (F)	Leiche f	corpse	—	cadavere m	cadáver m
cadeau (F)	Geschenk n	present	—	regalo m	regalo m
cadena (Es)	Kette f	chain	chaîne f	catena f	—
cadera (Es)	Hüfte f	hip	hanche f	fianco m	—
cadere[1] (I)	fallen	fall	tomber	—	caer
cadere[2] (I)	stürzen	fall	tomber	—	caer
cadere[3] (I)	umfallen	fall over	tomber	—	caerse
cadre (F)	Rahmen m	frame	—	cornice f	marco m
caducado (Es)	ungültig	invalid	non valable	non valido(a)	—
caduta[1] (I)	Absturz m	crash	chute f	—	caída f
caduta[2] (I)	Sturz m	fall	chute f	—	caída f
caer[1] (Es)	fallen	fall	tomber	cadere	—
caer[2] (Es)	stürzen	fall	tomber	cadere	—
caer a tierra (Es)	abstürzen	crash	faire une chute	precipitare	—
caerse (Es)	umfallen	fall over	tomber	cadere	—
Café (D)	—	café	café m	caffè m	café m
café (E)	Café n	—	café m	caffè m	café m
café[1] (Es)	Café n	café	café m	caffè m	—
café[2] (Es)	Kaffee m	coffee	café m	caffè m	—
café[1] (F)	Café n	café	—	caffè m	café m
café[2] (F)	Kaffee m	coffee	—	caffè m	café m
caffè[1] (I)	Café n	café	café m	—	café m
caffè[2] (I)	Kaffee m	coffee	café m	—	café m
cage (E)	Käfig m	—	cage f	gabbia f	jaula f
cage (F)	Käfig m	cage	—	gabbia f	jaula f
cahier (F)	Heft n	exercise book	—	quaderno m	cuaderno m

	D	E	F	I	Es
caída¹ (Es)	Absturz *m*	crash	chute *f*	caduta *f*	—
caída² (Es)	Sturz *m*	fall	chute *f*	caduta *f*	—
caisse¹ (F)	Kasse *f*	till	—	cassa *f*	caja *f*
caisse² (F)	Kiste *f*	box	—	cassetta *f*	caja *f*
caisse d'épargne (F)	Sparkasse *f*	savings bank	—	cassa di risparmio *f*	caja de ahorros *f*
caja¹ (Es)	Kasse *f*	till	caisse *f*	cassa *f*	—
caja² (Es)	Kiste *f*	box	caisse *f*	cassetta *f*	—
caja³ (Es)	Schachtel *f*	box	boîte *f*	scatola *f*	—
caja de ahorros (Es)	Sparkasse *f*	savings bank	caisse d'épargne *f*	cassa di risparmio *f*	—
cajón (Es)	Schublade *f*	drawer	tiroir *m*	cassetto *m*	
cake¹ (E)	Kuchen *m*	—	gâteau *m*	dolce *m*	pastel *m*
cake² (E)	Torte *f*	—	gâteau *m*	torta *f*	tarta *f*
cake shop (E)	Konditorei *f*	—	pâtisserie *f*	pasticceria *f*	pastelería *f*
calamar (Es)	Tintenfisch *m*	cuttlefish	seiche *f*	seppia *f*	—
calcetín (Es)	Socke *f*	sock	chaussette *f*	calzino *m*	—
calcolare (I)	berechnen	calculate	calculer	—	calcular
calcular¹ (Es)	berechnen	calculate	calculer	calcolare	—
calcular² (Es)	rechnen	calculate	calculer	fare i conti	—
calculate (E)	rechnen	—	calculer	fare i conti	calcular
calculer¹ (F)	berechnen	calculate	—	calcolare	calcular
calculer² (F)	rechnen	calculate	—	fare i conti	calcular
caldo (Es)	Brühe *f*	broth	bouillon *m*	brodo *m*	—
caldo¹ (I)	heiß	hot	chaud(e)	—	caliente
caldo² (I)	Hitze *f*	heat	chaleur *f*	—	calor *m*
caldo³ (I)	warm	warm	chaud(e)	—	caliente
calefacción (Es)	Heizung *f*	heating	chauffage *m*	riscaldamento *m*	—
calefacción central (Es)	Zentralheizung *f*	central heating	chauffage central *m*	riscaldamento centrale *m*	—
calendar (E)	Kalender *m*	—	calendrier *m*	calendario *m*	calendario *m*
calendario (Es)	Kalender *m*	calendar	calendrier *m*	calendario *m*	—
calendario (I)	Kalender *m*	calendar	calendrier *m*	—	calendario *m*
calendrier (F)	Kalender *m*	calendar	—	calendario *m*	calendario *m*
calentar¹ (Es)	heizen	heat	chauffer	riscaldare	—
calentar² (Es)	wärmen	warm	chauffer	riscaldare	—
calf (E)	Kalb *n*	—	veau *m*	vitello *m*	ternera *f*
caliente¹ (Es)	heiß	hot	chaud(e)	caldo(a)	—
caliente² (Es)	warm	warm	chaud(e)	caldo(a)	—
calificación (Es)	Note *f*	mark	note *f*	voto *m*	—
call¹ (E)	Anruf *m*	—	coup de téléphone *m*	chiamata *f*	llamada *f*
call² (E)	nennen	—	appeler	chiamare	nombrar
callar (Es)	schweigen	be silent	taire, se	tacere	—
calle (Es)	Straße *f*	street	rue *f*	strada *f*	—
calle central (Es)	Hauptstraße *f*	main street	grande rue *f*	strada principale *f*	—
calle de dirección única (Es)	Einbahnstraße *f*	one-way street	rue à sens unique *f*	senso unico *m*	—
callejear (Es)	bummeln	stroll	flâner	girellare	—
callejón (Es)	Gasse *f*	lane	ruelle *f*	vicolo *m*	—

	D	E	F	I	Es
call off (E)	abblasen	—	annuler	disdire	anular
calm[1] (E)	beruhigen	—	calmer, se	calmarsi	calmarse
calm[2] (E)	Ruhe f	—	calme m	silenzio m	quietud f
calmar (Es)	beruhigen	calm down	calmer, se	calmarsi	—
calmare (I)	beruhigen, sich	calm down	calmer, se	—	calmarse
calme[1] (F)	Ruhe f	calm	—	silenzio m	quietud f
calme[2] (F)	still	quiet	—	calmo(a)	tranquilo(a)
calmer, se (F)	beruhigen	calm down	—	calmare	calmar
calmo[1] (I)	ruhig	quiet	tranquille	—	quieto(a)
calmo[2] (I)	still	quiet	calme	—	tranquilo(a)
calor[1] (Es)	Hitze f	heat	chaleur f	caldo m	—
calor[2] (Es)	Wärme f	warmth	chaleur f	calore m	—
calore (I)	Wärme f	warmth	chaleur f	—	calor m
calvo (I)	kahl	bald	chauve	—	calvo(a)
calvo (Es)	kahl	bald	chauve	calvo(a)	—
calza (I)	Strumpf m	stocking	bas m	—	media f
calzada (Es)	Fahrbahn f	roadway	chaussée f	carreggiata f	—
calzamaglia (I)	Strumpfhose f	tights	collants m pl	—	leotardos m pl
calzino (I)	Socke f	sock	chausette f	—	calcetín m
calzolaio (I)	Schuster m	shoemaker	cordonnier m	—	zapatero m
calzoncillos (Es)	Unterhose f	underpants	slip m	mutande f pl	—
cama (Es)	Bett n	bed	lit m	letto m	—
camarada (Es)	Genosse m	comrade	camarade m	compagno m	—
camarade (F)	Genosse m	comrade	—	compagno m	camarada m
camarero (Es)	Kellner m/ Ober m	waiter	garçon m	cameriere m	—
cambiamento[1] (I)	Veränderung f	change	changement m	—	cambio m
cambiamento[2] (I)	Wechsel m	change	changement m	—	cambio m
cambiar[1] (Es)	ändern	change	changer	cambiare	—
cambiar[2] (Es)	austauschen	exchange	échanger	scambiare	—
cambiar[3] (Es)	tauschen	swap	échanger	scambiare	—
cambiar[4] (Es)	umtauschen	exchange	échanger	cambiare	—
cambiar[5] (Es)	umziehen	move	déménager	cambiare casa	—
cambiar[6] (Es)	umwechseln	change	changer	cambiare	—
cambiar[7] (Es)	vertauschen	exchange	échanger	scambiare	—
cambiar[8] (Es)	verändern	change	transformer	mutare	—
cambiar[9] (Es)	wechseln	change	changer	cambiare	—
cambiare[1] (I)	ändern	change	changer	—	cambiar
cambiare[2] (I)	umtauschen	exchange	échanger	—	cambiar
cambiare[3] (I)	umsteigen	change	changer (de train)	—	transbordar
cambiare[4] (I)	umwechseln	change	changer	—	cambiar
cambiare[5] (I)	wechseln	change	changer	—	cambiar
cambiare casa (I)	umziehen	move	déménager	—	cambiar
cambiarse (Es)	umziehen	change	changer, se	cambiarsi	—
cambiarse de ropa (Es)	umkleiden	change	changer de vêtements	cambiarsi	—
cambiarsi[1] (I)	umziehen	change	changer, se	—	cambiarse
cambiarsi[2] (I)	umkleiden	change	changer de vêtements	—	cambiarse de ropa

	D	E	F	I	Es
cambio¹ (Es)	Austausch *m*	exchange	échange *m*	scambio *m*	—
cambio² (Es)	Kleingeld *n*	small change	monnaie *f*	spiccioli *m pl*	—
cambio³ (Es)	Umbuchung *f*	alteration	transfert *m*	riporto *m*	—
cambio⁴ (Es)	Veränderung *f*	change	changement *m*	cambiamento *m*	—
cambio⁵ (Es)	Wechsel *m*	change	changement *m*	cambiamento *m*	—
cambrioler (F)	einbrechen	break in	—	fare irruzione	irrumpir
camera (E)	Fotoapparat *m*	—	appareil photo *m*	macchina fotografica *f*	máquina fotográfica *f*
camera (I)	Zimmer *n*	room	chambre *f*	—	habitación *f*
camera da letto (I)	Schlafzimmer *n*	bedroom	chambre à coucher *f*	—	dormitorio *m*
cameriere (I)	Kellner *m*/Ober *m*	waiter	garçon *m*	—	camarero *m*
camicetta (I)	Bluse *f*	blouse	chemisier *m*	—	blusa *f*
camicia (I)	Hemd *n*	shirt	chemise *f*	—	camisa *f*
camilla (Es)	Bahre *f*	stretcher	brancard *m*	barella *f*	—
camino (Es)	Weg *m*	way	chemin *m*	via *f*	—
camión (Es)	Lastwagen *m*	lorry	camion *m*	camion *m*	—
camion (F)	Lastwagen *m*	lorry	—	camion *m*	camión *m*
camion (I)	Lastwagen *m*	lorry	camion *m*	—	camión *m*
camionero (Es)	Fernfahrer *m*	long-distance driver	routier *m*	camionista *m*	—
camión grúa (Es)	Abschlepp-wagen *m*	breakdown van	dépanneuse *f*	carro attrezzi *m*	—
camionista (I)	Fernfahrer *m*	long-distance driver	routier *m*	—	camionero *m*
camisa (Es)	Hemd *n*	shirt	chemise *f*	camicia *f*	—
camiseta (Es)	Unterhemd *n*	vest	tricot *m*	canottiera *f*	—
camp (E)	zelten	—	camper	campeggiare	acampar
campana (Es)	Glocke *f*	bell	cloche *f*	campana *f*	—
campana (I)	Glocke *f*	bell	cloche *f*	—	campana *f*
campanello (I)	Klingel *f*	bell	sonnette *f*	—	timbre *m*
campeggiare (I)	zelten	camp	camper	—	acampar
campeggio¹ (I)	Camping *n*	camping	camping *m*	—	camping *m*
campeggio² (I)	Campingplatz *m*	campsite	terrain de camping *m*	—	camping *m*
camper (E)	Wohnmobil n	—	caravane f	camper m	caravana *f*
camper (F)	zelten	camp	—	campeggiare	acampar
camper (I)	Wohnmobil *n*	camper	caravane *f*	—	caravana *f*
campesino (Es)	Bauer *m*	farmer	paysan *m*	contadino *m*	—
Camping (D)	—	camping	camping *m*	campeggio *m*	camping *m*
camping (E)	Camping *n*	—	camping *m*	campeggio *m*	camping *m*
camping¹ (Es)	Campingplatz *m*	campsite	terrain de camping *m*	campeggio *m*	—
camping² (Es)	Camping *n*	camping	camping *m*	campeggio *m*	—
camping (F)	Camping *n*	camping	—	campeggio *m*	camping *m*
Campingplatz (D)	—	campsite	terrain de camping *m*	campeggio *m*	camping *m*
campione (I)	Muster *n*	sample	modèle *m*	—	muestra *f*
campo¹ (Es)	Acker *m*	field	champ *m*	campo *m*	—
campo² (Es)	Feld *n*	field	champ *m*	campo *m*	—
campo¹ (I)	Acker *m*	field	champ *m*	—	campo *m*

	D	E	F	I	Es
campo² (I)	Feld *n*	field	champ *m*	—	campo *m*
campo dei giochi (I)	Spielplatz *m*	playground	terrain de jeux *m*	—	campo de juego *m*
campo de juego (Es)	Spielplatz *m*	playground	terrain de jeux *m*	campo dei giochi *m*	—
campsite (E)	Campingplatz *m*	—	terrain de camping *m*	campeggio *m*	camping *m*
can (E)	können	—	pouvoir	sapere	saber
Canada (E)	Kanada *n*	—	Canada *m*	Canada *m*	Canadá *m*
Canadá (Es)	Kanada *n*	Canada	Canada *m*	Canada *m*	—
Canada (F)	Kanada *n*	Canada	—	Canada *m*	Canadá *m*
Canada (I)	Kanada *n*	Canada	Canada *m*	—	Canadá *m*
Canal de la Mancha (Es)	Ärmelkanal *m*	Channel	Manche *f*	Manica *f*	—
canapé¹ (F)	Couch *f*	couch	—	divano *m*	diván *m*
canapé² (F)	Sofa *n*	sofa	—	sofà *m*	sofá *m*
canard (F)	Ente *f*	duck	—	anatra *f*	pato *m*
cancel (E)	abbestellen	—	décommander	annullare	anular el pedido de
cancelliere federale (I)	Bundeskanzler *m*	Federal Chancellor	chancelier fédéral *m*	—	canciller federal *m*
cancer (E)	Krebs *m*	—	cancer *m*	cancro *m*	cáncer *m*
cáncer (Es)	Krebs *m*	cancer	cancer *m*	cancro *m*	—
cancer (F)	Krebs *m*	cancer	—	cancro *m*	cáncer *m*
canciller federal (Es)	Bundeskanzler *m*	Federal Chancellor	chancelier fédéral *m*	cancelliere federale *m*	—
canción (Es)	Lied *n*	song	chanson *f*	canzone *f*	—
cancro (I)	Krebs *m*	cancer	cancer *m*	—	cáncer *m*
candela (I)	Kerze *f*	candle	bougie *f*	—	vela *f*
candidature (F)	Bewerbung *f*	application	—	domanda d'impiego *f*	candidatura *f*
candle (E)	Kerze *f*	—	bougie *f*	candela *f*	vela *f*
cane (I)	Hund *m*	dog	chien *m*	—	perro *m*
cangrejo (Es)	Krebs *m*	crayfish	écrevisse *f*	gambero *m*	—
cannocchiale (I)	Fernglas *n*	binoculars	jumelles *f pl*	—	gemelos *m pl*
canoa (I)	Paddelboot *n*	canoe	canoë *m*	—	piragua *f*
canoe (E)	Paddelboot *n*	—	canoë *m*	canoa *f*	piragua *f*
canot pneumatique (F)	Schlauchboot *n*	(rubber) dinghy	—	canotto pneumatico *m*	bote neumático *m*
canottiera (I)	Unterhemd *n*	vest	tricot *m*	—	camiseta *f*
canotto pneumatico (I)	Schlauchboot *n*	(rubber) dinghy	canot pneumatique *m*	—	bote neumático *m*
cansado (Es)	müde	tired	fatigué(e)	stanco(a)	—
cansar¹ (Es)	anstrengen	make an effort	faire des efforts	affaticare	—
cansar² (Es)	ermüden	tire	fatiguer	stancare	—
cantante (Es)	Sänger *m*	singer	chanteur *m*	cantante *m*	—
cantante (I)	Sänger *m*	singer	chanteur *m*	—	cantante *m*
cantar (Es)	singen	sing	chanter	cantare	—
cantare (I)	singen	sing	chanter	—	cantar
cantidad¹ (Es)	Menge *f*	quantity	quantité *f*	quantità *f*	—
cantidad² (Es)	Quantität *f*	quantity	quantité *f*	quantità *f*	—
cantina (I)	Keller *m*	cellar	cave *f*	—	sótano *m*
canto (Es)	Gesang *m*	singing	chant *m*	canto *m*	—

	D	E	F	I	Es
canto (I)	Gesang *m*	singing	chant *m*	—	canto *m*
cantuccio (I)	Winkel *m*	corner	coin *m*	—	rincón *m*
canzone (I)	Lied *n*	song	chanson *f*	—	canción *f*
cap (E)	Mütze *f*	—	casquette *f*	berretto *m*	gorra *f*
capable (E)	fähig	—	capable	capace	hábil
capable¹ (F)	fähig	capable	—	capace	hábil
capable² (F)	imstande	able	—	capace	en condiciones
capace¹ (I)	fähig	capable	capable	—	hábil
capace² (I)	imstande	able	capable	—	en condiciones
capacidad (Es)	Fähigkeit *f*	ability	capacité *f*	capacità *f*	—
capacità (I)	Fähigkeit *f*	ability	capacité *f*	—	capacidad *f*
capacité (F)	Fähigkeit *f*	ability	—	capacità *f*	capacidad *f*
capanna (I)	Hütte *f*	hut	cabane *f*	—	cabaña *f*
capello (I)	Haar *n*	hair	cheveu *m*	—	pelo *m*
capilla (Es)	Kapelle *f*	chapel	chapelle *f*	cappella *f*	—
capire (I)	verstehen	understand	comprendre	—	entender
capitaine (F)	Kapitän *m*	captain	—	capitano *m*	capitán *m*
capital¹ (E)	Hauptstadt *f*	—	capitale *f*	capitale *f*	capital *f*
capital² (E)	Kapital *n*	—	capital *m*	capitale *m*	capital *m*
capital¹ (Es)	Hauptstadt *f*	capital	capitale *f*	capitale *f*	—
capital² (Es)	Kapital *n*	capital	capital *m*	capitale *m*	—
capital (F)	Kapital *n*	capital	—	capitale *m*	capital *m*
capitale (F)	Hauptstadt *f*	capital	—	capitale *f*	capital *f*
capitale¹ (I)	Hauptstadt *f*	capital	capitale *f*	—	capital *f*
capitale² (I)	Kapital *n*	capital	capital *m*	—	capital *m*
capitán (Es)	Kapitän *m*	captain	capitaine *m*	capitano *m*	—
capitano (I)	Kapitän *m*	captain	capitaine *m*	—	capitán *m*
capitolo (I)	Kapitel *n*	chapter	chapitre *m*	—	capítulo *m*
capítulo (Es)	Kapitel *n*	chapter	chapitre *m*	capitolo *m*	—
capo (I)	Chef *m*	boss	patron *m*	—	jefe *m*
Capodanno (I)	Neujahr *n*	New Year	nouvel an *m*	—	Año Nuevo *m*
capolinea (I)	Endstation *f*	terminus	terminus *m*	—	estación terminal *f*
cappella (I)	Kapelle *f*	chapel	chapelle *f*	—	capilla *f*
cappello (I)	Hut *m*	hat	chapeau *m*	—	sombrero *m*
cappotto (I)	Mantel *m*	coat	manteau *m*	—	abrigo *m*
cappuccio (I)	Kapuze *f*	hood	capuchon *m*	—	capucha *f*
capra (I)	Ziege *f*	goat	chèvre *f*	—	cabra *f*
capriolo (I)	Reh *n*	deer	chevreuil *m*	—	corzo *m*
captain (E)	Kapitän *m*	—	capitaine *m*	capitano *m*	capitán *m*
capucha (Es)	Kapuze *f*	hood	capuchon *m*	cappuccio *m*	—
capuchon (F)	Kapuze *f*	hood	—	cappuccio *m*	capucha *f*
car¹ (E)	Auto *n*	—	voiture *f*	automobile *f* / macchina *f*	coche *m*
car² (E)	Wagen *m*	—	voiture *f*	vettura *f*	coche *m*
car (F)	denn	for	—	perché	pues/porque
cara (Es)	Gesicht *n*	face	visage *m*	faccia *f*	—
car accident (E)	Autounfall *m*	—	accident de voiture *m*	incidente stradale *m*	accidente de automóvil *m*
carácter (Es)	Charakter *m*	character	caractère *m*	carattere *m*	—

	D	E	F	I	Es
caractère (F)	Charakter *m*	character	—	carattere *m*	carácter *m*
caramella (I)	Bonbon *n*	sweet	bonbon *m*	—	caramelo *m*
caramelo (Es)	Bonbon *n*	sweet	bonbon *m*	caramella *f*	—
carattere (I)	Charakter *m*	character	caractère *m*	—	carácter *m*
caratteristica (I)	Merkmal *n*	characteristic	signe *m*	—	rasgo *m*
caravan (E)	Wohnwagen *m*	—	caravane *f*	roulotte *f*	rulota *f*
caravana (Es)	Wohnmobil *n*	camper	caravane *f*	camper *m*	—
caravane¹ (F)	Wohnwagen *m*	caravan	—	roulotte *f*	rulota *f*
caravane² (F)	Wohnmobil *n*	camper	—	camper *m*	caravana *f*
carbón (Es)	Kohle *f*	coal	charbon *m*	carbone *m*	—
carbone (I)	Kohle *f*	coal	charbon *m*	—	carbón *m*
cárcel (Es)	Gefängnis *n*	prison	prison *f*	prigione *f*	—
card (E)	Karte *f*	—	carte *f*	cartolina *f*	postal *f*
cardboard (E)	Pappe *f*	—	carton *m*	cartone *m*	cartón *m*
cardboard box (E)	Karton *m*	—	carton *m*	cartone *m*	cartón *m*
cardigan (E)	Strickjacke *f*	—	veste en tricot *f*	giacca di maglia *f*	chaqueta de punto *f*
care (E)	Pflege *f*	—	soins *m pl*	cura *f*	cuidado *m*
career (E)	Karriere *f*	—	carrière *f*	carriera *f*	carrera *f*
careful¹ (E)	sorgfältig	—	soigneux(-euse)	accurato(a)	cuidadoso(a)
careful² (E)	vorsichtig	—	prudent(e)	prudente	cauto(a)
careless¹ (E)	leichtsinnig	—	étourdi(e)	spensierato(a)	imprudente
careless² (E)	unvorsichtig	—	imprudent(e)	imprudente	descuidado(a)
caretaker (E)	Hausmeister *m*	—	concierge *m*	portinaio *m*	portero *m*
carga (Es)	Ladung *f*	cargo	charge *f*	carico *m*	—
cargar¹ (Es)	aufladen	load	charger	caricare	—
cargar² (Es)	aufbürden	burden	charger	addossare	—
cargar³ (Es)	verladen	load	charger	caricare	—
cargo (E)	Ladung *f*	—	charge *f*	carico *m*	carga *f*
caricare¹ (I)	aufladen	load	charger	—	cargar
caricare² (I)	verladen	load	charger	—	cargar
carico¹ (I)	Ladung *f*	cargo	charge *f*	—	carga *f*
carico² (I)	Last *f*	load	charge *f*	—	peso *m*
cariño (Es)	Zärtlichkeit *f*	tenderness	tendresse *f*	tenerezza *f*	—
carino¹ (I)	hübsch	pretty	joli(e)	—	bonito(a)
carino² (I)	nett	nice	joli(e)	—	agradable
carino³ (I)	niedlich	sweet	mignon(ne)	—	gracioso(a)
carnation (E)	Nelke *f*	—	œillet *m*	garofano *m*	clavel *m*
carnaval (Es)	Karneval *m*/ Fasching *m*	carnival	carnaval *m*	carnevale *m*	—
carnaval (F)	Karneval *m*/ Fasching *m*	carnival	—	carnevale *m*	carnaval *m*
carne (Es)	Fleisch *n*	meat	viande *f*	carne *f*	—
carne (I)	Fleisch *n*	meat	viande *f*	—	carne *f*
carne de cerdo (Es)	Schweinefleisch *n*	pork	viande de porc *f*	carne di maiale *f*	—
carne de vaca (Es)	Rindfleisch *n*	beef	viande de bœuf *f*	carne di manzo *f*	—
carne di maiale (I)	Schweinefleisch *n*	pork	viande de porc *f*	—	carne de cerdo *f*
carne di manzo (I)	Rindfleisch *n*	beef	viande de bœuf *f*	—	carne de vaca *f*
carne picada (Es)	Hackfleisch *n*	minced meat	viande hachée *f*	carne tritata *f*	—

	D	E	F	I	Es
carnet de chèques (F)	Scheckbuch n	cheque book	—	libretto degli assegni m	talonario de cheques m
carne tritata (I)	Hackfleisch n	minced meat	viande hachée f	—	carne picada f
carnevale (I)	Karneval m/ Fasching m	carnival	carnaval m	—	carnaval m
carnicería (Es)	Metzgerei f	butcher's	boucherie f	macelleria f	—
carnicero (Es)	Metzger m	butcher	boucher m	macellaio m	—
carnival (E)	Karneval m/ Fasching m	—	carnaval m	carnevale m	carnaval m
caro¹ (I)	lieb	sweet	gentil(le)	—	amable
caro² (I)	teuer	expensive	cher(-ère)	—	caro(a)
caro (Es)	teuer	expensive	cher(-ère)	caro(a)	—
carota (I)	Karotte f/ Möhre f	carrot	carotte f	—	zanahoria f
carotte (F)	Karotte f/ Möhre f	carrot	—	carota f	zanahoria f
carpenter (E)	Tischler m	—	menuisier m	falegname m	carpintero m
carpet (E)	Teppich m	—	tapis m	tappeto m	alfombra f
carpeta (Es)	Mappe f	folder	serviette f	raccoglitore m	—
carpintero (Es)	Tischler m	carpenter	menuisier m	falegname m	—
carré¹ (F)	Quadrat n	square	—	quadrato m	cuadrado m
carré² (F)	viereckig	square	—	quadrato(a)	cuadrangular
carré³ (F)	quadratisch	square	—	quadrato(a)	cuadrado(a)
carreau (F)	Scheibe f	pane	—	vetro m	cristal m
carreggiata (I)	Fahrbahn f	roadway	chaussée f	—	calzada f
carrera (Es)	Karriere f	career	carrière f	carriera f	—
carretera de circulación rápida (Es)	Schnellstraße f	expressway	voie rapide f	superstrada f	—
carretera nacional¹ (Es)	Bundesstraße f	Federal Highway/ main road	route nationale f	strada statale f	—
carretera nacional² (Es)	Landstraße f	country road	route f	strada provinciale f	—
carriage (E)	Waggon m	—	wagon m	vagone m	vagón m
carrier (E)	Träger m	—	porteur m	facchino m	mozo m
carriera (I)	Karriere f	career	carrière f	—	carrera f
carrière (F)	Karriere f	career	—	carriera f	carrera f
carro attrezzi (I)	Abschlepp- wagen m	breakdown van	dépanneuse f	—	camión grúa m
carrocería (Es)	Karosserie f	body	carrosserie f	carrozzeria f	—
carrosserie (F)	Karosserie f	body	—	carrozzeria f	carrocería f
carrot (E)	Karotte f/ Möhre f	—	carotte f	carota f	zanahoria f
carrozzeria (I)	Karosserie f	body	carrosserie f	—	carrocería f
carry (E)	tragen	—	porter	portare	llevar
carry on (E)	weitermachen	—	continuer	continuare	continuar
carta (Es)	Brief m	letter	lettre f	lettera f	—
carta (I)	Papier n	paper	papier m	—	papel m
carta con acuse de recibo (Es)	Einschreibebrief m	recorded delivery letter	lettre recommandée f	lettera raccomandata f	—
carta de amor (Es)	Liebesbrief m	love letter	lettre d'amour f	lettera d'amore f	—
carta d'identità (I)	Personalausweis m	identity card	carte d'identité f	—	documento de identidad m
carta geografica (I)	Landkarte f	map	carte f	—	mapa m

	D	E	F	I	Es
carte¹ (F)	Karte f	card	—	cartolina f	postal f
carte² (F)	Landkarte f	map	—	carta geografica f	mapa m
carte d'identité (F)	Personalausweis m	identity card	—	carta d'identitá f	documento de identidad m
cartel (Es)	Plakat n	poster	affiche f	affisso m	—
cartella (I)	Aktenmappe f	file	porte-documents m	—	cartera f
carte postale¹ (F)	Ansichtskarte f	postcard	—	cartolina f	tarjeta postal f
carte postale² (F)	Postkarte f	postcard	—	cartolina f	postal f
cartera (Es)	Aktenmappe f	file	porte-documents m	cartella f	—
cartero (Es)	Postbote m	postman	facteur m	postino m	—
cartoleria (I)	Schreibwaren-handlung f	stationery shop	papeterie f	—	papelería f
cartolina¹ (I)	Ansichtskarte f	postcard	carte postale f	—	tarjeta postal f
cartolina² (I)	Karte f	card	carte f	—	postal f
cartolina³ (I)	Postkarte f	postcard	carte postale f	—	postal f
cartón¹ (Es)	Karton m	cardboard box	carton m	cartone m	—
cartón² (Es)	Pappe f	cardboard	carton m	cartone m	—
carton¹ (F)	Karton m	cardboard box	—	cartone m	cartón m
carton² (F)	Pappe f	cardboard	—	cartone m	cartón m
cartone¹ (I)	Karton m	cardboard box	carton m	—	cartón m
cartone² (I)	Pappe f	cardboard	carton m	—	cartón m
casa¹ (Es)	Haus n	house	maison f	casa f	—
casa² (Es)	Haushalt m	household	ménage m	casa f	—
casa¹ (I)	Haus n	house	maison f	—	casa f
casa² (I)	Haushalt m	household	ménage m	—	casa f
casa de cambio (Es)	Wechselstube f	bureau de change	bureau de change m	ufficio di cambio m	—
casado (Es)	verheiratet	married	marié(e)	sposato(a)	—
casalinga (I)	Hausfrau f	housewife	femme de maison f	—	ama de casa f
casarse (Es)	heiraten	marry	marier, se	sposarsi	—
casco (Es)	Helm m	helmet	casque m	casco m	—
casco (I)	Helm m	helmet	casque m	—	casco m
cas d'urgence (F)	Notfall m	emergency	—	caso di emergenza m	caso de urgencia m
cash (E)	Bargeld f	—	espèces f pl	contanti m pl	dinero al contado m
cash on delivery (E)	Nachnahme f	—	remboursement m	pagamento contro assegno m	entrega contro reembolso f
casi¹ (Es)	beinahe	nearly	presque	circa/quasi	—
casi² (Es)	fast	nearly	presque	quasi	—
casino (Es)	Kasino n	casino	casino m	casinò m	—
casino (F)	Kasino n	casino		casinò m	casino m
casinò (I)	Kasino n	casino	casino m	—	casino m
caso¹ (I)	Vorfall m	incident	incident m	—	suceso m
caso² (I)	Zufall m	chance	hasard m	—	casualidad f
caso de urgencia (Es)	Notfall m	emergency	cas d'urgence m	caso di emergenza m	
caso di emergenza (I)	Notfall m	emergency	cas d'urgence m	—	caso de urgencia m
cásquara (Es)	Schale f	peel	peau f	buccia f	—

	D	E	F	I	Es
casque (F)	Helm *m*	helmet	—	casco *m*	casco *m*
casquette (F)	Mütze *f*	cap	—	berretto *m*	gorra *f*
cassa (I)	Kasse *f*	till	caisse *f*	—	caja *f*
cassa di risparmio (I)	Sparkasse *f*	savings bank	caisse d'épargne *f*	—	caja de ahorros *f*
cassé (F)	kaputt	broken	—	rotto(a)	roto(a)
casse-croûte (F)	Imbiß *m*	snack	—	spuntino *m*	refrigerio *m*
casser[1] (F)	brechen/ zerbrechen	break	—	rompere	romper
casser[2] (F)	einschlagen	smash	—	rompere	romper
casserole[1] (F)	Kochtopf *m*	saucepan	—	pentola *f*	olla *f*
casserole[2] (F)	Topf *m*	pot	—	pentola *f*	olla *f*
cassetta[1] (I)	Kiste *f*	box	caisse *f*	—	caja *f*
cassetta[2] (I)	Kassette *f*	cassette	cassette *f*	—	cassette *f*
cassetta delle lettere (I)	Briefkasten *m*	letterbox	boîte aux lettres *f*	—	buzón *m*
cassette (E)	Kassette *f*	—	cassette *f*	cassetta *f*	cassette *f*
cassette (Es)	Kassette *f*	cassette	cassette *f*	cassetta *f*	—
cassette (F)	Kassette *f*	cassette	—	cassetta *f*	cassette *f*
cassetto (I)	Schublade *f*	drawer	tiroir *m*	—	cajón *m*
castello (I)	Schloß *n*	castle	château *m*	—	castillo *m*
castigar (Es)	strafen	punish	punir	punire	—
castigo (Es)	Strafe *f*	punishment	punition *f*	punizione *f*	—
castillo (Es)	Schloß *n*	castle	château *m*	castello *m*	—
castle (E)	Schloß *n*	—	château *m*	castello *m*	castillo *m*
casualidad (Es)	Zufall *m*	chance	hasard *m*	caso *m*	—
cat (E)	Katze *f*	—	chat *m*	gatto *m*	gato *m*
catarro (Es)	Erkältung *f*	cold	refroidissement *m*	raffreddore *m*	—
catch[1] (E)	erwischen	—	attraper	acchiappare	atrapar
catch[2] (E)	fangen	—	attraper	acchiappare	coger
catedral[1] (Es)	Dom *m*	cathedral	cathédrale *f*	duomo *m*	—
catedral[2] (Es)	Kathedrale *f*	cathedral	cathédrale *f*	cattedrale *f*	—
catena (I)	Kette *f*	chain	chaîne *f*	—	cadena *f*
catenaccio (I)	Riegel *m*	bolt	verrou *m*	—	cerrojo *m*
catering (E)	Verpflegung *f*	—	nourriture *f*	vitto *m*	alimentación *f*
cathedral[1] (E)	Dom *m*	—	cathédrale *f*	duomo *m*	catedral *f*
cathedral[2] (E)	Kathedrale *f*	—	cathédrale *f*	cattedrale *f*	catedral *f*
cathédrale[1] (F)	Dom *m*	cathedral	—	duomo *m*	catedral *f*
cathédrale[2] (F)	Kathedrale *f*	cathedral	—	cattedrale *f*	catedral *f*
catholic (E)	katholisch	—	catholique	cattolico(a)	católico(a)
catholique (F)	katholisch	catholic	—	cattolico(a)	católico(a)
católico (Es)	katholisch	catholic	catholique	cattolico(a)	—
catorce (Es)	vierzehn	fourteen	quatorze	quattordici	—
cattedrale (I)	Kathedrale *f*	cathedral	cathédrale *f*	—	catedral *f*
cattivo[1] (I)	böse	wicked	méchant(e)	—	malo(a)
cattivo[2] (I)	schlecht	bad	mauvais(e)	—	malo(a)
cattivo[3] (I)	übel	bad	mauvais(e)	—	malo(a)
cattolico (I)	katholisch	catholic	catholique	—	católico(a)
cauliflower (E)	Blumenkohl *m*	—	chou-fleur *m*	cavolfiore *m*	coliflor *f*
causa[1] (Es)	Anlaß *m*	occasion	occasion *f*	occasione *f*	—

	D	E	F	I	Es
causa² (Es)	Grund m	reason	raison f	causa f	—
causa³ (Es)	Ursache f	cause	cause f	causa f	—
causa¹ (I)	Grund m	reason	raison f	—	causa f
causa² (I)	Ursache f	cause	cause f	—	causa f
causare (I)	verursachen	cause	causer	—	ocasionar
cause¹ (E)	Anlaß m	—	occasion f	occasione f	ocasión f
cause² (E)	Ursache f	—	cause f	causa f	causa f
cause³ (E)	verursachen	—	causer	causare	ocasionar
cause (F)	Ursache f	cause	—	causa f	causa f
causer¹ (F)	plaudern	chat	—	chiacchierare	conversar
causer² (F)	verursachen	cause	—	causare	ocasionar
caution (E)	Vorsicht f	—	prudence f	prudenza f	cuidado m
cauto (Es)	vorsichtig	careful	prudent(e)	prudente	—
cavalcare (I)	reiten	ride	monter	—	cabalgar
cavallo (I)	Pferd n	horse	cheval m	—	caballo m
cavar (Es)	graben	dig	creuser	scavare	—
cavatappi (I)	Korkenzieher m	corkscrew	tire-bouchon m	—	sacacorchos m
cave (E)	Höhle f	—	grotte f	caverna f	cueva f
cave (F)	Keller m	cellar	—	cantina f	sótano m
caverna (I)	Höhle f	cave	grotte f	—	cueva f
caviglia (I)	Knöchel m	ankle	cheville f	—	tobillo m
cavo¹ (I)	hohl	hollow	creux(-euse)	—	hueco(a)
cavo² (I)	Kabel n	cable	câble m	—	cable m
cavolfiore (I)	Blumenkohl m	cauliflower	chou-fleur m	—	coliflor f
cavolo (I)	Kohl m	cabbage	chou m	—	col f
caza¹ (Es)	Jagd f	hunt	chasse f	caccia f	—
caza² (Es)	Wild n	game	gibier m	selvaggina f	—
cazar (Es)	jagen	hunt	chasser	cacciare	—
ce¹ (F)	diese(r,s)	this	—	questo(a)	esta, este, esto
ce² (F)	jene(r,s)	that	—	quello(a)	aquella, aquel, aquello
cebolla (Es)	Zwiebel f	onion	oignon m	cipolla f	—
Cecoslovacchia (I)	Tschecho-slowakei f	Czechoslovakia	Tchécoslovaquie f	—	Checoslovaquia f
ceder (Es)	nachgeben	yield	céder	cedere	—
céder¹ (F)	nachgeben	yield	—	cedere	ceder
céder² (F)	überschreiben	make over	—	cedere	transferir
cedere¹ (I)	nachgeben	yield	céder	—	ceder
cedere² (I)	überschreiben	make over	céder	—	transferir
ceinture¹ (F)	Gurt m	belt	—	cinghia f	cinturón m
ceinture² (F)	Gürtel m	belt	—	cintura f	cinturón m
celebrar (Es)	feiern	celebrate	fêter	festeggiare	—
celebrate (E)	feiern	—	fêter	festeggiare	celebrar
célèbre (F)	berühmt	famous	—	famoso(a)	famoso(a)
célibataire¹ (F)	ledig	single	—	celibe m/nubile f	soltero(a)
célibataire² (F)	Junggeselle m	bachelor	—	scapolo m	soltero m
celibe¹ (I)	ledig	single	célibataire	—	soltero(a)
celibe² (I)	unverheiratet	unmarried	non marié(e)	—	soltero(a)
cellar (E)	Keller m	—	cave f	cantina f	sótano m

	D	E	F	I	Es
celos (Es)	Eifersucht f	jealousy	jalousie f	gelosia f	—
cementerio (Es)	Friedhof m	cemetery	cimetière m	cimitero m	—
cemetery (E)	Friedhof m	—	cimetière m	cimitero m	cementerio m
cena (Es)	Abendessen n	supper	dîner m	cena f	—
cena (I)	Abendessen n	supper	dîner m	—	cena f
cenar (Es)	speisen	dine	manger	cenare	—
cendre (F)	Asche f	ash	—	cenere f	ceniza f
cendrier (F)	Aschenbecher m	ashtray	—	portacenere m	cenicero m
cenere (I)	Asche f	ash	cendre f	—	ceniza f
cenicero (Es)	Aschenbecher m	ashtray	cendrier m	portacenere m	—
ceniza (Es)	Asche f	ash	cendre f	cenere f	—
cent[1] (F)	einhundert	one hundred	—	cento	cien
cent[2] (F)	hundert	hundred	—	cento	cien
cento[1] (I)	einhundert	one hundred	cent	—	cien
cento[2] (I)	hundert	hundred	cent	—	cien
central (E)	zentral	—	central(e)	centrale	céntrico(a)
central (F)	zentral	central	—	centrale	céntrico(a)
centrale (I)	zentral	central	central(e)	—	céntrico(a)
central heating (E)	Zentralheizung f	—	chauffage central m	riscaldamento centrale m	calefacción central f
central station (E)	Hauptbahnhof m	—	gare centrale f	stazione centrale f	estación central f
centre (E)	Zentrum n	—	centre m	centro m	centro m
centre (F)	Zentrum n	centre	—	centro m	centro m
centre ville (F)	Innenstadt f	town centre	—	centro città m	centro de ciudad m
céntrico (Es)	zentral	central	central(e)	centrale	—
centro (Es)	Zentrum n	centre	centre m	centro m	—
centro[1] (I)	Mitte f	middle	milieu m	—	medio m
centro[2] (I)	Zentrum n	centre	centre m	—	centro m
centro città (I)	Innenstadt f	town centre	centre ville m	—	centro de ciudad m
centro de ciudad (Es)	Innenstadt f	town centre	centre ville m	centro città m	—
century (E)	Jahrhundert n	—	siècle m	secolo m	siglo m
cependant[1] (F)	dennoch	nevertheless	—	tuttavia	sin embargo
cependant[2] (F)	indessen	meanwhile	—	nel frattempo	en eso
cependant[3] (F)	jedoch	however	—	tuttavia	sin embargo
cepillo (Es)	Bürste f	brush	brosse f	spazzola f	—
cepillo de dientes (Es)	Zahnbürste f	toothbrush	brosse à dents f	spazzolino da denti m	—
cerca de (Es)	bei	at/near	chez/près de	da/presso	—
cercare (I)	suchen	look for	chercher	—	buscar
cerchio (I)	Kreis m	circle	cercle	—	círculo m
cercle (F)	Kreis m	circle	—	cerchio m	círculo m
cercueil (F)	Sarg m	coffin	—	bara f	ataúd m
cerdo (Es)	Schwein n	pig	cochon m	maiale m	—
cereal (E)	Getreide n	—	céréales f pl	cereali m pl	cereales m pl
cereales (Es)	Getreide n	grain	céréales f pl	cereali m pl	—
céréales (F)	Getreide n	grain	—	cereali m pl	cereales m pl
cereali (I)	Getreide n	grain	céréales f pl	—	cereales m pl
cerebro (Es)	Hirn n	brain	cerveau m	cervello m	—

	D	E	F	I	Es
cereza (Es)	Kirsche *f*	cherry	cerise *f*	ciliegia *f*	—
cerilla (Es)	Streichholz *n*	match	allumette *f*	fiammifero *m*	—
cerise (F)	Kirsche *f*	cherry	—	ciliegia *f*	cereza *f*
cero (Es)	Null *f*	zero	zéro	zero	—
cerotto (I)	Pflaster *n*	plaster	emplâtre *m*	—	esparadrapo *m*
cerrado (Es)	geschlossen	closed	fermé(e)	chiuso(a)	—
cerradura (Es)	Schloß *n*	lock	serrure *f*	serratura *f*	—
cerrar[1] (Es)	schließen	close	fermer	chiudere	—
cerrar[2] (Es)	zudrehen	turn off	fermer	chiudere	—
cerrar[3] (Es)	zumachen	shut	fermer	chiudere	—
cerrar con llave[1] (Es)	verschließen	lock (up)	fermer à clé	chiudere a chiave	—
cerrar con llave[2] (Es)	zuschließen	lock (up)	fermer à clé	chiudere a chiave	—
cerrojo (Es)	Riegel *m*	bolt	verrou *m*	catenaccio *m*	—
certain (F)	gewiß	certainely	—	certo(a)	cierto(a)
certain (E)	gewiß	—	certain(e)	certo(a)	cierto(a)
certainement (F)	bestimmt	definitely	—	certamente	ciertamente
certamente (I)	bestimmt	definitely	certainement	—	ciertamente
certificado[1] (Es)	Attest *n*	certificate	certificat *m*	certificato *m*	—
certificado[2] (Es)	Bescheinigung *f*	certificate	attestation *f*	certificato *m*	—
certificat (F)	Attest *n*	certificate	—	certificato *m*	certificado *m*
certificate[1] (E)	Attest *n*	—	certificat *m*	certificato *m*	certificado *m*
certificate[2] (E)	Bescheinigung *f*	—	attestation *f*	certificato *m*	certificado *m*
certificato[1] (I)	Attest *n*	certificate	certificat *m*	—	certificado *m*
certificato[2] (I)	Bescheinigung *f*	certificate	attestation *f*	—	certificado *m*
certify (E)	bescheinigen	—	attester	attestare	atestiguar
certo (I)	gewiß	certain(ly)	certain(e)	—	cierto
cerveau (F)	Hirn *n*	brain	—	cervello *m*	cerebro *m*
cervello (I)	Hirn *n*	brain	cerveau *m*	—	cerebro *m*
cerveza (Es)	Bier *n*	beer	bière *f*	birra *f*	—
césped (Es)	Rasen *m*	lawn	pelouse *f*	prato *m*	—
cespuglio (I)	Strauch *m*	bush	buisson *m*	—	arbusto *m*
cessare (I)	aufhören	stop	arrêter	—	terminar
cesta (Es)	Korb *m*	basket	panier *m*	cesto *m*	—
cesto (I)	Korb *m*	basket	panier *m*	—	cesta *f*
c'est pourquoi (F)	deshalb	therefore	—	perció	por eso
ceto (I)	Rang *m*	rank	rang *m*	—	clase *f*
cetriolo (I)	Gurke *f*	cucumber	concombre *m*	—	pepino *m*
chagrin (F)	Kummer *m*	grief	—	dolore *m*	pena *f*
chain (E)	Kette *f*	—	chaîne *f*	catena *f*	cadena *f*
chaîne (F)	Kette *f*	chain	—	catena *f*	cadena *f*
chair (E)	Stuhl *m*	—	chaise *f*	sedia *f*	silla *f*
chaise (F)	Stuhl *m*	chair	—	sedia *f*	silla *f*
chaise longue (F)	Liegestuhl *m*	deck chair	—	sedia a sdraio *f*	tumbona *f*
chal (Es)	Schal *m*	scarf	écharpe *f*	sciarpa *f*	—
chaleco salvavidas (Es)	Schwimmweste *f*	life jacket	gilet de sauvetage *m*	giubbotto di salvataggio *m*	—
chaleur[1] (F)	Hitze *f*	heat	—	caldo *m*	calor *m*

	D	E	F	I	Es
chaleur² (F)	Wärme f	warmth	—	calore m	calor m
chambre (F)	Zimmer n	room	—	camera f	habitación f
chambre à coucher (F)	Schlafzimmer n	bedroom	—	camera da letto f	dormitorio m
champ¹ (F)	Acker m	field	—	campo m	campo m
champ² (F)	Feld n	field	—	campo m	campo m
champagne (E)	Sekt m	—	champagne m	spumante m	champán m
champagne (F)	Sekt m	champagne	—	spumante m	champán m
champán (Es)	Sekt m	champagne	champagne m	spumante m	—
champignon (F)	Pilz m	mushroom	—	fungo m	hongo m
Chance (D)	—	chance	possibilité f	occasione f	oportunidad f
chance¹ (E)	Chance f	—	possibilité f	occasione f	oportunidad f
chance² (E)	Zufall m	—	hasard m	caso m	casualidad f
chance (F)	Glück n	luck	—	fortuna f	suerte f
chanceler (F)	wanken	stagger	—	barcollare	vacilar
chancelier fédéral (F)	Bundeskanzler m	Federal Chancellor	—	cancelliere federale m	canciller federal m
change¹ (E)	ändern	—	changer	cambiare	cambiar
change² (E)	umkleiden	—	changer de vêtements	cambiarsi	cambiarse de ropa
change³ (E)	umsteigen	—	changer (de train)	cambiare	transbordar
change⁴ (E)	umziehen	—	changer, se	cambiarsi	cambiarse
change⁵ (E)	umwechseln	—	changer	cambiare	cambiar
change⁶ (E)	verändern	—	transformer	mutare	cambiar
change⁷ (E)	Veränderung f	—	changement m	cambiamento m	cambio m
change⁸ (E)	wechseln	—	changer	cambiare	cambiar
change⁹ (E)	Wechsel m	—	changement m	cambiamento m	cambio m
changeable (E)	veränderlich	—	variable	variabile	variable
changement¹ (F)	Veränderung f	change	—	cambiamento m	cambio m
changement² (F)	Wechsel m	change	—	cambiamento m	cambio m
changer (de train) (F)	umsteigen	change	—	cambiare	transbordar
changer¹ (F)	ändern	change	—	cambiare	cambiar
changer² (F)	umwechseln	change	—	cambiare	cambiar
changer³ (F)	wechseln	change	—	cambiare	cambiar
changer, se (F)	umziehen	change	—	cambiarsi	cambiarse
changer de vêtements (F)	umkleiden	change	—	cambiarsi	cambiarse de ropa
Channel (E)	Ärmelkanal m	—	Manche f	Manica f	Canal de la Mancha m
chanson (F)	Lied n	song	—	canzone f	canción f
chant (F)	Gesang m	singing	—	canto m	canto m
chantage (F)	Erpressung f	blackmail	—	ricatto m	chantaje m
chantaje (Es)	Erpressung f	blackmail	chantage m	ricatto m	—
chanter (F)	singen	sing	—	cantare	cantar
chanteur (F)	Sänger m	singer	—	cantante m	cantante m
chapa (Es)	Blech n	sheet metal	tôle f	latta f	—
chapeau (F)	Hut m	hat	—	cappello m	sombrero m
chapel (E)	Kapelle f	—	chapelle f	cappella f	capilla f
chapelle (F)	Kapelle f	chapel	—	cappella f	capilla f
chapitre (F)	Kapitel n	chapter	—	capitolo m	capítulo m

	D	E	F	I	Es
chapter (E)	Kapitel n	—	chapitre m	capitolo m	capítulo m
chaque (F)	jede(r,s)	each/every	—	ogni/ognuno	cada
chaque fois (F)	jedesmal	each time	—	ogni volta	cada vez
chaqueta (Es)	Jacke f	jacket	veste f	giacca f	—
chaqueta de punto (Es)	Strickjacke f	cardigan	veste en tricot f	giacca di maglia f	—
character (E)	Charakter m	—	caractère m	carattere m	carácter m
characteristic (E)	Merkmal n	—	signe m	caratteristica f	rasgo m
Charakter (D)	—	character	caractère m	carattere m	carácter m
charbon (F)	Kohle f	coal	—	carbone m	carbón m
charco (Es)	Pfütze f	puddle	flaque f	pozzanghera f	—
charcuterie (F)	Aufschnitt m	cold meat	—	affettato m	fiambre m
charge[1] (E)	anrechnen	—	compter	mettere in conto	poner en cuenta
charge[2] (E)	berechnen	—	calculer	calcolare	calcular
charge (F)	Last f	load	—	carico m	peso m
charge for admission (E)	Eintritt m	—	entrée f	entrata f	entrada f
chargement (F)	Ladung f	cargo	—	carico m	carga f
charger[1] (F)	aufladen	load	—	caricare	cargar
charger[2] (F)	verladen	load	—	caricare	cargar
charger[3] (F)	aufbürden	burden	—	addossare	cargar
charger de (F)	beauftragen	instruct	—	incaricare	encargar
charlar (Es)	schwatzen	chatter	bavarder	chiacchierare	—
charmant (D)	—	charming	charmant(e)	affascinante	encantador(a)
charmant (F)	charmant	charming	—	affascinante	encantador(a)
charming (E)	charmant	—	charmant(e)	affascinante	encantador(a)
charwoman (E)	Putzfrau f	—	femme de ménage f	donna delle pulizie f	mujer de la limpieza f
chasse (F)	Jagd f	hunt	—	caccia f	caza f
chasser (F)	jagen	hunt	—	cacciare	cazar
chat (E)	plaudern	—	causer	chiacchierare	conversar
chat (F)	Katze f	cat	—	gatto m	gato m
château (F)	Schloß n	castle	—	castello m	castillo m
château fort (F)	Burg f	fortress	—	rocca f	fortaleza f
chatter (E)	schwatzen	—	bavarder	chiacchierare	charlar
chaud[1] (F)	heiß	hot	—	caldo(a)	caliente
chaud[2] (F)	warm	warm	—	caldo(a)	caliente
chauffage (F)	Heizung f	heating	—	riscaldamento m	calefacción f
chauffage central (F)	Zentralheizung f	central heating	—	riscaldamento centrale m	calefacción central f
chauffer[1] (F)	heizen	heat	—	riscaldare	calentar
chauffer[2] (F)	wärmen	warm	—	riscaldare	calentar
Chauffeur (D)	—	chauffeur	chauffeur m	autista m	chófer m
chauffeur (E)	Chauffeur m	—	chauffeur m	autista m	chófer m
chauffeur (F)	Chauffeur m	chauffeur	—	autista m	chófer m
chausette (F)	Socke f	sock	—	calzino m	calcetín m
chaussée (F)	Fahrbahn f	roadway	—	carreggiata f	calzada f
chaussure (F)	Schuh m	shoe	—	scarpa f	zapato m
chauve (F)	kahl	bald	—	calvo(a)	calvo(a)
che[1] (I)	daß	that	que	—	que

	D	E	F	I	Es
che[2] (I)	welch	what a	quel(le)	—	¿qué?
che[3] (I)	was	what	quoi/ qu'est-ce que	—	¿qué?
cheap (E)	billig	—	bon marché(e)	a buon mercato	barato(a)
cheat (E)	betrügen	—	tromper	ingannare	engañar
check[1] (E)	nachsehen	—	vérifier	controllare	examinar
check[2] (E)	nachprüfen	—	contrôler	controllare	comprobar
check[3] (E)	überprüfen	—	contrôler	esaminare	examinar
checked (E)	kariert	—	à carreaux	a quadretti	a cuadros
Checoslovaquia (Es)	Tschecho- slowakei f	Czechoslovakia	Tchécoslovaquie f	Cecoslovacchia f	—
cheek (E)	Wange f	—	joue f	guancia f	mejilla f
cheeky (E)	frech	—	insolent(e)	sfacciato(a)	atrevido(a)
cheers! (E)	prost!	—	santé!	salute!	¡salud!
cheese (E)	Käse m	—	fromage m	formaggio m	queso m
Chef (D)	—	boss	patron m	capo m	jefe m
chef d'orchestre (F)	Dirigent m	conductor	—	direttore d'orchestra m	director(de orquesta) m
chemical (E)	chemisch	—	chimique	chimico(a)	químico(a)
chemin (F)	Weg m	way	—	via f	camino m
chemin de fer (F)	Eisenbahn f	railway	—	ferrovia f	ferrocarril m
chemisch (D)	—	chemical	chimique	chimico(a)	químico(a)
chemise (F)	Hemd n	shirt	—	camicia f	camisa f
chemisier (F)	Bluse f	blouse	—	camicetta f	blusa f
chemist's[1] (E)	Apotheke f	—	pharmacie f	farmacia f	farmacia f
chemist's[2] (E)	Drogerie f	—	droguerie f	drogheria f	droguería f
cheque (E)	Scheck m	—	chèque m	assegno m	cheque m
cheque (Es)	Scheck m	cheque	chèque m	assegno m	—
chèque (F)	Scheck m	cheque	—	assegno m	cheque m
cheque book (E)	Scheckbuch n	—	carnet de chèques m	libretto degli assegni m	talonario de cheques m
cheque de viaje (Es)	Reisescheck m	traveller's cheque	cheque de voyage m	assegno turistico m	—
chèque de voyage (F)	Reisescheck m	traveller's cheque	—	assegno turistico m	cheque de viaje m
cher[1] (F)	wert	worth	—	che vale	valioso(a)
cher[2] (F)	teuer	expensive	—	caro(a)	caro(a)
chercher (F)	suchen	look for	—	cercare	buscar
chéri (F)	Liebling m	darling	—	tesoro m	querido m
cherry (E)	Kirsche f	—	cerise f	ciliegia f	cereza f
cheval (F)	Pferd n	horse	—	cavallo m	caballo m
che vale (I)	wert	worth	cher(-ère)	—	valioso(a)
cheveu (F)	Haar n	hair	—	capello m	pelo m
cheville (F)	Knöchel m	ankle	—	caviglia f	tobillo m
chèvre (F)	Ziege f	goat	—	capra f	cabra f
chevreuil (F)	Reh n	deer	—	capriolo m	corzo m
chew (E)	kauen	—	mâcher	masticare	masticar
chez (F)	bei	at/near	—	da/presso	cerca de/junto a
chi (I)	wer	who	qui	—	¿quién?
chiacchierare[1] (I)	plaudern	chat	causer	—	conversar
chiacchierare[2] (I)	schwatzen	chatter	bavarder	—	charlar

	D	E	F	I	Es
chiamare[1] (I)	nennen	call	appeler	—	nombrar
chiamare[2] (I)	rufen	shout	appeler	—	llamar
chiamare con cenni (I)	winken	wave	faire signe	—	llamar con gestos
chiamarsi (I)	heißen	be called	appeler, se	—	llamarse
chiamata (I)	Anruf m	call	coup de téléphone m	—	llamada f
chiaro[1] (I)	deutlich	clear	clair(e)	—	claro(a)
chiaro[2] (I)	klar	clear	clair(e)	—	claro(a)
chiaro[3] (I)	hell	bright	clair(e)	—	claro(a)
chiasso (I)	Krach m	noise	bruit m	—	ruido m
chiatta (I)	Kahn m	barge	barque f	—	barcaza f
chiave (I)	Schlüssel m	key	clé f	—	llave f
chic (F)	schick	stylish	—	elegante	elegante
chica (Es)	Mädchen n	girl	jeune fille f	ragazza f	—
chicken (E)	Huhn n	—	poule f	pollo m	gallina f
chico (Es)	Junge m	boy	garçon m	ragazzo m	—
chien (F)	Hund m	dog	—	cane m	perro m
chiesa (I)	Kirche f	church	église f	—	iglesia f
chiffre (F)	Zahl f	number	—	numero m	número m
child (E)	Kind n	—	enfant m	bambino m	niño m
childhood (E)	Kindheit f	—	enfance f	infanzia f	niñez f
chilogrammo (I)	Kilogramm n	kilogram	kilogramme m	—	kilogramo m
chilometro (I)	Kilometer m	kilometre	kilomètre m	—	kilómetro m
chimico (I)	chemisch	chemical	chimique	—	químico(a)
chimique (F)	chemisch	chemical	—	chimico(a)	químico(a)
chin (E)	Kinn n	—	menton m	mento m	barbilla f
chiodo (I)	Nagel m	nail	clou m	—	clavo m
Chirurg (D)	—	surgeon	chirurgien m	chirurgo m	cirujano m
chirurgien (F)	Chirurg m	surgeon	—	chirurgo m	cirujano m
chirurgo (I)	Chirurg m	surgeon	chirurgien m	—	cirujano m
chiste (Es)	Witz m	joke	plaisanterie f	barzelletta f	—
chitarra (I)	Gitarre f	guitar	guitare f	—	guitarra f
chiudere[1] (I)	schließen	close	fermer	—	cerrar
chiudere[2] (I)	verschließen	lock (up)	fermer à clé	—	cerrar con llave
chiudere[3] (I)	zumachen	shut	fermer	—	cerrar
chiudere[4] (I)	zudrehen	turn off	fermer	—	cerrar
chiudere a chiave (I)	zuschließen	lock (up)	fermer à clé	—	cerrar con llave
chiuso (I)	geschlossen	closed	fermé(e)	—	cerrado(a)
chiusura (I)	Verschluß m	lock	fermeture f	—	cierre m
chiusura lampo (I)	Reißverschluß m	zip	fermeture éclair f	—	cremallera f
chocolat (F)	Schokolade f	chocolate	—	cioccolato m	chocolate m
chocolate (E)	Schokolade f	—	chocolat m	cioccolato m	chocolate m
chocolate (Es)	Schokolade f	chocolate	chocolat m	cioccolato m	—
chœur (F)	Chor m	choir	—	coro m	coro m
chófer (Es)	Chauffeur m	chauffeur	chauffeur m	autista m	—
choice[1] (E)	Auswahl f	—	choix m	scelta f	elección f
choice[2] (E)	Wahl f	—	choix m	scelta f	opción f
choir (E)	Chor m	—	chœur m	coro m	coro m

	D	E	F	I	Es
choisir[1] (F)	auswählen	choose	—	scegliere	elegir
choisir[2] (F)	aussuchen	select	—	scegliere	escoger
choix[1] (F)	Auswahl f	choice	—	scelta f	elección f
choix[2] (F)	Wahl f	choice	—	scelta f	opción f
chômage (F)	Arbeitslosig-keit f	unemployment	—	disoccupazione f	desempleo m
choose (E)	auswählen	—	choisir	scegliere	elegir
Chor (D)	—	choir	chœur m	coro m	coro m
chose[1] (F)	Ding n	thing	—	cosa f	cosa f
chose[2] (F)	Sache f	thing	—	cosa f	cosa f
chou (F)	Kohl m	cabbage	—	cavolo m	col f
chou-fleur (F)	Blumenkohl m	cauliflower	—	cavolfiore m	coliflor f
chrétien (F)	Christ m	Christian	—	cristiano m	cristiano m
Christ (D)	—	Christian	chrétien m	cristiano m	cristiano m
christian (E)	Christ m	—	chrétien m	cristiano m	cristiano m
Christian name (E)	Vorname m	—	prénom m	nome di battesimo m	nombre m
Christmas (E)	Weihnachten n	—	Noël m	Natale m	Navidad(es) f (pl)
Christmas Eve (E)	Heiligabend m	—	nuit de Noël f	vigilia di Natale f	Nochebuena f
chuchoter (F)	flüstern	whisper	—	bisbigliare	cuchichear
chuleta (Es)	Kotelett n	cutlet	côtelette f	costoletta f	—
chupar (Es)	lutschen	suck	sucer	succhiare	—
church (E)	Kirche f	—	église f	chiesa f	iglesia f
chute[1] (F)	Absturz m	crash	—	caduta f	caída f
chute[2] (F)	Sturz m	fall	—	caduta f	caída f
ciao! (I)	tschüs!	bye!	salut!	—	¡hasta luego!
cibo[1] (I)	Kost f	food	nourriture f	—	alimento m
cibo[2] (I)	Speise f	food	aliment m	—	comida f
cicatrice (F)	Narbe f	scar	—	cicatrice f	cicatriz f
cicatrice (I)	Narbe f	scar	cicatrice f	—	cicatriz f
cicatriz (Es)	Narbe f	scar	cicatrice f	cicatrice f	—
cieco (I)	blind	blind	aveugle	—	ciego(a)
ciego (Es)	blind	blind	aveugle	cieco(a)	—
ciel (F)	Himmel m	sky	—	cielo m	cielo m
cielo (Es)	Himmel m	sky	ciel m	cielo m	—
cielo (I)	Himmel m	sky	ciel m	—	cielo m
cien[1] (Es)	einhundert	one hundred	cent	cento	—
cien[2] (Es)	hundert	hundred	cent	cento	—
ciencia (Es)	Wissenschaft f	science	science f	scienza f	—
científico (Es)	Wissen-schaftler m	scientist	scientifique m	scienziato m	—
cierre (Es)	Verschluß m	lock	fermeture f	chiusura f	—
ciertamente (Es)	bestimmt	definite	certainement	certamente	—
cierto (Es)	gewiß	certain	certain(e)	certo	—
cigar (E)	Zigarre f	—	cigare m	sigaro m	cigarro m
cigare (F)	Zigarre f	cigar	—	sigaro m	cigarro m
cigarette (E)	Zigarette f	—	cigarette f	sigaretta f	cigarrillo m
cigarette (F)	Zigarette f	cigarette	—	sigaretta f	cigarrillo m
cigarrillo (Es)	Zigarette f	cigarette	cigarette f	sigaretta f	—

	D	E	F	I	Es
cigarro (Es)	Zigarre f	cigar	cigare m	sigaro m	—
ciglia (I)	Wimper f	eyelash	cil m	—	pestaña f
cil (F)	Wimper f	eyelash	—	ciglia f	pestaña f
ciliegia (I)	Kirsche f	cherry	cerise f	—	cereza f
cima (I)	Gipfel m	peak	sommet m	—	cumbre f
cimetière (F)	Friedhof m	cemetery	—	cimitero m	cementerio m
cimitero (I)	Friedhof m	cemetery	cimetière m	—	cementerio m
cinco (Es)	fünf	five	cinq	cinque	—
cincuenta (Es)	fünfzig	fifty	cinquante	cinquanta	—
cine (Es)	Kino n	cinema	cinéma m	cinema m	—
cinema (E)	Kino n	—	cinéma m	cinema m	cine m
cinéma (F)	Kino n	cinema	—	cinema m	cine m
cinema (I)	Kino n	cinema	cinéma m	—	cine m
cinghia[1] (I)	Gurt m	belt	ceinture f	—	cinturón m
cinghia[2] (I)	Riemen m	strap	courroie f	—	correa f
cinq (F)	fünf	five	—	cinque	cinco
cinquanta (I)	fünfzig	fifty	cinquante	—	cincuenta
cinquante (F)	fünfzig	fifty	—	cinquanta	cincuenta
cinque (I)	fünf	five	cinq	—	cinco
cinta (Es)	Band n	ribbon	bandeau m	nastro m	—
cinta magnetofónica (Es)	Tonband n	tape	bande magnétique f	nastro magnetico m	—
cintura (I)	Gürtel m	belt	ceinture f	—	cinturón m
cinturón[1] (Es)	Gurt m	belt	ceinture f	cinghia f	—
cinturón[2] (Es)	Gürtel m	girdle	ceinture f	cintura f	—
cioccolato (I)	Schokolade f	chocolate	chocolat m	—	chocolate m
cioè (I)	nämlich	namely	à savoir	—	a saber
cipolla (I)	Zwiebel f	onion	oignon m	—	cebolla f
cipria (I)	Puder m	powder	poudre f	—	polvos m pl
cirage (F)	Schuhcreme f	shoe polish	—	lucido per scarpe m	betún m
circa (I)	beinahe	nearly	presque	—	casi
circle (E)	Kreis m	—	cercle	cerchio m	círculo m
circo (Es)	Zirkus m	circus	cirque m	circo m	—
circo (I)	Zirkus m	circus	cirque m	—	circo m
circolazione (I)	Kreislauf m	circulation	circulation f	—	circulación f
circondare (I)	umgeben	surround	entourer	—	rodear
circonstances (F)	Umstände pl	circumstances	—	circostanze f pl	circunstancias f pl
circostanze (I)	Umstände pl	circumstances	circonstances f pl	—	circunstancias f pl
circuit (F)	Rundfahrt f	round trip	—	giro m	gira f
circulación (Es)	Kreislauf m	circulation	circulation f	circolazione f	—
circulation (E)	Kreislauf m	—	circulation f	circolazione f	circulación f
circulation[1] (F)	Kreislauf m	circulation	—	circolazione f	circulación f
circulation[2] (F)	Verkehr m	traffic	—	traffico m	tráfico m
círculo (Es)	Kreis m	circle	cercle	cerchio m	—
circumstances (E)	Umstände m	—	circonstances f pl	circostanze f pl	circunstancias f pl
circunstancias (Es)	Umstände m	circumstances	circonstances f pl	circostanze f pl	—
circus (E)	Zirkus m	—	cirque m	circo m	circo m
cirque (F)	Zirkus m	circus	—	circo m	circo m

	D	E	F	I	Es
ciruela (Es)	Pflaume f	plum	prune f	prugna f	—
cirujano (Es)	Chirurg m	surgeon	chirurgien m	chirurgo m	—
ciseaux (F)	Schere f	pair of scissors	—	forbici f pl	tijeras f pl
cistifellea (I)	Galle f	gall	fiel m	—	bilis f
cita (Es)	Verabredung f	date	rendez-vous m	appuntamento m	—
citar (Es)	vorladen	summon	assigner	citare in giudizio	—
citare in giudizio (I)	vorladen	summon	assigner	—	citar
cité (F)	Siedlung f	settlement	—	agglomerato m	colonia f
citron (F)	Zitrone f	lemon	—	limone m	limón m
città (I)	Stadt f	town	ville f	—	ciudad f
cittadinanza (I)	Staatsangehörigkeit f	nationality	nationalité f	—	nacionalidad f
ciudad (Es)	Stadt f	town	ville f	città f	—
civil (E)	bürgerlich	—	civil(e)	civile	civil
civil (Es)	bürgerlich	civil	civil(e)	civile	—
civil (F)	bürgerlich	civil	—	civile	civil
civile (I)	bürgerlich	civil	civil(e)	—	civil
civilisation (E)	Zivilisation f	—	civilisation f	civiltà f	civilización f
civilisation (F)	Zivilisation f	civilisation	—	civiltà f	civilización f
civiltà (I)	Zivilisation f	civilisation	civilisation f	—	civilización f
civilización (Es)	Zivilisation f	civilisation	civilisation f	civiltà f	—
civil servant (E)	Beamter m	—	fonctionnaire m	impiegato statale m	funcionario m
clacson (I)	Hupe f	horn	claxon m	—	bocina f
clair[1] (F)	deutlich	clear	—	chiaro(a)	claro(a)
clair[2] (F)	hell	bright	—	chiaro(a)	claro(a)
clair[3] (F)	klar	clear	—	chiaro(a)	claro(a)
claro[1] (Es)	deutlich	clear	clair(e)	chiaro(a)	—
claro[2] (Es)	hell	bright	clair(e)	chiaro(a)	—
claro[3] (Es)	klar	clear	clair(e)	chiaro(a)	—
clase[1] (Es)	Klasse f	class	classe f	classe f	—
clase[2] (Es)	Rang m	rank	rang m	ceto m	—
clase[3] (Es)	Sorte f	sort	sorte f	specie f	—
clase[4] (Es)	Unterrichtsstunde f	lesson	leçon f	lezione f	—
clase[5] (Es)	Vorlesung f	lecture	cours magistral m	lezione f	—
clasificar (Es)	sortieren	sort	trier	assortire	—
class (E)	Klasse f	—	classe f	classe f	clase f
classe (F)	Klasse f	class	—	classe f	clase f
classe (I)	Klasse f	class	classe f	—	clase f
clavel (Es)	Nelke f	carnation	œillet m	garofano m	—
clavo (Es)	Nagel m	nail	clou m	chiodo m	—
claxon (F)	Hupe f	horn	—	clacson m	bocina f
clé (F)	Schlüssel m	key	—	chiave f	llave f
clean[1] (E)	putzen	—	nettoyer	pulire	limpiar
clean[2] (E)	reinigen	—	nettoyer	pulire	limpiar
clean[3] (E)	sauber	—	propre	pulito(a)	limpio(a)
cleaning (E)	Reinigung f	—	nettoyage m	pulitura f	limpieza f

	D	E	F	I	Es
clear[1] (E)	deutlich	—	clair(e)	chiaro(a)	claro(a)
clear[2] (E)	klar	—	clair(e)	chiaro(a)	claro(a)
clear away (E)	aufräumen	—	ranger	mettere in ordine	arreglar
clever[1] (E)	clever	—	futé(e)	abile	listo(a)
clever[2] (E)	klug	—	intelligent(e)	intelligente	inteligente
clever[3] (E)	schlau	—	astucieux(-euse)	astuto(a)	astuto(a)
client (F)	Kunde *m*	customer	—	cliente *m*	cliente *m*
cliente (Es)	Kunde *m*	customer	client *m*	cliente *m*	—
cliente (I)	Kunde *m*	customer	client *m*	—	cliente *m*
cliente abituale (I)	Stammgast *m*	regular	habitué *m*	—	cliente habitual *m*
cliente habitual (Es)	Stammgast *m*	regular	habitué *m*	cliente abituale *m*	—
clignoter (F)	blinken	flash	—	lampeggiare	relampaquear
clima (Es)	Klima *n*	climate	climat *m*	clima *m*	—
clima (I)	Klima *n*	climate	climat *m*	—	clima *m*
climat (F)	Klima *n*	climate	—	clima *m*	clima *m*
climate (E)	Klima *n*	—	climat *m*	clima *m*	clima *m*
climb[1] (E)	hinaufsteigen	—	monter	salire	subir
climb[2] (E)	klettern	—	grimper	arrampicarsi	escalar
clínica (Es)	Klinik *f*	hospital	clinique *f*	clinica *f*	—
clinica (I)	Klinik *f*	hospital	clinique *f*	—	clínica *f*
clinique (F)	Klinik *f*	hospital	—	clinica *f*	clínica *f*
cloche (F)	Glocke *f*	bell	—	campana *f*	campana *f*
close (E)	schließen	—	fermer	chiudere	cerrar
closed (E)	geschlossen	—	fermé(e)	chiuso(a)	cerrado(a)
closing day (E)	Ruhetag *m*	—	jour de repos *m*	giorno di riposo *m*	día de descanso *m*
cloth[1] (E)	Stoff *m*	—	tissu *m*	stoffa *f*	tela *f*
cloth[2] (E)	Tuch *n*	—	étoffe *f*	panno *m*	paño *m*
clothing (E)	Kleidung *f*	—	habits *m pl*	abbigliamento *m*	vestuario *m*
clôture (F)	Zaun *m*	fence	—	recinto *m*	valla *f*
clou (F)	Nagel *m*	nail	—	chiodo *m*	clavo *m*
cloud (E)	Wolke *f*	—	nuage *m*	nuvola *f*	nube *f*
cloudy (E)	bewölkt	—	couvert(e)	nuvoloso(a)	nublado(a)
club[1] (E)	Kasino *n*	—	casino *m*	casinò *m*	casino *m*
club[2] (E)	Verein *m*	—	association *f*	associazione *f*	asociación *f*
clumsy (E)	ungeschickt	—	maladroit(e)	impacciato(a)	torpe
coal (E)	Kohle *f*	—	charbon *m*	carbone *m*	carbón *m*
coarse (E)	grob	—	grossier(-ière)	rozzo(a)	tosco(a)
coast (E)	Küste *f*	—	côte *f*	costa *f*	costa *f*
coat (E)	Mantel *m*	—	manteau *m*	cappotto *m*	abrigo *m*
cobarde (Es)	feig	cowardly	lâche	vile	—
cobrar[1] (Es)	einkassieren	collect	recouvrer	incassare	—
cobrar[2] (Es)	kassieren	take	encaisser	incassare	—
coccio (I)	Scherbe *f*	broken piece	tesson *m*	—	pedazo *m*
cocer (Es)	backen	bake	faire cuire	cuocere (al forno)	—
coche[1] (Es)	Auto *n*	car	voiture *f*	automobile *f*/ macchina *f*	—
coche[2] (Es)	Wagen *m*	car	voiture *f*	vettura *f*	—
coche cama (Es)	Liegewagen *m*	couchette	wagon-couchette *m*	cuccetta *f*	—

	D	E	F	I	Es
cochon (F)	Schwein *n*	pig	—	maiale *m*	cerdo *m*
cocina[1] (Es)	Herd *m*	cooker	fourneau *m*	cucina *f*	—
cocina[2] (Es)	Küche *f*	kitchen	cuisine *f*	cucina *f*	—
cocinar (Es)	kochen	cook	cuire	cucinare	—
cocinera (Es)	Köchin *f*	cook	cuisinière *f*	cuoca *f*	—
cocinero (Es)	Koch *m*	cook	cuisinier *m*	cuoco *m*	—
cock (E)	Hahn *m*	—	coq *m*	gallo *m*	gallo *m*
coda (I)	Schwanz *m*	tail	queue *f*	—	rabo *m*
cœur (F)	Herz *n*	heart	—	cuore *m*	corazón *m*
coffee (E)	Kaffee *m*	—	café *m*	caffè *m*	café *m*
coffin (E)	Sarg *m*	—	cercueil *m*	bara *f*	ataúd *m*
coffre (F)	Kofferraum *m*	boot	—	portabagagli *m*	maletero *m*
coger[1] (Es)	ergreifen	seize	saisir	afferrare	—
coger[2] (Es)	fassen	grasp	saisir	prendere	—
coger[3] (Es)	fangen	catch	attraper	acchiappare	—
coger[4] (Es)	greifen	seize	saisir	afferrare	—
coger[5] (Es)	pflücken	pick	cueillir	cogliere	—
cogliere (I)	pflücken	pick	cueillir	—	coger
cognata (I)	Schwägerin *f*	sister-in-law	belle-sœur *f*	—	cuñada *f*
cognato (I)	Schwager *m*	brother-in-law	beau-frère *m*	—	cuñado *m*
cognome (I)	Nachname *m*	surname	nom de famille *m*	—	apellido *m*
coiffeur (F)	Friseur *m*	hairdresser	—	parrucchiere *m*	peluquero *m*
coiffure (F)	Frisur *f*	hairstyle	—	pettinatura *f*	peinado *m*
coin (E)	Münze *f*	—	pièce de monnaie *f*	moneta *f*	moneda *f*
coin[1] (F)	Ecke *f*	corner	—	angolo *m*	esquina *f*
coin[2] (F)	Winkel *m*	corner	—	cantuccio *m*	rincón *m*
coincidenza (I)	Anschluß *m*	connection	correspondance *f*	—	conexión *f*
cojín (Es)	Kissen *n*	cushion	coussin *m*	cuscino *m*	—
col (Es)	Kohl *m*	cabbage	chou *m*	cavolo *m*	—
col[1] (F)	Kragen *m*	collar	—	colletto *m*	cuello *m*
col[2] (F)	Paß *m*	pass	—	passo *m*	paso *m*
colador (Es)	Sieb *n*	sieve	tamis *m*	setaccio *m*	—
colazione (I)	Frühstück *n*	breakfast	petit-déjeuner *m*	—	desayuno *m*
colchón (Es)	Matratze *f*	mattress	matelas *m*	materasso *m*	—
colchoneta (Es)	Matte *f*	mat	natte *f*	stuoia *f*	—
cold[1] (E)	Erkältung *f*	—	refroidissement *m*	raffreddore *m*	catarro *m*
cold[2] (E)	kalt	—	froid(e)	freddo(a)	frío(a)
cold[3] (E)	Schnupfen *m*	—	rhume *m*	raffreddore *m*	resfriado *m*
cold meat (E)	Aufschnitt *m*	—	charcuterie *f*	affettato *m*	fiambre *m*
colección (Es)	Sammlung *f*	collection	collection *f*	raccolta *f*	—
coléoptère (F)	Käfer *m*	beetle	—	coleottero *m*	escarabajo *m*
coleottero (I)	Käfer *m*	beetle	coléoptère *m*	—	escarabajo *m*
colère (F)	Wut *f*	anger	—	rabbia *f*	rabia *f*
colgar[1] (Es)	aufhängen	hang up	accrocher	appendere	—
colgar[2] (Es)	hängen	hang	pendre	pendere	—
coliflor (Es)	Blumenkohl *m*	cauliflower	chou-fleur *m*	cavolfiore *m*	—
colina (Es)	Hügel *m*	hill	colline *f*	collina *f*	—

	D	E	F	I	Es
colla (I)	Klebstoff *m*	glue	colle *f*	—	adhesivo *m*
collants (F)	Strumpfhose *f*	tights	—	calzamaglia *f*	leotardos *m pl*
collapse¹ (E)	einstürzen	—	écrouler, se	crollare	derrumbarse
collapse² (E)	zusammenbrechen	—	éffondrer, se	crollare	desmayarse
collar (E)	Kragen *m*	—	col *m*	colletto *m*	cuello *m*
collaudare (I)	testen	test	tester	—	probar
colle (F)	Klebstoff *m*	glue	—	colla *f*	adhesivo *m*
collect¹ (E)	einkassieren	—	recouvrer	incassare	cobrar
collect² (E)	sammeln	—	collecter	raccogliere	recolectar
collecter (F)	sammeln	collect	—	raccogliere	recolectar
collection (E)	Sammlung *f*	—	collection *f*	raccolta *f*	colección *f*
collection (F)	Sammlung *f*	collection	—	raccolta *f*	colección *f*
collegio (I)	Internat *n*	boarding school	internat *m*	—	internado *m*
coller (F)	kleben	stick	—	incollare	pegar
colletto (I)	Kragen *m*	collar	col *m*	—	cuello *m*
collina (I)	Hügel *m*	hill	colline *f*	—	colina *f*
colline (F)	Hügel *m*	hill	—	collina *f*	colina *f*
collo (I)	Hals *m*	neck	cou *m*	—	cuello *m*
colloquial language (E)	Umgangssprache *f*	—	langue familière *f*	linguaggio familiare *m*	lenguaje coloquial *m*
colloquio (I)	Unterredung *f*	talk	entrevue *f*	—	entrevista *f*
colocar¹ (Es)	anbringen	fasten	fixer	fissare	—
colocar² (Es)	legen	lay	mettre	mettere	—
colocar³ (Es)	stellen	place	mettre	mettere	—
colocar⁴ (Es)	unterbringen	stow (away)	ranger	sistemare	—
colonia (Es)	Siedlung *f*	settlement	cité *f*	agglomerato *m*	—
colonna (I)	Säule *f*	pillar	colonne *f*	—	columna *f*
colonna vertebrale (I)	Wirbelsäule *f*	spine	colonne vertébrale *f*	—	columna vertebral *f*
colonne (F)	Säule *f*	pillar	—	colonna *f*	columna *f*
colonne vertébrale (F)	Wirbelsäule *f*	spine	—	colonna vertebrale *f*	columna vertebral *f*
color (Es)	Farbe *f*	colour	couleur *f*	colore *m*	—
colorato (I)	farbig	colourful	coloré(e)	—	de colores
colore (I)	Farbe *f*	colour	couleur *f*	—	color *m*
coloré¹ (F)	bunt	coloured	—	variopinto	de colores
coloré² (F)	farbig	colourful	—	colorato(a)	de colores
colorear (Es)	färben	dye	colorer	tingere	—
colorer (F)	färben	dye	—	tingere	colorear
colour (E)	Farbe *f*	—	couleur *f*	colore *m*	color *m*
coloured (E)	bunt	—	coloré(e)	variopinto(a)	de colores
colourful (E)	farbig	—	coloré(e)	colorato(a)	de colores
colpa (I)	Schuld *f*	fault	culpabilité *f*	—	culpa *f*
colpevole (I)	schuldig	guilty	coupable	—	culpable
colpire (I)	treffen	hit	toucher	—	alcanzar
colpo (I)	Schlag *m*	blow	coup *m*	—	golpe *m*
coltello (I)	Messer *n*	knife	couteau *m*	—	cuchillo *m*
coltivare (I)	anbauen	cultivate	cultiver	—	cultivar
columna (Es)	Säule *f*	pillar	colonne *f*	colonna *f*	—

	D	E	F	I	Es
columna vertebral (Es)	Wirbelsäule *f*	spine	colonne vertébrale *f*	colonna vertebrale *f*	—
columpiarse (Es)	schaukeln	swing	balancer, se	dondolare	—
comb[1] (E)	kämmen	—	peigner	pettinare	peinar
comb[2] (E)	Kamm *m*	—	peigne *m*	pettine *m*	peine *m*
combattere (I)	kämpfen	fight	battre, se	—	luchar
combien[1] (F)	wieviele	how many	—	quanti(e)	¿cuántos(as)?
combien[2] (F)	wieviel	how much	—	quanto	¿cuánto?
combinación (Es)	Unterrock *m*	slip	jupon *m*	sottoveste *f*	—
combustible para la calefacción (Es)	Heizöl *n*	fuel	mazout *m*	olio combustibile *m*	—
come (E)	kommen	—	venir	venire	venir
come (I)	wie	how	comment	—	¿cómo?
come back[1] (E)	wiederkommen	—	revenir	ritornare	venir de nuevo
come back[2] (E)	zurückkommen	—	revenir	ritornare	regresar
comedia (Es)	Komödie *f*	comedy	comédie *f*	commedia *f*	—
comédie (F)	Komödie *f*	comedy	—	commedia *f*	comedia *f*
comedor (Es)	Eßzimmer *n*	dining room	salle à manger *f*	sala da pranzo *f*	—
comedy (E)	Komödie *f*	—	comédie *f*	commedia *f*	comedia *f*
come mai (I)	wieso	why	pourquoi	—	¿por qué?
com'è noto (I)	bekanntlich	as is well known	comme on sait	—	como es sabido
comer (Es)	essen	eat	manger	mangiare	—
comercial (Es)	geschäftlich	on business	d'affaires	per affari	—
comerciante[1] (Es)	Händler *m*	dealer	commerçant *m*	commerciante *m*	—
comerciante[2] (Es)	Kaufmann *m*	businessman	commerçant *m*	commerciante *m*	—
comestible (Es)	eßbar	eatable	mangeable	commestibile	—
comestibles (Es)	Eßwaren *pl*	foodstuffs	produits alimentaires *m pl*	alimentari *m pl*	—
comfort (E)	trösten	—	consoler	consolare	consolar
comfortable[1] (E)	bequem	—	confortable	comodo(a)	cómodo(a)
comfortable[2] (E)	gemütlich	—	agréable	comodo(a)	cómodo(a)
comico (I)	komisch	funny	drôle	—	cómico(a)
cómico (Es)	komisch	funny	drôle	comico(a)	—
comida[1] (Es)	Essen *n*	food	repas *m*	alimentazione *f*	—
comida[2] (Es)	Mittagessen *n*	lunch	déjeuner *m*	pranzo *m*	—
comida[3] (Es)	Mahlzeit *f*	meal	repas *m*	pasto *m*	—
comida[4] (Es)	Speise *f*	food	aliment *m*	cibo *m*	—
cominciare[1] (I)	anfangen	start	commencer	—	empezar
cominciare[2] (I)	beginnen	begin	commencer	—	empezar
comisión (Es)	Provision *f*	commission	commission *f*	provvigione *f*	—
commander (F)	bestellen	order	—	ordinare	pedir
commedia (I)	Komödie *f*	comedy	comédie *f*	—	comedia *f*
commencement[1] (F)	Anfang *m*	beginning	—	inizio *m*	inicio *m*
commencement[2] (F)	Beginn *m*	beginning	—	inizio *m*	principio *m*
commencer[1] (F)	anfangen	start	—	cominciare	empezar
commencer[2] (F)	beginnen	begin	—	cominciare	empezar
comment (F)	wie	how	—	come	¿cómo?
comme on sait (F)	bekanntlich	as is well known	—	com'è noto	como es sabido
commerçant[1] (F)	Händler *m*	dealer	—	commerciante *m*	comerciante *m*

	D	E	F	I	Es
commerçant² (F)	Kaufmann m	businessman	—	commerciante m	comerciante m
commerciante¹ (I)	Händler m	dealer	commerçant m	—	comerciante m
commerciante² (I)	Kaufmann m	businessman	commerçant m	—	comerciante m
commestibile (I)	eßbar	eatable	mangeable	—	comestible
commission (E)	Provision f	—	commission f	provvigione f	comisión f
commission (F)	Provision f	commission	—	provvigione f	comisión f
communication interurbaine (F)	Ferngespräch n	long-distance call	—	telefonata interurbana f	llamada interurbana f
communication téléphonique (F)	Telefongespräch n	phone call	—	conversazione telefonica f	conversación telefónica f
commutare (I)	schalten	switch	connecter	—	conectar
como (Es)	als	when	quand	quando	—
cómo (Es)	wie	how	comment	come	—
comodidad (Es)	Bequemlichkeit f	convenience	confort m	comodità f	—
comodità (I)	Bequemlichkeit f	convenience	confort m	—	comodidad f
comodo¹ (I)	bequem	comfortable	confortable	—	cómodo(a)
comodo² (I)	gemütlich	comfortable	agréable	—	cómodo(a)
cómodo¹ (Es)	bequem	comfortable	confortable	comodo(a)	—
cómodo² (Es)	gemütlich	comfortable	agréable	comodo(a)	—
como es sabido (Es)	bekanntlich	as is well known	comme on sait	com'è noto	—
compadecerse de (Es)	bemitleiden	pity	plaindre	compatire	—
compagno¹ (I)	Genosse m	comrade	camarade m	—	camarada m
compagno² (I)	Lebensgefährte m	lifepartner	compagnon m	—	compañero en la vida m
compagnon (F)	Lebensgefährte m	lifepartner	—	compagno m	compañero en la vida m
compañero en la vida (Es)	Lebensgefährte m	lifepartner	compagnon m	compagno m	—
company¹ (E)	Firma f	—	firme f	ditta f	empresa f
company² (E)	Unternehmen n	—	entreprise f	impresa f	empresa f
comparación (Es)	Vergleich m	comparison	comparaison f	paragone m	—
comparaison (F)	Vergleich m	comparison	—	paragone m	comparación f
comparar (Es)	vergleichen	compare	comparer	paragonare	—
compare (E)	vergleichen	—	comparer	paragonare	comparar
comparer (F)	vergleichen	compare	—	paragonare	comparar
comparison (E)	Vergleich m	—	comparaison f	paragone m	comparación f
compartiment¹ (F)	Abteil n	compartment	—	scompartimento m	compartimiento m
compartiment² (F)	Fach n	compartment	—	scomparto m	compartimiento m
compartimiento¹ (Es)	Abteil n	compartment	compartiment m	scompartimento m	—
compartimiento² (Es)	Fach n	compartment	compartiment m	scomparto m	—
compartment¹ (E)	Abteil n	—	compartiment m	scompartimento m	compartimiento m
compartment² (E)	Fach n	—	compartiment m	scomparto m	compartimiento m
compasión¹ (Es)	Bedauern n	regret	regret m	dispiacere m	—
compasión² (Es)	Mitleid n	pity	compassion f	compassione f	—
compassion (F)	Mitleid n	pity	—	compassione f	compasión f
compassione (I)	Mitleid n	pity	compassion f	—	compasión f
compatire (I)	bemitleiden	pity	plaindre	—	compadecerse de
competent (E)	zuständig	—	compétent(e)	competente	competente
compétent (F)	zuständig	competent	—	competente	competente
competente (Es)	zuständig	competent	compétent(e)	competente	—

	D	E	F	I	Es
competente (I)	zuständig	competent	compétent(e)	—	competente
competition (E)	Wettbewerb *m*	—	concours *m*	concorso *m*	concurso *m*
complain[1] (E)	beschweren, sich	—	plaindre, se	lamentarsi	quejarse
complain[2] (E)	reklamieren	—	plaindre de, se	reclamare	reclamar
complaint[1] (E)	Beschwerde *f*	—	plainte *f*	reclamo *m*	reclamación *f*
complaint[2] (E)	Klage *f*	—	plainte *f*	lamento *m*	lamento *m*
complaint[3] (E)	Reklamation *f*	—	réclamation *f*	reclamo *m*	reclamación *f*
compleanno (I)	Geburtstag *m*	birthday	anniversaire *m*	—	cumpleaños *m*
complement (E)	ergänzen	—	compléter	completare	completar
complessivamente (I)	insgesamt	altogether	dans l'ensemble	—	en suma
complet[1] (F)	ausgebucht	fully booked	—	esaurito(a)	completo(a)
complet[2] (F)	vollständig	complete	—	completo(a)	completo(a)
completamente (Es)	völlig	completely	complètement	completamente	—
completamente (I)	völlig	completely	complètement	—	completamente
completar (Es)	ergänzen	complement	compléter	completare	—
completare (I)	ergänzen	complement	compléter	—	completar
complete (E)	vollständig	—	complet(-ète)	completo(a)	completo(a)
completely[1] (E)	völlig	—	complètement	completamente	completamente
completely[2] (E)	restlos	—	complètement	interamente	totalmente
complètement[1] (F)	restlos	completely	—	interamente	totalmente
complètement[2] (F)	völlig	completely	—	completamente	completamente
compléter (F)	ergänzen	complement	—	completare	completar
completo (I)	vollständig	complete	complet(-ète)	—	completo(a)
completo[1] (Es)	ausgebucht	fully booked	complet(-ète)	esaurito(a)	—
completo[2] (Es)	vollständig	complete	complet(-ète)	completo(a)	—
complicado[1] (Es)	kompliziert	complicated	compliqué(e)	complicato(a)	—
complicado[2] (Es)	umständlich	complicated	compliqué(e)	complicato(a)	—
complicated[1] (E)	kompliziert	—	compliqué(e)	complicato(a)	complicado(a)
complicated[2] (E)	umständlich	—	compliqué(e)	complicato(a)	complicado(a)
complicato[1] (I)	kompliziert	complicated	compliqué(e)	—	complicado(a)
complicato[2] (I)	umständlich	complicated	compliqué(e)	—	complicado(a)
compliqué (F)	kompliziert	complicated	—	complicato(a)	complicado(a)
complique[2] (F)	umständlich	complicated	—	complicato(a)	complicado(a)
comportamento (I)	Benehmen *n*	behaviour	conduite *f*	—	comportamiento *m*
comportamiento (Es)	Benehmen *n*	behaviour	conduite *f*	comportamento *m*	—
comportarse (Es)	benehmen, sich	behave	comporter, se	comportarsi	—
comportarsi (I)	benehmen, sich	behave	comporter, se	—	comportarse
comporter, se (F)	benehmen, sich	behave	—	comportarsi	comportarse
composer (E)	Komponist *m*	—	compositeur *m*	compositore *m*	compositor *m*
compositeur (F)	Komponist *m*	composer	—	compositore *m*	compositor *m*
compositor (Es)	Komponist *m*	composer	compositeur *m*	compositore *m*	—
compositore (I)	Komponist *m*	composer	compositeur *m*	—	compositor *m*
compra[1] (Es)	Einkauf *m*	shopping	achat *m*	spesa *f*	—
compra[2] (Es)	Kauf *m*	purchase	achat *m*	acquisto *m*	—
comprador (Es)	Käufer *m*	buyer	acheteur *m*	acquirente *m*	—
comprar (Es)	kaufen	buy	acheter	comprare	—
comprare (I)	kaufen	buy	acheter	—	comprar
comprehend (E)	begreifen	—	comprendre	comprendere	comprender

	D	E	F	I	Es
compréhension (F)	Verständnis *n*	understanding	—	comprensione *f*	comprensión *f*
comprender (Es)	begreifen	comprehend	comprendre	comprendere	—
comprendere (I)	begreifen	comprehend	comprendre	—	comprender
comprendre¹ (F)	begreifen	comprehend	—	comprendere	comprender
comprendre² (F)	verstehen	understand	—	capire	entender
comprensión (Es)	Verständnis *n*	understanding	compréhension *f*	comprensione *f*	—
comprensione (I)	Verständnis *n*	understanding	compréhension *f*	—	comprensión *f*
compreso (I)	inbegriffen	included	compris(e)	—	incluído(a)
compressa (I)	Tablette *f*	tablet	comprimé *m*	—	pastilla *f*
comprimé (F)	Tablette *f*	tablet	—	compressa *f*	pastilla *f*
compris (F)	inbegriffen	included	—	compreso(a)	incluído(a)
comprobar (Es)	nachprüfen	check	contrôler	controllare	—
comptabilité (F)	Buchhaltung *f*	book-keeping	—	contabilità *f*	contabilidad *f*
compte (F)	Konto *n*	account	—	conto *m*	cuenta *f*
compter¹ (F)	anrechnen	charge	—	mettere in conto	poner en cuenta
compter² (F)	zählen	count	—	contare	contar
comptoir (F)	Ladentisch *m*	counter	—	banco di vendita *m*	mostrador *m*
compulsion (E)	Zwang *m*	—	contrainte *f*	costrizione *f*	presión *f*
comrade (E)	Genosse *m*	—	camarade *m*	compagno *m*	camarada *m*
comune (I)	gemeinsam	together	ensemble	—	juntos(as)
comunicación¹ (Es)	Anschluß *m*	connection	correspondance *f*	coincidenza *f*	—
comunicación² (Es)	Mitteilung *f*	message	information *f*	comunicazione *f*	—
comunicar¹ (Es)	ausrichten	pass on a message	transmettre	riferire	—
comunicar² (Es)	mitteilen	inform s.o.	informer qn de qch	comunicare	—
comunicare (I)	mitteilen	inform s.o.	informer qn de qch	—	comunicar
comunicazione (I)	Mitteilung *f*	message	information *f*	—	comunicación *f*
con (Es)	mit	with	avec	con	—
con (I)	mit	with	avec	—	con
conceder (Es)	gewähren	grant	accorder	concedere	—
concedere (I)	gewähren	grant	accorder	—	conceder
conseil (F)	Rat *m*	advice	—	consiglio *m*	consejo *m*
concentrar (Es)	konzentrieren	concentrate	concentrer	concentrare	—
concentrare (I)	konzentrieren	concentrate	concentrer	—	concentrar
concentrate (E)	konzentrieren	—	concentrer	concentrare	concentrar
concentrer (F)	konzentrieren	concentrate	—	concentrare	concentrar
concern¹ (E)	betreffen	—	concerner	riguardare	concernir
concern² (E)	Sorge *f*	—	souci *m*	preoccupazione *f*	preocupación *f*
concerner (F)	betreffen	concern	—	riguardare	concernir
concernir (Es)	betreffen	concern	concerner	riguardare	
concert (E)	Konzert *n*	—	concert *m*	concerto *m*	concierto *m*
concert (F)	Konzert *n*	concert	· —	concerto *m*	concierto *m*
concertar una cita (Es)	verabreden	arrange to meet	prendre rendez-vous	darsi appuntamento	—
concerto (I)	Konzert *n*	concert	concert *m*	—	concierto *m*
conciencia (Es)	Gewissen *n*	conscience	conscience *f*	coscienza *f*	—
concienzudo (Es)	gewissenhaft	conscientious	consciencieux (-euse)	coscienzioso(a)	—
concierge¹ (F)	Hausmeister *m*	caretaker	—	portinaio *m*	portero *m*
concierge² (F)	Pförtner *m*	porter	—	portiere *m*	portero *m*

	D	E	F	I	Es
concierto (Es)	Konzert *n*	concert	concert *m*	concerto *m*	—
conclusión (Es)	Schluß *m*	end	fin *f*	fine *f*	—
concombre (F)	Gurke *f*	cucumber	—	cetriolo *m*	pepino *m*
concordare (I)	übereinstimmen	agree	être d'accord	—	estar de acuerdo
concorrere (I)	bewerben, sich	apply	poser sa candidature	—	presentarse
concorso (I)	Wettbewerb *m*	competition	concours *m*	—	concurso *m*
concours (F)	Wettbewerb *m*	competition	—	concorso *m*	concurso *m*
concurso (Es)	Wettbewerb *m*	competition	concours *m*	concorso *m*	—
condamner (F)	verurteilen	condemn	—	condannare	sentenciar
condannare (I)	verurteilen	condemn	condamner	—	sentenciar
condecoración (Es)	Orden *m*	decoration	décoration *f*	decorazione *f*	—
condemn (E)	verurteilen	—	condamner	condannare	condenar
condición (Es)	Bedingung *f*	condition	condition *f*	condizione *f*	—
condimentar (Es)	würzen	season	épicer	condire	—
condire (I)	würzen	season	épicer	—	condimentar
condition¹ (E)	Bedingung *f*	—	condition *f*	condizione *f*	condición *f*
condition² (E)	Zustand *m*	—	état *m*	stato *m*	estado *m*
condition (F)	Bedingung *f*	condition	—	condizione *f*	condición *f*
condizione (I)	Bedingung *f*	condition	condition *f*	—	condición *f*
condizioni (I)	Verfassung *f*	constitution	état *m*	—	estado *m*
condoglianza (I)	Beileid *n*	condolence	condoléances *f pl*	—	pésame *m*
condoléances (F)	Beileid *n*	condolence	—	condoglianza *f*	pésame *m*
condolence (E)	Beileid *n*	—	condoléances *f pl*	condoglianza *f*	pésame *m*
conducir (Es)	fahren	drive	conduire	andare	—
conducteur (F)	Fahrer *m*	driver	—	autista *m*	conductor *m*
conductor¹ (E)	Dirigent *m*	—	chef d'orchestre *m*	direttore d'orchestra *m*	director (de orquesta) *m*
conductor² (E)	Schaffner *m*	—	contrôleur *m*	bigliettaio *m*	revisor *m*
conductor (Es)	Fahrer *m*	driver	conducteur *m*	autista *m*	—
conduire¹ (F)	fahren	drive	—	andare	conducir
conduire² (F)	lenken	steer	—	guidare	encauzar
conduite (F)	Benehmen *n*	behaviour	—	comportamento *m*	comportamiento *m*
conduttura (I)	Leitung *f*	pipe	tuyau *m*	—	tubería *f*
conectar¹ (Es)	einschalten	switch on	allumer	accendere	—
conectar² (Es)	schalten	switch	connecter	commutare	—
con ello (Es)	damit	with it	avec cela	con questo	—
conference (E)	Konferenz *f*	—	conférence *f*	conferenza *f*	conferencia *f*
conférence (F)	Konferenz *f*	conference	—	conferenza *f*	conferencia *f*
conferencia (Es)	Konferenz *f*	conference	conférence *f*	conferenza *f*	—
conferenza (I)	Konferenz *f*	conference	conférence *f*	—	conferencia *f*
confermare (I)	bestätigen	confirm	confirmer	—	confirmar
confesar (Es)	gestehen	confess	avouer	confessare	—
confesión (Es)	Bekenntnis *n*	confession	confession *f*	confessione *f*	—
confess (E)	gestehen	—	avouer	confessare	confesar
confessare (I)	gestehen	confess	avouer	—	confesar
confession (E)	Bekenntnis *n*	—	confession *f*	confessione *f*	confesión *f*
confession (F)	Bekenntnis *n*	confession	—	confessione *f*	confesión *f*
confessione (I)	Bekenntnis *n*	confession	confession *f*	—	confesión *f*

	D	E	F	I	Es
confiance (F)	Vertrauen n	confidence	—	fiducia f	confianza f
confianza (Es)	Vertrauen n	confidence	confiance f	fiducia f	—
confiar (Es)	vertrauen	trust	avoir confiance	fidarsi	—
confidence (E)	Vertrauen n	—	confiance f	fiducia f	confianza f
confirm (E)	bestätigen	—	confirmer	confermare	confirmar
confirmar (Es)	bestätigen	confirm	confirmer	confermare	—
confirmer (F)	bestätigen	confirm	—	confermare	confirmar
confiture (F)	Marmelade f	jam	—	marmellata f	mermelada f
confondre (F)	verwechseln	confuse	—	scambiare	confundir
confort (F)	Bequemlich-keit f	convenience	—	comodità f	comodidad f
confortable (F)	bequem	comfortable	—	comodo(a)	cómodo(a)
confundido (Es)	verwirrt	confused	confus(e)	confuso(a)	—
confundir (Es)	verwechseln	confuse	confondre	scambiare	—
confus (F)	verwirrt	confused	—	confuso(a)	confundido(a)
confuse (E)	verwechseln	—	confondre	scambiare	confundir
confused (E)	verwirrt	—	confus(e)	confuso(a)	confundido(a)
confusion¹ (E)	Durcheinander n	—	désordre m	confusione f	confusión f
confusion² (E)	Verwirrung f	—	confusion f	confusione f	confusión f
confusión¹ (Es)	Durcheinander n	confusion	désordre m	confusione f	—
confusión² (Es)	Verwirrung f	confusion	confusion f	confusione f	—
confusion (F)	Verwirrung f	confusion	—	confusione f	confusión f
confusione¹ (I)	Durcheinander n	confusion	désordre m	—	confusión f
confusione² (I)	Verwirrung f	confusion	confusion f	—	confusión f
confuso (I)	verwirrt	confused	confus(e)	—	confundido(a)
congedare (I)	verabschieden	say goodbye to	prendre congé de	—	despedir
congratularsi (I)	gratulieren	congratulate	féliciter	—	felicitar
congratulate (E)	gratulieren	—	féliciter	congratularsi	felicitar
congratulations (E)	Glückwunsch m	—	félicitations f pl	auguri m pl	felicitaciones f pl
con gusto (Es)	gern	willingly	avec plaisir	volentieri	—
conifer (E)	Nadelbaum m	—	conifère m	conifero m	conífera f
conífera (Es)	Nadelbaum m	conifer	conifère m	conifero m	—
conifère (F)	Nadelbaum m	conifer	—	conifero m	conífera f
conifero (I)	Nadelbaum m	conifer	conifère m	—	conífera f
conmemorar (Es)	gedenken	remember	souvenir de, se	ricordare	—
connaissance¹ (F)	Bekannter m	acquaintance	—	conoscente m	conocido m
connaissance² (F)	Kenntnis f	knowledge	—	conoscenza f	conocimiento m
connaître (F)	kennen	know	—	conoscere	conocer
connaître, s'y (F)	auskennen, sich	know one's way about	—	conoscere	conocer a fondo
connect (E)	verbinden	—	relier	unire	unir
connecter (F)	schalten	switch	—	commutare	conectar
connection¹ (E)	Anschluß m	—	correspondance f	coincidenza f	conexión f
connection² (E)	Verbindung f	—	relation f	relazione f	relación f
connu (F)	bekannt	well known	—	conosciuto(a)	conocido(a)
conocer (Es)	kennen	know	connaître	conoscere	—
conocer a fondo (Es)	auskennen, sich	know one's way about	connaître, s'y	conoscere	—
conocido¹ (Es)	Bekannter m	acquaintance	ami m	conoscente m	

	D	E	F	I	Es
conocido² (Es)	bekannt	well known	connu(e)	conosciuto(a)	—
conocimiento (Es)	Kenntnis f	knowledge	connaissance f	conoscenza f	—
conoscente (I)	Bekannter m	acquaintance	ami m	—	conocido m
conoscenza (I)	Kenntnis f	knowledge	connaissance f	—	conocimiento m
conoscere¹ (I)	auskennen, sich	know one's way about	connaître, s'y	—	conocer a fondo
conoscere² (I)	kennen	know	connaître	—	conocer
conosciuto (I)	bekannt	well known	connu(e)	—	conocido(a)
con paciencia (Es)	geduldig	patient	patient(e)	paziente	—
con questo (I)	damit	with it	avec cela	—	con ello
conscience (E)	Gewissen n	—	conscience f	coscienza f	conciencia f
conscience (F)	Gewissen n	conscience	—	coscienza f	conciencia f
consciencieux (F)	gewissenhaft	conscientious	—	coscienzioso(a)	concienzudo(a)
conscientious (E)	gewissenhaft	—	consciencieux (-euse)	coscienzioso(a)	concienzudo(a)
consegnare¹ (I)	übergeben	hand over	remettre	—	transmitir
consegnare² (I)	überreichen	hand over	présenter	—	entregar
conseguenza (I)	Folge f	consequence	conséquence f	—	consecuencia f
conseguir¹ (Es)	besorgen	acquire	procurer	procurare	—
conseguir² (Es)	gelangen	attain	arriver à	arrivare a	—
conseiller (F)	raten	advise	—	consigliare	aconsejar
consejo (Es)	Rat m	advice	conseil m	consiglio m	—
consentir (Es)	zustimmen	agree	être d'accord	acconsentire	—
consequence (E)	Folge f	—	conséquence f	conseguenza f	consecuencia f
conservare (I)	aufbewahren	keep	garder	—	guardar
consider (E)	überlegen	—	réfléchir à	riflettere	pensar
considerable¹ (E)	beträchtlich	—	considérable	considerevole	notable
considerable² (E)	erheblich	—	considérable	rilevante	considerable
considerable (Es)	erheblich	considerable	considérable	rilevante	—
considérable¹ (F)	beträchtlich	considerable	—	considerevole	notable
considérable² (F)	erheblich	considerable	—	rilevante	considerable
considérer (F)	beachten	take notice of	—	osservare	prestar atención a
considerevole (I)	beträchtlich	considerable	considérable	—	notable
consigliare (I)	raten	advise	conseiller	—	aconsejar
consiglio (I)	Rat m	advice	conseil m	—	consejo m
consolar (Es)	trösten	comfort	consoler	consolare	—
consolare (I)	trösten	comfort	consoler	—	consolar
consolation (E)	Trost m	—	consolation f	consolazione f	consuelo m
consolation (F)	Trost m	consolation	—	consolazione f	consuelo m
consolato (I)	Konsulat n	consulate	consulat m	—	consulado m
consolazione (I)	Trost m	consolation	consolation f	—	consuelo m
consoler (F)	trösten	comfort	—	consolare	consolar
consommation (F)	Verbrauch m	consumption	—	consumo m	consumo m
consommer (F)	verbrauchen	consume	—	consumare	consumir
constitución (Es)	Verfassung f	constitution	constitution f	costituzione f	—
constitution¹ (E)	Verfassung f	—	état m	condizioni f pl	estado m
constitution² (E)	Verfassung f	—	constitution f	costituzione f	constitución f
constitution (F)	Verfassung f	constitution	—	costituzione f	constitución f
construcción (Es)	Bau m	construction	construction f	costruzione f	—

contenuto

	D	E	F	I	Es
construction (E)	Bau *m*	—	construction *f*	costruzione *f*	construcción *f*
construction[1] (F)	Anlage *f*	plant	—	impianto *m*	establecimiento *m*
construction[2] (F)	Bau *m*	construction	—	costruzione *f*	construcción *f*
construir (Es)	bauen	build	construire	costruire	—
construire (F)	bauen	build	—	costruire	construir
consuelo (Es)	Trost *m*	consolation	consolation *f*	consolazione *f*	—
consulado (Es)	Konsulat *n*	consulate	consulat *m*	consolato *m*	—
consulat (F)	Konsulat *n*	consulate	—	consolato *m*	consulado *m*
consulate (E)	Konsulat *n*	—	consulat *m*	consolato *m*	consulado *m*
consultation hour (E)	Sprechstunde *f*	—	heures de consultation *f pl*	ora di ricevimento *f*	hora de consulta *f*
consumare[1] (I)	abnutzen	wear out	user	—	desgastar
consumare[2] (I)	verbrauchen	consume	consommer	—	consumir
consume (E)	verbrauchen	—	consommer	consumare	consumir
consumir (Es)	verbrauchen	consume	consommer	consumare	—
consumo (Es)	Verbrauch *m*	consumption	consommation *f*	consumo *m*	—
consumo (I)	Verbrauch *m*	consumption	consommation *f*	—	consumo *m*
consumption (E)	Verbrauch *m*	—	consommation *f*	consumo *m*	consumo *m*
contabilidad (Es)	Buchhaltung *f*	book-keeping	comptabilité *f*	contabilità *f*	—
contabilità (I)	Buchhaltung *f*	book-keeping	comptabilité *f*	—	contabilidad
contact (E)	Kontakt *m*	—	contact *m*	contatto *m*	contacto *m*
contact (F)	Kontakt *m*	contact	—	contatto *m*	contacto *m*
contacto (Es)	Kontakt *m*	contact	contact *m*	contatto *m*	—
contadino (I)	Bauer *m*	farmer	paysan *m*	—	campesino *m*
contain (E)	enthalten	—	contenir	contenere	contener
container[1] (E)	Behälter *m*	—	récipient *m*	recipiente *m*	recipiente *m*
container[2] (E)	Gefäß *n*	—	récipient *m*	recipiente *m*	recipiente *m*
contanti (I)	Bargeld *n*	cash	espèces *f pl*	—	dinero al contado *m*
contar[1] (Es)	erzählen	tell	raconter	raccontare	—
contar[2] (Es)	zählen	count	compter	contare	—
contare (I)	zählen	count	compter	—	contar
contatto (I)	Kontakt *m*	contact	contact *m*	—	contacto *m*
contemporain (F)	zeitgenössisch	contemporary	—	contemporaneo(a)	contemporáneo(a)
contemporaneo[1] (I)	gleichzeitig	simultaneous	en même temps	—	a la vez
contemporaneo[2] (I)	zeitgenössisch	contemporary	contemporain(e)	—	contemporáneo(a)
contemporáneo (Es)	zeitgenössisch	contemporary	contemporain(e)	contemporaneo(a)	—
contemporary (E)	zeitgenössisch	—	contemporain(e)	contemporaneo(a)	contemporáneo(a)
contener (Es)	enthalten	contain	contenir	contenere	—
contenere (I)	enthalten	contain	contenir	—	contener
contenido (Es)	Inhalt *m*	contents	contenu *m*	contenuto *m*	—
contenir (F)	enthalten	contain	—	contenere	contener
content (F)	zufrieden	satisfied	—	contento(a)	satisfecho(a)
contento (I)	zufrieden	satisfied	content(e)	—	satisfecho(a)
contento[1] (Es)	erfreut	delighted	réjoui(e)	lieto(a)	—
contento[2] (Es)	froh	glad	content(e)	lieto(a)	—
contents (E)	Inhalt *m*	—	contenu *m*	contenuto *m*	contenido *m*
contenu (F)	Inhalt *m*	contents	—	contenuto *m*	contenido *m*
contenuto (I)	Inhalt *m*	contents	contenu *m*	—	contenido *m*

	D	E	F	I	Es
contiguo (Es)	nahe	near	près de	vicino(a) a	—
continent (E)	Kontinent *m*	—	continent *m*	continente *m*	continente *m*
continent[1] (F)	Festland *n*	mainland	—	terraferma *f*	tierra firme *f*
continent[2] (F)	Kontinent *m*	continent	—	continente *m*	continente *m*
continente (Es)	Kontinent *m*	continent	continent *m*	continente *m*	—
continente (I)	Kontinent *m*	continent	continent *m*	—	continente *m*
continuar (Es)	weitermachen	carry on	continuer	continuare	—
continuare[1] (I)	fortsetzen	continue	continuer	—	proseguir
continuare[2] (I)	weitermachen	carry on	continuer	—	continuar
continuare a dormire (I)	weiterschlafen	sleep on	continuer à dormir	—	seguir durmiendo
continue (E)	fortsetzen	—	continuer	continuare	proseguir
continuer[1] (F)	fortsetzen	continue	—	continuare	proseguir
continuer[2] (F)	weitermachen	carry on	—	continuare	continuar
continuer à dormir (F)	weiterschlafen	sleep on	—	continuare a dormire	seguir durmiendo
conto (I)	Konto n	account	compte m	—	cuenta f
contra[1] (Es)	dagegen	against it	contre cela	contro	—
contra[2] (Es)	gegen	against	contre	contro	—
contract (E)	Vertrag *m*	—	contrat *m*	contratto *m*	contrato *m*
contraddire (I)	widersprechen	contradict	contredire	—	contradecir
contradecir (Es)	widersprechen	contradict	contredire	contraddire	—
contradict (E)	widersprechen	—	contredire	contraddire	contradecir
contrainte (F)	Zwang *m*	compulsion	—	costrizione *f*	presión *f*
contraire (F)	Gegenteil *n*	opposite	—	contrario *m*	opuesto *m*
contrario (I)	Gegenteil *n*	opposite	contraire *m*	—	opuesto *m*
contrario (Es)	umgekehrt	vice versa	vice versa	inverso(a)	—
contrat (F)	Vertrag *m*	contract	—	contratto *m*	contrato *m*
contratiempo (Es)	Verlegenheit *f*	embarrassment	gêne *f*	imbarazzo *m*	—
contrato (Es)	Vertrag *m*	contract	contrat *m*	contratto *m*	—
contratto (I)	Vertrag *m*	contract	contrat *m*	—	contrato *m*
contre (F)	gegen	against	—	contro	contra
contre cela (F)	dagegen	against it	—	contro	contra
contredire (F)	widersprechen	contradict	—	contraddire	contradecir
contribution (E)	Beitrag *m*	—	contribution *f*	contributo *m*	cuota *f*
contribution (F)	Beitrag *m*	contribution	—	contributo *m*	cuota *f*
contributo (I)	Beitrag *m*	contribution	contribution *f*	—	cuota *f*
contro[1] (I)	dagegen	against it	contre cela	—	contra
contro[2] (I)	gegen	against	contre	—	contra
control (E)	Kontrolle *f*	—	contrôle *m*	controllo *m*	control *m*
control (Es)	Kontrolle *f*	control	contrôle *m*	controllo *m*	—
controlador (Es)	Kontrolleur *m*	inspector	contrôleur *m*	controllore *m*	—
control de radar (Es)	Radarkontrolle *f*	speed trap	contrôle radar *m*	controllo radar *m*	—
contrôle (F)	Kontrolle *f*	control	—	controllo *m*	control *m*
contrôler[1] (F)	nachprüfen	check	—	controllare	comprobar
contrôler[2] (F)	überprüfen	check	—	esaminare	examinar
contrôle radar (F)	Radarkontrolle *f*	speed trap	—	controllo radar *m*	control de radar *m*
contrôleur[1] (F)	Kontrolleur *m*	inspector	—	controllore *m*	controlador *m*

	D	E	F	I	Es
contrôleur² (F)	Schaffner m	conductor	—	bigliettaio m	revisor m
controllare¹ (I)	nachprüfen	check	contrôler	—	comprobar
controllare² (I)	nachsehen	check	vérifier	—	examinar
controllo (I)	Kontrolle f	control	contrôle m	—	control m
controllo radar (I)	Radarkontrolle f	speed trap	contrôle radar m	—	control de radar m
controllore (I)	Kontrolleur m	inspector	contrôleur m	—	controlador m
convaincre (F)	überzeugen	convince	—	convincere	convencer
convenable (F)	anständig	decent	—	decente	decente
convencer (Es)	überzeugen	convince	convaincre	convincere	—
convenience (E)	Bequemlich-keit f	—	confort m	comodità f	comodidad f
conveniente (I)	preiswert	inexpensive	bon marché	—	económico(a)
convenir¹ (Es)	ausmachen	agree	convenir	stabilire	—
convenir² (Es)	vereinbaren	agree upon	convenir de	fissare	—
convenir (F)	ausmachen	agree	—	stabilire	convenir
convenir de (F)	vereinbaren	agree upon	—	fissare	convenir
convenir pour (F)	taugen	be of use	—	servire	valer
convento (I)	Kloster n	monastery	couvent m	—	monasterio m
conversación¹ (Es)	Gespräch n	conversation	conversation f	conversazione f	—
conversación² (Es)	Unterhaltung f	conversation	entretien m	conversazione f	—
conversación telefónica (Es)	Telefongespräch n	phone call	communication téléphonique f	conversazione telefonica f	—
conversar¹ (Es)	plaudern	chat	causer	chiacchierare	—
conversar² (Es)	unterhalten, sich	talk	entretenir, se	conversare	—
conversare (I)	unterhalten, sich	talk	entretenir, se	—	conversar
conversation¹ (E)	Gespräch n	—	conversation f	conversazione f	conversación f
conversation² (E)	Unterhaltung f	—	entretien m	conversazione f	conversación f
conversation (F)	Gespräch n	conversation	—	conversazione f	conversación f
conversazione¹ (I)	Gespräch n	conversation	conversation f	—	conversación f
conversazione² (I)	Unterhaltung f	conversation	entretien m	—	conversación f
conversazione telefonica (I)	Telefongespräch n	phone call	communication téléphonique f	—	conversación telefónica f
convert (E)	umrechnen	—	convertir	convertire	convertir
convertir (Es)	umrechnen	convert	convertir	convertire	—
convertir (F)	umrechnen	convert	—	convertire	convertir
convertire (I)	umrechnen	convert	convertir	—	convertir
convey (E)	übermitteln	—	transmettre	trasmettere	transmitir
convince¹ (E)	überreden	—	persuader	persuadere	persuadir
convince² (E)	überzeugen	—	convaincre	convincere	convencer
convincere (I)	überzeugen	convince	convaincre	—	convencer
cook¹ (E)	kochen	—	cuire	cucinare	cocinar
cook² (E)	Koch m	—	cuisinier m	cuoco m	cocinero m
cook³ (E)	Köchin f	—	cuisinière f	cuoca f	cocinera f
cooker (E)	Herd m	—	fourneau m	cucina f	cocina f
cool (E)	kühl	—	frais (fraîche)	fresco(a)	fresco(a)
coperchio (I)	Deckel m	lid	couvercle m	—	tapa f
coperta (I)	Decke f	blanket	couverture f	—	techo m
coperto¹ (I)	bedeckt	covered	couvert(e)	—	cubierto(a)
coperto² (I)	Gedeck n	cover	couvert m	—	cubierto m

	D	E	F	I	Es
copia (Es)	Kopie f	copy	copie f	copia f	—
copia (I)	Kopie f	copy	copie f	—	copia f
copiar (Es)	kopieren	copy	copier	copiare	—
copiare (I)	kopieren	copy	copier	—	copiar
copie (F)	Kopie f	copy	—	copia f	copia f
copier (F)	kopieren	copy	—	copiare	copiar
coprire[1] (I)	bedecken	cover	couvrir	—	cubrir
coprire[2] (I)	zudecken	cover (up)	couvrir	—	tapar
copy[1] (E)	kopieren	—	copier	copiare	copiar
copy[2] (E)	Kopie f	—	copie f	copia f	copia f
coq (F)	Hahn m	cock	—	gallo m	gallo m
coquelicot (F)	Mohn m	poppy	—	papavero m	amapola f
coraggio (I)	Mut m	courage	courage m	—	coraje m
coraggioso (I)	tapfer	brave	courageux (-euse)	—	valiente
coraje (Es)	Mut m	courage	courage m	coraggio m	—
corazón (Es)	Herz n	heart	cœur m	cuore m	—
corbata (Es)	Krawatte f	tie	cravate f	cravatta f	—
corbeau (F)	Rabe m	raven	—	corvo m	cuervo m
corda[1] (I)	Schnur f	string	ficelle f	—	cordel m
corda[2] (I)	Strick m	rope	corde f	—	cuerda f
corde[1] (F)	Seil n	rope	—	fune f	soga f
corde[2] (F)	Strick m	rope	—	corda f	cuerda f
cordel (Es)	Schnur f	string	ficelle f	corda f	—
cordero (Es)	Lamm n	lamb	agneau m	agnello m	—
cordial (E)	herzlich	—	cordial(e)	cordiale	afectuoso(a)
cordial (F)	herzlich	cordial	—	cordiale	afectuoso(a)
cordiale (I)	herzlich	cordial	cordial(e)	—	afectuoso(a)
cordonnier (F)	Schuster m	shoemaker	—	calzolaio m	zapatero m
coriace (F)	zäh	tough	—	duro(a)	duro(a)
corkscrew (E)	Korkenzieher m	—	tire-bouchon m	cavatappi m	sacacorchos m
corn[1] (E)	Korn n	—	grain m	grano m	semilla f
corn[2] (E)	Mais m	—	maïs m	mais m	maíz m
corner[1] (E)	Ecke f	—	coin m	angolo m	esquina f
corner[2] (E)	Winkel m	—	coin m	cantuccio m	rincón m
cornice (I)	Rahmen m	frame	cadre m	—	marco m
coro (Es)	Chor m	choir	chœur m	coro m	—
coro (I)	Chor m	choir	chœur m	—	coro m
corpo (I)	Körper m	body	corps m	—	cuerpo m
corps (F)	Körper m	body	—	corpo m	cuerpo m
corpse (E)	Leiche f	—	cadavre m	cadavere m	cadáver m
correa (Es)	Riemen m	strap	courroie f	cinghia f	—
correct[1] (E)	korrekt	—	correct(e)	corretto(a)	correcto(a)
correct[2] (E)	richtig	—	juste	giusto(a)	correcto(a)
correct (F)	korrekt	correct	—	corretto(a)	correcto(a)
correcto[1] (Es)	korrekt	correct	correct(e)	corretto(a)	—
correcto[2] (Es)	richtig	correct	juste	giusto(a)	—
corredor[1] (Es)	Flur m	hall	entrée f	corridoio m	—

	D	E	F	I	Es
corredor² (Es)	Gang *m*	corridor	couloir *m*	corridoio *m*	—
corrente (I)	Strom *m*	current	courant *m*	—	corriente *f*
corrente d'aria (I)	Luftzug *m*	draught	courant d'air *m*	—	corriente de aire *f*
correo (Es)	Post *f*	post	poste *f*	posta *f*	—
correo aéreo (Es)	Luftpost *f*	air mail	poste aérienne *f*	posta aerea *f*	—
correr¹ (Es)	fließen	flow	couler	scorrere	—
correr² (Es)	laufen	run	courir	correre	—
correr³ (Es)	rennen	run	courir	correre	—
correr⁴ (Es)	vorziehen	draw	tirer	tirare in avanti	—
correre¹ (I)	laufen	run	courir	—	correr
correre² (I)	rennen	run	courir	—	correr
correspond (E)	entsprechen	—	correspondre à	corrispondere	corresponder
correspondance (F)	Anschluß *m*	connection	—	coincidenza *f*	conexión *f*
corresponder (Es)	entsprechen	correspond	correspondre à	corrispondere	—
correspondre à (F)	entsprechen	correspond	—	corrispondere	corresponder
corretto (I)	korrekt	correct	correct(e)	—	correcto(a)
corridoio¹ (I)	Diele *f*	hall	vestibule *m*	—	entrada *f*
corridoio² (I)	Flur *m*	hall	entrée *f*	—	corredor *m*
corridoio³ (I)	Gang *m*	corridor	couloir *m*	—	corredor *m*
corridoio⁴ (I)	Korridor *m*	corridor	corridor *m*	—	pasillo *m*
corridor¹ (E)	Gang *m*	—	couloir *m*	corridoio *m*	corredor *m*
corridor² (E)	Korridor *m*	—	corridor *m*	corridoio *m*	pasillo *m*
corridor (F)	Korridor *m*	corridor	—	corridoio *m*	pasillo *m*
corriente (Es)	Strom *m*	current	courant *m*	corrente *f*	—
corriente de aire (Es)	Luftzug *m*	draught	courant d'air *m*	corrente d'aria *f*	—
corriere (I)	Eilbote *m*	courier	courrier *m*	—	correo urgente *m*
corrispondere (I)	entsprechen	correspond	correspondre à	—	corresponder
corso (I)	Kurs *m*	rate	cours *m*	—	curso *m*
cortante (Es)	scharf	sharp	tranchant(e)	tagliente	—
cortar¹ (Es)	mähen	mow	faucher	falciare	—
cortar² (Es)	schneiden	cut	couper	tagliare	—
corte (Es)	Schnitt *m*	cut	coupe *f*	taglio *m*	—
cortés¹ (Es)	höflich	polite	poli(e)	cortese	—
cortés² (Es)	zuvorkommend	obliging	prévenant(e)	premuroso(a)	—
cortese (I)	höflich	polite	poli(e)	—	cortés
cortesía (Es)	Höflichkeit *f*	politeness	politesse *f*	cortesia *f*	—
cortesia (I)	Höflichkeit *f*	politeness	politesse *f*	—	cortesía *f*
cortile (I)	Hof *m*	yard	cour *f*	—	patio *m*
cortina¹ (Es)	Gardine *f*	curtain	rideau *m*	tenda *f*	—
cortina² (Es)	Vorhang *m*	curtain	rideau *m*	tenda *f*	—
corto (I)	kurz	short	court(e)	—	corto(a)
corto (Es)	kurz	short	court(e)	corto(a)	—
corvo (I)	Rabe *m*	raven	corbeau *m*	—	cuervo *m*
corzo (Es)	Reh *n*	deer	chevreuil *m*	capriolo *m*	—
cosa¹ (Es)	Ding *n*	thing	chose *f*	cosa *f*	—
cosa² (Es)	Sache *f*	thing	chose *f*	cosa *f*	—
cosa³ (Es)	Zeug *n*	stuff	truc *m*	cose *f pl*	—

	D	E	F	I	Es
cosa¹ (I)	Ding n	thing	chose f	—	cosa f
cosa² (I)	Sache f	thing	chose f	—	cosa f
coscienza (I)	Gewissen n	conscience	conscience f	—	conciencia f
coscienzioso (I)	gewissenhaft	conscientious	consciencieux (-euse)	—	concienzudo(a)
cose (I)	Zeug n	stuff	truc m	—	cosa f
cosecha (Es)	Ernte f	harvest	moisson f	raccolto m	—
coser (Es)	nähen	sew	coudre	cucire	—
così (I)	so	like this	ainsi	—	así
cost (E)	kosten	—	coûter	costare	costar
costa (Es)	Küste f	coast	côte f	costa f	—
costa (I)	Küste f	coast	côte f	—	costa f
costar (Es)	kosten	cost	coûter	costare	—
costare (I)	kosten	cost	coûter	—	costar
costas (Es)	Kosten pl	expenses	coût m	spese f pl	—
costilla (Es)	Rippe f	rib	côte f	costola f	—
costituzione (I)	Verfassung f	constitution	constitution f	—	constitución f
costola (I)	Rippe f	rib	côte f	—	costilla f
costoletta (I)	Kotelett n	cutlet	côtelette f	—	chuleta f
costoso (I)	kostspielig	expensive	coûteux(-euse)	—	costoso(a)
costoso (Es)	kostspielig	expensive	coûteux(-euse)	costoso(a)	—
costringere (I)	zwingen	force	forcer	—	obligar
costrizione (I)	Zwang m	compulsion	contrainte f	—	presión f
costruire (I)	bauen	build	construire	—	construir
costruzione (I)	Bau m	construction	construction f	—	construcción f
costumbre¹ (Es)	Gewohnheit f	habit	habitude f	abitudine f	—
costumbre² (Es)	Sitte f	custom	coutume f	usanza f	—
costume (E)	Kostüm n	—	costume m	tailleur m	vestido m
costume¹ (F)	Anzug m	suit	—	vestito m	traje m
costume² (F)	Kostüm n	costume	—	tailleur m	vestido m
costume da bagno¹ (I)	Badeanzug m	swimsuit	maillot de bain m	—	traje de baño m
costume da bagno² (I)	Badehose f	swimming trunks	slip de bain m	—	bañador m
côte¹ (F)	Küste f	coast	—	costa f	costa f
côte² (F)	Rippe f	rib	—	costola f	costilla f
côtelette (F)	Kotelett n	cutlet	—	costoletta f	chuleta f
cotidiano (Es)	täglich	daily	quotidien(ne)	quotidiano(a)	—
coton (F)	Baumwolle f	cotton	—	cotone m	algodón m
cotone (I)	Baumwolle f	cotton	coton m	—	algodón m
cotto (I)	gar	done	cuit(e)	—	estar a punto
cotton (E)	Baumwolle f	—	coton m	cotone m	algodón m
cotton wool (E)	Watte f	—	ouate f	ovatta f	algodón m
cou (F)	Hals m	neck	—	collo m	cuello m
Couch (D)	—	couch	canapé m	divano m	diván m
couch (E)	Couch f	—	canapé m	divano m	diván m
coucher du soleil (F)	Sonnenuntergang m	sunset	—	tramonto del sole m	puesta de sol f
couchette (E)	Liegewagen m	—	wagon-couchette m	cuccetta f	coche cama m

	D	E	F	I	Es
coudre (F)	nähen	sew	—	cucire	coser
cough¹ (E)	husten	—	tousser	tossire	toser
cough² (E)	Husten *m*	—	toux *m*	tosse *f*	tos *f*
couler¹ (F)	fließen	flow	—	scorrere	correr
couler² (F)	sinken	sink	—	affondare	hundirse
couleur (F)	Farbe *f*	colour	—	colore *m*	color *m*
couloir (F)	Gang *m*	corridor	—	corridoio *m*	corredor *m*
count (E)	zählen	—	compter	contare	contar
counter¹ (E)	Ladentisch *m*	—	comptoir *m*	banco di vendita *m*	mostrador *m*
counter² (E)	Schalter *m*	—	guichet *m*	sportello *m*	ventanilla *f*
country road (E)	Landstraße *f*	—	route *f*	strada provinciale *f*	carretera nacional *f*
coup¹ (F)	Stoß *m*	blow	—	spinta *f*	empujón *m*
coup² (F)	Schlag *m*	blow	—	colpo *m*	golpe *m*
coup³ (F)	Schuß *m*	shot	—	sparo *m*	disparo *m*
coupable (F)	schuldig	guilty	—	colpevole	culpable
coup de soleil (F)	Sonnenbrand *m*	sunburn	—	scottatura solare *f*	quemadura solar *f*
coup de téléphone¹ (F)	Anruf *m*	call	—	chiamata *f*	llamada *f*
coup de téléphone² (F)	Telefonanruf *m*	phone call	—	telefonata *f*	llamada telefónica *f*
coupe (F)	Schnitt *m*	cut	—	taglio *m*	corte *m*
couper (F)	schneiden	cut	—	tagliare	cortar
cour (F)	Hof *m*	yard	—	cortile *m*	patio *m*
courage (E)	Mut *m*	—	courage *m*	coraggio *m*	coraje *m*
courage (F)	Mut *m*	courage	—	coraggio *m*	coraje *m*
courageux (F)	tapfer	brave	—	coraggioso(a)	valiente
courant (F)	Strom *m*	current	—	corrente *f*	corriente *f*
courant d'air (F)	Luftzug *m*	draught	—	corrente d'aria *f*	corriente de aire *f*
courier (E)	Eilbote *m*	—	courrier *m*	corriere *m*	correo urgente *m*
courir¹ (F)	laufen	run	—	correre	correr
courir² (F)	rennen	run	—	correre	correr
courrier (F)	Eilbote *m*	courier	—	corriere *m*	correo urgente *m*
courroie (F)	Riemen *m*	strap	—	cinghia *f*	correa *f*
cours¹ (F)	Kurs *m*	rate	—	corso *m*	curso *m*
cours² (F)	Unterricht *m*	lessons	—	lezione *f*	enseñanza *f*
course (E)	Gang *m*	—	plat *m*	portata *f*	plato *m*
cours magistral (F)	Vorlesung *f*	lecture	—	lezione *f*	clase *f*
court (E)	Gericht *n*	—	tribunal *m*	tribunale *m*	tribunal *m*
court (F)	kurz	short	—	corto(a)	corto(a)
cousin¹ (E)	Cousine *f*	—	cousine *f*	cugina *f*	prima *f*
cousin² (E)	Vetter *m*	—	cousin *m*	cugino *m*	primo *m*
cousin (F)	Vetter *m*	cousin	—	cugino *m*	primo *m*
Cousine (D)	—	cousin	cousine *f*	cugina *f*	prima *f*
cousine (F)	Cousine *f*	cousin	—	cugina *f*	prima *f*
coussin (F)	Kissen *n*	cushion	—	cuscino *m*	cojín *m*
coût (F)	Kosten *pl*	expenses	—	spese *f pl*	costas *m pl*
couteau (F)	Messer *n*	knife	—	coltello *m*	cuchillo *m*

	D	E	F	I	Es
coûter (F)	kosten	cost	—	costare	costar
coûteux (F)	kostspielig	expensive	—	costoso(a)	costoso(a)
coutume (F)	Sitte *f*	custom	—	usanza *f*	costumbre *f*
couvent (F)	Kloster *n*	monastery	—	convento *m*	monasterio *m*
couvercle (F)	Deckel *m*	lid	—	coperchio *m*	tapa *f*
couvert[1] (F)	bedeckt	covered	—	coperto(a)	cubierto(a)
couvert[2] (F)	Gedeck *n*	cover	—	coperto *m*	cubierto *m*
couvert[3] (F)	bewölkt	cloudy	—	nuvoloso(a)	nublado(a)
couverture (F)	Decke *f*	blanket	—	coperta *f*	techo *m*
couvrir[1] (F)	bedecken	cover	—	coprire	cubrir
couvrir[2] (F)	zudecken	cover (up)	—	coprire	tapar
cover[1] (E)	bedecken	—	couvrir	coprire	cubrir
cover[2] (E)	beziehen	—	recouvrir	ricoprire	tapizar
cover[3] (E)	Gedeck *n*	—	couvert *m*	coperto *m*	cubierto *m*
covered (E)	bedeckt	—	couvert(e)	coperto(a)	cubierto(a)
cover (up) (E)	zudecken	—	couvrir	coprire	tapar
cow[1] (E)	Kuh *f*	—	vache *f*	mucca *f*	vaca *f*
cow[2] (E)	Rind *n*	—	bœuf *m*	manzo *m*	buey *m*
cowardly (E)	feig	—	lâche	vile	cobarde
cozza (I)	Muschel *m*	mussel	moule *f*	—	mejillón *m*
cracher (F)	spucken	spit	—	sputare	escupir
craft (E)	Handwerk *n*	—	métier *m*	artigianato *m*	artesanía *f*
craftsman (E)	Handwerker *m*	—	artisan *m*	artigiano *m*	artesano *m*
craindre[1] (F)	befürchten	fear	—	temere	temer
craindre[2] (F)	fürchten	fear	—	temere	temer
crâne (F)	Schädel *m*	skull	—	cranio *m*	cráneo *m*
cráneo (Es)	Schädel *m*	skull	crâne *m*	cranio *m*	—
cranio (I)	Schädel *m*	skull	crâne *m*	—	cráneo *m*
crash[1] (E)	abstürzen	—	faire une chute	precipitare	caer a tierra
crash[2] (E)	Absturz *m*	—	chute *f*	caduta *f*	caída *f*
cravate (F)	Krawatte *f*	tie	—	cravatta *f*	corbata *f*
cravatta (I)	Krawatte *f*	tie	cravate *f*	—	corbata *f*
crayfish (E)	Krebs *m*	—	écrevisse *f*	gambero *m*	cangrejo *m*
crayon[1] (F)	Bleistift *m*	pencil	—	matita *f*	lápiz *m*
crayon[2] (F)	Stift *m*	pencil	—	penna *f*	lápiz m
cream[1] (E)	Creme *f*	—	crème *f*	crema	crema *f*
cream[2] (E)	Sahne *f*	—	crème *f*	panna *f*	nata *f*
crear (Es)	schaffen	create	réussir à faire	creare	—
creare (I)	schaffen	create	réussir à faire	—	crear
create (E)	schaffen	—	réussir à faire	creare	crear
crecer[1] (Es)	größer werden	grow	grandir	crescere	—
crecer[2] (Es)	wachsen	grow	grandir	crescere	—
credere[1] (I)	glauben	believe	croire	—	creer
credere[2] (I)	meinen	think	penser	—	opinar
credit (E)	Kredit *m*	—	crédit *m*	credito *m*	crédito *m*
crédit (F)	Kredit *m*	credit	—	credito *m*	crédito *m*
crédito (Es)	Kredit *m*	credit	crédit *m*	credito *m*	—
credito (I)	Kredit *m*	credit	crédit *m*	—	crédito *m*

	D	E	F	I	Es
creer (Es)	glauben	believe	croire	credere	—
crema (Es)	Creme *f*	cream	crème *f*	crema	—
crema (I)	Creme *f*	cream	crème *f*	—	crema *f*
cremallera (Es)	Reißverschluß *m*	zip	fermeture éclair *f*	chiusura lampo *f*	—
Creme (D)	—	cream	crème *f*	crema	crema *f*
crème[1] (F)	Creme *f*	cream	—	crema	crema *f*
crème[2] (F)	Sahne *f*	cream	—	panna *f*	nata *f*
crescere[1] (I)	aufwachsen	grow up	grandir	—	criarse
crescere[2] (I)	größer werden	grow	grandir	—	crecer
crescere[3] (I)	wachsen	grow	grandir	—	crecer
creuser (F)	graben	dig	—	scavare	cavar
creux (F)	hohl	hollow	—	cavo(a)	hueco(a)
cri (F)	Schrei *m*	scream	—	grido *m*	grito *m*
criada (Es)	Hausmädchen *n*	maid	fille de service *f*	domestica *f*	—
crianza (Es)	Erziehung *f*	education	éducation *f*	educazione *f*	—
criar[1] (Es)	erziehen	educate	élever	educare	—
criar[2] (Es)	züchten	breed	élever	allevare	—
criarse (Es)	aufwachsen	grow up	grandir	crescere	—
crier[1] (F)	ausrufen	exclaim	—	esclamare	exclamar
crier[2] (F)	schreien	scream	—	gridare	gritar
crime[1] (E)	Untat *f*	—	méfait *m*	misfatto *m*	crimen *m*
crime[2] (E)	Verbrechen *n*	—	crime *m*	delitto *m*	crimen *m*
crime (F)	Verbrechen *n*	crime	—	delitto *m*	crimen *m*
crimen[1] (Es)	Untat *f*	crime	méfait *m*	misfatto *m*	—
crimen[2] (Es)	Verbrechen *n*	crime	crime *m*	delitto *m*	—
cristal (Es)	Scheibe *f*	pane	vitre *m*	vetro *m*	—
cristiano (I)	Christ *m*	Christian	chrétien *m*	—	cristiano *m*
cristiano (Es)	Christ *m*	Christian	chrétien *m*	cristiano *m*	—
criticar (Es)	kritisieren	criticize	critiquer	criticare	—
criticare (I)	kritisieren	criticize	critiquer	—	criticar
criticize (E)	kritisieren	—	critiquer	criticare	criticar
critiquer (F)	kritisieren	criticize	—	criticare	criticar
croce (I)	Kreuz *n*	cross	croix *f*	—	cruz *f*
crochet (F)	Haken *m*	hook	—	gancio *m*	gancho *m*
crockery (E)	Geschirr *n*	—	vaisselle *f*	stoviglie *f pl*	vajilla *f*
croire (F)	glauben	believe	—	credere	creer
croix (F)	Kreuz *n*	cross	—	croce *f*	cruz *f*
crollare[1] (I)	einstürzen	collapse	écrouler, se	—	derrumbarse
crollare[2] (I)	zusammenbrechen	collapse	éffondrer, se	—	desmayarse
crooked (E)	krumm	—	tordu(e)	storto(a)	torcido(a)
cross[1] (E)	Kreuz *n*	—	croix *f*	croce *f*	cruz *f*
cross[2] (E)	überqueren	—	traverser	attraversare	atravesar
crossing[1] (E)	Kreuzung *f*	—	intersection *f*	incrocio *m*	cruce *m*
crossing[2] (E)	Übergang *m*	—	passage *m*	passaggio *m*	paso *m*
crossing[3] (E)	Überfahrt *f*	—	traversée *f*	traversata *f*	travesía *f*
crowd (E)	Menschenmenge *f*	—	foule *f*	folla *f*	muchedumbre *f*
crowded (E)	überfüllt	—	bondé(e)	pieno(a) zeppo(a)	abarrotado(a)
cru (F)	roh	raw	—	crudo(a)	crudo(a)

	D	E	F	I	Es
cruce (Es)	Kreuzung *f*	crossing	intersection *f*	incrocio *m*	—
cruche (F)	Krug *m*	jug	—	brocca *f*	jarro(a) *m(f)*
crudele (I)	grausam	cruel	cruel(le)	—	cruel
crudo (I)	roh	raw	cru(e)	—	crudo(a)
crudo (Es)	roh	raw	cru(e)	crudo(a)	—
cruel (E)	grausam	—	cruel(le)	crudele	cruel
cruel (Es)	grausam	cruel	cruel(le)	crudele	—
cruel (F)	grausam	cruel	—	crudele	cruel
cruz (Es)	Kreuz *n*	cross	croix *f*	croce *f*	—
cry (E)	weinen	—	pleurer	piangere	llorar
cuaderno (Es)	Heft *n*	exercise book	cahier *m*	quaderno *m*	—
cuadrado[1] (Es)	Quadrat *n*	square	carré *m*	quadrato *m*	—
cuadrado[2] (Es)	quadratisch	square	carré(e)	quadrato(a)	—
cuadrangular (Es)	viereckig	square	carré(e)	quadrato(a)	—
cuadro[1] (Es)	Bild *n*	picture	image *f*	immagine *f*	—
cuadro[2] (Es)	Gemälde *n*	painting	tableau *m*	quadro *m*	—
¿cuál? (Es)	welche(r,s)	which	qui/que	il(la) quale	—
cualidad (Es)	Qualität *f*	quality	qualité *f*	qualità *f*	—
cualquiera[1] (Es)	irgendein(e)	some/any	quelconque	qualcuno(a)	—
cualquiera[2] (Es)	irgend	at all/some	d'une façon ou d'une autre	in qualche modo	—
cuando[1] (Es)	wenn	when/if	si/quand	se/quando	—
cuando[2] (Es)	wann	when	quand	quando	—
¿cuánto? (Es)	wieviel	how much	combien	quanto	—
¿cuántos? (Es)	wieviele	how many	combien	quanti(e)	—
cuarenta (Es)	vierzig	forty	quarante	quaranta	—
cuarteto (Es)	Quartett *n*	quartet	quatuor *m*	quartetto *m*	—
cuarto (Es)	Viertel *n*	a quarter	quart *m*	quarto *m*	—
cuarto de baño (Es)	Badezimmer *n*	bathroom	salle de bains *f*	stanza da bagno *f*	—
cuatro (Es)	vier	four	quatre	quattro	—
cubic metre (E)	Kubikmeter *m*	—	mètre cube *m*	metro cubo *m*	metro cúbico *m*
cubierta (Es)	Deck *n*	deck	pont *m*	ponte *m*	—
cubierto[1] (Es)	Gedeck *n*	cover	couvert *m*	coperto *m*	—
cubierto[2] (Es)	bedeckt	covered	couvert	coperto(a)	—
cubo (Es)	Eimer m	bucket	seau m	secchio m	—
cubo de la basura[1] (Es)	Abfalleimer *m*	bin	poubelle *f*	pattumiera *f*	—
cubo de la basura[2] (Es)	Mülleimer *m*	dustbin	poubelle *f*	secchio dei rifiuti *m*	—
cubrir (Es)	bedecken	cover	couvrir	coprire	—
cuccetta (I)	Liegewagen *m*	couchette	wagon-couchette *m*	—	coche cama *m*
cucchiaino da tè (I)	Teelöffel *m*	teaspoon	cuiller à thé *f*	—	cucharilla *f*
cucchiaio[1] (I)	Eßlöffel *m*	tablespoon	cuiller *f*	—	cuchara *f*
cucchiaio[2] (I)	Löffel *m*	spoon	cuiller *f*	—	cuchara *f*
cuchara[1] (Es)	Eßlöffel *m*	tablespoon	cuiller *f*	cucchiaio *m*	—
cuchara[2] (Es)	Löffel *m*	spoon	cuiller *f*	cucchiaio *m*	—
cucharilla (Es)	Teelöffel *m*	teaspoon	cuiller à thé *f*	cucchiaino da tè *m*	—
cuchichear (Es)	flüstern	whisper	chuchoter	bisbigliare	—

	D	E	F	I	Es
cuchilla (Es)	Klinge f	blade	lame f	lama f	—
cuchillo (Es)	Messer n	knife	couteau m	coltello m	—
cucina[1] (I)	Küche f	kitchen	cuisine f	—	cocina f
cucina[2] (I)	Herd m	cooker	fourneau m	—	cocina f
cucinare (I)	kochen	cook	cuire	—	cocinar
cucire (I)	nähen	sew	coudre	—	cocer
cucumber (E)	Gurke f	—	concombre m	cetriolo m	pepino m
cueillir (F)	pflücken	pick	—	cogliere	coger
cuello[1] (Es)	Hals m	neck	cou m	collo m	—
cuello[2] (Es)	Kragen m	collar	col m	colletto m	—
cuenta (Es)	Konto n	account	compte m	conto m	—
cuerda (Es)	Strick m	rope	corde f	corda f	—
cuero (Es)	Leder n	leather	cuir m	cuoio m	—
cuerpo (Es)	Körper m	body	corps m	corpo m	—
cuerpo de bomberos (Es)	Feuerwehr f	fire brigade	sapeurs pompiers m pl	vigili del fuoco m pl	—
cuervo (Es)	Rabe m	raven	corbeau m	corvo m	—
cuesta abajo (Es)	bergab	downhill	en descendant	in discesa	—
cuesta arriba (Es)	bergauf	uphill	en montant	in salita	—
cueva (Es)	Höhle f	cave	grotte f	caverna f	—
cugina (I)	Cousine f	cousin	cousine f	—	prima f
cugino (I)	Vetter m	cousin	cousin m	—	primo m
cuidado[1] (Es)	Vorsicht f	caution	prudence f	prudenza f	—
cuidado[2] (Es)	gepflegt	looked-after	soigné(e)	curato(a)	—
cuidadoso (Es)	sorgfältig	careful(ly)	soigneux(-euse)	accurato(a)	—
cuidar (Es)	pflegen	look after	soigner	curare	—
cuiller[1] (F)	Eßlöffel m	tablespoon	—	cucchiaio m	cuchara f
cuiller[2] (F)	Löffel m	spoon	—	cucchiaio m	cuchara f
cuiller à thé (F)	Teelöffel m	teaspoon	—	cucchiaino da tè m	cucharilla f
cuir (F)	Leder n	leather	—	cuoio m	cuero m
cuire (F)	kochen	cook	—	cucinare	cocinar
cuisine (F)	Küche f	kitchen	—	cucina f	cocina f
cuisinier (F)	Koch m	cook	—	cuoco m	cocinero m
cuisinière (F)	Köchin f	cook	—	cuoca f	cocinera f
cuit (F)	gar	done	—	cotto(a)	a punto
culpa (Es)	Schuld f	fault	culpabilité f	colpa f	—
culpabilité (F)	Schuld f	fault	—	colpa f	culpa f
culpable (Es)	schuldig	guilty	coupable	colpevole	—
cultivar (Es)	anbauen	cultivate	cultiver	coltivare	—
cultivate (E)	anbauen	—	cultiver	coltivare	cultivar
cultiver (F)	anbauen	cultivate	—	coltivare	cultivar
cultura (Es)	Kultur f	culture	culture f	cultura f	—
cultura (I)	Kultur f	culture	culture f	—	cultura f
culture (E)	Kultur f	—	culture f	cultura f	cultura f
culture (F)	Kultur f	culture	—	cultura f	cultura f
cumbre (Es)	Gipfel m	peak	sommet m	cima f	—
cumpleaños (Es)	Geburtstag m	birthday	anniversaire m	compleanno m	—
cuñada (Es)	Schwägerin f	sister-in-law	belle-sœur f	cognata f	—

	D	E	F	I	Es
cuñado (Es)	Schwager *m*	brother-in-law	beau-frère *m*	cognato *m*	—
cuoca (I)	Köchin *f*	cook	cuisinière *f*	—	cocinera *f*
cuocere (al forno) (I)	backen	bake	faire cuire	—	cocer (al horno)
cuoco (I)	Koch *m*	cook	cuisinier *m*	—	cocinero *m*
cuoio (I)	Leder *n*	leather	cuir *m*	—	cuero *m*
cuore (I)	Herz *n*	heart	cœur *m*	—	corazón *m*
cuota (Es)	Beitrag *m*	contribution	contribution *f*	contributo *m*	—
cup (E)	Tasse *f*	—	tasse *f*	tazza *f*	taza *f*
cupboard (E)	Schrank *m*	—	armoire *f*	armadio *m*	armario *m*
cura (Es)	Kur *f*	treatment	cure *f*	cura *f*	—
cura¹ (I)	Kur *f*	treatment	cure *f*	—	cura *f*
cura² (I)	Pflege *f*	care	soins *m pl*	—	aseo *m*
curar (Es)	heilen	heal	guérir	curare	—
curare¹ (I)	heilen	heal	guérir	—	curar
curare² (I)	pflegen	look after	soigner	—	cuidar
curato (I)	gepflegt	looked-after	soigné(e)	—	cuidado(a)
curd cheese (E)	Quark *m*	—	fromage blanc *m*	ricotta *f*	requesón *m*
cure (F)	Kur *f*	treatment	—	cura *f*	cura *f*
curé (F)	Pfarrer *m*	priest	—	parroco *m*	párroco *m*
curieux¹ (F)	merkwürdig	strange	—	curioso(a)	curioso(a)
curieux² (F)	neugierig	curious	—	curioso(a)	curioso(a)
curiosità (I)	Sehenswürdig-keit *f*	sight	curiosité *f*	—	lugares de interés *m pl*
curiosité (F)	Sehenswürdig-keit *f*	sight	—	curiosità *f*	lugares de interés *m pl*
curioso¹ (I)	merkwürdig	strange	curieux(-euse)	—	curioso(a)
curioso² (I)	neugierig	curious	curieux(-euse)	—	curioso(a)
curioso¹ (Es)	merkwürdig	strange	curieux(-euse)	strano(a)	—
curioso² (Es)	neugierig	curious	curieux(-euse)	curioso(a)	—
curious (E)	neugierig	—	curieux(-euse)	curioso(a)	curioso(a)
curl (E)	Locke *f*	—	boucle *f*	riccio *m*	rizo *m*
currant (E)	Johannisbeere *f*	—	groseille *f*	ribes *m*	grosella *f*
currency (E)	Währung *f*	—	monnaie *f*	valuta *f*	moneda *f*
current (E)	Strom *m*	—	courant *m*	corrente *f*	corriente *f*
curriculum vitae (E)	Lebenslauf *m*	—	curriculum vitae *m*	curriculum vitae *m*	curriculum vitae *m*
curriculum vitae (Es)	Lebenslauf *m*	curriculum vitae	curriculum vitae *m*	curriculum vitae *m*	—
curriculum vitae (F)	Lebenslauf *m*	curriculum vitae	—	curriculum vitae *m*	curriculum vitae *m*
curriculum vitae (I)	Lebenslauf *m*	curriculum vitae	curriculum vitae *m*	—	curriculum vitae *m*
curso (Es)	Kurs *m*	rate	cours *m*	corso *m*	—
curtain¹ (E)	Gardine *f*	—	rideau *m*	tenda *f*	cortina *f*
curtain² (E)	Vorhang *m*	—	rideau *m*	tenda *f*	cortina *f*
curva (Es)	Kurve *f*	bend	virage *m*	curva *f*	—
curva (I)	Kurve *f*	bend	virage *m*	—	curva *f*
cuscino (I)	Kissen *n*	cushion	coussin *m*	—	cojín *m*
cushion (E)	Kissen *n*	—	coussin *m*	cuscino *m*	cojín *m*
custode¹ (I)	Aufseher *m*	guard	gardien *m*	—	vigilante *m*

	D	E	F	I	Es
custode[2] (I)	Wärter m	attendant	gardien m	—	guarda m
custom[1] (E)	Gebrauch m	—	usage m	uso m	uso m
custom[2] (E)	Sitte f	—	coutume f	usanza f	costumbre f
customer (E)	Kunde m	—	client m	cliente m	cliente m
customs (E)	Zoll m	—	douane f	dogana f	aduana f
cut[1] (E)	schneiden	—	couper	tagliare	cortar
cut[2] (E)	Schnitt m	—	coupe f	taglio m	corte m
cutlet (E)	Kotelett n	—	côtelette f	costoletta f	chuleta f
cuttlefish (E)	Tintenfisch m	—	seiche f	seppia f	calamar m
Czechoslovakia (E)	Tschecho-slowakei f	—	Tchécoslovaquie f	Cecoslovacchia f	Checoslovaquia f
da (D)	—	there	là/ici	qui/là	allí
da[1] (I)	ab	off	à partir de/dès	—	a partir de/de
da[2] (I)	seit	since/for	depuis	—	de/desde
da[3] (I)	aus	off/from/out of	de/par/hors de	—	de/por
da[4] (I)	zu	to	de/à	—	para
da[5] (I)	bei	at/near	chez/près de	—	cerca de/junto a
d'abord[1] (F)	erst	first	—	dapprima	primero
d'abord[2] (F)	zuerst	at first	—	dapprima	primero
d'accord (F)	einverstanden	agreed	—	d'accordo	de acuerdo
d'accordo (I)	einverstanden	agreed	d'accord	—	de acuerdo
Dach (D)	—	roof	toit m	tetto m	techo m
dado (Es)	Würfel m	dice	dé m	dado m	—
dado (I)	Würfel m	dice	dé m	—	dado m
da dove (I)	woher	where from	d'où	—	¿de dónde?
d'affaires (F)	geschäftlich	on business	—	per affari	comercial
daft (E)	doof	—	bête	scemo(a)	estúpido(a)
dafür[1] (D)	—	for it	pour cela	per questo	para ello
dafür[2] (D)	—	instead	en échange	invece	en su lugar
dagegen (D)	—	against it	contre cela	contro	contra
daheim (D)	—	at home	à la maison	a casa	en casa
dahinter (D)	—	behind it	derrière	dietro	detrás
d'ailleurs (F)	übrigens	by the way	—	del resto	por lo demás
daily (E)	täglich	—	quotidien(ne)	quotidiano(a)	cotidiano(a)
dall'altra parte (I)	drüben	over there	de l'autre côté	—	al otro lado
d'altra parte (I)	andererseits	on the other hand	d'autre part	—	por otra parte
damage[1] (E)	beschädigen	—	endommager	danneggiare	deteriorar
damage[2] (E)	Beschädigung f	—	endommage-ment m	danno m	deterioro m
damage[3] (E)	schaden	—	nuire	nuocere	dañar
damage[4] (E)	Schaden m	—	dommage m	danno m	daño m
damals (D)	—	at that time	alors	allora	entonces
Dame (D)	—	lady	dame f	signora f	señora f
dame (F)	Dame f	lady	—	signora f	señora f
damit (D)	—	with it	avec cela	con questo	con ello
dämmern (D)	—	dawn	poindre	spuntare	amanecer
da molto (I)	längst	a long time ago	depuis bien longtemps	—	hace mucho
damp (E)	feucht	—	humide	umido(a)	húmedo(a)

	D	E	F	I	Es
Dampf (D)	—	steam	vapeur f	vapore m	vapor m
danach (D)	—	afterwards	après	poi/dopo	después
dañar (Es)	schaden	damage	nuire	nuocere	—
dance[1] (E)	tanzen	—	danser	ballare	bailar
dance[2] (E)	Tanz m	—	danse f	ballo m	baile f
da nessuna parte (I)	nirgends	nowhere	nulle part	—	en ninguna parte
danger (E)	Gefahr f	—	danger m	pericolo m	peligro m
danger (F)	Gefahr f	danger	—	pericolo m	peligro m
dangereux (F)	gefährlich	dangerous	—	pericoloso(a)	peligroso(a)
dangerous (E)	gefährlich	—	dangereux(-euse)	pericoloso(a)	peligroso(a)
Dank (D)	—	thanks	remerciement m	ringraziamento m	agradecimiento m
dankbar (D)	—	grateful	reconnaissant(e)	grato(a)	agradecido(a)
danke (D)	—	thank you	merci	grazie	¡gracias!
danken (D)	—	thank	remercier	ringraziare	agradecer
dann (D)	—	then	ensuite	in seguito	luego
danneggiare (I)	beschädigen	damage	endommager	—	deteriorar
danno[1] (I)	Beschädigung f	damage	endommage-ment m	—	deterioro m
danno[2] (I)	Schaden m	damage	dommage m	—	daño m
daño (Es)	Schaden m	damage	dommage m	danno m	—
dans[1] (F)	hinein	in	—	dentro	dentro
dans[2] (F)	in	in/into	—	in/a/tra/fra	en/a
danse (F)	Tanz m	dance	—	ballo m	baile f
danser (F)	tanzen	dance	—	ballare	bailar
dans l'ensemble (F)	insgesamt	altogether	—	complesivamente	en suma
da piccolo borghese (I)	spießig	bourgeois	bourgeois(e)	—	pequeño(a) burgués(-esa)
dappertutto (I)	überall	everywhere	partout	—	por todas partes
dapprima[1] (I)	erst	first	d'abord	—	primero
dapprima[2] (I)	zunächst	first of all	pour l'instant	—	en primer lugar
dapprima[3] (I)	zuerst	at first	d'abord	—	primero
da questa parte (I)	herüber	over	par ici	—	a este lado
darauf (D)	—	afterwards/on it	dessus/ensuite	dopo/su	después/encima
dare (E)	wagen	—	oser	osare	atreverse
dare (I)	geben	give	donner	—	dar
dare del tu (I)	duzen	use the familiar form	tutoyer	—	tutear
dare in prestito (I)	ausleihen	lend	prêter	—	prestar
dare le dimissioni (I)	zurücktreten	retire	démissionner	—	dimitir
dare nell'occhio (I)	auffallen	be noticeable	faire remarquer, se	—	llamar la atención por algo
d'argent (F)	silbern	silver	—	d'argento	plateado(a)
dar gritos de alegría (Es)	jubeln	rejoice	pousser des cris de joie	giubilare	—
d'argento (I)	silbern	silver	d'argent	—	plateado(a)
dark[1] (E)	dunkel	—	sombre	scuro(a)	oscuro(a)
dark[2] (E)	finster	—	sombre	buio(a)	oscuro(a)
darkness (E)	Finsternis f	—	obscurité f	buio m	oscuridad f
darling (E)	Liebling m	—	chéri m	tesoro m	querido m
Darm (D)	—	intestine	intestin m	intestino m	intestino m

	D	E	F	I	Es
darse cuenta (Es)	bemerken	notice	remarquer	notare	—
darse prisa¹ (Es)	beeilen, sich	hurry up	dépêcher, se	affrettarsi	—
darse prisa² (Es)	eilen	hurry	dépêcher, se	andare in fretta	—
darsi appuntamento (I)	verabreden	arrange to meet	prendre rendez-vous	—	concertar una cita
darstellen (D)	—	represent	représenter	rappresentare	representar
darüber (D)	—	above	au dessus	sopra	por encima
darunter (D)	—	underneath	au dessous	sotto	por debajo
dar vuelta (Es)	herumdrehen	turn around	tourner	girare	—
das (D)	—	that/which	le/la	il/la	lo
Dasein (D)	—	existence	existence *f*	esistenza *f*	existencia *f*
daß (D)	—	that	que	che	que
dasselbe (D)	—	the same	la même chose	lo stesso	lo mismo
data (I)	Datum *n*	date	date *f*	—	fecha *f*
date¹ (E)	Datum *n*	—	date *f*	data *f*	fecha *f*
date² (E)	Termin *m*	—	terme *m*	termine *m*	fecha *f*
date³ (E)	Verabredung *f*	—	rendez-vous *m*	appuntamento *m*	cita *f*
date (F)	Datum *n*	date	—	data *f*	fecha *f*
dated (E)	altertümlich	—	antique	antico(a)	antiguo(a)
Datum (D)	—	date	date *f*	data *f*	fecha *f*
Dauer (D)	—	duration	durée *f*	durata *f*	duración *f*
dauern (D)	—	last	durer	durare	durar
daughter (E)	Tochter *f*	—	fille *f*	figlia *f*	hija *f*
Daumen (D)	—	thumb	pouce *m*	pollice *m*	pulgar *m*
da un lato (I)	einerseits	on one hand	d'une part	—	por un lado
d'autre part (F)	andererseits	on the other hand	—	d'altra parte	por otra parte
davanti (I)	vorn(e)	at the front	devant	—	delante
davanti a (I)	vor	before/ in front of	devant/avant	—	delante de
davon (D)	—	of it	en/de cela	di la/ne	de ello
dawn (E)	dämmern	—	poindre	spuntare	amanecer
day (E)	Tag *m*	—	jour *m*	giorno *m*	día *m*
day after tomorrow (E)	übermorgen	—	après-demain	dopodomani	pasado mañana
day before yesterday (E)	vorgestern	—	avant-hier	l'altro ieri	anteayer
dazio (I)	Zoll *m*	duty	droits de douane *m pl*	—	arbitrio *m*
dazwischen (D)	—	inbetween	entre	in mezzo	entre
de¹ (Es)	aus	off/from/out of	de/par/hors de	da/di	—
de² (Es)	seit	since/for	depuis	da	—
de³ (Es)	von	from/by	de	di/da	—
de¹ (F)	aus	off/from/out of	—	da/di	de/por
de² (F)	von	from/by	—	di/da	de
de³ (F)	zu	to	—	da/di/a	para
dé (F)	Würfel *m*	dice	—	dado *m*	dado *m*
de acuerdo (Es)	einverstanden	agreed	d'accord	d'accordo	—
dead (E)	tot	—	mort(e)	morto(a)	muerto(a)
deaf (E)	taub	—	sourd(e)	sordo(a)	sordo(a)
dealer (E)	Händler *m*	—	commerçant *m*	commerciante *m*	comerciante *m*

	D	E	F	I	Es
de alguna manera (Es)	irgendwie	somehow	n'importe comment	in qualche modo	—
death (E)	Tod *m*	—	mort *f*	morte *f*	muerte *f*
debajo de (Es)	unter	under	sous	al di sotto di	—
deber¹ (Es)	müssen	have to	devoir	dovere	—
deber² (Es)	sollen	have to	devoir	dovere	—
deber³ (Es)	schulden	owe	devoir qch à qn	dovere	—
débil (Es)	schwach	weak	faible	debole	—
debilidad (Es)	Schwäche *f*	weakness	faiblesse *f*	debolezza *f*	—
debiti (I)	Schulden *pl*	debt	dette *f*	—	deudas *f pl*
debole (I)	schwach	weak	faible	—	débil
debolezza (I)	Schwäche *f*	weakness	faiblesse *f*	—	debilidad *f*
debt (E)	Schulden *pl*	—	dette *f*	debiti *m pl*	deudas *f pl*
débutant (F)	Anfänger *m*	beginner	—	principiante *m*	principante *m*
de camino (Es)	unterwegs	on the way	en route	per strada	—
deceive (E)	täuschen	—	tromper	ingannare	engañar
December (E)	Dezember *m*	—	décembre *m*	dicembre *m*	diciembre *m*
décembre (F)	Dezember *m*	December	—	dicembre *m*	diciembre *m*
decent (E)	anständig	—	convenable	decente	decente
decente (Es)	anständig	decent	convenable	decente	—
decente (I)	anständig	decent	convenable	—	decente
décevoir (F)	enttäuschen	disappoint	—	deludere	defraudar
décharger¹ (F)	ausladen	unload	—	scaricare	descargar
décharger² (F)	abladen	unload	—	scaricare	descargar
déchets (F)	Abfall *m*	rubbish	—	immondizia *f*	basura *f*
déchirer (F)	zerreißen	rip	—	strappare	romper
déchirer, se (F)	reißen	tear	—	strappare	desgarrarse
decide¹ (E)	beschließen	—	décider	decidere	decidir
decide² (E)	entschließen, sich	—	décider, se	decidere	decidirse
decide³ (E)	entscheiden	—	décider	decidere	decidir
décider¹ (F)	beschließen	decide	—	decidere	decidir
décider² (F)	entscheiden	decide	—	decidere	decidir
décider, se (F)	entschließen, sich	decide	—	decidere	decidirse
decidere¹ (I)	beschließen	decide	décider	—	decidir
decidere² (I)	entschließen, sich	decide	décider, se	—	decidirse
decidere³ (I)	entscheiden	decide	décider	—	decidir
decidir¹ (Es)	beschließen	decide	décider	decidere	—
decidir² (Es)	entscheiden	decide	décider	decidere	—
decidirse (Es)	entschließen, sich	decide	décider, se	decidere	—
decir (Es)	sagen	say	dire	dire	—
decision¹ (E)	Entschluß *m*	—	décision *f*	decisione *f*	decisión *f*
decision² (E)	Entscheidung *f*	—	décision *f*	decisione *f*	decisión *f*
decisión¹ (Es)	Entschluß *m*	decision	décision *f*	decisione *f*	—
decisión² (Es)	Entscheidung *f*	decision	décision *f*	decisione *f*	—
décision¹ (F)	Entschluß *m*	decision	—	decisione *f*	decisión *f*
décision² (F)	Entscheidung *f*	decision	—	decisione *f*	decisión *f*
decisione¹ (I)	Entschluß *m*	decision	décision *f*	—	decisión *f*

defective

	D	E	F	I	Es
decisione² (I)	Entscheidung f	decision	décision f	—	decisión f
Deck (D)	—	deck	pont m	ponte m	cubierta f
deck (E)	Deck n	—	pont m	ponte m	cubierta f
deck chair (E)	Liegestuhl m	—	chaise longue f	sedia a sdraio f	tumbona f
Decke (D)	—	blanket	couverture f	coperta f	techo m
Deckel (D)	—	lid	couvercle m	coperchio m	tapa f
declarar¹ (Es)	behaupten	assert	affirmer	affermare	—
declarar² (Es)	melden	report	annoncer	annunciare	—
declarar en la aduana (Es)	verzollen	declare	dédouaner	sdoganare	—
déclaration (F)	Aussage f	statement	—	dichiarazione f	afirmación f
declare (E)	verzollen	—	dédouaner	sdoganare	declarar en la aduana
décollage (F)	Abflug m	take-off	—	decollo m	despegue m
de colores¹ (Es)	bunt	coloured	coloré(e)	variopinto(a)	—
de colores² (Es)	farbig	colourful	coloré(e)	colorato(a)	—
decollo (I)	Abflug m	take-off	décollage m	—	despegue m
de color lila (Es)	lila	purple	mauve	lilla	—
de color rosa (Es)	rosa	pink	rose	rosa	—
décombres (F)	Trümmer pl	ruins	—	macerie f pl	escombros m pl
décommander (F)	abbestellen	cancel	—	annullare	anular el pedido de
de confianza (Es)	zuverlässig	reliable	sûr(e)	affidabile	—
de congé (F)	schulfrei	holiday	—	vacanza f	sin colegio
déconseiller (F)	abraten	warn	—	sconsigliare	desaconsejar
decorate (E)	garnieren	—	garnir	guarnire	guarnecer
decoration (E)	Orden m	—	décoration f	decorazione f	condecoración f
décoration (F)	Orden m	decoration	—	decorazione f	condecoración f
decorazione (I)	Orden m	decoration	décoration f	—	condecoración f
découvrir (F)	entdecken	discover	—	scoprire	descubrir
décrire (F)	beschreiben	describe	—	descrivere	describir
décrocher (F)	abnehmen	take away	—	staccare	descolgar
déçu (F)	enttäuscht	disappointed	—	deluso(a)	defraudado(a)
dedicar (Es)	widmen	dedicate	dédier	dedicare	—
dedicare (I)	widmen	dedicate	dédier	—	dedicar
dedicate (E)	widmen	—	dédier	dedicare	dedicar
dédier (F)	widmen	dedicate	—	dedicare	dedicar
dedo (Es)	Finger m	finger	doigt m	dito m	—
dedo del pie (Es)	Zehe f	toe	doigt de pied m	dito del piede m	—
de dónde (Es)	woher	where from	d'où	da dove	—
dédouaner (F)	verzollen	declare	—	sdoganare	declarar en la aduana
deed (E)	Tat f	—	action f	azione f	acción f
de ello (Es)	davon	of it	en/de cela	di la/ne	—
deep (E)	tief	—	profond(e)	profondo(a)	profundo(a)
deer (E)	Reh n	—	chevreuil m	capriolo m	corzo m
défaire (F)	auspacken	unpack	—	disfare	deshacer
défaite (F)	Niederlage f	defeat	—	sconfitta f	derrota f
defeat (E)	Niederlage f	—	défaite f	sconfitta f	derrota f
defective (E)	defekt	—	défectueux(-euse)	guasto(a)	defectuoso(a)

	D	E	F	I	Es
défectueux (F)	defekt	defective	—	guasto(a)	defectuoso(a)
defectuoso (Es)	defekt	defective	défectueux(-euse)	guasto(a)	—
defekt (D)	—	defective	défectueux(-euse)	guasto(a)	defectuoso(a)
defence (E)	Verteidigung f	—	défense f	difesa f	defensa f
defend[1] (E)	verteidigen	—	défendre	difendere	defender
defend[2] (E)	wehren, sich	—	défendre, se	difendersi	defenderse
defender (Es)	verteidigen	defend	défendre	difendere	—
defenderse (Es)	wehren, sich	defend	défendre, se	difendersi	—
défendre[1] (F)	verteidigen	defend	—	difendere	defender
défendre[2] (F)	verbieten	forbid	—	proibire	prohibir
défendre, se (F)	wehren, sich	defend	—	difendersi	defenderse
defensa (Es)	Verteidigung f	defence	défense f	difesa f	—
défense[1] (F)	Verteidigung f	defence	—	difesa f	defensa f
défense[2] (F)	Verbot n	prohibition	—	divieto m	prohibición f
défense de stationner (F)	Parkverbot n	no parking	—	divieto di parcheggio m	estacionamiento prohibido m
definitely (E)	bestimmt	—	certainement	certamente	ciertamente
defraudado (Es)	enttäuscht	disappointed	déçu(e)	deluso(a)	—
defraudar (Es)	enttäuschen	disappoint	décevoir	deludere	—
dégoutter (F)	tropfen	drip	—	gocciolare	gotear
degré (F)	Grad m	degree	—	grado m	grado m
degree (E)	Grad m	—	degré m	grado m	grado m
dehors[1] (F)	draußen	outside	—	fuori	afuera
dehors[2] (F)	heraus	out	—	fuori	hacia afuera
dehors[3] (F)	hinaus	out	—	fuori	hacia afuera
deinetwegen (D)	—	for your sake	pour toi	per te	por ti
déjà (F)	bereits	already	—	già	ya
dejar[1] (Es)	hinterlassen	leave	laisser	lasciare	—
dejar[2] (Es)	lassen	let	laisser	lasciare	—
dejar[3] (Es)	übriglassen	leave	laisser	lasciare	—
dejar[4] (Es)	verlassen	leave	abandonner	lasciare	—
dejar libre (Es)	loslassen	let go of	lâcher	mollare	—
déjeuner (F)	Mittagessen n	lunch	—	pranzo m	comida f
delante[1] (Es)	hervor	forth	au-dehors	fuori	—
delante[2] (Es)	voraus	ahead	en avant	avanti	—
delante[3] (Es)	vorn(e)	at the front	devant	davanti	—
delante de (Es)	vor	before/ in front of	devant/avant	davanti a	—
de l'autre côté[1] (F)	drüben	over there	—	dall'altra parte	al otro lado
de l'autre côté[2] (F)	hinüber	across	—	di là	hacia el otro lado
de l'autre côté[3] (F)	jenseits	beyond	—	al di là	al otro lado
delay (E)	Verspätung f	—	retard m	ritardo m	retraso m
delega (I)	Vollmacht f	authority	procuration f	—	poder m
deleite (Es)	Genuß m	pleasure	plaisir m	piacere m	—
deletrear (Es)	buchstabieren	spell	épeler	sillabare	—
delgado[1] (Es)	dünn	thin	mince	magro(a)	—
delgado[2] (Es)	mager	skinny	maigre	magro(a)	—
delgado[3] (Es)	schlank	slim	mince	snello(a)	—
deliberate (E)	bewußt	—	délibéré(e)	intenzionale	intencionado(a)

	D	E	F	I	Es
délibéré (F)	bewußt	deliberate	—	intenzionale	intencionado(a)
delicious (E)	köstlich	—	savoureux (-euse)	squisito(a)	exquisito(a)
délier (F)	losbinden	free	—	sciogliere	desatar
delight (E)	Lust f	—	plaisir m	piacere m	ganas f pl
delighted[1] (E)	erfreut	—	réjoui(e)	lieto(a)	contento(a)
delighted[2] (E)	entzückt	—	ravi(e)	affascinato(a)	encantado(a)
delightful (E)	entzückend	—	ravissant(e)	affascinante	encantador(a)
delitto (I)	Verbrechen n	crime	crime m	—	crimen m
deliver[1] (E)	liefern	—	livrer	fornire	suministrar
deliver[2] (E)	überbringen	—	remettre	portare	transmitir
delivery (E)	Lieferung f	—	livraison f	fornitura f	suministro m
del norte (Es)	nördlich	northern	du nord	a nord	—
de l'ouest (F)	westlich	western	—	ad ovest	del oeste
del resto (I)	übrigens	by the way	d'ailleurs	—	por lo demás
deludere (I)	enttäuschen	disappoint	décevoir	—	defraudar
de lujo (Es)	luxuriös	luxurious	luxueux(-euse)	lussuoso(a)	—
deluso (I)	enttäuscht	disappointed	déçu(e)	—	defraudado(a)
demain (F)	morgen	tomorrow	—	domani	mañana
de mala gana (Es)	ungern	reluctantly	de mauvaise grâce	malvolentieri	—
demand[1] (E)	fordern	—	exiger	esigere	exigir
demand[2] (E)	Forderung f	—	exigence f	esigenza f	exigencia f
demand[3] (E)	Nachfrage f	—	demande f	domanda f	demanda f
demand[4] (E)	verlangen	—	demander	richiedere	exigir
demanda (Es)	Nachfrage f	demand	demande f	domanda f	—
demande[1] (F)	Antrag m	application	—	domanda f	solicitud f
demande[2] (F)	Bitte f	request	—	domanda f	ruego m
demande[3] (F)	Nachfrage f	demand	—	domanda f	demanda f
demander[1] (F)	anfordern	request	—	esigere	pedir
demander[2] (F)	bitten	request	—	pregare	rogar
demander[3] (F)	fragen	ask	—	domandare	preguntar
demander[4] (F)	verlangen	demand	—	richiedere	exigir
démanger (F)	jucken	itch	—	prudere	picar
démarrer (F)	starten	start	—	partire	partir
demasiado (Es)	zuviel	too much	trop	troppo	—
demasiado poco (Es)	zuwenig	too little	trop peu	troppo poco	—
demasiados (Es)	zuviele	too many	trop	troppi(e)	—
de mauvaise grâce (F)	ungern	reluctantly	—	malvolentieri	de mala gana
de memoria (Es)	auswendig	by heart	par cœur	a memoria	—
déménagement (F)	Umzug m	move	—	trasloco m	mudanza f
déménager[1] (F)	ausziehen	move out	—	sloggiare	mudarse
déménager[2] (F)	umziehen	move	—	cambiare casa	cambiar
démentir (F)	widerrufen	retract	—	revocare	revocación f
demi (F)	halb	half	—	mezzo(a)	medio(a)
demi-pension (F)	Halbpension f	half board	—	mezza pensione f	media pensión f
démissionner (F)	zurücktreten	retire	—	dare le dimissioni	dimitir
demnächst (D)	—	shortly	prochainement	presto	próximamente

	D	E	F	I	Es
democracia (Es)	Demokratie *f*	democracy	démocratie *f*	democrazia *f*	—
democracy (E)	Demokratie *f*	—	démocratie *f*	democrazia *f*	democracia *f*
démocratie (F)	Demokratie *f*	democracy	—	democrazia *f*	democracia *f*
democrazia (I)	Demokratie *f*	democracy	démocratie *f*	—	democracia *f*
démodé (F)	altmodisch	old-fashioned	—	fuori moda	pasado(a) de moda
Demokratie (D)	—	democracy	démocratie *f*	democrazia *f*	democracia *f*
Demonstration (D)	—	demonstration	manifestation *f*	manifestazione *f*	manifestación *f*
demonstration (E)	Demonstration *f*	—	manifestation *f*	manifestazione *f*	manifestación *f*
demostración (Es)	Demonstration *f*	demonstration	manifestation *f*	manifestazione *f*	—
denaro (I)	Geld *n*	money	argent *m*	—	dinero *m*
denaro per le piccole spese (I)	Taschengeld *n*	pocket money	argent de poche *f*	—	dinero de bolsillo *m*
denken (D)	—	think	penser	pensare	pensar
Denkmal (D)	—	monument	monument *m*	monumento *m*	monumento *m*
denn (D)	—	for/than	car	perchè	pues/porque
dennoch (D)	—	nevertheless	cependant	tuttavia	sin embargo
dénonciation (F)	Anzeige *f*	denunciation	—	denuncia *f*	denuncia *f*
de nos jours (F)	heutzutage	nowadays	—	oggigiorno	hoy en día
dénouer (F)	auflösen	dissolve	—	sciogliere	deshacer
de nouveau (F)	wieder	again	—	di nuovo	de nuevo
dense (E)	dicht	—	épais(se)	denso(a)	espeso(a)
denso (I)	dicht	dense	épais(se)	—	espeso(a)
dent (F)	Zahn *m*	tooth	—	dente *m*	diente *m*
dentadura (Es)	Gebiß *n*	teeth	dents *f pl*	denti *m pl*	—
dente (I)	Zahn *m*	tooth	dent *f*	—	diente *m*
denti (I)	Gebiß *n*	teeth	dents *f pl*	—	dentadura *f*
dentifrice (F)	Zahnpasta *f*	toothpaste	—	dentifricio *m*	pasta dentífrica *f*
dentifricio (I)	Zahnpasta *f*	toothpaste	dentifrice *m*	—	pasta dentífrica *f*
dentist (E)	Zahnarzt *m*	—	dentiste *m*	dentista *m*	dentista *m*
dentista (Es)	Zahnarzt *m*	dentist	dentiste *m*	dentista *m*	—
dentista (I)	Zahnarzt *m*	dentist	dentiste *m*	—	dentista *m*
dentiste (F)	Zahnarzt *m*	dentist	—	dentista *m*	dentista *m*
dentro¹ (Es)	hinein	in	dans	dentro	—
dentro² (Es)	innen	inside	à l'intérieur	dentro	—
dentro¹ (I)	hinein	in	dans	—	dentro
dentro² (I)	herein	in	vers l'intérieur	—	adentro
dentro³ (I)	innen	inside	à l'intérieur	—	dentro
dentro de (Es)	innerhalb	within	à l'intérieur de	entro	—
dents (F)	Gebiß *n*	teeth	—	denti *m pl*	dentadura *f*
de nuevo (Es)	wieder	again	de nouveau	di nuovo	—
de nuit (F)	nachts	at nighttime	—	di notte	por la noche
denuncia (Es)	Anzeige *f*	denunciation	dénonciation *f*	denuncia *f*	—
denuncia (I)	Anzeige *f*	denunciation	dénonciation *f*	—	denuncia *f*
denunciation (E)	Anzeige *f*	—	dénonciation *f*	denuncia *f*	denuncia *f*
deny (E)	leugnen	—	nier	negare	negar
de oro (Es)	golden	golden	d'or	d'oro	—
dépanneuse (F)	Abschleppwagen *m*	breakdown van	—	carro attrezzi *m*	camión grúa *m*
depart (E)	abfahren	—	partir (de)	partire	salir

	D	E	F	I	Es
départ[1] (F)	Abreise *f*	departure	—	partenza *f*	salida *f*
départ[2] (F)	Ausreise *f*	departure	—	partenza *f*	salida *f*
départ[3] (F)	Abfahrt *f*	departure	—	partenza *f*	salida *f*
départ[4] (F)	Start *m*	start	—	partenza *f*	partida *f*
departamento (Es)	Abteilung *f*	department	section *f*	reparto *m*	—
department (E)	Abteilung *f*	—	section *f*	reparto *m*	departamento *m*
department store (E)	Kaufhaus *n*	—	grand magasin *m*	grande magazzino *m*	grandes almacenes *m pl*
departure[1] (E)	Ausreise *f*	—	départ *m*	partenza *f*	salida *f*
departure[2] (E)	Abfahrt *f*	—	départ *m*	partenza *f*	salida *f*
departure[3] (E)	Abreise *f*	—	départ *m*	partenza *f*	salida *f*
dépêcher, se[1] (F)	beeilen, sich	hurry up	—	affrettarsi	darse prisa
dépêcher, se[2] (F)	eilen	hurry	—	andare in fretta	darse prisa
depend (E)	abhängen	—	dépendre	dipendere	depender
depender (Es)	abhängen	depend	dépendre	dipendere	—
dépendre (F)	abhängen	depend	—	dipendere	depender
déplacer (F)	rücken	move	—	muovere	mover
dépliant (I)	Prospekt *m*	brochure	prospectus *m*	—	prospecto *m*
deplorare (I)	bedauern	regret	regretter	—	lamentar
deplore (E)	beklagen	—	plaindre de, se	lamentare	quejarse
deporte (Es)	Sport *m*	sport	sport *m*	sport *m*	—
déposer (F)	hinterlegen	deposit	—	depositare	depositar
deposit[1] (E)	Anzahlung *f*	—	acompte *m*	acconto *m*	primer pago *m*
deposit[2] (E)	hinterlegen	—	déposer	depositare	depositar
depositar (Es)	hinterlegen	deposit	déposer	depositare	—
depositare (I)	hinterlegen	deposit	déposer	—	depositar
depth (E)	Tiefe *f*	—	profondeur *f*	profondità *f*	profundidad *f*
depuis (F)	seit	since/for	—	da	de/desde
depuis bien longtemps (F)	längst	a long time ago	—	da molto	hace mucho
de qui (F)	wessen	whose	—	di chi	¿de quién?
de quién (Es)	wessen	whose	de qui	di chi	—
der, die, das (D)	—	the	le, la	il, la	el, la, lo
déranger (F)	stören	disturb	—	disturbare	molestar
derecho[1] (Es)	Jura	law	droit *m*	giurisprudenza *f*	—
derecho[2] (Es)	Recht *n*	right	droit *m*	diritto *m*	—
derecho[3] (Es)	aufrecht	upright	droit(e)	diritto(a)	—
derecho[4] (Es)	gerade	straight	droit(e)	diritto(a)	—
de repente (Es)	plötzlich	suddenly	tout à coup	di colpo	—
de retour (F)	zurück	back	—	indietro	atrás
deridere (I)	auslachen	laugh at	rire de qn	—	reírse de
dernier[1] (F)	vergangene(r,s)	past	—	passato(a)	pasada(o)
dernier[2] (F)	letzte(r,s)	last	—	ultimo(a)	último(a)
derribar (Es)	umschmeißen	throw over	renverser	rovesciare	—
derrière[1] (F)	dahinter	behind it	—	dietro	detrás
derrière[2] (F)	hinten	behind	—	dietro	detrás
derrota (Es)	Niederlage *f*	defeat	défaite *f*	sconfitta *f*	—
derrumbarse (Es)	einstürzen	collapse	écrouler, se	crollare	—
derselbe (D)	—	the same	le même	lo stesso	el mismo

	D	E	F	I	Es
desaconsejar (Es)	abraten	warn	déconseiller	sconsigliare	—
desacostumbrado (Es)	ungewöhnlich	unusual	exceptionnel(le)	insolito(a)	—
desagradable[1] (Es)	lästig	troublesome	importun(e)	molesto(a)	—
desagradable[2] (Es)	peinlich	embarrassing	gênant(e)	imbarazzante	—
desagradable[3] (Es)	unangenehm	unpleasant	désagréable	spiacevole	—
desagradecido (Es)	undankbar	ungrateful	ingrat(e)	ingrato(a)	—
désagréable[1] (F)	ungemütlich	uncomfortable	—	poco accogliente	incómodo(a)
désagréable[2] (F)	unangenehm	unpleasant	—	spiacevole	desagradable
desaparecer (Es)	verschwinden	disappear	disparaître	sparire	—
désapprouver (F)	mißbilligen	disapprove	—	disapprovare	desaprobar
desaprobar (Es)	mißbilligen	disapprove	désapprouver	disapprovare	—
desarmar (Es)	abrüsten	disarm	désarmer	disarmare	—
désarmer (F)	abrüsten	disarm	—	disarmare	desarmar
desarrollar (Es)	entwickeln	develop	développer	sviluppare	—
desarrollo (Es)	Entwicklung f	development	développement m	sviluppo m	—
desatar[1] (Es)	losbinden	free	délier	sciogliere	—
desatar[2] (Es)	lösen	solve	résoudre	sciogliere	—
désavantage (F)	Nachteil m	disadvantage	—	svantaggio m	desventaja f
désavantager (F)	benachteiligen	disadvantage	—	svantaggiare	perjudicar
desayuno (Es)	Frühstück n	breakfast	petit-déjeuner m	colazione f	—
descansar[1] (Es)	ausruhen	rest	reposer, se	riposare	—
descansar[2] (Es)	ruhen	rest	reposer, se	riposare	—
descanso[1] (Es)	Erholung f	recovery	repos m	riposo m	—
descanso[2] (Es)	Ruhestand m	retirement	retraite f	pensione f	—
descargar[1] (Es)	ausladen	unload	décharger	scaricare	—
descargar[2] (Es)	abladen	unload	décharger	scaricare	—
descend (E)	hinuntergehen	—	descendre	scendere	bajar
descender[1] (Es)	absteigen	dismount	descendre	scendere	—
descender[2] (Es)	abstammen	be descended	descendre	discendere	—
descendre[1] (F)	aussteigen	get off	—	scendere	bajar
descendre[2] (F)	abstammen	be descended	—	discendere	descender
descendre[3] (F)	absteigen	dismount	—	scendere	descender
descendre[4] (F)	hinuntergehen	descend	—	scendere	bajar
descolgar (Es)	abnehmen	take away	décrocher	staccare	—
desconectar[1] (Es)	abschalten	switch off	éteindre	spegnere	—
desconectar[2] (Es)	ausschalten	switch off	arrêter	spegnere	—
desconectar[3] (Es)	abstellen	turn off	arrêter	spegnere	—
desconfianza (Es)	Mißtrauen n	distrust	méfiance f	sfiducia f	—
desconfiar (Es)	mißtrauen	mistrust	méfier, se	non fidarsi	—
desconocido (Es)	unbekannt	unknown	inconnu(e)	sconosciuto(a)	—
descontento (Es)	unzufrieden	dissatisfied	mécontent(e)	scontento(a)	—
descortés[1] (Es)	unhöflich	impolite	impoli(e)	scortese	—
descortés[2] (Es)	unfreundlich	unfriendly	peu aimable	sgarbato(a)	—
describe (E)	beschreiben	—	décrire	descrivere	describir
describir (Es)	beschreiben	describe	décrire	descrivere	—
descrivere (I)	beschreiben	describe	décrire	—	describir
descubrir (Es)	entdecken	discover	découvrir	scoprire	—

	D	E	F	I	Es
descuidado (Es)	unvorsichtig	careless	imprudent(e)	imprudente	—
descuidar (Es)	vernachlässigen	neglect	négliger	trascurare	—
desear (Es)	wünschen	wish	souhaiter	desiderare	—
desembocadura (Es)	Mündung f	mouth	embouchure f	sbocco m	—
desempleado (Es)	arbeitslos	unemployed	en chômage	disoccupato(a)	—
desempleo (Es)	Arbeitslosigkeit f	unemployment	chômage m	disoccupazione f	—
deseo (Es)	Wunsch m	wish	souhait m	desiderio m	—
desert (E)	Wüste f	—	désert m	deserto m	desierto m
désert[1] (F)	öde	waste	—	deserto(a)	desierto(a)
désert[2] (F)	Wüste f	desert	—	deserto m	desierto m
desert (I)	Nachtisch m	dessert	dessert m	—	postre m
deserto[1] (I)	öde	waste	désert(e)	—	desierto(a)
deserto[2] (I)	Wüste f	desert	désert m	—	desierto m
desesperado (Es)	verzweifelt	desperate	désespéré(e)	disperato(a)	—
désespéré (F)	verzweifelt	desperate	—	disperato(a)	desesperado(a)
desgarrarse (Es)	reißen	tear	déchirer, se	strappare	—
desgastar (Es)	abnutzen	wear out	user	consumare	—
desgracia (Es)	Unglück n	misfortune	malheur m	disgrazia f	—
desgraciadamente (Es)	leider	unfortunately	malheureusement	purtroppo	—
desgraciado (Es)	unglücklich	unhappy	malheureux (-euse)	sfortunato(a)	—
deshacer[1] (Es)	auspacken	unpack	défaire	disfare	—
deshacer[2] (Es)	auflösen	dissolve	dénouer	sciogliere	—
deshalb (D)	—	therefore	c'est pourquoi	perció	por eso
deshelar (Es)	tauen	thaw	fondre	sciogliersi	—
deshonra (Es)	Schande f	disgrace	honte f	vergogna f	—
desiderare (I)	wünschen	wish	souhaiter	—	desear
desiderio (I)	Wunsch m	wish	souhait m	—	deseo m
desierto[1] (Es)	Wüste f	desert	désert m	deserto m	—
desierto[2] (Es)	öde	waste	désert(e)	deserto(a)	—
desmayarse (Es)	zusammenbrechen	collapse	s'éffondrer	crollare	—
desmayo (Es)	Ohnmacht f	faint	évanouissement m	svenimento m	—
desnudo (Es)	nackt	naked	nu(e)	nudo(a)	—
desocupado (Es)	unbesetzt	unoccupied	vacant(e)	libero(a)	—
desorden (Es)	Unordnung f	mess	désordre m	disordine m	—
desordenado (Es)	unordentlich	untidy	désordonné(e)	disordinato(a)	—
désordonné (F)	unordentlich	untidy	—	disordinato(a)	desordenado(a)
désordre[1] (F)	Durcheinander n	confusion	—	confusione f	confusión f
désordre[2] (F)	Unordnung f	mess		disordine m	desorden m
despacio (Es)	langsam	slow	lent(e)	lento(a)	—
despedida (Es)	Abschied m	parting	adieux m pl	addio m	—
despedir[1] (Es)	entlassen	release	renvoyer	licenziare	—
despedir[2] (Es)	kündigen	sack	résilier	licenziare	—
despedir[3] (Es)	verabschieden	say goodbye to	prendre congé de	congedare	—
despegue (Es)	Abflug m	take-off	décollage m	decollo m	—
desperate (E)	verzweifelt	—	désespéré(e)	disperato(a)	desesperado(a)
desperdiciar (Es)	verschwenden	waste	gaspiller	sprecare	—
despertador (Es)	Wecker m	alarm clock	réveil m	sveglia f	—

	D	E	F	I	Es
despertar¹ (Es)	aufwecken	wake up	réveiller	svegliare	—
despertar² (Es)	erwachen	wake up	réveiller, se	svegliarsi	—
despertar³ (Es)	wecken	wake (up)	réveiller	svegliare	—
despertarse (Es)	aufwachen	wake up	réveiller, se	svegliarsi	—
despierto (Es)	wach	awake	réveillé(e)	sveglio(a)	—
despite (E)	trotz	—	malgré	nonostante	a pesar de
después¹ (Es)	danach	afterwards	après	poi/dopo	—
después² (Es)	darauf	afterwards	dessus/ensuite	dopo	—
después³ (Es)	nachher	afterwards	ensuite	dopo	—
después que (Es)	nachdem	after	après que	dopo que (di)	—
dès que (F)	sobald	as soon as	—	appena	tan pronto como
desserré (F)	locker	loose	—	lento(a)	flojo(a)
dessert (E)	Nachtisch *m*	—	dessert *m*	desert *m*	postre *m*
dessert (F)	Nachtisch *m*	dessert	—	desert *m*	postre *m*
dessin (F)	Zeichnung *f*	drawing	—	disegno *m*	dibujo *m*
dessiner (F)	zeichnen	draw	—	disegnare	dibujar
dessous (F)	unten	downstairs	—	sotto/giù	abajo
dessus (F)	darauf	afterwards/on it	—	dopo/su	encima
d'est (F)	östlich	eastern	—	ad est	al este
destin (F)	Schicksal *n*	fate	—	destino *m*	destino *m*
destinataire (F)	Empfänger *m*	receiver	—	destinatario *m*	destinatario *m*
destinatario (Es)	Empfänger *m*	receiver	destinataire *f*	destinatario *m*	—
destinatario (I)	Empfänger *m*	receiver	destinataire *f*	—	destinatario *m*
destino (Es)	Schicksal *n*	fate	destin *m*	destino *m*	—
destino (I)	Schicksal *n*	fate	destin *m*	—	destino *m*
destornillador (Es)	Schrauben- zieher *m*	screwdriver	tournevis *m*	cacciavite *m*	—
destroy¹ (E)	vernichten	—	détruire	distruggere	destruir
destroy² (E)	zerstören	—	détruire	distruggere	destruir
destruir¹ (Es)	vernichten	destroy	détruire	distruggere	—
destruir² (Es)	zerstören	destroy	détruire	distruggere	—
desvalijar (Es)	plündern	loot	piller	saccheggiare	—
desventaja (Es)	Nachteil *m*	disadvantage	désavantage *m*	svantaggio *m*	—
desviación (Es)	Umleitung *f*	diversion	déviation *f*	deviazione *f*	—
desviar (Es)	ablenken	distract	distraire	distrarre	—
detail (E)	Einzelheit *f*	—	détail *m*	dettaglio *m*	detalle *f*
détail (F)	Einzelheit *f*	detail	—	dettaglio *m*	detalle *f*
detailed (E)	ausführlich	—	détaillé(e)	dettagliato(a)	detallado(a)
détaillé (F)	ausführlich	detailed	—	dettagliato(a)	detallado(a)
detallado (Es)	ausführlich	detailed	détaillé(e)	dettagliato(a)	—
detalle (Es)	Einzelheit *f*	detail	détail *m*	dettaglio *m*	—
detener (Es)	verhaften	arrest	arrêter	arrestare	—
detergent (E)	Waschmittel *n*	—	lessive *f*	detersivo *m*	detergente *m*
detergente (Es)	Waschmittel *n*	detergent	lessive *f*	detersivo *m*	—
deteriorar (Es)	beschädigen	damage	endommager	danneggiare	—
deterioro (Es)	Beschädigung *f*	damage	endommage- ment *m*	danno *m*	—
detersivo (I)	Waschmittel *n*	detergent	lessive *f*	—	detergente *m*
détester (F)	hassen	hate	—	odiare	odiar

	D	E	F	I	Es
detour (E)	Umweg m	—	détour m	deviazione f	rodeo m
détour (F)	Umweg m	detour	—	deviazione f	rodeo m
detrás[1] (Es)	dahinter	behind it	derrière	dietro	—
detrás[2] (Es)	hinten	behind	derrière	dietro	—
détresse (F)	Not f	trouble	—	miseria f	necesidad f
détruire[1] (F)	vernichten	destroy	—	distruggere	destruir
détruire[2] (F)	verderben	ruin	—	rovinare	arrruinar
détruire[3] (F)	zerstören	destroy	—	distruggere	destruir
dettagliato (I)	ausführlich	detailed	détaillé(e)	—	detallado(a)
dettaglio (I)	Einzelheit f	detail	détail m	—	detalle f
dette (F)	Schulden pl	debt	—	debiti m pl	deudas f pl
deudas (Es)	Schulden pl	debt	dette f	debiti m pl	—
de un solo color (Es)	einfarbig	all one colour	uni(e)	monocolore	—
deutlich (D)	—	clear	clair(e)	chiaro(a)	claro(a)
deutsch (D)	—	German	allemand(e)	tedesco(a)	alemán(-ana)
Deutscher (D)	—	German	Allemand m	tedesco	alemán m
Deutschland (D)	—	Germany	Allemagne f	Germania f	Alemania f
deux (F)	zwei	two	—	due	dos
deux fois (F)	zweimal	twice	—	due volte	dos veces
devant[1] (F)	vorn(e)	at the front	—	davanti	delante
devant[2] (F)	vor	before/in front of	—	davanti a	delante de
develop (E)	entwickeln	—	développer	sviluppare	desarrollar
development (E)	Entwicklung f	—	développement m	sviluppo m	desarrollo m
développement (F)	Entwicklung f	development	—	sviluppo m	desarrollo m
développer (F)	entwickeln	develop	—	sviluppare	desarrollar
devenir (F)	werden	become	—	diventare	llegar
déviation (F)	Umleitung f	diversion	—	deviazione f	desviación f
deviazione[1] (I)	Umleitung f	diversion	déviation f	—	desviación f
deviazione[2] (I)	Umweg m	detour	détour m	—	rodeo m
devil (E)	Teufel m	—	diable m	diavolo m	diablo m
deviner (F)	raten	guess	—	indovinare	adivinar
devinette (F)	Rätsel n	riddle	—	enigma m	adivinanza f
devoir[1] (F)	müssen	have to		dovere	deber
devoir[2] (F)	Pflicht f	duty	—	dovere m	obligación f
devoir[3] (F)	sollen	have to	—	dovere	deber
devoir[4] (F)	schulden	owe	—	dovere	deber
devolver[1] (Es)	wiedergeben	return	rendre	restituire	—
devolver[2] (Es)	zurückbringen	bring back	rapporter	riportare	—
devolver[3] (Es)	zurückzahlen	pay back	rembourser	rimborsare	—
devolver[4] (Es)	zurückgeben	give back	rendre	restituire	—
devorar (Es)	fressen	eat	bouffer	mangiare	—
devoto (I)	fromm	pious	pieux(-euse)	—	religioso(a)
Dezember (D)	—	December	décembre m	dicembre m	diciembre m
di (I)	von	from/by	de	—	de
Dia (D)	—	slide	diapositive f	diapositiva f	diapositiva f
día (Es)	Tag m	day	jour m	giorno m	—
diable (F)	Teufel m	devil	—	diavolo m	diablo m
diablo (Es)	Teufel m	devil	diable m	diavolo m	—

	D	E	F	I	Es
día de descanso (Es)	Ruhetag m	closing day	jour de repos m	giorno di riposo m	—
día de fiesta (Es)	Feiertag m	holiday	jour férié m	giorno festivo m	—
día laborable (Es)	Werktag m	working day	jour ouvrable m	giorno feriale m	—
dialling code (E)	Vorwahl f	—	indicatif téléphonique m	prefisso m	prefijo m
diapositiva (Es)	Dia n	slide	diapositive f	diapositiva f	—
diapositiva (I)	Dia n	slide	diapositive f	—	diapositiva f
diapositive (F)	Dia n	slide	—	diapositiva f	diapositiva f
Diät (D)	—	diet	diète f	dieta f	dieta f
diavolo (I)	Teufel m	devil	diable m	—	diablo m
dibujar (Es)	zeichnen	draw	dessiner	disegnare	—
dibujo (Es)	Zeichnung f	drawing	dessin m	disegno m	—
diccionario[1] (Es)	Lexikon n	encyclopaedia	encyclopédie f	enciclopedia f	—
diccionario[2] (Es)	Wörterbuch n	dictionary	dictionnaire m	dizionario m	—
dice (E)	Würfel m	—	dé m	dado m	dado m
dicembre (I)	Dezember m	December	décembre m	—	diciembre m
dichi (I)	wessen	whose	de qui	—	¿de quién?
dichiarazione (I)	Aussage f	statement	déclaration f	—	declaración f
dicht (D)	—	dense	épais(se)	denso(a)	espeso(a)
Dichter (D)	—	poet	poète m	poeta m	poeta m
diciannove (I)	neunzehn	nineteen	dix-neuf	—	diecinueve
diciassette (I)	siebzehn	seventeen	dix-sept	—	diecisiete
diciembre (Es)	Dezember m	December	décembre m	dicembre m	—
diciotto (I)	achtzehn	eighteen	dix-huit	—	dieciocho
dick (D)	—	fat	gros(se)	grasso(a)	grueso(a)
di colpo (I)	plötzlich	suddenly	tout à coup	—	de repente
dictionary (E)	Wörterbuch n	—	dictionnaire m	dizionario m	diccionario m
dictionnaire (F)	Wörterbuch n	dictionary	—	dizionario m	diccionario m
die (E)	sterben	—	mourir	morire	morir
Dieb (D)	—	thief	voleur m	ladro m	ladrón m
dieci (I)	zehn	ten	dix	—	diez
diecinueve (Es)	neunzehn	nineteen	dix-neuf	diciannove	—
dieciocho (Es)	achtzehn	eighteen	dix-huit	diciotto	—
dieciseis (Es)	sechzehn	sixteen	seize	sedici	—
diecisiete (Es)	siebzehn	seventeen	dix-sept	diciassette	—
Diele (D)	—	hall	vestibule m	corridoio m	entrada f
dienen (D)	—	serve	servir	servire	servir
Dienst (D)	—	service	service m	servizio m	servicio m
Dienstag (D)	—	Tuesday	mardi m	martedì m	martes m
diente (Es)	Zahn m	tooth	dent f	dente m	—
diese (D)	—	this	ce, cette	questo(a)	esta, este, esto
diet (E)	Diät f	—	diète f	dieta f	dieta f
dieta (Es)	Diät f	diet	diète f	dieta f	—
dieta (I)	Diät f	diet	diète f	—	dieta f
diète (F)	Diät f	diet	—	dieta f	dieta f
dietro[1] (I)	dahinter	behind it	derrière	—	detrás
dietro[2] (I)	hinten	behind	derrière	—	detrás
Dieu (F)	Gott m	God	—	Dio m	Dios m

dimenticare

	D	E	F	I	Es
diez (Es)	zehn	ten	dix	dieci	—
difendere (I)	verteidigen	defend	défendre	—	defender
difendersi (I)	wehren, sich	defend	défendre, se	—	defenderse
diferencia (Es)	Unterschied *m*	difference	différence *f*	differenza *f*	—
diferente¹ (Es)	anders	different	différent(e)	differente	—
diferente² (Es)	verschieden	different	différent(e)	diverso(a)	—
difesa³ (I)	Verteidigung *f*	defence	défense *f*	—	defensa *f*
difference (E)	Unterschied *m*	—	différence *f*	differenza *f*	diferencia *f*
différence (F)	Unterschied *m*	difference	—	differenza *f*	diferencia *f*
different¹ (E)	anders	—	différent(e)	differente	diferente
different² (E)	unterschiedlich	—	différent(e)	diverso(a)	distinto(a)
different³ (E)	verschieden	—	différent(e)	diverso(a)	diferente
différent¹ (F)	anders	different	—	differente	diferente
différent² (F)	unterschiedlich	different	—	diverso(a)	distinto(a)
différent³ (F)	verschieden	different	—	diverso(a)	diferente
differente (I)	anders	different	différent(e)	—	diferente
differenza (I)	Unterschied *m*	difference	différence *f*	—	diferencia *f*
difficile (F)	schwierig	difficult	—	difficile	dificil
difficile (I)	schwierig	difficult	difficile	—	dificil
difficoltà (I)	Schwierigkeit *f*	difficulty	difficulté *f*	—	dificultad *f*
difficult (E)	schwierig	—	difficile	difficile	dificil
difficulté (F)	Schwierigkeit *f*	difficulty	—	difficoltà *f*	dificultad *f*
difficulty (E)	Schwierigkeit *f*	—	difficulté *f*	difficoltà *f*	dificultad *f*
diffondere (I)	verbreiten	spread	propager	—	difundir
diffusion (F)	Sendung *f*	transmission	—	trasmissione *f*	emisión *f*
dificil (Es)	schwierig	difficult	difficile	difficile	—
dificultad (Es)	Schwierigkeit *f*	difficulty	difficulté *f*	difficoltà *f*	—
di fronte (I)	gegenüber	opposite	en face de	—	en frente
difundir (Es)	verbreiten	spread	propager	diffondere	—
dig (E)	graben	—	creuser	scavare	cavar
¡diga! (Es)	hallo!	hello!	allô!	pronto!	—
digérer (F)	verdauen	digest	—	digerire	digerir
digerir (Es)	verdauen	digest	digérer	digerire	—
digerire (I)	verdauen	digest	digérer	—	digerir
digest (E)	verdauen	—	digérer	digerire	digerir
digiunare (I)	fasten	fast	jeûner	—	ayunar
di là¹ (I)	hinüber	across	de l'autre côté	—	hacia el otro lado
di la² (I)	davon	of it	en/de cela	—	de ello
diligent (E)	fleißig	—	travailleur (-euse)	diligente	activo(a)
diligente (Es)	eifrig	keen	zélé(e)	diligente	—
diligente¹ (I)	eifrig	keen	zélé(e)	—	diligente
diligente² (I)	fleißig	diligent	travailleur (-euse)	—	activo(a)
dimagrire (I)	abnehmen	lose weight	maigrir	—	adelgazar
dimanche (F)	Sonntag m	Sunday	—	domenica f	domingo m
di mattina (I)	vormittags	in the morning	le matin	—	por la mañana
di meno (I)	weniger	less	moins	—	menos
dimenticare (I)	vergessen	forget	oublier	—	olvidar

	D	E	F	I	Es
dimezzare (I)	halbieren	halve	partager en deux	—	dividir por la mitad
diminuer (F)	verringern	reduce	—	diminuire	disminuir
diminuire[1] (I)	herabsetzen	lower	baisser	—	rebajar
diminuire[2] (I)	verringern	reduce	diminuer	—	disminuir
dimitir (Es)	zurücktreten	retire	démissionner	dare le dimissioni	—
dindon (F)	Truthahn m	turkey	—	tacchino m	pavo m
dine (E)	speisen	—	manger	mangiare	comer
dîner (F)	Abendessen n	supper	—	cena f	cena f
dinero (Es)	Geld n	money	argent m	denaro m	—
dinero al contado (Es)	Bargeld n	cash	espèces f pl	contanti m	—
dinero de bolsillo (Es)	Taschengeld n	pocket money	argent de poche f	denaro per le piccole spese m	—
Ding (D)	—	thing	chose f	cosa f	cosa f
dining car (E)	Speisewagen m	—	wagon-restaurant m	vagone ristorante m	vagón restaurante m
dining room (E)	Eßzimmer n	—	salle à manger f	sala da pranzo f	comedor m
di notte (I)	nachts	at nighttime	la nuit	—	por la noche
dintorni (I)	Umgebung f	surroundings	environs m pl	—	alrededores m pl
di nuovo[1] (I)	nochmals	again	encore une fois	—	otra vez
di nuovo[2] (I)	wieder	again	de nouveau	—	de nuevo
Dio (I)	Gott m	God	Dieu m	—	Dios m
Dios (Es)	Gott m	God	Dieu m	Dio m	—
dipendere da (I)	abhängen	depend	dépendre	—	dejar atrás
dipingere (I)	malen	paint	peindre	—	pintar
di pomeriggio (I)	nachmittags	in the afternoon	l'aprés-midi	—	por la tarde
dire (F)	sagen	say	—	dire	decir
dire (I)	sagen	say	dire	—	decir
dirección[1] (Es)	Anschrift f / Adresse f	address	adresse f	indirizzo m	—
dirección[2] (Es)	Leitung f	direction	direction f	direzione f	—
dirección[3] (Es)	Richtung f	direction	direction f	direzione f	—
direct (F)	direkt	direct	—	diretto(a)	directo(a)
direct (E)	direkt	—	direct(e)	diretto(a)	directo(a)
directeur (F)	Direktor m	director	—	direttore m	director m
direction[1] (E)	Leitung f	—	direction f	direzione f	dirección f
direction[2] (E)	Richtung f	—	direction f	direzione f	dirección f
direction[1] (F)	Leitung f	direction	—	direzione f	dirección f
direction[2] (F)	Richtung f	direction	—	direzione f	dirección f
directo[1] (Es)	direkt	direct	direct(e)	diretto(a)	—
directo[2] (Es)	unmittelbar	immediate	immédiat(e)	immediato(a)	—
director[1] (E)	Direktor m	—	directeur m	direttore m	director m
director[2] (E)	Regisseur m	—	réalisateur m	regista m	director m
director[1] (Es)	Direktor m	director	directeur m	direttore m	—
director[2] (Es)	Regisseur m	director	réalisateur m	regista m	—
director (de orquesta) (Es)	Dirigent m	conductor	chef d'orchestre m	direttore d'orchestra m	—
direct to (E)	richten	—	diriger	dirigere	dirigir
direkt (D)	—	direct	direct(e)	diretto(a)	directo(a)
Direktor (D)	—	director	directeur m	direttore m	director m

discusión

	D	E	F	I	Es
direttissimo (I)	D-Zug *m*	through train	express *m*	—	tren expreso *m*
diretto (I)	direkt	direct	direct(e)	—	directo(a)
direttore (I)	Direktor *m*	director	directeur *m*	—	director *m*
direttore d'orchestra (I)	Dirigent *m*	conductor	chef d'orchestre *m*	—	director (de orquesta) *m*
direzione[1] (I)	Leitung *f*	direction	direction *f*	—	dirección *f*
direzione[2] (I)	Richtung *f*	direction	direction *f*	—	dirección *f*
Dirigent (D)	—	conductor	chef d'orchestre *m*	direttore d'orchestra *m*	director (de orquesta) *m*
diriger (F)	richten	direct to	—	dirigere	dirigir
dirigere (I)	richten	direct to	diriger	—	dirigir
dirigir[1] (Es)	führen	lead	guider	guidare	—
dirigir[2] (Es)	regeln	regulate	régler	regolare	—
dirigir[3] (Es)	richten	direct to	diriger	dirigere	—
diritto[1] (I)	aufrecht	upright	droit(e)	—	derecho(a)
diritto[2] (I)	Recht *n*	right	droit *m*	—	derecho *m*
diritto[3] (I)	gerade	straight	droit(e)	—	derecho(a)
dirt (E)	Schmutz *m*	—	saleté *f*	sporcizia *f*	suciedad *f*
dirty[1] (E)	dreckig	—	sale	sporco(a)	sucio(a)
dirty[2] (E)	schmutzig	—	sale	sporco(a)	sucio(a)
disadvantage[1] (E)	benachteiligen	—	désavantager	svantaggiare	perjudicar
disadvantage[2] (E)	Nachteil *m*	—	désavantage *m*	svantaggio *m*	desventaja *f*
disappear (E)	verschwinden	—	disparaître	sparire	desaparecer
disappoint (E)	enttäuschen	—	décevoir	deludere	defraudar
disappointed (E)	enttäuscht	—	déçu(e)	deluso(a)	defraudado(a)
disapprovare (I)	mißbilligen	disapprove	désapprouver	—	desaprobar
disapprove (E)	mißbilligen	—	désapprouver	disapprovare	desaprobar
disarm (E)	abrüsten	—	désarmer	disarmare	desarmar
disarmare (I)	abrüsten	disarm	désarmer	—	desarmar
disc (E)	Scheibe *f*	—	disque *m*	disco *m*	disco *m*
discendere (I)	abstammen	be descended	descendre	—	descender
disco[1] (Es)	Platte *f*	record	disque *m*	disco *m*	—
disco[2] (Es)	Scheibe *f*	disc	disque *m*	disco *m*	—
disco[3] (Es)	Schallplatte *f*	record	disque *m*	disco *m*	—
disco[1] (I)	Platte *f*	record	disque *m*	—	disco *m*
disco[2] (I)	Schallplatte *f*	record	disque *m*	—	disco *m*
disco[3] (I)	Scheibe *f*	disc	disque *m*	—	disco *m*
discorso (I)	Rede *f*	speech	discours *m*	—	discurso *m*
discoteca (Es)	Diskothek *f*	discotheque	discothèque *f*	discoteca *f*	—
discoteca (I)	Diskothek *f*	discotheque	discothèque *f*	discoteca *f*	discoteca *f*
discotheque (E)	Diskothek *f*	—	discothèque *f*	discoteca *f*	discoteca *f*
discothèque (F)	Diskothek *f*	discotheque	—	discoteca *f*	discoteca *f*
discount (E)	Rabatt *m*	—	rabais *m*	sconto *m*	rebaja *f*
discours (F)	Rede *f*	speech	—	discorso *m*	discurso *m*
discover (E)	entdecken	—	découvrir	scoprire	descubrir
disculpa (Es)	Entschuldigung *f*	apology	excuse *f*	scusa *f*	—
disculparse (Es)	entschuldigen, sich	apologize	excuser, se	scusarsi	—
discurso (Es)	Rede *f*	speech	discours *m*	discorso *m*	—
discusión (Es)	Aussprache *f*	discussion	discussion *f*	discussione *f*	—

	D	E	F	I	Es
discuss (E)	besprechen	—	discuter	discutere	discutir
discussion (E)	Aussprache f	—	discussion f	discussione f	discusión f
discussion (F)	Aussprache f	discussion	—	discussione f	discusión f
discussione (I)	Aussprache f	discussion	discussion f	—	discusión f
discuter (F)	besprechen	discuss	—	discutere	discutir
discutere (I)	besprechen	discuss	discuter	—	discutir
discutir[1] (Es)	besprechen	discuss	discuter	discutere	—
discutir[2] (Es)	streiten	quarrel	disputer, se	litigare	—
disdire (I)	abblasen	call off	souffler	—	anular
disegnare (I)	zeichnen	draw	dessiner	—	dibujar
disegno (I)	Zeichnung f	drawing	dessin m	—	dibujo m
di sera (I)	abends	in the evening	le soir	—	por la tarde
disfare (I)	auspacken	unpack	défaire	—	deshacer
disfrutar (Es)	genießen	enjoy	jouir	godere	—
disgrace (E)	Schande f	—	honte f	vergogna f	deshonra f
disgrazia (I)	Unglück n	misfortune	malheur m	—	desgracia f
disgusting (E)	widerlich	—	repoussant(e)	ripugnante	repugnante
disgustoso (I)	abscheulich	abominable	affreux(-euse)	—	horrible
dish (E)	Gericht n	—	plat m	piatto m	comida f
Diskothek (D)	—	discotheque	discothèque f	discoteca f	discoteca f
disminuir (Es)	verringern	reduce	diminuer	diminuire	—
dismount (E)	absteigen	—	descendre	scendere	descender
disoccupato (I)	arbeitslos	unemployed	en chômage	—	desempleado(a)
disoccupazione (I)	Arbeitslosigkeit f	unemployment	chômage m	—	desempleo m
di solito (I)	meistens	generally	généralement	—	por lo común
disordinato (I)	unordentlich	untidy	désordonné(e)	—	desordenado(a)
disordine (I)	Unordnung f	mess	désordre m	—	desorden m
disparaître (F)	verschwinden	disappear	—	sparire	desaparecer
disparar (Es)	schießen	shoot	tirer	sparare	—
dispari (I)	ungerade	uneven	impair(e)	—	impar
disparo (Es)	Schuß m	shot	coup m	sparo m	—
disperato (I)	verzweifelt	desperate	désespéré(e)	—	desesperado(a)
dispersé (F)	zerstreut	scattered	—	disperso(a)	disperso(a)
disperso (Es)	zerstreut	scattered	dispersé(e)	disperso(a)	—
disperso (I)	zerstreut	scattered	dispersé(e)	—	disperso(a)
dispiacere (I)	Bedauern n	regret	regret m	—	compasión f
disponer (Es)	verfügen	order	disposer de	disporre	—
disponibile (I)	vorhanden	available	présent(e)	—	presente
disporre (I)	verfügen	order	disposer de	—	disponer
disposer de (F)	verfügen	order	—	disporre	disponer
disposition (E)	Gemüt n	—	disposition f	animo m	ánimo m
disposition (F)	Gemüt n	disposition	—	animo m	ánimo m
dispuesto (Es)	bereit	ready	prêt(e)	pronto(a)	—
disputa (Es)	Streit m	argument	dispute f	lite f	—
dispute (F)	Streit m	argument	—	lite f	disputa f
disputer, se (F)	streiten	quarrel	—	litigare	discutir
disque[1] (F)	Platte f	record	—	disco m	disco m
disque[2] (F)	Schallplatte f	record	—	disco m	disco m

	D	E	F	I	Es
disque³ (F)	Scheibe *f*	disc	—	disco *m*	disco *m*
dissatisfied (E)	unzufrieden	—	mécontent(e)	scontento(a)	descontento(a)
dissimuler (F)	verbergen	hide	—	nascondere	esconder
dissolve (E)	auflösen	—	dénouer	sciogliere	deshacer
distance¹ (E)	Abstand *m*	—	distance *f*	distanza *f*	distancia *f*
distance² (E)	Entfernung *f*	—	distance *f*	distanza *f*	distancia *f*
distance³ (E)	Ferne *f*	—	lointain *m*	distanza *f*	lejanía *f*
distance¹ (F)	Abstand *m*	distance	—	distanza *f*	distancia *f*
distance² (F)	Entfernung *f*	distance	—	distanza *f*	distancia *f*
distancia¹ (Es)	Abstand *m*	distance	distance *f*	distanza *f*	—
distancia² (Es)	Entfernung *f*	distance	distance *f*	distanza *f*	—
distant (E)	entfernt	—	éloigné(e)	distante	distante
distante (Es)	entfernt	distant	éloigné(e)	distante	—
distante (I)	entfernt	distant	éloigné(e)	—	distante
distanza¹ (I)	Abstand *m*	distance	distance *f*	—	distancia *f*
distanza² (I)	Entfernung *f*	distance	distance *f*	—	distancia *f*
distanza³ (I)	Ferne *f*	distance	lointain *m*	—	lejanía *f*
distingué (F)	vornehm	distinguished	—	distinto(a)	distinguido(a)
distinguer (F)	unterscheiden	distinguish	—	distinguere	distinguir
distinguere (I)	unterscheiden	distinguish	distinguer	—	distinguir
distinguido (Es)	vornehm	distinguished	distingué(e)	distinto(a)	—
distinguir (Es)	unterscheiden	distinguish	distinguer	distinguere	—
distinguish (E)	unterscheiden	—	distinguer	distinguere	distinguir
distinguished (E)	vornehm	—	distingué(e)	distinto(a)	distinguido(a)
distinto (Es)	unterschiedlich	different	différent(e)	diverso(a)	—
distinto (I)	vornehm	distinguished	distingué(e)	—	distinguido(a)
distract (E)	ablenken	—	distraire	distrarre	desviar
distraire (F)	ablenken	distract	—	distrarre	desviar
distrarre (I)	ablenken	distract	distraire	—	desviar
distretto (I)	Revier *n*	district	district *m*	—	distrito *m*
distribuer¹ (F)	austeilen	distribute	—	distribuire	distribuir
distribuer² (F)	verteilen	distribute	—	distribuire	repartir
distribuidor automático (Es)	Automat *m*	vending machine	distributeur automatique *m*	distributore automatico *m*	—
distribuir (Es)	austeilen	distribute	distribuer	distribuire	—
distribuire¹ (I)	austeilen	distribute	distribuer	—	distribuir
distribuire² (I)	verteilen	distribute	distribuer	—	repartir
distribute¹ (E)	austeilen	—	distribuer	distribuire	distribuir
distribute² (E)	verteilen	—	distribuer	distribuire	repartir
distributeur automatique (F)	Automat *m*	vending machine	—	distributore *m*	distribuidor automático *m*
distributore automatico (I)	Automat *m*	vending machine	distributeur automatique *m*	—	distribuidor automático *m*
distributore di benzina (I)	Tankstelle *f*	filling station	station-service *f*	—	gasolinera *f*
district (E)	Revier *n*	—	district *m*	distretto *m*	distrito *m*
district (F)	Revier *n*	district	—	distretto *m*	distrito *m*
distrito (Es)	Revier *n*	district	district *m*	distretto *m*	—
distruggere¹ (I)	vernichten	destroy	détruire	—	destruir
distruggere² (I)	zerstören	destroy	détruire	—	destruir

	D	E	F	I	Es
distrust (E)	Mißtrauen n	—	méfiance f	sfiducia f	desconfianza f
disturb¹ (E)	beunruhigen	—	inquiéter	preoccupare	inquietar
disturb² (E)	stören	—	déranger	disturbare	molestar
disturbare (I)	stören	disturb	déranger	—	molestar
disturbo (I)	Störung f	interference	trouble m	—	molestia f
dito (I)	Finger m	finger	doigt m	—	dedo m
dito del piede (I)	Zehe f	toe	doigt de pied m	—	dedo del pie m
di trasverso¹ (I)	quer	across	en travers	—	al través
di trasverso² (I)	Transport m	transport	transport m	—	transporte m
ditta (I)	Firma f	company	firme f	—	empresa f
diván (Es)	Couch f	couch	canapé m	divano m	—
divano (I)	Couch f	couch	canapé m	—	diván m
dive (E)	tauchen	—	plonger	immergere	bucear
diventare (I)	werden	become	devenir	—	llegar
diversion (E)	Umleitung f	—	déviation f	deviazione f	desviación f
diverso¹ (I)	unterschiedlich	different	différent(e)	—	distinto(a)
diverso² (I)	verschieden	different	différent(e)	—	diferente
divertido (Es)	lustig	funny	marrant(e)	allegro(a)	—
divertimento (I)	Vergnügen n	pleasure	plaisir m	—	placer m
divertire (I)	unterhalten	entertain	entretenir	—	entretener
divertirse (Es)	amüsieren, sich	enjoy o.s.	amuser, se	divertirsi	—
divertirsi (I)	amüsieren, sich	enjoy o.s.	amuser, se	—	divertirse
dividere (I)	teilen	share	partager	—	partir
dividir por la mitad (Es)	halbieren	halve	partager en deux	dimezzare	—
divieto (I)	Verbot n	prohibition	défense f	—	prohibición f
divieto di parcheggio (I)	Parkverbot n	no parking	défense de stationner f	—	estacionamiento prohibido m
divisa (I)	Uniform f	uniform	uniforme m	—	uniforme m
dix (F)	zehn	ten	—	dieci	diez
dix-huit (F)	achtzehn	eighteen	—	diciotto	dieciocho
dix-neuf (F)	neunzehn	nineteen	—	diciannove	diecinueve
dix-sept (F)	siebzehn	seventeen	—	diciassette	diecisiete
dizionario (I)	Wörterbuch n	dictionary	dictionnaire m	—	diccionario m
do (E)	tun	—	faire	fare	hacer
doblar¹ (Es)	biegen	bend	plier	piegare	—
doblar² (Es)	einbiegen	turn	tourner	svoltare	—
doble¹ (Es)	doppelt	double	double	doppio(a)	—
doble² (Es)	zweifach	double	double	duplice	—
d'occasion (F)	gebraucht	used	—	usato(a)	usado(a)
doccia (I)	Dusche f	shower	douche f	—	ducha f
doce (Es)	zwölf	twelve	douze	dodici	—
docena (Es)	Dutzend n	dozen	douzaine f	dozzina f	—
doch (D)	—	still	si	si	sin embargo
docteur (F)	Doktor m	doctor	—	dottore m	doctor m
doctor¹ (E)	Arzt m	—	médecin m	medico m	médico(a) m(f)
doctor² (E)	Doktor m	—	docteur m	dottore m	doctor m
doctor (Es)	Doktor m	doctor	docteur m	dottore m	—
document (E)	Urkunde f	—	document m	documento m	documento m
document (F)	Urkunde f	document	—	documento m	documento m

	D	E	F	I	Es
documento (Es)	Urkunde *f*	document	document *m*	documento *m*	—
documento (I)	Urkunde *f*	document	document *m*	—	documento *m*
documento de identidad (Es)	Personalausweis *m*	identity card	carte d'identité *f*	carta d'identitá *f*	—
documento d'identità (I)	Ausweis *m*	passport	pièce d'identité *f*	—	documento de identidad *m*
dodici (I)	zwölf	twelve	douze	—	doce
dog (E)	Hund *m*	—	chien *m*	cane *m*	perro *m*
dogana (I)	Zoll *m*	customs	douane *f*	—	aduana *f*
do gymnastic exercises (E)	turnen	—	faire de la gymnastique	fare ginnastica	hacer gimnasia
doigt (F)	Finger *m*	finger	—	dito *m*	dedo *m*
doigt de pied (F)	Zehe *f*	toe	—	dito del piede *m*	dedo del pie *m*
Doktor (D)	—	doctor	docteur *m*	dottore *m*	doctor *m*
dolce¹ (I)	Kuchen *m*	cake	gâteau *m*	—	pastel *m*
dolce² (I)	süß	sweet	sucré(e)	—	dulce
dolce³ (I)	sanft	gentle	doux(douce)	—	dulce
dolente (I)	weh	hurt	douloureux (-euse)	—	doloroso(a)
doll (E)	Puppe *f*	—	poupée *f*	bambola *f*	muñeca *f*
Dolmetscher (D)	—	interpreter	interprète *m/f*	interprete *m*	intérprete *m(f)*
dolor (Es)	Schmerz *m*	pain	douleur *f*	dolore *m*	—
dolor de cabeza (Es)	Kopf- schmerzen *pl*	headache	mal de tête *m*	mal di testa *m*	—
dolor de estómago (Es)	Magen- schmerzen *pl*	stomach-ache	mal d'estomac *m*	mal di stomaco *m*	—
dolor de garganta (Es)	Hals- schmerzen *pl*	sore throat	mal de gorge *m*	mal di gola *m*	—
dolor de muelas (Es)	Zahn- schmerzen *pl*	toothache	mal de dents *m*	mal di denti *m*	—
dolor de oídos (Es)	Ohren- schmerzen *pl*	earache	mal d'oreilles *m*	mal d'orecchi *m*	—
dolore¹ (I)	Kummer *m*	grief	chagrin *m*	—	pesar *m*
dolore² (I)	Schmerz *m*	pain	douleur *f*	—	dolor *m*
doloroso (I)	schmerzhaft	painful	douloureux (-euse)	—	doloroso(a)
doloroso¹ (Es)	schmerzhaft	painful	douloureux (-euse)	doloroso(a)	—
doloroso² (Es)	weh	hurt	douloureux (-euse)	dolente	—
Dom (D)	—	cathedral	cathédrale *f*	duomo *m*	catedral *f*
domaine (F)	Anwesen *n*	premises	—	podere *m*	posesión *f*
domanda¹ (I)	Antrag *m*	application	demande *f*	—	solicitud *f*
domanda² (I)	Bitte *f*	request	demande *f*	—	ruego *m*
domanda³ (I)	Frage *f*	question	question *f*	—	pregunta *f*
domanda⁴ (I)	Nachfrage *f*	demand	demande *f*	—	demanda *f*
domanda d'impiego (I)	Bewerbung *f*	application	candidature *f*	—	solicitud *f*
domandare (I)	fragen	ask	demander	—	preguntar
domani (I)	morgen	tomorrow	demain	—	mañana
domenica (I)	Sonntag *m*	Sunday	dimanche *m*	—	domingo *m*
domestica (I)	Hausmädchen *n*	maid	fille de service *f*	—	criada *f*
domicile (E)	Wohnort *m*	—	domicile *m*	residenza *f*	residencia *f*
domicile (F)	Wohnort *m*	domicile	—	residenza *f*	residencia *f*

	D	E	F	I	Es
dominare (I)	herrschen	rule	régner	—	mandar
domingo (Es)	Sonntag *m*	Sunday	dimanche *m*	domenica *f*	—
dommage (F)	Schaden *m*	damage	—	danno *m*	daño *m*
don (F)	Spende *f*	donation	—	donazione *f*	donativo *m*
donation (E)	Spende *f*	—	don *m*	donazione *f*	donativo *m*
donativo (Es)	Spende *f*	donation	don *m*	donazione *f*	—
donazione (I)	Spende *f*	donation	don *m*	—	donativo *m*
donc (F)	also	therefore	—	dunque/ quindi	así
¿dónde? (Es)	wo	where	où	dove	—
dondolare (I)	schaukeln	swing	balancer, se	—	columpiarse
done (E)	gar	—	cuit(e)	cotto(a)	estar a punto
donkey (E)	Esel *m*	—	âne *m*	asino *m*	burro *m*
donna (I)	Frau *f*	woman	femme *f*	—	mujer *f*
donna delle pulizie (I)	Putzfrau *f*	charwoman	femme de ménage *f*	—	mujer de la limpieza *f*
Donner (D)	—	thunder	tonnerre *m*	tuono *m*	trueno *m*
donner (F)	geben	give	—	dare	andar
Donnerstag (D)	—	Thursday	jeudi *m*	giovedì *m*	jueves *m*
doof (D)	—	daft	bête	scemo(a)	estúpido(a)
door (E)	Tür *f*	—	porte *f*	porta *f*	puerta *f*
dopo[1] (I)	darauf	afterwards	dessus/ensuite	—	encima
dopo[2] (I)	nachher	afterwards	ensuite	—	después
dopo[3] (I)	nachdem	after	après que	—	después que
dopodomani (I)	übermorgen	day after tomorrow	après-demain	—	pasado mañana
doppelt (D)	—	double	double	doppio(a)	doble
doppio (I)	doppelt	double	double	—	doble
d'or (F)	golden	golden	—	d'oro	de oro
Dorf (D)	—	village	village *m*	paese *m*	pueblo *m*
dormir (Es)	schlafen	sleep	dormir	dormire	—
dormir (F)	schlafen	sleep	—	dormire	dormir
dormire (I)	schlafen	sleep	dormir	—	dormir
dormitorio (Es)	Schlafzimmer *n*	bedroom	chambre à coucher *f*	camera da letto *f*	—
d'oro (I)	golden	golden	d'or	—	de oro
dort (D)	—	there	là/y	là	allí
dos (Es)	zwei	two	deux	due	—
dos (F)	Rücken *m*	back	—	schiena *f*	espalda *m*
Dose (D)	—	tin	boîte *f*	scatola *f*	lata *f*
dos veces (Es)	zweimal	twice	deux fois	due volte	—
dotado (Es)	begabt	gifted	doué(e)	dotato(a)	—
dotato (I)	begabt	gifted	doué(e)	—	dotado(a)
dottore (I)	Doktor *m*	doctor	docteur *m*	—	doctor *m*
douane (F)	Zoll *m*	customs	—	dogana *f*	aduana *f*
d'où (F)	woher	where from	—	da dove	¿de dónde?
double[1] (E)	doppelt	—	double	doppio(a)	doble
double[2] (E)	zweifach	—	double	duplice	doble
double[1] (F)	doppelt	double	—	doppio(a)	doble
double[2] (F)	zweifach	double	—	duplice	doble

	D	E	F	I	Es
doubler (F)	überholen	overtake	—	sorpassare	adelantar
doubt[1] (E)	zweifeln	—	douter	dubitare	dudar
doubt[2] (E)	Zweifel *m*	—	doute *m*	dubbio *m*	duda *f*
doubtful (E)	zweifelhaft	—	douteux(-euse)	dubbioso(a)	dudoso(a)
doubtless (E)	zweifellos	—	sans doute	senza dubbio	sin duda
douche (F)	Dusche *f*	shower	—	doccia *f*	ducha *f*
doué (F)	begabt	gifted	—	dotato(a)	dotado(a)
dough (E)	Teig *m*	—	pâte *f*	pasta *f*	masa *f*
douleur (F)	Schmerz *m*	pain	—	dolore *m*	dolor *m*
douloureux[1] (F)	schmerzhaft	painful	—	doloroso(a)	doloroso(a)
douloureux[2] (F)	weh	hurt	—	dolente	doloroso(a)
doute (F)	Zweifel *m*	doubt	—	dubbio *m*	duda *f*
douter (F)	zweifeln	doubt	—	dubitare	dudar
douter, se (F)	ahnen	suspect	—	supporre	suponer
douteux (F)	zweifelhaft	doubtful	—	dubbioso(a)	dudoso(a)
doux[1] (F)	zart	soft	—	tenero(a)	suave
doux[2] (F)	mild	mild	—	mite	agradable
doux[3] (F)	sanft	gentle	—	dolce	dulce
doux[4] (F)	weich	soft	—	morbido(a)	tierno(a)
douzaine (F)	Dutzend *n*	dozen	—	dozzina *f*	docena *f*
douze (F)	zwölf	twelve	—	dodici	doce
dove[1] (I)	wo	where	où	—	¿dónde?
dove[2] (I)	wohin	where to	où	—	a dónde
dovere[1] (I)	müssen	have to	devoir	—	deber
dovere[2] (I)	Pflicht *f*	duty	devoir *m*	—	obligación *f*
dovere[3] (I)	schulden	owe	devoir qch à qn	—	deber
dovere[4] (I)	sollen	have to	devoir	—	deber
do without (E)	entbehren	—	passer de, se	fare a meno di	pasarse sin
down[1] (E)	herunter	—	en bas	giù	abajo
down[2] (E)	herab/hinab	—	vers le bas	giù	hacia abajo
downhill (E)	bergab	—	en descendant	in discesa	cuesta abajo
downstairs (E)	unten	—	dessous	sotto/giù	abajo
downwards (E)	abwärts	—	en bas	in giù	hacia abajo
dozen (E)	Dutzend *n*	—	douzaine *f*	dozzina *f*	docena *f*
dozzina (I)	Dutzend *n*	dozen	douzaine *f*	—	docena *f*
Draht (D)	—	wire	fil de fer *m*	filo metallico *m*	alambre *m*
drap (F)	Laken *n*	sheet	—	lenzuolo *m*	sábana *f*
drapeau (F)	Fahne *f*	flag	—	bandiera *f*	bandera *f*
draught (E)	Luftzug *m*	—	courant d'air *m*	corrente d'aria *f*	corriente de aire *f*
draußen (D)	—	outside	dehors	fuori	afuera
draw[1] (E)	vorziehen	—	tirer	tirare in avanti	correr
draw[2] (E)	zeichnen	—	dessiner	disegnare	dibujar
drawer (E)	Schublade *f*	—	tiroir *m*	cassetto *m*	cajón *m*
drawing (E)	Zeichnung *f*	—	dessin *m*	disegno *m*	dibujo *m*
dream[1] (E)	träumen	—	rêver	sognare	soñar
dream[2] (E)	Traum *m*	—	rêve *m*	sogno *m*	sueño *m*
dreckig (D)	—	dirty	sale	sporco(a)	sucio(a)
drehen (D)	—	turn	tourner	girare	girar

	D	E	F	I	Es
drei (D)	—	three	trois	tre	tres
dreißig (D)	—	thirty	trente	trenta	treinta
dreizehn (D)	—	thirteen	treize	tredici	trece
dress¹ (E)	kleiden	—	habiller	vestire	vestir
dress² (E)	Kleid n	—	robe f	vestito m	vestido m
dringend (D)	—	urgent	urgent(e)	urgente	urgente
drink¹ (E)	Getränk n	—	boisson f	bevanda f	bebida f
drink² (E)	trinken	—	boire	bere	beber
drinkable (E)	trinkbar	—	potable	potabile	potable
drinking water (E)	Trinkwasser n	—	eau potable f	acqua potabile f	agua potable f
drinnen (D)	—	inside	à l'intérieur	dentro	dentro
drip (E)	tropfen	—	dégoutter	gocciolare	gotear
dritte (D)	—	third	troisième	terzo(a)	tercera(o)
Drittel (D)	—	a third	tiers m	terzo m	tercio m
dritto (I)	geradeaus	straight ahead	tout droit	—	todo derecho
drive¹ (E)	Auffahrt f	—	allée f	salita d'ingresso f	entrada f
drive² (E)	fahren	—	conduire	andare	conducir
drive³ (E)	treiben	—	mener	spingere	estimular
drive back (E)	zurückfahren	—	retourner	tornare indietro	retroceder
driver (E)	Fahrer m	—	conducteur m	autista m	conductor m
driving licence (E)	Führerschein m	—	permis de conduire m	patente f	permiso de conducir m
droga (Es)	Droge f	drug	drogue f	droga f	—
droga (I)	Droge f	drug	drogue f	—	droga f
Droge (D)	—	drug	drogue f	droga f	droga f
Drogerie (D)	—	chemist's	droguerie f	drogheria f	droguería f
drogheria (I)	Drogerie f	chemist's	droguerie f	—	droguería f
drogue (F)	Droge f	drug	—	droga f	droga f
droguería (Es)	Drogerie f	chemist's	droguerie f	drogheria f	—
droguerie (F)	Drogerie f	chemist's	—	drogheria f	droguería f
drohen (D)	—	threaten	menacer	minacciare	amenazar (a alguien)
droit¹ (F)	Gebühr f	fee	—	tassa f	tarifa f
droit² (F)	Jura	law	—	giurisprudenza f	derecho m
droit³ (F)	Recht n	right	—	diritto m	derecho m
droit⁴ (F)	aufrecht	upright	—	diritto(a)	derecho(a)
droit⁵ (F)	gerade	straight	—	diritto(a)	derecho(a)
droits de douane (F)	Zoll m	duty	—	dazio m	arbitrio m
drôle (F)	komisch	funny	—	comico(a)	cómico(a)
drop (E)	Tropfen m	—	goutte f	goccia f	gota f
drown (E)	ertrinken	—	noyer, se	annegare	ahogarse
drüben (D)	—	over there	de l'autre côté	dall'altra parte	al otro lado
drücken (D)	—	press	presser	premere	apretar
drug (E)	Droge f	—	drogue f	droga f	droga f
drunk (E)	betrunken	—	soûl(e)	ubriaco(a)	borracho(a)
dry¹ (E)	trocknen	—	sécher	asciugare	secar
dry² (E)	trocken	—	sec(sèche)	asciutto(a)	seco(a)
du (D)	—	you	tu/toi	tu	tú

	D	E	F	I	Es
dubbio (I)	Zweifel *m*	doubt	doute *m*	—	duda *f*
dubbioso (I)	zweifelhaft	doubtful	douteux (-euse)	—	dudoso(a)
dubitare (I)	zweifeln	doubt	douter	—	dudar
ducha (Es)	Dusche *f*	shower	douche *f*	doccia *f*	—
duck (E)	Ente *f*	—	canard *m*	anatra *f*	pato *m*
duda (Es)	Zweifel *m*	doubt	doute *m*	dubbio *m*	—
dudar (Es)	zweifeln	doubt	douter	dubitare	—
dudoso (Es)	zweifelhaft	doubtful	douteux (-euse)	dubbioso(a)	—
due (I)	zwei	two	deux	—	dos
dueño (Es)	Wirt *m*	landlord	patron *m*	oste *m*	—
due volte (I)	zweimal	twice	deux fois	—	dos veces
Duft (D)	—	scent	odeur *f*	profumo *m*	aroma *m*
dulce¹ (Es)	süß	sweet	sucré(e)	dolce	—
dulce² (Es)	sanft	gentle	doux(douce)	dolce	—
dull¹ (E)	fade	—	fade	insipido(a)	soso(a)
dull² (E)	trüb	—	trouble	torbido(a)	turbio(a)
dumb (E)	stumm	—	muet(te)	muto(a)	mudo(a)
dumm (D)	—	stupid	bête	stupido(a)	tonto(a)
d'une façon ou d'une autre (F)	irgend	at all/some	—	in qualche modo	cualquiera
d'une part (F)	einerseits	on one hand	—	da un lato	por un lado
dunkel (D)	—	dark	sombre	scuro(a)	oscuro(a)
dünn (D)	—	thin	mince	magro(a)	delgado(a)
du nord (F)	nördlich	northern	—	a nord	del norte
dunque (I)	also	therefore	donc	—	así
duomo (I)	Dom *m*	cathedral	cathédrale *f*	—	catedral *f*
duplice (I)	zweifach	double	double	—	doble
dur (F)	hart	hard	—	duro(a)	duro(a)
durable (E)	haltbar	—	résistant(e)	durevole	duradero
duración (Es)	Dauer *f*	duration	durée *f*	durata *f*	—
duradero (Es)	haltbar	durable	résistant(e)	durevole	—
durante (Es)	während	during	pendant	durante	—
durante (I)	während	during	pendant	—	durante
durar (Es)	dauern	last	durer	durare	—
durare (I)	dauern	last	durer	—	durar
durata (I)	Dauer *f*	duration	durée *f*	—	duración *f*
duration (E)	Dauer *f*	—	durée *f*	durata *f*	duración *f*
durch (D)	—	through	par	per	por
durcheinander (D)	—	in a muddle	pêle-mêle	sottosopra	en desorden
Durcheinander (D)	—	confusion	désordre *m*	confusione *f*	confusión *f*
Durchfahrt (D)	—	transit	passage *m*	passaggio *m*	paso *m*
Durchgang (D)	—	passage	passage *m*	passaggio *m*	paso *m*
durchgehen (D)	—	go through	passer à travers	passare	pasar
Durchreise (D)	—	passing through	passage *m*	transito *m*	paso *m*
durchschnittlich (D)	—	average	moyen(ne)	medio(a)	medio(a)
durée (F)	Dauer *f*	duration	—	durata *f*	duración *f*
durer (F)	dauern	last	—	durare	durar

	D	E	F	I	Es
durevole (I)	haltbar	durable	résistant(e)	—	duradero
dürfen (D)	—	be allowed	avoir le droit	potere	poder
dürftig (D)	—	needy	nécessiteux	misero(a)	escaso(a)
during (E)	während	—	pendant	durante	durante
during the week (E)	wochentags	—	en semaine	nei giorni feriali	entre semana
duro[1] (Es)	hart	hard	dur(e)	duro(a)	—
duro[2] (Es)	zäh	tough	coriace	duro(a)	—
duro[1] (I)	hart	hard	dur(e)	—	duro(a)
duro[2] (I)	zäh	tough	coriace	—	duro(a)
dürr (D)	—	skinny	maigre	secco(a)	árido(a)
Durst (D)	—	thirst	soif *f*	sete *f*	sed *f*
durstig (D)	—	thirsty	assoiffé(e)	assetato(a)	sediento(a)
Dusche (D)	—	shower	douche *f*	doccia *f*	ducha *f*
dust (E)	Staub *m*	—	poussière *f*	polvere *f*	polvo *m*
dustbin (E)	Mülleimer *m*	—	poubelle *f*	secchio dei rifiuti *m*	cubo de la basura *m*
dusty (E)	staubig	—	poussiéreux (-euse)	polveroso(a)	polvoriento(a)
du sud (F)	südlich	southern	—	a sud	al sur
duty[1] (E)	Pflicht *f*	—	devoir *m*	dovere *m*	obligación *f*
duty[2] (E)	Zoll *m*	—	droits de douane *m pl*	dazio *m*	arbitrio *m*
Dutzend (D)	—	dozen	douzaine *f*	dozzina *f*	docena *f*
duzen (D)	—	use the familiar form	tutoyer	dare del tu	tutear
dye (E)	färben	—	colorer	tingere	colorear
D-Zug (D)	—	through train	express *m*	direttissimo *m*	tren expreso *m*
e (I)	und	and	et	—	y
each (E)	jede(r,s)	—	chaque	ogni/ognuno	cada
each time (E)	jedesmal	—	chaque fois	ogni volta	cada vez
eagle (E)	Adler *m*	—	aigle *m*	aquila *f*	águila *f*
ear (E)	Ohr *n*	—	oreille *f*	orecchio *m*	oreja *f*
earache (E)	Ohrenschmerzen *pl*	—	mal d'oreilles *m*	mal d'orecchi *m*	dolor de oídos *m*
earlier (E)	früher	—	autrefois	prima	antes
early (E)	früh	—	tôt	presto	temprano(a)
earn (E)	verdienen	—	gagner	guadagnare	ganar
ear specialist (E)	Ohrenarzt *m*	—	spécialiste de l'oreille *m*	otoiatra *m*	médico del oído *m*
earth (E)	Erde *f*	—	terre *f*	terra *f*	tierra *f*
earthquake (E)	Erdbeben *n*	—	tremblement de terre *m*	terremoto *m*	terremoto *m*
east (E)	Osten *m*	—	est *m*	est *m*	este *m*
Easter (E)	Ostern *n*	—	Pâques *f pl*	Pasqua *f*	Pascua *f*
eastern (E)	östlich	—	d'est	ad est	al este
easy (E)	leicht	—	facile	semplice	ligero(a)
eat[1] (E)	essen	—	manger	mangiare	comer
eat[2] (E)	fressen	—	bouffer	mangiare	devorar
eatable (E)	eßbar	—	mangeable	commestibile	comestible
eau (F)	Wasser *n*	water	—	acqua *f*	agua *f*
eau-de-vie (F)	Schnaps *m*	spirits	—	acquavite *f*	aguardiente *m*

	D	E	F	I	Es
eau minérale (F)	Mineralwasser *n*	mineral water	—	acqua minerale *f*	agua mineral *f*
eau potable (F)	Trinkwasser *n*	drinking water	—	acqua potabile *f*	agua potable *f*
eaux (F)	Gewässer *n*	waters	—	acque *f pl*	aguas *f pl*
Ebbe (D)	—	low tide	marée basse *f*	bassa marea *f*	marea baja *f*
eben (D)	—	even	plan(e)	piano(a)	plano(a)
Ebene (D)	—	plain	plaine *f*	pianura *f*	llanura *f*
ebenfalls (D)	—	likewise	aussi	altrettanto	también
ebreo (I)	Jude *m*	Jew	juif *m*	—	judío *m*
eccellente[1] (I)	ausgezeichnet	excellent	excellent(e)	—	excelente
eccellente[2] (I)	hervorragend	excellent	excellent(e)	—	extraordinario(a)
eccetto[1] (I)	ausgenommen	except	exepté	—	excepto
eccetto[2] (I)	außer	except	hors de	—	salvo
eccezione (I)	Ausnahme *f*	exception	exeption *f*	—	excepción *f*
eccitante (I)	aufregend	exciting	énervant(e)	—	emocionante
eccitato (I)	aufgeregt	excited	agité(e)	—	excitado(a)
échange (F)	Austausch *m*	exchange	—	scambio *m*	cambio *m*
échanger[1] (F)	austauschen	exchange	—	scambiare	cambiar
échanger[2] (F)	tauschen	swap	—	scambiare	cambiar
échanger[3] (F)	umtauschen	exchange	—	cambiare	cambiar
échanger[4] (F)	vertauschen	exchange	—	scambiare	cambiar
échapper (F)	entkommen	escape	—	scappare	escapar
échapper, se (F)	entfliehen	escape	—	scappare	huir
echar[1] (Es)	einwerfen	post	poster	imbucare	—
echar[2] (Es)	eingießen	pour	verser	versare	—
echar de menos (Es)	vermissen	miss	manquer	sentire la mancanza	—
echar en cara (Es)	vorwerfen	blame	reprocher	rimproverare	—
écharpe[1] (F)	Halstuch *n*	scarf	—	sciarpa *f*	pañuelo para el cuello *m*
écharpe[2] (F)	Schal *m*	scarf	—	sciarpa *f*	chal *m*
échec (F)	Mißerfolg *m*	failure	—	insuccesso *m*	fracaco *m*
échelle (F)	Leiter *f*	ladder	—	scala *f*	escalera *f*
echt (D)	—	genuine	vrai(e)	vero(a)	verdadero(a)
Ecke (D)	—	corner	coin *m*	angolo *m*	esquina *f*
éclair (F)	Blitz *m*	lightning	—	lampo *m*	rayo *m*
éclairage (F)	Beleuchtung *f*	lighting	—	illuminazione *f*	iluminación *f*
éclairer (F)	beleuchten	illuminate	—	illuminare	iluminar
éclater (F)	platzen	burst	—	scoppiare	reventar
école (F)	Schule *f*	school	—	scuola *f*	escuela *f*
économe (F)	sparsam	economical		parsimonioso(a)	económico(a)
economical (E)	sparsam	—	économe	parsimonioso(a)	económico(a)
económico[1] (Es)	preiswert	inexpensive	bon marché	conveniente	—
económico[2] (Es)	sparsam	economical	économe	parsimonioso(a)	—
économiser (F)	sparen	save	—	risparmiare	ahorrar
écouter (F)	zuhören	listen	—	ascoltare	escuchar
écraser[1] (F)	überfahren	run over	—	investire	atropellar
écraser[2] (F)	zerdrücken	squash	—	sgualcire	aplastar
écrevisse (F)	Krebs *m*	crayfish	—	gambero *m*	cangrejo *m*
écrire (F)	schreiben	write	—	scrivere	escribir

	D	E	F	I	Es
écrit (F)	schriftlich	written	—	scritto(a)	por escrito
écriture (F)	Schrift f	writing	—	scrittura f	escritura f
écrivain (F)	Schriftsteller m	writer	—	scrittore m	escritor m
écrouler, se (F)	einstürzen	collapse	—	crollare	derrumbarse
écume (F)	Schaum m	foam	—	schiuma f	espuma f
edad (Es)	Alter n	age	âge m	età f	—
edificio (Es)	Gebäude n	building	bâtiment m	edificio m	—
edificio (I)	Gebäude n	building	bâtiment m	—	edificio m
editar (Es)	herausgeben	publish	éditer	pubblicare	—
éditer (F)	herausgeben	publish	—	pubblicare	editar
educación (Es)	Bildung f	education	éducation f	educazione f	—
educare (I)	erziehen	educate	élever	—	educar
educate[1] (E)	ausbilden	—	former	addestrare	instruir
educate[2] (E)	erziehen	—	élever	educare	educar
education[1] (E)	Ausbildung f	—	formation f	addestramento m	formación f
education[2] (E)	Bildung f	—	éducation f	istruzione f	educación f
education[3] (E)	Erziehung f	—	éducation f	educazione f	crianza f
éducation[1] (F)	Bildung f	education	—	istruzione f	educación f
éducation[2] (F)	Erziehung f	education	—	educazione f	crianza f
educazione (I)	Erziehung f	education	éducation f	—	crianza f
efecto (Es)	Wirkung f	effect	effet m	effetto m	—
effacer (F)	tilgen	erase	—	estinguere	anular
effect (E)	Wirkung f	—	effet m	effetto m	efecto m
effective (E)	wirksam	—	efficace	efficace	eficaz
effet (F)	Wirkung f	effect	—	effetto m	efecto m
effetto (I)	Wirkung f	effect	effet m	—	efecto m
efficace (F)	wirksam	effective	—	efficace	eficaz
efficace (I)	wirksam	effective	efficace	—	eficaz
éffondrer, se (F)	zusammen-brechen	collapse	—	crollare	desmayarse
efforcer, se (F)	bemühen, sich	make an effort	—	sforzarsi	esforzarse
effort[1] (E)	Bemühung f	—	effort m	sforzo m	esfuerzo m
effort[2] (E)	Mühe f	—	peine f	fatica f	esfuerzo m
effort[1] (F)	Anstrengung f	strain	—	fatica f	esfuerzo m
effort[2] (F)	Bemühung f	effort	—	sforzo m	esfuerzo m
effrayer (F)	erschrecken	frighten	—	spaventare	asustar
eficaz (Es)	wirksam	effective	efficace	efficace	—
egal (D)	—	all the same	égal(e)	uguale	igual
égal[1] (F)	egal	all the same	—	uguale	igual
égal[2] (F)	gleich	same	—	identico(a)	idéntico(a)
égarer (F)	verlegen	mislay	—	perdere	extraviar
egg (E)	Ei n	—	œuf m	uovo m	huevo m
église (F)	Kirche f	church	—	chiesa f	iglesia f
égoïsme (F)	Selbstsucht f	selfishness	—	egoismo m	egoísmo m
egoísmo (Es)	Selbstsucht f	selfishness	égoïsme m	egoismo m	—
egoismo (I)	Selbstsucht f	selfishness	égoïsme m	—	egoísmo m
ehe (D)	—	before	avant que	prima che	antes que
Ehe (D)	—	marriage	mariage m	matrimonio m	matrimonio m

	D	E	F	I	Es
Ehefrau (D)	—	wife	épouse *f*	moglie *f*	mujer *f*
Ehemann (D)	—	husband	mari *m*	marito *m*	marido *m*
eher (D)	—	sooner	plus tôt	prima	antes
Ehre (D)	—	honour	honneur *m*	onore *m*	honor *m*
ehrlich (D)	—	honest	honnête	onesto(a)	honesto(a)
Ei (D)	—	egg	œuf *m*	uovo *m*	huevo *m*
Eifersucht (D)	—	jealousy	jalousie *f*	gelosia *f*	celos *m pl*
eifrig (D)	—	keen	zélé(e)	diligente	diligente
eigen (D)	—	own	propre	proprio(a)	propio(a)
eigenartig (D)	—	strange	singulier(-ère)	strano(a)	extraño(a)
Eigenschaft (D)	—	quality	qualité *f*	qualità *f*	atributo *m*
eigentlich (D)	—	actually	en fait	in fondo	en realidad
Eigentümer (D)	—	owner	propriétaire *m*	proprietario *m*	propietario *m*
eight (E)	acht	—	huit	otto	ocho
eighteen (E)	achtzehn	—	dix-huit	diciotto	dieciocho
eighty (E)	achtzig	—	quatre-vingts	ottanta	ochenta
Eilbote (D)	—	courier	courrier *m*	corriere *m*	correo urgente *m*
Eile (D)	—	haste	hâte *f*	fretta *f*	prisa *f*
eilen (D)	—	hurry	dépêcher, se	andare in fretta	darse prisa
eilig (D)	—	hurried	pressé(e)	frettoloso(a)	rápido(a)
Eilzug (D)	—	limited stop train	express *m*	treno diretto *m*	tren expreso *m*
Eimer (D)	—	bucket	seau *m*	secchio *m*	cubo *m*
Einbahnstraße (D)	—	one-way street	rue à sens unique *f*	senso unico *m*	calle de dirección única *f*
einbehalten (D)	—	keep	retenir	trattenere	retener
einbiegen (D)	—	turn	tourner	svoltare	doblar
einbilden, sich (D)	—	imagine	imaginer, se	immaginarsi	imaginarse
einbrechen (D)	—	break in	cambrioler	rubare	robar
einbüßen (D)	—	lose	perdre	perdere	perder
eindeutig (D)	—	unequivocal	incontestable	univoco(a)	evidente
Eindruck (D)	—	impression	impression *f*	impressione *f*	impresión *f*
eine (D)	—	one	un(e)	un(a)	una/un/uno
einerseits (D)	—	on one hand	d'une part	da un lato	por un lado
einfach (D)	—	simple	simple	semplice	sencillo(a)
Einfahrt (D)	—	entrance	entrée *f*	ingresso *m*	entrada *f*
einfarbig (D)	—	all one colour	uni(e)	monocolore	de un solo color
Einfluß (D)	—	influence	influence *f*	influenza *f*	influencia *f*
Einfuhr (D)	—	import	importation *f*	importazione *f*	importación *f*
Eingang (D)	—	entrance	entrée *f*	entrata *f*	entrada *f*
eingießen (D)	—	pour	verser	versare	echar
eingreifen (D)	—	intervene	intervenir	intervenire	intervenir
einheimisch (D)	—	native	indigène	indigeno(a)	nativo
einhundert (D)	—	one hundred	cent	cento	cien
einige (D)	—	some	quelques	alcuni(e)	algunos(as)
einigen, sich (D)	—	agree	mettre d'accord, se	accordarsi	ponerse de acuerdo
einkassieren (D)	—	call in	recouvrer	incassare	cobrar
Einkauf (D)	—	shopping	achat *m*	spesa *f*	compra *f*
einkaufen gehen (D)	—	go shopping	faire les courses	fare la spesa	ir de compras

	D	E	F	I	Es
Einkaufstasche (D)	—	shopping bag	sac à provision *m*	borsa della spesa *f*	bolsa de compra *f*
Einkommen (D)	—	income	revenu *m*	entrate *f pl*	ingresos *m pl*
einladen (D)	—	invite	inviter	invitare	invitar
Einladung (D)	—	invitation	invitation *f*	invito *m*	invitación *f*
einleben, sich (D)	—	settle down	acclimater, se	ambientarsi	familiarizarse
Einleitung (D)	—	introduction	introduction *f*	introduzione *f*	introducción *f*
einmal (D)	—	once	une fois	una volta	una vez
einreisen (D)	—	enter	entrer dans un pays	entrare (in un paese)	entrar(en un país)
einrichten (D)	—	fit out	aménager	arredare	equipar
Einrichtung (D)	—	furnishing	ameublement *m*	arredamento *m*	mobiliario *m*
eins (D)	—	one	un	uno	uno(a)
einsam (D)	—	lonely	solitaire	solitario(a)	solitario(a)
einschalten (D)	—	switch on	allumer	accendere	conectar
einschlafen (D)	—	falling asleep	endormir, se	addormentarsi	adormecerse
einschlagen (D)	—	smash	casser	rompere	romper
einschließen (D)	—	lock up	renfermer	rinchiudere	encerrar
einschließlich (D)	—	including	y compris	incluso(a)	incluso
Einschreibebrief (D)	—	recorded delivery letter	lettre recommandée *f*	lettera raccomandata *f*	carta con acuse de recibo *f*
einschreiben (D)	—	enrol	inscrire	iscrivere	inscribir
einseitig (D)	—	one-sided	partial(e)	unilaterale	unilateral
einsteigen (D)	—	get in	monter	salire	subir a
einstellen[1] (D)	—	adjust	régler	regolare	ajustar
einstellen[2] (D)	—	employ	recruter	assumere	emplear
Einstellung (D)	—	attitude	attitude *f*	atteggiamento *m*	actitud *f*
einstürzen (D)	—	collapse	écrouler, se	crollare	derrumbarse
eintreffen (D)	—	arrive	arriver	arrivare	llegar
eintreten (D)	—	enter	entrer	entrare	entrar
Eintritt (D)	—	charge for admission	entrée *f*	entrata *f*	entrada *f*
einverstanden (D)	—	agreed	d'accord	d'accordo	de acuerdo
einwerfen (D)	—	post	poster	imbucare	echar
einwickeln (D)	—	wrap up	envelopper	avvolgere	envolver
Einwohner (D)	—	inhabitant	habitant *m*	abitante *m*	habitante *m*
Einzelheit (D)	—	detail	détail *m*	dettaglio *m*	detalle *f*
einzeln (D)	—	single	seul(e)	singolo(a)	singular
einziehen (D)	—	move in	emménager	prendere alloggio	instalarse
einzig (D)	—	only	seul(e)	unico(a)	único(a)
Eis (D)	—	ice	glace *f*	gelato *m*	hielo *m*
Eisen (D)	—	iron	fer *m*	ferro *m*	hierro *m*
Eisenbahn (D)	—	railway	chemin de fer *m*	ferrovia *f*	ferrocarril *m*
Eisschrank (D)	—	freezer	réfrigérateur *m*	frigorifero *m*	refrigerador *m*
eitel (D)	—	vain	vaniteux(-euse)	vanitoso(a)	vanidoso(a)
either...or (E)	entweder...oder	—	ou....ou	o...o	o...o
ejemplo (Es)	Beispiel *n*	example	exemple *m*	esempio *m*	—
ejercer (Es)	ausüben	practise	exercer	esercitare	—
ejercicio (Es)	Übung *f*	exercise	exercice *m*	esercizio *f*	—
él (Es)	er	he	il	lui/egli/esso	—

	D	E	F	I	Es
el, la, lo (Es)	der, die, das	the	le, la	il, la	—
elder (E)	ältere(r,s)	—	aîné(e)	maggiore	mayor
elección[1] (Es)	Auswahl f	choice	choix m	scelta f	—
elección[2] (Es)	Wahl f	election	élection f	elezioni f pl	—
elect (E)	wählen	—	élire	eleggere	elegir
election (E)	Wahl f	—	élection f	elezioni f pl	elección f
élection (F)	Wahl f	election	—	elezioni f pl	elección f
electric (E)	elektrisch	—	électrique	elettrico(a)	eléctrico(a)
electrician (E)	Elektriker m	—	électricien m	elettricista m	electricista m
electricidad (Es)	Elektrizität f	electricity	électricité f	elettricità f	—
électricien (F)	Elektriker m	electrician	—	elettricista m	electricista m
electricista (Es)	Elektriker m	electrician	électricien m	elettricista m	—
électricité (F)	Elektrizität f	electricity	—	elettricità f	electricidad f
electricity (E)	Elektrizität f	—	électricité f	elettricità f	electricidad f
eléctrico (Es)	elektrisch	electric	électrique	elettrico(a)	—
électrique (F)	elektrisch	electric	—	elettrico(a)	eléctrico(a)
Elefant (D)	—	elephant	éléphant m	elefante m	elefante m
elefante (Es)	Elefant m	elephant	éléphant m	elefante m	—
elefante (I)	Elefant m	elephant	éléphant m	—	elefante m
elegant (D)	—	elegant	élégant(e)	elegante	elegante
elegant (E)	elegant	—	élégant(e)	elegante	elegante
élégant (F)	elegant	elegant	—	elegante	elegante
elegante[1] (Es)	elegant	elegant	élégant(e)	elegante	—
elegante[2] (Es)	schick	stylish	chic	elegante	—
elegante[1] (I)	elegant	elegant	élégant(e)	—	elegante
elegante[2] (I)	schick	stylish	chic	—	elegante
eleggere (I)	wählen	elect	élire	—	elegir
elegir (Es)	wählen	elect	élire	eleggere	—
Elektriker (D)	—	electrician	électricien m	elettricista m	electricista m
elektrisch (D)	—	electric	électrique	elettrico(a)	eléctrico(a)
Elektrizität (D)	—	electricity	électricité f	elettricità f	electricidad f
elemosina (I)	Almosen n	alms	aumône f	—	limosna f
elenco (I)	Verzeichnis n	list	registro m	—	lista f
elenco telefonico (I)	Telefonbuch n	phone book	annuaire du téléphone m	—	guía telefónica f
Elend (D)	—	misery	misère f	miseria f	miseria f
elephant (E)	Elefant m	—	éléphant m	elefante m	elefante m
éléphant (F)	Elefant m	elephant	—	elefante m	elefante m
elettricista (I)	Elektriker m	electrician	électricien m	—	electricista m
elettricità (I)	Elektrizität f	electricity	électricité f	—	electricidad f
elettrico (I)	elektrisch	electric	électrique	—	eléctrico(a)
elevar[1] (Es)	erhöhen	raise	augmenter	innalzare	—
elevar[2] (Es)	erheben	raise	lever	alzare	—
elevator (E)	Fahrstuhl m/ Lift m	—	ascenseur m	ascensore m	ascensor m
élève (F)	Schüler m	pupil	—	scolaro m	alumno m
eleven (E)	elf	—	onze	undici	once
élever[1] (F)	erziehen	educate	—	educare	criar
élever[2] (F)	züchten	breed	—	allevare	criar

	D	E	F	I	Es
elezioni (I)	Wahl *f*	election	élection *f*	—	elección *f*
elf (D)	—	eleven	onze	undici	once
elegir (Es)	auswählen	choose	choisir	scegliere	—
élire (F)	wählen	elect	—	eleggere	elegir
ella (Es)	sie	she	elle	lei	—
elle (F)	sie	she	—	lei	ella
ellos, ellas (Es)	sie *pl*	they	ils/elles	loro	—
el mismo (Es)	derselbe	the same	le même	lo stesso	—
elogiar (Es)	loben	praise	louer	lodare	—
éloigné[1] (F)	entfernt	distant	—	distante	distante
éloigné[2] (F)	fern	far away	—	lontano(a)	lejos
éloigné[3] (F)	weit	far	—	largo(a)	ancho(a)
éloigner (F)	entfernen	remove	—	allontanare	quitar
elsewhere (E)	woanders	—	ailleurs	altrove	en otra parte
Eltern (D)	—	parents	parents *m pl*	genitori *m pl*	padres *m pl*
embajada (Es)	Botschaft *f*	embassy	ambassade *f*	ambasciata *f*	—
emballer (F)	verpacken	pack	—	impacchettare	empaquetar
embarazada (Es)	schwanger	pregnant	enceinte	incinta	—
embarrassing (E)	peinlich	—	gênant(e)	imbarazzante	desagradable
embarrassment (E)	Verlegenheit *f*	—	gêne *f*	imbarazzo *m*	contratiempo *m*
embassy (E)	Botschaft *f*	—	ambassade *f*	ambasciata *f*	embajada *f*
embezzle (E)	unterschlagen	—	soustraire	sottrarre	sustraer
emborracharse (Es)	betrinken, sich	get drunk	enivrer, se	ubriacarsi	—
embotella-miento (Es)	Stau *m*	traffic jam	embouteillage *m*	ingorgo *m*	—
embouchure (F)	Mündung *f*	mouth	—	sbocco *m*	desembocadura *f*
embouteillage (F)	Stau *m*	traffic jam	—	ingorgo *m*	embotella-miento *m*
embrace (E)	umarmen	—	embrasser	abbracciare	abrazar
embrasser[1] (F)	küssen	kiss	—	baciare	besar
embrasser[2] (F)	umarmen	embrace	—	abbracciare	abrazar
embutido (Es)	Wurst *f*	sausage	saucisse *f*	salsiccia *f*	—
emerald (E)	Smaragd *m*	—	émeraude *f*	smeraldo *m*	esmeralda *f*
émeraude (F)	Smaragd *m*	emerald	—	smeraldo *m*	esmeralda *f*
emergency (E)	Notfall *m*	—	cas d'urgence *m*	caso di emergenza *m*	caso de urgencia *m*
emergency exit (E)	Notausgang *m*	—	sortie de secours *f*	uscita di sicurezza *f*	salida de emergencia *f*
émetteur (F)	Sender *m*	station	—	trasmettitore *m*	emisora *f*
emicrania (I)	Migräne *f*	migraine	migraine *f*	—	jaqueca *f*
emigrar (Es)	auswandern	emigrate	émigrer	emigrare	—
emigrare (I)	auswandern	emigrate	émigrer	—	emigrar
emigrate (E)	auswandern	—	émigrer	emigrare	emigrar
émigrer[1] (F)	auswandern	emigrate	—	emigrare	emigrar
émigrer[2] (F)	übersiedeln	move	—	trasferirsi	transladarse
emisión (Es)	Sendung *f*	transmission	diffusion *f*	trasmissione *f*	—
emisora (Es)	Sender *m*	station	émetteur *m*	trasmettitore *m*	—
emitir reflejos (Es)	blinken	flash	clignoter	lampeggiare	—
emménager (F)	einziehen	move in	—	prendere alloggio	instalarse
emmener (F)	mitnehmen	take along	—	prendere con sé	llevar consigo

	D	E	F	I	Es
emocionante (Es)	aufregend	exciting	énervant(e)	eccitante	—
empanada (Es)	Pastete f	pie	pâté m	vol-au-vent m	—
empaquetar (Es)	verpacken	pack	emballer	impacchettare	—
emparentado (Es)	verwandt	related	parent(e)	imparentato(a)	—
empêché (F)	verhindert	unable to make it	—	impedito(a)	impedido(a)
empêcher[1] (F)	hindern	hinder	—	impedire	impedir
empêcher[2] (F)	verhindern	prevent	—	impedire	evitar
emperador (Es)	Kaiser m	emperor	empereur m	imperatore m	—
empereur (F)	Kaiser m	emperor	—	imperatore m	emperador m
emperor (E)	Kaiser m	—	empereur m	imperatore m	emperador m
empezar[1] (Es)	anfangen	start	commencer	cominciare	—
empezar[2] (Es)	beginnen	begin	commencer	cominciare	—
Empfang (D)	—	reception	réception f	ricezione f	recepción f
empfangen (D)	—	receive	recevoir	ricevere	recibir
Empfänger (D)	—	receiver	destinataire f	destinatario m	destinatario m
empfehlen (D)	—	recommend	recommander	raccomandare	recomendar
Empfehlung (D)	—	recommendation	recommandation f	raccomandazione f	recomendación f
empfindlich (D)	—	sensitive	sensible	sensibile	sensible
emplâtre (F)	Pflaster n	plaster	—	cerotto m	esparadrapo m
empleado (Es)	Angestellter m	employee	employé m	impiegato m	—
emplear (Es)	einstellen	employ	recruter	assumere	—
emploi (F)	Verwendung f	use	—	uso m	utilización f
employ (E)	einstellen	—	recruter	assumere	emplear
employé (F)	Angestellter m	employee	—	impiegato m	empleado(a) m(f)
employee (E)	Angestellter m	—	employé m	impiegato m	empleado(a) m(f)
employer[1] (F)	anwenden	apply	—	impiegare	usar
employer[2] (F)	verwenden	use	—	usare	utilizar
empört (D)	—	indignant	révolté(e)	indignato(a)	indignado(a)
emprender (Es)	unternehmen	undertake	entreprendre	intraprendere	—
empresa[1] (Es)	Firma f	company	firme f	ditta f	—
empresa[2] (Es)	Unternehmen n	company	entreprise f	impresa f	—
empty (E)	leer	—	vide	vuoto(a)	vacío(a)
empujar[1] (Es)	anstoßen	bump	heurter	urtare	—
empujar[2] (Es)	stoßen	push	pousser	spingere	—
empujar[3] (Es)	schieben	push	pousser	spingere	—
empujón (Es)	Stoß m	blow	coup m	spinta f	—
en (Es)	in	in/into	dans/à/en	in/a/tra/fra	—
en (F)	davon	of it	—	di la/ne	de ello
en alguna parte (Es)	irgendwo	somewhere	n'importe où	in qualche posto	—
enamorado (Es)	verliebt	in love	amoureux(-euse)	innamorato(a)	—
enamorarse (Es)	verlieben	fall in love	tomber amoureux(-euse)	innamorarsi	—
en arrière (F)	rückwärts	backwards	—	in dietro	marcha atrás
en avant[1] (F)	voraus	ahead	—	avanti	delante
en avant[2] (F)	vorwärts	forward(s)	—	avanti	adelante
en bas[1] (F)	abwärts	downwards	—	in giù	hacia abajo
en bas[2] (F)	herunter	down	—	giù	abajo
encaisser (F)	kassieren	take	—	incassare	cobrar

	D	E	F	I	Es
encantado (Es)	entzückt	delighted	ravi(e)	affascinato(a)	—
encantador[1] (Es)	entzückend	delightful	ravissant(e)	affascinante	—
encantador[2] (Es)	charmant	charming	charmant(e)	affascinante	—
encargar (Es)	beauftragen	instruct	charger de	incaricare	—
en casa (Es)	daheim	at home	à la maison	a casa	—
en caso de que (Es)	falls	in case	au cas où	qualora	—
encauzar (Es)	lenken	steer	conduire	guidare	—
enceinte (F)	schwanger	pregnant	—	incinta	embarazada
encender[1] (Es)	anzünden	light	allumer	accendere	—
encender[2] (Es)	anmachen	put on	allumer	accendere	—
encender[3] (Es)	zünden	ignite	allumer, se	accendersi	—
encerrar (Es)	einschließen	lock up	renfermer	rinchiudere	—
en chômage (F)	arbeitslos	unemployed	—	disoccupato(a)	desempleado(a)
enchufe (Es)	Steckdose *f*	socket	prise électrique *f*	presa *f*	—
enciclopedia (I)	Lexikon *n*	encyclopaedia	encyclopédie *f*	—	diccionario *m*
en condiciones (Es)	imstande	able	capable	capace	—
encontrar[1] (Es)	begegnen	meet	rencontrer	incontrare	—
encontrar[2] (Es)	finden	find	trouver	trovare	—
encontrar[3] (Es)	treffen	meet	rencontrer	incontrare	—
encontrarse (Es)	befinden, sich	be situated	trouver, se	trovarsi	—
encore (F)	noch	still	—	ancora	aún/todavía
encore une fois (F)	nochmals	again	—	di nuovo	otra vez
en cualquier caso (Es)	jedenfalls	in any case	en tout cas	in ogni caso	—
encuentro (Es)	Treffen *n*	meeting	rencontre *f*	incontro *m*	—
encuesta (Es)	Umfrage *f*	poll	enquête *f*	inchiesta *f*	—
encyclopaedia (E)	Lexikon *n*	—	encyclopédie *f*	enciclopedia *f*	diccionario *m*
encyclopédie (F)	Lexikon *n*	encyclopaedia	—	enciclopedia *f*	diccionario *m*
end[1] (E)	enden	—	finir	finire	acabar
end[2] (E)	Ende *n*	—	fin *f*	fine *f*	fin *m*
end[3] (E)	Schluß *m*	—	fin *f*	fine *f*	conclusión *f*
Ende (D)	—	end	fin *f*	fine *f*	fin *m*
enden (D)	—	end	finir	finire	acabar
en descendant (F)	bergab	downhill	—	in discesa	cuesta abajo
en desorden (Es)	durcheinander	in a muddle	pêle-mêle	sottosopra	—
en dessous (F)	darunter	underneath	—	sotto	por debajo
en dessus (F)	darüber	above	—	sopra	por encima
endlich (D)	—	at last	enfin	finalmente	finalmente
endommage-ment (F)	Beschädigung *f*	damage	—	danno *m*	deterioro *m*
endommager (F)	beschädigen	damage	—	danneggiare	deteriorar
endormir, se (F)	einschlafen	fall asleep	—	addormentarsi	adormecerse
endroit (F)	Ort *m*	place	—	luogo *m*	lugar *m*
Endstation (D)	—	terminus	terminus *m*	capolinea *m*	estación terminal *f*
en échange (F)	dafür	instead	—	invece	en su lugar
en el futuro (Es)	zukünftig	future	futur(e)	futuro(a)	—
enemigo (Es)	Feind *m*	enemy	ennemi *m*	nemico *m*	—
enemy (E)	Feind *m*	—	ennemi *m*	nemico *m*	enemigo *m*
enero (Es)	Januar *m*	January	janvier *m*	gennaio *m*	—

	D	E	F	I	Es
énervant (F)	aufregend	exciting	—	eccitante	emocionante
énerver (F)	aufregen	excite	—	agitare	agitar
en eso (Es)	indessen	meanwhile	cependant	nel frattempo	—
en face de (F)	gegenüber	opposite	—	di fronte (a)	en frente
enfadado (Es)	ärgerlich	angry	fâché(e)	arrabbiato(a)	—
enfadarse (Es)	ärgern	annoy	fâcher	arrabbiare	—
en fait (F)	eigentlich	actually	—	in fondo	en realidad
enfance (F)	Kindheit f	childhood	—	infanzia f	niñez f
enfant (F)	Kind n	child	—	bambino m	niño m
enfer (F)	Hölle f	hell	—	inferno m	infierno m
enfermar (Es)	erkranken	get ill	tomber malade	ammalarsi	—
enfermedad (Es)	Krankheit f	illness	maladie f	malattia f	—
enfermera (Es)	Kranken-schwester f	nurse	infirmière f	infermiera f	—
enfermero (Es)	Kranken-pfleger m	nursing orderly	infirmier m	infermiere m	—
enfermizo (Es)	ungesund	unhealthy	malsain(e)	malsano(a)	—
enfermo (Es)	krank	ill	malade	malato(a)	—
enfin (F)	endlich	at last	—	finalmente	finalmente
enflé (F)	geschwollen	swollen	—	gonfio(a)	hinchado(a)
enfoncer (F)	stecken	insert	—	inserire	introducir
enfoncer, se (F)	versinken	sink	—	affondare	hundirse
en frente (Es)	gegenüber	opposite	en face de	di fronte(a)	—
eng (D)	—	narrow	étroit(e)	stretto(a)	estrecho(a)
engaged (E)	besetzt	—	occupé(e)	occupato(a)	ocupado(a)
engañar[1] (Es)	betrügen	cheat	tromper	ingannare	—
engañar[2] (Es)	täuschen	deceive	tromper	ingannare	—
engañar[3] (Es)	verführen	seduce	séduire	sedurre	—
engaño (Es)	Betrug m	fraud	tromperie f	inganno m	—
Engel (D)	—	angel	ange m	angelo m	ángel m
en general (Es)	überhaupt	at all	en général	in genere	—
en général (F)	überhaupt	at all	—	in genere	en general
engineer (E)	Mechaniker m	—	mécanicien m	meccanico m	mecánico m
England (D)		England	Angleterre f	Inghilterra f	Inglaterra f
England (E)	England n	—	Angleterre f	Inghilterra f	Inglaterra f
Engländer (D)	—	Englishman	Anglais m	inglese m	inglés m
englisch (D)	—	English	anglais(e)	inglese	inglés(-esa)
English (E)	englisch	—	anglais(e)	inglese	inglés(a)
Englishman (E)	Engländer m	—	Anglais m	inglese m	inglés m
en haut (F)	oben	above	—	sopra	arriba
enigma (I)	Rätsel n	riddle	devinette f	—	adivinanza f
enivrer, se (F)	betrinken, sich	get drunk	—	ubriacarsi	emborracharse
enjoy (E)	genießen	—	jouir	godere	disfrutar
enjoy o.s. (E)	amüsieren, sich	—	amuser, se	divertirsi	divertirse
Enkel (D)	—	grandson	petit-fils m	nipote m	nieto m
Enkelin (D)	—	granddaughter	petite-fille f	nipote f	nieta f
Enkelkind (D)	—	grandchild	petit-enfant m	nipote m/f	nieto m
enlarge (E)	vergrößern	—	agrandir	ingrandire	agrandar
enlever[1] (F)	ausziehen	take off	—	levare	quitarse

	D	E	F	I	Es
enlever² (F)	wegnehmen	take away	—	togliere	quitar
en medio (Es)	mitten	in the middle	au milieu	in mezzo(a)	—
en medio de (Es)	inmitten	in the middle of	au milieu de	in mezza	—
en même temps (F)	gleichzeitig	simultaneous	—	contemporaneo(a)	a la vez
en modo alguno (Es)	keineswegs	not at all	pas du tout	non affatto	—
en montant (F)	bergauf	uphill	—	in salita	cuesta arriba
ennemi (F)	Feind m	enemy	—	nemico m	enemigo m
en ninguna parte (Es)	nirgends	nowhere	nulle part	da nessuna parte	—
ennuyer, se (F)	langweilen, sich	get bored	—	annoiarsi	aburrirse
ennuyeux (F)	langweilig	boring	—	noioso(a)	aburrido(a)
enorme (Es)	riesig	huge	énorme	enorme	—
énorme¹ (F)	gewaltig	tremendous	—	enorme	formidable
énorme² (F)	riesig	huge	—	enorme	enorme
enorme¹ (I)	gewaltig	tremendous	énorme	—	formidable
enorme² (I)	riesig	huge	énorme	—	enorme
en otra parte (Es)	woanders	elsewhere	ailleurs	altrove	—
enough (E)	genug	—	assez	abbastanza	bastante
en outre (F)	außerdem	besides	—	inoltre	además
en parte (Es)	teilweise	partly	en partie	in parte	—
en partie (F)	teilweise	partly	—	in parte	en parte
en persona (Es)	persönlich	personal	personnel(le)	personale	—
en primer lugar (Es)	zunächst	first of all	pour l'instant	dapprima	—
en principio (Es)	grundsätzlich	fundamental	par principe	basilare	—
enquête (F)	Umfrage f	poll	—	inchiesta f	encuesta f
en realidad (Es)	eigentlich	actually	en fait	in fondo	—
enregistrement des bagages (F)	Gepäckannahme f	luggage desk	—	accettazione bagagli f	recepción de equipajes f
enregistrer (F)	verzeichnen	list	—	registrare	hacer una lista
enrol (E)	einschreiben	—	inscrire	iscrivere	inscribir
enrouler (F)	wickeln	wind	—	avvolgere	envolver
en route (F)	unterwegs	on the way	—	per strada	en camino
ensalada (Es)	Salat m	salad	salade f	insalata f	—
en seguida (Es)	sofort	immediately	immédiatement	subito	—
enseigner (F)	lehren	teach	—	insegnare	enseñar
en semaine (F)	wochentags	during the week	—	nei giorni feriali	entre semana
ensemble¹ (F)	miteinander	together	—	insieme	juntos
ensemble² (F)	zusammen	together	—	insieme	juntos
ensemble³ (F)	gemeinsam	together	—	comune	juntos
enseñanza (Es)	Unterricht m	lessons	cours m	lezione f	—
enseñar (Es)	lehren	teach	enseigner	insegnare	—
ensoleillé (F)	sonnig	sunny	—	sereno(a)	soleado(a)
ensuite¹ (F)	dann	then	—	in seguito	luego
ensuite² (F)	nachher	afterwards	—	dopo	después
en su lugar (Es)	dafür	instead	en échange	invece	—
en suma (Es)	insgesamt	altogether	dans l'ensemble	complessivamente	—
en tanto que (Es)	solange	as long	tant que	finché	—

	D	E	F	I	Es
entarimado (Es)	Parkett n	stalls	parquet m	parquet m	—
entbehren (D)	—	do without	passer de, se	fare a meno di	pasarse sin
entdecken (D)	—	discover	découvrir	scoprire	descubrir
Ente (D)	—	duck	canard m	anatra f	pato m
entender (Es)	verstehen	understand	comprendre	capire	—
entendre (F)	hören	hear	—	sentire	oír
enter[1] (E)	betreten	—	entrer dans	entrare in	entrar en
enter[2] (E)	eintreten	—	entrer	entrare	entrar
enter[3] (E)	einreisen	—	entrer dans un pays	entrare (in un paese)	entrar (en un país)
enterarse (Es)	erfahren	learn	apprendre	venire a sapere	—
entero[1] (Es)	ganz	whole	tout(e)	intero(a)	—
entero[2] (Es)	gesamt	entire	tout(e)	totale	—
enterrement (F)	Beerdigung f	funeral	—	funerale m	entierro m
entertain (E)	unterhalten	—	entretenir	divertire	entretener
entfernen (D)	—	remove	éloigner	allontanare	quitar
entfernt (D)	—	distant	éloigné(e)	distante	distante
Entfernung (D)	—	distance	distance f	distanza f	distancia f
entfliehen (D)	—	escape	échapper, se	scappare	huir
entgegengesetzt (D)	—	opposite	opposé(e)	opposto(a)	opuesto(a)
entgegen-kommen (D)	—	approach	venir à la rencontre	venire incontro	venir al encuentro
enthalten (D)	—	contain	contenir	contenere	contener
enthousiasmer (F)	begeistern	inspire	—	entusiasmare	entusiasmar
enthousiaste (F)	begeistert	inspired	—	entusiasta	entusiasta
entierro (Es)	Beerdigung f	funeral	enterrement m	funerale m	—
entire (E)	gesamt	—	tout(e)	totale	entero(a)
entkommen (D)	—	escape	échapper	scappare	escapar
entlang (D)	—	along	le long de	lungo	a lo largo de
entlassen (D)	—	release	renvoyer	licenziare	despedir
entonces (Es)	damals	at that time	alors	allora	—
entourer (F)	umgeben	surround	—	circondare	rodear
en tout cas (F)	jedenfalls	in any case	—	in ogni caso	en cualquier caso
entrada[1] (Es)	Eingang m	entrance	entrée f	entrata f	—
entrada[2] (Es)	Eintritt m	charge for admission	entrée f	entrata f	—
entrada[3] (Es)	Einfahrt f	entrance	entrée f	ingresso m	—
entrada[4] (Es)	Zugang m	access	accès m	entrata f	—
entrambi (I)	beide	both	tous/ toutes les deux	—	ambos(as)
entrance[1] (E)	Eingang m	—	entrée f	entrata f	entrada f
entrance[2] (E)	Einfahrt f	—	entrée f	ingresso m	entrada f
entrar (Es)	eintreten	enter	entrer	entrare	—
entrar en (Es)	betreten	enter	entrer dans	entrare in	—
entrare[1] (I)	betreten	enter	entrer dans	—	entrar
entrare[2] (I)	eintreten	enter	entrer	—	entrar
entrare (in un paese) (I)	einreisen	enter	entrer dans un pays	—	entrar (en un país)
entrar (en un país) (Es)	einreisen	enter	entrer dans un pays	entrare (in un paese)	—
entrata[1] (I)	Auffahrt f	slip road	bretelle d'accès f	—	vía de acceso f

	D	E	F	I	Es
entrata² (I)	Eingang m	entrance	entrée f	—	entrada f
entrata³ (I)	Eintritt m	charge for admission	entrée f	—	entrada f
entrata⁴ (I)	Zugang m	access	accès m	—	entrada f
entrate (I)	Einkommen n	income	revenu m	—	ingresos m pl
en travers (F)	quer	across	—	di trasverso	al través
entre¹ (Es)	dazwischen	in between	entre	in mezzo	—
entre² (Es)	zwischen	between	entre	tra/fra	—
entre¹ (F)	dazwischen	in between	—	in mezzo	entre
entre² (F)	zwischen	between	—	tra/fra	entre
entrée¹ (F)	Eingang m	entrance	—	entrata f	entrada f
entrée² (F)	Eintritt m	charge for admission	—	entrata f	entrada f
entrée³ (F)	Einfahrt f	entrance	—	ingresso m	entrada f
entrée⁴ (F)	Flur m	hall	—	corridoio m	corredor m
entregar (Es)	überreichen	hand over	présenter	consegnare	—
entreprendre (F)	unternehmen	undertake	—	intraprendere	emprender
entreprise (F)	Unternehmen n	company	—	impresa f	empresa f
entrer (F)	eintreten	enter	—	entrare	entrar
entrer dans (F)	betreten	enter	—	entrare	entrar
entrer dans un pays (F)	einreisen	enter	—	entrare (in un paese)	entrar (en un país)
entre semana (Es)	wochentags	during the week	en semaine	nei giorni feriali	—
entretemps (F)	inzwischen	meanwhile	—	frattanto	mientras tanto
entretener (Es)	unterhalten	entertain	entretenir	divertire	—
entretenir (F)	unterhalten	entertain	—	divertire	entretener
entretenir, se (F)	unterhalten, sich	talk	—	conversare	conversar
entretien (F)	Unterhaltung f	conversation	—	conversazione f	conversación f
entrevista¹ (Es)	Interview n	interview	interview f	intervista f	—
entrevista² (Es)	Unterredung f	talk	entrevue f	colloquio m	—
entrevue (F)	Unterredung f	talk	—	colloquio m	entrevista f
entro (I)	innerhalb	within	à l'intérieur de	—	dentro de
entscheiden (D)	—	decide	décider	decidere	decidir
Entscheidung (D)	—	decision	décision f	decisione f	decisión f
entschließen, sich (D)	—	decide	décider, se	decidere	decidirse
Entschluß (D)	—	decision	décision f	decisione f	decisión f
entschuldigen, sich (D)	—	apologize	excuser, se	scusarsi	disculparse
Entschuldigung (D)	—	apology	excuse f	scusa f	disculpa f
entsprechen (D)	—	correspond	correspondre à	corrispondere	corresponder
entstehen (D)	—	arise	naître	nascere	surgir
enttäuschen (D)	—	disappoint	décevoir	deludere	defraudar
enttäuscht (D)	—	disappointed	déçu(e)	deluso(a)	defraudado(a)
entusiasmar (Es)	begeistern	inspire	enthousiasmer	entusiasmare	—
entusiasmare (I)	begeistern	inspire	enthousiasmer	—	entusiasmar
entusiasta (Es)	begeistert	inspired	enthousiaste	entusiasta	—
entusiasta (I)	begeistert	inspired	enthousiaste	entusiasta	—
entweder...oder (D)	—	either...or	ou...ou	o...o	o...o
entwickeln (D)	—	develop	développer	sviluppare	desarrollar

	D	E	F	I	Es
Entwicklung (D)	—	development	développement *m*	sviluppo *m*	desarrollo *m*
Entwurf (D)	—	outline	esquisse *f*	abbozzo *m*	proyecto *m*
entzückend (D)	—	delightful	ravissant(e)	affascinante	encantador(a)
entzückt (D)	—	delighted	ravi(e)	affascinato(a)	encantado(a)
Entzündung (D)	—	inflammation	inflammation *f*	infiammazione *f*	inflamación *f*
en vain (F)	umsonst	for nothing	—	per niente	en vano
en valoir la peine (F)	lohnen	be worth while	—	valere la pena	valer la pena
en vano (Es)	umsonst	for nothing	en vain	per niente	—
envelope (E)	Umschlag *m*	—	enveloppe *f*	busta *f*	sobre *m*
enveloppe (F)	Umschlag *m*	envelope	—	busta *f*	sobre *m*
envelopper (F)	einwickeln	wrap up	—	avvolgere	envolver
en vente (F)	erhältlich	available	—	acquistabile	que puede adquirirse
en vez de[1] (Es)	anstatt	instead of	au lieu de	invece di	—
en vez de[2] (Es)	statt	instead	au lieu de	invece di	—
enviar (Es)	übersenden	send	envoyer	spedire	—
enviar a la nueva dirección (Es)	nachsenden	send on	faire suivre	inoltrare	—
envidia (Es)	Neid *m*	envy	jalousie *f*	invidia *f*	—
envidiar (Es)	beneiden	envy	envier	invidiare	—
envidioso (Es)	neidisch	envious	envieux(-euse)	invidioso(a)	—
envier (F)	beneiden	envy	—	invidiare	envidiar
envieux (F)	neidisch	envious	—	invidioso(a)	envidioso(a)
envious (E)	neidisch	—	envieux(-euse)	invidioso(a)	envidioso(a)
environ[1] (F)	etwa	about	—	pressappoco	unos
environ[2] (F)	ungefähr	about	—	pressappoco	aproximadamente
environment (E)	Umwelt *f*	—	environnement *m*	ambiente *m*	medioambiente *m*
environnement (F)	Umwelt *f*	environment	—	ambiente *m*	medioambiente *m*
environs[1] (F)	Nähe *f*	proximity	—	vicinanza *f*	proximidad *f*
environs[2] (F)	Umgebung *f*	surroundings	—	dintorni *m pl*	alrededores *m pl*
envolver[1] (Es)	einwickeln	wrap up	enchvelopper	avvolgere	—
envolver[2] (Es)	wickeln	wind	enrouler	avvolgere	—
envoyer[1] (F)	schicken	send	—	inviare	mandar
envoyer[2] (F)	übersenden	send	—	spedire	enviar
envy[1] (E)	beneiden	—	envier	invidiare	envidiar
envy[2] (E)	Neid *m*	—	jalousie *f*	invidia *f*	envidia *f*
épais (F)	dicht	dense	—	denso(a)	espeso(a)
épaule (F)	Schulter *f*	shoulder	—	spalla *f*	hombro *m*
épeler (F)	buchstabieren	spell	—	sillabare	deletrear
épice (F)	Gewürz *n*	spice	—	spezia *f*	especia *f*
épicé[1] (F)	scharf	hot	—	piccante	picante
épicé[2] (F)	würzig	spicy	—	aromatico(a)	aromático(a)
épicer (F)	würzen	season	—	condire	condimentar
épinard (F)	Spinat *m*	spinach	—	spinaci *m pl*	espinacas *f pl*
éplucher (F)	schälen	peel	—	sbucciare	pelar
éponge (F)	Schwamm *m*	sponge	—	spugna *f*	esponja *f*
épouse (F)	Ehefrau *f*	wife	—	moglie *f*	mujer *f*
épuisé[1] (F)	ausverkauft	sold out	—	esaurito(a)	vendido(a)

	D	E	F	I	Es
épuisé² (F)	erschöpft	exhausted	—	esausto(a)	agotado(a)
equipaje (Es)	Gepäck n	luggage	bagages m pl	bagaglio m	—
equipaje de mano (Es)	Handgepäck n	hand-luggage	bagage à main m	bagaglio a mano m	—
equipar (Es)	einrichten	fit out	aménager	arredare	—
équipe (F)	Mannschaft f	team	—	squadra f	equipo m
equipo (Es)	Mannschaft f	team	équipe f	squadra f	—
equivocado (Es)	verkehrt	wrong	faux(fausse)	sbagliato(a)	—
equivocarse (Es)	irren	be mistaken	tromper, se	sbagliare	—
equivoco (I)	Mißverständnis n	misunderstanding	malentendu m	—	malentendido m
er (D)	—	he	il	lui/egli/esso	él
erase (E)	tilgen	—	effacer	estinguere	anular
erba (I)	Gras n	grass	herbe f	—	hierba f
erben (D)	—	inherit	hériter	ereditare	heredar
Erbse (D)	—	pea	pois m	pisello m	guisante m
Erdbeben (D)	—	earthquake	tremblement de terre m	terremoto m	terremoto m
Erdbeere (D)	—	strawberry	fraise f	fragola f	fresa f
Erde (D)	—	earth	terre f	terra f	tierra f
Erdgeschoß (D)	—	ground floor	rez-de-chaussée m	pianterreno m	planta baja f
Erdöl (D)	—	oil	pétrole m	petrolio m	petróleo m
ereditare¹ (I)	beerben	inherit from	hériter	—	heredar
ereditare² (I)	erben	inherit	hériter	—	heredar
Ereignis (D)	—	event	événement m	avvenimento m	suceso m
erfahren (D)	—	learn	apprendre	venire a sapere	enterarse
Erfahrung (D)	—	experience	expérience f	esperienza f	experiencia f
erfinden (D)	—	invent	inventer	inventare	inventar
Erfolg (D)	—	success	succès m	successo m	éxito m
erfolgreich (D)	—	successful	avec succès	pieno(a) di successi	afortunado(a)
erforderlich (D)	—	necessary	nécessaire	necessario(a)	necesario(a)
erfreut (D)	—	delighted	réjoui(e)	lieto(a)	contento(a)
erfrieren (D)	—	freeze to death	mourir de froid	morire di freddo	morirse de frío
Erfrischung (D)	—	refreshment	rafraîchissement m	rinfresco m	refresco m
erfüllen (D)	—	fulfil	remplir	esaudire	conceder
ergänzen (D)	—	supplement	compléter	completare	completar
Ergebnis (D)	—	result	résultat m	risultato m	resultado m
ergreifen (D)	—	seize	saisir	afferrare	coger
erhalten (D)	—	receive	recevoir	ricevere	obtener
erhältlich (D)	—	available	en vente	acquistabile	que puede adquirirse
erheben (D)	—	raise	lever	alzare	elevar
erheblich (D)	—	considerable	considérable	rilevante	considerable
erhöhen (D)	—	raise	augmenter	innalzare	elevar
erholen, sich (D)	—	recover	reposer, se	rimettersi	recuperarse
Erholung (D)	—	recovery	repos m	riposo m	descanso m
erinnern (D)	—	remember	souvenir	ricordare	recordar
Erinnerung (D)	—	memory	souvenir m	ricordo m	memoria f

	D	E	F	I	Es
erkältet (D)	—	have a cold	avoir un rhume	essere raffreddato(a)	estar acatarrado(a)
Erkältung (D)	—	cold	refroidissement *m*	raffreddore *m*	catarro *m*
erkennen (D)	—	recognize	reconnaître	riconoscere	reconocer
erklären (D)	—	explain	expliquer	spiegare	explicar
erkranken (D)	—	get ill	tomber malade	ammalarsi	enfermar
erkundigen, sich (D)	—	inquire	renseigner, se	informarsi	informarse
erlauben (D)	—	allow	permettre	permettere	permitir
Erlaubnis (D)	—	permission	permission *f*	permesso *m*	permiso *m*
erleben (D)	—	experience	être témoin de	vivere	experimentar
erledigen (D)	—	take care of	régler	sbrigare	acabar
Ermäßigung (D)	—	reduction	réduction *f*	riduzione *f*	rebaja *f*
ermöglichen (D)	—	make possible	rendre possible	rendere possibile	facilitar
ermüden (D)	—	tire	fatiguer	stancarsi	cansar
ernähren (D)	—	feed	nourrir	nutrire	alimentar
Ernährung (D)	—	nourishment	nourriture *f*	alimentazione *f*	alimentación *f*
erneuern (D)	—	renew	rénover	rinnovare	renovar
ernst (D)	—	serious	sérieux(-ieuse)	serio(a)	serio(a)
Ernst (D)	—	seriousness	sérieux *m*	serietà *f*	seriedad *f*
Ernte (D)	—	harvest	moisson *f*	raccolto *m*	cosecha *f*
eroe (I)	Held *m*	hero	héros *m*	—	héroe *m*
Eröffnung (D)	—	opening	ouverture *f*	apertura *f*	abertura *f*
Erpressung (D)	—	blackmail	chantage *m*	ricatto *m*	chantaje *m*
erreichen (D)	—	reach	atteindre	raggiungere	alcanzar
erreur (F)	Irrtum *m*	mistake	—	errore *m*	error *m*
error (Es)	Irrtum *m*	mistake	erreur *f*	errore *m*	—
errore (I)	Irrtum *m*	mistake	erreur *f*	—	error *m*
Ersatz (D)	—	substitute	remplacement *m*	sostituzione *f*	sustitución *f*
erscheinen (D)	—	appear	apparaître	apparire	aparecer
erschöpft (D)	—	exhausted	épuisé(e)	esausto(a)	agotado(a)
erschrecken (D)	—	frighten	effrayer	spaventare	asustar
ersetzen (D)	—	replace	remplacer	sostituire	sustituir
erst (D)	—	first	d'abord	dapprima	primero
erste (D)	—	first	premier(-ière)	primo(a)	primero(a)
ertragen (D)	—	bear	supporter	sopportare	soportar
ertrinken (D)	—	drown	noyer, se	annegare	ahogarse
erwachen (D)	—	wake up	réveiller, se	svegliarsi	despertar
erwachsen (D)	—	grown up	adulte	adulto(a)	adulto(a)
Erwachsener (D)	—	adult	adulte *m*	adulto *m*	adulto *m*
erwähnen (D)	—	mention	mentionner	menzionare	mencionar
erwarten (D)	—	expect	attendre	aspettare	esperar
erwerben (D)	—	acquire	acquérir	acquistare	adquirir
erwischen (D)	—	catch	attraper	acchiappare	atrapar
erzählen (D)	—	tell	raconter	raccontare	contar
erzeugen (D)	—	produce	produire	fabbricare	generar
Erzeugnis (D)	—	product	produit *m*	prodotto *m*	producto *m*
erziehen (D)	—	educate	élever	educare	educar
Erziehung (D)	—	education	éducation *f*	educazione *f*	crianza *f*

	D	E	F	I	Es
erzwingen (D)	—	obtain by force	forcer	ottenere con la forza	forzar
esagerare (I)	übertreiben	exaggerate	exagérer	—	exagerar
esagerato (I)	übertrieben	exaggerated	exagéré(e)	—	exagerado(a)
esagerazione (I)	Übertreibung f	exaggeration	exagération f	—	exageración f
esame (I)	Prüfung f	examination	examen m	—	examen m
esaminare[1] (I)	prüfen	test	tester	—	examinar
esaminare[2] (I)	untersuchen	examine	examiner	—	examinar
esaminare[3] (I)	überprüfen	check	contrôler	—	examinar
esaudire (I)	erfüllen	fulfil	remplir	—	conceder
esaurito[1] (I)	ausverkauft	sold out	épuisé(e)	—	vendido(a)
esaurito[2] (I)	ausgebucht	fully booked	complet(-ète)	—	completo(a)
esausto (I)	erschöpft	exhausted	épuisé(e)	—	agotado(a)
escala (Es)	Zwischen-landung f	intermediate landing	escale f	scalo intermedio m	—
escalar (Es)	klettern	climb	grimper	arrampicarsi	—
escalator (E)	Rolltreppe f	—	escalier roulant m	scala mobile f	escalera mecánica f
escale (F)	Zwischen-landung f	intermediate landing	—	scalo intermedio m	escala f
escalera[1] (Es)	Leiter f	ladder	échelle f	scala f	—
escalera[2] (Es)	Treppe f	stairs	escalier m	scala f	—
escalera mecánica (Es)	Rolltreppe f	escalator	escalier roulant m	scala mobile f	—
escalier (F)	Treppe f	stairs	—	scala f	escalera f
escalier roulant (F)	Rolltreppe f	escalator	—	scala mobile f	escalera mecánica f
escalón (Es)	Stufe f	step	marche f	gradino m	—
escándalo (Es)	Skandal m	scandal	scandale m	scandalo m	—
Escandinavia (Es)	Skandinavien	Scandinavia	Scandinavie f	Scandinavia f	—
escapar (Es)	entkommen	escape	échapper	scappare	—
escaparate (Es)	Schaufenster n	shop window	vitrine f	vetrina f	—
escape[1] (E)	entkommen	—	échapper	scappare	escapar
escape[2] (E)	entfliehen	—	échapper, se	scappare	huir
escarabajo (Es)	Käfer m	beetle	coléoptère m	coleottero m	—
escasez (Es)	Mangel m	lack	manque m	mancanza f	—
escaso (Es)	dürftig	needy	nécessiteux	misero(a)	—
escenario (Es)	Bühne f	stage	scène f	palcoscenico m	—
escenificar (Es)	inszenieren	stage	mettre en scène	mettere in scena	—
esclamare (I)	ausrufen	exclaim	crier	—	exclamar
esclave (F)	Sklave m	slave	—	schiavo m	esclavo m
esclavo (Es)	Sklave m	slave	esclave m	schiavo m	—
escluso (I)	ausgeschlossen	impossible	hors de question	—	imposible
escoba (Es)	Besen m	broom	balai m	scopa f	—
escoger (Es)	aussuchen	select	choisir	scegliere	—
escombros (Es)	Trümmer pl	ruins	décombres m pl	macerie f pl	—
esconder (Es)	verbergen	hide	dissimuler	nascondere	—
escorpión (Es)	Skorpion m	scorpion	scorpion m	scorpione m	—
escribir (Es)	schreiben	write	écrire	scrivere	—
escribir a máquina (Es)	tippen	type	taper (à la machine)	battere a macchina	—

	D	E	F	I	Es
escritor (Es)	Schriftsteller *m*	writer	écrivain *m*	scrittore *m*	—
escritura (Es)	Schrift *f*	writing	écriture *f*	scrittura *f*	—
escuchar (Es)	zuhören	listen	écouter	ascoltare	—
escudo (Es)	Schild *n*	shield	bouclier *m*	scudo *m*	—
escuela (Es)	Schule *f*	school	école *f*	scuola *f*	—
escuela superior (Es)	Hochschule *f*	university	université *f*	istituto superiore *m*	—
escultor (Es)	Bildhauer *m*	sculptor	sculpteur *m*	scultore *m*	—
escultura (Es)	Skulptur *f*	sculpture	sculpture *f*	scultura *f*	—
escupir (Es)	spucken	spit	cracher	sputare	—
Esel (D)	—	donkey	âne *m*	asino *m*	burro *m*
esempio (I)	Beispiel *n*	example	exemple *m*	—	ejemplo *m*
esencial (Es)	wesentlich	essential	essentiel(-le)	essenziale	—
esercitare (I)	ausüben	practise	exercer	—	ejercer
esercitare la magia (I)	zaubern	practise magic	faire de la magie	—	hacer magia
esercitarsi (I)	üben	practise	étudier	—	practicar
esercizio (I)	Übung *f*	exercise	exercice *m*	—	ejercicio *m*
esforzarse (Es)	bemühen, sich	make an effort	efforcer, se	sforzarsi	—
esfuerzo[1] (Es)	Anstrengung *f*	strain	effort *m*	fatica *f*	—
esfuerzo[2] (Es)	Bemühung *f*	effort	effort *m*	sforzo *m*	—
esfuerzo[3] (Es)	Mühe *f*	effort	peine *f*	fatica *f*	—
esibire (I)	vorzeigen	show	montrer	—	presentar
esigenza (I)	Forderung *f*	demand	exigence *f*	—	exigencia *f*
esigere[1] (I)	anfordern	request	demander	—	pedir
esigere[2] (I)	fordern	demand	exiger	—	exigir
esistenza (I)	Dasein *n*	existence	existence *f*	—	existencia *f*
esistere (I)	existieren	exist	exister	—	existir
esitare (I)	zögern	hesitate	hésiter	—	vacilar
esmeralda (Es)	Smaragd *m*	emerald	émeraude *f*	smeraldo *m*	—
espacio (Es)	Lücke *f*	gap	lacune *f*	lacuna *f*	—
espace (F)	Zwischenraum *m*	space	—	spazio *m*	espacio intermedio *m*
espacio intermedio (Es)	Zwischenraum *m*	space	espace *m*	spazio *m*	—
espacioso (Es)	geräumig	spacious	spacieux(-euse)	spazioso(a)	—
Espagne (F)	Spanien *n*	Spain	—	Spagna *f*	España *f*
Espagnol (F)	Spanier *m*	Spaniard	—	spagnolo *m*	español *m*
espagnol (F)	spanisch	Spanish	—	spagnolo(a)	español(a)
espalda (Es)	Rücken *m*	back	dos *m*	schiena *f*	—
España (Es)	Spanien *n*	Spain	Espagne *f*	Spagna *f*	—
español[1] (Es)	Spanier *m*	Spaniard	Espagnol *m*	spagnolo *m*	—
español[2] (Es)	spanisch	Spanish	espagnol(e)	spagnolo(a)	—
espantoso (Es)	schauderhaft	horrible	horrible	spaventoso(a)	—
esparadrapo (Es)	Pflaster *n*	plaster	emplâtre *m*	cerotto *m*	—
espatrio (I)	Ausreise *f*	departure	départ *m*	—	salida *f*
espèce (F)	Art *f*	species	—	specie *f*	especie *f*
espèces (F)	Bargeld *n*	cash	—	contanti *m pl*	dinero al contado *m*
especia (Es)	Gewürz *n*	spice	épice *f*	spezia *f*	—

	D	E	F	I	Es
especial (Es)	speziell	special	spécial(e)	speciale	—
especially (E)	besonders	—	surtout	particolarmente	sobre todo
especie (Es)	Art *f*	species	espèce *f*	specie *f*	—
espectáculo (Es)	Schauspiel *n*	play	spectacle *m*	spettacolo *m*	—
espectador (Es)	Zuschauer *m*	spectator	spectateur *m*	spettatore *m*	—
espejo (Es)	Spiegel *m*	mirror	miroir *m*	specchio *m*	—
esperar¹ (Es)	erwarten	expect	attendre	aspettare	—
esperar² (Es)	hoffen	hope	espérer	sperare	—
esperar³ (Es)	warten	wait	attendre	aspettare	—
espérer (F)	hoffen	hope	—	sperare	esperar
esperienza (I)	Erfahrung *f*	experience	expérience *f*	—	experiencia *f*
espérons (F)	hoffentlich	hopefully	—	speriamo que	espero que
espero que (Es)	hoffentlich	hopefully	espérons	speriamo que	—
espeso (Es)	dicht	dense	épais(se)	denso(a)	—
espinacas (Es)	Spinat *m*	spinach	épinard *m*	spinaci *m pl*	—
espíritu (Es)	Geist *m*	spirit	esprit *m*	spirito *m*	—
esponja (Es)	Schwamm *m*	sponge	éponge *f*	spugna *f*	—
esporre (I)	ausstellen	exhibit	exposer	—	exponer
esportare (I)	ausführen	export	exporter	—	exportar
esportazione¹ (I)	Ausfuhr *f*	export	exportation *f*	—	exportación *f*
esportazione² (I)	Export *m*	export	exportation *f*	—	exportación *f*
esposizione (I)	Ausstellung *f*	exhibition	exposition *f*	—	exposición *f*
espressione (I)	Ausdruck *m*	expression	expression *f*	—	término *m*
espresso (I)	ausdrücklich	explicit	exprès(-esse)	—	explícito(a)
esprit (F)	Geist *m*	spirit	—	spirito *m*	espíritu *m*
espuma (Es)	Schaum *m*	foam	écume *f*	schiuma *f*	—
esquí (Es)	Ski *m*	ski	ski *m*	sci *m*	—
esquina (Es)	Ecke *f*	corner	coin *m*	angolo *m*	—
esquisse¹ (F)	Entwurf *m*	outline	—	abbozzo *m*	proyecto *m*
esquisse² (F)	Skizze *f*	sketch	—	schizzo *m*	boceto *m*
essai¹ (F)	Probe *f*	test	—	prova *f*	prueba *f*
essai² (F)	Versuch *m*	try	—	tentativo *m*	intento *m*
essayer¹ (F)	anprobieren	try on	—	provare	probar
essayer² (F)	probieren	try	—	assaggiare	probar
essayer³ (F)	versuchen	try	—	provare	probar
eßbar (D)	—	eatable	mangeable	commestibile	comestible
essen (D)	—	eat	manger	mangiare	comer
Essen (D)	—	food	repas *m*	alimentazione *f*	comida *f*
essence (F)	Benzin *n*	petrol	—	benzina	gasolina *f*
essential (E)	wesentlich	—	essentiel(-le)	essenziale	esencial
essentiale (I)	wesentlich	essential	essentiel(-le)	—	esencial
essentiel (F)	wesentlich	essential	—	essenziale	esencial
essere¹ (I)	sein	be	être	—	ser/estar
essere² (I)	Wesen *n*	being	être *m*	—	ser *m*
essere portato (I)	taugen	be of use	convenir pour	—	valer
essere raffreddato (I)	erkältet	have a cold	avoir un rhume	—	estar acatarrado(a)
essere umano (I)	Mensch *m*	human being	homme *m*	—	persona *f*
Essig (D)	—	vinegar	vinaigre *m*	aceto *m*	vinagre *m*

	D	E	F	I	Es
Eßlöffel (D)	—	tablespoon	cuiller *f*	cucchiaio *m*	cuchara *f*
essuyer (F)	wischen	wipe	—	pulire	fregar
Eßwaren (D)	—	victuals	produits alimentaires *m pl*	alimentari *m pl*	comestibles *m pl*
Eßzimmer (D)	—	dining room	salle à manger *f*	sala da pranzo *f*	comedor *m*
est (F)	Osten *m*	east	—	est *m*	este *m*
est (I)	Osten *m*	east	est *m*	—	este *m*
esta (Es)	diese(r,s)	this	ce, cette	questo(a)	—
establecimiento (Es)	Anlage *f*	plant	édifices *m pl*	impianto *m*	—
estación[1] (Es)	Bahnhof *m*	station	gare *f*	stazione *f*	—
estación[2] (Es)	Station *f*	station	station *f*	stazione *f*	—
estacionamiento prohibido (Es)	Parkverbot *n*	no parking	défense de stationner	divieto di parcheggio	—
estación central (Es)	Hauptbahnhof *m*	central station	gare centrale *f*	stazione centrale *f*	—
estación del año (Es)	Jahreszeit *f*	time of year	saison *f*	stagione *f*	—
estación terminal (Es)	Endstation *f*	terminus	terminus *m*	capolinea *m*	—
estado[1] (Es)	Stand *m*	position	état *m*	stato *m*	—
estado[2] (Es)	Staat *m*	state	état *m*	stato *m*	—
estado[3] (Es)	Verfassung *f*	constitution	état *m*	condizioni *f pl*	—
estado[4] (Es)	Zustand *m*	condition	état *m*	stato *m*	—
Estados Unidos (Es)	Vereinigte Staaten *pl*	United States	Etats-Unis *m pl*	Stati Uniti *m pl*	—
estancia (Es)	Aufenthalt *m*	stay	séjour *m*	soggiorno *m*	—
estanque (Es)	Teich *m*	pond	étang *m*	stagno *m*	—
estantería (Es)	Regal *n*	shelves	étagère *f*	scaffale *m*	—
estar acatarrado (Es)	erkältet sein	have a cold	avoir un rhume	essere raffreddato(a)	—
estar a punto (Es)	gar	done	cuit(e)	cotto(a)	—
estar de acuerdo (Es)	übereinstimmen	agree	être d'accord	concordare	—
estar de pie (Es)	stehen	stand	être debout	stare in piedi	—
estar sentado (Es)	sitzen	sit	être assis(e)	stare seduto(a)	—
estar tumbado (Es)	liegen	lie	trouver, se	giacere	—
estate (I)	Sommer *m*	summer	été *m*	—	verano *m*
este (Es)	Osten *m*	east	est *m*	est *m*	—
esterno (I)	äußerlich	external	externe	—	superficial
estero (I)	Ausland *n*	abroad	étranger *m*	—	extranjero *m*
estimado (Es)	beliebt	popular	populaire	popolare	—
estimar (Es)	schätzen	estimate	estimer	stimare	—
estimate (E)	schätzen	—	estimer	stimare	estimar
estimer (F)	schätzen	estimate	—	stimare	estimar
estimular (Es)	treiben	drive	mener	spingere	—
estinguere[1] (I)	auslöschen	extinguish	éteindre	—	apagar
estinguere[2] (I)	tilgen	erase	effacer	—	anular
estomac (F)	Magen *m*	stomach	—	stomaco *m*	estómago *m*
estómago (Es)	Magen *m*	stomach	estomac *m*	stomaco *m*	—
estornudar (Es)	niesen	sneeze	éternuer	starnutire	—
estraneo (I)	fremd	foreign	étranger(-ère)	—	extranjero(a)

	D	E	F	I	Es
estrecho¹ (Es)	eng	narrow	étroit(e)	stretto(a)	—
estrecho² (Es)	knapp	tight	étroit(e)	scarso(a)	—
estrella (Es)	Stern *m*	star	étoile *f*	stella *f*	—
estudiante (Es)	Student *m*	student	étudiant *m*	studente *m*	—
estudiar (Es)	studieren	study	étudier	studiare	—
estudio (Es)	Studium *n*	studies	études *f pl*	studi *m pl*	—
estufa (Es)	Ofen *m*	oven	poêle *m*	stufa *f*	—
estúpido (Es)	doof	daft	bête	scemo(a)	—
et (F)	und	and	—	e	y
età (I)	Alter *n*	age	âge *m*	—	edad *f*
Etage (D)	—	floor	étage *m*	piano *m*	piso *m*
étage (F)	Etage *f*	floor	—	piano *m*	piso *m*
étagère (F)	Regal *n*	shelves	—	scaffale *m*	estantería *f*
étang (F)	Teich *m*	pond	—	stagno *m*	estanque *m*
état¹ (F)	Stand *m*	position	—	stato *m*	estado *m*
état² (F)	Staat *m*	state	—	stato *m*	estado *m*
état³ (F)	Verfassung *f*	constitution	—	condizioni *f pl*	estado *m*
état⁴ (F)	Zustand *m*	condition	—	stato *m*	estado *m*
Etats-Unis (F)	Vereinigte Staaten *pl*	United States	—	Stati Uniti *m pl*	Estados Unidos *m pl*
été (F)	Sommer *m*	summer	—	estate *f*	verano *m*
éteindre¹ (F)	ausmachen	switch off	—	spegnere	apagar
éteindre² (F)	abschalten	switch off	—	spegnere	desconectar
éteindre³ (F)	auslöschen	extinguish	—	estinguere	apagar
éteindre⁴ (F)	löschen	extinguish	—	spengere	apagar
eternal (E)	ewig	—	éternel(le)	eterno(a)	eterno(a)
éternel (F)	ewig	eternal	—	eterno(a)	eterno(a)
eterno (I)	ewig	eternal	éternel(le)	—	eterno(a)
eterno (Es)	ewig	eternal	éternel(le)	eterno(a)	—
éternuer (F)	niesen	sneeze	—	starnutire	estornudar
etliche (D)	—	several	quelques	alcuni(e)	algunos(as)
étoffe (F)	Tuch *n*	cloth	—	panno *m*	paño *m*
étoile (F)	Stern *m*	star	—	stella *f*	estrella *f*
étonner (F)	wundern	wonder	—	stupire	asombrar
étonner, se (F)	staunen	be astonished	—	stupirsi	asombrarse
étourdi (F)	leichtsinnig	careless	—	spensierato(a)	imprudente
étranger¹ (F)	ausländisch	foreign	—	straniero(a)	extranjero(a)
étranger² (F)	Ausland *n*	abroad	—	estero *m*	extranjero *m*
étranger³ (F)	Ausländer *m*	foreigner	—	straniero *m*	extranjero *m*
étranger⁴ (F)	fremd	foreign	—	estraneo(a)	extranjero(a)
étranger⁵ (F)	Fremder *m*	foreigner	—	straniero *m*	extranjero *m*
être¹ (F)	sein	be	—	essere	ser/estar
être² (F)	Wesen *n*	being	—	essere *m*	ser *m*
être assis (F)	sitzen	sit	—	stare seduto(a)	estar sentado(a)
être d'accord¹ (F)	übereinstimmen	agree	—	concordare	estar de acuerdo
être d'accord² (F)	zustimmen	agree	—	acconsentire	consentir
être debout (F)	stehen	stand	—	stare in piedi	estar en pie
être en retard (F)	verspäten	be late	—	ritardare	llevar retraso

	D	E	F	I	Es
être heureux (F)	freuen, sich	be glad	—	rallegrarsi	alegrarse
être témoin de (F)	erleben	experience	—	vivere	experimentar
être vaincu par qn (F)	unterliegen	be defeated	—	soccombere	sucumbir
étroit[1] (F)	eng	narrow	—	stretto(a)	estrecho(a)
étroit[2] (F)	knapp	tight	—	scarso(a)	estrecho(a)
études (F)	Studium *n*	studies	—	studi *m pl*	estudio *m*
étudiant (F)	Student *m*	student	—	studente *m*	estudiante *m(f)*
étudier[1] (F)	studieren	study	—	studiare	estudiar
étudier[2] (F)	üben	practise	—	esercitarsi	practicar
etwa (D)	—	about	environ	pressappoco	unos
etwas (D)	—	something	quelque chose	qualcosa	algo
Europa (D)	—	Europe	Europe *f*	Europa *f*	Europa *f*
Europa (Es)	Europa *n*	Europe	Europe *f*	Europa *f*	—
Europa (I)	Europa *n*	Europe	Europe *f*	—	Europa *f*
Europäer (D)	—	European	Européen *m*	europeo *m*	europeo *m*
europäisch (D)	—	European	européen(ne)	europeo(a)	europeo(a)
Europe (E)	Europa *n*	—	Europe *f*	Europa *f*	Europa *f*
Europe (F)	Europa *n*	Europe	—	Europa *f*	Europa *f*
European[1] (E)	europäisch	—	européen(ne)	europeo(a)	europeo(a)
European[2] (E)	Europäer *m*	—	Européen *m*	europeo *m*	europeo *m*
européen (F)	europäisch	European	—	europeo(a)	europeo(a)
Européen (F)	Europäer *m*	European	—	europeo *m*	europeo *m*
europeo[1] (I)	europäisch	European	européen(ne)	—	europeo(a)
europeo[2] (I)	Europäer *m*	European	Européen *m*	—	europeo *m*
europeo[1] (Es)	europäisch	European	européen(ne)	europeo(a)	—
europeo[2] (Es)	Europäer *m*	European	Européen *m* •	europeo *m*	—
evangelisch (D)	—	Protestant	protestant(e)	protestante	protestante
évanouissement (F)	Ohnmacht *f*	faint	—	svenimento *m*	desmayo *m*
éveillé (F)	munter	lively	—	vivace	alegre
even[1] (E)	eben	—	plan(e)	piano(a)	plano(a)
even[2] (E)	gerade	—	pair(e)	pari	par
even[3] (E)	sogar	—	même	perfino	incluso
événement (F)	Ereignis *n*	event	—	avvenimento *m*	suceso *m*
evening (E)	Abend *m*	—	soir *m*	sera *f*	noche *f*
evening before (E)	Vorabend *m*	—	veille *f*	vigilia *f*	víspera *f*
event[1] (E)	Ereignis *n*	—	événement *m*	avvenimento *m*	suceso *m*
event[2] (E)	Veranstaltung *f*	—	manifestation *f*	manifestazione *f*	manifestación *f*
éventé (F)	windig	windy	—	ventoso(a)	ventoso(a)
eventual (Es)	eventuell	possible	éventuel(le)	eventuale	—
eventuale (I)	eventuell	possible	éventuel(le)	—	eventual
éventuel (F)	eventuell	possible	—	eventuale	eventual
eventuell (D)	—	possible	éventuel(le)	eventuale	eventual
ever (E)	jemals	—	jamais	mai	jamás
everyday life (E)	Alltag *m*	—	vie quotidienne *f*	vita quotidiana *f*	vida cotidiana *f*
everything (E)	alles	—	tout	tutto	todo
everywhere (E)	überall	—	partout	dappertutto	por todas partes
évidemment (F)	selbstverständlich	of course	—	naturalmente	por supuesto

	D	E	F	I	Es
evidente[1] (Es)	eindeutig	unequivocal	incontestable	univoco(a)	—
evidente[2] (Es)	offensichtlich	obvious	manifeste	evidente	—
evidente (I)	offensichtlich	obvious	manifeste	—	evidente
evitar[1] (Es)	meiden/ vermeiden	avoid	éviter	evitare	—
evitar[2] (Es)	verhindern	prevent	empêcher	impedire	—
evitare (I)	meiden/ vermeiden	avoid	éviter	—	evitar
éviter (F)	meiden/ vermeiden	avoid	—	evitare	evitar
ewig (D)	—	eternal	éternel(le)	eterno(a)	eterno(a)
exact (F)	genau	exact	—	preciso(a)	exacto(a)
exact (E)	genau	—	exact(e)	preciso(a)	exacto(a)
exactitud (Es)	Genauigkeit f	accuracy	exactitude f	precisione f	—
exactitude (F)	Genauigkeit f	accuracy	—	precisione f	exactitud f
exacto (Es)	genau	exact	exact(e)	preciso(a)	—
exageración (Es)	Übertreibung f	exaggeration	exagération f	esagerazione f	—
exagerado (Es)	übertrieben	exaggerated	exagéré(e)	esagerato(a)	—
exagerar (Es)	übertreiben	exaggerate	exagérer	esagerare	—
exagération (F)	Übertreibung f	exaggeration	—	esagerazione f	exageración f
exagéré (F)	übertrieben	exaggerated	—	esagerato(a)	exagerado(a)
exagérer (F)	übertrieben	exaggerate	—	esagerare	exagerar
exaggerate (E)	übertreiben	—	exagérer	esagerare	exagerar
exaggerated (E)	übertrieben	—	exagéré(e)	esagerato(a)	exagerado(a)
exaggeration (E)	Übertreibung f	—	exagération f	esagerazione f	exageración f
examen (Es)	Prüfung f	examination	examen m	esame m	—
examen (F)	Prüfung f	examination	—	esame m	examen m
examinar[1] (Es)	nachsehen	check	vérifier	controllare	—
examinar[2] (Es)	prüfen	test	tester	esaminare	—
examinar[3] (Es)	untersuchen	examine	examiner	esaminare	—
examinar[4] (Es)	überprüfen	check	contrôler	esaminare	—
examination (E)	Prüfung f	—	examen m	esame m	examen m
examine (E)	untersuchen	—	examiner	esaminare	examinar
examiner (F)	untersuchen	examine	—	esaminare	examinar
example (E)	Beispiel n	—	exemple m	esempio m	ejemplo m
excelente (Es)	ausgezeichnet	excellent	excellent(e)	eccellente	—
excellent[1] (E)	ausgezeichnet	—	excellent(e)	eccellente	excelente
excellent[2] (E)	hervorragend	—	excellent(e)	eccellente	extraordinario(a)
excellent[1] (F)	ausgezeichnet	excellent	—	eccellente	excelente
excellent[2] (F)	hervorragend	excellent	—	eccellente	extraordinario(a)
excepción (Es)	Ausnahme f	exception	exception f	eccezione f	—
excepcional (Es)	außergewöhnlich	exceptional	exceptionnel(le)	straordinario(a)	—
except[1] (E)	außer	—	hors de	eccetto	salvo
except[2] (E)	ausgenommen	—	excepté	eccetto	excepto
excepté (F)	ausgenommen	except	—	eccetto	excepto
exception (E)	Ausnahme f	—	exception f	eccezione f	excepción f
exception (F)	Ausnahme f	exception	—	eccezione f	excepción f
exceptional (E)	außergewöhnlich	—	exceptionnel(le)	straordinario(a)	excepcional

	D	E	F	I	Es
exceptionnel (F)	ungewöhnlich	unusual	—	insolito(a)	desacostumbrado(a)
excepto (Es)	ausgenommen	except	excepté	eccetto	—
exchange¹ (E)	austauschen	—	échanger	scambiare	cambiar
exchange² (E)	Austausch *m*	—	échange *m*	scambio *m*	cambio *m*
exchange³ (E)	umtauschen	—	échanger	cambiare	cambiar
exchange⁴ (E)	vertauschen	—	échanger	scambiare	cambiar
excitado (Es)	aufgeregt	excited	agité(e)	eccitato(a)	—
excite (E)	aufregen	—	énerver	agitare	agitar
excited (E)	aufgeregt	—	agité(e)	eccitato(a)	excitado(a)
exciting (E)	aufregend	—	énervant(e)	eccitante	emocionante
exclaim (E)	ausrufen	—	crier	esclamare	exclamar
exclamar (Es)	ausrufen	exclaim	crier	esclamare	—
excursión¹ (Es)	Ausflug *m*	outing	excursion *f*	gita *f*	—
excursión² (Es)	Tour *f*	tour	excursion *f*	giro *m*	—
excursion¹ (F)	Ausflug *m*	outing	—	gita *f*	excursión *f*
excursion² (F)	Tour *f*	tour	—	giro *m*	excursión *f*
excuse (F)	Entschuldigung *f*	apology	—	scusa *f*	disculpar
excuser, se (F)	entschuldigen, sich	apologize	—	scusarsi	disculparse
exemple (F)	Beispiel *n*	example	—	esempio *m*	ejemplo *m*
exercer (F)	ausüben	exercise	—	esercitare	ejercer
exercice (F)	Übung *f*	exercise	—	esercizio *f*	ejercicio *m*
exercise (E)	Übung *f*	—	exercice *m*	esercizio *f*	ejercicio *m*
exercise book (E)	Heft *n*	—	cahier *m*	quaderno *m*	cuaderno *m*
exhausted (E)	erschöpft	—	épuisé(e)	esausto(a)	agotado(a)
exhibit (E)	ausstellen	—	exposer	esporre	exponer
exhibition (E)	Ausstellung *f*	—	exposition *f*	esposizione *f*	exposición *f*
exhorter (F)	mahnen	warn	—	ammonire	notificar
exigence (F)	Forderung *f*	demand	—	esigenza *f*	exigencia *f*
exigencia (Es)	Forderung *f*	demand	exigence *f*	esigenza *f*	—
exiger¹ (F)	fordern	demand	—	esigere	exigir
exiger² (F)	zumuten	expect	—	pretendere	exigir
exigir¹ (Es)	auffordern	ask	inviter	invitare	—
exigir² (Es)	fordern	demand	exiger	esigere	—
exigir³ (Es)	verlangen	demand	demander	richiedere	—
exigir⁴ (Es)	zumuten	expect	exiger	pretendere	—
exist (E)	existieren	—	exister	esistere	existir
existence (E)	Dasein *n*	—	existence *f*	esistenza *f*	existencia *f*
existence (F)	Dasein *n*	existence	—	esistenza *f*	existencia *f*
existencia (Es)	Dasein *n*	existence	existence *f*	esistenza *f*	—
exister¹ (F)	existieren	exist	—	esistere	existir
exister² (F)	vorkommen	occur	—	accadere	suceder
existieren (D)	—	exist	exister	esistere	existir
existir (Es)	existieren	exist	exister	esistere	—
exit (E)	Ausgang *m*	—	sortie *f*	uscita *f*	salida *f*
éxito (Es)	Erfolg *m*	success	succès *m*	successo *m*	—
expect¹ (E)	erwarten	—	attendre	aspettare	esperar
expect² (E)	zumuten	—	exiger	pretendere	exigir

	D	E	F	I	Es
expéditeur (F)	Absender *m*	sender	—	mittente *m*	remitente *m*
expenses[1] (E)	Kosten *pl*	—	coûts *m pl*	spese *f pl*	costas *m pl*
expenses[2] (E)	Spesen *pl*	—	frais *m pl*	spese *f pl*	gastos *m pl*
expenses[3] (E)	Unkosten *pl*	—	frais *m pl*	spese *f pl*	gastos *m pl*
expensive[1] (E)	kostspielig	—	coûteux(-euse)	costoso(a)	costoso(a)
expensive[2] (E)	teuer	—	cher(-ère)	caro(a)	caro(a)
experience[1] (E)	erleben	—	être témoin de	vivere	experimentar
experience[2] (E)	Erfahrung *f*	—	expérience *f*	esperienza *f*	experiencia *f*
expérience (F)	Erfahrung *f*	experience	—	esperienza *f*	experiencia *f*
experiencia (Es)	Erfahrung *f*	experience	expérience *f*	esperienza *f*	—
experimentar (Es)	erleben	experience	être témoin de	vivere	—
explain (E)	erklären	—	expliquer	spiegare	explicar
explicar (Es)	erklären	explain	expliquer	spiegare	—
explicit (E)	ausdrücklich	—	exprès(-esse)	espresso(a)	explícito(a)
explícito (Es)	ausdrücklich	explicit	exprès(-esse)	espresso(a)	—
expliquer (F)	erklären	explain	—	spiegare	explicar
exponer (Es)	ausstellen	exhibit	exposer	esporre	—
Export (D)	—	export	exportation *f*	esportazione *f*	exportación *f*
export[1] (E)	ausführen	—	exporter	esportare	exportar
export[2] (E)	Ausfuhr *f*	—	exportation *f*	esportazione *f*	exportación *f*
export[3] (E)	Export *m*	—	exportation *f*	esportazione *f*	exportación *f*
exportación[1] (Es)	Ausfuhr *f*	export	exportation *f*	esportazione *f*	—
exportación[2] (Es)	Export *m*	export	exportation *f*	esportazione *f*	—
exportar (Es)	ausführen	export	exporter	esportare	—
exportation[1] (F)	Ausfuhr *f*	export	—	esportazione *f*	exportación *f*
exportation[2] (F)	Export *m*	export	—	esportazione *f*	exportación *f*
exporter (F)	ausführen	export	—	esportare	exportar
exposer (F)	ausstellen	exhibit	—	esporre	exponer
exposición (Es)	Ausstellung *f*	exhibition	exposition *f*	esposizione *f*	—
exposition (F)	Ausstellung *f*	exhibition	—	esposizione *f*	exposición *f*
exprès[1] (F)	absichtlich	intentionally	—	apposta	adrede
exprès[2] (F)	ausdrücklich	explicit	—	espresso(a)	explícito(a)
express[1] (F)	D-Zug *m*	through train	—	direttissimo *m*	tren expreso *m*
express[2] (F)	Eilzug *m*	limited stop train	—	treno diretto *m*	tren expreso *m*
expression[1] (E)	Ausdruck *m*	—	expression *f*	espressione *f*	término *m*
expression[2] (E)	Miene *f*	—	mine *f*	aspetto *m*	expresión *f*
expression (F)	Ausdruck *m*	expression	—	espressione *f*	término *m*
express train (E)	Schnellzug *m*	—	rapide *m*	treno direttissimo *m*	tren expreso *m*
expressway (E)	Schnellstraße *f*	—	voie rapide *f*	superstrada *f*	carretera de circulación rápida *f*
exquisito (Es)	köstlich	delicious	savoureux(-euse)	squisito(a)	—
extend (E)	verlängern	—	prolonger	allungare	alargar
extensión (Es)	Breite *f*	width	largeur *f*	larghezza *f*	—
external (E)	äußerlich	—	externe	esterno(a)	superficial
externe (F)	äußerlich	external	—	esterno(a)	superficial
extinguish[1] (E)	auslöschen	—	éteindre	estinguere	apagar
extinguish[2] (E)	löschen	—	éteindre	spegnere	apagar
extra (D)	—	extra	à part	a parte	separado(a)

	D	E	F	I	Es
extra (E)	extra	—	à part	a parte	separado(a)
extra charge (E)	Zuschlag *m*	—	supplément *m*	supplemento *m*	suplemento *m*
extranjero[1] (Es)	Ausland *n*	abroad	étranger *m*	estero *m*	—
extranjero[2] (Es)	Fremder *m*	foreigner	étranger *m*	straniero *m*	—
extranjero[3] (Es)	ausländisch	foreign	étranger(-ère)	straniero(a)	—
extranjero[4] (Es)	Ausländer *m*	foreigner	étranger *m*	straniero *m*	—
extranjero[5] (Es)	fremd	foreign	étranger(-ère)	estraneo(a)	—
extraño[1] (Es)	eigenartig	strange	singulier(-ère)	strano(a)	—
extraño[2] (Es)	seltsam	strange	bizarre	strano(a)	—
extraordinaire[1] (F)	außergewöhnlich	exceptional	—	straordinario(a)	excepcional
extraordinaire[2] (F)	außerordentlich	extraordinary	—	straordinario(a)	extraordinario(a)
extraordinario[1] (Es)	außerordentlich	extraordinary	extraordinaire	straordinario(a)	—
extraordinario[2] (Es)	besondere(r,s)	special	spécial(e)	straordinario(a)	—
extraordinario[3] (Es)	hervorragend	excellent	excellent(e)	eccellente	—
extraordinary (E)	außerordentlich	—	exceptionnel(le)	straordinario(a)	extraordinario(a)
extraviar (Es)	verlegen	mislay	égarer	perdere	—
eye (E)	Auge *n*	—	œil *m* (yeux *pl*)	occhio *m*	ojo *m*
eyelash (E)	Wimper *f*	—	cil *m*	ciglia *f*	pestaña *f*
eye specialist (E)	Augenarzt *m*	—	oculiste *m*	oculista *m*	oculista *m*
fabbrica (I)	Fabrik *f*	factory	usine *f*	—	fábrica *f*
fabbricare[1] (I)	erzeugen	produce	produire	—	producir
fabbricare[2] (I)	herstellen	manufacture	produire	—	producir
fabric (E)	Gewebe *n*	—	tissu *m*	tessuto *m*	tela *f*
fábrica (Es)	Fabrik *f*	factory	usine *f*	fabbrica *f*	—
Fabrik (D)	—	factory	usine *f*	fabbrica *f*	fábrica *f*
façade (E)	Fassade *f*	—	façade *f*	facciata *f*	fachada *f*
façade (F)	Fassade *f*	façade	—	facciata *f*	fachada *f*
facchino (I)	Träger *m*	carrier	porteur *m*	—	mozo *m*
faccia (I)	Gesicht *n*	face	visage *m*	—	cara *f*
facciata (I)	Fassade *f*	façade	façade *f*	—	fachada *f*
face (E)	Gesicht *n*	—	visage *m*	faccia *f*	cara *f*
Fach[1] (D)	—	compartment	compartiment *m*	scomparto *m*	compartimiento *m*
Fach[2] (D)	—	subject	matière *f*	materia *f*	materia *f*
fachada (Es)	Fassade *f*	façade	façade *f*	facciata *f*	—
fâché (F)	ärgerlich	angry	—	arrabbiato(a)	enfadado(a)
fâcher (F)	ärgern	annoy	—	arrabbiare	enfadar
facile (F)	leicht	easy	—	semplice	ligero(a)
facilitar (Es)	ermöglichen	make possible	rendre possible	rendere possibile	—
fact (E)	Tatsache *f*	—	fait *m*	fatto *m*	hecho *m*
facteur (F)	Postbote *m*	postman	—	postino *m*	cartero *m*
factory (E)	Fabrik *f*	—	usine *f*	fabbrica *f*	fábrica *f*
factura (Es)	Rechnung *f*	bill	facture *f*	fattura *f*	—
facture (F)	Rechnung *f*	bill	—	fattura *f*	factura *f*
fade (D)	—	dull	fade	insipido(a)	soso(a)
fade (F)	fade	dull	—	insipido(a)	soso(a)
Faden (D)	—	thread	fil *m*	filo *m*	hilo *m*
fagiolo (I)	Bohne *f*	bean	haricot *m*	—	judía *f*
fähig (D)	—	capable	capable	capace	hábil

	D	E	F	I	Es
Fähigkeit (D)	—	ability	capacité f	capacità f	capacidad f
Fahne (D)	—	flag	drapeau m	bandiera f	bandera f
Fahrbahn (D)	—	carriageway	chaussée f	corsia f	calzada f
Fähre (D)	—	ferry	bac m	traghetto m	transbordador m
fahren (D)	—	drive	conduire	andare	conducir
Fahrer (D)	—	driver	conducteur m	autista m	conductor m
Fahrgast (D)	—	passenger	passager m	passeggero m	pasajero m
Fahrkarte (D)	—	ticket	billet m	biglietto m	billete m
Fahrplan (D)	—	timetable	horaire m	orario m	horario m
Fahrrad (D)	—	bicycle	bicyclette f	bicicletta f	bicicleta f
Fahrschein (D)	—	ticket	ticket m	biglietto m	billete m
Fahrstuhl (D)	—	elevator	ascenseur m	ascensore m	ascensor m
Fahrt (D)	—	journey	voyage f	viaggio m	viaje m
Fahrzeug (D)	—	vehicle	véhicule m	veicolo m	vehículo m
faible (F)	schwach	weak	—	debole	débil
faiblesse (F)	Schwäche f	weakness	—	debolezza f	debilidad f
failure (E)	Mißerfolg m	—	échec m	insuccesso m	fracaso m
faim (F)	Hunger m	hunger	—	fame f	hambre m
faint (E)	Ohnmacht f	—	évanouissement m	svenimento m	desmayo m
fair¹ (E)	Jahrmarkt m	—	foire f	fiera f	feria f
fair² (E)	Messe f	—	foire f	fiera f	feria f
faire¹ (F)	machen	make/do	—	fare	hacer
faire² (F)	tun	do	—	fare	hacer
faire attention¹ (F)	aufpassen	pay attention	—	fare attenzione	prestar atención
faire attention² (F)	achtgeben	take care	—	badare	atender
faire cuire (F)	backen	bake	—	cuocere (al forno)	cocer (al horno)
faire de la gymnastique (F)	turnen	do gymnastic exercises	—	fare ginnastica	hacer gimnasia
faire de la magie (F)	zaubern	practise magic	—	esercitare la magia	hacer magia
faire de la publicité (F)	werben	advertise	—	fare propaganda	hacer propaganda
faire de la voile (F)	segeln	sail	—	andare a vela	navegar a vela
faire des efforts (F)	anstrengen	make an effort	—	affaticare	cansar
faire grève (F)	streiken	be on strike	—	scioperare	hacer huelga
faire la vaisselle (F)	abspülen	wash up	—	sciacquare	lavar
faire les malles (F)	packen	pack	—	fare le valigie	hacer la maleta
faire les courses (F)	einkaufen gehen	go shopping	—	fare la spesa	ir de compras
faire passer (F)	herumreichen	pass around	—	far circolare	pasar de mano en mano
faire remarquer, se (F)	auffallen	be noticeable	—	dare nell'occhio	llamar la atención por algo
faire signe (F)	winken	wave	—	chiamare con cenni	llamar con gestos
faire suivre (F)	nachsenden	send on	—	inoltrare	enviar a la nueva dirección
faire une chute (F)	abstürzen	crash	—	precipitare	caer a tierra
faire un rapport (F)	berichten	report	—	riferire	informar
faire un signe de tête (F)	nicken	nod	—	annuire	inclinar la cabeza
fait (F)	Tatsache f	fact	—	fatto m	hecho m

	D	E	F	I	Es
faithful (E)	treu	—	fidèle	fedele	fiel
faja (Es)	Binde f	bandage	bandage m	fascia f	—
fake (E)	unecht	—	imité(e)	falso(a)	falso(a)
falciare (I)	mähen	mow	faucher	—	cortar
falda (Es)	Rock m	skirt	jupe f	gonna f	—
falegname (I)	Tischler m	carpenter	menuisier m	—	carpintero m
fall¹ (E)	fallen		tomber	cadere	caer
fall² (E)	stürzen	—	tomber	cadere	caer
fall³ (E)	Sturz m	—	chute f	caduta f	caída f
fall asleep (E)	einschlafen	—	endormir, se	addormentarsi	adormecerse
fallen (D)	—	fall	tomber	cadere	caer
fall in love (E)	verlieben	—	tomber amoureux(-euse)	innamorarsi	enamorarse
fallito (I)	pleite	penniless	fauché(e)	—	sin dinero
fall over (E)	umfallen	—	tomber	cadere	caerse
falls (D)	—	in case	au cas où	qualora	en caso de que
falsch (D)	—	wrong	faux(fausse)	falso(a)	falso(a)
falso¹ (I)	falsch	wrong	faux(fausse)	—	falso(a)
falso² (I)	unecht	fake	imité(e)	—	falso(a)
falso¹ (Es)	falsch	wrong	faux(fausse)	falso(a)	—
falso² (Es)	unecht	fake	imité(e)	falso(a)	—
falta (Es)	Fehler m	mistake	faute f	sbaglio m	—
faltar (Es)	fehlen	miss	manquer	mancare	—
fame (I)	Hunger m	hunger	faim f	—	hambre m
famiglia (I)	Familie f	family	famille f	—	familia f
familia (Es)	Familie f	family	famille f	famiglia f	—
familiarizarse (Es)	einleben, sich	settle down	acclimater, se	ambientarsi	—
Familie (D)	—	family	famille f	famiglia f	familia f
famille (F)	Familie f	family	—	famiglia f	familia f
family (E)	Familie f	—	famille f	famiglia f	familia f
famoso (I)	berühmt	famous	célèbre	—	famoso(a)
famoso (Es)	berühmt	famous	célèbre	famoso(a)	—
famous (E)	berühmt	—	célèbre	famoso(a)	famoso(a)
faner, se (F)	welken	wither	—	appassire	marchitarse
fangen (D)	—	catch	attraper	acchiappare	coger
fango (I)	Schlamm m	mud	boue f	—	barro m
far (E)	weit	—	éloigné(e)	largo(a)	ancho(a)
far away (E)	fern	—	éloigné(e)	lontano(a)	lejos
Farbe (D)	—	colour	couleur f	colore m	color m
färben (D)	—	dye	colorer	tingere	colorear
farbig (D)	—	colourful	coloré(e)	colorato(a)	de colores
far circolare (I)	herumreichen	pass around	faire passer	—	pasar de mano en mano
fare¹ (I)	machen	make/do	faire	—	hacer
fare² (I)	tun	do	faire	—	hacer
fare a meno di (I)	entbehren	do without	passer de, se	—	pasarse sin
fare attenzione (I)	aufpassen	pay attention	faire attention	—	prestar atención
fare benzina (I)	tanken	fill up with petrol	prendre de l'essence	—	llenar de gasolina

	D	E	F	I	Es
fare escursioni a piedi (I)	wandern	hike	marcher	—	hacer excursiones
fare ginnastica (I)	turnen	do gymnastic exercises	faire de la gymnastique	—	hacer gimnasia
fare i conti (I)	rechnen	calculate	calculer	—	calcular
fare il bagno (I)	baden	bathe	baigner, se	—	bañarse
fare la barba (I)	rasieren	shave	raser	—	afeitar
fare la spesa (I)	einkaufen gehen	go shopping	faire les courses	—	ir de compras
fare la valigie (I)	packen	pack	faire les malles	—	hacer la maleta
fare propaganda (I)	werben	advertise	faire de la publicité	—	hacer propaganda
fare una radiografia (I)	röntgen	X-ray	radiographier	—	radiografiar
farfalla (I)	Schmetterling *m*	butterfly	papillon *m*	—	mariposa *f*
farina (I)	Mehl *n*	flour	farine *f*	—	harina *f*
farine (F)	Mehl *n*	flour	—	farina *f*	harina *f*
faringe (I)	Rachen *m*	throat	gorge *f*	—	garganta *f*
farmacia (Es)	Apotheke *f*	chemist's	pharmacie *f*	farmacia *f*	—
farmacia (I)	Apotheke *f*	chemist's	pharmacie *f*	—	farmacia *f*
farmer[1] (E)	Bauer *m*	—	paysan *m*	contadino *m*	campesino *m*
farmer[2] (E)	Landwirt *m*	—	agriculteur *m*	agricoltore *m*	agricultor *m*
farmhouse (E)	Bauernhof *m*	—	ferme *f*	fattoria *f*	granja *f*
farola (Es)	Laterne *f*	street light	réverbère *m*	lampione *m*	—
Fasching (D)	—	carnival	carnaval *m*	carnevale *m*	carnaval *m*
fascia (I)	Binde *f*	bandage	bandage *m*	—	faja *f*
fashion (E)	Mode *f*	—	mode *f*	moda *f*	moda *f*
Fassade (D)	—	façade	façade *f*	facciata *f*	fachada *f*
fassen (D)	—	grasp	saisir	prendere	coger
fast (D)	—	nearly	presque	quasi	casi
fast[1] (E)	fasten	—	jeûner	digiunare	ayunar
fast[2] (E)	schnell	—	rapide	veloce	rápido(a)
fasten (D)	—	fast	jeûner	digiunare	ayunar
fasten[1] (E)	anbringen	—	fixer	fissare	colocar
fasten[2] (E)	befestigen	—	fixer	fissare	sujetar
fat[1] (E)	dick	—	gros(se)	grasso(a)	grueso(a)
fat[2] (E)	fett	—	gras(se)	grasso(a)	graso(a)
fat[3] (E)	Fett *n*	—	graisse *f*	grasso *m*	grasa *f*
fate (E)	Schicksal *n*	—	destin *m*	destino *m*	destino *m*
father (E)	Vater *m*	—	père *m*	padre *m*	padre *m*
fatica[1] (I)	Anstrengung *f*	strain	effort *m*	—	esfuerzo *m*
fatica[2] (I)	Mühe *f*	effort	peine *f*	—	esfuerzo *m*
faticoso (I)	anstrengend	tiring	fatigant(e)	—	fatigoso(a)
fatigant (F)	anstrengend	tiring	—	faticoso(a)	fatigoso(a)
fatigoso (Es)	anstrengend	tiring	fatigant(e)	faticoso(a)	—
fatigué (F)	müde	tired	—	stanco(a)	cansado(a)
fatiguer (F)	ermüden	tire	—	stancarsi	cansar
fatto (I)	Tatsache *f*	fact	fait *m*	—	hecho *m*
fattoria (I)	Bauernhof *m*	farmhouse	ferme *f*	—	granja *f*
fattura (I)	Rechnung *f*	bill	facture *f*	—	factura *f*
faubourg (F)	Vorort *m*	suburb	—	sobborgo *m*	suburbio *m*

	D	E	F	I	Es
fauché (F)	pleite	penniless	—	fallito(a)	sin dinero
faucher (F)	mähen	mow	—	falciare	cortar
faul (D)	—	lazy	paresseux(-euse)	pigro(a)	perezoso(a)
fault (E)	Schuld *f*	—	culpabilité *f*	colpa *f*	culpa *f*
Faust (D)	—	fist	poing *m*	pugno *m*	puño *m*
faute (F)	Fehler *m*	mistake	—	sbaglio *m*	falta *f*
fauteuil (F)	Sessel *m*	armchair	—	poltrona *f*	sillón *m*
faux[1] (F)	falsch	wrong	—	falso(a)	falso(a)
faux[2] (F)	verkehrt	wrong	—	sbagliato(a)	equivocado(a)
favor[1] (Es)	Gefallen *m*	favour	service *m*	favore *m*	—
favor[2] (Es)	Gefälligkeit *f*	favour	obligeance *f*	favore *m*	—
favorable (Es)	günstig	favourable	favorable	favorevole	—
favorable (F)	günstig	favourable	—	favorevole	favorable
favore[1] (I)	Gefälligkeit *f*	favour	obligeance *f*	—	favor *m*
favore[2] (I)	Gefallen *m*	favour	service *m*	—	favor *m*
favorevole (I)	günstig	favourable	favorable	—	favorable
favour[1] (E)	Gefälligkeit *f*	—	obligeance *f*	favore *m*	favor *m*
favour[2] (E)	Gefallen *m*	—	service *m*	favore *m*	favor *m*
favourable (E)	günstig	—	favorable	favorevole	favorable
fazzoletto (I)	Taschentuch *n*	handkerchief	mouchoir *m*	—	pañuelo *m*
fear[1] (E)	Angst *f*	—	peur *f*	paura *f*	miedo *m*
fear[2] (E)	befürchten	—	craindre	temere	temer
fear[3] (E)	fürchten	—	craindre	temere	temer
fearful (E)	ängstlich	—	peureux(-euse)	pauroso(a)	miedoso(a)
feather (E)	Feder *f*	—	plume *f*	piuma *f*	pluma *f*
febbraio (I)	Februar *m*	February	février *m*	—	febrero *m*
febbre (I)	Fieber *n*	fever	fièvre *f*	—	fiebre *m*
febrero (Es)	Februar *m*	February	février *m*	febbraio *m*	—
fébrile (F)	hektisch	hectic	—	nervoso(a)	inquieto(a)
Februar (D)	—	February	février *m*	febbraio *m*	febrero *m*
February (E)	Februar *m*	—	février *m*	febbraio *m*	febrero *m*
fecha[1] (Es)	Datum *n*	date	date *f*	data *f*	—
fecha[2] (Es)	Termin *m*	date	terme *m*	termine *m*	—
fedele (I)	treu	faithful	fidèle	—	fiel
Feder[1] (D)	—	pen nib	plume *f*	penna *f*	pluma *f*
Feder[2] (D)	—	feather	plume *f*	piuma *f*	pluma *f*
Federal Chancellor (E)	Bundeskanzler *m*	—	chancelier fédéral *m*	cancelliere federale *m*	canciller federal *m*
Federal Highway (E)	Bundesstraße *f*	—	route nationale *f*	strada statale *f*	carretera nacional *f*
fee (E)	Gebühr *f*	—	droit *m*	tassa *f*	tarifa *f*
feed (E)	ernähren	—	nourrir	nutrire	alimentar
feel[1] (E)	befinden, sich	—	trouver, se	trovarsi	encontrarse
feel[2] (E)	fühlen	—	sentir	sentire	sentir
feeling (E)	Gefühl *n*	—	sentiment *m*	sensazione *f*	sentimiento *m*
fegato (I)	Leber *f*	liver	foie *m*	—	hígado *m*
fegen (D)	—	sweep	balayer	scopare	barrer
fehlen (D)	—	miss	manquer	mancare	faltar
Fehler (D)	—	mistake	faute *f*	sbaglio *m*	falta *f*

feiern

	D	E	F	I	Es
feiern (D)	—	celebrate	fêter	festeggiare	celebrar
Feiertag (D)	—	holiday	jour férié *m*	giorno festivo *m*	día de fiesta *m*
feig (D)	—	cowardly	lâche	vile	cobarde
Feige (D)	—	fig	figue *f*	fico *m*	higo *m*
fein (D)	—	fine	fin(e)	sottile	fino(a)
Feind (D)	—	enemy	ennemi *m*	nemico *m*	enemigo *m*
Feld (D)	—	field	champ *m*	campo *m*	campo *m*
felice (I)	glücklich	happy	heureux(-euse)	—	feliz
felicitaciónes (Es)	Glückwunsch *m*	congratulations	félicitations *f pl*	auguri *m pl*	—
felicitar (Es)	gratulieren	congratulate	féliciter	congratularsi	—
félicitations (F)	Glückwunsch *m*	congratulations	—	auguri *m pl*	felicitaciónes *f pl*
féliciter (F)	gratulieren	congratulate	—	congratularsi	felicitar
feliz (Es)	glücklich	happy	heureux(-euse)	felice	—
fellow (E)	Bursche *m*	—	garçon *m*	ragazzo *m*	chico *m*
femenino (Es)	weiblich	feminine	féminin(e)	femminile	—
féminin (F)	weiblich	feminine	—	femminile	femenino(a)
feminine (E)	weiblich	—	féminin(e)	femminile	femenino(a)
femme (F)	Frau *f*	woman	—	donna *f*	mujer *f*
femme de maison (F)	Hausfrau *f*	housewife	—	casalinga *f*	ama de casa *f*
femme de ménage (F)	Putzfrau *f*	charwoman	—	donna delle pulizie *f*	mujer de la limpieza *f*
femminile (I)	weiblich	feminine	féminin(e)	—	femenino(a)
fence (E)	Zaun *m*	—	clôture *f*	recinto *m*	valla *f*
fenêtre (F)	Fenster *n*	window	—	finestra *f*	ventana *f*
Fenster (D)	—	window	fenêtre *f*	finestra *f*	ventana *f*
feo (Es)	häßlich	ugly	laid(e)	brutto(a)	—
fer (F)	Eisen *n*	iron	—	ferro *m*	hierro *m*
fer à repasser (F)	Bügeleisen *n*	iron	—	ferro da stiro *m*	plancha *f*
feria¹ (Es)	Jahrmarkt *m*	fair	foire *f*	fiera *f*	—
feria² (Es)	Messe *f*	fair	foire *f*	fiera *f*	—
Ferien (D)	—	holidays	vacances *f pl*	vacanze *f pl*	vacaciones *f pl*
ferire¹ (I)	verwunden	wound	blesser	—	herir
ferire² (I)	verletzen	injure	blesser	—	herir
ferita¹ (I)	Verletzung *f*	injury	blessure *f*	—	herida *f*
ferita² (I)	Wunde *f*	wound	blessure *f*	—	herida *f*
fermare (I)	anhalten	stop	arrêter	—	parar
fermata (I)	Haltestelle *f*	stop	arrêt *m*	—	parada *f*
ferme (F)	Bauernhof *m*	farmhouse	—	fattoria *f*	granja *f*
fermé (F)	geschlossen	closed	—	chiuso	cerrado(a)
fermer¹ (F)	schließen	close	—	chiudere	cerrar
fermer² (F)	zumachen	shut	—	chiudere	cerrar
fermer³ (F)	zudrehen	turn off	—	chiudere girando	cerrar
fermer à clé¹ (F)	verschließen	lock (up)	—	chiudere a chiave	cerrar con llave
fermer à clé² (F)	zuschließen	lock (up)	—	chiudere a chiave	cerrar con llave
fermeture (F)	Verschluß *m*	lock	—	chiusura *f*	cierre *m*
fermeture éclair (F)	Reißverschluß *m*	zip	—	chiusura lampo *f*	cremallera *f*
fern (D)	—	far away	éloigné(e)	lontano(a)	lejos
Ferne (D)	—	distance	lointain *m*	distanza *f*	lejanía *f*

	D	E	F	I	Es
Fernfahrer (D)	—	long-distance driver	routier *m*	camionista *m*	camionero *m*
Ferngespräch (D)	—	long-distance call	communication interurbaine *f*	telefonata interurbana *f*	llamada interurbana *f*
Fernglas (D)	—	binoculars	jumelles *f pl*	cannocchiale *m*	gemelos *m pl*
fernsehen (D)	—	watch television	regarder la télévision	guardare la TV	ver la televisión
Fernsehen (D)	—	television	télévision *f*	televisione *f*	televisión *f*
Fernseher (D)	—	television set	poste de télévision *m*	televisore *m*	televisor *m*
ferro (I)	Eisen *n*	iron	fer *m*	—	hierro *m*
ferrocarril (Es)	Eisenbahn *f*	railway	chemin de fer *m*	ferrovia *f*	—
ferro da stiro (I)	Bügeleisen *n*	iron	fer à repasser *m*	—	plancha *f*
ferrovia (I)	Eisenbahn *f*	railway	chemin de fer *m*	—	ferrocarril *m*
ferry (E)	Fähre *f*	—	bac *m*	traghetto *m*	transbordador *m*
fertig (D)	—	ready	prêt(e)	pronto(a)	listo(a)
fest (D)	—	solid	solide	solido(a)	firme
Fest (D)	—	party	fête *f*	festa *f*	fiesta *f*
festa¹ (I)	Fest *n*	party	fête *f*	—	fiesta *f*
festa² (I)	Party *f*	party	fête *f*	—	fiesta *f*
festeggiare (I)	feiern	celebrate	fêter	—	celebrar
festhalten (D)	—	seize	tenir ferme	tener fermo	sujetar
Festland (D)	—	mainland	continent *m*	terraferma *f*	tierra firme *f*
festsetzen (D)	—	fix	fixer	stabilire	fijar
fetch¹ (E)	bringen	—	porter	portare	llevar
fetch² (E)	holen	—	aller chercher	andare a prendere	traer
fête¹ (F)	Fest *n*	party	—	festa *f*	fiesta *f*
fête² (F)	Party *f*	party	—	festa *f*	fiesta *f*
fêter (F)	feiern	celebrate	—	festeggiare	celebrar
fett (D)	—	fat	gras(se)	grasso(a)	graso(a)
Fett (D)	—	fat	graisse *f*	grasso *m*	grasa *f*
fette biscottate (I)	Zwieback *m*	rusk	biscotte *f*	—	bizcocho *m*
feu (F)	Feuer *n*	fire	—	fuoco *m*	fuego *m*
feucht (D)	—	damp	humide	umido(a)	húmedo(a)
feu d'artifice (F)	Feuerwerk *n*	fireworks	—	fuoco d'artificio *m*	fuegos artificiales *m pl*
Feuer (D)	—	fire	feu *m*	fuoco *m*	fuego *m*
feuergefährlich (D)	—	inflammable	inflammable	infiammabile	inflamable
Feuerwehr (D)	—	fire brigade	sapeurs pompiers *m pl*	vigili del fuoco *m pl*	cuerpo de bomberos *m*
Feuerwerk (D)	—	fireworks	feu d'artifice *m*	fuoco d'artificio *m*	fuegos artificiales *m pl*
Feuerzeug (D)	—	lighter	briquet *m*	accendino *m*	mechero *m*
feuille (F)	Blatt *n*	leaf	—	foglia *m*	hoja *f*
feux (F)	Ampel *f*	traffic lights	—	semaforo *m*	semáforo *m*
fever (E)	Fieber *n*	—	fièvre *f*	febbre *f*	fiebre *m*
février (F)	Februar *m*	February	—	febbraio *m*	febrero *m*
few (E)	wenige	—	peu	pochi	pocos(as)
fiambre (Es)	Aufschnitt *m*	cold meat	charcuterie *f*	affettato *m*	—
fiamma (I)	Flamme *f*	flame	flamme *f*	—	llama *f*

	D	E	F	I	Es
fiammifero (I)	Streichholz n	match	allumette f	—	cerilla f
fiancé (E)	Verlobter m	—	fiancé m	fidanzato m	prometido m
fiancé (F)	Verlobter m	fiancé	—	fidanzato m	prometido m
fiancer, se (F)	verloben	get engaged	—	fidanzarsi	prometerse
fianco (I)	Hüfte f	hip	hanche f	—	cadera f
fiato (I)	Atem m	breath	respiration f	—	respiro m
ficelle (F)	Schnur f	string	—	corda f	cordel m
fico (I)	Feige f	fig	figue f	—	higo m
fidanzarsi (I)	verloben	get engaged	fiancer, se	—	prometerse
fidanzato (I)	Verlobter m	fiancé	fiancé m	—	prometido m
fidarsi (I)	vertrauen	trust	avoir confiance	—	confiar
fidèle (F)	treu	faithful	—	fedele	fiel
fiducia (I)	Vertrauen n	confidence	confiance f	—	confianza f
Fieber (D)	—	fever	fièvre f	febbre f	fiebre m
fiebre (Es)	Fieber n	fever	fièvre f	febbre f	—
fiel (Es)	treu	faithful	fidèle	fedele	—
fiel (F)	Galle f	gall	—	cistifellea f	bilis f
field[1] (E)	Acker m	—	champ m	campo m	campo m
field[2] (E)	Feld n	—	champ m	campo m	campo m
fier (F)	stolz	proud	—	orgoglioso(a)	orgulloso(a)
fiera[1] (I)	Messe f	fair	foire f	—	feria f
fiera[2] (I)	Jahrmarkt m	fair	foire f	—	feria f
fierce (E)	heftig	—	violent(e)	violento(a)	fuerte
fiesta[1] (Es)	Fest n	party	fête f	festa f	—
fiesta[2] (Es)	Party f	party	fête f	festa f	—
fièvre (F)	Fieber n	fever	—	febbre f	fiebre m
fifteen (E)	fünfzehn	—	quinze	quindici	quince
fifty (E)	fünfzig	—	cinquante	cinquanta	cincuenta
fig (E)	Feige f	—	figue f	fico m	higo m
fight (E)	kämpfen	—	battre, se	combattere	luchar
figlia (I)	Tochter f	daughter	fille f	—	hija f
figlio (I)	Sohn m	son	fils m	—	hijo m
figue (F)	Feige f	fig	—	fico m	higo m
fijar (Es)	festsetzen	fix	fixer	stabilire	—
fijo (Es)	starr	rigid	rigide	rigido(a)	—
fil (F)	Faden m	thread	—	filo m	hilo m
fila (Es)	Reihe f	row	rangée f	fila f	—
fila (I)	Reihe f	row	rangée f	—	fila f
fil de fer (F)	Draht m	wire	—	filo metallico m	alambre m
file (E)	Aktenmappe f	—	porte-documents m	cartella f	cartera f
filet (F)	Netz n	net	—	rete f	red f
Filiale (D)	—	branch	succursale f	filiale f	sucursal f
filiale (I)	Filiale f	branch	succursale f	—	sucursal f
fill (E)	füllen	—	remplir	riempire	llenar
fille (F)	Tochter f	daughter	—	figlia f	hija f
fille de service (F)	Hausmädchen n	maid	—	domestica f	criada f
fill in (E)	ausfüllen	—	remplir	riempire	llenar

	D	E	F	I	Es
filling station (E)	Tankstelle *f*	—	station-service *f*	distributore di benzina *m*	gasolinera *f*
fill up with petrol (E)	tanken	—	prendre de l'essence	fare benzina	llenar de gasolina
Film (D)	—	film	film *m*	film *m*	película *f*
film (E)	Film *m*	—	film *m*	film *m*	película *f*
film (F)	Film *m*	film	—	film *m*	película *f*
film (I)	Film *m*	film	film *m*	—	película *f*
filo (I)	Faden *m*	thread	fil *m*	—	hilo *m*
filo metallico (I)	Draht *m*	wire	fil de fer *m*	—	alambre *m*
fils (F)	Sohn *m*	son	—	figlio *m*	hijo *m*
fin (Es)	Ende *n*	end	fin *f*	fine *f*	—
fin¹ (F)	Ende *n*	end	—	fine *f*	fin *m*
fin² (F)	fein	fine	—	sottile	fino(a)
fin³ (F)	Schluß *m*	end	—	fine *f*	conclusión *f*
finalement¹ (F)	schließlich	finally	—	finalmente	finalmente
finalement² (F)	zuletzt	finally	—	infine	por último
finalidad (Es)	Zweck *m*	purpose	but *m*	scopo *m*	—
finally¹ (E)	schließlich	—	finalement	finalmente	finalmente
finally² (E)	zuletzt	—	finalement	infine	por último
finalmente¹ (Es)	endlich	at last	enfin	finalmente	—
finalmente² (Es)	schließlich	finally	finalement	finalmente	—
finalmente¹ (I)	endlich	at last	enfin	—	finalmente
finalmente² (I)	schließlich	finally	finalement	—	finalmente
finché (I)	solange	as long	tant que	—	en tanto que
find (E)	finden	—	trouver	trovare	encontrar
finden (D)	—	find	trouver	trovare	encontrar
fin de semana (Es)	Wochenende *n*	weekend	week-end *m*	fine settimana *m*	—
find one's way (E)	zurechtfinden, sich	—	retrouver, se	orientarsi	orientarse
fin dove (I)	soweit	as far as	autant que	—	hasta tanto
fine (E)	fein	—	fin(e)	sottile	fino(a)
fine¹ (I)	Ende *n*	end	fin *f*	—	fin *m*
fine² (I)	Schluß *m*	end	fin *f*	—	conclusión *f*
fine settimana (I)	Wochenende *n*	weekend	week-end *m*	—	fin de semana *m*
finestra (I)	Fenster *n*	window	fenêtre *f*	—	ventana *f*
Finger (D)	—	finger	doigt *m*	dito *m*	dedo *m*
finger (E)	Finger *m*	—	doigt *m*	dito *m*	dedo *m*
finir (F)	enden	end	—	finire	acabar
finir de payer (F)	abbezahlen	pay off	—	saldare	saldar
finire (I)	enden	end	finir	—	acabar
fino (Es)	fein	fine	fin(e)	sottile	—
fino a (I)	bis	until	jusqu'à	—	hasta
finora (I)	bisher	so far	jusqu'à présent	—	hasta ahora
finster (D)	—	dark	sombre	buio(a)	oscuro(a)
Finsternis (D)	—	darkness	obscurité *f*	buio *m*	oscuridad *f*
fiore (I)	Blume *f*	flower	fleur *f*	—	flor *f*
fiorire (I)	blühen	bloom	fleurir	—	florecer
fire¹ (E)	Brand *m*	—	incendie *m*	incendio *m*	incendio *m*

	D	E	F	I	Es
fire² (E)	Feuer n	—	feu m	fuoco m	fuego m
fire brigade (E)	Feuerwehr f	—	sapeurs pompiers m pl	vigili del fuoco m pl	cuerpo de bomberos m
fireworks (E)	Feuerwerk n	—	feu d'artifice m	fuoco d'artificio m	fuegos artificiales m pl
Firma (D)	—	company	firme f	ditta f	empresa f
firma (Es)	Unterschrift f	signature	signature f	firma f	—
firma (I)	Unterschrift f	signature	signature f	—	firma f
firmar (Es)	unterschreiben	sign	signer	firmare	—
firmare (I)	unterschreiben	sign	signer	—	firmar
firme (Es)	fest	solid	solide	solido(a)	—
firme (F)	Firma f	company	---	ditta f	empresa f
first¹ (E)	erst	—	d'abord	dapprima	primero
first² (E)	erste(r,s)	—	premier(-ière)	primo(a)	primero(a)
first of all (E)	zunächst	—	pour l'instant	dapprima	en primer lugar
Fisch (D)	—	fish	poisson m	pesce m	pez m
fischen (D)	—	fish	pêcher	pescare	pescar
Fischer (D)	—	fisher	pêcheur m	pescatore m	pescador m
fischietto (I)	Pfeife f	whistle	sifflet m	—	silbato m
fish¹ (E)	fischen	—	pêcher	pescare	pescar
fish² (E)	Fisch m	—	poisson m	pesce m	pez m
fish³ (E)	angeln	—	pêcher	pescare	pescar con caña
fisher (E)	Fischer m	—	pêcheur m	pescatore m	pescador m
fissare¹ (I)	anbringen	fasten	fixer	—	colocar
fissare² (I)	befestigen	fasten	fixer	—	sujetar
fissare³ (I)	vereinbaren	agree upon	convenir de	—	convenir
fisso (I)	ständig	permanent	permanent(e)	—	permanente
fist (E)	Faust f	—	poing m	pugno m	puño m
fit out (E)	einrichten	—	aménager	arredare	equipar
fiume (I)	Fluß m	river	fleuve m	—	rio m
five (E)	fünf	—	cinq	cinque	cinco
fix (E)	festsetzen	—	fixer	stabilire	fijar
fixer¹ (F)	anbringen	fasten	—	fissare	colocar
fixer² (F)	befestigen	fasten	—	fissare	sujetar
fixer³ (F)	festsetzen	fix	—	stabilire	fijar
flach (D)	—	flat	plat(e)	piatto(a)	llano(a)
Fläche (D)	—	area	surface f	area f	área f
flag¹ (E)	Fahne f	—	drapeau m	bandiera f	bandera f
flag² (E)	Flagge f	—	pavillon m	bandiera f	bandera f
Flagge (D)	—	flag	pavillon m	bandiera f	bandera f
flame (E)	Flamme f	—	flamme f	fiamma f	llama f
Flamme (D)	—	flame	flamme f	fiamma f	llama f
flamme (F)	Flamme f	flame	—	fiamma f	llama f
flan (Es)	Pudding m	pudding	flan m	budino m	—
flan (F)	Pudding m	pudding	—	budino m	flan m
flâner (F)	bummeln	stroll	—	girellare	callejear
flaque (F)	Pfütze f	puddle	—	pozzanghera f	charco m
Flasche (D)	—	bottle	bouteille f	bottiglia f	botella f

	D	E	F	I	Es
Flaschenöffner (D)	—	bottle opener	ouvre-bouteilles *m*	apribottiglie *m*	abrebotellas *m*
flash (E)	blinken	—	clignoter	lampeggiare	emitir reflejos
flat[1] (E)	flach	—	plat(e)	piatto(a)	llano(a)
flat[2] (E)	Wohnung *f*	—	appartement *m*	abitazione *f*	piso *m*
flauta (Es)	Flöte *f*	flute	flûte *f*	flauto *m*	—
flauto (I)	Flöte *f*	flute	flûte *f*	—	flauta *f*
flea (E)	Floh *m*	—	puce *f*	pulce *f*	pulga *f*
fleamarket (E)	Flohmarkt *m*	—	marché aux puces *m*	mercato delle pulci *m*	rastro *m*
flecha (Es)	Pfeil *m*	arrow	flèche *f*	freccia *f*	—
flèche (F)	Pfeil *m*	arrow	—	freccia *f*	flecha *f*
Fleck (D)	—	stain	tache *f*	macchia *f*	mancha *f*
Fleisch (D)	—	meat	viande *f*	carne *f*	carne *f*
fleißig (D)	—	diligent	travailleur(-euse)	diligente	activo(a)
fleur (F)	Blume *f*	flower	—	fiore *m*	flor *f*
fleurir (F)	blühen	bloom	—	fiorire	florecer
fleuve (F)	Fluß *m*	river	—	fiume *m*	rio *m*
Fliege (D)	—	fly	mouche *f*	mosca *f*	mosca *f*
fliegen (D)	—	fly	voler	volare	volar
fließen (D)	—	flow	couler	scorrere	correr
flight[1] (E)	Flug *m*	—	vol *m*	volo *m*	vuelo *m*
flight[2] (E)	Flucht *f*	—	fuite *f*	fuga *f*	fuga *f*
Flitterwochen (D)	—	honeymoon	lune de miel *f*	luna di miele *f*	luna de miel *f*
Floh (D)	—	flea	puce *f*	pulce *f*	pulga *f*
Flohmarkt (D)	—	fleamarket	marché aux puces *m*	mercato delle pulci *m*	rastro *m*
flojo (Es)	locker	loose	desserré(e)	lento(a)	—
flood (E)	Überschwemmung *f*	—	inondation *f*	inondazione *f*	inundación *f*
floor[1] (E)	Boden *m*	—	terre *f*	terra *f*	suelo *m*
floor[2] (E)	Etage *f*	—	étage *m*	piano *m*	piso *m*
floor[3] (E)	Fußboden *m*	—	sol *m*	pavimento *m*	suelo *m*
flor (Es)	Blume *f*	flower	fleur *f*	fiore *m*	—
florecer (Es)	blühen	bloom	fleurir	fiorire	—
florero (Es)	Vase *f*	vase	vase *m*	vaso *m*	—
Flöte (D)	—	flute	flûte *f*	flauto *m*	flauta *f*
flour (E)	Mehl *n*	—	farine *f*	farina *f*	harina *f*
flow (E)	fließen	—	couler	scorrere	correr
flower (E)	Blume *f*	—	fleur *f*	fiore *m*	flor *f*
flu (E)	Grippe *f*	—	grippe *f*	influenza *f*	gripe *f*
Flucht (D)	—	flight	fuite *f*	fuga *f*	fuga *f*
Flug (D)	—	flight	vol *m*	volo *m*	vuelo *m*
Flügel (D)	—	wing	aile *f*	ala *f*	ala *f*
Flughafen (D)	—	airport	aéroport *m*	aeroporto *m*	aeropuerto *m*
Flugzeug (D)	—	aeroplane	avion *m*	aereo *m*	avión *m*
fluid (E)	flüssig	—	liquide	liquido(a)	liquido(a)
Flur (D)	—	hall	entrée *f*	corridoio *m*	corredor *m*
Fluß (D)	—	river	fleuve *m*	fiume *m*	rio *m*
flüssig (D)	—	fluid	liquide	liquido(a)	líquido(a)

	D	E	F	I	Es
flüstern (D)	—	whisper	chuchoter	bisbigliare	cuchichear
Flut (D)	—	high tide	marée haute f	alta marea f	marea alta f
flute (E)	Flöte f	—	flûte f	flauto m	flauta f
flûte (F)	Flöte f	flute	—	flauto m	flauta f
fly[1] (E)	fliegen	—	voler	volare	volar
fly[2] (E)	Fliege f	—	mouche f	mosca f	mosca f
foam (E)	Schaum m	—	écume f	schiuma f	espuma f
foca (Es)	Robbe f	seal	phoque m	foca f	—
foca (I)	Robbe f	seal	phoque m	—	foca f
fog (E)	Nebel m	—	brouillard m	nebbia f	niebla f
foglia (I)	Blatt n	leaf	feuille f	—	hoja f
foie (F)	Leber f	liver	—	fegato m	hígado m
foire[1] (F)	Jahrmarkt m	fair	—	fiera f	feria f
foire[2] (F)	Messe f	fair	—	fiera f	feria f
folder (E)	Mappe f	—	serviette f	raccoglitore m	carpeta f
Folge (D)	—	consequence	suite f	conseguenza f	serie f
folgen (D)	—	follow	suivre	seguire	seguir
folgend (D)	—	following	suivant(e)	seguente	siguiente
folla (I)	Menschen-menge f	crowd	foule f	—	muchedumbre f
follow (E)	folgen	—	suivre	seguire	seguir
following (E)	folgend	—	suivant(e)	seguente	siguiente
fonctionnaire (F)	Beamter m	civil servant	—	impiegato statale m	funcionario m
fonctionner (F)	funktionieren	work	—	funzionare	funcionar
fondare (I)	gründen	found	fonder	—	fundar
fonder (F)	gründen	found	—	fondare	fundar
fondre (F)	tauen	thaw	—	sciogliersi	deshelar
fontaine (F)	Brunnen m	fountain	—	fontana f	fuente f
fontana (I)	Brunnen m	fountain	fontaine f	—	fuente f
food[1] (E)	Essen n	—	repas m	alimentazione f	comida f
food[2] (E)	Kost f	—	nourriture f	cibo m	alimento m
food[3] (E)	Lebensmittel n	—	alimentation f	alimentari m pl	alimentos m pl
food[4] (E)	Nahrung f	—	nourriture f	alimentazione f	nutrición f
food[5] (E)	Speise f	—	aliment m	cibo m	comida f
fool (E)	Narr m	—	fou m	pazzo m	loco m
foolish (E)	albern	—	sot(te)	sciocco(a)	tonto(a)
foot (E)	Fuß m	—	pied m	piede m	pie m
football (E)	Fußball m	—	football m	pallone m	fútbol m
football (F)	Fußball m	football	—	pallone m	fútbol m
for[1] (E)	für	—	pour	per	por/para
for[2] (E)	denn	—	car	perché	pues/porque
forbici (I)	Schere f	pair of scissors	ciseaux m pl	—	tijeras f pl
forbid[1] (E)	untersagen	—	interdire qch à qn	proibire	prohibir
forbid[2] (E)	verbieten	—	défendre	proibire	prohibir
forbidden (E)	verboten	—	interdit(e)	vietato(a)	prohibido(a)
force[1] (E)	Gewalt f	—	force f	forza f	poder m
force[2] (E)	zwingen	—	forcer	costringere	obligar
force[1] (F)	Gewalt f	force	—	forza f	poder m

	D	E	F	I	Es
force² (F)	Kraft f	strength	—	forza f	fuerza f
forcer¹ (F)	erzwingen	obtain by force	—	ottenere con la forza	forzar
forcer² (F)	zwingen	force	—	costringere	obligar
forchetta (I)	Gabel f	fork	fourchette f	—	tenedor m
fordern (D)	—	demand	exiger	esigere	exigir
Forderung (D)	—	demand	exigence f	esigenza f	exigencia f
forehead (E)	Stirn f	—	front m	fronte f	frente f
foreign¹ (E)	ausländisch	—	étranger(-ère)	straniero(a)	extranjero(a)
foreign² (E)	fremd	—	étranger(-ère)	estraneo(a)	extranjero(a)
foreigner¹ (E)	Ausländer m	—	étranger m	straniero m	extranjero m
foreigner² (E)	Fremder m	—	étranger m	straniero m	extranjero m
foreign language (E)	Fremdsprache f	—	langue étrangère f	lingua straniera f	idioma extranjero m
Forelle (D)	—	trout	truite f	trota f	trucha f
forest¹ (E)	Forst m	—	forêt f	foresta f	bosque m
forest² (E)	Wald m	—	forêt f	bosco m	bosque m
foresta (I)	Forst m	forest	forêt f	—	bosque m
forêt¹ (F)	Forst m	forest	—	foresta f	bosque m
forêt² (F)	Wald m	forest	—	bosco m	bosque m
forget (E)	vergessen	—	oublier	dimenticare	olvidar
forgive (E)	verzeihen	—	pardonner	perdonare	perdonar
forgiveness (E)	Verzeihung f	—	pardon m	perdono m	perdón m
forgo (E)	verzichten	—	renoncer	rinunciare	renunciar
for it (E)	dafür	—	pour cela	per questo	para ello
fork (E)	Gabel f	—	fourchette f	forchetta f	tenedor m
Form (D)	—	form	forme f	forma f	forma f
form¹ (E)	bilden	—	former	formare	formar
form² (E)	Formular n	—	formulaire m	modulo m	formulario m
form³ (E)	Form f	—	forme f	forma f	forma f
forma (Es)	Form f	form	forme f	forma f	—
forma (I)	Form f	form	forme f	—	forma f
formación¹ (Es)	Ausbildung f	education	formation f	addestramento m	—
formación² (Es)	Bildung f	formation	formation f	formazione f	—
formaggio (I)	Käse m	cheese	fromage m	—	queso m
formal (E)	formell	—	formel(le)	formale	formal
formal (Es)	formell	formal	formel(le)	formale	—
formale (I)	formell	formal	formel(le)	—	formal
formar (Es)	bilden	form	former	formare	—
formare (I)	bilden	form	former	—	formar
formation (E)	Bildung f	—	formation f	formazione f	formación f
formation¹ (F)	Ausbildung f	education	—	addestramento m	formación f
formation² (F)	Bildung f	formation	—	formazione f	formación f
formazione (I)	Bildung f	formation	formation f	—	formación f
forme (F)	Form f	form	—	forma f	forma f
formel (F)	formell	formal	—	formale	formal
formell (D)	—	formal	formel(le)	formale	formal
former¹ (F)	ausbilden	educate	—	addestrare	instruir
former² (F)	bilden	form	—	formare	formar

	D	E	F	I	Es
formidable (Es)	gewaltig	tremendous	énorme	enorme	—
formidable (F)	großartig	magnificent	—	grandioso(a)	magnífico(a)
formulaire (F)	Formular n	form	—	modulo m	formulario m
Formular (D)	—	form	formulaire m	modulo m	formulario m
formulario (Es)	Formular n	form	formulaire m	modulo m	—
fornire (I)	liefern	deliver	fournir	—	suministrar
fornitura (I)	Lieferung f	delivery	livraison f	—	suministro m
for nothing (E)	umsonst	—	en vain	per niente	en vano
forschen (D)	—	research	rechercher	ricercare	investigar
forse (I)	vielleicht	maybe	peut-être	—	tal vez
Forst (D)	—	forest	forêt f	foresta f	bosque m
fort (D)	—	away	parti	via	lejos
fort[1] (F)	kräftig	strong	—	forte	fuerte
fort[2] (F)	laut	loud	—	rumoroso(a)	fuerte
fort[3] (F)	stark	strong	—	forte	fuerte
fortaleza (Es)	Burg f	fortress	château fort m	rocca f	—
forte[1] (I)	kräftig	strong	fort(e)	—	fuerte
forte[2] (I)	stark	strong	fort(e)	—	fuerte
forth (E)	hervor	—	au-dehors	fuori	delante
fortress (E)	Burg f	—	château fort m	rocca f	fortaleza f
Fortschritt (D)	—	progress	progrès m	progresso m	progreso m
fortsetzen (D)	—	continue	continuer	continuare	proseguir
fortuna (I)	Glück n	luck	chance f	—	suerte f
forty (E)	vierzig	—	quarante	quaranta	cuarenta
forward (E)	vorwärts	—	en avant	avanti	adelante
for your sake (E)	deinetwegen	—	pour toi	per te	por ti
forza[1] (I)	Gewalt f	force	force f	—	poder m
forza[2] (I)	Kraft f	strength	force f	—	fuerza f
forza[3] (I)	Stärke f	strength	puissance f	—	fuerza f
forzar (Es)	erzwingen	obtain by force	forcer	ottenere con la forza	—
Foto (D)	—	photo	photo f	foto f	foto f
foto (Es)	Foto n	photo	photo f	foto f	—
foto (I)	Foto n	photo	photo f	—	foto f
Fotoapparat (D)	—	camera	appareil photo m	macchina fotografica f	máquina fotográfica f
fotocopia (Es)	Fotokopie f	photocopy	photocopie f	fotocopia f	—
fotocopia (I)	Fotokopie f	photocopy	photocopie f	—	fotocopia f
fotografare[1] (I)	aufnehmen	photograph	photographier	—	fotografiar
fotografare[2] (I)	fotografieren	take pictures	photographier	—	fotografiar
fotografía (Es)	Aufnahme f	photograph	photographie f	fotografia f	—
fotografia (I)	Aufnahme f	photograph	photographie f	—	fotografía f
fotografiar[1] (Es)	aufnehmen	photograph	photographier	fotografare	—
fotografiar[2] (Es)	fotografieren	take pictures	photographier	fotografare	—
fotografieren (D)	—	take pictures	photographier	fotografare	fotografiar
Fotokopie (D)	—	photocopy	photocopie f	fotocopia f	fotocopia f
fou[1] (F)	Narr m	fool	—	pazzo m	loco m
fou[2] (F)	verrückt	mad	—	pazzo(a)	loco(a)
fouiller (F)	wühlen	scrabble	—	rovistare	revolver

	D	E	F	I	Es
foule (F)	Menschen-menge f	crowd	—	folla f	muchedumbre f
found (E)	gründen	—	fonder	fondare	fundar
fountain (E)	Brunnen m	—	fontaine f	fontana f	fuente f
fountain pen (E)	Füller m	—	stylo m	penna stilografica f	pluma f
four (E)	vier	—	quatre	quattro	cuatro
fourchette (F)	Gabel f	fork	—	forchetta f	tenedor m
fourneau (F)	Herd m	cooker	—	cucina f	cocina f
fournir en (F)	versorgen	provide	—	approvvigionare	proveer
fourrure (F)	Pelz m	fur	—	pelliccia f	piel f
fourteen (E)	vierzehn	—	quatorze	quattordici	catorce
fox (E)	Fuchs m	—	renard m	volpe f	zorro m
fracaso[1] (Es)	Mißerfolg m	failure	échec m	insuccesso m	—
fracaso[2] (Es)	Niete f	blank	mauvais numéro m	biglietto non vincente m	—
Frage (D)	—	question	question f	domanda f	pregunta f
fragen (D)	—	ask	demander	domandare	preguntar
frágil (Es)	zerbrechlich	fragile	fragile	fragile	—
fragile (E)	zerbrechlich	—	fragile	fragile	frágil
fragile (F)	zerbrechlich	fragile	—	fragile	frágil
fragile (I)	zerbrechlich	fragile	fragile	—	frágil
fragola (I)	Erdbeere f	strawberry	fraise f	—	fresa f
frais[1] (F)	frisch	fresh	—	fresco(a)	fresco(a)
frais[2] (F)	Spesen pl	expenses	—	spese f pl	gastos m pl
frais[3] (F)	Unkosten pl	expenses	—	spese f pl	gastos m pl
frais[4] (F)	kühl	cool	—	fresco(a)	fresco(a)
fraise (F)	Erdbeere f	strawberry	—	fragola f	fresa f
framboise (F)	Himbeere f	raspberry	—	lampone m	frambuesa f
frambuesa (Es)	Himbeere f	raspberry	framboise f	lampone m	—
frame (E)	Rahmen m	—	cadre m	cornice f	marco m
français (F)	französisch	French	—	francese	francés(-esa)
Français (F)	Franzose m	Frenchman	—	francese	francés m
France (E)	Frankreich n	—	France f	Francia f	Francia f
France (F)	Frankreich n	France	—	Francia f	Francia f
francés[1] (Es)	Franzose m	Frenchman	Français	francese m	—
francés[2] (Es)	französisch	French	français(e)	francese	—
francese[1] (I)	französisch	French	français(e)	—	francés(-esa)
francese[2] (I)	Franzose m	Frenchman	Français	—	francés m
Francia (Es)	Frankreich n	France	France f	Francia f	—
Francia (I)	Frankreich n	France	France f	—	Francia f
francobollo (I)	Briefmarke f	stamp	timbre m	—	sello m
frankieren (D)	—	stamp	affranchir	affrancare	franquear
Frankreich (D)	—	France	France f	Francia f	Francia f
franquear (Es)	frankieren	stamp	affranchir	affrancare	—
franqueo (Es)	Porto n	postage	port m	affrancatura f	—
Franzose (D)	—	Frenchman	Français	francese m	francés m
französisch (D)	—	French	français(e)	francese	francés(-esa)
frapper[1] (F)	klopfen	knock	—	bussare	golpear
frapper[2] (F)	pochen	knock	—	battere	golpear

	D	E	F	I	Es
frase (I)	Satz *m*	sentence	phrase *f*	—	oración *f*
fratelli (I)	Geschwister *pl*	brothers and sisters	frère(s) et sœur(s) *pl*	—	hermanos *m pl*
fratello (I)	Bruder *m*	brother	frère *m*	—	hermano *m*
frattanto (I)	inzwischen	meanwhile	entretemps	—	mientras tanto
Frau (D)	—	woman	femme *f*	donna *f*	mujer *f*
fraud (E)	Betrug *m*	—	tromperie *f*	inganno *m*	engaño *m*
Fräulein (D)	—	Miss	mademoiselle *f*	signorina *f*	señorita *f*
freccia (I)	Pfeil *m*	arrow	flèche *f*	—	flecha *f*
frech (D)	—	cheeky	insolent(e)	sfacciato(a)	atrevido(a)
frecuente (Es)	häufig	frequent	fréquent(e)	frequente	—
freddo (I)	kalt	cold	froid(e)	—	frío(a)
free[1] (E)	frei	—	libre	libero(a)	libre
free[2] (E)	kostenlos	—	gratuit(e)	gratuito(a)	gratis
free[3] (E)	losbinden	—	délier	sciogliere	desatar
freedom (E)	Freiheit *f*	—	liberté *f*	libertà *f*	libertad *f*
free of charge (E)	gratis	—	gratuit(e)	gratuito(a)	gratis
free time (E)	Freizeit *f*	—	loisirs *m pl*	tempo libero	tiempo libre *m*
freezer (E)	Eisschrank *m*	—	réfrigérateur *m*	frigorifero *m*	refrigerador *m*
freeze to death (E)	erfrieren	—	mourir de froid	morire di freddo	morirse de frío
fregar (Es)	wischen	wipe	essuyer	pulire	—
frei (D)	—	free	libre	libero(a)	libre
Freibad (D)	—	open-air swimming pool	piscine en plein air *f*	piscina all'aperto *f*	piscina al aire libre *f*
Freiheit (D)	—	freedom	liberté *f*	libertà *f*	libertad *f*
freilassen (D)	—	release	libérer	mettere in libertà	poner en libertad
frein (F)	Bremse *f*	brake	—	freno *m*	freno *m*
freiner (F)	bremsen	brake	—	frenare	frenar
Freitag (D)	—	Friday	vendredi *m*	venerdì *m*	viernes *m*
freiwillig (D)	—	voluntary	volontaire	volontario(a)	voluntario(a)
Freizeit (D)	—	free time	loisirs *m pl*	tempo libero	tiempo libre *m*
fremd (D)	—	foreign	étranger(-ère)	estraneo(a)	extranjero(a)
Fremder (D)	—	foreigner	étranger(-ère) *m(f)*	straniero *m*	extranjero *m*
Fremdsprache (D)	—	foreign-language	langue étrangère *f*	lingua straniera *f*	idioma extranjero *m*
frenar (Es)	bremsen	brake	freiner	frenare	—
frenare (I)	bremsen	brake	freiner	—	frenar
French (E)	französisch	—	français(e)	francese	francés(-esa)
french fries (E)	Pommes frites *pl*	—	frites *f pl*	patate fritte *f pl*	patatas fritas *f pl*
Frenchman (E)	Franzose *m*	—	Français	francese *m*	francés *m*
freno (Es)	Bremse *f*	brake	frein *m*	freno *m*	—
freno (I)	Bremse *f*	brake	frein *m*	—	freno *m*
frente (Es)	Stirn *f*	forehead	front *m*	fronte *f*	—
frequent (E)	häufig	—	fréquent(e)	frequente	frecuente
fréquent (F)	häufig	frequent	—	frequente	frecuente
frequente (I)	häufig	frequent	fréquent(e)	—	frecuente
frère (F)	Bruder *m*	brother	—	fratello *m*	hermano *m*
frère(s) et sœur(s) (F)	Geschwister *pl*	brothers and sisters	—	fratelli *m pl*	hermanos *m pl*

	D	E	F	I	Es
fresa (Es)	Erdbeere f	strawberry	fraise f	fragola f	—
fresco¹ (I)	frisch	fresh	frais(fraîche)	—	fresco(a)
fresco² (I)	kühl	cool	frais(fraîche)	—	fresco(a)
fresco¹ (Es)	frisch	fresh	frais(fraîche)	fresco(a)	—
fresco² (Es)	kühl	cool	frais(fraîche)	fresco(a)	—
fresh (E)	frisch	—	frais(fraîche)	fresco(a)	fresco(a)
fressen (D)	—	eat	bouffer	mangiare	devorar
fretta (I)	Eile f	haste	hâte f	—	prisa f
frettoloso (I)	eilig	hurried	pressé(e)	—	rápido(a)
Freude (D)	—	joy	joie f	gioia f	alegría f
freuen, sich (D)	—	be glad	être heureux(-euse)	rallegrarsi	alegrarse
Freund (D)	—	friend	ami m	amico m	amigo m
freundlich (D)	—	friendly	aimable	gentile	amistoso(a)
Freundschaft (D)	—	friendship	amitié f	amicizia f	amistad f
Friday (E)	Freitag m	—	vendredi m	venerdì m	viernes m
fridge (E)	Kühlschrank m	—	réfrigérateur m	frigorifero m	nevera f
fried (E)	gebraten	—	rôti(e)	arrostito(a)	asado(a)
Friede (D)	—	peace	paix f	pace f	paz f
Friedhof (D)	—	cemetery	cimetière m	cimitero m	cementerio m
friedlich (D)	—	peaceful	paisible	pacifico(a)	pacifico(a)
friend (E)	Freund m	—	ami m	amico m	amigo m
friendly¹ (E)	befreundet	—	ami(e) de	amico(a)	amigo(a) de
friendly² (E)	freundlich	—	aimable	gentile	amistoso(a)
friendship (E)	Freundschaft f	—	amitié f	amicizia f	amistad f
frieren (D)	—	be cold	avoir froid	avere freddo	tener frío
frighten (E)	erschrecken	—	effrayer	spaventare	asustar
frigorifero¹ (I)	Eisschrank m	freezer	réfrigérateur m	—	refrigerador m
frigorifero² (I)	Kühlschrank m	fridge	réfrigérateur m	—	nevera f
frío (Es)	kalt	cold	froid(e)	freddo(a)	—
frisch (D)	—	fresh	frais(fraîche)	fresco(a)	fresco(a)
Friseur (D)	—	hairdresser	coiffeur m	parrucchiere m	peluquero m
Frisur (D)	—	hairstyle	coiffure f	pettinatura f	peinado m
frites (F)	Pommes frites pl	french fries	—	patate fritte f pl	patatas fritas f pl
frittata (I)	Omelett n	omelette	omelette f	—	tortilla f
frog (E)	Frosch m	—	grenouille f	rana f	rana f
froh (D)	—	glad	content(e)	lieto(a)	contento(a)
froid (F)	kalt	cold	—	freddo(a)	frío(a)
from (E)	von	—	de	di/da	de
fromage (F)	Käse m	cheese	—	formaggio m	queso m
fromage blanc (F)	Quark m	curd cheese	—	ricotta f	requesón m
fromm (D)	—	pious	pieux(-euse)	devoto(a)	religioso(a)
front (F)	Stirn f	forehead	—	fronte f	frente f
fronte (I)	Stirn f	forehead	front m	—	frente f
frontera (Es)	Grenze f	frontier	frontière f	trontiera f	—
frontier (E)	Grenze f	—	frontière f	frontiera f	frontera f
frontiera (I)	Grenze f	frontier	frontière f	—	frontera f
frontière (F)	Grenze f	frontier	—	frontiera f	frontera f

Frosch

	D	E	F	I	Es
Frosch (D)	—	frog	grenouille f	rana f	rana f
Frost (D)	—	frost	gelée f	gelo m	helada f
frost (E)	Frost m	—	gelée f	gelo m	helada f
frotar (Es)	reiben	rub	frotter	sfregare	—
frotter (F)	reiben	rub	—	sfregare	frotar
Frucht (D)	—	fruit	fruit m	frutto m	fruto m
früh (D)	—	early	tôt	presto	temprano(a)
früher (D)	—	earlier	autrefois	prima	antes
Frühjahr (D)	—	spring	printemps m	primavera f	primavera f
Frühstück (D)	—	breakfast	petit-déjeuner m	colazione f	desayuno m
fruit¹ (E)	Frucht f	—	fruit m	frutto m	fruto m
fruit² (E)	Obst n	—	fruits m pl	frutta f	fruta f
fruit (F)	Frucht f	fruit	—	frutto m	fruto m
fruits (F)	Obst n	fruit	—	frutta f	fruta f
fruta (Es)	Obst n	fruit	fruits m pl	frutta f	—
frumento (I)	Weizen m	wheat	blé m	—	trigo m
fruto (Es)	Frucht f	fruit	fruit m	frutto m	—
frutta (I)	Obst n	fruit	fruits m pl	—	fruta f
frutto (I)	Frucht f	fruit	fruit m	—	fruto m
Fuchs (D)	—	fox	renard m	volpe f	zorro m
fuego (Es)	Feuer n	fire	feu m	fuoco m	—
fuegos artificiales (Es)	Feuerwerk n	fireworks	feu d'artifice m	fuoco d'artificio m	—
fuel (E)	Heizöl n	—	mazout m	olio combustibile m	combustible para la calefacción m
fuente¹ (Es)	Brunnen m	well	fontaine f	fontana f	
fuente² (Es)	Quelle f	spring	source f	sorgente f	—
fuente³ (Es)	Schüssel m	bowl	jatte f	scodella f	—
fuera¹ (Es)	auswärts	outwards	à l'extérieur	fuori	—
fuera² (Es)	weg	away	pas là	via	—
fuera de (Es)	außerhalb	out of	hors de	fuori di	—
fuerte¹ (Es)	heftig	fierce	violent(e)	violento(a)	—
fuerte² (Es)	kräftig	strong	fort(e)	forte	—
fuerte³ (Es)	laut	loud	fort(e)	rumoroso(a)	—
fuerte⁴ (Es)	stark	strong	fort(e)	forte	—
fuerza¹ (Es)	Kraft f	strength	force f	forza f	—
fuerza² (Es)	Stärke f	strength	puissance f	forza f	—
fuga (Es)	Flucht f	flight	fuite f	fuga f	—
fuga (I)	Flucht f	flight	fuite f	—	fuga f
fühlen (D)	—	feel	sentir	sentire	sentir
führen (D)	—	lead	guider	guidare	dirigir
Führer (D)	—	leader	guide m	guida f	guía m
Führerschein (D)	—	driving licence	permis de conduire m	patente f	permiso de conducir m
Führung (D)	—	guided tour	visite guidée f	visita guidata f	visita guiada f
fuite (F)	Flucht f	flight	—	fuga f	fuga f
fulfil (E)	erfüllen	—	remplir	esaudire	conceder
full¹ (E)	satt	—	rassasié(e)	sazio(a)	satisfecho(a)
full² (E)	voll	—	plein(e)	pieno(a)	lleno(a)

	D	E	F	I	Es
full board (E)	Vollpension *f*	—	pension complète *f*	pensione completa *f*	pensión completa *f*
füllen (D)	—	fill	remplir	riempire	llenar
Füller (D)	—	fountain pen	stylo *m*	penna stilografica *f*	pluma *f*
fully booked (E)	ausgebucht	—	complet(-ète)	esaurito(a)	completo(a)
fumador (Es)	Raucher *m*	smoker	fumeur *m*	fumatore *m*	—
fumar (Es)	rauchen	smoke	fumer	fumare	—
fumare (I)	rauchen	smoke	fumer	—	fumar
fumatore (I)	Raucher *m*	smoker	fumeur *m*	—	fumador *m*
fumée (F)	Rauch *m*	smoke	—	fumo *m*	humo *m*
fumer (F)	rauchen	smoke	—	fumare	fumar
fumeur (F)	Raucher *m*	smoker	—	fumatore *m*	fumador *m*
fumo (I)	Rauch *m*	smoke	fumée *f*	—	humo *m*
fun (E)	Spaß *m*	—	plaisir *m*	scherzo *m*	broma *f*
funcionar (Es)	funktionieren	work	fonctionner	funzionare	—
funcionario (Es)	Beamter *m*	civil servant	fonctionnaire *m*	impiegato statale *m*	—
fundamental (E)	grundsätzlich	—	par principe	basilare	por principio
fundar (Es)	gründen	found	fonder	fondare	—
Fundbüro (D)	—	lost property office	bureau des objets trouvés *m*	ufficio oggetti smarriti *m*	oficina de objetos perdidos *f*
fune (I)	Seil *n*	rope	corde *f*	—	soga *f*
funeral (E)	Beerdigung *f*	—	enterrement *m*	funerale *m*	entierro *m*
funerale (I)	Beerdigung *f*	funeral	enterrement *m*	—	entierro *m*
fünf (D)	—	five	cinq	cinque	cinco
fünfzehn (D)	—	fifteen	quinze	quindici	quince
fünfzig (D)	—	fifty	cinquante	cinquanta	cincuenta
fungo (I)	Pilz *m*	mushroom	champignon *m*	—	hongo *m*
funktionieren (D)	—	work	fonctionner	funzionare	funcionar
funny[1] (E)	komisch	—	drôle	comico(a)	cómico(a)
funny[2] (E)	lustig	—	marrant(e)	allegro(a)	divertido(a)
funzionare (I)	funktionieren	work	fonctionner	—	funcionar
fuoco (I)	Feuer *n*	fire	feu *m*	—	fuego *m*
fuoco d'artificio (I)	Feuerwerk *n*	fireworks	feu d'artifice *m*	—	fuegos artificiales *m pl*
fuori[1] (I)	auswärts	out(wards)	à l'extérieur	—	fuera
fuori[2] (I)	außen	outside	au dehors	—	afuera
fuori[3] (I)	draußen	outside	dehors	—	afuera
fuori[4] (I)	hervor	forth	au-dehors	—	delante
fuori[5] (I)	hinaus	out	dehors	—	hacia afuera
fuori[6] (I)	heraus	out	dehors	—	hacia afuera
fuori di (I)	außerhalb	out of	hors de	—	fuera de
fuori moda (I)	altmodisch	old-fashioned	démodé	—	pasado(a) de moda
für (D)	—	for	pour	per	por/para
fur (E)	Pelz *m*	—	fourrure *f*	pelliccia *f*	piel *f*
furieux (F)	wütend	furious	—	arrabbiato(a)	furioso(a)
fürchten (D)	—	fear	craindre	temere	temer
fürchterlich (D)	—	terrible	terrible	terribile	terrible
furioso (Es)	wütend	furious	furieux(-euse)	arrabbiato(a)	—

	D	E	F	I	Es
furious (E)	wütend	—	furieux(-euse)	arrabbiato(a)	furioso(a)
furnish (E)	möblieren	—	meubler	ammobiliare	amueblar
furnished (E)	möbliert	—	meublé(e)	ammobiliato(a)	amueblado(a)
furnishing (E)	Einrichtung f	—	ameublement m	arredamento m	mobiliario m
furniture (E)	Möbel n	—	meuble m	mobile m	mueble m
Fürst (D)	—	prince	prince m	principe m	príncipe m
further (E)	weiter	—	plus éloigné(e)	più ampio(a)	adelante
Fuß (D)	—	foot	pied m	piede m	pie m
Fußball (D)	—	football	football m	pallone m	fútbol m
Fußboden (D)	—	floor	sol m	pavimento m	suelo m
Fußgänger (D)	—	pedestrian	piéton m	pedone m	peatón m
fútbol (Es)	Fußball m	football	football m	pallone m	—
futé (F)	clever	clever	—	abile	listo(a)
futur (F)	zukünftig	future	—	futuro(a)	en el futuro
future[1] (E)	zukünftig	—	futur(e)	futuro(a)	en el futuro
future[2] (E)	Zukunft f	—	avenir m	futuro m	futuro m
futuro (Es)	Zukunft f	future	avenir m	futuro m	—
futuro[1] (I)	zukünftig	future	futur(e)	—	en el futuro
futuro[2] (I)	Zukunft f	future	avenir m	—	futuro m
gabbia (I)	Käfig m	cage	cage f	—	jaula f
gabbiano (I)	Möwe f	seagull	mouette f	—	gaviota f
Gabel (D)	—	fork	fourchette f	forchetta f	tenedor m
gabinetto (I)	Klosett n	lavatory	cabinets m pl	—	retrete m
gafas (Es)	Brille f	glasses	lunettes f pl	occhiali m pl	—
gafas de sol (Es)	Sonnenbrille f	sunglasses	lunettes de soleil f pl	occhiali da sole m pl	—
gage (F)	Pfand n	piedge	—	pegno m	prenda f
gagner[1] (F)	gewinnen	win	—	vincere	ganar
gagner[2] (F)	siegen	win	—	vincere	vencer
gagner[3] (F)	verdienen	earn	—	guadagnare	ganar
gain (F)	Gewinn m	profit	—	guadagno m	ganancia f
gall (E)	Galle f	—	fiel m	cistifellea f	bilis f
Galle (D)	—	gall	fiel m	cistifellea f	bilis f
galleria (I)	Tunnel m	tunnel	tunnel m	—	túnel m
galleta (Es)	Keks m	biscuit	biscuit m	biscotto m	—
gallina[1] (Es)	Henne f	hen	poule f	gallina f	—
gallina[2] (Es)	Huhn n	chicken	poule f	pollo m	—
gallina (I)	Henne f	hen	poule f	—	gallina f
gallo (Es)	Hahn m	cock	coq m	gallo m	—
gallo (I)	Hahn m	cock	coq m	—	gallo m
gamba (I)	Bein n	leg	jambe f	—	pierna f
gambero (I)	Krebs m	crayfish	écrevisse f	—	cangrejo m
game[1] (E)	Spiel n	—	jeu m	gioco m	juego m
game[2] (E)	Wild n	—	gibier m	selvaggina f	caza f
ganancia[1] (Es)	Gewinn m	profit	gain m	guadagno m	—
ganancia[2] (Es)	Verdienst m	income	revenus m pl	guadagno m	—
ganar[1] (Es)	gewinnen	win	gagner	vincere	—
ganar[2] (Es)	verdienen	earn	gagner	guadagnare	—

	D	E	F	I	Es
ganas (Es)	Lust *f*	delight	plaisir *m*	piacere *m*	—
gancho (Es)	Haken *m*	hook	crochet *m*	gancio *m*	—
gancio (I)	Haken *m*	hook	crochet *m*	—	gancho *m*
Gang¹ (D)	—	course	plat *m*	portata *f*	plato *m*
Gang² (D)	—	corridor	couloir *m*	corridoio *m*	corredor *m*
Gang³ (D)	—	gear	vitesse *f*	marcia *f*	marcha *f*
Gans (D)	—	goose	oie *f*	oca *f*	ganso *m*
ganso (Es)	Gans *f*	goose	oie *f*	oca *f*	—
gant (F)	Handschuh *m*	glove	—	guanto *m*	guante *m*
ganz (D)	—	whole	tout(e)	intero(a)	entero(a)
Ganze (D)	—	lot	le tout	insieme *m*	todo *m*
gap (E)	Lücke *f*	—	lacune *f*	lacuna *f*	espacio *m*
gar (D)	—	done	cuit(e)	cotto(a)	estar a punto
Garage (D)	—	garage	garage *m*	garage *m*	garaje *m*
garage (E)	Garage *f*	—	garage *m*	garage *m*	garaje *m*
garage (F)	Garage *f*	garage	—	garage *m*	garaje *m*
garage (I)	Garage *f*	garage	garage *m*	—	garaje *m*
garaje (Es)	Garage *f*	garage	garage *m*	garage *m*	—
garantía¹ (Es)	Garantie *f*	guarantee	garantie *f*	garanzia *f*	—
garantía² (Es)	Gewähr *f*	guarantee	garantie *f*	garanzia *f*	—
Garantie (D)	—	guarantee	garantie *f*	garanzia *f*	garantía *f*
garantie¹ (F)	Garantie *f*	guarantee	—	garanzia *f*	garantía *f*
garantie² (F)	Gewähr *f*	guarantee	—	garanzia *f*	garantía *f*
garanzia¹ (I)	Gewähr *f*	guarantee	garantie *f*	—	garantía *f*
garanzia² (I)	Garantie *f*	guarantee	garantie *f*	—	garantía *f*
garçon¹ (F)	Bursche *m*	fellow	—	ragazzo *m*	chico *m*
garçon² (F)	Junge *m*	boy	—	ragazzo *m*	chico *m*
garçon³ (F)	Kellner *m*/ Ober *m*	waiter	—	cameriere *m*	camarero *m*
garden (E)	Garten *m*	—	jardin *m*	giardino *m*	jardín *m*
gardener (E)	Gärtner *m*	—	jardinier *m*	giardiniere *m*	jardinero *m*
garder¹ (F)	aufbewahren	keep	—	conservare	guardar
garder² (F)	bewachen	guard	—	sorvegliare	vigilar
garder³ (F)	behalten	keep	—	tenere	retener
Garderobe (D)	—	wardrobe	vestiaire *m*	guardaroba *m*	guardaropa *m*
garderobe (F)	Kleiderschrank *m*	wardrobe	—	armadio *m*	armario ropero *m*
gardien¹ (F)	Aufseher *m*	guard	—	custode *m*	vigilante *m*
gardien² (F)	Wärter *m*	attendant	—	custode *m*	guarda *m*
Gardine (D)	—	curtain	rideau *m*	tenda *f*	cortina *f*
gare (F)	Bahnhof *m*	station	—	stazione *f*	estación *f*
gare centrale (F)	Hauptbahnhof *m*	central station	—	stazione centrale *f*	estación central *f*
garer (F)	parken	park	—	parcheggiare	aparcar
garganta (Es)	Rachen *m*	throat	gorge *f*	faringe *m*	—
garlic (E)	Knoblauch *m*	—	ail *m*	aglio *m*	ajo *m*
garnieren (D)		decorate	garnir	guarnire	guarnecer
garnir (F)	garnieren	decorate	—	guarnire	guarnecer
garofano (I)	Nelke *f*	carnation	œillet *m*	—	clavel *m*
Garten (D)	—	garden	jardin *m*	giardino *m*	jardín *m*

	D	E	F	I	Es
Gärtner (D)	—	gardener	jardinier *m*	giardiniere *m*	jardinero *m*
gaseosa (Es)	Limonade *f*	lemonade	limonade *f*	limonata *f*	—
gasolina (Es)	Benzin *n*	petrol	essence *f*	benzina	—
gasolinera (Es)	Tankstelle *f*	filling station	station-service *f*	distributore di benzina *m*	—
gaspiller (F)	verschwenden	waste	—	sprecare	desperdiciar
Gasse (D)	—	lane	ruelle *f*	vicolo *m*	callejón *m*
Gast (D)	—	guest	hôte *m/f*	ospite *m*	invitado *m*
gastfreundlich (D)	—	hospitable	hospitalier(-ière)	ospitale	hospitalario(a)
Gastfreund-schaft (D)	—	hospitality	hospitalité *f*	ospitalità *f*	hospitalidad *f*
Gastgeber (D)	—	host	hôte *m*	ospite *m*	anfitrión *m*
Gasthaus (D)	—	hotel	auberge *f*	osteria *m*	posada *f*
gastos[1] (Es)	Spesen *pl*	expenses	frais *m pl*	spese *f pl*	—
gastos[2] (Es)	Unkosten *pl*	expenses	frais *m pl*	spese *f pl*	—
gate (E)	Tor *n*	—	porte *f*	porta *f*	puerta *f*
gâteau[1] (F)	Kuchen *m*	cake	—	dolce *m*	pastel *m*
gâteau[2] (F)	Torte *f*	cake	—	torta *f*	tarta *f*
gâter (F)	verwöhnen	spoil	—	viziare	mimar
gato (Es)	Katze *f*	cat	chat *m*	gatto *m*	—
gatto (I)	Katze *f*	cat	chat *m*	—	gato *m*
gaviota (Es)	Möwe *f*	seagull	mouette *f*	gabbiano *m*	—
gear (E)	Gang *m*	—	vitesse *f*	marcia *f*	marcha *f*
Gebäck (D)	—	pastry	pâtisserie *f*	biscotti *m pl*	pastas *f pl*
gebären (D)	—	give birth to	mettre au monde	partorire	parir
Gebäude (D)	—	building	bâtiment *m*	edificio *m*	edificio *m*
geben (D)	—	give	donner	dare	andar
Gebet (D)	—	prayer	prière *f*	preghiera *f*	oración *f*
Gebiet (D)	—	region	région *f*	regione *f*	zona *f*
Gebirge (D)	—	mountain chain	montagne *f*	montagna *f*	montañas *f pl*
Gebiß (D)	—	teeth	dents *f pl*	denti *m pl*	dentadura *f*
geboren (D)	—	born	né(e)	nato(a)	nacido(a)
gebraten (D)	—	fried	rôti(e)	arrostito(a)	asado(a)
Gebrauch (D)	—	custom	usage *m*	uso *m*	uso *m*
gebrauchen (D)	—	use	utiliser	usare	usar
gebraucht (D)	—	used	d'occasion	usato(a)	usado(a)
Gebühr (D)	—	fee	droit *m*	tassa *f*	tarifa *f*
Geburt (D)	—	birth	naissance *f*	nascita *f*	nacimiento *m*
Geburtstag (D)	—	birthday	anniversaire *m*	compleanno *m*	cumpleaños *m*
Gedächtnis (D)	—	memory	mémoire *f*	memoria *f*	memoria *f*
Gedanke (D)	—	thought	pensée *f*	pensiero *m*	pensamiento *m*
Gedeck (D)	—	cover	couvert *m*	coperto *m*	cubierto *m*
gedenken (D)	—	remember	souvenir de, se	ricordare	conmemorar
Gedicht (D)	—	poem	poème *m*	poesia *f*	poema *m*
Geduld (D)	—	patience	patience *f*	pazienza *f*	paciencia *f*
geduldig (D)	—	patient	patient(e)	paziente	con paciencia
geeignet (D)	—	suitable	approprié(e)	adatto(a)	indicado(a)
Gefahr (D)	—	danger	danger *m*	pericolo *m*	peligro *m*
gefährlich (D)	—	dangerous	dangereux(-euse)	pericoloso(a)	peligroso(a)

	D	E	F	I	Es
gefallen (D)	—	please	plaire	piacere	gustar
Gefallen (D)	—	favour	service *m*	favore *m*	favor *m*
Gefälligkeit (D)	—	favour	obligeance *f*	favore *m*	favor *m*
Gefängnis (D)	—	prison	prison *f*	prigione *f*	cárcel *f*
Gefäß (D)	—	container	récipient *m*	recipiente *m*	recipiente *m*
Geflügel (D)	—	poultry	volaille *f*	pollame *m*	aves *f pl*
Gefühl (D)	—	feeling	sentiment *m*	sensazione *f*	sentimiento *m*
gegen (D)	—	against	contre	contro	contra
Gegend (D)	—	region	région *f*	regione *f*	región *f*
Gegenstand (D)	—	object	objet *m*	oggetto *m*	objeto *m*
Gegenteil (D)	—	opposite	contraire *m*	contrario *m*	opuesto *m*
gegenüber (D)	—	opposite	en face de	di fronte(a)	en frente
Gegenwart (D)	—	present	présent *m*	presente *m*	presente *m*
Gegner (D)	—	opponent	adversaire *m*	avversario *m*	adversario *m*
Gehalt (D)	—	salary	salaire *m*	stipendio *m*	sueldo *m*
geheim (D)	—	secret	secret(-ète)	segreto(a)	secreto(a)
Geheimnis (D)	—	secret	secret *m*	segreto *m*	secreto *m*
gehen (D)	—	go	aller	andare	andar
Gehör (D)	—	hearing	ouïe *f*	udito *m*	oreja *f*
gehorchen (D)	—	obey	obéir	ubbidire	obedecer
gehören (D)	—	belong	appartenir	appartenere	pertenecer
gehorsam (D)	—	obedient	obéissant(e)	ubbidiente	obediente
Gehweg (D)	—	pavement	trottoir *m*	marciapiede *m*	acera *f*
Geige (D)	—	violin	violon *m*	violino *m*	violín *m*
Geist (D)	—	spirit	esprit *m*	spirito *m*	espíritu *m*
geizig (D)	—	mean	avare	avaro(a)	avaro(a)
Gelächter (D)	—	laughter	rires *m pl*	risata *f*	risa *f*
gelähmt (D)	—	paralysed	paralysé(e)	paralizzato(a)	paralítico(a)
Gelände (D)	—	terrain	terrain	terreno *m*	terreno *m*
gelangen (D)	—	attain	arriver à	arrivare a	conseguir
gelato (I)	Eis *n*	ice	glace *f*	—	hielo *m*
gelb (D)	—	yellow	jaune	giallo(a)	amarillo(a)
Geld (D)	—	money	argent *m*	denaro *m*	dinero *m*
gelée (F)	Frost *m*	frost	—	gelo *m*	helada *f*
Gelegenheit (D)	—	occasion	occasion *f*	occasione *f*	oportunidad *f*
gelegentlich (D)	—	occasional	occasionnel(le)	occasionale	ocasional
gelingen (D)	—	succeed	réussir	riuscire	acertar
gelo (I)	Frost *m*	frost	gelée *f*	—	helada *f*
gelosia (I)	Eifersucht *f*	jealousy	jalousie *f*	—	celos *m pl*
gelten (D)	—	be worth	valoir	valere	valer
Gemälde (D)	—	painting	tableau *m*	quadro *m*	cuadro *m*
gemein (D)	—	mean	méchant(e)	volgare	vulgar
gemeinsam (D)	—	together	ensemble	comune	juntos(as)
gemelli (I)	Zwillinge *pl*	twins	jumeaux *m pl*	—	gemelos *m pl*
gemelos[1] (Es)	Fernglas *n*	binoculars	jumelles *f pl*	cannocchiale *m*	—

	D	E	F	I	Es
gemelos² (Es)	Zwillinge pl	twins	jumeaux m pl	gemelli m pl	—
Gemüse (D)	—	vegetables	légumes m pl	verdura f	legumbres f pl
Gemüt (D)	—	disposition	disposition f	animo m	ánimo m
gemütlich (D)	—	comfortable	agréable	comodo(a)	cómodo(a)
gênant (F)	peinlich	embarrassing	—	imbarazzante	desagradable
genau (D)	—	exact	exact(e)	preciso(a)	exacto(a)
Genauigkeit (D)	—	accuracy	exactitude f	precisione f	exactitud f
gêne (F)	Verlegenheit f	embarrassment	—	imbarazzo m	contratiempo m
genehmigen (D)	—	approve	autoriser	approvare	permitir
Genehmigung (D)	—	authorization	autorisation f	permesso m	permiso m
General (D)	—	General	général m	generale m	general m
general (E)	allgemein	—	général(e)	generale	general
General (E)	General m	—	général m	generale m	general m
general¹ (Es)	allgemein	general	général(e)	generale	—
general² (Es)	General m	General	général m	generale m	—
général¹ (F)	General m	General	—	generale m	general m
général² (F)	allgemein	general	—	generale	general
generale¹ (I)	allgemein	general	général(e)	—	general
generale² (I)	General m	General	général m	—	general m
généralement (F)	meistens	generally	—	di solito	por lo común
generally (E)	meistens	—	généralement	di solito	por lo común
généreux (F)	großzügig	generous	—	generoso(a)	generoso(a)
generoso (I)	großzügig	generous	généreux(-euse)	—	generoso(a)
generoso (Es)	großzügig	generous	généreux(-euse)	generoso(a)	—
generous (E)	großzügig	—	généreux(-euse)	generoso(a)	generoso(a)
genießen (D)	—	enjoy	jouir	godere	disfrutar
genitori (I)	Eltern pl	parents	parents m pl	—	padres m pl
gennaio (I)	Januar m	January	janvier m	—	enero m
Genosse (D)	—	comrade	camarade m	compagno m	camarada m
genou (F)	Knie n	knee	—	ginocchio m	rodilla f
gens (F)	Leute f	people	—	gente f	gente f
gente (Es)	Leute f	people	gens m pl	gente f	—
gente (I)	Leute f	people	gens m pl	—	gente f
gentil (Es)	liebenswürdig	kind	aimable	gentile	—
gentil¹ (F)	lieb	sweet	—	caro(a)	amable
gentil² (F)	brav	good	—	bravo(a)	bueno(a)
gentile¹ (I)	freundlich	friendly	aimable	—	amistoso(a)
gentile² (I)	liebenswürdig	kind	aimable	—	gentil
gentle (E)	sanft	—	doux(douce)	dolce	dulce
gentleman (E)	Herr m	—	monsieur m	signore m	señor m
genug (D)	—	enough	assez	abbastanza	bastante
genügen (D)	—	suffice	suffire	bastare	bastar
genuine (E)	echt	—	vrai(e)	vero(a)	verdadero(a)
Genuß (D)	—	pleasure	plaisir m	piacere m	deleite m

	D	E	F	I	Es
geöffnet (D)	—	open	ouvert(e)	aperto(a)	abierto(a)
Gepäck (D)	—	luggage	bagages *m pl*	bagaglio *m*	equipaje *m*
Gepäckannahme (D)	—	luggage desk	enregistrement des bagages *m*	accettazione bagagli *f*	recepción de equipajes *f*
gepflegt (D)	—	looked-after	soigné(e)	curato(a)	cuidado(a)
gerade[1] (D)	—	even	pair(e)	pari	par
gerade[2] (D)	—	straight	droit(e)	diritto(a)	derecho(a)
geradeaus (D)	—	straight ahead	tout droit	dritto	todo derecho
gérant (F)	Geschäftsführer *m*	manager	—	gerente *m*	gerente *m*
Gerät (D)	—	appliance	appareil *m*	apparecchio *m*	utensilio *m*
geräumig (D)	—	spacious	spacieux(-euse)	spazioso(a)	espacioso(a)
Geräusch (D)	—	sound	bruit *m*	rumore *m*	ruido *m*
gerecht (D)	—	just	juste	giusto(a)	justo(a)
gerente (Es)	Geschäftsführer *m*	manager	gérant *m*	gerente *m*	—
gerente (I)	Geschäftsführer *m*	manager	gérant *m*	—	gerente *m*
Gericht[1] (D)	—	court	tribunal *m*	tribunale *m*	tribunal *m*
Gericht[2] (D)	—	dish	plat *m*	piatto *m*	comida *f*
gering (D)	—	slight	minime	poco(a)	pequeño(-ana)
German[1] (E)	deutsch	—	allemand	tedesco(a)	alemán(-ana)
German[2] (E)	Deutscher *m*	—	Allemand *m*	tedesco(a)	alemán *m*
Germania (I)	Deutschland *n*	Germany	Allemagne *f*	—	Alemania *f*
German school leaving examinations (E)	Abitur *n*	—	baccalauréat *m*	maturità *f*	bachillerato *m*
Germany (E)	Deutschland *n*	—	Allemagne *f*	Germania *f*	Alemania *f*
gern (D)	—	willingly	avec plaisir	volentieri	con gusto
Geruch (D)	—	smell	odeur *f*	odore *m*	olor *m*
Gerücht (D)	—	rumour	rumeur *f*	voce *f*	rumor *m*
gesamt (D)	—	entire	tout(e)	totale	entero(a)
Gesang (D)	—	singing	chant *m*	canto *m*	canto *m*
Geschäft (D)	—	shop	magasin *m*	negozio *m*	tienda *f*
geschäftlich (D)	—	on business	d'affaires	per affari	comercial
Geschäftsführer (D)	—	manager	gérant *m*	gerente *m*	gerente *m*
geschehen (D)	—	happen	arriver	accadere	ocurrir
Geschenk (D)	—	present	cadeau *m*	regalo *m*	regalo *m*
Geschichte (D)	—	history	histoire *f*	storia *f*	historia *f*
geschickt (D)	—	skilful	habile	abile	mañoso(a)
Geschirr (D)	—	crockery	vaiselle *f*	stoviglie *f pl*	vajilla *f*
Geschlecht (D)	—	sex	sexe *m*	sesso *m*	sexo *m*
geschlossen (D)	—	closed	fermé(e)	chiuso(a)	cerrado(a)
Geschmack (D)	—	taste	goût *m*	gusto *m*	sabor *m*
Geschwindigkeit (D)	—	speed	vitesse *f*	velocità *f*	velocidad *f*
Geschwister (D)	—	brothers and sisters	frère(s) et sœur(s) *pl*	fratelli *m pl*	hermanos *m pl*
geschwollen (D)	—	swollen	enflé(e)	gonfio(a)	hinchado(a)
Gesellschaft (D)	—	society	société *f*	società *f*	sociedad *f*

	D	E	F	I	Es
Gesetz (D)	—	law	loi f	legge f	ley f
gesetzlich (D)	—	legal	légal(e)	legale	legal
gesetzwidrig (D)	—	illegal	illégal(e)	illegale	ilegal
Gesicht (D)	—	face	visage m	faccia f	cara f
gespannt (D)	—	tense	tendu(e)	teso(a)	tenso(a)
Gespräch (D)	—	conversation	conversation f	conversazione f	conversación f
gestatten (D)	—	allow	permettre	permettere	permitir
gestehen (D)	—	confess	avouer	confessare	confesar
gestern (D)	—	yesterday	hier	ieri	ayer
gesund (D)	—	healthy	sain(e)	sano(a)	sano(a)
Gesundheit (D)	—	health	santé f	salute f	salud f
get[1] (E)	beschaffen	—	procurer	procurare	proporcionar
get[2] (E)	bekommen	—	recevoir	ricevere	recibir
get bored (E)	langweilen, sich	—	ennuyer, se	annoiarsi	aburrirse
get drunk (E)	betrinken, sich	—	enivrer, se	ubriacarsi	emborracharse
get engaged (E)	verloben	—	fiancer, se	fidanzarsi	prometerse
get ill (E)	erkranken	—	tomber malade	ammalarsi	enfermar
get in (E)	einsteigen	—	monter	salire	subir a
get lost (E)	verlaufen	—	perdre, se	perdersi	perderse
get off (E)	aussteigen	—	descendre	scendere	bajar
Getränk (D)	—	drink	boisson f	bevanda f	bebida f
Getreide (D)	—	cereals	céréales $f\,pl$	cereali $m\,pl$	cereales $m\,pl$
getrennt (D)	—	separate	séparé(e)	separato(a)	separado(a)
get up (E)	aufstehen	—	lever, se	alzarsi	levantarse
get used to (E)	gewöhnen, sich	—	habituer, se	abituare	acostumbrarse
Gewähr (D)	—	guarantee	garantie f	garanzia f	garantía f
gewähren (D)	—	grant	accorder	concedere	conceder
Gewalt (D)	—	force	force f	forza f	poder m
gewaltig (D)	—	tremendous	énorme	enorme	formidable
Gewässer (D)	—	waters	eaux $f\,pl$	acque $f\,pl$	aguas $f\,pl$
Gewebe (D)	—	fabric	tissu m	tessuto m	tela f
Gewerkschaft (D)	—	trade union	syndicat m	sindacato m	sindicato m
Gewicht (D)	—	weight	poids m	peso m	peso m
Gewinn (D)	—	profit	gain m	guadagno m	ganancia f
gewinnen (D)	—	win	gagner	guadagnare	ganar
gewiß (D)	—	certain	certain(e)	certo(a)	cierto
Gewissen (D)	—	conscience	conscience f	coscienza f	conciencia f
gewissenhaft (D)	—	conscientious	consciencieux (-euse)	coscienzioso(a)	concienzudo(a)
Gewitter (D)	—	thunderstorm	orage m	temporale m	tormenta f
gewöhnen, sich (D)	—	get used to	habituer	abituare	acostumbrarse
Gewohnheit (D)	—	habit	habitude f	abitudine f	costumbre f
gewöhnlich (D)	—	usual	habituel(le)	abituale	habitual
Gewürz (D)	—	spice	épice f	spezia f	especia f

giro

	D	E	F	I	Es
già (I)	bereits, schon	already	déjà	—	ya
giacca (I)	Jacke *f*	jacket	veste *f*	—	chaqueta *f*
giacca di maglia (I)	Strickjacke *f*	cardigan	veste en tricot *f*	—	chaqueta de punto *f*
giacere (I)	liegen	lie	trouver, se	—	estar tumbado(a)
giallo (I)	gelb	yellow	jaune	—	amarillo(a)
giardiniere (I)	Gärtner *m*	gardener	jardinier *m*	—	jardinero *m*
giardino (I)	Garten *m*	garden	jardin *m*	—	jardín *m*
gibier (F)	Wild *n*	game	—	selvaggina *f*	caza *f*
gießen (D)	—	water	arroser	annaffiare	regar
Gift (D)	—	poison	poison *m*	veleno *m*	veneno *m*
gifted (E)	begabt	—	doué(e)	dotato(a)	dotado(a)
giftig (D)	—	poisonous	toxique	velenoso(a)	venenoso(a)
gilet de sauvetage (F)	Schwimmweste *f*	life jacket	—	giubbotto di salvataggio *m*	chaleco salvavidas *m*
ginocchio (I)	Knie *n*	knee	genou *m*	—	rodilla *f*
giocare (I)	spielen	play	jouer	—	jugar
giocatore (I)	Spieler *m*	player	joueur *m*	—	jugador *m*
gioco (I)	Spiel *n*	game	jeu *m*	—	juego *m*
gioia (I)	Freude *f*	joy	joie *f*	—	alegría *f*
gioielli (I)	Schmuck *m*	jewellery	bijoux *m pl*	—	joyas *f pl*
gioielliere (I)	Juwelier *m*	jeweller	bijoutier *m*	—	joyero *m*
gioiello (I)	Juwel *n*	jewel	joyau *m*	—	joya *f*
giornale (I)	Zeitung *f*	newspaper	journal *m*	—	periódico *m*
giornale radio (I)	Nachrichten *pl*	news	informations *f pl*	—	noticiario *m*
giornalista (I)	Journalist *m*	journalist	journaliste *m*	—	periodista *m*
giorno (I)	Tag *m*	day	jour *m*	—	día *m*
giorno di riposo (I)	Ruhetag *m*	closing day	jour de repos *m*	—	día de descanso *m*
giorno feriale (I)	Werktag *m*	working day	jour ouvrable *m*	—	día laborable *m*
giorno festivo (I)	Feiertag *m*	holiday	jour férié *m*	—	día de fiesta *m*
giostra (I)	Karussell *n*	roundabout	manège *m*	—	tíovivo *m*
giovane (I)	jung	young	jeune	—	joven
giovedì (I)	Donnerstag *m*	Thursday	jeudi *m*	—	jueves *m*
gioventù (I)	Jugend *f*	youth	jeunesse *f*	—	juventud *f*
Gipfel (D)	—	peak	sommet *m*	cima *f*	cumbre *f*
gira (Es)	Rundfahrt *f*	round trip	circuit *m*	giro *m*	—
giradischi (I)	Plattenspieler *m*	record player	tourne-disque *m*	—	tocadiscos *m*
girar (Es)	drehen	turn	tourner	girare	—
girare¹ (I)	drehen	turn	tourner	—	girar
girare² (I)	herumdrehen	turn around	tourner	—	dar vuelta
girare³ (I)	umdrehen	turn around	tourner	—	volver
girellare (I)	bummeln	stroll	flâner	—	callejear
girl (E)	Mädchen *n*	—	jeune fille *f*	ragazza *f*	chica *f*
giro¹ (I)	Rundfahrt *f*	round trip	circuit *m*	—	circuito *m*
giro² (I)	Tour *f*	tour	excursion *f*	—	excursión *f*

	D	E	F	I	Es
gita (I)	Ausflug *m*	outing	excursion *f*	—	excursión *f*
Gitarre (D)	—	guitar	guitare *f*	chitarra *f*	guitarra *f*
giù¹ (I)	herab/hinab	down	vers le bas	—	hacia abajo
giù² (I)	herunter	down	en bas	—	abajo
giubbotto di salvataggio (I)	Schwimmweste *f*	life jacket	gilet de sauvetage *m*	—	chaleco salvavidas *m*
giubilare (I)	jubeln	rejoice	pousser des cris de joie	—	dar gritos de alegría
giudicare¹ (I)	beurteilen	judge	juger	—	juzgar
giudicare² (I)	urteilen	judge	juger	—	juzgar
giudice (I)	Richter *m*	judge	juge *m*	—	juez *m*
giudizio (I)	Urteil *n*	judgement	jugement *m*	—	juicio *m*
giugno (I)	Juni *m*	June	juin *m*	—	junio *m*
giurare (I)	schwören	swear	jurer	—	jurar
giurisprudenza (I)	Jura	law	droit *m*	—	derecho *m*
giusto¹ (I)	gerecht	just	juste	—	justo(a)
giusto² (I)	richtig	correct	juste	—	correcto(a)
give¹ (E)	geben	—	donner	dare	dar
give² (E)	schenken	—	offrir	regalare	regalar
give back (E)	zurückgeben	—	rendre	restituire	devolver
give birth to (E)	gebären	—	mettre au monde	partorire	parir
give in one's notice (E)	kündigen	—	résilier	licenziare	despedir
give up (E)	aufgeben	—	abandonner	rinunciare	renunciar
glace (F)	Eis *n*	ice	—	gelato *m*	hielo *m*
glad (E)	froh	—	content(e)	lieto(a)	contento(a)
glänzen (D)	—	shine	briller	splendere	brillar
Glas (D)	—	glass	verre *m*	bicchiere *m*	vaso *m*
glass (E)	Glas *n*	—	verre *m*	bicchiere *m*	vaso *m*
glasses (E)	Brille *f*	—	lunettes *f pl*	occhiali *m pl*	gafas *f pl*
glatt (D)	—	smooth	lisse	liscio(a)	liso(a)
glauben (D)	—	believe	croire	credere	creer
gleich (D)	—	same	égal(e)	identico(a)	idéntico(a)
gleichzeitig (D)	—	simultaneous	en même temps	contemporaneo (a)	a la vez
Gleis (D)	—	track	voie *f*	binario *m*	vía *f*
glisser (F)	rutschen	slide	—	scivolare	resbalar
Glocke (D)	—	bell	cloche *f*	campana *f*	campana *f*
glove (E)	Handschuh *m*	—	gant *m*	guanto *m*	guante *m*
Glück (D)	—	luck	chance *f*	fortuna *f*	suerte *f*
glücklich (D)	—	happy	heureux(-euse)	felice	feliz
Glückwunsch (D)	—	congratulations	félicitations *f pl*	auguri *m pl*	felicitaciones *f pl*
glue (E)	Klebstoff *m*	—	colle *f*	colla *f*	adhesivo *m*
Glühbirne (D)	—	light bulb	ampoule *f*	lampadina *f*	lámpara *f*
go (E)	gehen	—	aller	andare	andar
go ahead (E)	vorangehen	—	marcher devant	andare avanti	pasar adelante

	D	E	F	I	Es
goal (E)	Ziel n	—	but m	meta f	intención f
go along with (E)	mitgehen	—	accompagner	accompagnare	acompañar
goat (E)	Ziege f	—	chèvre f	capra f	cabra f
go away[1] (E)	verreisen	—	partir en voyage	partire in viaggio	irse de viaje
go away[2] (E)	weggehen	—	s'en aller	andare via	marcharse
gobierno (Es)	Regierung f	government	gouvernement m	governo m	—
goccia (I)	Tropfen m	drop	goutte f	—	gota f
gocciolare (I)	tropfen	drip	dégoutter	—	gotear
God (E)	Gott m	—	Dieu m	Dio m	Dios m
godere (I)	genießen	enjoy	jouir	—	disfrutar
godfather (E)	Pate m	—	parrain m	padrino m	padrino m
godmother (E)	Patin f	—	marraine f	madrina f	madrina f
go for a walk (E)	spazierengehen	—	promener, se	passeggiare	ir de paseo
Gold (D)	—	gold	or m	oro m	oro m
gold (E)	Gold n	—	or m	oro m	oro m
golden (D)	—	golden	d'or	d'oro	de oro
golden (E)	golden	—	d'or	d'oro	de oro
golpe (Es)	Schlag m	blow	coup m	colpo m	—
golpear[1] (Es)	klopfen	knock	frapper	bussare	—
golpear[2] (Es)	pochen	knock	frapper	battere	—
golpear[3] (Es)	schlagen	hit	battre	battere	—
goma (Es)	Gummi m	rubber	gomme f	gomma f	—
gomma (I)	Gummi m	rubber	gomme f	—	goma f
gomme (F)	Gummi m	rubber	—	gomma f	goma f
gonfio (I)	geschwollen	swollen	enflé(e)	—	hinchado(a)
gonna (I)	Rock m	skirt	jupe f	—	falda f
good[1] (E)	brav	—	gentil(-le)	bravo(a)	bueno(a)
good[2] (E)	gut	—	bon(ne)/bien	buono(a)/bene	bueno(a)/bien
good-bye![1] (E)	wiederhören!	—	au revoir!	a risentirci!	¡adiós!
good-bye![2] (E)	wiedersehen!	—	au revoir!	arrivederci!	¡adiós!
goods[1] (E)	Güter pl	—	marchandises f pl	beni m pl	bienes f pl
goods[2] (E)	Ware f	—	marchandise f	merce f	mercancía f
go on (E)	weitergehen	—	aller plus loin	proseguire	proseguir
goose (E)	Gans f	—	oie f	oca f	ganso m
go out[1] (E)	ausgehen	—	sortir	uscire	salir
go out[2] (E)	hinausgehen	—	sortir	uscire	salir afuera
gorge (F)	Rachen m	throat	—	faringe m	garganta f
gorra (Es)	Mütze f	cap	casquette f	berretto m	—
go shopping (E)	einkaufen gehen	—	faire les courses	fare la spesa	ir de compras
gota (Es)	Tropfen m	drop	goutte f	goccia f	—
gotear (Es)	tropfen	drip	dégoutter	gocciolare	—
go through (E)	durchgehen	—	passer à travers	passare	pasar
Gott (D)	—	God	Dieu m	Dio m	Dios m
Gottesdienst (D)	—	service	office divin m	messa f	servicio religioso m

	D	E	F	I	Es
go up (E)	steigen	—	monter	salire	subir
goût (F)	Geschmack *m*	taste	—	gusto *m*	sabor *m*
goutte (F)	Tropfen *m*	drop	—	goccia *f*	gota *f*
gouvernement (F)	Regierung *f*	government	—	governo *m*	gobierno *m*
government (E)	Regierung *f*	—	gouvernement *m*	governo *m*	gobierno *m*
governo (I)	Regierung *f*	government	gouvernement *m*	—	gobierno *m*
Grab (D)	—	grave	tombe *f*	tomba *f*	tumba *f*
graben (D)	—	dig	creuser	scavare	cavar
gracias (Es)	danke	thank you	merci	grazie	—
gracioso (Es)	niedlich	sweet	mignon(ne)	carino(a)	—
Grad¹ (D)	—	degree	degré *m*	grado *m*	grado *m*
Grad² (D)	—	rank	grade *m*	rango *m*	título *m*
grade (F)	Grad *m*	rank	—	rango *m*	título *m*
gradevole (I)	angenehm	pleasant	agréable	—	agradable
gradino (I)	Stufe *f*	step	marche *f*	—	escalón *m*
grado (Es)	Grad *m*	degree	degré *m*	grado *m*	—
grado (I)	Grad *m*	degree	degré *m*	—	grado *m*
gradual (E)	allmählich	—	graduel(le)	graduale	gradual
gradual (Es)	allmählich	gradual	graduel(le)	graduale	—
graduale (I)	allmählich	gradual	graduel(le)	—	gradual
graduel (F)	allmählich	gradual	—	graduale	gradual
grain (F)	Korn *n*	corn	—	grano *m*	semilla *f*
graisse (F)	Fett *n*	fat	—	grasso *m*	grasa *f*
gram (E)	Gramm *n*	—	gramme *m*	grammo *m*	gramo *m*
Gramm (D)	—	gram	gramme *m*	grammo *m*	gramo *m*
grammar school (E)	Gymnasium *n*	—	lycée *m*	liceo *m*	instituto de enseñanza media *m*
gramme (F)	Gramm *n*	gram	—	grammo *m*	gramo *m*
grammo (I)	Gramm *n*	gram	gramme *m*	—	gramo *m*
gramo (Es)	Gramm *n*	gram	gramme *m*	grammo *m*	—
grand (F)	groß	big/large	—	grande	grande
grandchild (E)	Enkelkind *n*	—	petit-enfant *m*	nipote *m*	nieto *m*
granddaughter (E)	Enkelin *f*	—	petite-fille *f*	nipote *f*	nieta *f*
grande (Es)	groß	big/large	grand(e)	grande	—
grande (I)	groß	big/large	grand(e)	—	grande
grande città (I)	Großstadt *f*	large town	grande ville *f*	—	gran ciudad *f*
grande magazzino (I)	Kaufhaus *n*	department store	grand magasin *m*	—	grandes almacenes *m pl*
grandes almacenes (Es)	Kaufhaus *n*	department store	grand magasin *m*	grande magazzino *m*	—
grandeur (F)	Größe *f*	greatness	—	grandezza *f*	grandeza *f*
grande ville (F)	Großstadt *f*	large town	—	grande città *f*	gran ciudad *f*
grandeza (Es)	Größe *f*	greatness	grandeur *f*	grandezza *f*	—
grandezza (I)	Größe *f*	greatness	grandeur *f*	—	grandeza *f*
grandfather (E)	Großvater *m*	—	grand-père *m*	nonno *m*	abuelo *m*

	D	E	F	I	Es
grandinare (I)	hageln	hail	grêler	—	granizar
grandine (I)	Hagel *m*	hail	grêle *f*	—	granizo *m*
grandioso (I)	großartig	magnificent	formidable	—	magnífico(a)
grandir¹ (F)	aufwachsen	grow up	—	crescere	criarse
grandir² (F)	größer werden	grow	—	crescere	crecer
grandir³ (F)	wachsen	grow	—	crescere	crecer
grand magasin (F)	Kaufhaus *n*	department store	—	grande magazzino *m*	grandes almacenes *m pl*
grand-mère (F)	Großmutter *f*	grandmother	—	nonna *f*	abuela *f*
grandmother (E)	Großmutter *f*	—	grand-mère *f*	nonna *f*	abuela *f*
grandparents (E)	Großeltern *pl*	—	grands-parents *m pl*	nonni *m pl*	abuelos *m pl*
grand-père (F)	Großvater *m*	grandfather	—	nonno *m*	abuelo *m*
grand propriétaire (F)	Großgrundbesitzer *m*	landowner	—	latifondista *m*	latifundista *m*
grand-rue (F)	Hauptstraße *f*	main street	—	strada principale *f*	calle central *f*
grandson (E)	Enkel *m*	—	petit-fils *m*	nipote *m*	nieto *m*
grands-parents (F)	Großeltern *pl*	grandparents	—	nonni *m pl*	abuelos *m pl*
granizar (Es)	hageln	hail	grêler	grandinare	—
granizo (Es)	Hagel *m*	hail	grêle *f*	grandine *f*	—
granja (Es)	Bauernhof *m*	farmhouse	ferme *f*	fattoria *f*	—
grano (I)	Korn *n*	corn	grain *m*	—	semilla *f*
grant (E)	gewähren	—	accorder	concedere	conceder
grape (E)	Traube *f*	—	grappe *f*	uva *f*	uva *f*
grapefruit (E)	Pampelmuse *f*	—	pamplemousse *m*	pompelmo *m*	pomelo *m*
grappe (F)	Traube *f*	grape	—	uva *f*	uva *f*
Gras (D)	—	grass	herbe *f*	erba *f*	hierba *f*
gras (F)	fett	fat	—	grasso(a)	graso(a)
grasa (Es)	Fett *n*	fat	graisse *f*	grasso *m*	—
graso (Es)	fett	fat	gras(se)	grasso(a)	—
grasp (E)	fassen	—	saisir	prendere	coger
grass (E)	Gras *n*	—	herbe *f*	erba *f*	hierba *f*
grasso¹ (I)	dick	fat	gros(se)	—	grueso(a)
grasso² (I)	fett	fat	gras(se)	—	graso(a)
grasso³ (I)	Fett *n*	fat	graisse *f*	—	grasa *f*
grateful (E)	dankbar	—	reconnaissant(e)	grato(a)	agradecido(a)
gratis (D)	—	free of charge	gratuit(e)	gratuito(a)	gratis
gratis¹ (Es)	gratis	free of charge	gratuit(e)	gratuito(a)	—
gratis² (Es)	kostenlos	free	gratuit(e)	gratuito(a)	—
grato (I)	dankbar	grateful	reconnaissant(e)	—	agradecido(a)
gratuit¹ (F)	gratis	free of charge	—	gratuito(a)	gratis
gratuit² (F)	kostenlos	free	—	gratuito(a)	gratis
gratuito¹ (I)	gratis	free of charge	gratuit(e)	—	gratis
gratuito² (I)	kostenlos	free	gratuit(e)	—	gratis
gratulieren (D)	—	congratulate	féliciter	congratularsi	felicitar

	D	E	F	I	Es
grau (D)	—	grey	gris(e)	grigio(a)	gris
grausam (D)	—	cruel	cruel(le)	crudele	cruel
grave (E)	Grab *n*	—	tombe *f*	tomba *f*	tumba *f*
grazie (I)	danke	thank you	merci	—	¡gracias!
great-grandparents (E)	Urgroßeltern *pl*	—	arrière-grands-parents *m pl*	bisnonni *m pl*	bisabuelos *m pl*
greatness (E)	Größe *f*	—	grandeur *f*	grandezza *f*	grandeza *f*
Grèce (F)	Griechenland *n*	Greece	—	Grecia *f*	Grecia *f*
Grecia (Es)	Griechenland *n*	Greece	Grèce *f*	Grecia *f*	—
Grecia (I)	Griechenland *n*	Greece	Grèce *f*	—	Grecia *f*
Greece (E)	Griechenland *n*	—	Grèce *f*	Grecia *f*	Grecia *f*
green (E)	grün	—	vert(e)	verde	verde
greet[1] (E)	begrüßen	—	saluer	salutare	saludar
greet[2] (E)	grüßen	—	saluer	salutare	saludar
greeting (E)	Gruß *m*	—	salut *m*	saluto *m*	saludo *m*
greifen (D)	—	seize	saisir	afferrare	coger
grêle (F)	Hagel *m*	hail	—	grandine *f*	granizo *m*
grêler (F)	hageln	hail	—	grandinare	granizar
grenouille (F)	Frosch *m*	frog	—	rana *f*	rana *f*
Grenze (D)	—	frontier	frontière *f*	frontiera *f*	frontera *f*
grève (F)	Streik *m*	strike	—	sciopero *m*	huelga *f*
grey (E)	grau	—	gris(e)	grigio(a)	gris
gridare (I)	schreien	scream	crier	—	gritar
grido (I)	Schrei *m*	scream	cri *m*	—	grito *m*
Griechenland (D)	—	Greece	Grèce *f*	Grecia *f*	Grecia *f*
grief (E)	Kummer *m*	—	chagrin *m*	dolore *m*	pesar *m*
Griff (D)	—	handle	poignée *f*	maniglia *f*	asidero *m*
grigio (I)	grau	grey	gris	—	gris
griller (F)	rösten	roast	—	abbrustolire	tostar
grimper (F)	klettern	climb	—	arrampicarsi	escalar
gripe (Es)	Grippe *f*	flu	grippe *f*	influenza *f*	—
Grippe (D)	—	flu	grippe *f*	influenza *f*	gripe *f*
grippe (F)	Grippe *f*	flu	—	influenza *f*	gripe *f*
gris (Es)	grau	grey	gris(e)	grigio(a)	—
gris (F)	grau	grey	—	grigio(a)	gris
gritar (Es)	schreien	scream	crier	gridare	—
grito (Es)	Schrei *m*	scream	cri *m*	grido *m*	—
grob (D)	—	coarse	grossier(-ière)	rozzo(a)	tosco(a)
grocer's (E)	Lebensmittelgeschäft *n*	—	magasin d'alimentation *m*	negozio di alimentari *m*	tienda de comestibles *f*
gronder (F)	schimpfen	scold	—	imprecare	insultar
gros (F)	dick	fat	—	grasso(a)	grueso(a)
groseille (F)	Johannisbeere *f*	currant	—	ribes *m*	grosella *f*
grosella (Es)	Johannisbeere *f*	currant	groseille *f*	ribes *m*	—
groß (D)	—	big/large	grand(e)	grande	grande

	D	E	F	I	Es
großartig (D)	—	magnificent	formidable	grandioso(a)	magnifico(a)
Größe[1] (D)	—	greatness	grandeur f	grandezza f	grandeza f
Größe[2] (D)	—	size	taille f	taglia f	talla f
Großeltern (D)	—	grandparents	grands-parents m pl	nonni m pl	abuelos m pl
größer werden (D)	—	grow	grandir	crescere	crecer
Großgrundbesitzer (D)	—	landowner	grand propriétaire m	latifondista m	latifundista m
grossier (F)	grob	coarse	—	rozzo(a)	tosco(a)
Großmutter (D)	—	grandmother	grand-mère f	nonna f	abuela f
Großstadt (D)	—	large town	grande ville f	grande città f	gran ciudad f
Großvater (D)	—	grandfather	grand-père m	nonno m	abuelo m
großzügig (D)	—	generous	généreux(-euse)	generoso(a)	generoso(a)
grotte (F)	Höhle f	cave	—	caverna f	cueva f
ground floor[1] (E)	Erdgeschoß n	—	rez-de-chaussée m	pianterreno m	planta baja f
ground floor[2] (E)	Parterre n	—	rez-de chaussée m	pianterreno m	planta baja f
group (E)	Gruppe f	—	groupe m	gruppo m	grupo m
groupe (F)	Gruppe f	group	—	gruppo m	grupo m
grow[1] (E)	größer werden	—	grandir	crescere	crecer
grow[2] (E)	wachsen	—	grandir	crescere	crecer
grown up (E)	erwachsen	—	adulte	adulto(a)	adulto(a)
grow up (E)	aufwachsen	—	grandir	crescere	criarse
grueso (Es)	dick	fat	gros(se)	grasso(a)	—
grün (D)	—	green	vert(e)	verde	verde
Grund (D)	—	reason	raison f	causa f	causa f
gründen (D)	—	found	fonder	fondare	fundar
Grundfläche (D)	—	base	base f	base f	base f
gründlich (D)	—	thorough	à fond	a fondo	a fondo
grundsätzlich (D)	—	fundamental	par principe	basilare	en principio
grupo[1] (Es)	Gruppe f	group	groupe m	gruppo m	—
grupo[2] (Es)	Schar f	band	bande f	schiera f	—
Gruppe (D)	—	group	groupe m	gruppo m	grupo m
gruppo (I)	Gruppe f	group	groupe m	—	grupo m
Gruß (D)	—	greeting	salut m	saluto m	saludo m
grüßen (D)	—	greet	saluer	salutare	saludar
guadagnare (I)	verdienen	earn	gagner	—	ganar
guadagno[1] (I)	Gewinn m	profit	gain m	—	ganancia f
guadagno[2] (I)	Verdienst m	income	revenus m pl	—	ganancia f
guancia (I)	Wange f	cheek	joue f	—	mejilla f
guanciale (I)	Kopfkissen n	pillow	oreiller m	—	almohada f
guante (Es)	Handschuh m	glove	gant m	guanto m	—
guanto (I)	Handschuh m	glove	gant m	—	guante m
guarantee[1] (E)	Gewähr f	—	garantie f	garanzia f	garantía f
guarantee[2] (E)	Garantie f	—	garantie f	garanzia f	garantía f
guard[1] (E)	Aufseher m	—	gardien m	custode m	vigilante m

guard

	D	E	F	I	Es
guard² (E)	bewachen	—	garder	sorvegliare	vigilar
guarda (Es)	Wärter *m*	attendant	gardien *m*	custode *m*	—
guardar (Es)	aufbewahren	keep	garder	conservare	—
guardare¹ (I)	anschauen	look at	regarder	—	mirar
guardare² (I)	ansehen	look at	regarder	—	mirar
guardare³ (I)	blicken	look	regarder	—	mirar
guardare⁴ (I)	schauen	look	regarder	—	mirar
guardare la TV (I)	fernsehen	watch television	regarder la télévision	—	ver la televisión
guardaroba (I)	Garderobe *f*	wardrobe	vestiaire *m*	—	guardaropa *m*
guardaropa (Es)	Garderobe *f*	wardrobe	vestiaire *m*	guardaroba *m*	—
guardia notturna (I)	Nachtwächter *m*	night-watchman	veilleur de nuit *m*	—	sereno *m*
guarnecer (Es)	garnieren	decorate	garnir	guarnire	—
guarnire (I)	garnieren	decorate	garnir	—	guarnecer
guasto (I)	defekt	defect	défectueux (-euse)	—	defecto(a)
guêpe (F)	Wespe *f*	wasp	—	vespa *f*	avispa *f*
guérir (F)	heilen	heal	—	curare	curar
guerra (Es)	Krieg *m*	war	guerre *f*	guerra *f*	—
guerra (I)	Krieg *m*	war	guerre *f*	—	guerra *f*
guerre (F)	Krieg *m*	war	—	guerra *f*	guerra *f*
guess (E)	raten	—	deviner	indovinare	adivinar
guest (E)	Gast *m*	—	hôte *m/f*	ospite *m*	invitado *m*
gueule (F)	Maul *n*	mouth	—	muso *m*	hocico *m*
guía¹ (Es)	Führer *m*	leader	guide *m*	guida *f*	—
guía² (Es)	Reiseführer *m*	guide	guide *m*	guida *f*	—
guía telefónica (Es)	Telefonbuch *n*	phone book	annuaire du téléphone *m*	elenco telefonico *m*	—
guichet (F)	Schalter *m*	counter	—	sportello *m*	ventanilla *f*
guida¹ (I)	Führer *m*	leader	guide *m*	—	guía *m*
guida² (I)	Reiseführer *m*	guide	guide *m*	—	guía *m*
guidare¹ (I)	führen	lead	guider	—	dirigir
guidare² (I)	lenken	steer	conduire	—	encauzar
guide (E)	Reiseführer *m*	—	guide *m*	guida *f*	guía *m*
guide¹ (F)	Führer *m*	leader	—	guida *f*	guía *m*
guide² (F)	Reiseführer *m*	guide	—	guida *f*	guía *m*
guided tour (E)	Führung *f*	—	visite guidée *f*	visita guidata *f*	visita guiada *f*
guider² (F)	führen	lead	—	guidare	dirigir
guilty (E)	schuldig	—	coupable	colpevole	culpable
guisante (Es)	Erbse *f*	pea	pois *m*	pisello *m*	—
guitar (E)	Gitarre *f*	—	guitare *f*	chitarra *f*	guitarra *f*
guitare (F)	Gitarre *f*	guitar	—	chitarra *f*	guitarra *f*
guitarra (Es)	Gitarre *f*	guitar	guitare *f*	chitarra *f*	—
gültig (D)	—	valid	valable	valido(a)	válido(a)
Gültigkeit (D)	—	validity	validité *f*	validità *f*	validez *f*
Gummi (D)	—	rubber	gomme *f*	gomma *f*	goma *f*

	D	E	F	I	Es
günstig (D)	—	favourable	favorable	favorevole	favorable
Gurke (D)	—	cucumber	concombre *m*	cetriolo *m*	pepino *m*
Gurt (D)	—	belt	ceinture *f*	cinghia *f*	cinturón *m*
Gürtel (D)	—	belt	ceinture *f*	cintura *f*	cinturón *m*
gustar[1] (Es)	gefallen	please	plaire	piacere	—
gustar[2] (Es)	schmecken	taste	sentir	piacere	—
gusto (I)	Geschmack *m*	taste	goût *m*	—	sabor *m*
gut (D)	—	good/well	bon(ne)/bien	buono(a)/bene	bueno(a)/bien
Güter (D)	—	goods	marchandises *f pl*	beni *m pl*	bienes *f pl*
Gutschein (D)	—	voucher	bon *m*	buono *m*	vale *m*
Gymnasium (D)	—	grammar school	lycée *m*	liceo *m*	instituto de enseñanza media *m*
Haar (D)	—	hair	cheveu *m*	capello *m*	pelo *m*
haben (D)	—	have	avoir	avere	tener
hábil (Es)	fähig	capable	capable	capace	—
habile (F)	geschickt	skilful	—	abile	mañoso(a)
habiller (F)	kleiden	dress	—	vestire	vestir
habit (E)	Gewohnheit *f*	—	habitude *f*	abitudine *f*	costumbre *f*
habitación[1] (Es)	Raum *m*	room	pièce *f*	stanza *f*	—
habitación[2] (Es)	Zimmer *n*	room	chambre *f*	camera *f*	—
habitant[1] (F)	Bewohner *m*	inhabitant	—	abitante *m*	habitante *m(f)*
habitant[2] (F)	Einwohner *m*	inhabitant	—	abitante *m*	habitante *m*
habitante[1] (Es)	Bewohner *m*	inhabitant	habitant *m*	abitante *m*	—
habitante[2] (Es)	Einwohner *m*	inhabitant	habitant *m*	abitante *m*	—
habiter (F)	wohnen	live	—	abitare	vivir
habits (F)	Kleidung *f*	clothing	—	abbigliamento *m*	vestuario *m*
habitual (Es)	gewöhnlich	usual	habituel(le)	abituale	—
habitude (F)	Gewohnheit *f*	habit	—	abitudine *f*	costumbre *f*
habitué (F)	Stammgast *m*	regular	—	cliente abituale *m*	cliente habitual *m*
habituel[1] (F)	gewöhnlich	usual	—	abituale	habitual
habituel[2] (F)	üblich	usual	—	solito(a)	usual
habituer, se (F)	gewöhnen, sich	get used to	—	abituare	acostumbrarse
hablar[1] (Es)	reden	talk	parler	parlare	—
hablar[2] (Es)	sprechen	speak	parler	parlare	—
hace mucho (Es)	längst	a long time ago	depuis bien longtemps	da molto	—
hacer[1] (Es)	machen	make/do	faire	fare	—
hacer[2] (Es)	tun	do	faire	fare	—
hacer excursiones (Es)	wandern	hike	marcher	fare escursioni a piedi	—
hacer gimnasia (Es)	turnen	do gymnastic exercises	faire de la gymnastique	fare ginnastica	—
hacer huelga (Es)	streiken	be on strike	faire grève	scioperare	—
hacer la maleta (Es)	packen	pack	faire les malles	fare le valigie	—
hacer magia (Es)	zaubern	practise magic	faire de la magie	esercitare la magia	—

	D	E	F	I	Es
hacer propaganda (Es)	werben	advertise	faire de la publicité	fare propaganda	—
hacer punto (Es)	stricken	knit	tricoter	lavorare a maglia	—
hacer reservar (Es)	vorbestellen	book	réserver	prenotare	—
hacer una foto (Es)	knipsen	take a snap	photographier	scattare	—
hacer una lista (Es)	verzeichnen	list	enregistrer	registrare	—
hacia abajo[1] (Es)	abwärts	downwards	en bas	in giù	—
hacia abajo[2] (Es)	herab/hinab	down	vers le bas	giù	—
hacia afuera[1] (Es)	heraus	out	dehors	fuori	—
hacia afuera[2] (Es)	hinaus	out	dehors	fuori	—
hacia allá (Es)	hin	there	jusqu'à/vers	là	—
hacia arriba[1] (Es)	aufwärts	upwards	vers le haut	in su	—
hacia arriba[2] (Es)	hinauf	up	montez	su	—
hacia arriba[3] (Es)	herauf	up	vers le haut	su	—
hacia el otro lado (Es)	hinüber	across	de l'autre côté	di là	—
Hackfleisch (D)	—	minced meat	viande hachée *f*	carne tritata *f*	carne picada *f*
Hafen (D)	—	port	port *m*	porto *m*	puerto *m*
Hagel (D)	—	hail	grêle *f*	grandine *f*	granizo *m*
hageln (D)	—	hail	grêler	grandinare	granizar
Hahn (D)	—	cock	coq *m*	gallo *m*	gallo *m*
Hai (D)	—	shark	requin *m*	pescecane *m*	tiburón *m*
hail[1] (E)	hageln	—	grêler	grandinare	granizar
hail[2] (E)	Hagel *m*	—	grêle *f*	grandine *f*	granizo *m*
haine (F)	Haß *m*	hate	—	odio *m*	odio *m*
hair (E)	Haar *n*		cheveu *m*	capello *m*	pelo *m*
hairdresser (E)	Friseur *m*	—	coiffeur *m*	parrucchiere *m*	peluquero *m*
hairstyle (E)	Frisur *f*	—	coiffure *f*	pettinatura *f*	peinado *m*
Haken (D)	—	hook	crochet *m*	gancio *m*	gancho *m*
halb (D)	—	half	demi(e)	mezzo(a)	medio(a)
halbieren (D)	—	halve	partager en deux	dimezzare	dividir por la mitad
Halbinsel (D)	—	peninsula	presqu'île *f*	penisola *f*	península *f*
Halbpension (D)	—	half board	demi-pension *f*	mezza pensione *f*	media pensión *f*
half[1] (E)	halb	—	demi(e)	mezzo(a)	medio(a)
half[2] (E)	Hälfte *f*	—	moitié *f*	metà *f*	mitad *f*
half board (E)	Halbpension *f*	—	demi-pension *f*	mezza pensione *f*	media pensión *f*
halfcaste (E)	Mischling *m*	—	métis *m*	sangue misto *m*	mestizo *m*
Hälfte (D)	—	half	moitié *f*	metà *f*	mitad *f*
hall[1] (E)	Diele *f*	—	vestibule *m*	corridoio *m*	tabla *f*
hall[2] (E)	Flur *m*	—	entrée *f*	corridoio *m*	corredor *m*
hall[3] (E)	Saal *m*	—	salle *f*	sala *f*	sala *f*
Hallenbad (D)	—	indoor swimming pool	piscine *f*	piscina coperta *f*	piscina cubierta *f*
hallo! (D)	—	hello!	allô!	pronto!	¡diga!
Hals (D)	—	neck	cou *m*	collo *m*	cuello *m*

	D	E	F	I	Es
Halsschmerzen (D)	—	sore throat	mal de gorge *m*	mal di gola *m*	dolor de garganta *m*
Halstuch (D)	—	scarf	écharpe *f*	sciarpa *f*	pañuelo para el cuello *m*
halt! (D)	—	stop!	stop!	alt!	¡alto!
haltbar (D)	—	durable	résistant(e)	durevole	duradero
halten (D)	—	hold	tenir	tenere	sujetar
Haltestelle (D)	—	stop	arrêt *m*	fermata *f*	parada *f*
halve (E)	halbieren	—	partager en deux	dimezzare	dividir por la mitad
ham (E)	Schinken *m*	—	jambon *m*	prosciutto *m*	jamón *m*
hambre (Es)	Hunger *m*	hunger	faim *f*	fame *f*	—
hambriento (Es)	hungrig	hungry	affamé(e)	affamato(a)	—
Hammer (D)	—	hammer	marteau *m*	martello *m*	martillo *m*
hammer (E)	Hammer *m*	—	marteau *m*	martello *m*	martillo *m*
hanche (F)	Hüfte *f*	hip	—	fianco *m*	cadera *f*
Hand (D)	—	hand	main *f*	mano *f*	mano *f*
hand (E)	Hand *f*	—	main *f*	mano *f*	mano *f*
handbag (E)	Handtasche *f*	—	sac à main *m*	borsetta *f*	bolso *m*
handeln (D)	—	act	agir	agire	obrar
Handgepäck (D)	—	hand-luggage	bagage à main	bagaglio a mano *m*	equipaje de mano *m*
handkerchief (E)	Taschentuch *n*	—	mouchoir *m*	fazzoletto *m*	pañuelo *m*
handle (E)	Griff *m*	—	poignée *f*	maniglia *f*	asidero *m*
Händler (D)	—	dealer	commerçant *m*	commerciante *m*	comerciante *m*
hand-luggage (E)	Handgepäck *n*	—	bagage à main *m*	bagaglio a mano *m*	equipaje de mano *m*
hand over[1] (E)	übergeben	—	remettre	consegnare	transmitir
hand over[2] (E)	überreichen	—	présenter	consegnare	entregar
Handschuh (D)	—	glove	gant *m*	guanto *m*	guante *m*
Handtasche (D)	—	handbag	sac à main *m*	borsetta *f*	bolso *m*
Handtuch (D)	—	towel	serviette *f*	asciugamano *m*	pañuelo *m*
Handwerk (D)	—	craft	métier *m*	artigianato *m*	artesanía *f*
Handwerker (D)	—	craftsman	artisan *m*	artigiano *m*	artesano *m*
Hang (D)	—	slope	versant *m*	pendio *m*	pendiente *m*
hang (E)	hängen	—	pendre	pendere	colgar
hängen (D)	—	hang	pendre	pendere	colgar
hang up (E)	aufhängen	—	accrocher	appendere	colgar
happen[1] (E)	geschehen	—	arriver	accadere	ocurrir
happen[2] (E)	passieren	—	arriver	succedere	pasar
happy (E)	glücklich	—	heureux(-euse)	felice	feliz
hard (E)	hart	—	dur(e)	duro(a)	duro(a)
hardly (E)	kaum	—	à peine	appena	apenas
hare (E)	Hase *m*	—	lièvre *m*	lepre *f*	liebre *m*
haricot (F)	Bohne *f*	bean	—	fagiolo *m*	judía *f*
harina (Es)	Mehl *n*	flour	farine *f*	farina *f*	—
harmful (E)	schädlich	—	nuisible	nocivo(a)	nocivo(a)

	D	E	F	I	Es
harmless (E)	harmlos	—	inoffensif(-ive)	inoffensivo(a)	inofensivo(a)
harmlos (D)	—	harmless	inoffensif(-ive)	inoffensivo(a)	inofensivo(a)
Harn (D)	—	urine	urine f	urina f	orina f
hart (D)	—	hard	dur(e)	duro(a)	duro(a)
harvest (E)	Ernte f	—	moisson f	raccolto m	cosecha f
hasard (F)	Zufall m	chance	—	caso m	casualidad f
Hase (D)	—	hare	lièvre m	lepre f	liebre m
Haß (D)	—	hate	haine f	odio m	odio m
hassen (D)	—	hate	détester	odiare	odiar
häßlich (D)	—	ugly	laid(e)	brutto(a)	feo(a)
hasta (Es)	bis	until	jusqu'à	fino a	—
hasta ahora (Es)	bisher	so far	jusqu'à présent	finora	—
¡hasta luego! (Es)	tschüs	bye	salut	ciao	—
hasta tanto (Es)	soweit	as far as	autant que	fin dove	—
haste (E)	Eile f	—	hâte f	fretta f	prisa f
hat (E)	Hut m	—	chapeau m	cappello m	sombrero m
hate[1] (E)	hassen	—	détester	odiare	odiar
hate[2] (E)	Haß m	—	haine f	odio m	odio m
hâte (F)	Eile f	haste	—	fretta f	prisa f
Haufen (D)	—	heap	tas m	mucchio m	montón m
häufig (D)	—	frequent	fréquent(e)	frequente	frecuente
Hauptbahnhof (D)	—	central station	gare centrale f	stazione centrale f	estación central f
hauptsächlich (D)	—	mainly	surtout	principalmente	principalmente
Hauptstadt (D)	—	capital	capitale f	capitale f	capital f
Hauptstraße (D)	—	main street	grand-rue f	strada principale f	calle central f
Haus (D)	—	house	maison f	casa f	casa f
Hausfrau (D)	—	housewife	femme de maison f	casalinga f	ama de casa f
Haushalt (D)	—	household	ménage m	casa f	casa f
Hausmädchen (D)	—	maid	fille de service f	domestica f	criada f
Hausmeister (D)	—	caretaker	concierge m	portinaio m	portero m
Haut (D)	—	skin	peau f	pelle f	piel f
haut (F)	hoch	up/high	—	alto(a)	alto(a)
haute montage (F)	Hochgebirge n	high mountain-chain	—	alta montagna f	montañas elevadas f pl
hauteur (F)	Höhe f	height	—	altezza f	altura f
haut-parleur (F)	Lautsprecher m	loudspeaker	—	altoparlante m	altavoz m
have (E)	haben	—	avoir	avere	tener
have a cold (E)	erkältet sein	—	avoir un rhume	essere raffreddato(a)	estar acatarrado(a)
have a look at (E)	besichtigen	—	visiter	visitare	visitar
have on (E)	anhaben	—	porter	indossare	llevar
have to[1] (E)	müssen	—	devoir	dovere	deber
have to[2] (E)	sollen	—	devoir	dovere	deber
he (E)	er	—	il	lui/egli/esso	él
head (E)	Kopf m	—	tête f	testa f	cabeza f

	D	E	F	I	Es
headache (E)	Kopfschmerzen pl	—	mal de tête m	mal di testa m	dolor de cabeza m
heading (E)	Überschrift f	—	titre m	titolo m	título m
headline (E)	Schlagzeile f	—	manchette f	titolo m	titular m
heal (E)	heilen	—	guérir	curare	curar
health (E)	Gesundheit f	—	santé f	salute f	salud f
health food shop (E)	Reformhaus n	—	magasin diététique m	negozio di prodotti dietetici m	tienda de productos dietéticos f
healthy (E)	gesund	—	sain(e)	sano(a)	sano(a)
heap (E)	Haufen m	—	tas m	mucchio m	montón m
hear (E)	hören	—	entendre	sentire	oír
hearing (E)	Gehör n	—	ouïe f	udito m	oído m
heart (E)	Herz n	—	cœur m	cuore m	corazón m
heat¹ (E)	heizen	—	chauffer	riscaldare	calentar
heat² (E)	Hitze f	—	chaleur f	caldo m	calor m
heating (E)	Heizung f	—	chauffage m	riscaldamento m	calefacción f
heavy (E)	schwer	—	lourd(e)	pesante	pesado(a)
hebdomadaire (F)	wöchentlich	weekly	—	settimanale	semanal
heben (D)	—	lift	soulever	alzare	levantar
hecho (Es)	Tatsache f	fact	fait m	fatto m	—
hectic (E)	hektisch	—	fébrile	nervoso(a)	inquieto(a)
Heft (D)	—	exercise book	cahier m	quaderno m	cuaderno m
heftig (D)	—	fierce	violent(e)	violento(a)	fuerte
height (E)	Höhe f	—	hauteur	altezza f	altura f
heilen (D)	—	heal	guérir	curare	curar
heilig (D)	—	holy	saint(e)	santo(a)	santo(a)
Heiligabend (D)	—	Christmas Eve	nuit de Noël f	vigilia di Natale f	Nochebuena f
Heimat (D)	—	home	patrie f	patria f	patria f
heimlich (D)	—	secret	secret(-ète)	segreto(a)	oculto(a)
Heimweh (D)	—	homesickness	mal du pays m	nostalgia f	nostalgia f
Heirat (D)	—	marriage	mariage m	matrimonio m	boda f
heiraten (D)	—	marry	marier	sposarsi	casarse
heiß (D)	—	hot	chaud(e)	caldo(a)	caliente
heißen (D)	—	be called	appeler, se	chiamarsi	llamarse
heizen (D)	—	heat	chauffer	riscaldare	calentar
Heizöl (D)	—	fuel	mazout m	olio combustibile m	combustible para la calefacción m
Heizung (D)	—	heating	chauffage m	riscaldamento m	calefacción f
hektisch (D)	—	hectic	fébrile	nervoso(a)	inquieto(a)
helada (Es)	Frost m	frost	gelée f	gelo m	—
Held (D)	—	hero	héros m	eroe m	héroe m
helfen (D)	—	help	aider	aiutare	ayudar
hell (D)	—	bright	clair(e)	chiaro(a)	claro(a)
hell (E)	Hölle f	—	enfer m	inferno m	infierno m
hello! (E)	hallo!	—	allô!	pronto!	¡diga!

	D	E	F	I	Es
Helm (D)	—	helmet	casque *m*	casco *m*	casco *m*
helmet (E)	Helm *m*	—	casque *m*	casco *m*	casco *m*
help¹ (E)	helfen	—	aider	aiutare	ayudar
help² (E)	Hilfe *f*	—	aide *f*	aiuto *m*	ayuda *f*
help s.b. (E)	behilflich sein	—	aider qn	aiutare	ayudar a alguien
Hemd (D)	—	shirt	chemise *f*	camicia *f*	camisa *f*
hen (E)	Henne *f*	—	poule *f*	gallina *f*	gallina *f*
Henne (D)	—	hen	poule *f*	gallina *f*	gallina *f*
her (D)	—	here/ago	ici	qua/qui/da	aquí
herab (D)	—	down	vers le bas	giù	hacia abajo
herabsetzen (D)	—	lower	baisser	diminuire	rebajar
herauf (D)	—	up	vers le haut	su	hacia arriba
heraus (D)	—	out	dehors	fuori	hacia afuera
herausgeben (D)	—	publish	éditer	pubblicare	editar
heraustreten (D)	—	step out	sortir	uscire fuori	salir
herb (D)	—	bitter	amer(-ère)	amaro(a)	amargo(a)
herbe (F)	Gras *n*	grass	—	erba *f*	hierba *f*
Herbst (D)	—	autumn	automne *m*	autunno *m*	otoño *m*
Herd (D)	—	cooker	fourneau *m*	cucina *f*	cocina *f*
here¹ (E)	hier	—	ici	qui	aquí
here² (E)	her	—	ici	qua/qui/da	aquí
heredar¹ (Es)	beerben	inherit from	hériter	ereditare	—
heredar² (Es)	erben	inherit	hériter	ereditare	—
herein (D)	—	in	vers l'intérieur	dentro	adentro
herida¹ (Es)	Verletzung *f*	injury	blessure *f*	ferita *f*	—
herida² (Es)	Wunde *f*	wound	blessure *f*	ferita *f*	—
herir¹ (Es)	verwunden	wound	blesser	ferire	—
herir² (Es)	verletzen	injure	blesser	ferire	—
hériter¹ (F)	beerben	inherit from	—	ereditare	heredar
hériter² (F)	erben	inherit	—	ereditare	heredar
hermana (Es)	Schwester *f*	sister	sœur *f*	sorella *f*	—
hermano (Es)	Bruder *m*	brother	frère *m*	fratello *m*	—
hermanos (Es)	Geschwister *pl*	brothers and sisters	frère(s) et sœur(s) *pl*	fratelli *m pl*	—
hermoso (Es)	schön	beautiful	beau, bel, belle	bello(a)	—
hero (E)	Held *m*	—	héros *m*	eroe *m*	héroe *m*
héroe (Es)	Held *m*	hero	héros *m*	eroe *m*	—
héros (F)	Held *m*	hero	—	eroe *m*	héroe *m*
Herr (D)	—	gentleman	monsieur *m*	signore *m*	señor *m*
herramienta (Es)	Werkzeug *n*	tool	outil *m*	utensile *m*	—
herrlich (D)	—	marvellous	magnifique	stupendo(a)	maravilloso(a)
herrschen (D)	—	rule	régner	dominare	mandar
herstellen (D)	—	manufacture	produire	fabbricare	producir
Hersteller (D)	—	manufacturer	producteur *m*	produttore *m*	productor *m*
herüber (D)	—	over	par ici	da questa parte	a este lado

	D	E	F	I	Es
herum (D)	—	around	autour	intorno	alrededor
herumdrehen (D)	—	turn around	tourner	girare	dar vuelta
herumreichen (D)	—	pass around	faire passer	far circolare	pasar de mano en mano
herunter (D)	—	down	en bas	giù	abajo
hervor (D)	—	forth	au-dehors	fuori	delante
hervorragend (D)	—	excellent	excellent(e)	eccellente	extraordinario(a)
Herz (D)	—	heart	cœur *m*	cuore *m*	corazón *m*
herzlich (D)	—	cordial	cordial(e)	cordiale	afectuoso(a)
hesitate (E)	zögern	—	hésiter	esitare	vacilar
hésiter (F)	zögern	hesitate	—	esitare	vacilar
heure (F)	Stunde *f*	hour	—	ora *f*	hora *f*
heure d'été (F)	Sommerzeit *f*	summertime	—	ora legale *f*	temporada de verano *f*
heures de consultation (F)	Sprechstunde *f*	consultation hour	—	ora di ricevimento *f*	hora de consulta *f*
heures d'ouverture (F)	Öffnungszeiten *pl*	business hours	—	orario di apertura *m pl*	horario de abertura *m*
heureux (F)	glücklich	happy	—	felice	feliz
heurter (F)	anstoßen	bump	—	urtare	empujar
heute (D)	—	today	aujourd'hui	oggi	hoy
heutzutage (D)	—	nowadays	de nos jours	oggigiorno	hoy en día
Hexe (D)	—	witch	sorcière *f*	strega *f*	bruja *f*
hide[1] (E)	verstecken	—	cacher	nascondere	ocultar
hide[2] (E)	verbergen	—	dissimuler	nascondere	esconder
hielo (Es)	Eis *n*	ice	glace *f*	gelato *m*	—
hier (D)	—	here	ici	qui	aquí
hier (F)	gestern	yesterday	—	ieri	ayer
hierba (Es)	Gras *n*	grass	herbe *f*	erba *f*	—
hierbleiben (D)	—	stay here	rester	restare qui	quedarse aquí
hierher (D)	—	over here	par ici	qua	para acá
hierro (Es)	Eisen *n*	iron	fer *m*	ferro *m*	—
hígado (Es)	Leber *f*	liver	foie *m*	fegato *m*	—
high mountain-chain (E)	Hochgebirge *n*	—	haute montage *f*	alta montagna *f*	montañas elevadas *f pl*
high season (E)	Hochsaison *f*	—	pleine saison *f*	alta stagione *f*	temporada alta *f*
high tide (E)	Flut *f*	—	marée haute *f*	altamarea *f*	marea alta *f*
higo (Es)	Feige *f*	fig	figue *f*	fico *m*	—
hija (Es)	Tochter *f*	daughter	fille *f*	figlia *f*	—
hijo (Es)	Sohn *m*	son	fils *m*	figlio *m*	—
hike (E)	wandern	—	marcher	fare escursioni a piedi	hacer excursiones
Hilfe (D)	—	help	aide *f*	aiuto *m*	ayuda *f*
hill (E)	Hügel *m*	—	colline *f*	collina *f*	colina *f*
hilo (Es)	Faden *m*	thread	fil *m*	filo *m*	—
Himbeere (D)	—	raspberry	framboise *f*	lampone *m*	frambuesa *f*

	D	E	F	I	Es
Himmel (D)	—	sky	ciel m	cielo m	cielo m
hin (D)	—	there	jusqu'à/vers	là	hacia allá/hasta
hinab (D)	—	down	vers le bas	giù	hacia abajo
hinauf (D)	—	up	montez	su	hacia arriba
hinaufsteigen (D)	—	climb	monter	salire	subir
hinaus (D)	—	out	dehors	fuori	hacia afuera
hinausgehen (D)	—	go out	sortir	uscire	salir afuera
hinchado (Es)	geschwollen	swollen	enflé(e)	gonfio(a)	—
hinder (E)	hindern	—	empêcher	impedire	impedir
hindern (D)	—	hinder	empêcher	impedire	impedir
hindurch (D)	—	through	à travers	attraverso	a través de
hinein (D)	—	in	dans	dentro	dentro
hinlegen (D)	—	put down	poser	posare	poner
hinsetzen (D)	—	sit down	asseoir, se	sedersi	sentarse
hint (E)	Hinweis m	—	indication f	indicazione f	indicación f
hinten (D)	—	behind	derrière	dietro	detrás
hintereinander (D)	—	one after the other	l'un derrière l'autre	uno dopo l'altro	uno detras de otro
hinterlassen (D)	—	leave	laisser	lasciare	dejar
hinterlegen (D)	—	deposit	déposer	depositare	depositar
hinüber (D)	—	across	de l'autre côté	di là	hacia el otro lado
hinunter (D)	—	down	vers le bas	giù	hacia abajo
hinuntergehen (D)	—	descend	descendre	scendere	bajar
Hinweis (D)	—	hint	indication f	indicazione f	indicación f
hinzufügen (D)	—	add	ajouter	aggiungere	añadir
hip (E)	Hüfte f	—	hanche f	fianco m	cadera f
Hirn (D)	—	brain	cerveau m	cervello m	cerebro m
histoire (F)	Geschichte f	history	—	storia f	historia f
historia (Es)	Geschichte f	history	histoire f	storia f	—
history (E)	Geschichte f	—	histoire f	storia f	historia f
hit[1] (E)	schlagen	—	battre	battere	golpear
hit[2] (E)	treffen	—	toucher	colpire	alcanzar
hitch-hiker (E)	Anhalter m	—	auto-stoppeur m	autostoppista m	autoestopista m
Hitze (D)	—	heat	chaleur f	caldo m	calor m
hiver (F)	Winter m	winter	—	inverno m	invierno m
hoch (D)	—	up/high	haut(e)	alto(a)	alto(a)
Hochgebirge (D)	—	high mountain-chain	haute montage f	alta montagna f	montañas elevadas $f\,pl$
Hochsaison (D)	—	high season	pleine saison f	alta stagione f	temporada alta f
Hochschule (D)	—	university	université f	istituto supériore m	escuela superior f
höchstens (D)	—	at the most	tout au plus	al massimo	a lo sumo
Höchstgeschwindigkeit (D)	—	maximum speed	vitesse maximum f	velocità massima f	velocidad máxima f
Höchstpreis (D)	—	maximum price	prix plafond m	prezzo massimo m	precio máximo m
Hochzeit (D)	—	wedding	mariage m	nozze $f\,pl$	boda f

	D	E	F	I	Es
hocico (Es)	Maul *n*	mouth	gueule *f*	muso *m*	—
Hof (D)	—	yard	cour *f*	cortile *m*	patio *m*
hoffen (D)	—	hope	espérer	sperare	esperar
hoffentlich (D)	—	hopefully	espérons	speriamo que	espero que
höflich (D)	—	polite	poli(e)	cortese	cortés
Höflichkeit (D)	—	politeness	politesse *f*	cortesia *f*	cortesía *f*
Höhe (D)	—	height	hauteur	altezza *f*	altura *f*
hohl (D)	—	hollow	creux(-euse)	cavo	hueco(a)
Höhle (D)	—	cave	grotte *f*	caverna *f*	cueva *f*
hoja (Es)	Blatt *n*	leaf	feuille *f*	foglia *f*	—
hold (E)	halten	—	tenir	tenere	sujetar
hole (E)	Loch *n*	—	trou *m*	buco *m*	agujero *m*
holen (D)	—	fetch	aller chercher	andare a prendere	traer
holiday[1] (E)	Feiertag *m*	—	jour férié *m*	giorno festivo *m*	día de fiesta *m*
holiday[2] (E)	schulfrei	—	de congé	vacanza *f*	sin colegio
holidays (E)	Ferien *pl*	—	vacances *f pl*	vacanze *f pl*	vacaciones *f pl*
Hölle (D)	—	hell	enfer *m*	inferno *m*	infierno *m*
hollow (E)	hohl	—	creux(-euse)	cavo(a)	hueco(a)
holy (E)	heilig	—	saint(e)	santo(a)	santo(a)
Holy week (E)	Osterwoche *f*	—	semaine sainte *f*	settimana santa *f*	Semana Santa *f*
Holz (D)	—	wood	bois *m*	legno *m*	madera *f*
hombre (Es)	Mann *m*	man	homme *m*	uomo *m*	—
hombro (Es)	Schulter *f*	shoulder	épaule *f*	spalla *f*	—
home[1] (E)	Heimat *f*	—	patrie *f*	patria *f*	patria *f*
home[2] (E)	nach Hause	—	à la maison	a casa	a casa
homesickness (E)	Heimweh *n*	—	mal du pays *m*	nostalgia *f*	nostalgia *f*
homme[1] (F)	Mensch *m*	human being	—	essere umano *m*	persona *f*
homme[2] (F)	Mann *m*	man	—	uomo *m*	hombre *m*
honest[1] (E)	aufrichtig	—	sincère	onesto(a)	sincero(a)
honest[2] (E)	ehrlich	—	honnête	onesto(a)	honesto(a)
honesto (Es)	ehrlich	honest	honnête	onesto(a)	—
honey (E)	Honig *m*	—	miel *m*	miele *m*	miel *f*
honeymoon (E)	Flitterwochen *pl*	—	lune de miel *f*	luna di miele *f*	luna de miel *f*
hongo (Es)	Pilz *m*	mushroom	champignon *m*	fungo *m*	—
Honig (D)	—	honey	miel *m*	miele *m*	miel *f*
honnête (F)	ehrlich	honest	—	onesto(a)	honesto(a)
honneur (F)	Ehre *f*	honour	—	onore *m*	honor *m*
honor (Es)	Ehre *f*	honour	honneur *m*	onore *m*	—
honour (E)	Ehre *f*	—	honneur *m*	onore *m*	honor *m*
honte (F)	Schande *f*	disgrace	—	vergogna *f*	deshonra *f*
hood (E)	Kapuze *f*	—	capuchon *m*	cappuccio *m*	capucha *f*
hook (E)	Haken *m*	—	crochet *m*	gancio *m*	gancho *m*
hope (E)	hoffen	—	espérer	sperare	esperar
hopefully (E)	hoffentlich	—	espérons	speriamo que	espero que

	D	E	F	I	Es
hôpital (F)	Krankenhaus n	hospital	—	ospedale m	hospital m
hora (Es)	Stunde f	hour	heure f	ora f	—
horación (Es)	Gebet n	prayer	prière f	preghiera f	—
hora de consulta (Es)	Sprechstunde f	consultation hour	heures de consultation f pl	ora di ricevimento f	—
horaire (F)	Fahrplan m	timetable	—	orario m	horario m
horario (Es)	Fahrplan m	timetable	horaire m	orario m	—
horario de abertura (Es)	Öffnungszeiten pl	opening times	heures d'ouverture f pl	orario di apertura m pl	—
hören (D)	—	hear	entendre	sentire	oír
Hörer[1] (D)	—	listener	auditeur m	ascoltatore m	oyente m
Hörer[2] (D)	—	receiver	récepteur m	ricevitore m	auricular m
horizontal (E)	waagrecht	—	horizontal(e)	orizzontale	horizontal
horizontal (Es)	waagrecht	horizontal	horizontal(e)	orizzontale	—
horizontal (F)	waagrecht	horizontal	—	orizzontale	horizontal
horn (E)	Hupe f	—	claxon m	clacson m	bocina f
horrible (E)	schauderhaft	—	horrible	spaventoso(a)	espantoso(a)
horrible[1] (Es)	abscheulich	abominable	affreux(-euse)	disgustoso(a)	—
horrible[2] (Es)	schrecklich	terrible	terrible	spaventoso(a)	—
horrible (F)	schauderhaft	horrible	—	spaventoso(a)	espantoso(a)
hors de[1] (F)	außerhalb	out of	—	fuori di	fuera de
hors de[2] (F)	außer	except	—	eccetto	salvo
hors de question (F)	ausgeschlossen	impossible	—	escluso	imposible
hors-d'œuvre (F)	Vorspeise f	appetizer	—	antipasto m	primer plato m
horse (E)	Pferd n	—	cheval m	cavallo m	caballo m
Hose (D)	—	trousers	pantalon m	pantaloni m pl	pantalón m
hospedaje (Es)	Unterkunft f	accommodation	logement m	alloggio m	—
hospitable (E)	gastfreundlich	—	hospitalier(-ière)	ospitale	hospitalario(a)
hospital[1] (E)	Krankenhaus n	—	hôpital m	ospedale m	hospital m
hospital[2] (E)	Klinik f	—	clinique f	clinica f	clínica f
hospital (Es)	Krankenhaus n	hospital	hôpital m	ospedale m	—
hospitalario (Es)	gastfreundlich	hospitable	hospitalier(-ière)	ospitale	—
hospitalidad (Es)	Gastfreundschaft f	hospitality	hospitalité f	ospitalità f	—
hospitalier (F)	gastfreundlich	hospitable	—	ospitale	hospitalario(a)
hospitalité (F)	Gastfreundschaft f	hospitality	—	ospitalità f	hospitalidad f
hospitality (E)	Gastfreundschaft f	—	hospitalité f	ospitalità f	hospitalidad f
host (E)	Gastgeber m	—	hôte m	ospite m	anfitrión m
hostess (I)	Stewardeß f	stewardess	hôtesse de l'air f	—	azafata f
hot[1] (E)	heiß	—	chaud(e)	caldo	caliente
hot[2] (E)	scharf	—	épicé(e)	piccante	picante
hôte[1] (F)	Gast m	guest	—	ospite m	invitado m
hôte[2] (F)	Gastgeber m	host	—	ospit m	anfitrión m
Hotel (D)	—	hotel	hôtel m	albergo m	hotel m
hotel[1] (E)	Gasthaus n	—	auberge f	osteria f	posada f
hotel[2] (E)	Hotel n	—	hôtel m	albergo m	hotel m

hundred

	D	E	F	I	Es
hotel (Es)	Hotel *n*	hotel	hôtel *m*	albergo *m*	—
hôtel (F)	Hotel *n*	hotel	—	albergo *m*	hotel *m*
hôtesse de l'air (F)	Stewardeß *f*	stewardess	—	hostess *f*	azafata *f*
hour (E)	Stunde *f*	—	heure *f*	ora *f*	hora *f*
hourly (E)	stündlich	—	toutes les heures	ogni ora	cada hora
house (E)	Haus *n*	—	maison *f*	casa *f*	casa *f*
household (E)	Haushalt *m*	—	ménage *m*	casa *f*	casa *f*
housewife (E)	Hausfrau *f*	—	femme de maison *f*	casalinga *f*	ama de casa *f*
how (E)	wie	—	comment	come	cómo
however (E)	jedoch	—	cependant	tutta via	sin embargo
how many (E)	wieviele	—	combien	quanti(e)	cuántos(as)
how much (E)	wieviel	—	combien	quanto	cuánto
hoy (Es)	heute	today	aujourd'hui	oggi	—
hoy en día (Es)	heutzutage	nowadays	de nos jour	oggigiorno	—
hübsch (D)	—	pretty	joli(e)	carino(a)	bonito(a)
hueco (Es)	hohl	hollow	creux(-euse)	cavo(a)	—
huelga (Es)	Streik *m*	strike	grève *f*	sciopero *m*	—
huérfano (Es)	Waise *f*	orphan	orphelin *m*	orfano *m*	—
hueso[1] (Es)	Kern *m*	pip	noyau *m*	nocciolo *m*	—
hueso[2] (Es)	Knochen *m*	bone	os *m*	osso *m*	—
huevo (Es)	Ei *n*	egg	œuf *m*	uovo *m*	—
Hüfte (D)	—	hip	hanche *f*	fianco *m*	cadera *f*
huge (E)	riesig	—	énorme	enorme	enorme
Hügel (D)	—	hill	colline *f*	collina *f*	colina *f*
Huhn (D)	—	chicken	poule *f*	pollo *m*	gallina *f*
huile (F)	Öl *n*	oil	—	olio *m*	aceite *m*
huir (Es)	entfliehen	escape	échapper, se	scappare	—
huit (F)	acht	eight	—	otto	ocho
huître (F)	Auster *f*	oyster	—	ostrica *f*	ostra *f*
humain (F)	menschlich	human	—	umano(a)	humano(a)
human (E)	menschlich	—	humain(e)	umano(a)	humano(a)
human being (E)	Mensch *m*	—	homme *m*	essere umano *m*	persona *f*
humano (Es)	menschlich	human	humain(e)	umano(a)	—
húmedo[1] (Es)	feucht	damp	humide	umido(a)	—
húmedo[2] (Es)	naß	wet	mouillé(e)	bagnato(a)	—
humeur (F)	Laune *f*	mood	—	umore *m*	humor *m*
humide (F)	feucht	damp	—	umido(a)	húmedo(a)
humo (Es)	Rauch *m*	smoke	fumée *f*	fumo *m*	—
humor (Es)	Laune *f*	mood	humeur *f*	umore *m*	—
Hund (D)	—	dog	chien *m*	cane *m*	perro *m*
hundert (D)	—	hundred	cent	cento	cien
hundirse[1] (Es)	sinken	sink	couler	affondare	—
hundirse[2] (Es)	versinken	sink	enfoncer, se	affondare	—
hundred (E)	hundert	—	cent	cento	cien

	D	E	F	I	Es
Hunger (D)	—	hunger	faim *f*	fame *f*	hambre *m*
hunger (E)	Hunger *m*	—	faim *f*	fame *f*	hambre *m*
hungrig (D)	—	hungry	affamé(e)	affamato(a)	hambriento(a)
hungry (E)	hungrig	—	affamé(e)	affamato(a)	hambriento(a)
hunt¹ (E)	jagen	—	chasser	cacciare	cazar
hunt² (E)	Jagd *f*	—	chasse *f*	caccia *f*	caza *f*
Hupe (D)	—	horn	claxon *m*	clacson *m*	bocina *f*
hüpfen (D)	—	jump	sautiller	saltellare	saltar
hurried (E)	eilig	—	pressé(e)	frettoloso(a)	rápido(a)
hurry (E)	eilen	—	dépêcher, se	andare in fretta	darse prisa
hurry up (E)	beeilen, sich	—	dépêcher, se	affrettarsi	darse prisa
hurt (E)	weh	—	douloureux(-euse)	dolente	doloroso(a)
husband (E)	Ehemann *m*	—	mari *m*	marito *m*	marido *m*
husten (D)	—	cough	tousser	tossire	toser
Husten (D)	—	cough	toux *m*	tosse *f*	tos *f*
Hut (D)	—	hat	chapeau *m*	cappello *m*	sombrero *m*
hut (E)	Hütte *f*	—	cabane *f*	capanna *f*	cabaña *f*
Hütte (D)	—	hut	cabane *f*	capanna *f*	cabaña *f*
I (E)	ich	—	je/moi	io	yo
ice (E)	Eis *n*	—	glace *f*	gelato *m*	hielo *m*
ich (D)	—	I	je/moi	io	yo
ici¹ (F)	her	here	—	qua/qui/da	aquí
ici² (F)	hier	here	—	qui	aquí
idea¹ (E)	Idee *f*	—	idée *f*	idea *f*	idea *f*
idea² (E)	Vorstellung *f*	—	idée *f*	idea *f*	idea *f*
idea¹ (Es)	Idee *f*	idea	idée *f*	idea *f*	—
idea² (Es)	Vorstellung *f*	idea	idée *f*	idea *f*	—
idea¹ (I)	Idee *f*	idea	idée *f*	—	idea *f*
idea² (I)	Vorstellung *f*	idea	idée *f*	—	idea *f*
ideal (D)	—	ideal	idéal(e)	ideale	ideal
ideal¹ (E)	ideal	—	idéal(e)	ideale	ideal
ideal² (E)	Vorbild *n*	—	modèle *m*	modello *m*	modelo *m*
ideal (Es)	ideal	ideal	idéal(e)	ideale	—
idéal (F)	ideal	ideal	—	ideale	ideal
ideale (I)	ideal	ideal	idéal(e)	—	ideal
Idee (D)	—	idea	idée *f*	idea *f*	idea *f*
idée (F)	Idee *f*	idea	—	idea *f*	idea *f*
idéntico (Es)	gleich	same	égal(e)	identico(a)	—
identico (I)	gleich	same	égal(e)	—	idéntico(a)
identity card (E)	Personalausweis *m*	—	carte d'identité *f*	carta d'identitá *f*	documento de identidad *m*
idioma extranjero (Es)	Fremdsprache *f*	foreign language	langue étrangère *f*	lingua straniera *f*	—
ieri (I)	gestern	yesterday	hier	—	ayer
if (E)	ob	—	si	se	si

imbarazzo

	D	E	F	I	Es
iglesia (Es)	Kirche *f*	church	église *f*	chiesa *f*	—
ignite (E)	zünden	—	allumer, se	accendersi	encender
ignorar (Es)	ignorieren	ignore	ignorer	ignorare	—
ignorare (I)	ignorieren	ignore	ignorer	—	ignorar
ignore[1] (E)	ignorieren	—	ignorer	ignorare	ignorar
ignore[2] (E)	übersehen	—	ignorer	non vedere	no ver
ignorer[1] (F)	ignorieren	ignore	—	ignorare	ignorar
ignorer[2] (F)	übersehen	ignore	—	non vedere	no ver
ignorieren (D)	—	ignore	ignorer	ignorare	ignorar
igual (Es)	egal	all the same	égal(e)	uguale	—
ihr (D)	—	you	vous	voi	vosotros
il (F)	er	he	—	lui/egli/esso	él
il, la[1] (I)	der, die, das	the	le, la	—	el, la, lo
il, la[2] (I)	das	that/which	le, la	—	lo
île (F)	Insel *f*	island	—	isola *f*	isla *f*
ilegal (Es)	gesetzwidrig	illegal	illégal(e)	illegale	—
ilegítimo (Es)	unrechtmäßig	unlawful	illégitime	illegale	—
ilimitado (Es)	unbegrenzt	unlimited	illimité(e)	illimitato(a)	—
ill (E)	krank	—	malade	malato(a)	enfermo(a)
illegal (E)	gesetzwidrig	—	illégal(e)	illegale	ilegal
illégal (F)	gesetzwidrig	illegal	—	illegale	ilegal
illegale[1] (I)	gesetzwidrig	illegal	illégal(e)	—	ilegal
illegale[2] (I)	unrechtmäßig	unlawful	illégitime	—	ilegítimo(a)
illégitime (F)	unrechtmäßig	unlawful	—	illegale	ilegítimo(a)
illimitato (I)	unbegrenzt	unlimited	illimité(e)	—	ilimitado(a)
illimité (F)	unbegrenzt	unlimited	—	illimitato(a)	ilimitado(a)
illness (E)	Krankheit *f*	—	maladie *f*	malattia *f*	enfermedad *f*
illuminare (I)	beleuchten	illuminate	éclairer	—	iluminar
illuminate (E)	beleuchten	—	éclairer	illuminare	iluminar
illuminazione (I)	Beleuchtung *f*	lighting	éclairage *m*	—	iluminación *f*
il lunedì (I)	montags	Mondays	le lundi	—	los lunes
illustré (F)	Illustrierte *f*	illustrated magazine	—	rivista *f*	revista
Illustrierte (D)	—	illustrated magazine	illustré *m*	rivista *f*	revista
il quale (I)	welche(r,s)	which	qui/que	—	¿cual?
ils (F)	sie	they	—	loro	ellos, ellas
iluminación (Es)	Beleuchtung *f*	lighting	éclairage *m*	illuminazione *f*	—
iluminar (Es)	beleuchten	illuminate	éclairer	illuminare	—
image (F)	Bild *n*	picture	—	immagine *f*	cuadro *m*
imaginarse (Es)	einbilden, sich	imagine	imaginer, se	immaginarsi	—
imagine (E)	einbilden, sich	—	imaginer, se	immaginarsi	imaginarse
imaginer, se (F)	einbilden, sich	imagine	—	immaginarsi	imaginarse
imbarazzante (I)	peinlich	embarrassing	gênant(e)	—	desagradable
imbarazzo (I)	Verlegenheit *f*	embarrassment	gêne *f*	—	contratiempo *m*

	D	E	F	I	Es
Imbiß (D)	—	snack	casse-croûte *m*	spuntino *m*	refrigerio *m*
imbucare (I)	einwerfen	post	poster	—	echar
imitar (Es)	nachahmen	imitate	imiter	imitare	—
imitare (I)	nachahmen	imitate	imiter	—	imitar
imitate (E)	nachahmen	—	imiter	imitare	imitar
imité (F)	unecht	fake	—	falso(a)	falso(a)
imiter (F)	nachahmen	imitate	—	imitare	imitar
immaginarsi (I)	einbilden, sich	imagine	imaginer, se	—	imaginarse
immagine (I)	Bild *n*	picture	image *f*	—	cuadro *m*
immédiat (F)	unmittelbar	immediate	—	inmediato(a)	directo(a)
immediate (E)	unmittelbar	—	immédiat(e)	inmediato(a)	directo(a)
immediately (E)	sofort	—	immédiatement	subito	en seguida
immédiatement (F)	sofort	immediately	—	subito	en seguida
immediato (I)	unmittelbar	immediate	immédiat(e)	—	directo(a)
immer (D)	—	always	toujours	sempre	siempre
immergere (I)	tauchen	dive	plonger	—	bucear
immobile (F)	bewegungslos	motionless	—	immobile	inmóvil
immobile (I)	bewegungslos	motionless	immobile	—	inmóvil
immondizia (I)	Abfall *m*	rubbish	déchets *m pl*	—	basura *f*
impacchettare (I)	verpacken	pack	emballer	—	empaquetar
impacciato (I)	ungeschickt	clumsy	maladroit(e)	—	torpe
impair (F)	ungerade	uneven	—	dispari	impar
impar (Es)	ungerade	uneven	impair(e)	dispari	—
imparare (I)	lernen	learn	apprendre	—	aprender
imparentato (I)	verwandt	related	parent(e)	—	emparentado(a)
impatient (E)	ungeduldig	—	impatient(e)	impaziente	impaciente
impatient (F)	ungeduldig	impatient	—	impaziente	impaciente
impaziente (I)	ungeduldig	impatient	impatient(e)	—	impaciente
impedido (Es)	verhindert	unable to make it	empêché(e)	impedito(a)	—
impedir (Es)	hindern	hinder	empêcher	impedire	—
impedire[1] (I)	hindern	hinder	empêcher	—	impedir
impedire[2] (I)	verhindern	prevent	empêcher	—	evitar
impedito (I)	verhindert	unable to make it	empêché(e)	—	impedido(a)
imperatore (I)	Kaiser *m*	emperor	empereur *m*	—	emperador *m*
impermeabile (I)	Regenmantel *m*	raincoat	imperméable *m*	—	impermeable *m*
impermeable (Es)	Regenmantel *m*	raincoat	imperméable *m*	impermeabile *m*	—
imperméable (F)	Regenmantel *m*	raincoat	—	impermeabile *m*	impermeable *m*
impfen (D)	—	vaccinate	vacciner	vaccinare	vacunar
Impfung (D)	—	vaccination	vaccination *f*	vaccinazione *f*	vacunación *f*
impianto (I)	Anlage *f*	plant	construction *f*	—	establecimiento *m*
impiegare (I)	anwenden	apply	employer	—	usar
impiegato (I)	Angestellter *m*	employee	employé *m*	—	empleado *m*
impiegato statale (I)	Beamter *m*	civil servant	fonctionnaire *m*	—	funcionario *m*
impoli (F)	unhöflich	impolite	—	scortese	descortés

imprudente

	D	E	F	I	Es
impolite (E)	unhöflich	—	impoli(e)	scortese	descortés
Import (D)	—	import	importation f	importazione f	importación f
import[1] (E)	Einfuhr f	—	importation f	importazione f	importación f
import[2] (E)	Import m	—	importation f	importazione f	importación f
importación[1] (Es)	Einfuhr f	import	importation f	importazione f	—
importación[2] (Es)	Import m	import	importation f	importazione f	—
important (E)	wichtig	—	important(e)	importante	importante
important[1] (F)	bedeutend	significant	—	importante	importante
important[2] (F)	wichtig	important	—	importante	importante
importante[1] (Es)	bedeutend	significant	important(e)	importante	—
importante[2] (Es)	wichtig	important	important(e)	importante	—
importante[1] (I)	bedeutend	significant	important(e)	—	importante
importante[2] (I)	wichtig	important	important(e)	—	importante
importation[1] (F)	Einfuhr f	import	—	importazione f	importación f
importation[2] (F)	Import m	import	—	importazione f	importación f
importazione[1] (I)	Einfuhr f	import	importation f	—	importación f
importazione[2] (I)	Import m	import	importation f	—	importación f
importe (Es)	Betrag m	amount	montant m	somma f	—
importun (F)	lästig	troublesome	—	molesto(a)	desagradable
importunare (I)	belästigen	annoy	importuner	—	molestar
importuner (F)	belästigen	annoy	—	importunare	molestar
imposible[1] (Es)	ausgeschlossen	impossible	hors de question	escluso(a)	—
imposible[2] (Es)	unmöglich	impossible	impossible	impossibile	—
impossibile (I)	unmöglich	impossible	impossible	—	imposible
impossible[1] (E)	ausgeschlossen	—	hors de question	escluso(a)	imposible
impossible[2] (E)	unmöglich	—	impossible	impossibile	imposible
impossible (F)	unmöglich	impossible	—	impossibile	imposible
imposta sul'valore aggiunto (I)	Mehrwertsteuer f	value added tax	taxe sur la valeur ajoutée f	—	impuesto sobre el valor añadido m
imposte (I)	Steuern pl	tax	impôt m	—	impuesto m
impôt (F)	Steuern pl	tax	—	imposte f pl	impuesto m
imprecare (I)	schimpfen	scold	gronder	—	insultar
impreciso (I)	ungenau	inaccurate	inexact(e)	—	inexacto(a)
impresa (I)	Unternehmen n	company	entreprise f	—	empresa f
impresión (Es)	Eindruck m	impression	impression f	impressione f	—
impression (E)	Eindruck m	—	impression f	impressione f	impresión f
impression (F)	Eindruck m	impression	—	impressione f	impresión f
impressione (I)	Eindruck m	impression	impression f	—	impresión f
improbabile (I)	unwahrscheinlich	unlikely	invraisemblable	—	improbable
improbable (Es)	unwahrscheinlich	unlikely	invraisemblable	improbabile	—
improve (E)	verbessern	—	améliorer	migliorare	mejorar
improvement (E)	Besserung f	—	amélioration f	miglioramento m	restablecimiento m
improvviso (I)	abrupt	abrupt	subit(e)	—	súbito(a)
imprudent (F)	unvorsichtig	careless	—	imprudente	descuidado(a)
imprudente (Es)	leichtsinnig	careless	étourdi(e)	spensierato(a)	—

	D	E	F	I	Es
imprudente (I)	unvorsichtig	careless	imprudent(e)	—	descuidado(a)
impuesto (Es)	Steuern *pl*	tax	impôt *m*	imposte *f pl*	—
impuesto sobre el valor añadido (Es)	Mehrwertsteuer *f*	value added tax	taxe sur la valeur ajoutée *f*	imposta sul'valore aggiunto *f*	—
impulsivo (Es)	rasch	quick	rapide	rapido(a)	—
imstande (D)	—	able	capable	capace	en condiciones
in (D)	—	in/into	dans/à/en	in/a/tra/fra	en/a
in[1] (E)	herein	—	vers l'intérieur	dentro	adentro
in[2] (E)	hinein	—	dans	dentro	dentro
in[3] (E)	in	—	dans/à/en	in/a/tra/fra	en/a
in (I)	in	in/into	dans/à/en	—	en/a
inaccurate (E)	ungenau	—	inexact(e)	impreciso(a)	inexacto(a)
in addition (E)	zusätzlich	—	supplémentaire	supplementare	adicional
inadecuado (Es)	unpassend	inappropriate	mal à propos	sconveniente	—
inaguantable (Es)	unerträglich	unbearable	insupportable	insopportabile	—
in a muddle (E)	durcheinander	—	pêle-mêle	sottosopra	en desorden
in any case (E)	jedenfalls	—	en tout cas	in ogni caso	en cualquier caso
inappropriate (E)	unpassend	—	mal à propos	sconveniente	inadecuado(a)
inatteso (I)	unerwartet	unexpected	inattendu(e)	—	inesperado(a)
in basso (I)	nieder	inferior	bas(se)	—	abajo
inbegriffen (D)	—	included	compris	compreso(a)	incluído(a)
inbetween (E)	dazwischen	—	entre	in mezzo	entre
inborn (E)	angeboren	—	inné(e)	innato(a)	innato(a)
incapable (E)	unfähig	—	incapable	incapace	incapaz
incapable[1] (F)	untauglich	unfit	—	incapace	inútil
incapable[2] (F)	unfähig	incapable	—	incapace	incapaz
incapace[1] (I)	untauglich	unfit	incapable	—	inútil
incapace[2] (I)	unfähig	incapable	incapable	—	incapaz
incapaz (Es)	unfähig	incapable	incapable	incapace	—
incaricare (I)	beauftragen	instruct	charger de	—	encargar
incarico (I)	Aufgabe *f*	task	tâche *f*	—	tarea *f*
in case (E)	falls	—	au cas où	qualora	en caso de que
incassare[1] (I)	einkassieren	collect	recouvrer	—	cobrar
incassare[2] (I)	kassieren	take	encaisser	—	cobrar
incendie (F)	Brand *m*	fire	—	incendio *m*	incendio *m*
incendio (Es)	Brand *m*	fire	incendie *m*	incendio *m*	—
incendio (I)	Brand *m*	fire	incendie *m*	—	incendio *m*
incertain[1] (F)	unsicher	uncertain	—	incerto(a)	inseguro(a)
incertain[2] (F)	ungewiß	uncertain	—	incerto(a)	incierto(a)
incerto[1] (I)	ungewiß	uncertain	incertain(e)	—	incierto(a)
incerto[2] (I)	unsicher	uncertain	incertain(e)	—	inseguro(a)
incerto[3] (I)	unbestimmt	uncertain	indéfini(e)	—	indeterminado(a)
inchiesta (I)	Umfrage *f*	poll	enquête *f*	—	encuesta *f*
inciampare (I)	stolpern	stumble	trébucher	—	tropezar
incident (E)	Vorfall *m*	—	incident *m*	caso *m*	suceso *m*

	D	E	F	I	Es
incident (F)	Vorfall *m*	incident	—	caso *m*	suceso *m*
incidente (I)	Unfall *m*	accident	accident *m*	—	accidente *m*
incidente stradale (I)	Autounfall *m*	car accident	accident de voiture *m*	—	accidente de automóvil *m*
incierto (Es)	ungewiß	uncertain	incertain(e)	incerto(a)	—
incinta (I)	schwanger	pregnant	enceinte	—	embarazada
inclinado (Es)	steil	steep	raide	ripido(a)	—
inclinar (Es)	nicken	nod	faire un signe de tête	annuire	—
included (E)	inbegriffen	—	compris	compreso(a)	incluído(a)
including (E)	einschließlich	—	y compris	incluso(a)	incluído
incluído (Es)	inbegriffen	included	compris	compreso(a)	—
incluso[1] (Es)	einschließlich	including	y compris	incluso(a)	—
incluso[2] (Es)	sogar	even	même	perfino	—
incluso (I)	einschließlich	including	y compris	—	incluído
incollare (I)	kleben	stick	coller	—	pegar
income[1] (E)	Einkommen *n*	—	revenu *m*	entrate *f pl*	ingresos *m pl*
income[2] (E)	Verdienst *m*	—	revenus *m pl*	guadagno *m*	ganancia *f*
incómodo[1] (Es)	ungemütlich	uncomfortable	désagréable	poco accogliente	—
incómodo[2] (Es)	unbequem	uncomfortable	inconfortable	scomodo(a)	—
incomplet (F)	unvollständig	incomplete	—	incompleto(a)	incompleto(a)
incomplete (E)	unvollständig	—	incomplet(-ète)	incompleto(a)	incompleto(a)
incompleto (I)	unvollständig	incomplete	incomplet(-ète)	—	incompleto(a)
incompleto (Es)	unvollständig	incomplete	incomplet(-ète)	incompleto(a)	—
inconfortable (F)	unbequem	uncomfortable	—	scomodo(a)	incómodo(a)
inconnu (F)	unbekannt	unknown	—	sconosciuto(a)	desconocido(a)
incontestable (F)	eindeutig	unequivocal	—	univoco(a)	evidente
incontrare[1] (I)	begegnen	meet	rencontrer	—	encontrar
incontrare[2] (I)	treffen	meet	rencontrer	—	encontrar
incontro (I)	Treffen *n*	meeting	rencontre *f*	—	encuentro *m*
increase[1] (E)	vermehren	—	augmenter	aumentare	aumentar
increase[2] (E)	zunehmen	—	augmenter	aumentare	aumentar
incredibile (I)	unglaublich	incredible	incroyable	—	increíble
incredible (E)	unglaublich	—	incroyable	incredibile	increíble
increíble (Es)	unglaublich	incredible	incroyable	incredibile	—
incrocio (I)	Kreuzung *f*	crossing	intersection *f*	—	cruce *m*
incroyable (F)	unglaublich	incredible	—	incredibile	increíble
indecent (E)	unanständig	—	indécent(e)	indecente	inmoral
indécent (F)	unanständig	indecent	—	indecente	inmoral
indecente (I)	unanständig	indecent	indécent(e)	—	inmoral
indeciso (I)	unentschlossen	undecided	irrésolu(e)	—	irresoluto(a)
indéfini (F)	unbestimmt	uncertain	—	incerto(a)	indeterminado(a)
indépendant[1] (F)	selbständig	independent	—	indipendente	independiente
indépendant[2] (F)	unabhängig	independent	—	indipendente	independiente
independent[1] (E)	selbständig	—	indépendant(e)	indipendente	independiente

	D	E	F	I	Es
independent[2] (E)	unabhängig	—	indépendant(e)	indipendente	independiente
independiente[1] (Es)	selbständig	independent	indépendant(e)	indipendente	—
independiente[2] (Es)	unabhängig	independent	indépendant(e)	indipendente	—
indeseado (Es)	unerwünscht	unwelcome	inopportun(e)	indesiderato(a)	—
indesiderato (I)	unerwünscht	unwelcome	inopportun(e)	—	indeseado(a)
indessen (D)	—	meanwhile	cependant	nel frattempo	en eso
indeterminado (Es)	unbestimmt	uncertain	indéfini(e)	incerto(a)	—
Indianer (D)	—	Red Indian	Indien m	indiano m	indio m
indiano (I)	Indianer m	Red Indian	Indien m	—	indio m
indicación (Es)	Hinweis m	hint	indication f	indicazione f	—
indicado (Es)	geeignet	suitable	approprié(e)	adatto(a)	—
indicar (Es)	zeigen	show	montrer	mostrare	—
indicatif téléphonique (F)	Vorwahl f	dialling code	—	prefisso m	prefijo m
indicazione[1] (I)	Angabe f	information	information f	—	información f
indicazione[2] (I)	Hinweis m	hint	indication f	—	indicación f
índice (Es)	Inhalts-verzeichnis n	table of contents	table des matières f	indice m	—
indice (I)	Inhalts-verzeichnis n	table of contents	table des matières f	—	índice m
Indien (F)	Indianer m	Red Indian	—	indiano m	indio m
in dietro (I)	rückwärts	backwards	en arrière	—	marcha atrás
indietro (I)	zurück	back	de retour	—	atrás
indigène (F)	einheimisch	native	—	indigeno(a)	nativo
indigeno (I)	einheimisch	native	indigène	—	nativo
indignado (Es)	empört	indignant	révolté(e)	indignato(a)	—
indignant (E)	empört	—	révolté(e)	indignato(a)	indignado(a)
indignato (I)	empört	indignant	révolté(e)	—	indignado(a)
indio (Es)	Indianer m	Red Indian	Indien m	indiano m	—
indipendente[1] (I)	selbständig	independent	indépendant(e)	—	independiente
indipendente[2] (I)	unabhängig	independent	indépendant(e)	—	independiente
indirizzare (I)	adressieren	address	adresser	—	poner las señas en
indirizzo (I)	Anschrift f / Adresse f	address	adresse f	—	dirección f
in discesa (I)	bergab	downhill	en descendant	—	cuesta abajo
indispensabile (I)	unentbehrlich	indispensable	indispensable	—	indispensable
indispensable (E)	unentbehrlich	—	indispensable	indispensabile	indispensable
indispensable (Es)	unentbehrlich	indispensable	indispensable	indispensabile	—
indispensable (F)	unentbehrlich	indispensable	—	indispensabile	indispensable
indisposé (F)	unwohl	unwell	—	indisposto(a)	indispuesto(a)
indisposto (I)	unwohl	unwell	indisposé(e)	—	indispuesto(a)
indispuesto (Es)	unwohl	unwell	indisposé(e)	indisposto(a)	—
indoor swimming pool (E)	Hallenbad n	—	piscine f	piscina coperta f	piscina cubierta f
indossare[1] (I)	anhaben	have on	porter	—	llevar
indossare[2] (I)	anziehen	dress	mettre	—	ponerse

	D	E	F	I	Es
indovinare (I)	raten	guess	deviner	—	adivinar
industria (Es)	Industrie f	industry	industrie f	industria f	—
industria (I)	Industrie f	industry	industrie f	—	industria f
Industrie (D)	—	industry	industrie f	industria f	industria f
industrie (F)	Industrie f	industry	—	industria f	industria f
industry (E)	Industrie f	—	industrie f	industria f	industria f
ineinander (D)	—	into one another	l'un dans l'autre	l'uno nell'altro	uno en otro
inesperado (Es)	unerwartet	unexpected	inattendu(e)	inatteso(a)	—
inesperto (I)	unerfahren	inexperienced	inexpérimenté(e)	—	inexperto(a)
inevitabile (I)	unvermeidlich	inevitable	inévitable	—	inevitable
inevitable (E)	unvermeidlich	—	inévitable	inevitabile	inevitable
inevitable (Es)	unvermeidlich	inevitable	inévitable	inevitabile	—
inévitable (F)	unvermeidlich	inevitable	—	inevitabile	inevitable
inexact (F)	ungenau	inaccurate	—	impreciso(a)	inexacto(a)
inexacto (Es)	ungenau	inaccurate	inexact(e)	impreciso(a)	—
inexpensive (E)	preiswert	—	bon marché	conveniente	económico(a)
inexperienced (E)	unerfahren	—	inexpérimenté(e)	inesperto(a)	inexperto(a)
inexpérimenté (F)	unerfahren	inexperienced	—	inesperto(a)	inexperto(a)
inexperto (Es)	unerfahren	inexperienced	inexpérimenté(e)	inesperto(a)	—
infanzia (I)	Kindheit f	childhood	enfance f	—	niñez f
inférieur (F)	unterste(r,s)	lowest	-—	inferiore	inferior(a)
inferior (E)	nieder	—	bas(se)	in basso	abajo
inferior (Es)	unterste(r,s)	lowest	inférieur(e)	inferiore	—
inferiore (I)	unterste(r,s)	lowest	inférieur(e)	—	inferior(a)
infermiera (I)	Kranken- schwester f	nurse	infirmière f	—	enfermera f
infermiere (I)	Kranken- pfleger m	nursing orderly	infirmier m	—	enfermero m
inferno (I)	Hölle f	hell	enfer m	—	infierno m
infiammabile (I)	feuergefährlich	inflammable	inflammable	—	inflamable
infiammazione (I)	Entzündung f	inflammation	inflammation f	—	inflamación f
infierno (Es)	Hölle f	hell	enfer m	inferno m	—
infine (I)	zuletzt	finally	finalement	—	por último
infirmier (F)	Kranken- pfleger m	nursing orderly	—	infermiere m	enfermero m
infirmière (F)	Kranken- schwester f	nurse	—	infermiera f	enfermera f
inflamable (Es)	feuergefährlich	inflammable	inflammable	infiammabile	—
inflamación (Es)	Entzündung f	inflammation	inflammation f	infiammazione f	—
inflammable (E)	feuergefährlich	—	inflammable	infiammabile	inflamable
inflammable (F)	feuergefährlich	inflammable	—	infiammabile	inflamable
inflammation (E)	Entzündung f	—	inflammation f	infiammazione f	inflamación f
inflammation (F)	Entzündung f	inflammation	—	infiammazione f	inflamación f
influence¹ (E)	beeinflussen	—	influencer	influenzare	influir
influence² (E)	Einfluß m	—	influence f	influenza f	influencia f
influence (F)	Einfluß m	influence	—	influenza f	influencia f

	D	E	F	I	Es
influencer (F)	beeinflussen	influence	—	influenzare	influir
influencia (Es)	Einfluß *m*	influence	influence *f*	influenza *f*	—
influenza¹ (I)	Einfluß *m*	influence	influence *f*	—	influencia *f*
influenza² (I)	Grippe *f*	flu	grippe *f*	—	gripe *f*
influenzare (I)	beeinflussen	influence	influencer	—	influir
influir (Es)	beeinflussen	influence	influencer	influenzare	—
infolge (D)	—	as a result of	par suite de	in seguito a	por
in fondo (I)	eigentlich	actually	en fait	—	en realidad
inform¹ (E)	benachrichtigen	—	informer	informare	avisar
inform² (E)	informieren	—	informer	informare	informar
inform³ (E)	verständigen	—	prévenir	informare	informar
inform s.o. (E)	mitteilen	—	informer qn de qch	comunicare	comunicar
información¹ (Es)	Auskunft *f*	information	renseigne-ment *m*	informazione *f*	—
información² (Es)	Angabe *f*	information	information *f*	indicazione *f*	—
informar¹ (Es)	berichten	report	faire un rapport	riferire	—
informar² (Es)	informieren	inform	informer	informare	—
informar³ (Es)	verständigen	inform	prévenir	informare	—
informare¹ (I)	benachrichtigen	inform	informer	—	avisar
informare² (I)	informieren	inform	informer	—	informar
informare³ (I)	verständigen	inform	prévenir	—	informar
informarse (Es)	erkundigen, sich	inquire	renseigner, se	informarsi	—
informarsi (I)	erkundigen, sich	inquire	renseigner, se	—	informarse
information¹ (E)	Angabe *f*	—	information *f*	indicazione *f*	información *f*
information² (E)	Auskunft *f*	—	renseignement *m*	informazione *f*	información *f*
information¹ (F)	Angabe *f*	information	—	indicazione *f*	información *f*
information² (F)	Mitteilung *f*	message	—	comunicazione *f*	comunicación *f*
informations (F)	Nachrichten *pl*	news	—	giornale radio *m*	noticiario *m*
informazione (I)	Auskunft *f*	information	renseignement *m*	—	información *f*
informe (Es)	Zeugnis *n*	report	bulletin *m*	pagella *f*	—
informe metereológico (Es)	Wetterbericht *m*	weather report	bulletin météorologique *m*	bollettino meteorologico *m*	—
informer¹ (F)	benachrichtigen	inform	—	informare	avisar
informer² (F)	informieren	inform	—	informare	informar
informer qn de qch (F)	mitteilen	inform s.o.	—	comunicare	comunicar
informieren (D)	—	inform	informer	informare	informar
ingannare¹ (I)	betrügen	cheat	tromper	—	engañar
ingannare² (I)	täuschen	deceive	tromper	—	engañar
inganno (I)	Betrug *m*	fraud	tromperie *f*	—	engaño *m*
in genere (I)	überhaupt	at all	en général	—	en general
Inghilterra (I)	England *n*	England	Angleterre *f*	—	Inglaterra *f*
inghiottire (I)	schlucken	swallow	avaler	—	tragar
in giù (I)	abwärts	downwards	en bas	—	hacia abajo
ingiustizia (I)	Ungerechtigkeit *f*	injustice	injustice *f*	—	injusticia *f*

	D	E	F	I	Es
ingiusto (I)	ungerecht	unjust	injuste	—	injusto(a)
Inglaterra (Es)	England *n*	England	Angleterre *f*	Inghilterra *f*	—
inglés¹ (Es)	englisch	English	anglais(e)	inglese	—
inglés² (Es)	Engländer *m*	Englishman	Anglais *m*	inglese *m*	—
inglese¹ (I)	englisch	English	anglais(e)	—	inglés(-esa)
inglese² (I)	Engländer *m*	Englishman	Anglais *m*	—	inglés *m*
ingorgo (I)	Stau *m*	traffic jam	embouteillage *m*	—	embotella-miento *m*
ingrandire (I)	vergrößern	enlarge	agrandir	—	agrandar
ingrat (F)	undankbar	ungrateful	—	ingrato(a)	desagradecido(a)
ingrato (I)	undankbar	ungrateful	ingrat(e)	—	desagradecido(a)
ingraziamento (I)	Dank *m*	thanks	remerciement *m*	—	agradecimiento *m*
ingresos (Es)	Einkommen *n*	income	revenu *m*	entrate *f pl*	—
ingresso (I)	Einfahrt *f*	entrance	entrée *f*	—	entrada *f*
Inhaber (D)	—	owner	propriétaire *m*	proprietario *m*	propietario *m*
inhabitant¹ (E)	Bewohner *m*	—	habitant *m*	abitante *m*	habitante *m*
inhabitant² (E)	Einwohner *m*	—	habitant *m*	abitante *m*	habitante *m*
Inhalt (D)	—	contents	contenu *m*	contenuto *m*	contenido *m*
Inhalts-verzeichnis (D)	—	table of contents	table des matières *f*	indice *m*	índice *m*
inherit (E)	erben	—	hériter	ereditare	heredar
inherit from (E)	beerben	—	hériter	ereditare	heredar
inicio (Es)	Anfang *m*	beginning	commencement *m*	inizio *m*	—
iniezione (I)	Spritze *f*	injection	piqûre *f*	—	inyección *f*
inizio¹ (I)	Anfang *m*	beginning	commencement *m*	—	inicio *m*
inizio² (I)	Beginn *m*	beginning	commencement *m*	—	principio *m*
injection (E)	Spritze *f*	—	piqûre *f*	iniezione *f*	inyección *f*
injure (E)	verletzen	—	blesser	ferire	herir
injury (E)	Verletzung *f*	—	blessure *f*	ferita *f*	herida *f*
injuste (F)	ungerecht	unjust	—	ingiusto(a)	injusto(a)
injustice (E)	Ungerechtigkeit *f*	—	injustice *f*	ingiustizia *f*	injusticia *f*
injustice¹ (F)	Ungerechtigkeit *f*	injustice	—	ingiustizia *f*	injusticia *f*
injustice² (F)	Unrecht *n*	wrong	—	torto *m*	injusticia *f*
injusticia¹ (Es)	Unrecht *n*	wrong	injustice *f*	torto *m*	—
injusticia² (Es)	Ungerechtigkeit *f*	injustice	injustice *f*	ingiustizia *f*	—
injusto (Es)	ungerecht	unjust	injuste	ingiusto(a)	—
Inland (D)	—	inland	intérieur *m*	territorio nazionale *m*	territorio nacional *m*
inland (E)	Inland *n*	—	intérieur *m*	territorio nazionale *m*	territorio nacional *m*
in love (E)	verliebt	—	amoureux(-euse)	innamorato(a)	enamorado(a)
in mezzo¹ (I)	dazwischen	in between	entre	—	entre
in mezzo² (I)	mitten	in the middle	au milieu	—	en medio
in mezzo a (I)	inmitten	in the middle of	au milieu de	—	en medio de
inmitten (D)	—	in the middle of	au milieu de	in mezzo a	en medio de
inmoral (Es)	unanständig	indecent	indécent(e)	indecente	—

	D	E	F	I	Es
inmóvil (Es)	bewegungslos	motionless	immobile	immobile	—
inn (E)	Wirtshaus n	—	auberge f	osteria f	restaurante m
innalzare (I)	erhöhen	raise	augmenter	—	elevar
innamorarsi (I)	verlieben	fall in love	tomber amoureux(-euse)	—	enamorarse
innamorato (I)	verliebt	in love	amoureux(-euse)	—	enamorado(a)
innato (I)	angeboren	inborn	inné(e)	—	innato(a)
innato (Es)	angeboren	inborn	inné(e)	innato(a)	—
innattendu (F)	unerwartet	unexpected	—	inatteso(a)	inesperado(a)
inné (F)	angeboren	inborn	—	innato(a)	innato(a)
innen (D)	—	inside	à l'intérieur	dentro	dentro
Innenstadt (D)	—	town centre	centre ville m	centro città m	centro de la ciudad m
innere (D)	—	internal	intérieur(e)	interno(a)	interior
innerhalb (D)	—	within	à l'intérieur de	entro	dentro de
innocent (E)	unschuldig	—	innocent(e)	innocente	inocente/puro(a)
innocent (F)	unschuldig	innocent	—	innocente	inocente/puro(a)
innocente (I)	unschuldig	innocent	innocent(e)	—	inocente/puro(a)
inocente (Es)	unschuldig	innocent	innocent(e)	innocente	—
inofensivo (Es)	harmlos	harmless	inoffensif(-ive)	inoffensivo(a)	—
inoffensif (F)	harmlos	harmless	—	inoffensivo(a)	inofensivo(a)
inoffensivo (I)	harmlos	harmless	inoffensif(-ive)	—	inofensivo(a)
in ogni caso (I)	jedenfalls	in any case	en tout cas	—	en cualquier caso
inoltrare (I)	nachsenden	send on	faire suivre	—	enviar a la nueva dirección
inoltre (I)	außerdem	besides	en outre	—	además
inondation (F)	Über-schwemmung f	flood	—	inondazione f	inundación f
inondazione (I)	Über-schwemmung f	flood	inondation f	—	inundación f
inopportun (F)	unerwünscht	unwelcome	—	indesiderato(a)	indeseado(a)
inpaciente (Es)	ungeduldig	impatient	impatient(e)	impaziente	—
in parte (I)	teilweise	partly	en partie	—	en parte
in qualche modo[1] (I)	irgendwie	somehow	n'importe comment	—	de alguna manera
in qualche modo[2] (I)	irgend	at all/some	d'une façon ou d'une autre	—	cualquiera
in qualche posto (I)	irgendwo	somewhere	n'importe où	—	en alguna parte
inquiet (F)	unruhig	restless	—	inquieto(a)	intranquilo(a)
inquietar (Es)	beunruhigen	disturb	inquiéter	preoccupare	—
inquiéter (F)	beunruhigen	disturb	—	preoccupare	inquietar
inquieto (I)	unruhig	restless	inquiet(-ète)	—	intranquilo(a)
inquieto (Es)	hektisch	hectic	fébrile	nervoso(a)	—
inquilino (Es)	Mieter m	tenant	locataire m	inquilino m	—
inquilino (I)	Mieter m	tenant	locataire m	—	inquilino m
inquire (E)	erkundigen, sich	—	renseigner, se	informarsi	informarse
insalata (I)	Salat m	salad	salade f	—	ensalada f

	D	E	F	I	Es
in salita (I)	bergauf	uphill	en montant	—	cuesta arriba
inscribir (Es)	einschreiben	enrol	inscrire	iscrivere	—
inscrire (F)	einschreiben	enrol	—	iscrivere	inscribir
insect (E)	Insekt n	—	insecte m	insetto m	insecto m
insecte (F)	Insekt n	insect	—	insetto m	insecto m
insecto (Es)	Insekt n	insect	insecte m	insetto m	—
insegnare (I)	lehren	teach	enseigner	—	enseñar
inseguire (I)	verfolgen	pursue	poursuivre	—	perseguir
in seguito (I)	dann	then	ensuite	—	luego
in seguito a (I)	infolge	as a result of	par suite de	—	por
inseguro (Es)	unsicher	uncertain	incertain(e)	incerto(a)	—
Insekt (D)	—	insect	insecte m	insetto m	insecto m
Insel (D)	—	island	île f	isola f	isla f
insensato (I)	unsinnig	nonsensical	insensé(e)	—	absurdo(a)
insensé[1] (F)	unsinnig	nonsensical	—	insensato(a)	absurdo(a)
insensé[2] (F)	sinnlos	senseless	—	assurdo(a)	inútil
Inserat (D)	—	advertisement	annonce f	inserzione f	anuncio m
inserire (I)	stecken	insert	enfoncer	—	introducir
insert (E)	stecken	—	enfoncer	inserire	introducir
inserzione (I)	Inserat n	advertisement	annonce f	—	anuncio m
insetto (I)	Insekt n	insect	insecte m	—	insecto m
insgesamt (D)	—	altogether	dans l'ensemble	complessiva-mente	en suma
inside (E)	innen	—	à l'intérieur	dentro	dentro
insieme[1] (I)	Ganze(s) n	lot	le tout	—	todo m
insieme[2] (I)	miteinander	together	ensemble	—	juntos
insieme[3] (I)	zusammen	together	ensemble	—	juntos
insipido (I)	fade	dull	fade	—	soso(a)
insolent (F)	frech	cheeky	—	sfacciato(a)	atrevido(a)
insolito (I)	ungewöhnlich	unusual	exceptionnel(le)	—	desacostum-brado(a)
insopportabile (I)	unerträglich	unbearable	insupportable	—	inaguantable
inspector (E)	Kontrolleur m	—	contrôleur m	controllore m	controlador m
inspire (E)	begeistern	—	enthousiasmer	entusiasmare	entusiasmar
inspired (E)	begeistert	—	enthousiaste	entusiasta	entusiasta
instalarse[1] (Es)	einziehen	move in	emménager	prendere alloggio	—
instalarse[2] (Es)	niederlassen	settle down	installer, se	stabilirsi	—
installer, se (F)	niederlassen	settle down	—	stabilirsi	instalarse
instalment (E)	Rate f	—	quote-part f	rata f	plazo m
instant (F)	Augenblick m	moment	—	attimo m	momento m
instantané (F)	augenblicklich	instantaneous	—	instantaneo(a)	instantáneo(a)
instantaneo (I)	augenblicklich	immediately	instantané(e)	—	inmediato(a)
instantáneo (Es)	augenblicklich	at the moment	instantané(e)	immediato(a)	—
instantaneous (E)	augenblicklich	—	instantané(e)	instantaneo(a)	instantáneo(a)
instead[1] (E)	dafür	—	en échange	invece	en su lugar

	D	E	F	I	Es
instead² (E)	statt	—	au lieu de	invece di	en vez de
instead of (E)	anstatt	—	au lieu de	invece di	en vez de
instituto de enseñanza media (Es)	Gymnasium n	grammar school	lycée m	liceo m	—
instruct (E)	beauftragen	—	charger de	incaricare	encargar
instruir (Es)	ausbilden	educate	former	addestrare	—
Instrument (D)	—	instrument	instrument m	strumento m	instrumento m
instrument (E)	Instrument n	—	instrument m	strumento m	instrumento m
instrument (F)	Instrument n	instrument	—	strumento m	instrumento m
instrumento (Es)	Instrument n	instrument	instrument m	strumento m	—
in su (I)	aufwärts	upwards	vers le haut	—	hacia arriba
insuccesso (I)	Mißerfolg m	failure	échec m	—	fracaso m
insufficient (E)	ungenügend	—	insuffisant(e)	insufficiente	insuficiente
insufficiente (I)	ungenügend	insufficient	insuffisant(e)	—	insuficiente
insuffisant (F)	ungenügend	insufficient	—	insufficiente	insuficiente
insuficiente (Es)	ungenügend	insufficient	insuffisant(e)	insufficiente	—
insult¹ (E)	beleidigen	—	offenser	offendere	ofender
insult² (E)	Beleidigung f	—	offense f	offesa f	ofensa f
insultar (Es)	schimpfen	scold	gronder	imprecare	—
insupportable (F)	unerträglich	unbearable	—	insopportabile	inaguantable
insurance (E)	Versicherung f	—	assurance f	assicurazione f	seguro m
insurrezione (I)	Aufstand m	rebellion	soulèvement m	—	revuelta f
inszenieren (D)	—	stage	mettre en scène	mettere in scena	escenificar
inteligente¹ (Es)	intelligent	intelligent	intelligent(e)	intelligente	—
inteligente² (Es)	klug	clever	intelligent(e)	intelligente	—
intelligence (E)	Verstand m	—	intelligence f	intelligenza f	razón f
intelligence (F)	Verstand m	intelligence	—	intelligenza f	razón f
intelligent (D)	—	intelligent	intelligent(e)	intelligente	inteligente
intelligent (E)	intelligent	—	intelligent(e)	intelligente	inteligente
intelligent¹ (F)	intelligent	intelligent	—	intelligente	inteligente
intelligent² (F)	klug	clever	—	intelligente	inteligente
intelligente¹ (I)	intelligent	intelligent	intelligent(e)	—	inteligente
intelligente² (I)	klug	clever	intelligent(e)	—	inteligente
intelligenza (I)	Verstand m	intelligence	intelligence f	—	razón f
in tempo (I)	rechtzeitig	in time	à temps	—	a tiempo
intención¹ (Es)	Absicht f	intention	intention f	intenzione f	—
intención² (Es)	Ziel n	goal	but m	meta f	—
intencionado (Es)	bewußt	deliberate	délibéré(e)	intenzionale	—
intend¹ (E)	beabsichtigen	—	avoir l'intention de	avere (l')intenzione di	proyectar
intend² (E)	vorhaben	—	avoir l'intention de	avere intenzione di	tener la intención de
intention (E)	Absicht f	—	intention f	intenzione f	intención f
intention (F)	Absicht f	intention	—	intenzione f	intención f

	D	E	F	I	Es
intentionally (E)	absichtlich	—	exprès	apposta	adrede
intento (Es)	Versuch *m*	try	essai *m*	tentativo *m*	—
intenzionale (I)	bewußt	deliberate	délibéré(e)	—	intencionado(a)
intenzione (I)	Absicht *f*	intention	intention *f*	—	intención *f*
interamente (I)	restlos	completely	complètement	—	totalmente
interdire (F)	untersagen	forbid	—	proibire	prohibir
interdit (F)	verboten	forbidden	—	vietato(a)	prohibido(a)
interés (Es)	Interesse *n*	interest	intérêt *m*	interesse *m*	—
interesante (Es)	interessant	interesting	intéressant(e)	interessante	—
interesar (Es)	interessieren	interest	intéresser	interessare	—
interessant (D)	—	interesting	intéressant(e)	interessante	interesante
intéressant (F)	interessant	interesting	—	interessante	interesante
interessante (I)	interessant	interesting	intéressant(e)	—	interesante
interessare (I)	interessieren	interest	intéresser	—	interesar
interessarsi di (I)	kümmern, sich	look after	occuper de, se	—	ocuparse de
Interesse (D)	—	interest	intérêt *m*	interesse *m*	interés *m*
interesse (I)	Interesse *n*	interest	intérêt *m*	—	interés *m*
intéresser (F)	interessieren	interest	—	interessare	interesar
interessieren (D)	—	interest	intéresser	interessare	interesar
interest[1] (E)	interessieren	—	intéresser	interessare	interesar
interest[2] (E)	Interesse *n*	—	intérêt *m*	interesse *m*	interés *m*
interesting (E)	interessant	—	intéressant(e)	interessante	interesante
intérêt (F)	Interesse *n*	interest	—	interesse *m*	interés *m*
interference (E)	Störung *f*	—	trouble *m*	disturbo *m*	molestia *f*
intérieur[1] (F)	innere	internal	—	interno(a)	interior
intérieur[2] (F)	Inland *n*	inland	—	territorio nazionale *m*	territorio nacional *m*
interior (Es)	innere	internal	intérieur(e)	interno(a)	—
intermediate landing (E)	Zwischenlandung *f*	—	escale *f*	scalo intermedio *m*	escala *f*
internacional (Es)	international	international	international(e)	internazionale	—
internado (Es)	Internat *n*	boarding school	internat *m*	collegio *m*	—
internal (E)	innere	—	intérieur(e)	interno(a)	interior
Internat (D)	—	boarding school	internat *m*	collegio *m*	internado *m*
internat (F)	Internat *n*	boarding school	—	collegio *m*	internado *m*
international (D)	—	international	international(e)	internazionale	internacional
international (E)	international	—	international(e)	internazionale	internacional
international (F)	international	international	—	internazionale	internacional
internazionale (I)	international	international	international(e)	—	internacional
interno (I)	innere	internal	intérieur(e)	—	interior
intero (I)	ganz	whole	tout(e)	—	entero(a)
intérprete (Es)	Dolmetscher *m*	interpreter	interprète *m*	interprete *m*	—
interprete (I)	Dolmetscher *m*	interpreter	interprète *m*	—	intérprete *m(f)*
interprète (F)	Dolmetscher *m*	interpreter	—	interprete *m*	intérprete *m(f)*
interpreter (E)	Dolmetscher *m*	—	interprète *m*	interprete *m*	intérprete *m*

	D	E	F	I	Es
interrompere (I)	unterbrechen	interrupt	interrompre	—	interrumpir
interrompre (F)	unterbrechen	interrupt	—	interrompere	interrumpir
interrumpir (Es)	unterbrechen	interrupt	interrompre	interrompere	—
interrupción (Es)	Unterbrechung *f*	interruption	interruption *f*	interruzione *f*	—
interrupt (E)	unterbrechen	—	interrompre	interrompere	interrumpir
interrupteur (F)	Lichtschalter *m*	light switch	—	inerruttore *m*	interruptor *m*
interruption (E)	Unterbrechung *f*	—	interruption *f*	interruzione *f*	interrupción *f*
interruption (F)	Unterbrechung *f*	interruption	—	interruzione *f*	interrupción *f*
interruptor (Es)	Lichtschalter *m*	light switch	interrupteur *m*	interruttore *m*	—
interruttore (I)	Lichtschalter *m*	light switch	interrupteur *m*	—	interruptor *m*
interruzione (I)	Unterbrechung *f*	interruption	interruption *f*	—	interrupción *f*
intersecting road (E)	Querstraße *f*	—	rue transversale *f*	traversa *f*	travesía *f*
intersection (F)	Kreuzung *f*	crossing	—	incrocio *m*	cruce *m*
intervene (E)	eingreifen	—	intervenir	intervenire	intervenir
intervenir (Es)	eingreifen	intervene	intervenir	intervenire	—
intervenir (F)	eingreifen	intervene	—	intervenire	intervenir
intervenire (I)	eingreifen	intervene	intervenir	—	intervenir
Interview (D)	—	interview	interview *f*	intervista *f*	entrevista *f*
interview (E)	Interview *n*	—	interview *f*	intervista *f*	entrevista *f*
interview (F)	Interview *n*	interview	—	intervista *f*	entrevista *f*
intervista (I)	Interview *n*	interview	interview *f*	—	entrevista *f*
intestin (F)	Darm *m*	intestine	—	intestino *m*	intestino *m*
intestine (E)	Darm *m*	—	intestin *m*	intestino *m*	intestino *m*
intestino (Es)	Darm *m*	intestine	intestin *m*	intestino *m*	—
intestino (I)	Darm *m*	intestine	intestin *m*	—	intestino *m*
in the afternoon (E)	nachmittags	—	l'après-midi	di pomeriggio	por la tarde
in the evening (E)	abends	—	le soir *m*	di sera	por la tarde
in the middle (E)	mitten	—	au milieu	in mezzo	en medio
in the middle of (E)	inmitten	—	au milieu de	in mezzo a	en medio de
in the morning (E)	vormittags	—	le matin	di mattina	por la mañana
in time (E)	rechtzeitig	—	à temps	in tempo	a tiempo
into one another (E)	ineinander	—	l'un dans l'autre	l'uno nell'altro	uno en otro
intorno (I)	herum	around	autour	—	alrededor
intorno a (I)	um	at/around	autour de/à	—	alrededor de/a las
intranquilo (Es)	unruhig	restless	inquiet(-ète)	inquieto(a)	—
intraprendere (I)	unternehmen	undertake	entreprendre	—	emprender
introducción (Es)	Einleitung *f*	introduction	introduction *f*	introduzione *f*	—
introduce (E)	vorstellen	—	présenter	presentare	presentar
introducir (Es)	stecken	insert	enfoncer	inserire	—
introduction (E)	Einleitung *f*	—	introduction *f*	introduzione *f*	introducción *f*
introduction (F)	Einleitung *f*	introduction	—	introduzione *f*	introducción *f*
introduzione (I)	Einleitung *f*	introduction	introduction *f*	—	introducción *f*
inundación (Es)	Überschwemmung *f*	flood	inondation *f*	inondazione *f*	—

	D	E	F	I	Es
inútil¹ (Es)	nutzlos	useless	inutile	inutile	—
inútil² (Es)	sinnlos	senseless	insensé(e)	assurdo(a)	—
inútil³ (Es)	unnötig	unnecessary	inutile	inutile	—
inútil⁴ (Es)	untauglich	unfit	incapable	incapace	—
inútil⁵ (Es)	zwecklos	pointless	inutile	inutile	—
inutile¹ (F)	nutzlos	useless	—	inutile	inútil
inutile² (F)	unnötig	unnecessary	—	inutile	inútil
inutile³ (F)	zwecklos	pointless	—	inutile	inútil
inutile³ (I)	zwecklos	pointless	inutile	—	inútil
inutile² (I)	nutzlos	useless	inutile	—	inútil
inutile³ (I)	unnötig	unnecessary	inutile	—	inútil
invalid (E)	ungültig	—	non valable	non valido(a)	caducado(a)
invece (I)	dafür	instead	en échange	—	en su lugar
invece di¹ (I)	anstatt	instead of	au lieu de	—	en vez de
invece di² (I)	statt	instead	au lieu de	—	en vez de
invent (E)	erfinden	—	inventer	inventare	inventar
inventar (Es)	erfinden	invent	inventer	inventare	—
inventare (I)	erfinden	invent	inventer	—	inventar
inventer (F)	erfinden	invent	—	inventare	inventar
inverno (I)	Winter *m*	winter	hiver *m*	—	invierno *m*
inverso (I)	umgekehrt	vice versa	vice versa	—	contrario(a)
investigar (Es)	forschen	research	rechercher	ricercare	—
investire (I)	überfahren	run over	écraser	—	atropellar
inviare (I)	schicken	send	envoyer	—	mandar
invidia (I)	Neid *m*	envy	jalousie *f*	—	envidia *f*
invidiare (I)	beneiden	envy	envier	—	envidiar
invidioso (I)	neidisch	envious	envieux(-euse)	—	envidioso(a)
invierno (Es)	Winter *m*	winter	hiver *m*	inverno *m*	—
invitación (Es)	Einladung *f*	invitation	invitation *f*	invito *m*	—
Invitado (Es)	Gast *m*	guest	hôte *m*	ospite *m*	—
invitar (Es)	einladen	invite	inviter	invitare	—
invitare¹ (I)	auffordern	ask	inviter	—	exigir
invitare² (I)	einladen	invite	inviter	—	invitar
invitation (E)	Einladung *f*	—	invitation *f*	invito *m*	invitación *f*
invitation (F)	Einladung *f*	invitation	—	invito *m*	invitación *f*
invite (E)	einladen	—	inviter	invitare	invitar
inviter¹ (F)	auffordern	ask	—	invitare	exigir
inviter² (F)	einladen	invite	—	invitare	invitar
invito (I)	Einladung *f*	invitation	invitation *f*	—	invitación *f*
invraisemblable (F)	unwahrscheinlich	unlikely	—	improbabile	improbable
inyección (Es)	Spritze *f*	injection	piqûre *f*	iniezione *f*	—
inzwischen (D)	—	meanwhile	entretemps	frattanto	mientras tanto
io (I)	ich	I	je/moi	—	yo
ir de compras (Es)	einkaufen gehen	go shopping	faire les courses	fare la spesa	—

	D	E	F	I	Es
ir de paseo (Es)	spazierengehen	go for a walk	promener, se	passeggiare	—
irgend (D)	—	at all/some	d'une façon ou d'une autre	in qualche modo	cualquiera
irgendein (D)	—	some/any	quelconque	qualcuno(a)	cualquiera
irgend etwas (D)	—	something	n'importe quoi	qualsiasi cosa	algo
irgend jemand (D)	—	somebody	n'importe qui	qualcuno	alguno(a)
irgendwie (D)	—	somehow	n'importe comment	in qualche modo	de alguna manera
irgendwo (D)	—	somewhere	n'importe où	in qualche posto	en alguna parte
iron¹ (E)	bügeln	—	repasser	stirare	planchar
iron² (E)	Bügeleisen *n*	—	fer à repasser *m*	ferro da stiro *m*	plancha *f*
iron³ (E)	Eisen *n*	—	fer *m*	ferro *m*	hierro *m*
irregolare (I)	unregelmäßig	irregular	irrégulier(-ère)	—	irregular
irregular (E)	unregelmäßig	—	irrégulier(-ère)	irregolare	irregular
irregular (Es)	unregelmäßig	irregular	irrégulier(-ère)	irregolare	—
irrégulier (F)	unregelmäßig	irregular	—	irregolare	irregular
irren (D)	—	be mistaken	tromper, se	sbagliare	equivocarse
irrésolu (F)	unentschlossen	undecided	—	indeciso(a)	irresoluto(a)
irresoluto (Es)	unentschlossen	undecided	irrésolu(e)	indeciso(a)	—
Irrtum (D)	—	mistake	erreur *f*	errore *m*	error *m*
irse de viaje (Es)	verreisen	go away	partir en voyage	partire in viaggio	—
iscrivere (I)	einschreiben	enrol	inscrire	—	inscribir
isla (Es)	Insel *f*	island	île *f*	isola *f*	—
island (E)	Insel *f*	—	île *f*	isola *f*	isla *f*
isola (I)	Insel *f*	island	île *f*	—	isla *f*
istituto superiore (I)	Hochschule *f*	university	université *f*	—	escuela superior *f*
istruzione (I)	Bildung *f*	education	éducation *f*	—	educación *f*
Italia (Es)	Italien *n*	Italy	Italie *f*	Italia *f*	—
Italia (I)	Italien *n*	Italy	Italie *f*	—	Italia *f*
Italian¹ (E)	italienisch	—	italien(ne)	italiano(a)	italiano(a)
Italian² (E)	Italiener *m*	—	Italien *m*	italiano *m*	italiano *m*
italiano¹ (Es)	Italiener *m*	Italian	Italien *m*	italiano *m*	—
italiano² (Es)	italienisch	Italian	italien(ne)	italiano(a)	—
italiano¹ (I)	italienisch	Italian	italien(ne)	—	italiano(a)
italiano² (I)	Italiener *m*	Italian	Italien *m*	—	italiano *m*
Italie (F)	Italien *n*	Italy	—	Italia *f*	Italia *f*
Italien (D)	—	Italy	Italie *f*	Italia *f*	Italia *f*
italien¹ (F)	italienisch	Italian	—	italiano(a)	italiano(a)
Italien² (F)	Italiener *m*	Italian	—	italiano *m*	italiano *m*
Italiener (D)	—	Italian	Italien *m*	italiano *m*	italiano *m*
italienisch (D)	—	Italian	italien(ne)	italiano(a)	italiano(a)
Italy (E)	Italien *n*	—	Italie *f*	Italia *f*	Italia *f*
itch (E)	jucken	—	démanger	prudere	picar
itinéraire (F)	Reiseroute *f*	route	—	itinerario *m*	itinerario *m*
itinerario (Es)	Reiseroute *f*	route	itinéraire *m*	itinerario *m*	—

	D	E	F	I	Es
itinerario (I)	Reiseroute f	route	itinéraire m	—	itinerario m
ja (D)	—	yes	oui	sì	sí
jabón (Es)	Seife f	soap	savon m	sapone m	—
Jacht (D)	—	yacht	yacht m	panfilo m	yate m
Jacke (D)	—	jacket	veste f	giacca f	chaqueta f
jacket (E)	Jacke f	—	veste f	giacca f	chaqueta f
Jagd (D)	—	hunt	chasse f	caccia f	caza f
jagen (D)	—	hunt	chasser	cacciare	cazar
Jahr (D)	—	year	année f	anno m	año m
Jahreszeit (D)	—	time of year	saison f	stagione f	estación del año f
Jahrhundert (D)	—	century	siècle m	secolo m	siglo m
jährlich (D)	—	annual	annuel(le)	annuale	anualmente
Jahrmarkt (D)	—	fair	foire f	fiera f	feria f
jalousie[1] (F)	Eifersucht f	jealousy	—	gelosia f	celos m pl
jalousie[2] (F)	Neid m	envy	—	invidia f	envidia f
jam (E)	Marmelade f	—	confiture f	marmellata f	mermelada f
jamais (F)	jemals	ever	—	mai	jamás
jamás[1] (Es)	jemals	ever	jamais	mai	—
jamás[2] (Es)	niemals	never	ne...jamais	mai	—
jambe (F)	Bein n	leg	—	gamba f	pierna f
jambon (F)	Schinken m	ham	—	prosciutto m	jamón m
jamón (Es)	Schinken m	ham	jambon m	prosciutto m	—
Januar (D)	—	January	janvier m	gennaio m	enero m
January (E)	Januar m	—	janvier m	gennaio m	enero m
janvier (F)	Januar m	January	—	gennaio m	enero m
jaqueca (Es)	Migräne f	migraine	migraine f	emicrania f	—
jardín (Es)	Garten m	garden	jardin m	giardino m	—
jardin (F)	Garten m	garden	—	giardino m	jardín m
jardín de infancia (Es)	Kindergarten m	nursery school	jardin d'enfants m	asilo (infantile) m	—
jardin d'enfants (F)	Kindergarten m	nursery school	—	asilo (infantile) m	jardín de infancia m
jardinero (Es)	Gärtner m	gardener	jardinier m	giardiniere m	—
jardinier (F)	Gärtner m	gardener	—	giardiniere m	jardinero m
jarro (Es)	Krug m	jug	cruche f	brocca f	—
jatte (F)	Schüssel f	bowl	—	scodella f	fuente f
jaula (Es)	Käfig m	cage	cage f	gabbia f	—
jaune (F)	gelb	yellow	—	giallo(a)	amarillo(a)
je (F)	ich	I	—	io	yo
jealousy (E)	Eifersucht f	—	jalousie f	gelosia f	celos m pl
jede (D)	—	each/every	chaque	ogni, ognuno	cada
jedenfalls (D)	—	in any case	en tout cas	in ogni caso	en cualquier caso
jedesmal (D)	—	each time	chaque fois	ogni volta	cada vez
jedoch (D)	—	however	cependant	tuttavia	sin embargo
jefe (Es)	Chef m	boss	patron m	capo m	—

	D	E	F	I	Es
jemals (D)	—	ever	jamais	mai	jamás
jemand (D)	—	somebody	quelqu'un	qualcuno	alguien
jene (D)	—	that	ce, cette	quello(a)	aquella, aquel, aquello
jenseits (D)	—	beyond	de l'autre côté	al di là	al otro lado
jersey (Es)	Pullover m	pullover	pull-over m	pullover m	—
jetzt (D)	—	now	maintenant	adesso	ahora
jeu (F)	Spiel n	game	—	gioco m	juego m
jeudi (F)	Donnerstag m	Thursday	—	giovedì m	jueves m
jeune (F)	jung	young	—	giovane	joven
jeune fille (F)	Mädchen n	girl	—	ragazza f	chica f
jeûner (F)	fasten	fast	—	digiunare	ayunar
jeunesse (F)	Jugend f	youth	—	gioventù f	juventud f
jeux olympiques (F)	Olympische Spiele pl	Olympic Games	—	Olimpiadi f pl	Juegos Olímpicos m pl
Jew (E)	Jude m	—	juif m	ebreo m	judío m
jewel (E)	Juwel n	—	joyau m	gioiello m	joya f
jeweller (E)	Juwelier m	—	bijoutier m	gioielliere m	joyero m
jewellery (E)	Schmuck m	—	bijoux m pl	gioielli m pl	joyas f pl
Joghurt (D)	—	yogurt	yaourt m	yoghurt m	yogur(t) m
Johannisbeere (D)	—	currant	groseille f	ribes m	grosella f
joie (F)	Freude f	joy	—	gioia f	alegría f
joke[1] (E)	spaßen	—	plaisanter	scherzare	bromear
joke[2] (E)	Scherz m	—	plaisanterie f	scherzo m	broma f
joke[3] (E)	Witz m	—	plaisanterie f	barzelletta f	chiste m
joli[1] (F)	hübsch	pretty	—	carino(a)	bonito(a)
joli[2] (F)	nett	nice	—	carino(a)	agradable
joue (F)	Wange f	cheek	—	guancia f	mejilla f
jouer (F)	spielen	play	—	giocare	jugar
joueur (F)	Spieler m	player	—	giocatore m	jugador m
jouir (F)	genießen	enjoy	—	godere	disfrutar
jour (F)	Tag m	day	—	giorno m	día m
jour de repos (F)	Ruhetag m	closing day	—	giorno di riposo m	día de descanso m
jour férié (F)	Feiertag m	holiday	—	giorno festivo m	día de fiesta m
journal (F)	Zeitung f	newspaper	—	giornale m	periódico m
Journalist (D)	—	journalist	journaliste m	giornalista m	periodista m
journalist (E)	Journalist m	—	journaliste m	giornalista m	periodista m
journaliste (F)	Journalist m	journalist	—	giornalista m	periodista m
journey[1] (E)	Fahrt f	—	voyage m	viaggio m	viaje m
journey[2] (E)	Reise f	—	voyage m	viaggio m	viaje m
jour ouvrable (F)	Werktag m	working day	—	giorno feriale m	día laborable m
joven (Es)	jung	young	jeune	giovane	—
joy (E)	Freude f	—	joie f	gioia f	alegría f
joya (Es)	Juwel n	jewel	joyau m	gioiello m	—
joyas (Es)	Schmuck m	jewellery	bijoux m pl	gioielli m pl	—

	D	E	F	I	Es
joyau (F)	Juwel n	jewel	—	gioiello m	joya f
joyero (Es)	Juwelier m	jeweller	bijoutier m	gioielliere m	—
joyeux (F)	froh	glad	—	lieto(a)	contento(a)
jubeln (D)	—	rejoice	pousser des cris de joie	giubilare	dar gritos de alegría
jucken (D)	—	itch	démanger	prudere	picar
Jude (D)	—	Jew	juif m	ebreo m	judío m
judge[1] (E)	beurteilen	—	juger	giudicare	juzgar
judge[2] (E)	Richter m	—	juge m	giudice m	juez m
judge[3] (E)	urteilen	—	juger	giudicare	juzgar
judgement (E)	Urteil n	—	jugement m	giudizio m	juicio m
judía (Es)	Bohne f	bean	haricot m	fagiolo m	—
judío (Es)	Jude m	Jew	juif m	ebreo m	—
juego (Es)	Spiel n	game	jeu m	gioco m	—
Juegos Olímpicos (Es)	Olympische Spiele pl	Olympic Games	jeux olympiques m pl	Olimpiadi f pl	—
jueves (Es)	Donnerstag m	Thursday	jeudi m	giovedì m	—
juez (Es)	Richter m	judge	juge m	giudice m	—
jug (E)	Krug m	—	cruche f	brocca f	jarro m
jugador (Es)	Spieler m	player	joueur m	giocatore m	—
jugar (Es)	spielen	play	jouer	giocare	—
juge (F)	Richter m	judge	—	giudice m	juez m
jugement (F)	Urteil n	judgement	—	giudizio m	juicio m
Jugend (D)	—	youth	jeunesse f	gioventù f	juventud f
juger[1] (F)	beurteilen	judge	—	giudicare	juzgar
juger[2] (F)	urteilen	judge	—	giudicare	juzgar
juice (E)	Saft m	—	jus m	succo m	zumo m
juicio (Es)	Urteil n	judgement	jugement m	giudizio m	—
juif (F)	Jude m	Jew	—	ebreo m	judío m
juillet (F)	Juli m	July	—	luglio m	julio m
juin (F)	Juni m	June	—	giugno m	junio m
Juli (D)	—	July	juillet m	luglio m	julio m
julio (Es)	Juli m	July	juillet m	luglio m	—
July (E)	Juli m	—	juillet m	luglio m	julio m
jumeaux (F)	Zwillinge pl	twins	—	gemelli m pl	gemelos m pl
jumelles (F)	Fernglas n	binoculars	—	cannocchiale m	gemelos m pl
jump[1] (E)	hüpfen	—	sautiller	saltellare	saltar
jump[2] (E)	springen	—	sauter	saltare	saltar
jump[3] (E)	Sprung m	—	saut m	salto m	salto m
June (E)	Juni m	—	juin m	giugno m	junio m
jung (D)	—	young	jeune	giovane	joven
Junge (D)	—	boy	garçon m	ragazzo m	chico m
Jungfrau (D)	—	virgin	vierge f	vergine f	virgen f
Junggeselle (D)	—	bachelor	célibataire m	scapolo m	soltero m
Juni (D)	—	June	juin m	giugno m	junio m

	D	E	F	I	Es
junio (Es)	Juni *m*	June	juin *m*	giugno *m*	—
junto (Es)	an	at/on/by	à/près de	a/in/su	—
juntos[1] (Es)	gemeinsam	together	ensemble	comune	—
juntos[2] (Es)	miteinander	together	ensemble	insieme	—
juntos[3] (Es)	zusammen	together	ensemble	insieme	—
jupe (F)	Rock *m*	skirt	—	gonna *f*	falda *f*
jupon (F)	Unterrock *m*	slip	—	sottoveste *f*	combinación *f*
Jura (D)	—	law	droit *m*	giurisprudenza *f*	derecho *m*
jurar (Es)	schwören	swear	jurer	giurare	—
jurer (F)	schwören	swear	—	giurare	jurar
jus (F)	Saft *m*	juice	—	succo *m*	zumo *m*
jusqu'à[1] (F)	bis	until	—	fino a	hasta
jusqu'à[2] (F)	hin	there	—	là	hacia allá/hasta
jusqu'à présent (F)	bisher	so far	—	finora	hasta ahora
just (E)	gerecht	—	juste	giusto(a)	justo(a)
juste (F)	gerecht	just	—	giusto(a)	justo(a)
juste (F)	richtig	correct	—	giusto(a)	correcto(a)
just now (E)	soeben	—	à l'instant même	poco fa	ahora mismo
justo (Es)	gerecht	just	juste	giusto(a)	—
juventud (Es)	Jugend *f*	youth	jeunesse *f*	gioventù *f*	—
Juwel (D)	—	jewel	joyau *m*	gioiello *m*	joya *f*
Juwelier (D)	—	jeweller	bijoutier *m*	gioielliere *m*	joyero *m*
juzgar[1] (Es)	beurteilen	judge	juger	giudicare	—
juzgar[2] (Es)	urteilen	judge	juger	giudicare	—
Kabel (D)	—	cable	câble *m*	cavo *m*	cable *m*
Kabine (D)	—	cabin	cabine *f*	cabina *f*	cabina *f*
Käfer (D)	—	beetle	coléoptère *m*	coleottero *m*	escarabajo *m*
Kaffee (D)	—	coffee	café *m*	caffè *m*	café *m*
Käfig (D)	—	cage	cage *f*	gabbia *f*	jaula *f*
kahl (D)	—	bald	chauve	calvo(a)	calvo(a)
Kahn (D)	—	barge	barque *f*	chiatta *f*	barcaza *f*
Kaiser (D)	—	emperor	empereur *m*	imperatore *m*	emperador *m*
Kalb (D)	—	calf	veau *m*	vitello *m*	ternera *f*
Kalender (D)	—	calendar	calendrier *m*	calendario *m*	calendario *m*
kalt (D)	—	cold	froid(e)	freddo(a)	frío(a)
Kamm (D)	—	comb	peigne *m*	pettine *m*	peine *m*
kämmen (D)	—	comb	peigner	pettinare	peinar
kämpfen (D)	—	fight	battre, se	combattere	luchar
Kanada (D)	—	Canada	Canada *m*	Canada *m*	Canadá *m*
Kapelle[1] (D)	—	chapel	chapelle *f*	cappella *f*	capilla *f*
Kapelle[2] (D)	—	band	orchestre *m*	banda *f*	banda *f*
Kapital (D)	—	capital	capital *m*	capitale *m*	capital *m*
Kapitän (D)	—	captain	capitaine *m*	capitano *m*	capitán *m*
Kapitel (D)	—	chapter	chapitre *m*	capitolo *m*	capítulo *m*

	D	E	F	I	Es
kaputt (D)	—	broken	cassé(e)	rotto(a)	roto(a)
Kapuze (D)	—	hood	capuchon *m*	cappuccio *m*	capucha *f*
kariert (D)	—	checked	à carreaux	a quadretti	a cuadros
Karneval (D)	—	carnival	carnaval *m*	carnevale *m*	carnaval *m*
Karosserie (D)	—	body	carrosserie *f*	carrozzeria *f*	carrocería *f*
Karotte (D)	—	carrot	carotte *f*	carota *f*	zanahoria *f*
Karriere (D)	—	career	carrière *f*	carriera *f*	carrera *f*
Karte (D)	—	card	carte *f*	cartolina *f*	postal *f*
Kartoffel (D)	—	potato	pomme de terre *f*	patata *f*	patata *f*
Karton (D)	—	cardboard box	carton *m*	cartone *m*	cartón *m*
Karussell (D)	—	roundabout	manège *m*	giostra *f*	tíovivo *m*
Käse (D)	—	cheese	fromage *m*	formaggio *m*	queso *m*
Kasino (D)	—	club	casino *m*	casinò *m*	casino *m*
Kasse (D)	—	till	caisse *f*	cassa *f*	caja *f*
Kassette (D)	—	cassette	cassette *f*	cassetta *f*	cassette *f*
kassieren (D)	—	take	encaisser	incassare	cobrar
Kathedrale (D)	—	cathedral	cathédrale *f*	cattedrale *f*	catedral *f*
katholisch (D)	—	catholic	catholique	cattolico(a)	católico(a)
Katze (D)	—	cat	chat *m*	gatto *m*	gato *m*
kauen (D)	—	chew	mâcher	masticare	masticar
Kauf (D)	—	purchase	achat *m*	acquisto *m*	compra *f*
kaufen (D)	—	buy	acheter	comprare	comprar
Käufer (D)	—	buyer	acheteur *m*	acquirente *m*	comprador *m*
Kaufhaus (D)	—	department store	grand magasin *m*	grande magazzino *m*	grandes almacenes *m pl*
Kaufmann (D)	—	businessman	commerçant *m*	commerciante *m*	comerciante *m*
kaum (D)	—	hardly	à peine	appena	apenas
keen (E)	eifrig	—	zélé(e)	diligente	diligente
keep[1] (E)	aufbewahren	—	garder	conservare	guardar
keep[2] (E)	behalten	—	garder	tenere	retener
keep[3] (E)	einbehalten	—	retenir	trattenere	retener
kehren (D)	—	sweep	balayer	scopare	barrer
keine (D)	—	none	aucun(e)	nessuno(a)	ninguno(a)
keineswegs (D)	—	not at all	pas du tout	non affatto	en modo alguno
Keks (D)	—	biscuit	biscuit *m*	biscotto *m*	galleta *f*
Keller (D)	—	cellar	cave *f*	cantina *f*	sótano *m*
Kellner (D)	—	waiter	garçon *m*	cameriere *m*	camarero *m*
kennen (D)	—	know	connaître	conoscere	conocer
Kenntnis (D)	—	knowledge	connaissance *f*	conoscenza *f*	conocimiento *m*
Kern (D)	—	pip	noyau *m*	nocciolo *m*	hueso *m*
Kerze (D)	—	candle	bougie *f*	candela *f*	vela *f*
Kette (D)	—	chain	chaîne *f*	catena *f*	cadena *f*
key (E)	Schlüssel *m*	—	clé *f*	chiave *f*	llave *f*

	D	E	F	I	Es
keyhole (E)	Schlüsselloch n	—	trou de la serrure m	buco della chiave m	ojo de la cerradura m
kidney (E)	Niere f	—	rein m	rene m	riñón m
kill[1] (E)	töten	—	tuer	uccidere	matar
kill[2] (E)	umbringen	—	tuer	uccidere	matar
kilogram (E)	Kilogramm n	—	kilogramme m	chilogrammo m	kilógramo m
Kilogramm (D)	—	kilogram	kilogramme m	chilogrammo m	kilógramo m
kilogramme (F)	Kilogramm n	kilogram	—	chilogrammo m	kilógramo m
kilogramo (Es)	Kilogramm n	kilogram	kilogramme m	chilogrammo m	—
Kilometer (D)	—	kilometre	kilomètre m	chilometro m	kilómetro m
kilometre (E)	Kilometer m	—	kilomètre m	chilometro m	kilómetro m
kilomètre (F)	Kilometer m	kilometre	—	chilometro m	kilómetro m
kilómetro (Es)	Kilometer m	kilometre	kilomètre m	chilometro m	—
Kind (D)	—	child	enfant m	bambino m	niño m
kind (E)	liebenswürdig	—	aimable	gentile	gentil
Kindergarten (D)	—	nursery school	jardin d'enfants m	asilo (infantile) m	jardín de infancia m
Kindheit (D)	—	childhood	enfance f	infanzia f	niñez f
king (E)	König m	—	roi m	re m	rey m
Kinn (D)	—	chin	menton m	mento m	barbilla f
Kino (D)	—	cinema	cinéma m	cinema m	cine m
Kirche (D)	—	church	église f	chiesa f	iglesia f
Kirsche (D)	—	cherry	cerise f	ciliegia f	cereza f
kiss[1] (E)	küssen	—	embrasser	baciare	besar
kiss[2] (E)	Kuß m	—	baiser m	bacio m	beso m
Kissen (D)	—	cushion	coussin m	cuscino m	cojín m
Kiste (D)	—	box	caisse f	cassetta f	caja f
kitchen (E)	Küche f	—	cuisine f	cucina f	cocina f
Klage (D)	—	complaint	plainte f	lamento m	lamento m
Klang (D)	—	sound	son m	suono m	sonido m
klar (D)	—	clear	clair(e)	chiaro(a)	claro(a)
Klasse (D)	—	class	classe f	classe f	clase f
klatschen (D)	—	applaud	applaudir	battere le mani	aplaudir
Klavier (D)	—	piano	piano m	pianoforte m	piano m
kleben (D)	—	stick	coller	incollare	pegar
Klebstoff (D)	—	glue	colle f	colla f	adhesivo m
Kleid (D)	—	dress	robe f	vestito m	vestido m
kleiden (D)	—	dress	habiller	vestire	vestir
Kleiderschrank (D)	—	wardrobe	garde-robe f	armadio m	armario ropero m
Kleidung (D)	—	clothing	habits m pl	abbigliamento m	vestuario m
klein (D)	—	small/little	petit(e)	piccolo(a)	pequeño(a)
Kleingeld (D)	—	small change	monnaie f	spiccioli m pl	cambio m
klettern (D)	—	climb	grimper	arrampicarsi	escalar
Klima (D)	—	climate	climat m	clima m	clima m
Klinge (D)	—	blade	lame f	lama f	cuchilla f

	D	E	F	I	Es
Klingel (D)	—	bell	sonnette f	campanello m	timbre m
klingeln (D)	—	ring the bell	sonner	suonare	tocar el timbre
Klinik (D)	—	hospital	clinique f	clinica f	clínica f
klopfen (D)	—	knock	frapper	bussare	golpear
Klosett (D)	—	lavatory	cabinets m pl	gabinetto m	retrete m
Kloster (D)	—	monastery	couvent m	convento m	monasterio m
klug (D)	—	clever	intelligent(e)	intelligente	inteligente
knapp (D)	—	tight	étroit(e)	scarso(a)	escaso(a)
knee (E)	Knie n	—	genou m	ginocchio m	rodilla f
Kneipe (D)	—	pub	bistro m	osteria f	tasca f
Knie (D)	—	knee	genou m	ginocchio m	rodilla f
knife (E)	Messer n	—	couteau m	coltello m	cuchillo m
knipsen (D)	—	take a snap	photographier	scattare una foto	hacer una foto
knit (E)	stricken	—	tricoter	lavorare a maglia	hacer punto
Knoblauch (D)	—	garlic	ail m	aglio m	ajo m
Knöchel (D)	—	ankle	cheville f	caviglia f	tobillo m
Knochen (D)	—	bone	os m	osso m	hueso m
knock[1] (E)	klopfen	—	frapper	bussare	golpear
knock[2] (E)	pochen	—	frapper	battere	golpear
Knopf (D)	—	button	bouton m	bottone m	botón m
Knospe (D)	—	bud	bourgeon m	bocciolo m	yema f
knot (E)	Knoten m	—	nœud m	nodo m	nudo m
Knoten (D)	—	knot	nœud m	nodo m	nudo m
know[1] (E)	kennen	—	connaître	conoscere	conocer
know[2] (E)	wissen	—	savoir	sapere	saber
knowledge[1] (E)	Kenntnis f	—	connaissance f	conoscenza f	conocimiento m
knowledge[2] (E)	Wissen n	—	savoir m	sapere m	saber m
know one's way about (E)	auskennen, sich	—	connaître, s'y	conoscere	conocer a fondo
Koch (D)	—	cook	cuisinier m	cuoco m	cocinero m
kochen (D)	—	cook	cuire	cucinare	cocinar
Köchin (D)	—	cook	cuisinière f	cuoca f	cocinera f
Kochtopf (D)	—	saucepan	casserole f	pentola f	olla f
Koffer (D)	—	suitcase	valise f	valigia f	maleta f
Kofferraum (D)	—	boot	coffre m	portabagagli m	maletero m
Kohl (D)	—	cabbage	chou m	cavolo m	col f
Kohle (D)	—	coal	charbon m	carbone m	carbón m
komisch (D)	—	funny	drôle	comico(a)	cómico(a)
kommen (D)	—	come	venir	venire	venir
Komödie (D)	—	comedy	comédie f	commedia f	comedia f
kompliziert (D)	—	complicated	compliqué(e)	complicato(a)	complicado(a)
Komponist (D)	—	composer	compositeur m	compositore m	compositor m
Konditorei (D)	—	cake shop	pâtisserie f	pasticceria f	pastelería f
Konferenz (D)	—	conference	conférence f	conferenza f	conferencia f

	D	E	F	I	Es
König (D)	—	king	roi *m*	re *m*	rey *m*
Königin (D)	—	queen	reine *f*	regina *f*	reina *f*
können (D)	—	can	pouvoir	sapere	saber
Konsulat (D)	—	consulate	consulat *m*	consolato *m*	consulado *m*
Kontakt (D)	—	contact	contact *m*	contatto *m*	contacto *m*
Kontinent (D)	—	continent	continent *m*	continente *m*	continente *m*
Konto (D)	—	account	compte *m*	conto *m*	cuenta *f*
Kontrolle (D)	—	control	contrôle *m*	controllo *m*	control *m*
Kontrolleur (D)	—	inspector	contrôleur *m*	controllore *m*	controlador *m*
konzentrieren (D)	—	concentrate	concentrer	concentrare	concentrar
Konzert (D)	—	concert	concert *m*	concerto *m*	concierto *m*
Kopf (D)	—	head	tête *f*	testa *f*	cabeza *f*
Kopfkissen (D)	—	pillow	oreiller *m*	guanciale *m*	almohada *f*
Kopfschmerzen (D)	—	headache	mal de tête *m*	mal di testa *m*	dolor de cabeza *m*
Kopie (D)	—	copy	copie *f*	copia *f*	copia *f*
kopieren (D)	—	copy	copier	copiare	copiar
Korb (D)	—	basket	panier *m*	cesto *m*	cesta *f*
Korkenzieher (D)	—	corkscrew	tire-bouchon *m*	cavatappi *m*	sacacorchos *m*
Korn (D)	—	corn	grain *m*	grano *m*	semilla *f*
Körper (D)	—	body	corps *m*	corpo *m*	cuerpo *m*
korrekt (D)	—	correct	correct(e)	corretto(a)	correcto(a)
Korridor (D)	—	corridor	corridor *m*	corridoio *m*	pasillo *m*
Kost (D)	—	food	nourriture *f*	cibo *m*	alimento *m*
kostbar (D)	—	precious	précieux(-euse)	prezioso(a)	valioso(a)
kosten (D)	—	cost	coûter	costare	costar
Kosten (D)	—	expenses	coûts *m pl*	spese *f pl*	costas *f pl*
kostenlos (D)	—	free	gratuit(e)	gratuito(a)	gratis
köstlich (D)	—	delicious	savoureux(-euse)	squisito(a)	exquisito(a)
kostspielig (D)	—	expensive	coûteux(-euse)	costoso(a)	costoso(a)
Kostüm (D)	—	costume	costume *m*	tailleur *m*	vestido *m*
Kotelett (D)	—	cutlet	côtelette *f*	costoletta *f*	chuleta *f*
Krach (D)	—	noise	bruit *m*	chiasso *m*	ruido *m*
kräftig (D)	—	strong	fort(e)	forte	fuerte
Kraft (D)	—	strength	force *f*	forza *f*	fuerza *f*
Kragen (D)	—	collar	col *m*	colletto *m*	cuello *m*
krank (D)	—	ill	malade	malato(a)	enfermo(a)
Krankenhaus (D)	—	hospital	hôpital *m*	ospedale *m*	hospital *m*
Krankenpfleger (D)	—	nursing orderly	infirmier *m*	infermiere *m*	enfermero *m*
Kranken-schwester (D)	—	nurse	infirmière *f*	infermiera *f*	enfermera *f*
Krankenwagen (D)	—	ambulance	ambulance *f*	ambulanza *f*	ambulancia *f*
Krankheit (D)	—	illness	maladie *f*	malattia *f*	enfermedad *f*
Krawatte (D)	—	tie	cravate *f*	cravatta *f*	corbata *f*
Krebs¹ (D)	—	crayfish	écrevisse *f*	gambero *m*	cangrejo *m*

	D	E	F	I	Es
Krebs² (D)	—	cancer	cancer *m*	cancro *m*	cáncer *m*
Kredit (D)	—	credit	crédit *m*	credito *m*	crédito *m*
Kreis (D)	—	circle	cercle	cerchio *m*	círculo *m*
Kreislauf (D)	—	circulation	circulation *f*	circolazione *f*	circulación *f*
Kreuz (D)	—	cross	croix *f*	croce *f*	cruz *f*
Kreuzung (D)	—	crossing	intersection *f*	incrocio *m*	cruce *m*
Krieg (D)	—	war	guerre *f*	guerra *f*	guerra *f*
kritisieren (D)	—	criticize	critiquer	criticare	criticar
Krug (D)	—	jug	cruche *f*	brocca *f*	jarro *m*
krumm (D)	—	crooked	tordu(e)	storto(a)	torcido(a)
Kubikmeter (D)	—	cubic metre	mètre cube	metro cubo *m*	metro cúbico *m*
Küche (D)	—	kitchen	cuisine *f*	cucina *f*	cocina *f*
Kuchen (D)	—	cake	gâtcau *m*	dolce *m*	pastel *m*
Kugelschreiber (D)	—	biro	stylo à bille *m*	biro *f*	bolígrafo *m*
Kuh (D)	—	cow	vache *f*	mucca *f*	vaca *f*
kühl (D)	—	cool	frais (fraîche)	fresco(a)	fresco(a)
Kühlschrank (D)	—	fridge	réfrigérateur *m*	frigorifero *m*	nevera *f*
Kultur (D)	—	culture	culture *f*	cultura *f*	cultura *f*
Kummer (D)	—	grief	chagrin *m*	dolore *m*	pesar *m*
kümmern, sich (D)	—	look after	occuper de, se	interessarsi di	ocuparse de
Kunde (D)	—	customer	client *m*	cliente *m*	cliente *m*
kündigen (D)	—	sack	résilier	licenziare	despedir
Kunst (D)	—	art	art *m*	arte *f*	arte *m*
Künstler (D)	—	artist	artiste *m*	artista *m*	artista *m*
künstlich (D)	—	artificial	artificiel(le)	artificiale	artificial
Kur (D)	—	treatment	cure *f*	cura *f*	cura *f*
Kurs (D)	—	rate	cours *m*	corso *m*	curso *m*
Kurve (D)	—	bend	virage *m*	curva *f*	curva *f*
kurz (D)	—	short	court(e)	corto(a)	corto(a)
kürzlich (D)	—	lately	récemment	recente	reciente
Kuß (D)	—	kiss	baiser *m*	bacio *m*	beso *m*
küssen (D)	—	kiss	embrasser	baciare	besar
Küste (D)	—	coast	côte *f*	costa *f*	costa *f*
la¹ (I)	dort	there	là/y	—	allí
là² (I)	hin	there	jusqu'à/ vers	—	hacia allá/ hasta
là¹ (F)	da	there	—	qui/là	allí
là² (F)	dort	there	—	là	allí
labbro (I)	Lippe *f*	lip	lèvre *f*	—	labio *m*
labio (Es)	Lippe *f*	lip	lèvre *f*	labbro *m*	—
lac (F)	See *m*	lake	—	lago *m*	lago *m*
lâche (F)	feig	cowardly	—	vile	cobarde
lächeln (D)	—	smile	sourire	sorridere	sonreír
Lächeln (D)	—	smile	sourire *m*	sorriso *m*	sonrisa *f*

	D	E	F	I	Es
lachen (D)	—	laugh	rire	ridere	reír
Lachen (D)	—	laughter	rire *m*	riso *m*	risa *f*
lâcher (F)	loslassen	let go of	—	mollare	dejar libre
lächerlich (D)	—	ridiculous	ridicule	ridicolo(a)	ridículo(a)
Lachs (D)	—	salmon	saumon *m*	salmone *m*	salmón *m*
lack (E)	Mangel *m*	—	manque *m*	mancanza *f*	escasez *f*
lacrima (I)	Träne *f*	tear	larme *f*	—	lágrima *f*
lacuna (I)	Lücke *f*	gap	lacune *f*	—	espacio *m*
lacune (F)	Lücke *f*	gap	—	lacuna *f*	espacio *m*
ladder (E)	Leiter *f*	—	échelle *f*	scala *f*	escalera *f*
Laden (D)	—	shop	magasin *m*	negozio *m*	tienda *f*
Ladentisch (D)	—	counter	comptoir *m*	banco di vendita *m*	mostrador *m*
ladrillo (Es)	Ziegel *m*	brick	brique *f*	mattone *m*	—
ladro (I)	Dieb *m*	thief	voleur *m*	—	ladrón *m*
ladrón (Es)	Dieb *m*	thief	voleur *m*	ladro *m*	—
Ladung (D)	—	cargo	charge *f*	carico *m*	carga *f*
lady (E)	Dame *f*	—	dame *f*	signora *f*	señora *f*
Lage (D)	—	situation	situation *f*	situazione *f*	situación *f*
Lager (D)	—	store	magasin *m*	magazzino *m*	almacén *m*
lago (Es)	See *m*	lake	lac *m*	lago *m*	—
lago (I)	See *m*	lake	lac *m*	—	lago *m*
lágrima (Es)	Träne *f*	tear	larme *f*	lacrima *f*	—
laid (F)	häßlich	ugly	—	brutto(a)	feo(a)
laine (F)	Wolle *f*	wool	—	lana *f*	lana *f*
laisser¹ (F)	hinterlassen	leave	—	lasciare	dejar
laisser² (F)	lassen	let	—	lasciare	dejar
laisser³ (F)	übriglassen	leave	—	lasciare	dejar
lait (F)	Milch *f*	milk	—	latte *m*	leche *f*
lake (E)	See *m*	—	lac *m*	lago *m*	lago *m*
Laken (D)	—	sheet	drap *m*	lenzuolo *m*	sábana *f*
l'altro ieri (I)	vorgestern	day before yesterday	avant-hier	—	anteayer
lama (I)	Klinge *f*	blade	lame *f*	—	cuchilla *f*
la mayor parte de (Es)	meist	most	la plupart de	nella maggior parte di	—
lamb (E)	Lamm *n*	—	agneau *m*	agnello *m*	cordero *m*
lame (F)	Klinge *f*	blade	—	lama *f*	cuchilla *f*
la même chose (F)	dasselbe	the same	—	lo stesso	lo mismo
lamentar (Es)	bedauern	regret	regretter	deplorare	—
lamentare (I)	beklagen	deplore	plaindre de, se	—	quejarse
lamentarsi (I)	beschweren, sich	complain	plaindre, se	—	quejarse
lamento (Es)	Klage *f*	complaint	plainte *f*	lamento *m*	—
lamento (I)	Klage *f*	complaint	plainte *f*	—	lamento *m*
Lamm (D)	—	lamb	agneau *m*	agnello *m*	cordero *m*
lamp (E)	Lampe *f*	—	lampe *f*	lampada *f*	lámpara *f*

	D	E	F	I	Es
lampada (I)	Lampe *f*	lamp	lampe *f*	—	lámpara *f*
lampadina (I)	Glühbirne *f*	light bulb	ampoule *f*	—	lámpara *f*
lampadina tascabile (I)	Taschenlampe *f*	torch	lampe de poche *f*	—	linterna *f*
lámpara¹ (Es)	Glühbirne *f*	light bulb	ampoule *f*	lampadina *f*	—
lámpara² (Es)	Lampe *f*	lamp	lampe *f*	lampada *f*	—
Lampe (D)	—	lamp	lampe *f*	lampada *f*	lámpara *f*
lampe (F)	Lampe *f*	lamp	—	lampada *f*	lámpara *f*
lampe de poche (F)	Taschenlampe *f*	torch	—	lampadina tascabile *f*	linterna *f*
lampeggiare (I)	blinken	flash	clignoter	—	relampagnear
lampione (I)	Laterne *f*	street light	réverbère *f*	—	farola *f*
lampo (I)	Blitz *m*	lightning	éclair *m*	—	rayo *m*
lampone (I)	Himbeere *f*	raspberry	framboise *f*	—	frambuesa *f*
lana (Es)	Wolle *f*	wool	laine *f*	lana *f*	—
lana (I)	Wolle *f*	wool	laine *f*	—	lana *f*
lancer (F)	werfen	throw	—	lanciare	tirar
lanciare (I)	werfen	throw	lancer	—	tirar
Land (D)	—	land	pays *m*	paese *m*	país *m*
land¹ (E)	landen	—	atterrir	atterrare	aterrizar
land² (E)	Land *n*	—	pays *m*	paese *m*	país *m*
landen (D)	—	land	atterrir	atterrare	aterrizar
landing (E)	Landung *f*	—	atterrissage *m*	atterraggio *m*	aterrizajc *m*
Landkarte (D)	—	map	carte *f*	carta geografica *f*	mapa *m*
landlord (E)	Wirt *m*	—	patron *m*	oste *m*	dueño *m*
landowner (E)	Großgrund-besitzer *m*	—	grand propriétaire *m*	latifondista *m*	latifundio *m*
landscape (E)	Landschaft *f*	—	paysage *m*	paesaggio *m*	paisaje *m*
Landschaft (D)	—	landscape	paysage *m*	paesaggio *m*	paisaje *m*
Landstraße (D)	—	country road	route *f*	strada provinciale *f*	carretera nacional *f*
Landung (D)	—	landing	atterrissage *m*	atterraggio *m*	aterrizaje *m*
Landwirt (D)	—	farmer	agriculteur *m*	agricoltore *m*	agricultor *m*
lane (E)	Gasse *f*	—	ruelle *f*	vicolo *m*	callejón *m*
lang (D)	—	long	long(ue)	lungo(a)	largo(a)
langage (F)	Sprache *f*	language	—	lingua *f*	lengua *f*
lange (D)	—	long time	longtemps	molto tempo	mucho tiempo
Länge (D)	—	length	longueur *f*	lunghezza *f*	longitud *f*
lange (F)	Windel *f*	nappy	—	pannolino *m*	pañal *m*
langsam (D)	—	slow	lent(e)	lento(a)	despacio(a)
längst (D)	—	a long time ago	depuis bien longtemps	da molto	hace mucho
language (E)	Sprache *f*	—	langage *m*	lingua *f*	lengua *f*
langue (F)	Zunge *f*	tongue	—	lingua *f*	lengua *f*
langue étrangère (F)	Fremdsprache *f*	foreign-language	—	lingua straniera *f*	idioma extranjero *m*

	D	E	F	I	Es
langue familière (F)	Umgangssprache *f*	colloquial language	—	linguaggio corrente	lenguaje coloquial *m*
langue internationale (F)	Weltsprache *f*	world language	—	lingua mondiale *f*	lengua universal *f*
langue maternelle (F)	Muttersprache *f*	native language	—	lingua madre *f*	lengua materna *f*
langweilen, sich (D)	—	get bored	ennuyer, se	annoiarsi	aburrirse
langweilig (D)	—	boring	ennuyeux (-euse)	noioso(a)	aburrido(a)
lápiz[1] (Es)	Bleistift *m*	pencil	crayon *m*	matita *f*	—
lápiz[2] (Es)	Stift *m*	pencil	crayon *m*	penna *f*	—
la plupart de (F)	meist	most	—	nella maggior parte di	la mayor parte de
l'après-midi (F)	nachmittags	in the afternoon	—	di pomeriggio	por la tarde
lard (F)	Speck *m*	bacon	—	lardo *m*	tocino *m*
lardo (I)	Speck *m*	bacon	lard *m*	—	tocino *m*
large (F)	breit	broad	—	largo(a)	amplio(a)
large town (E)	Großstadt *f*	—	grande ville *f*	grande città *f*	gran ciudad *f*
largeur (F)	Breite *f*	width	—	larghezza *f*	extensión *f*
larghezza (I)	Breite *f*	width	largeur *f*	—	extensión *f*
largo (I)	breit	broad	large	—	amplio(a)
largo (Es)	lang	long	long(ue)	lungo(a)	—
Lärm (D)	—	noise	bruit *m*	rumore *m*	ruido *m*
larme (F)	Träne *f*	tear	—	lacrima *f*	lágrima *f*
lasciare[1] (I)	hinterlassen	leave	laisser	—	dejar
lasciare[2] (I)	lassen	let	laisser	—	dejar
lasciare[3] (I)	übriglassen	leave	laisser	—	dejar
lasciare[4] (I)	verlassen	leave	abandonner	—	dejar
lasciare in eredità (I)	vererben	bequeath	léguer	—	transmitir hereditariamente
lassen (D)	—	let	laisser	lasciare	dejar
Last (D)	—	load	charge *f*	carico *m*	peso *m*
last[1] (E)	dauern	—	durer	durare	durar
last[2] (E)	letzte(r,s)	—	dernier(-ière)	ultimo(a)	última(o)
lästig (D)	—	troublesome	importun(e)	molesto(a)	desagradable
lastricato (I)	Pflaster *n*	pavement	pavé *m*	—	adoquinado *m*
Lastwagen (D)	—	lorry	camion *m*	camion *m*	camión *m*
lata (Es)	Dose *f*	tin	boîte *f*	scatola *f*	—
late (E)	spät	—	tard	tardi	tarde
lately (E)	kürzlich	—	récemment	recente	reciente
later (E)	später	—	plus tard	piú tardi	más tarde
Laterne (D)	—	street light	réverbère *f*	lampione *m*	farola *f*
latifondista (I)	Großgrund-besitzer *m*	landowner	grand propriétaire *m*	—	latifundista *m*
latifundista (Es)	Großgrund-besitzer *m*	landowner	grand propriétaire *m*	latifondista *m*	—
latta (I)	Blech *n*	sheet metal	tôle *f*	—	chapa *f*
latte (I)	Milch *f*	milk	lait *m*	—	leche *f*

	D	E	F	I	Es
laufen (D)	—	run	courir	correre	correr
laugh (E)	lachen	—	rire	ridere	reír
laugh at (E)	auslachen	—	rire de qn	deridere	reírse de
laughter[1] (E)	Gelächter n	—	rires m pl	risata f	risa f
laughter[2] (E)	Lachen n	—	rire m	riso m	risa f
laundry (E)	Wäscherei f	—	blanchisserie f	lavanderia f	lavandería f
Laune (D)	—	mood	humeur f	umore m	humor m
laut (D)	—	loud	fort(e)	rumoroso(a)	fuerte
läuten (D)	—	ring	sonner	suonare	tocar
l'autre jour (F)	neulich	recently	—	recentemente	recientemente
Lautsprecher (D)	—	loudspeaker	haut-parleur m	altoparlante m	altavoz m
lauwarm (D)	—	lukewarm	tiède	tiepido(a)	templado(a)
lavabile (I)	waschbar	washable	lavable	—	lavable
lavable (Es)	waschbar	washable	lavable	lavabile	—
lavable (F)	waschbar	washable	—	lavabile	lavable
lavabo[1] (Es)	Toilette f	toilet	toilette f	toilette f	—
lavabo[2] (Es)	Waschbecken n	wash-basin	lavabo m	lavandino m	—
lavabo (F)	Waschbecken n	wash-basin	—	lavandino m	lavabo m
lavadora (Es)	Waschmaschine f	washing machine	machine à laver f	lavatrice f	—
lavandería (Es)	Wäscherei f	laundry	blanchisserie f	lavanderia f	—
lavanderia (I)	Wäscherei f	laundry	blanchisserie f	—	lavandería f
lavandino (I)	Waschbecken n	wash-basin	lavabo m	—	lavabo m
lavar[1] (Es)	abwaschen	wash off	laver	lavar via	—
lavar[2] (Es)	abspülen	wash up	faire la vaisselle	sciacquare	—
lavar[3] (Es)	waschen	wash	laver	lavare	—
lavare (I)	waschen	wash	laver	—	lavar
lavar via (I)	abwaschen	wash off	laver	—	lavar
lavatory (E)	Klosett n	—	cabinets m pl	gabinetto m	retrete m
lavatrice (I)	Waschmaschine f	washing machine	machine à laver f	—	lavadora f
laver[1] (F)	abwaschen	wash off	—	lavar via	lavar
laver[2] (F)	waschen	wash	—	lavare	lavar
lavorare (I)	arbeiten	work	travailler	—	trabajar
lavorare a maglia (I)	stricken	knit	tricoter	—	hacer punto
lavoro (I)	Arbeit f	work	travail m	—	trabajo m
law[1] (E)	Gesetz n	—	loi f	legge f	ley f
law[2] (E)	Jura	—	droit m	giurisprudenza f	derecho m
lawn (E)	Rasen m	—	pelouse f	prato m	césped m
lawyer (E)	Rechtsanwalt m	—	avocat m	avvocato m	abogado m
lay (E)	legen	—	mettre	mettere	colocar
lazy (E)	faul	—	paresseux(-euse)	pigro(a)	perezoso(a)
le, la (F)	der, die, das	the	—	il, la	el, la, lo
lead (E)	führen	—	guider	guidare	dirigir
leader (E)	Führer m	—	guide m	guida f	guía m

	D	E	F	I	Es
leaf (E)	Blatt *n*	—	feuille *f*	foglia *f*	hoja *f*
learn¹ (E)	erfahren	—	apprendre	venire a sapere	enterarse
learn² (E)	lernen	—	apprendre	imparare	aprender
lease out (E)	verpachten	—	affermer	affittare	arrendar
leather (E)	Leder *n*	—	cuir *m*	cuoio *m*	cuero *m*
leave¹ (E)	abreisen	—	partir	partire	salir
leave² (E)	hinterlassen	—	laisser	lasciare	dejar
leave³ (E)	verlassen	—	abandonner	lasciare	dejar
leave⁴ (E)	übriglassen	—	laisser	lasciare	dejar
leben (D)	—	live	vivre	vivere	vivir
Leben (D)	—	life	vie *f*	vita *f*	vida *f*
lebendig (D)	—	alive	vivant(e)	vivo(a)	vivo(a)
Lebensgefährte (D)	—	life partner	compagnon *m*	compagno *m*	compañero en la vida *m*
Lebenslauf (D)	—	curriculum vitae	curriculum vitae *m*	curriculum vitae *m*	curriculum vitae *m*
Lebensmittel (D)	—	food	alimentation *f*	alimentari *m pl*	alimentos *m pl*
Lebensmittel-geschäft (D)	—	grocer's	magasin d'alimentation *m*	negozio di alimentari *m*	tienda de comestibles *f*
Leber (D)	—	liver	foie *m*	fegato *m*	hígado *m*
lebhaft (D)	—	lively	vif(vive)	vivace	vivaz
leche (Es)	Milch *f*	milk	lait *m*	latte *m*	—
leçon (F)	Unterrichts-stunde *f*	lesson	—	lezione *f*	clase *f*
lecture (E)	Vorlesung *f*	—	cours magistral *m*	lezione *f*	clase *f*
Leder (D)	—	leather	cuir *m*	cuoio *m*	cuero *m*
ledig (D)	—	single	célibataire	celibe m/nubile *f*	soltero(a)
leer (D)	—	empty	vide	vuoto(a)	vacío(a)
leer (Es)	lesen	read	lire	leggere	—
left¹ (E)	links	—	à gauche	a sinistra	a la izquierda
left² (E)	übrig	—	restant(e)	restante	restante
leg (E)	Bein *n*	—	jambe *f*	gamba *f*	pierna *f*
legal (E)	gesetzlich	—	légal(e)	legale	legal
legal (Es)	gesetzlich	legal	légal(e)	legale	—
légal (F)	gesetzlich	legal	—	legale	legal
legale (I)	gesetzlich	legal	légal(e)	—	legal
legare (I)	binden	bind	attacher	—	atar
legen (D)	—	lay	mettre	mettere	colocar
léger (F)	leicht	light	—	leggero(a)	sencillo(a)
legge (I)	Gesetz *n*	law	loi *f*	—	ley *f*
leggere (I)	lesen	read	lire	—	leer
leggero (I)	leicht	light	léger(-ère)	—	sencillo(a)
legno (I)	Holz *n*	wood	bois *m*	—	madera *f*
léguer (F)	vererben	bequeath	—	lasciare in eredità	transmitir hereditariamente
legumbres (Es)	Gemüse *n*	vegetables	légumes *m pl*	verdura *f*	—
légumes (F)	Gemüse *n*	vegetables	—	verdura *f*	legumbres *f pl*

lento

	D	E	F	I	Es
lehren (D)	—	teach	enseigner	insegnare	enseñar
Lehrer (D)	—	teacher	professeur *m*	maestro *m*	profesor *m*
Lehrling (D)	—	apprentice	apprenti *m*	apprendista *m*	aprendiz *m*
lei (I)	sie	she	elle	—	ella
Leiche (D)	—	corpse	cadavre *m*	cadavere *m*	cadáver *m*
leicht¹ (D)	—	easy	facile	semplice	ligero(a)
leicht² (D)	—	light	léger(-ère)	leggero(a)	sencillo(a)
leichtsinnig (D)	—	careless	étourdi(e)	spensierato(a)	imprudente
leiden (D)	—	suffer	souffrir	soffrire	sufrir
Leidenschaft (D)	—	passion	passion *f*	passione *f*	pasión *f*
leider (D)	—	unfortunately	malheureuse-ment	purtroppo	desgraciadamente
leihen (D)	—	lend	prêter	prestare	prestar
leise (D)	—	quietly	à voix basse	a bassa voce	sin ruido
Leiter (D)	—	ladder	échelle *f*	scala *f*	escalera *f*
Leitung¹ (D)	—	direction	direction *f*	direzione *f*	dirección *f*
Leitung² (D)	—	pipe	tuyau *m*	conduttura *f*	tubería *f*
lejanía (Es)	Ferne *f*	distance	lointain *m*	distanza *f*	—
lejos¹ (Es)	fort	away	parti	via	—
lejos² (Es)	fern	far away	éloigné(e)	lontano(a)	—
lejos³ (Es)	auseinander	apart	séparé(e)	separato(a)	—
le long de (F)	entlang	along	—	lungo	a lo largo de
le lundi (F)	montags	Mondays	—	il lunedì	los lunes
le matin (F)	vormittags	in the morning	—	di mattina	por la mañana
le même (F)	derselbe	the same	—	lo stesso	el mismo
le mien (F)	meine(r,s)	mine/my	—	mio(a)	mío(a)
lemon (E)	Zitrone *f*	—	citron *m*	limone *m*	limón *m*
lemonade (E)	Limonade *f*	—	limonade *f*	limonata *f*	gaseosa *f*
lend¹ (E)	ausleihen	—	prêter	dare in prestito	prestar
lend² (E)	leihen	—	prêter	prestare	prestar
lend³ (E)	verleihen	—	prêter	prestare	prestar
lend⁴ (E)	borgen	—	prêter	prestare	prestar
length (E)	Länge *f*	—	longueur *f*	lunghezza *f*	longitud *f*
lengua¹ (Es)	Sprache *f*	language	langage *m*	lingua *f*	—
lengua² (Es)	Zunge *f*	tongue	langue *f*	lingua *f*	—
lenguado (Es)	Seezunge *f*	sole	sole *f*	sogliola *f*	—
lenguaje coloquial (Es)	Umgangssprache *f*	colloquial language	langue familière *f*	linguaggio corrente *m*	—
lengua materna (Es)	Muttersprache *f*	native language	langue maternelle *f*	lingua madre *f*	—
lengua universal (Es)	Weltsprache *f*	world language	langue internationale *f*	lingua mondiale *f*	—
lenken (D)	—	steer	conduire	guidare	encauzar
Lenkrad (D)	—	steering wheel	volant *m*	volante *m*	volante *m*
lent (F)	langsam	slow	—	lento(a)	despacio(a)
lento¹ (I)	langsam	slow	lent(e)	—	despacio(a)

	D	E	F	I	Es
lento² (I)	locker	loose	desserré(e)	—	flojo(a)
lenzuolo (I)	Laken *n*	sheet	drap *m*	—	sábana *f*
león (Es)	Löwe *m*	lion	lion *m*	leone *m*	—
leone (I)	Löwe *m*	lion	lion *m*	—	león *m*
Leopard (D)	—	leopard	léopard *m*	leopardo *m*	leopardo *m*
leopard (E)	Leopard *m*	—	léopard *m*	leopardo *m*	leopardo *m*
léopard (F)	Leopard *m*	leopard	—	leopardo *m*	leopardo *m*
leopardo (Es)	Leopard *m*	leopard	léopard *m*	leopardo *m*	—
leopardo (I)	Leopard *m*	leopard	léopard *m*	—	leopardo *m*
leotardos (Es)	Strumpfhose *f*	tights	collants *m pl*	calzamaglia *f*	—
lepre (I)	Hase *m*	hare	lièvre *m*	—	liebre *m*
lernen (D)	—	learn	apprendre	imparare	aprender
lesen (D)	—	read	lire	leggere	leer
les jours ouvrables (F)	werktags	on working days	—	nei giorni feriali	los días laborables
le soir (F)	abends	in the evening	—	di sera	por la tarde
less (E)	weniger	—	moins	di meno	menos
lessive (F)	Waschmittel *n*	detergent	—	detersivo *m*	detergente *m*
lesson (E)	Unterrichts- stunde *f*	—	leçon *f*	lezione *f*	clase *f*
lessons (E)	Unterricht *m*	—	cours	lezione *f*	enseñanza *f*
let (E)	lassen	—	laisser	lasciare	dejar
let go of (E)	loslassen	—	lâcher	mollare	dejar libre
le tout (F)	Ganze(s) *n*	lot	—	insieme *m*	todo *m*
letra (Es)	Buchstabe *m*	letter	lettre *f*	lettera *f*	—
letter¹ (E)	Buchstabe *m*	—	lettre *f*	lettera *f*	letra *f*
letter² (E)	Brief *m*	—	lettre *f*	lettera *f*	carta *f*
lettera¹ (I)	Buchstabe *m*	letter	lettre *f*	—	letra *f*
lettera² (I)	Brief *m*	letter	lettre *f*	—	carta *f*
lettera d'amore (I)	Liebesbrief *m*	love letter	lettre d'amour *f*	—	carta de amor *f*
lettera raccomandata (I)	Einschreibe- brief *m*	recorded delivery letter	lettre recommandée *f*	—	carta con acuse de recibo *f*
letterbox (E)	Briefkasten *m*	—	boîte aux lettres *f*	cassetta postale *f*	buzón *m*
letto (I)	Bett *n*	bed	lit *m*	—	cama *f*
lettre¹ (F)	Brief *m*	letter	—	lettera *f*	carta *f*
lettre² (F)	Buchstabe *m*	letter	—	lettera *f*	letra *f*
lettre d'amour (F)	Liebesbrief *m*	love letter	—	lettera d'amore *f*	carta de amor *f*
lettre recommandée (F)	Einschreibe- brief *m*	recorded delivery letter	—	lettera raccomandata *f*	carta con acuse de recibo *f*
letzte (D)	—	last	dernier(-ière)	ultimo(a)	último(a)
leugnen (D)	—	deny	nier	negare	negar
Leute (D)	—	people	gens *m pl*	gente *f*	gente *f*
levantar (Es)	heben	lift	soulever	alzare	—
levantarse (Es)	aufstehen	get up	lever, se	alzarsi	—
levare (I)	ausziehen	take off	enlever	—	quitarse
lever (F)	erheben	raise	—	alzare	elevar

	D	E	F	I	Es
lever, se (F)	aufstehen	get up	—	alzarsi	levantarse
lever du soleil (F)	Sonnenaufgang m	sunrise	—	sorgere del sole m	salida del sol f
lèvre (F)	Lippe f	lip	—	labbro m	labio m
Lexikon (D)	—	dictionary	encyclopédie f	enciclopedia f	diccionario m
ley (Es)	Gesetz n	law	loi f	legge f	—
lezione[1] (I)	Unterrichts-stunde f	lesson	leçon f	—	clase f
lezione[2] (I)	Unterricht m	lessons	cours m	—	enseñanza f
lezione (I)	Vorlesung f	lecture	cours magistral m	—	clase f
libérer (F)	freilassen	release	—	mettere in libertà	poner en libertad
libero[1] (I)	frei	free	libre	—	libre
libero[2] (I)	unbesetzt	unoccupied	vacant(e)	—	desocupado(a)
libertà (I)	Freiheit f	freedom	liberté f	—	libertad f
libertad (Es)	Freiheit f	freedom	liberté f	libertà f	—
liberté (F)	Freiheit f	freedom	—	libertà f	libertad f
libra (Es)	Pfund n	pound	livre f	mezzo chilo m	—
librairie (F)	Buchhandlung f	bookshop	—	libreria f	librería f
libre (Es)	frei	free	libre	libero(a)	—
libre (F)	frei	free	—	libero(a)	libre
librería (Es)	Buchhandlung f	bookshop	librairie f	libreria f	—
libreria (I)	Buchhandlung f	bookshop	librairie f	—	librería f
libre-service (F)	Selbstbedienung f	self service	—	self-service m	autoservicio m
libreta de ahorro (Es)	Sparbuch n	savings book	livret de caisse d'épargne m	libretto di risparmio m	
libretto degli assegni (I)	Scheckbuch n	cheque book	carnet de chèques m	—	talonario de cheques m
libretto di risparmio (I)	Sparbuch n	savings book	livret de caisse d'épargne m	—	libreta de ahorro f
libro (Es)	Buch n	book	livre m	libro m	—
libro (I)	Buch n	book	livre m	—	libro m
licenziare[1] (I)	entlassen	release	renvoyer	—	despedir
licenziare[2] (I)	kündigen	sack	résilier	—	despedir
liceo (I)	Gymnasium n	grammar school	lycée m	—	instituto de enseñanza media m
Licht (D)	—	light	lumière f	luce f	luz f
Lichtschalter (D)	—	light switch	interrupteur m	interruttore m	interruptor m
licor (Es)	Likör m	liqueur	liqueur f	liquore m	—
lid (E)	Deckel m	—	couvercle m	coperchio m	tapa f
lie[1] (E)	lügen	—	mentir	mentire	mentir
lie[2] (E)	liegen	—	trouver, se	giacere	estar tumbado(a)
lieb (D)	—	sweet	gentil(le)	caro(a)	amable
Liebe (D)	—	love	amour m	amore m	amor m
lieben (D)	—	love	aimer	amare	amar
liebenswürdig (D)	—	kind	aimable	gentile	gentil
lieber (D)	—	rather	mieux	piuttosto	más bien
Liebesbrief (D)	—	love letter	lettre d'amour f	lettera d'amore f	carta de amor f

	D	E	F	I	Es
Liebling (D)	—	darling	chéri *m*	tesoro *m*	querido *m*
liebre (Es)	Hase *m*	hare	lièvre *m*	lepre *f*	—
Lied (D)	—	song	chanson *f*	canzone *f*	canción *f*
liefern (D)	—	deliver	livrer	fornire	suministrar
Lieferung (D)	—	delivery	livraison *f*	fornitura *f*	suministro *m*
liegen (D)	—	lie	trouver, se	giacere	estar tumbado(a)
Liegestuhl (D)	—	deck chair	chaise longue *f*	sedia a sdraio *f*	tumbona *f*
Liegewagen (D)	—	couchette	wagon-couchette *m*	cuccetta *f*	coche cama *m*
lieto[1] (I)	erfreut	delighted	réjoui(e)	—	contento(a)
lieto[2] (I)	froh	glad	content(e)	—	contento(a)
lièvre (F)	Hase *m*	hare	—	lepre *f*	liebre *m*
life (E)	Leben *n*	—	vie *f*	vita *f*	vida *f*
lifebelt (E)	Rettungsring *m*	—	bouée de sauvetage *f*	salvagente *m*	salvavidas *m*
life jacket (E)	Schwimmweste *f*	—	gilet de sauvetage *m*	giubbetto di salvataggio *m*	chaleco salvavidas *m*
life partner (E)	Lebensgefährte *m*	—	compagnon *m*	compagno *m*	compañero en la vida *m*
Lift (D)	—	elevator	ascenseur *m*	ascensore *m*	ascensor *m*
lift (E)	heben	—	soulever	alzare	levantar
ligero (Es)	leicht	easy	facile	semplice	—
light[1] (E)	anzünden	—	allumer	accendere	encender
light[2] (E)	leicht	—	léger(-ère)	leggero(a)	sencillo(a)
light[3] (E)	Licht *n*	—	lumière *f*	luce *f*	luz *f*
light[4] (E)	Schein *m*	—	lumière *f*	luce *f*	luz *f*
light bulb (E)	Glühbirne *f*	—	ampoule *f*	lampadina *f*	lámpara *f*
lighter (E)	Feuerzeug *n*	—	briquet *m*	accendino *m*	mechero *m*
lighting (E)	Beleuchtung *f*	—	éclairage *m*	illuminazione *f*	iluminación *f*
lightning (E)	Blitz *m*	—	éclair *m*	lampo *m*	rayo *m*
light switch (E)	Lichtschalter *m*	—	interrupteur *m*	interruttore *m*	interruptor *m*
ligne[1] (F)	Linie *f*	line	—	linea *f*	línea *f*
ligne[2] (F)	Zeile *f*	line	—	riga *f*	línea *f*
like (E)	mögen	—	aimer	piacere	querer
likeable (E)	sympathisch	—	sympathique	simpatico(a)	simpático(a)
like this (E)	so	—	ainsi	così	así
likewise (E)	ebenfalls	—	aussi	altrettanto	también
Likör (D)	—	liqueur	liqueur *f*	liquore *m*	licor *m*
lila (D)	—	purple	mauve	lilla	de color lila
lilla (I)	lila	purple	mauve	—	de color lila
limit (E)	begrenzen	—	limiter	limitare	limitar
limitar (Es)	begrenzen	limit	limiter	limitare	—
limitare (I)	begrenzen	limit	limiter	—	limitar
limited stop train (E)	Eilzug *m*	—	express *m*	treno diretto *m*	tren expreso *m*
limiter (F)	begrenzen	limit	—	limitare	limitar
limón (Es)	Zitrone *f*	lemon	citron *m*	limone *m*	—

	D	E	F	I	Es
Limonade (D)	—	lemonade	limonade f	limonata f	gaseosa f
limonade (F)	Limonade f	lemonade	—	limonata f	gaseosa f
limonata (I)	Limonade f	lemonade	limonade f	—	gaseosa f
limone (I)	Zitrone f	lemon	citron m	—	limón m
limosna (Es)	Almosen n	alms	aumône f	elemosina f	—
limpiar¹ (Es)	putzen	clean	nettoyer	pulire	—
limpiar² (Es)	reinigen	clean	nettoyer	pulire	—
limpieza (Es)	Reinigung f	cleaning	nettoyage m	pulitura f	—
limpio (Es)	sauber	clean	propre	pulito(a)	—
line¹ (E)	Linie f	—	ligne f	linea f	línea f
line² (E)	Strich m	—	trait m	linea f	línea f
line³ (E)	Zeile f	—	ligne f	riga f	línea f
línea¹ (Es)	Linie f	line	ligne f	linea f	—
línea² (Es)	Strich m	line	trait m	linea f	—
línea³ (Es)	Zeile f	line	ligne f	riga f	—
linea¹ (I)	Linie f	line	ligne f	—	línea f
linea² (I)	Strich m	line	trait m	—	línea f
Lineal (D)	—	ruler	règle f	riga f	regla f
linge (F)	Wäsche f	washing	—	biancheria f	ropa f
lingua¹ (I)	Sprache f	language	langage m	—	lengua f
lingua² (I)	Zunge f	tongue	langue f	—	lengua f
linguaggio corrente (I)	Umgangssprache f	colloquial language	langue familière f	—	lenguaje coloquial m
lingua madre (I)	Muttersprache f	native language	langue maternelle f	—	lengua materna f
lingua mondiale (I)	Weltsprache f	world language	langue internationale f	—	lengua universal f
lingua straniera (I)	Fremdsprache f	foreign language	langue étrangère f	—	idioma extranjero m
Linie (D)	—	line	ligne f	linea f	línea f
links (D)	—	left	à gauche	a sinistra	a la izquierda
linterna (Es)	Taschenlampe f	torch	lampe de poche f	lampadina tascabile f	—
lion (E)	Löwe m	—	lion m	leone m	león m
lion (F)	Löwe m	lion	—	leone m	león m
lip (E)	Lippe f	—	lèvre f	labbro m	labio m
Lippe (D)	—	lip	lèvre f	labbro m	labio m
liqueur (E)	Likör m	—	liqueur f	liquore m	licor m
liqueur (F)	Likör m	liqueur	—	liquore m	licor m
liquidación (Es)	Ausverkauf m	sale	soldes m pl	saldi m pl	—
liquide (F)	flüssig	fluid	—	liquido(a)	líquido(a)
liquido (I)	flüssig	fluid	liquide	—	líquido(a)
líquido (Es)	flüssig	fluid	liquide	liquido(a)	—
liquore (I)	Likör m	liqueur	liqueur f	—	licor m
lire (F)	lesen	read	—	leggere	leer
liscio (I)	glatt	smooth	lisse	—	liso(a)
liso (Es)	glatt	smooth	lisse	liscio	—

	D	E	F	I	Es
lisse (F)	glatt	smooth	—	liscio(a)	liso(a)
list¹ (E)	Liste *f*	—	liste *f*	lista *f*	lista *f*
list² (E)	verzeichnen	—	enregistrer	registrare	hacer una lista
list³ (E)	Verzeichnis *n*	—	registre *m*	elenco *m*	lista *f*
lista¹ (Es)	Liste *f*	list	liste *f*	lista *f*	—
lista² (Es)	Verzeichnis *n*	list	registre *m*	elenco *m*	—
lista (I)	Liste *f*	list	liste *f*	—	lista *f*
lista de platos (Es)	Speisekarte *f*	menu	menu *m*	menu *m*	—
Liste (D)	—	list	liste *f*	lista *f*	lista *f*
liste (F)	Liste *f*	list	—	lista *f*	lista *f*
listen (E)	zuhören	—	écouter	ascoltare	escuchar
listener (E)	Hörer *m*	—	auditeur *m*	ascoltatore *m*	oyente *m*
listo¹ (Es)	clever	clever	futé(e)	abile	—
listo² (Es)	fertig	ready	prêt(e)	pronto(a)	—
lit (F)	Bett *n*	bed	—	letto *m*	cama *f*
lite (I)	Streit *m*	argument	dispute *f*	—	disputa *f*
Liter (D)	—	litre	litre *m*	litro *m*	litro *m*
litigare (I)	streiten	quarrel	disputer, se	—	discutir
litre (E)	Liter *n*	—	litre *m*	litro *m*	litro *m*
litre (F)	Liter *n*	litre	—	litro *m*	litro *m*
litro (Es)	Liter *n*	litre	litre *m*	litro *m*	—
litro (I)	Liter *n*	litre	litre *m*	litro *m*	—
little (E)	wenig	—	peu de	poco(a)	poco(a)
live¹ (E)	leben	—	vivre	vivere	vivir
live² (E)	wohnen	—	habiter	abitare	vivir
livello del mare (I)	Meeresspiegel *m*	sea level	niveau de la mer *m*	—	nivel del mar *m*
lively¹ (E)	lebhaft	—	vif(vive)	vivace	vivaz
lively² (E)	munter	—	éveillé(e)	vivace	alegre
lively³ (E)	belebt	—	animé(e)	animato(a)	animado(a)
liver (E)	Leber *f*	—	foie *m*	fegato *m*	hígado *m*
living room (E)	Wohnzimmer *n*	—	salle de séjour *f*	salotto *m*	sala de estar *f*
livraison (F)	Lieferung *f*	delivery	—	fornitura *f*	suministro *m*
livre¹ (F)	Buch *n*	book	—	libro *m*	libro *m*
livre² (F)	Pfund *n*	pound	—	mezzo chilo *m*	libra *f*
livrer (F)	liefern	deliver	—	fornire	suministrar
livret de caisse d'épargne (F)	Sparbuch *n*	savings book	—	libretto di risparmio *m*	libreta de ahorro *f*
llama (Es)	Flamme *f*	flame	flamme *f*	fiamma *f*	—
llamada (Es)	Anruf *m*	call	coup de téléphone *m*	chiamata *f*	—
llamada interurbana (Es)	Ferngespräch *n*	long-distance call	communication interurbaine *f*	telefonata interurbana *f*	—
llamada telefónica (Es)	Telefonanruf *m*	phone call	coup de téléphone *m*	telefonata *f*	—
llamar (Es)	rufen	shout	appeler	chiamare	—
llamar con gestos (Es)	winken	wave	faire signe	chiamare con cenni	—

	D	E	F	I	Es
llamar la atención por algo (Es)	auffallen	be noticeable	faire remarquer, se	dare nell'occhio	—
llamar por teléfono[1] (Es)	anrufen	ring up	téléphoner	telefonare	—
llamar por teléfono[2] (Es)	telefonieren	telephone	téléphoner	telefonare	—
llamarse (Es)	heißen	be called	appeler, se	chiamarsi	—
llano (Es)	flach	flat	plat(e)	piatto(a)	—
llanura[1] (Es)	Ebene f	plain	plaine f	pianura f	—
llanura[2] (Es)	Fläche f	area	surface f	area f	—
llave (Es)	Schlüssel m	key	clé f	chiave f	—
llegada (Es)	Ankunft f	arrival	arrivée f	arrivo m	—
llegar[1] (Es)	ankommen	arrive	arriver	arrivare	—
llegar[2] (Es)	eintreffen	arrive	arriver	arrivare	—
llegar a ser (Es)	werden	become	devenir	diventare	—
llenar[1] (Es)	ausfüllen	fill in	remplir	riempire	—
llenar[2] (Es)	erfüllen	fulfil	remplir	esaudire	—
llenar[3] (Es)	füllen	fill	remplir	riempire	—
llenar de gasolina (Es)	tanken	fill up with petrol	prendre de l'essence	fare benzina	—
lleno (Es)	voll	full	plein(e)	pieno(a)	—
llevar[1] (Es)	anhaben	have on	porter	indossare	—
llevar[2] (Es)	bringen	fetch	porter	portare	—
llevar[3] (Es)	tragen	carry	porter	portare	—
llevar a cabo (Es)	verwirklichen	realize	réaliser	realizzare	—
llevar consigo (Es)	mitnehmen	take along	emmener	prendere con sè	—
llevar retraso (Es)	verspäten	be late	être en retard	ritardare	—
llorar (Es)	weinen	cry	pleurer	piangere	—
llover (Es)	regnen	rain	pleuvoir	piovere	—
lluvia (Es)	Regen m	rain	pluie f	pioggia f	—
lo (Es)	das	that/which	le/la	il/la	—
load[1] (E)	aufladen	—	charger	caricare	cargar
load[2] (E)	Last f	—	charge f	carico m	peso m
load[3] (E)	verladen	—	charger	caricare	cargar
loben (D)	—	praise	louer	lodare	elogiar
local (E)	örtlich	—	local(e)	locale	local
local[1] (Es)	Lokal n	pub	restaurant m	locale m	—
local[2] (Es)	örtlich	local	local(e)	locale	—
local (F)	örtlich	local	—	locale	local
locale[1] (I)	Lokal n	pub	restaurant m	—	local m
locale[2] (I)	örtlich	local	local(e)	—	local
local nocturno (Es)	Nachtlokal n	(night) club	boîte de nuit f	night m	—
locataire (F)	Mieter m	tenant	—	inquilino m	inquilino m
location (F)	Vorverkauf m	advance booking	—	prevendita f	venta anticipada f
Loch (D)	—	hole	trou m	buco m	agujero m
lock[1] (E)	Schloß n	—	serrure f	serratura f	cerradura f

lock

	D	E	F	I	Es
lock² (E)	Verschluß m	—	fermeture f	chiusura f	cierre m
Locke (D)	—	curl	boucle f	riccio m	rizo m
locken (D)	—	attract	attirer	attirare	atraer
locker (D)	—	loose	desserré(e)	lento(a)	flojo(a)
lock (up)¹ (E)	verschließen	—	fermer à clé	chiudere a chiave	cerrar con llave
lock (up)² (E)	zuschließen	—	fermer à clé	chiudere a chiave	cerrar con llave
lock up³ (E)	einschließen	—	renfermer	rinchiudere	encerrar
loco¹ (Es)	Narr m	fool	fou m	pazzo m	—
loco² (Es)	verrückt	mad	fou (folle)	pazzo(a)	—
lodare (I)	loben	praise	louer	—	elogiar
Löffel (D)	—	spoon	cuiller f	cucchiaio m	cuchara f
Loge (D)	—	box	loge f	palco m	palco m
loge (F)	Loge f	box	—	palco m	palco m
logement (F)	Unterkunft f	accommodation	—	alloggio m	hospedaje m
logement pour une nuit (F)	Übernachtung f	overnight stay	—	pernottamento m	pernoctación f
Lohn (D)	—	wages	salaire m	salario m	salario m
lohnen (D)	—	be worth while	en valoir la peine	valere la pena	valer la pena
loi (F)	Gesetz n	law	—	legge f	ley f
lointain (F)	Ferne f	distance	—	distanza f	lejanía f
loisirs (F)	Freizeit f	free time	—	tempo libero m	tiempo libre m
Lokal (D)	—	pub	restaurant m	locale m	local m
lo mismo (Es)	dasselbe	the same	la même chose	lo stesso	—
lonely (E)	einsam	—	solitaire	solitario(a)	solitario(a)
long (E)	lang	—	long(ue)	lungo(a)	largo(a)
long (F)	lang	long	—	lungo(a)	largo(a)
long-distance call (E)	Ferngespräch n	—	communication interurbaine f	telefonata interurbana f	llamada interurbana f
long-distance driver (E)	Fernfahrer m	—	routier m	camionista m	camionero m
longitud (Es)	Länge f	length	longueur f	lunghezza f	—
longtemps (F)	lange	long time	—	molto tempo	mucho tiempo
long time (E)	lange	—	longtemps	molto tempo	mucho tiempo
longueur (F)	Länge f	length	—	lunghezza f	longitud f
lontano (I)	fern	far away	éloigné(e)	—	lejos
look¹ (E)	aussehen	—	avoir l'air	avere l'aspetto	parecer
look² (E)	blicken	—	regarder	guardare	mirar
look³ (E)	Blick m	—	regard m	sguardo m	vista f
look⁴ (E)	schauen	—	regarder	guardare	mirar
look after¹ (E)	kümmern, sich	—	occuper de, se	interessarsi di	ocuparse de
look after² (E)	pflegen	—	soigner	curare	cuidar
look at¹ (E)	ansehen	—	regarder	guardare	mirar
look at² (E)	anschauen	—	regarder	guardare	mirar
looked-after (E)	gepflegt	—	soigné(e)	curato(a)	cuidado(a)
look for (E)	suchen	—	chercher	cercare	buscar

	D	E	F	I	Es
loose (E)	locker	—	desserré(e)	lento(a)	flojo(a)
loot (E)	plündern	—	piller	saccheggiare	desvalijar
loro (I)	sie	they	ils/elles	—	ellos, ellas
lorry (E)	Lastwagen *m*	—	camion *m*	camion *m*	camión *m*
los! (D)	—	off!	allons-y!	avanti!	¡adelante!
losbinden (D)	—	free	délier	sciogliere	desatar
löschen (D)	—	extinguish	éteindre	spegnere	apagar
los días laborables (Es)	werktags	on working days	les jours ouvrables	nei giorni feriali	—
lösen (D)	—	solve	résoudre	sciogliere	desatar
lose[1] (E)	einbüßen	—	perdre	perdere	perder
lose[2] (E)	verlieren	—	perdre	perdere	perder
lose weight (E)	abnehmen	—	maigrir	dimagrire	adelgazar
loslassen (D)	—	let go of	lâcher	mollare	dejar libre
los lunes (Es)	montags	Mondays	le lundi	il lunedì	—
los Países Bajos (Es)	Niederlande *f*	Netherlands	Pays-Bas *m pl*	Paesi Bassi *m pl*	—
loss (E)	Verlust *m*	—	perte *f*	perdita *f*	pérdida *f*
lo stesso[1] (I)	dasselbe	the same	la même chose	—	lo mismo
lo stesso[2] (I)	derselbe	the same	le même	—	el mismo
lost property office (E)	Fundbüro *n*	—	bureau des objets trouvés *m*	ufficio oggetti smarriti *m*	oficina de objetos perdidos *f*
Lösung (D)	—	solution	solution *f*	soluzione *f*	solución *f*
lot (E)	Ganze(s) *n*	—	le tout	insieme *m*	todo *m*
loud (E)	laut	—	fort(e)	rumoroso(a)	fuerte
loudspeaker (E)	Lautsprecher *m*	—	haut-parleur *m*	altoparlante *m*	altavoz *m*
louer[1] (F)	loben	praise	—	lodare	elogiar
louer[2] (F)	mieten	rent	—	affittare	alquilar
louer[3] (F)	vermieten	rent	—	affittare	alquilar
lourd[1] (F)	schwül	sultry	—	afoso(a)	sofocante
lourd[2] (F)	schwer	heavy	—	pesante	pesado(a)
love[1] (E)	lieben	—	aimer	amare	amar
love[2] (E)	Liebe *f*	—	amour *m*	amore *m*	amor *m*
love letter (E)	Liebesbrief *m*	—	lettre d'amour *f*	lettera d'amore *f*	carta de amor *f*
low (E)	niedrig	—	bas(se)	basso(a)	bajo
Löwe (D)	—	lion	lion *m*	leone *m*	león *m*
lower[1] (E)	herabsetzen	—	baisser	diminuire	rebajar
lower[2] (E)	senken	—	baisser	abbassare	bajar
lowest (E)	unterste(r,s)	—	inférieur(e)	inferiore	inferior(a)
low season (E)	Vorsaison *f*	—	basse saison *f*	bassa stagione *f*	pretemporada *f*
low tide (E)	Ebbe *f*	—	marée basse *f*	bassa marea *f*	marea baja *f*
loyer (F)	Miete *f*	rent	—	affitto *m*	alquiler *m*
luce[1] (I)	Licht *n*	light	lumière *f*	—	luz *f*
luce[2] (I)	Schein *m*	light	lumière *f*	—	luz *f*
luchar (Es)	kämpfen	fight	battre, se	combattere	—
lucidare (I)	polieren	polish	astiquer	—	pulir

	D	E	F	I	Es
lucido per scarpe (I)	Schuhcreme f	shoe polish	cirage m	—	betún m
luck (E)	Glück n	—	chance f	fortuna f	suerte f
Lücke (D)	—	gap	lacune f	lacuna f	espacio m
luego (Es)	dann	then	ensuite	in seguito	—
Luft (D)	—	air	air m	aria f	aire m
lüften (D)	—	air	aérer	arieggiare	ventilar
Luftpost (D)	—	air mail	poste aérienne f	posta aerea f	correo aéreo m
Luftzug (D)	—	draught	courant d'air m	corrente d'aria f	corriente de aire f
lugar (Es)	Ort m	place	endroit m	luogo m	—
lugares de interés (Es)	Sehenswürdig-keit f	sight	curiosité f	curiosità f	—
lügen (D)	—	lie	mentir	mentire	mentir
luggage (E)	Gepäck n	—	bagages m pl	bagaglio m	equipaje m
luggage desk (E)	Gepäckannahme f	—	enregistrement des bagages m	accettazione bagagli f	recepción de equipajes f
luglio (I)	Juli m	July	juillet m	—	julio m
lui/egli/esso (I)	er	he	il	—	él
lujo (Es)	Luxus m	luxury	luxe m	lusso m	—
lukewarm (E)	lauwarm	—	tiède	tiepido(a)	templado(a)
lumière[1] (F)	Licht n	light	—	luce f	luz f
lumière[2] (F)	Schein m	light	—	luce f	luz f
luna (Es)	Mond m	moon	lune f	luna f	—
luna (I)	Mond m	moon	lune f	—	luna f
luna de miel (Es)	Flitterwochen pl	honeymoon	lune de miel f	luna di miele f	—
luna di miele (I)	Flitterwochen pl	honeymoon	lune de miel f	—	luna de miel f
lunch (E)	Mittagessen n	—	déjeuner m	pranzo m	comida f
l'un dans l'autre (F)	ineinander	into one another	—	l'uno nell'altro	uno en otro
l'un derrière l'autre (F)	hintereinander	one after the other	—	uno dopo l'altro	uno detrás de otro
lundi (F)	Montag m	Monday	—	lunedì m	lunes m
lune (F)	Mond m	moon	—	luna f	luna f
lune de miel (F)	Flitterwochen pl	honeymoon	—	luna di miele f	luna de miel f
lunedì (I)	Montag m	Monday	lundi m	—	lunes m
lunes (Es)	Montag m	Monday	lundi m	lunedì m	—
l'un(e) sur l'autre (F)	übereinander	one upon the other	—	uno sopra l'altro	uno sobre otro
lunettes (F)	Brille f	glasses	—	occhiali m pl	gafas f pl
lunettes de soleil (F)	Sonnenbrille f	sunglasses	—	occhiali da sole m pl	gafas de sol f pl
lung (E)	Lunge f	—	poumon m	polmone m	pulmón m
Lunge (D)	—	lung	poumon m	polmone m	pulmón m
lunghezza (I)	Länge f	length	longueur f	—	longitud f
lungo[1] (I)	entlang	along	le long de	—	a lo largo de
lungo[2] (I)	lang	long	long(ue)	—	largo(a)
l'uno nell'altro (I)	ineinander	into one another	l'un dans l'autre	—	uno en otro
luogo[3] (I)	Ort m	place	endroit m	—	lugar m
lusso (I)	Luxus m	luxury	luxe m	—	lujo m

	D	E	F	I	Es
lussuoso (I)	luxuriös	luxurious	luxueux(-euse)	—	de lujo
Lust (D)	—	delight	plaisir m	piacere m	ganas f pl
lustig (D)	—	funny	marrant(e)	allegro(a)	divertido(a)
lutschen (D)	—	suck	sucer	succhiare	chupar
luxe (F)	Luxus m	luxury	—	lusso m	lujo m
luxueux (F)	luxuriös	luxurious	—	lussuoso(a)	de lujo
luxuriös (D)	—	luxurious	luxueux(-euse)	lussuoso(a)	de lujo
luxurious (E)	luxuriös	—	luxueux(-euse)	lussuoso(a)	de lujo
luxury (E)	Luxus m	—	luxe m	lusso m	lujo m
Luxus (D)	—	luxury	luxe m	lusso m	lujo m
luz¹ (Es)	Licht n	light	lumière f	luce f	—
luz² (Es)	Schein m	light	lumière f	luce f	—
lycée (F)	Gymnasium n	grammar school	—	liceo m	instituto de enseñanza media m
ma¹ (I)	aber	but	mais	—	pero
ma² (I)	sondern	but	mais	—	sino
macchia (I)	Fleck m	stain	tache f	—	mancha f
macchina¹ (I)	Auto n	car	voiture f	—	coche m
macchina² (I)	Maschine f	machine	machine f	—	máquina f
macchina da scrivere (I)	Schreibmaschine f	typewriter	machine à écrire f	—	máquina de escribir f
macchina fotografica (I)	Fotoapparat m	camera	appareil-photo m	—	máquina fotográfica f
macellaio (I)	Metzger m	butcher	boucher m	—	carnicero m
macelleria (I)	Metzgerei f	butcher's	boucherie f	—	carnicería f
macerie (I)	Trümmer pl	ruins	décombres m pl	—	escombros m pl
machen (D)	—	make/do	faire	fare	hacer
mâcher (F)	kauen	chew	—	masticare	masticar
machine (E)	Maschine f	—	machine f	macchina f	máquina f
machine (F)	Maschine f	machine	—	macchina f	máquina f
machine à écrire (F)	Schreibmaschine f	typewriter	—	macchina da scrivere f	máquina de escribir f
machine à laver (F)	Waschmaschine f	washing machine	—	lavatrice f	lavadora f
machitarse (Es)	welken	wither	faner, se	appassire	—
Macht (D)	—	power	pouvoir m	potere m	poder m
mad (E)	verrückt	—	fou (folle)	pazzo	loco(a)
Mädchen (D)	—	girl	jeune fille f	ragazza f	chica f
mademoiselle (F)	Fräulein n	Miss	—	signorina f	señorita f
madera (Es)	Holz n	wood	bois m	legno m	—
madre (Es)	Mutter f	mother	mère f	madre f	—
madre (I)	Mutter f	mother	mère f	—	madre f
madrina (Es)	Patin f	godmother	marraine f	madrina f	—
madrina (I)	Patin f	godmother	marraine f	—	madrina f
maduro (Es)	reif	ripe	mûr(e)	maturo(a)	—
maestro (Es)	Meister m	master	maître m	maestro m	—

	D	E	F	I	Es
maestro¹ (I)	Lehrer *m*	teacher	professeur *m*	—	profesor *m*
maestro² (I)	Meister *m*	master	maître *m*	—	maestro *m*
magasin¹ (F)	Geschäft *n*	shop	—	negozio *m*	tienda *f*
magasin² (F)	Laden *m*	shop	—	negozio *m*	tienda *f*
magasin³ (F)	Lager *n*	store	—	magazzino *m*	almacén *m*
magasin d'alimentation (F)	Lebensmittel-geschäft *n*	grocer's	—	negozio di alimentari *m*	tienda de comestibles *f*
magasin de chaussures (F)	Schuhgeschäft *n*	shoeshop	—	negozio di scarpe *m*	zapatería *f*
magasin diététique (F)	Reformhaus *n*	health food shop	—	negozio di prodotti dietetici *m*	tienda de productos dietéticos *f*
magazine (E)	Zeitschrift *f*	—	revue *f*	rivista *f*	revista *f*
magazzino (I)	Lager *n*	store	magasin *m*	—	almacén *m*
Magen (D)	—	stomach	estomac *m*	stomaco *m*	estómago *m*
Magen-schmerzen (D)	—	stomach-ache	mal d'estomac *m*	mal di stomaco *m*	dolor de estómago
mager (D)	—	skinny	maigre	magro(a)	delgado(a)
maggio (I)	Mai *m*	May	mai *m*	—	mayo *m*
maggioranza (I)	Mehrheit *f*	majority	majorité *f*	—	mayoría *f*
maggiorenne (I)	volljährig	of age	majeur(e)	—	mayor de edad
magician (E)	Zauberer *m*	—	magicien *m*	mago *m*	mago *m*
magicien (F)	Zauberer *m*	magician	—	mago *m*	mago *m*
magnificent (E)	großartig	—	formidable	grandioso(a)	magnífico(a)
magnífico¹ (Es)	großartig	magnificent	formidable	grandioso(a)	—
magnífico² (Es)	prächtig	splendid	magnifique	meraviglioso(a)	—
magnifique¹ (F)	herrlich	marvellous	—	stupendo(a)	maravilloso(a)
magnifique² (F)	prächtig	splendid	—	meraviglioso(a)	magnífico(a)
mago (Es)	Zauberer *m*	magician	magicien *m*	mago *m*	—
mago (I)	Zauberer *m*	magician	magicien *m*	—	mago *m*
magro¹ (I)	dünn	thin	mince	—	delgado(a)
magro² (I)	mager	skinny	maigre	—	delgado(a)
mähen (D)	—	mow	faucher	falciare	cortar
Mahlzeit (D)	—	meal	repas *m*	pasto *m*	comida *f*
mahnen (D)	—	warn	exhorter	ammonire	notificar
Mai (D)	—	May	mai *m*	maggio *m*	mayo *m*
mai (F)	Mai *m*	May	—	maggio *m*	mayo *m*
mai¹ (I)	jemals	ever	jamais	—	jamás
mai² (I)	niemals	never	ne...jamais	—	jamás
maiale (I)	Schwein *n*	pig	cochon *m*	—	cerdo *m*
maid (E)	Hausmädchen *n*	—	fille de service *f*	domestica *f*	criada *f*
maigre¹ (F)	dürr	skinny	—	secco(a)	árido(a)
maigre² (F)	mager	skinny	—	magro(a)	delgado(a)
maigrir (F)	abnehmen	lose weight	—	dimagrire	adelgazar
maillot de bain (F)	Badeanzug *m*	swimsuit	—	costume da bagno *m*	traje de baño *m*
main (F)	Hand *f*	hand	—	mano *f*	mano *f*

	D	E	F	I	Es
mainland (E)	Festland n	—	continent m	terraferma f	tierra firme f
mainly (E)	hauptsächlich	—	surtout	principalmente	principalmente
main street (E)	Hauptstraße f	—	grand-rue f	strada principale f	calle central f
maintenant¹ (F)	jetzt	now	—	adesso	ahora
maintenant² (F)	nun	now	—	adesso	actualmente
maire (F)	Bürgermeister m	mayor	—	sindaco m	alcalde m
mairie (F)	Rathaus n	town hall	—	municipio m	ayuntamiento m
Mais (D)	—	corn	maïs m	mais m	maíz m
mais¹ (F)	aber	but	—	ma	pero
mais² (F)	sondern	but	—	ma/bensì	sino
maïs (F)	Mais m	corn	—	mais m	maíz m
mais (I)	Mais m	corn	maïs m	—	maíz m
maison (F)	Haus n	house	—	casa f	casa f
maître (F)	Meister m	master	—	maestro m	maestro m
maître baigneur (F)	Bademeister m	baths attendant	—	bagnino m	bañero m
maíz (Es)	Mais m	corn	maïs m	mais m	—
majeur (F)	volljährig	of age	—	maggiorenne	mayor de edad
majorité (F)	Mehrheit f	majority	—	maggioranza f	mayoría f
majority (E)	Mehrheit f	—	majorité f	maggioranza f	mayoría f
make (E)	machen	—	faire	fare	hacer
make an effort¹ (E)	anstrengen	—	faire des efforts	affaticare	cansar
make an effort² (E)	bemühen, sich	—	efforcer, se	sforzarsi	esforzarse
make over (E)	überschreiben	—	céder	cedere	transferir
make possible (E)	ermöglichen	—	rendre possible	rendere possibile	facilitar
make smaller (E)	verkleinern	—	réduire	ridurre	reducir
make-up (E)	Schminke f	—	maquillage m	trucco m	maquillaje m
make up for (E)	wiedergut-machen	—	réparer	riparare	subsanar
Mal (D)	—	mark	marque f	segno m	marca f
malade (F)	krank	ill	—	malato(a)	enfermo(a)
maladie (F)	Krankheit f	illness	—	malattia f	enfermedad f
maladroit (F)	ungeschickt	clumsy	—	impacciato(a)	torpe
mal à propos (F)	unpassend	inappropriate	—	sconveniente	inadecuado(a)
mala suerte (Es)	Pech n	bad luck	malchance f	sfortuna f	—
malato (I)	krank	ill	malade	—	enfermo(a)
malattia (I)	Krankheit f	illness	maladie f	—	enfermedad f
malchance (F)	Pech n	bad luck	—	sfortuna f	mala suerte f
mal de dents (F)	Zahn-schmerzen pl	toothache	—	mal di denti m	dolor de muelas m
mal de gorge (F)	Hals-schmerzen pl	sore throat	—	mal di gola m	dolor de garganta m
mal d'estomac (F)	Magen-schmerzen pl	stomach-ache	—	mal di stomaco m	dolor de estómago
mal de tête (F)	Kopfschmerzen pl	headache	—	mal di testa m	dolor de cabeza m
mal di denti (I)	Zahn-schmerzen pl	toothache	mal de dents m	—	dolor de muelas m

	D	E	F	I	Es
mal di gola (I)	Hals-schmerzen *pl*	sore throat	mal de gorge *m*	—	dolor de garganta *m*
mal di stomaco (I)	Magen-schmerzen *pl*	stomach-ache	mal d'estomac *m*	—	dolor de estómago *m*
mal di testa (I)	Kopf-schmerzen *pl*	headache	mal de tête *m*	—	dolor de cabeza *m*
mal d'orecchi (I)	Ohren-schmerzen *pl*	earache	mal d'oreilles *m*	—	dolor de oídos
mal d'oreilles (F)	Ohren-schmerzen *pl*	earache	—	mal d'orecchi *m*	dolor de oídos
mal du pays (F)	Heimweh *n*	homesickness	—	nostalgia *f*	nostalgía *f*
malen (D)	—	paint	peindre	dipingere	pintar
malentendido (Es)	Mißverständnis *n*	misunderstanding	malentendu *m*	equivoco *m*	—
malentendu (F)	Mißverständnis *n*	misunderstanding	—	equivoco *m*	malentendido *m*
Maler (D)	—	painter	peintre *m*	pittore *m*	pintor *m*
Malerei (D)	—	painting	peinture *f*	pittura *f*	pintura *f*
malerisch (D)	—	picturesque	pittoresque	pittoresco(a)	pintoresco(a)
maleta (Es)	Koffer *m*	suitcase	valise *f*	valigia *f*	—
maletero (Es)	Kofferraum *m*	boot	coffre *m*	portabagagli *m*	—
malgré (F)	trotz	despite	—	nonostante	a pesar de
malgré tout (F)	trotzdem	nevertheless	—	tuttavia	no obstante
malheur (F)	Unglück *n*	misfortune	—	disgrazia *f*	desgracia *f*
malheureuse-ment (F)	leider	unfortunately	—	purtroppo	desgraciadamente
malheureux (F)	unglücklich	unhappy	—	sfortünato(a)	desgraciado(a)
malo[1] (Es)	böse	wicked	méchant(e)	cattivo(a)	—
malo[2] (Es)	schlecht	bad	mauvais(e)	cattivo(a)	—
malo[3] (Es)	übel	bad	mauvais(e)	cattivo(a)	—
malsain (F)	ungesund	unhealthy	—	malsano(a)	enfermizo(a)
malsano (I)	ungesund	unhealthy	malsain(e)	—	enfermizo(a)
maltempo (I)	Unwetter *n*	thunderstorm	tempête *f*	—	tormenta *f*
malvolentieri (I)	ungern	reluctantly	de mauvaise grâce	—	de mala gana
man (E)	Mann *m*	—	homme *m*	uomo *m*	hombre *m*
manager (E)	Geschäftsführer *m*	—	gérant *m*	gerente *m*	gerente *m*
mañana[1] (Es)	morgen	tomorrow	demain	domani	—
mañana[2] (Es)	Morgen *m*	morning	matin *m*	mattino *m*	—
mañana[3] (Es)	Vormittag *m*	before noon	matinée *f*	mattina *f*	—
mancanza (I)	Mangel *m*	lack	manque *m*	—	escasez *f*
mancare (I)	fehlen	miss	manquer	—	faltar
mancha (Es)	Fleck *m*	stain	tache *f*	macchia *f*	—
manche (F)	Ärmel *m*	sleeve	—	manica *f*	manga *f*
Manche (F)	Ärmelkanal *m*	Channel	—	Manica *f*	Canal de la Mancha *m*
manchette (F)	Schlagzeile *f*	headline	—	titolo *m*	titular *m*
manchmal (D)	—	sometimes	quelquefois	talvolta	a veces
mancia (I)	Trinkgeld *n*	tip	pourboire *m*	—	propina *f*
mandar[1] (Es)	herrschen	rule	régner	dominare	—
mandar[2] (Es)	schicken	send	envoyer	inviare	—
mandarin (E)	Mandarine *f*	—	mandarine *f*	mandarino *m*	mandarina *f*
mandarina (Es)	Mandarine *f*	mandarin	mandarine *f*	mandarino *m*	—
Mandarine (D)	—	mandarin	mandarine *f*	mandarino *m*	mandarina *f*

	D	E	F	I	Es
mandarine (F)	Mandarine *f*	mandarin	—	mandarino *m*	mandarina *f*
mandarino (I)	Mandarine *f*	mandarin	mandarine *f*	—	mandarina *f*
Mandel (D)	—	almond	amande *f*	mandorla *f*	almendra *f*
mando¹ (Es)	Befehl *m*	order	ordre *m*	ordine *m*	—
mando² (Es)	Führung *f*	leadership	visite guidée *f*	visita guidata *f*	—
mandorla (I)	Mandel *f*	almond	amande *f*	—	almendra *f*
manège (F)	Karussell *n*	roundabout	—	giostra *f*	tíovivo *m*
manera¹ (Es)	Art *f*	way	manière *f*	modo *m*	—
manera² (Es)	Weise *f*	way	manière *f*	maniera *f*	—
manga (Es)	Ärmel *m*	sleeve	manche *f*	manica *f*	—
mangeable (F)	eßbar	eatable	—	commestibile	comestible
Mangel (D)	—	lack	manque *m*	mancanza *f*	escasez *f*
manger¹ (F)	essen	eat	—	mangiare	comer
manger² (F)	speisen	dine	—	mangiare	comer
mangiare¹ (I)	essen	eat	manger	—	comer
mangiare² (I)	fressen	eat	bouffer	—	devorar
mangiare³ (I)	speisen	dine	manger	—	comer
Manica (I)	Ärmel *m*	sleeve	manche *f*	—	manga *f*
manica (I)	Ärmelkanal *m*	Channel	Manche *f*	—	Canal de la Mancha *m*
maniera (I)	Weise *f*	way	manière *f*	—	manera *f*
manière¹ (F)	Art *f*	way	—	modo *m*	manera *f*
manière² (F)	Weise *f*	way	—	maniera *f*	manera *f*
manifestation¹ (F)	Demonstration *f*	demonstration	—	manifestazione *f*	manifestación *f*
manifestation² (F)	Veranstaltung *f*	event	—	manifestazione *f*	representación *f*
manifestazione¹ (I)	Demonstration *f*	demonstration	manifestation *f*	—	manifestación *f*
manifestazione² (I)	Veranstaltung *f*	event	manifestation *f*	—	representación *f*
manifeste (F)	offensichtlich	obvious	—	evidente	evidente
maniglia (I)	Griff *m*	handle	poignée *f*	—	asidero *m*
Mann (D)	—	man	homme *m*	uomo *m*	hombre *m*
männlich (D)	—	masculine	masculin(e)	maschile	masculino *m*
Mannschaft (D)	—	team	équipe *f*	squadra *f*	equipo *m*
mano (Es)	Hand *f*	hand	main *f*	mano *f*	—
mano (I)	Hand *f*	hand	main *f*	—	mano *f*
mañoso (Es)	geschickt	skilful	habile	abile	—
manque (F)	Mangel *m*	lack	—	mancanza *f*	escasez *f*
manquer¹ (F)	fehlen	miss	—	mancare	faltar
manquer² (F)	versäumen	miss	—	perdere	perder
manquer³ (F)	vermissen	miss	—	sentire la mancanza	echar de menos
manteau (F)	Mantel *m*	coat	—	cappotto *m*	abrigo *m*
Mantel (D)	—	coat	manteau *m*	cappotto *m*	abrigo *m*
mantequilla (Es)	Butter *f*	butter	beurre *m*	burro *m*	—
manufacture (E)	herstellen	—	produire	fabbricare	producir
manufacturer (E)	Hersteller *m*	—	producteur *m*	produttore *m*	productor *m*
many (E)	viele	—	beaucoup de	molti(e)	muchos(as)
manzana (Es)	Apfel *m*	apple	pomme *f*	mela *f*	—
manzo (I)	Rind *n*	cow	bœuf *m*	—	buey *m*
map (E)	Landkarte *f*	—	carte *f*	carta geografica *f*	mapa *m*

	D	E	F	I	Es
mapa (Es)	Landkarte f	map	carte f	carta geografica f	—
Mappe (D)	—	folder	serviette f	raccoglitore m	carpeta f
maquillage (F)	Schminke f	make-up	—	trucco m	maquillaje m
maquillaje (Es)	Schminke f	make-up	maquillage m	trucco m	—
máquina (Es)	Maschine f	machine	machine f	macchina f	—
máquina de afeitar (Es)	Rasierapparat m	shaver	rasoir m	rasoio m	—
máquina de escribir (Es)	Schreibmaschine f	typewriter	machine à écrire f	macchina da scrivere f	—
máquina fotográfica (Es)	Fotoapparat m	camera	appareil-photo m	macchina fotografica f	—
mar (Es)	Meer n	sea	mer f	mare m	—
maravilloso[1] (Es)	herrlich	marvellous	magnifique	stupendo(a)	—
maravilloso[2] (Es)	wunderbar	wonderful	miraculeux(-euse)	meraviglioso(a)	—
marca[1] (Es)	Marke f	brand	marque f	marca f	—
marca[2] (Es)	Mal n	mark	marque f	segno m	—
marca (I)	Marke f	brand	marque f	—	marca f
March (E)	März m	—	mars m	marzo m	marzo m
marcha (Es)	Gang m	gear	vitesse f	marcia f	—
marcha atrás (Es)	rückwärts	backwards	en arrière	in dietro	—
marchandise (F)	Ware f	goods	—	merce f	mercancía f
marchandises (F)	Güter pl	goods	—	beni m pl	bienes f pl
marcharse (Es)	weggehen	go away	s'en aller	andare via	—
marché (F)	Markt m	market	—	mercato m	mercado m
marche (F)	Stufe f	step	—	gradino m	escalón m
marché aux puces (F)	Flohmarkt m	fleamarket	—	mercato delle pulci m	rastro m
marcher (F)	wandern	hike	—	fare escursioni a piedi	hacer excursiones
marcher devant (F)	vorangehen	go ahead	—	andare avanti	pasar adelante
marcia (I)	Gang m	gear	vitesse f	—	marcha f
marciapiede (I)	Gehweg m	pavement	trottoir m	—	acera f
marco[1] (Es)	Mark f	mark	mark m	marco m	—
marco[2] (Es)	Rahmen m	frame	cadre m	cornice f	—
marco (I)	Mark f	mark	mark m	—	marco m
mar del norte (Es)	Nordsee f	North Sea	mer du Nord f	Mare del Nord m	—
mardi (F)	Dienstag m	Tuesday	—	martedì m	martes m
mare (I)	Meer n	sea	mer f	—	mar m
marea alta (Es)	Flut f	high tide	marée haute f	alta marea f	—
marea baja (Es)	Ebbe f	low tide	marée basse f	bassa marea f	—
Mare del Nord (I)	Nordsee f	North Sea	mer du Nord f	—	mar del norte m
marée basse (F)	Ebbe f	low tide	—	bassa marea f	marea baja f
marée haute (F)	Flut f	high tide	—	alta marea f	marea alta f
margine (I)	Rand m	brim	bord m	—	borde m
mari (F)	Ehemann m	husband	—	marito m	marido m
mariage[1] (F)	Ehe f	marriage	—	matrimonio m	matrimonio m
mariage[2] (F)	Hochzeit f	wedding	—	nozze f pl	boda f
mariage[3] (F)	Heirat f	marriage	—	matrimonio m	boda f
marido (Es)	Ehemann m	husband	mari m	marito m	—
marié (F)	verheiratet	married	—	sposato(a)	casado(a)

	D	E	F	I	Es
mariée (F)	Braut *f*	bride	—	sposa *f*	novia *f*
marier, se (F)	heiraten	marry	—	sposarsi	casarse
marinaio (I)	Matrose *m*	sailor	matelot *m*	—	marinero *m*
marinero (Es)	Matrose *m*	sailor	matelot *m*	marinaio *m*	—
mariposa (Es)	Schmetterling *m*	butterfly	papillon *m*	farfalla *f*	—
marito (I)	Ehemann *m*	husband	mari *m*	—	marido *m*
Mark (D)	—	mark	mark *m*	marco *m*	marco *m*
mark¹ (E)	Mark *f*	—	mark *m*	marco *m*	marco *m*
mark² (E)	Mal *n*	—	marque *f*	segno *m*	marca *f*
mark³ (E)	Note *f*	—	note *f*	voto *m*	calificación *f*
mark (F)	Mark *f*	mark	—	marco *m*	marco *m*
Marke (D)	—	brand	marque *f*	marca *f*	marca *f*
market (E)	Markt *m*	—	marché *m*	mercato *m*	mercado *m*
Markt (D)	—	market	marché *m*	mercato *m*	mercado *m*
mar mediterráneo (Es)	Mittelmeer *n*	Mediterranean	Méditerranée *f*	Mediterraneo *m*	—
Marmelade (D)	—	jam	confiture *f*	marmellata *f*	mermelada *f*
marmelade (E)	Orangen-marmelade *f*	—	marmelade d'oranges *f*	marmellata d'arancia *f*	mermelada de naranja *f*
marmellata (I)	Marmelade *f*	jam	confiture *f*	—	mermelada *f*
marque¹ (F)	Mal *n*	mark	—	segno *m*	marca *f*
marque² (F)	Marke *f*	brand	—	marca *f*	marca *f*
marraine (F)	Patin *f*	godmother	—	madrina *f*	madrina *f*
marrant (F)	lustig	funny	—	allegro(a)	divertido(a)
marriage¹ (E)	Ehe *f*	—	mariage *m*	matrimonio *m*	matrimonio *m*
marriage² (E)	Heirat *f*	—	mariage *m*	matrimonio *m*	boda *f*
married (E)	verheiratet	—	marié(e)	sposato(a)	casado(a)
marrón (Es)	braun	brown	marron	marrone	—
marron (F)	braun	brown	—	marrone	marrón
marrone (I)	braun	brown	marron	—	marrón
marry (E)	heiraten	—	marier, se	sposarsi	casarse
mars (F)	März *m*	March	—	marzo *m*	marzo *m*
marteau (F)	Hammer *m*	hammer	—	martello *m*	martillo *m*
martedì (I)	Dienstag *m*	Tuesday	mardi *m*	—	martes *m*
martello (I)	Hammer *m*	hammer	marteau *m*	—	martillo *m*
martes (Es)	Dienstag *m*	Tuesday	mardi *m*	martedì *m*	—
martillo (Es)	Hammer *m*	hammer	marteau *m*	martello *m*	—
marvellous (E)	herrlich	—	magnifique	stupendo(a)	maravilloso(a)
März (D)	—	March	mars *m*	marzo *m*	marzo *m*
marzo (Es)	März *m*	March	mars *m*	marzo *m*	—
marzo (I)	März *m*	March	mars *m*	—	marzo *m*
más¹ (Es)	mehr	more	plus	più	—
más² (Es)	plus	plus	plus	più	—
masa (Es)	Teig *m*	dough	pâte *f*	pasta *f*	—
masaje (Es)	Massage *f*	massage	massage *m*	massaggio *m*	—
más bien (Es)	lieber	rather	mieux	piuttosto	—
máscara (Es)	Maske *f*	mask	masque *m*	maschera *f*	—
maschera (I)	Maske *f*	mask	masque *m*	—	másquera *f*
maschile (I)	männlich	masculine	masculin(e)	—	masculino *m*

	D	E	F	I	Es
Maschine (D)	—	machine	machine *f*	macchina *f*	máquina *f*
masculin (F)	männlich	masculine	—	maschile	masculino *m*
masculine (E)	männlich	—	masculin(e)	maschile	masculino *m*
masculino (Es)	männlich	masculine	masculin(e)	maschile	—
Masern (D)	—	measles	rougeole *f*	morbillo *m*	sarampión *m*
mask (E)	Maske *f*	—	masque *m*	maschera *f*	másquera *f*
Maske (D)	—	mask	masque *m*	maschera *f*	másquera *f*
masque (F)	Maske *f*	mask	—	maschera *f*	másquera *f*
Maß (D)	—	measure	mesure *f*	misura *f*	medida *f*
Massage (D)	—	massage	massage *m*	massaggio *m*	masaje *m*
massage (E)	Massage *f*	—	massage *m*	massaggio *m*	masaje *m*
massage (F)	Massage *f*	massage	—	massaggio *m*	masaje *m*
massaggio (I)	Massage *f*	massage	massage *m*	—	masaje *m*
mäßig (D)	—	moderate	modéré(e)	moderato(a)	moderado(a)
massimo (I)	Maximum *n*	maximum	maximum *m*	—	máximo *m*
más tarde (Es)	später	later	plus tard	piú tardi	—
master (E)	Meister *m*	—	maître *m*	maestro *m*	maestro *m*
masticar (Es)	kauen	chew	mâcher	masticare	—
masticare (I)	kauen	chew	mâcher	—	mastigar
mat (E)	Matte *f*	—	natte *f*	stuoia *f*	colchoneta *f*
matar[1] (Es)	töten	kill	tuer	uccidere	—
matar[2] (Es)	umbringen	kill	tuer	uccidere	—
match (E)	Streichholz *n*	—	allumette *f*	fiammifero *m*	cerilla *f*
matelas (F)	Matratze *f*	mattress	—	materasso *m*	colchón *m*
matelot (F)	Matrose *m*	sailor	—	marinaio *m*	marinero *m*
materasso (I)	Matratze *f*	mattress	matelas *m*	—	colchón *m*
materia (Es)	Fach *n*	subject	matière *f*	materia *f*	—
materia (I)	Fach *n*	subject	matière *f*	—	materia *f*
Material (D)	—	material	matériel *m*	materiale *m*	material *m*
material (E)	Material *n*	—	matériel *m*	materiale *m*	material *m*
material (Es)	Material *n*	material	matériel *m*	materiale *m*	—
materiale (I)	Material *n*	material	matériel *m*	—	material *m*
matériel (F)	Material *n*	material	—	materiale *m*	material *m*
matière (F)	Fach *n*	subject	—	materia *f*	materia *f*
matin (F)	Morgen *m*	morning	—	mattino *m*	mañana *f*
matinée (F)	Vormittag *m*	before noon	—	mattina *f*	mañana *f*
matita (I)	Bleistift *m*	pencil	crayon *m*	—	lápiz *m*
Matratze (D)	—	mattress	matelas *m*	materasso *m*	colchón *m*
matrícula (Es)	Nummernschild *n*	number plate	plaque d'immatriculation *f*	targa *f*	—
matrimonio (Es)	Ehe *f*	marriage	mariage *m*	matrimonio *m*	—
matrimonio[1] (I)	Ehe *f*	marriage	mariage *m*	—	matrimonio *m*
matrimonio[2] (I)	Heirat *f*	marriage	mariage *m*	—	boda *f*
Matrose (D)	—	sailor	matelot *m*	marinaio *m*	marinero *m*
Matte (D)	—	mat	natte *f*	stuoia *f*	colchoneta *f*
mattina (I)	Vormittag *m*	before noon	matinée *f*	—	mañana *f*
mattino (I)	Morgen *m*	morning	matin *m*	—	mañana *f*
mattone (I)	Ziegel *m*	brick	brique *f*	—	ladrillo *m*

	D	E	F	I	Es
mattress (E)	Matratze f	—	matelas m	materasso m	colchón m
maturità (I)	Abitur n	German school leaving examinations	baccalauréat m	—	bachillerato m
maturo (I)	reif	ripe	mûr(e)	—	maduro(a)
Mauer (D)	—	wall	mur m	muro m	muro m
Maul (D)	—	mouth	gueule f	muso m	hocico m
Maus (D)	—	mouse	souris f	topo m	ratón m
mauvais¹ (F)	schlecht	bad	—	cattivo(a)	malo(a)
mauvais² (F)	übel	bad	—	cattivo(a)	malo(a)
mauvais numéro (F)	Niete f	blanc	—	biglietto non vincente m	número sin premio m
mauve (F)	lila	purple	—	lilla	de color lila
máximo (Es)	Maximum n	maximum	maximum m	massimo m	—
Maximum (D)	—	maximum	maximum m	massimo m	máximo m
maximum (E)	Maximum n	—	maximum m	massimo m	máximo m
maximum (F)	Maximum n	maximum	—	massimo m	máximo m
maximum price (E)	Höchstpreis m	—	prix plafond m	prezzo massimo m	precio máximo m
maximum speed (E)	Höchst-geschwindigkeit f	—	vitesse maximum f	velocità massima f	velocidad máxima f
May (E)	Mai m	—	mai m	maggio m	mayo m
maybe (E)	vielleicht	—	peut-être	forse	tal vez
mayo (Es)	Mai m	May	mai m	maggio m	—
mayor (E)	Bürgermeister m	—	maire m	sindaco m	alcalde m
mayor (Es)	ältere(r,s)	elder	aîné(e)	maggiore	—
mayor de edad (Es)	volljährig	of age	majeur(e)	maggiorenne	—
mayoría (Es)	Mehrheit f	majority	majorité f	maggioranza f	—
mazout (F)	Heizöl n	fuel	—	olio combustibile m	combustible para la calefacción m
mazzo (I)	Strauß m	bunch	bouquet m	—	ramo m
meadow (E)	Wiese f	—	pré m	prato m	prado m
meal (E)	Mahlzeit f	—	repas m	pasto m	comida f
mean¹ (E)	bedeuten	—	signifier	significare	significar
mean² (E)	geizig	—	avare	avaro(a)	avaro(a)
mean³ (E)	gemein	—	méchant(e)	volgare	vulgar
meaning (E)	Bedeutung f	—	signification f	significato m	significado m
means (E)	Mittel n	—	moyen m	mezzo m	medio m
meanwhile¹ (E)	inzwischen	—	entretemps	frattanto	mientras tanto
meanwhile² (E)	indessen	—	cependant	nel frattempo	en eso
measles (E)	Masern pl	—	rougeole f	morbillo m	sarampión m
measurable (E)	meßbar	—	mesurable	misurabile	mensurable
measure¹ (E)	messen	—	mesurer	misurare	medir
measure² (E)	Maß n	—	mesure f	misura f	medida f
meat (E)	Fleisch n	—	viande f	carne f	carne f
mécanicien (F)	Mechaniker m	engineer	—	meccanico m	mecánico m
mecánico (Es)	Mechaniker m	engineer	mécanicien m	meccanico m	—
meccanico (I)	Mechaniker m	engineer	mécanicien m	—	mecánico m
Mechaniker (D)	—	engineer	mécanicien m	meccanico m	mecánico m
méchant¹ (F)	böse	wicked	—	cattivo(a)	malo(a)
méchant² (F)	gemein	mean	—	volgare	vulgar

	D	E	F	I	Es
mechero (Es)	Feuerzeug *n*	lighter	briquet *m*	accendino *m*	—
mécontent (F)	unzufrieden	dissatisfied	—	scontento(a)	descontento(a)
médecin (F)	Arzt *m*	doctor	—	medico *m*	médico *m*
médecine (F)	Medizin *f*	medicine	—	medicina *f*	medicina *f*
media (Es)	Strumpf *m*	stocking	bas *m*	calza *f*	—
medianoche (Es)	Mitternacht *f*	midnight	minuit *m*	mezzanotte *f*	—
media pensión (Es)	Halbpension *f*	half board	demi-pension *f*	mezza pensione *f*	—
medicament (E)	Medikament *n*	—	médicament *m*	medicamento *m*	medicamento *m*
médicament[1] (F)	Arznei *f*	medicine	—	medicina *f*	medicina *f*
médicament[2] (F)	Medikament *n*	medicament	—	medicamento *m*	medicamento *m*
medicamento (Es)	Medikament *n*	medicament	médicament *m*	medicamento *m*	—
medicamento (I)	Medikament *n*	medicament	médicament *m*	—	medicamento *m*
medicina[1] (Es)	Arznei *f*	medicine	médicament *m*	medicina *f*	—
medicina[2] (Es)	Medizin *f*	medicine	médecine *f*	medicina *f*	—
medicina[1] (I)	Arznei *f*	medicine	médicament *m*	—	medicina *f*
medicina[2] (I)	Medizin *f*	medicine	médecine *f*	—	medicina *f*
medicine[1] (E)	Arznei *f*	—	médicament *m*	medicina *f*	medicina *f*
medicine[2] (E)	Medizin *f*	—	médecine *f*	medicina *f*	medicina *f*
medico (I)	Arzt *m*	doctor	médecin *m*	—	médico *m*
médico (Es)	Arzt *m*	doctor	médecin *m*	medico *m*	—
médico del oído (Es)	Ohrenarzt *m*	ear specialist	spécialiste de l'oreille *m*	otoiatra *m*	—
medida (Es)	Maß *n*	measure	mesure *f*	misura *f*	—
Medikament (D)	—	medicament	médicament *m*	medicamento *m*	medicamento *m*
medio[1] (Es)	Mitte *f*	middle	milieu *m*	centro *m*	—
medio[2] (Es)	Mittel *n*	means	moyen *m*	mezzo *m*	—
medio[3] (Es)	halb	half	demi(e)	mezzo(a)	—
medio (I)	durchschnittlich	average	moyen(ne)	—	medio(a)
medio ambiente (Es)	Umwelt *f*	environment	environnement *m*	ambiente *m*	—
mediodía[1] (Es)	mittags	midday	à midi	a mezzogiorno	—
mediodía[2] (Es)	Mittag *m*	midday	midi *m*	mezzogiorno *m*	—
medir (Es)	messen	measure	mesurer	misurare	—
Mediterranean (E)	Mittelmeer *n* ˜	—	Méditerranée *f*	Mediterraneo *m*	mar mediterráneo *m*
Méditerranée (F)	Mittelmeer *n*	Mediterranean	—	Mediterraneo *m*	mar mediterráneo *m*
Mediterraneo (I)	Mittelmeer *n*	Mediterranean	Méditerranée *f*	—	mar mediterráneo *m*
Medizin (D)	—	medicine	médecine *f*	medicina *f*	medicina *f*
Meer (D)	—	sea	mer *f*	mare *m*	mar *m*
Meeresspiegel (D)	—	sea level	niveau de la mer *m*	livello del mare *m*	nivel del mar *m*
meet[1] (E)	begegnen	—	rencontrer	incontrare	encontrar
meet[2] (E)	treffen	—	rencontrer	incontrare	encontrar
meeting[1] (E)	Sitzung *f*	—	séance *f*	seduta *f*	reunión *f*
meeting[2] (E)	Treffen *n*	—	rencontre *f*	incontro *m*	encuentro *m*
méfait (F)	Untat *f*	crime	—	misfatto *m*	crimen *m*
méfiance (F)	Mißtrauen *n*	distrust	—	sfiducia *f*	desconfianza *f*
méfier, se (F)	mißtrauen	mistrust	—	non fidarsi	desconfiar
meglio (I)	besser	better	meilleur(e)	—	mejor

	D	E	F	I	Es
Mehl (D)	—	flour	farine f	farina f	harina f
mehr (D)	—	more	plus	più	más
mehrere (D)	—	several	plusieurs	parecchi	muchos(as)
Mehrheit (D)	—	majority	majorité f	maggioranza f	mayoría f
Mehrwertsteuer (D)	—	value added tax	taxe sur la valeur ajoutée f	imposta sul'valore aggiunto f	impuesto sobre el valor añadido m
Mehrzahl (D)	—	plural	pluriel m	plurale m	plural m
meiden (D)	—	avoid	éviter	evitare	evitar
Meile (D)	—	mile	mille m	miglio m	milla f
meilleur[1] (F)	beste(r,s)	best	—	migliore	óptimo(a)
meilleur[2] (F)	besser	better	—	meglio	mejor
meine (D)	—	my/mine	le(la) mien(ne)	mio(a)	mío(a)
meinen (D)	—	think	penser	credere	opinar
Meinung (D)	—	opinion	opinion f	opinione f	opinión f
meist (D)	—	most	la plupart de	nella maggior parte di	la mayor parte de
meistens (D)	—	generally	généralement	di solito	por lo común
Meister (D)	—	master	maître m	maestro m	maestro m
Méjico (Es)	Mexiko	Mexico	Mexique m	Messico m	—
mejilla (Es)	Wange f	cheek	joue f	guancia f	—
mejillón (Es)	Muschel f	mussel	moule f	cozza f	—
mejor (Es)	besser	better	meilleur(e)	meglio	—
mejorar (Es)	verbessern	improve	améliorer	migliorare	—
mela (I)	Apfel m	apple	pomme f	—	manzana f
mélanger (F)	mischen	mix	—	mescolare	mezclar
melden (D)	—	report	annoncer	annunciare	declarar
Meldung (D)	—	report	annonce f	annuncio m	aviso m
melocotón (Es)	Pfirsich m	peach	pêche f	pesca f	—
melodía (Es)	Melodie f	melody	mélodie f	melodia f	—
melodia (I)	Melodie f	melody	mélodie f	—	melodía f
Melodie (D)	—	melody	mélodie f	melodia f	melodía f
mélodie (F)	Melodie f	melody	—	melodia f	melodía f
melody (E)	Melodie f	—	mélodie f	melodia f	melodía f
melon (E)	Melone f	—	melon m	melone m	melón m
melón (Es)	Melone f	melon	melon m	melone m	—
melon (F)	Melone f	melon	—	melone m	melón m
Melone (D)	—	melon	melon m	melone m	melón m
melone (I)	Melone f	melon	melon m	—	melón m
member (E)	Mitglied n	—	membre m	membro m	miembro m
membre (F)	Mitglied n	member	—	membro m	miembro m
membro (I)	Mitglied n	member	membre m	—	miembro m
même (F)	sogar	even	—	perfino	incluso
mémoire (F)	Gedächtnis n	memory	—	memoria f	memoria f
memoria[1] (Es)	Andenken n	souvenir	souvenir m	ricordo m	—
memoria[2] (Es)	Erinnerung f	memory	souvenir m	ricordo m	—
memoria[3] (Es)	Gedächtnis n	memory	mémoire f	memoria f	—
memoria (I)	Gedächtnis n	memory	mémoire f	—	memoria f
memory[1] (E)	Erinnerung f	—	souvenir m	ricordo m	recuerdo m
memory[2] (E)	Gedächtnis n	—	mémoire f	memoria f	memoria f

	D	E	F	I	Es
menacer¹ (F)	androhen	threaten s.b.	—	minacciare	amenazar
menacer² (F)	bedrohen	threaten	—	minacciare	amenazar
menacer³ (F)	drohen	threaten	—	minacciare	amenazar (a alguien)
ménage (F)	Haushalt *m*	household	—	casa *f*	casa *f*
mencionar (Es)	erwähnen	mention	mentionner	menzionare	—
mener (F)	treiben	drive	—	spingere	estimular
Menge (D)	—	quantity	quantité *f*	quantità *f*	cantidad *f*
meno (I)	minus	minus	moins	—	menos
menos¹ (Es)	minus	minus	moins	meno	—
menos² (Es)	weniger	less	moins	di meno	—
mensaje (Es)	Botschaft *f*	message	message *m*	messaggio *m*	—
mensajero (Es)	Eilbote *m*	courier	courrier *m*	corriere *m*	—
Mensch (D)	—	human being	homme *m*	essere umano *m*	persona *f*
Menschen-menge (D)	—	crowd	foule *f*	folla *f*	muchedumbre *f*
menschlich (D)	—	human	humain(e)	umano(a)	humano(a)
mensile (I)	monatlich	monthly	mensuel(le)	—	mensual
mensual (Es)	monatlich	monthly	mensuel(le)	mensile	—
mensuel (F)	monatlich	monthly	—	mensile	mensual
mensurable (Es)	meßbar	measurable	mesurable	misurabile	—
mention (E)	erwähnen	—	mentionner	menzionare	mencionar
mentionner (F)	erwähnen	mention	—	menzionare	mencionar
mentir (Es)	lügen	lie	mentir	mentire	—
mentir (F)	lügen	lie	—	mentire	mentir
mentire (I)	lügen	lie	mentir	—	mentir
mento (I)	Kinn *n*	chin	menton *m*	—	barbilla *f*
menton (F)	Kinn *n*	chin	—	mento *m*	barbilla *f*
menu (E)	Speisekarte *f*	—	menu *m*	menu *m*	lista de platos *f*
menu (F)	Speisekarte *f*	menu	—	menu *m*	lista de platos *f*
menu (I)	Speisekarte *f*	menu	menu *m*	—	lista de platos *f*
menuisier (F)	Tischler *m*	carpenter	—	falegname *m*	carpintero *m*
menzionare (I)	erwähnen	mention	mentionner	—	mencionar
mer (F)	Meer *n*	sea	—	mare *m*	mar *m*
meraviglioso¹ (I)	prächtig	splendid	magnifique	—	magnífico(a)
meraviglioso² (I)	wunderbar	wonderful	miraculeux (-euse)	—	maravilloso(a)
mercado (Es)	Markt *m*	market	marché *m*	mercato *m*	—
mercancía (Es)	Ware *f*	goods	marchandise *f*	merce *f*	—
mercato (I)	Markt *m*	market	marché *m*	—	mercado *m*
mercato delle pulci (I)	Flohmarkt *m*	fleamarket	marché aux puces *m*	—	rastro *m*
merce (I)	Ware *f*	goods	marchandise *f*	—	mercancía *f*
merci (F)	danke	thank you	—	grazie	¡gracias!
mercoledì (I)	Mittwoch *m*	Wednesday	mercredi *m*	—	miércoles *m*
mercredi (F)	Mittwoch *m*	Wednesday	—	mercoledì *m*	miércoles *m*
mercure (F)	Quecksilber *n*	mercury	—	mercurio *m*	mercurio *m*
mercurio (Es)	Quecksilber *n*	mercury	mercure *m*	mercurio *m*	—
mercurio (I)	Quecksilber *n*	mercury	mercure *m*	—	mercurio *m*
mercury (E)	Quecksilber *n*	—	mercure *m*	mercurio *m*	mercurio *m*

	D	E	F	I	Es
mer du Nord (F)	Nordsee f	North Sea	—	mare del Nord m	mar del norte m
mère (F)	Mutter f	mother	—	madre f	madre f
merit (E)	Verdienst n	—	mérite m	merito m	mérito m
mérite (F)	Verdienst n	merit	—	merit m	mérito m
mérito (Es)	Verdienst n	merit	mérite m	merito m	—
merito (I)	Verdienst n	merit	mérite m	—	mérito m
merken (D)	—	notice	remarquer	accorgersi di	notar
Merkmal (D)	—	characteristic	signe m	caratteristica f	rasgo m
merkwürdig (D)	—	strange	curieux(-euse)	curioso(a)	curioso(a)
mermelada (Es)	Marmelade f	jam	confiture f	marmellata f	—
mero (Es)	pur	pure	pur(e)	puro(a)	—
mes (Es)	Monat m	month	mois m	mese m	—
mesa (Es)	Tisch m	table	table f	tavolo m	—
mescolare (I)	mischen	mix	mélanger	—	mezclar
mese (I)	Monat m	month	mois m	—	mes m
mess (E)	Unordnung f	—	désordre m	disordine m	desorden m
messa (I)	Gottesdienst m	service	office divin m	—	servicio religioso m
message[1] (E)	Botschaft f	—	message m	messaggio m	mensaje m
message[2] (E)	Mitteilung f	—	information f	comunicazione f	comunicación f
message[3] (E)	Nachricht f	—	nouvelle f	notizia f	noticia f
message (F)	Botschaft f	message	—	messaggio m	mensaje m
messaggio (I)	Botschaft f	message	message m	—	mensaje m
meßbar (D)	—	measurable	mesurable	misurabile	mesurable
Messe (D)	—	fair	foire f	fiera f	feria f
messen (D)	—	measure	mesurer	misurare	medir
Messer (D)	—	knife	couteau m	coltello m	cuchillo m
Messico (I)	Mexiko	Mexico	Mexique m	—	Méjico m
mestizo (Es)	Mischling m	halfcaste	métis m	sangue misto m	—
mesurable (F)	meßbar	measurable	—	misurabile	mesurable
mesure (F)	Maß n	measure	—	misura f	medida f
mesurer (F)	messen	measure	—	misurare	medir
meta (I)	Ziel n	goal	but m	—	intención f
metà (I)	Hälfte f	half	moitié f	—	mitad f
metal (E)	Metall n	—	métal m	metallo m	metal m
metal (Es)	Metall n	metal	métal m	metallo m	—
métal (F)	Metall n	metal	—	metallo m	metal m
Metall (D)	—	metal	métal m	metallo m	metal m
metallo (I)	Metall n	metal	métal m	—	metal m
Meter (D)	—	metre	mètre m	metro m	metro m
method (E)	Methode f	—	méthode f	metodo m	método m
Methode (D)	—	method	méthode f	metodo m	método m
méthode (F)	Methode f	method	—	metodo m	método m
métier (F)	Handwerk n	craft	—	artigianato m	artesanía f
métis (F)	Mischling m	halfcaste	—	sangue misto m	mestizo m
método (Es)	Methode f	method	méthode f	metodo m	—
metodo (I)	Methode f	method	méthode f	—	método m
metre (E)	Meter m	—	mètre m	metro m	metro m
mètre (F)	Meter m	metre	—	metro m	metro m

	D	E	F	I	Es
mètre carré (F)	Quadratmeter n	square metre	—	metro quadrato m	metro cuadrado m
mètre cube (F)	Kubikmeter m	cubic metre	—	metro cubo m	metro cúbico m
metro¹ (Es)	Meter m	metre	mètre m	metro m	—
metro² (Es)	U-Bahn f	underground	métro m	metropolitana f	—
métro (F)	U-Bahn f	underground	—	metropolitana f	metro m
metro (I)	Meter m	metre	mètre m	—	metro m
metro cuadrado (Es)	Quadratmeter m	square metre	mètre carré m	metro quadrato m	—
metro cúbico (Es)	Kubikmeter m	cubic metre	mètre cube m	metro cubo m	—
metro cubo (I)	Kubikmeter m	cubic metre	mètre cube m	—	metro cúbico m
metropolitana (I)	U-Bahn f	underground	métro m	—	metro m
metro quadrato (I)	Quadratmeter m	square metre	mètre carré m	—	metro cuadrado m
mettere¹ (I)	legen	lay	mettre	—	colocar
mettere² (I)	stellen	place	mettre	—	colocar
mettere³ (I)	setzen	put	mettre	—	poner
mettere in conto (I)	anrechnen	charge	compter	—	poner en cuenta
mettere in libertà (I)	freilassen	release	libérer	—	poner en libertad
mettere in ordine (I)	aufräumen	clear away	ranger	—	arreglar
mettere in scena (I)	inszenieren	stage	mettre en scène	—	escenificar
mettre¹ (F)	anziehen	dress	—	indossare	ponerse
mettre² (F)	legen	lay	—	mettere	colocar
mettre³ (F)	setzen	put	—	mettere	poner
mettre⁴ (F)	stellen	place	—	mettere	colocar
mettre au monde (F)	gebären	give birth to	—	partorire	parir
mettre d'accord, se (F)	einigen, sich	agree	—	accordarsi	ponerse de acuerdo
mettre en marche (F)	anstellen	turn on	—	accendere	poner
mettre en scène (F)	inszenieren	stage	—	mettere in scena	escenificar
mettre le pied sur (F)	treten	step	—	pestare	pisar
Metzger (D)	—	butcher	boucher m	macellaio m	carnicero m
Metzgerei (D)	—	butcher's	boucherie f	macelleria f	carnicería f
meuble (F)	Möbel n	furniture	—	mobile m	mueble m
meublé (F)	möbliert	furnished	—	ammobiliato(a)	amueblado(a)
meubler (F)	möblieren	furnish	—	ammobiliare	amueblar
meurtre (F)	Mord m	murder	—	assassinio m	asesinato m
Mexico (E)	Mexiko	—	Mexique m	Messico m	Méjico m
Mexiko (D)	—	Mexico	Mexique m	Messico m	Méjico m
Mexique (F)	Mexiko	Mexico	—	Messico m	Méjico m
mezclar (Es)	mischen	mix	mélanger	mescolare	—
mezzanotte (I)	Mitternacht f	midnight	minuit m	—	medianoche f
mezza pensione (I)	Halbpension f	half board	demi-pension f	—	media pensión f
mezzo¹ (I)	halb	half	demi(e)	—	medio(a)
mezzo² (I)	Mittel n	means	moyen m	—	medio m
mezzo chilo (I)	Pfund n	pound	livre f	—	libra f
mezzogiorno (I)	Mittag m	midday	midi m	—	mediodía m
mío (Es)	meine(r,s)	mine	le(la) mien(ne)	mio(a)	—
midday (E)	Mittag m	—	midi m	mezzogiorno m	mediodía m
middle (E)	Mitte f	—	milieu m	centro m	medio m

	D	E	F	I	Es
midi (F)	Mittag *m*	midday	—	mezzogiorno *m*	mediodía *m*
midnight (E)	Mitternacht *f*	—	minuit *m*	mezzanotte *f*	medianoche *f*
miedo (Es)	Angst *f*	fear	peur *f*	paura *f*	—
miedoso (Es)	ängstlich	fearful	peureux(-euse)	pauroso(a)	—
miel (Es)	Honig *m*	honey	miel *m*	miele *m*	—
miel (F)	Honig *m*	honey	—	miele *m*	miel *f*
miele (I)	Honig *m*	honey	miel *m*	—	miel *f*
miembro (Es)	Mitglied *n*	member	membre *m*	membro *m*	—
Miene (D)	—	expression	mine *f*	aspetto *m*	expresión *f*
mientras tanto (Es)	inzwischen	meanwhile	entretemps	frattanto	—
miércoles (Es)	Mittwoch *m*	Wednesday	mercredi *m*	mercoledì *m*	—
Miete (D)	—	rent	loyer *m*	affitto *m*	alquiler *m*
mieten (D)	—	rent	louer	affittare	alquilar
Mieter (D)	—	tenant	locataire *m*	inquilino *m*	inquilino *m*
mieux (F)	lieber	rather	—	piuttosto	más bien
miglio (I)	Meile *f*	mile	mille *m*	—	milla *f*
miglioramento (I)	Besserung *f*	improvement	amélioration *f*	—	restablecimiento *m*
migliorare (I)	verbessern	improve	améliorer	—	mejorar
migliore (I)	beste(r,s)	best	meilleur(e)	—	óptimo(a)
mignon (F)	niedlich	sweet	—	carino(a)	gracioso(a)
migraine (E)	Migräne *f*	—	migraine *f*	emicrania *f*	jaqueca *f*
migraine (F)	Migräne *f*	migraine	—	emicrania *f*	jaqueca *f*
Migräne (D)	—	migraine	migraine *f*	emicrania *f*	jaqueca *f*
mil (Es)	tausend	thousand	mille	mille	—
milagro (Es)	Wunder *n*	miracle	miracle *m*	miracolo *m*	—
Milch (D)	—	milk	lait *m*	latte *m*	leche *f*
mild (D)	—	mild	doux(douce)	mite	agradable
mild (E)	mild	—	doux(douce)	mite	agradable
mile (E)	Meile *f*	—	mille *m*	miglio *m*	milla *f*
miliardo (I)	Milliarde *f*	billion	milliard *m*	—	mil millones *m*
milieu (F)	Mitte *f*	middle	—	centro *m*	medio *m*
milione (I)	Million *f*	million	million *m*	—	millón *m*
militaires (F)	Militär *n*	military	—	militari *m pl*	militar *m*
Militär (D)	—	military	militaires *m pl*	militari *m pl*	militar *m*
militar (Es)	Militär *n*	military	militaires *m pl*	militari *m pl*	—
militari (I)	Militär *n*	military	militaires *m pl*	—	militar *m*
military (E)	Militär *n*	—	militaires *m pl*	militari *m pl*	militar *m*
milk (E)	Milch *f*	—	lait *m*	latte *m*	leche *f*
milla (Es)	Meile *f*	mile	mille *m*	miglio *m*	—
mille[1] (F)	Meile *f*	mile	—	miglio *m*	milla *f*
mille[2] (F)	tausend	thousand	—	mille	mil
mille (I)	tausend	thousand	mille	—	mil
milliard (F)	Milliarde *f*	billion	—	miliardo *m*	mil millones *m*
Milliarde (D)	—	billion	milliard *m*	miliardo *m*	mil millones *m*
Million (D)	—	million	million *m*	milione *m*	millón *m*
million (E)	Million *f*	—	million *m*	milione *m*	millón *m*
million (F)	Million *f*	million	—	milione *m*	millón *m*
millón (Es)	Million *f*	million	million *m*	milione *m*	—

	D	E	F	I	Es
mil millones (Es)	Milliarde *f*	billion	milliard *m*	miliardo *m*	—
mimar (Es)	verwöhnen	spoil	gâter	viziare	—
minacciare[1] (I)	androhen	threaten s.b.	menacer	—	amenazar
minacciare[2] (I)	drohen	threaten	menacer	—	amenazar (a alguien)
minacciare[3] (I)	bedrohen	threaten	menacer	—	amenazar
mince[1] (F)	dünn	thin	—	magro(a)	delgado(a)
mince[2] (F)	schlank	slim	—	snello(a)	delgado(a)
minced meat (E)	Hackfleisch *n*	—	viande hachée *f*	carne tritata *f*	carne picada *f*
Minderheit (D)	—	minority	minorité *f*	minoranza *f*	minoría *f*
mindestens (D)	—	at least	au moins	almeno	por lo menos
mine (E)	meine(r,s)	—	le(la) mien(ne)	mio(a)	mío(a)
mine (F)	Miene *f*	expression	—	aspetto *m*	expresión *f*
Mineralwasser (D)	—	mineral water	eau minérale *f*	acqua minerale *f*	agua mineral *f*
mineral water (E)	Mineralwasser *n*	—	eau minérale *f*	acqua minerale *f*	agua mineral *f*
minime (F)	gering	slight	—	poco(a)	pequeño(a)
mínimo (Es)	Minimum *n*	minimum	minimum *m*	minimo *m*	—
minimo (I)	Minimum *n*	minimum	minimum *m*	—	mínimo *m*
Minimum (D)	—	minimum	minimum *m*	minimo *m*	mínimo *m*
minimum (E)	Minimum *n*	—	minimum *m*	minimo *m*	mínimo *m*
minimum (F)	Minimum *n*	minimum	—	minimo *m*	mínimo *m*
Minister (D)	—	minister	ministre *m*	ministro *m*	ministro *m*
minister (E)	Minister *m*	—	ministre *m*	ministro *m*	ministro *m*
ministre (F)	Minister *m*	minister	—	ministro *m*	ministro *m*
ministro (Es)	Minister *m*	minister	ministre *m*	ministro *m*	—
ministro (I)	Minister *m*	minister	ministre *m*	—	ministro *m*
minoranza[1] (I)	Minorität *f*	minority	minorité *f*	—	minoría *f*
minoranza[2] (I)	Minderheit *f*	minority	minorité *f*	—	minoría *f*
minoría[1] (Es)	Minorität *f*	minority	minorité *f*	minoranza *f*	—
minoría[2] (Es)	Minderheit *f*	minority	minorité *f*	minoranza *f*	—
Minorität (D)	—	minority	minorité *f*	minoranza *f*	minoría *f*
minorité[1] (F)	Minorität *f*	minority	—	minoranza *f*	minoría *f*
minorité[2] (F)	Minderheit *f*	minority	—	minoranza *f*	minoría *f*
minority[1] (E)	Minorität *f*	—	minorité *f*	minoranza *f*	minoría *f*
minority[2] (E)	Minderheit *f*	—	minorité *f*	minoranza *f*	minoría *f*
minuit (F)	Mitternacht *f*	midnight	—	mezzanotte *f*	medianoche *f*
minus (D)	—	minus	moins	meno	menos
minus (E)	minus	—	moins	meno	menos
Minute (D)	—	minute	minute *f*	minuto *m*	minuto *m*
minute (E)	Minute *f*	—	minute *f*	minuto *m*	minuto *m*
minute (F)	Minute *f*	minute	—	minuto *m*	minuto *m*
minuto (Es)	Minute *f*	minute	minute *f*	minuto *m*	—
minuto (I)	Minute *f*	minute	minute *f*	—	minuto *m*
mio (I)	meine(r,s)	mine	le(la) mien(ne)	—	mía(o)
miracle (E)	Wunder *n*	—	miracle *m*	miracolo *m*	milagro *m*
miracle (F)	Wunder *n*	miracle	—	miracolo *m*	milagro *m*
miracolo (I)	Wunder *n*	miracle	miracle *m*	—	milagro *m*
miraculeux (F)	wunderbar	wonderful	—	meraviglioso(a)	maravilloso(a)

	D	E	F	I	Es
mirar¹ (Es)	ansehen	look at	regarder	guardare	—
mirar² (Es)	anschauen	look at	regarder	guardare	—
mirar³ (Es)	blicken	look	regarder	guardare	—
mirar⁴ (Es)	schauen	look	regarder	guardare	—
mirar⁵ (Es)	zusehen	watch	regarder	stare a guardare	—
mirar⁶ (Es)	zuschauen	watch	regarder	stare a guardare	—
miroir (F)	Spiegel *m*	mirror	—	specchio *m*	espejo *m*
mirror (E)	Spiegel *m*	—	miroir *m*	specchio *m*	espejo *m*
mischen (D)	—	mix	mélanger	mescolare	mezclar
Mischling (D)	—	halfcaste	métis *m*	sangue misto *m*	mestizo *m*
misère (F)	Elend *n*	misery	—	miseria *f*	miseria *f*
miseria (Es)	Elend *n*	misery	misère *f*	miseria *f*	—
miseria¹ (I)	Elend *n*	misery	misère *f*	—	miseria *f*
miseria² (I)	Not *f*	trouble	détresse *f*	—	necesidad *f*
misero (I)	dürftig	needy	nécessiteux	—	escaso(a)
misery (E)	Elend *n*	—	misère *f*	miseria *f*	miseria *f*
misfatto (I)	Untat *f*	crime	méfait *m*	—	crimen *m*
misfortune (E)	Unglück *n*	—	malheur *m*	disgrazia *f*	desgracia *f*
mislay (E)	verlegen	—	égarer	perdere	extraviar
miss¹ (E)	fehlen	—	manquer	mancare	faltar
miss² (E)	versäumen	—	manquer	perdere	perder
miss³ (E)	vermissen	—	manquer	sentire la mancanza	echar de menos
Miss (E)	Fräulein *n*	—	mademoiselle *f*	signorina *f*	señorita *f*
mißbilligen (D)	—	disapprove	désapprouver	disapprovare	desaprobar
Mißbrauch (D)	—	abuse	abus *m*	abuso *m*	abuso *m*
mißbrauchen (D)	—	abuse	abuser de	abusare	abusar
Mißerfolg (D)	—	failure	échec *m*	insuccesso *m*	fracaso *m*
mißtrauen (D)	—	mistrust	méfier, se	non fidarsi	desconfiar
Mißtrauen (D)	—	distrust	méfiance *f*	sfiducia *f*	desconfianza *f*
Mißverständnis (D)	—	misunderstanding	malentendu *m*	equivoco *m*	malentendido *m*
mistake¹ (E)	Fehler *m*	—	faute *f*	shaglio *m*	falta *f*
mistake² (E)	Irrtum *m*	—	erreur *f*	errore *m*	error *m*
mistrust (E)	mißtrauen	—	méfier, se	non fidarsi	desconfiar
misunder-standing (E)	Mißverständnis *n*	—	malentendu *m*	equivoco *m*	malentendido *m*
misura (I)	Maß *n*	measure	mesure *f*	—	medida *f*
misurabile (I)	meßbar	measurable	mesurable	—	mensurable
misurare (I)	messen	measure	mesurer	—	medir
mit (D)	—	with	avec	con	con
mitad (Es)	Hälfte *f*	half	moitié *f*	metà *f*	—
mitbringen (D)	—	bring (along)	apporter	portare con sè	traer
mite (I)	mild	mild	doux(douce)	—	agradable
miteinander (D)	—	together	ensemble	insieme	juntos
mitgehen (D)	—	go along with	accompagner	accompagnare	acompañar
Mitglied (D)	—	member	membre *m*	membro *m*	miembro *m*
Mitleid (D)	—	pity	compassion *f*	compassione *f*	compasión *f*
mitnehmen (D)	—	take along	emmener	prendere con sè	llevar consigo
Mittag (D)	—	at midday	midi *m*	mezzogiorno *m*	a mediodía *m*

	D	E	F	I	Es
Mittagessen (D)	—	lunch	déjeuner *m*	pranzo *m*	comida *f*
mittags (D)	—	at midday	à midi	a mezzogiorno	a mediodía
Mitte (D)	—	middle	milieu *m*	centro *m*	medio *m*
mitteilen (D)	—	inform s.o.	informer qn de qch	comunicare	comunicar
Mitteilung (D)	—	message	information *f*	comunicazione *f*	comunicación *f*
Mittel (D)	—	means	moyen *m*	mezzo *m*	medio *m*
Mittelmeer (D)	—	Mediterranean	Méditerranée *f*	Mediterraneo *m*	mar mediterráneo *m*
mitten (D)	—	in the middle	au milieu	in mezzo	en medio
mittente (I)	Absender *m*	sender	expéditeur *m*	—	remitente *m*
Mitternacht (D)	—	midnight	minuit *m*	mezzanotte *f*	medianoche *f*
Mittwoch (D)	—	Wednesday	mercredi *m*	mercoledì *m*	miércoles *m*
mix (E)	mischen	—	mélanger	mescolare	mezclar
Möbel (D)	—	furniture	meuble *m*	mobile *m*	mueble *m*
mobile (I)	Möbel *n*	furniture	meuble *m*	—	mueble *m*
mobiliario (Es)	Einrichtung *f*	furnishing	ameublement *m*	arredamento *m*	—
möblieren (D)	—	furnish	meubler	ammobiliare	amueblar
möbliert (D)	—	furnished	meublé(e)	ammobiliato(a)	amueblado(a)
mochila (Es)	Rucksack *m*	rucksack	sac à dos *m*	zaino *m*	—
moda (Es)	Mode *f*	fashion	mode *f*	moda *f*	—
moda (I)	Mode *f*	fashion	mode *f*	—	moda *f*
Mode (D)	—	fashion	mode *f*	moda *f*	moda *f*
mode (F)	Mode *f*	fashion	—	moda *f*	moda *f*
model (E)	Modell *n*	—	modèle *m*	modello *m*	modelo *m*
modèle¹ (F)	Muster *n*	sample	—	campione *m*	modelo *m*
modèle² (F)	Modell *n*	model	—	modello *m*	modelo *m*
modèle³ (F)	Vorbild *n*	ideal	—	modello *m*	modelo *m*
Modell (D)	—	model	modèle *m*	modello *m*	modelo *m*
modello¹ (I)	Modell *n*	model	modèle *m*	—	modelo *m*
modello² (I)	Vorbild *n*	ideal	modèle *m*	—	modelo *m*
modelo¹ (Es)	Muster *n*	sample	modèle *m*	campione *m*	—
modelo² (Es)	Modell *n*	model	modèle *m*	modello *m*	—
modelo³ (Es)	Vorbild *n*	ideal	modèle *m*	modello *m*	—
moderado¹ (Es)	bescheiden	modest	modeste	modesto(a)	—
moderado² (Es)	mäßig	moderate	modéré(e)	moderato(a)	—
moderate (E)	mäßig	—	modéré(e)	moderato(a)	moderado(a)
moderato (I)	mäßig	moderate	modéré(e)	—	moderado(a)
modéré (F)	mäßig	moderate	—	moderato(a)	moderado(a)
modern (D)	—	modern	moderne	moderno(a)	moderno(a)
modern (E)	modern	—	moderne	moderno(a)	moderno(a)
moderne (F)	modern	modern	—	moderno(a)	moderno(a)
moderno (I)	modern	modern	moderne	—	moderno(a)
moderno (Es)	modern	modern	moderne	moderno(a)	—
modest (E)	bescheiden	—	modeste	modesto(a)	moderado(a)
modeste (F)	bescheiden	modest	—	modesto(a)	moderado(a)
modesto (I)	bescheiden	modest	modeste	—	moderado(a)
modo (I)	Art *f*	way	manière *f*	—	manera *f*
modulo (I)	Formular *n*	form	formulaire *m*	—	formulario *m*

	D	E	F	I	Es
mögen (D)	—	like	aimer	piacere	querer
möglich (D)	—	possible	possible	possibile	posible
Möglichkeit (D)	—	possibility	possibilité f	possibilità f	posibilidad f
moglie (I)	Ehefrau f	wife	épouse f	—	mujer f
Mohn (D)	—	poppy	coquelicot m	papavero m	amapola f
Möhre (D)	—	carrot	carotte f	carota f	zanahoria f
molne (F)	Mönch m	monk	—	monaco m	monje m
moins[1] (F)	minus	minus	—	meno	menos
moins[2] (F)	weniger	less	—	di meno	menos
mois (F)	Monat m	month	—	mese m	mes m
moisson (F)	Ernte f	harvest	—	raccolto m	cosecha f
moitié (F)	Hälfte f	half	—	metà f	mitad f
molestar[1] (Es)	belästigen	annoy	importuner	importunare	—
molestar[2] (Es)	stören	disturb	déranger	disturbare	—
molestia (Es)	Störung f	interference	trouble m	disturbo m	—
molesto (I)	lästig	troublesome	importun(e)	—	desagradable
mollare (I)	loslassen	let go of	lâcher	—	dejar libre
molti (I)	viele	many/a lot of	beaucoup de	—	muchos(as)
molto[1] (I)	sehr	very	très	—	mucho/muy
molto[2] (I)	viel	a lot of	beaucoup de	—	mucho(a)
molto tempo (I)	lange	long time	longtemps	—	mucho tiempo
Moment (D)	—	moment	moment m	momento m	momento m
moment[1] (E)	Augenblick m	—	instant m	attimo m	momento m
moment[2] (E)	Moment m	—	moment m	momento m	momento m
moment[1] (F)	Moment m	moment	—	momento m	momento m
moment[2] (F)	Weile f	while	—	momento m	rato m
momento[1] (Es)	Augenblick m	moment	instant m	attimo m	—
momento[2] (Es)	Moment m	moment	moment m	momento m	—
momento[1] (I)	Moment m	moment	moment m	—	momento m
momento[2] (I)	Weile f	while	moment m	—	rato m
monaco (I)	Mönch m	monk	moine m	—	monje m
monasterio (Es)	Kloster n	monastery	couvent m	convento m	—
monastery (E)	Kloster n	—	couvent m	convento m	monasterio m
Monat (D)	—	month	mois m	mese m	mes m
monatlich (D)	—	monthly	mensuel(le)	mensile	mensual
Mönch (D)	—	monk	moine m	monaco m	monje m
Mond (D)	—	moon	lune f	luna f	luna f
Monday (E)	Montag m	—	lundi m	lunedì m	lunes m
Mondays (E)	montags	—	le lundi	il lunedì	los lunes
monde (F)	Welt f	world	—	mondo m	mundo m
mondo (I)	Welt f	world	monde m	—	mundo m
moneda[1] (Es)	Münze f	coin	pièce de monnaie f	moneta f	—
moneda[2] (Es)	Währung f	currency	monnaie f	valuta f	—
moneta (I)	Münze f	coin	pièce de monnaie f	—	moneda f
money (E)	Geld n	—	argent m	denaro m	dinero m
monja (Es)	Nonne f	nun	religieuse f	suora f	—
monje (Es)	Mönch m	monk	moine m	monaco m	—

	D	E	F	I	Es
monk (E)	Mönch *m*	—	moine *m*	monaco *m*	monje *m*
monnaie[1] (F)	Kleingeld *n*	small change	—	spiccioli *m pl*	cambio *m*
monnaie[2] (F)	Währung *f*	currency	—	valuta *f*	moneda *f*
mono (Es)	Affe *m*	ape	singe *m*	scimmia *f*	—
monocolore (I)	einfarbig	all one colour	uni(e)	—	de un solo color
monsieur (F)	Herr *m*	gentleman	—	signore *m*	señor *m*
mont (F)	Berg *m*	mountain	—	monte *m*	montaña *f*
Montag (D)	—	Monday	lundi *m*	lunedì *m*	lunes *m*
montagna (I)	Gebirge *n*	mountain chain	montagne *f*	—	montañas *f pl*
montagne (F)	Gebirge *n*	mountain chain	—	montagna *f*	montañas *f pl*
montags (D)	—	Mondays	le lundi	il lunedì	los lunes
montaña (Es)	Berg *m*	mountain	mont *m*	monte *m*	—
montañas (Es)	Gebirge *n*	mountain chain	montagne *f*	montagna *f*	—
montañas elevadas (Es)	Hochgebirge *n*	high mountain-chain	haute montage *f*	alta montagna *f*	—
montant (F)	Betrag *m*	amount	—	somma *f*	importe *m*
monte (I)	Berg *m*	mountain	mont *m*	—	montaña *f*
montée (F)	Aufgang *m*	staircase	—	scala *f*	subida *f*
monter[1] (F)	aufsteigen	ascend	—	salire	subir
monter[2] (F)	einsteigen	get in	—	salire	subir a
monter[3] (F)	hinaufsteigen	climb	—	salire	subir
monter[4] (F)	reiten	ride	—	cavalcare	cabalgar
monter[5] (F)	steigen	go up	—	salire	subir
month (E)	Monat *m*	—	mois *m*	mese *m*	mes *m*
monthly (E)	monatlich	—	mensuel(le)	mensile	mensual
montón (Es)	Haufen *m*	heap	tas *m*	mucchio *m*	—
montre (F)	Uhr *f*	watch	—	orologio *m*	reloj *m*
montrer[1] (F)	vorzeigen	show	—	esibire	presentar
montrer[2] (F)	zeigen	show	—	mostrare	indicar
monument (E)	Denkmal *n*	—	monument *m*	monumento *m*	monumento *m*
monument (F)	Denkmal *n*	monument	—	monumento *m*	monumento *m*
monumento (Es)	Denkmal *n*	monument	monument *m*	monumento *m*	—
monumento (I)	Denkmal *n*	monument	monument *m*	—	monumento *m*
mood (E)	Laune *f*	—	humeur *f*	umore *m*	humor *m*
moon (E)	Mond *m*	—	lune *f*	luna *f*	luna *f*
mora (I)	Brombeere *f*	blackberry	mûre *f*	—	zarzamora *f*
Moral (D)	—	morality	morale *f*	morale *f*	moral *f*
moral (E)	sittlich	—	moral(e)	morale	moral
moral[1] (Es)	Moral *f*	morality	morale *f*	morale *f*	—
moral[2] (Es)	sittlich	moral	moral(e)	morale	—
moral (F)	sittlich	moral	—	morale	moral
morale (F)	Moral *f*	morality	—	morale *f*	moral *f*
morale[1] (I)	Moral *f*	morality	morale *f*	—	moral *f*
morale[2] (I)	sittlich	moral	moral(e)	—	moral
morality (E)	Moral *f*	—	morale *f*	morale *f*	moral *f*
morbido (I)	weich	soft	doux(douce)	—	tierno(a)
morbillo (I)	Masern *pl*	measles	rougeole *f*	—	sarampión *m*
morceau (F)	Stück *n*	piece	—	pezzo *m*	parte *f*

	D	E	F	I	Es
Mord (D)	—	murder	meurtre *m*	assassinio *m*	asesinato *m*
morder (Es)	beißen	bite	mordre	mordere	—
mordere (I)	beißen	bite	mordre	—	morder
mordre (F)	beißen	bite	—	mordere	morder
more (E)	mehr	—	plus	più	más
morgen (D)	—	tomorrow	demain	domani	mañana
Morgen (D)	—	morning	matin *m*	mattino *m*	mañana *f*
morir (Es)	sterben	die	mourir	morire	—
morir de hambre (Es)	verhungern	starve	mourir de faim	morire di fame	—
morire (I)	sterben	die	mourir	—	morir
morire di fame (I)	verhungern	starve	mourir de faim	—	morir de hambre
morire di freddo (I)	erfrieren	freeze to death	mourir de froid	—	morirse de frío
morirse de frío (Es)	erfrieren	freeze to death	mourir de froid	morire di freddo	—
mormorare (I)	rauschen	rush	bruire	—	susurrar
morning (E)	Morgen *m*	—	matin *m*	mattino *m*	mañana *f*
mort[1] (F)	Tod *m*	death	—	morte *f*	muerte *f*
mort[2] (F)	tot	dead	—	morto(a)	muerto(a)
morte (I)	Tod *m*	death	mort *f*	—	muerte *f*
morto (I)	tot	dead	mort(e)	—	muerto(a)
mosca (Es)	Fliege *f*	fly	mouche *f*	mosca *f*	—
mosca (I)	Fliege *f*	fly	mouche *f*	—	mosca *f*
mosquito (E)	Mücke *f*	—	moustique *m*	zanzara *f*	mosquito *m*
mosquito (Es)	Mücke *f*	mosquito	moustique *m*	zanzara *f*	—
most (E)	meist	—	la plupart de	nella maggior parte di	la mayor parte de
mostaza (Es)	Senf *m*	mustard	moutarde *f*	senape *f*	—
mostrador (Es)	Ladentisch *m*	counter	comptoir *m*	banco di vendita *m*	—
mostrare (I)	zeigen	show	montrer	—	indicar
mot (F)	Wort *n*	word	—	parola *f*	palabra *f*
moteur (F)	Motor *m*	motor	—	motore *m*	motor *m*
mother (E)	Mutter *f*	—	mère *f*	madre *f*	madre *f*
mother-in-law (E)	Schwiegermutter *f*	—	belle-mère *f*	suocera *f*	suegra *f*
motionless (E)	bewegungslos	—	immobile	immobile	inmóvil
moto (F)	Motorrad *n*	motorbike	—	motocicletta *f*	motocicleta *f*
motocicleta (Es)	Motorrad *n*	motorbike	moto *f*	motocicletta *f*	—
motocicletta (I)	Motorrad *n*	motorbike	moto *f*	—	motocicleta *f*
Motor (D)	—	motor	moteur *m*	motore *m*	motor *m*
motor (E)	Motor *m*	—	moteur *m*	motore *m*	motor *m*
motor (Es)	Motor *m*	motor	moteur *m*	motore *m*	—
motorbike (E)	Motorrad *n*	—	moto *f*	motocicletta *f*	motocicleta *f*
motore (I)	Motor *m*	motor	moteur *m*	—	motor *m*
Motorrad (D)	—	motorbike	moto *f*	motocicletta *f*	motocicleta *f*
motorway (E)	Autobahn *f*	—	autoroute *f*	autostrada *f*	autopista *f*

	D	E	F	I	Es
mouche (F)	Fliege *f*	fly	—	mosca *f*	mosca *f*
mouchoir (F)	Taschentuch *n*	handkerchief	—	fazzoletto *m*	pañuelo *m*
mouette (F)	Möwe *f*	seagull	—	gabbiano *m*	gaviota *f*
mouillé (F)	naß	wet	—	bagnato(a)	húmedo(a)
moule (F)	Muschel *f*	mussel	—	cozza *f*	mejillón *m*
mountain (E)	Berg *m*	—	mont *m*	monte *m*	montaña *f*
mountain chain (E)	Gebirge *n*	—	montagne *f*	montagna *f*	montañas *f pl*
mountaineer (E)	Bergsteiger *m*	—	alpiniste *m*	alpinista *m*	alpinista *m*
mourir (F)	sterben	die	—	morire	morir
mourir de faim (F)	verhungern	starve	—	morire di fame	morir de hambre
mourir de froid (F)	erfrieren	freeze to death	—	morire di freddo	morirse de frío
mouse (E)	Maus *f*	—	souris *f*	topo *m*	ratón *m*
moustache (E)	Schnurrbart *m*	—	moustache *f*	baffi *m pl*	bigote *m*
moustache (F)	Schnurrbart *m*	moustache	—	baffi *m pl*	bigote *m*
moustique (F)	Mücke *f*	mosquito	—	zanzara *f*	mosquito *m*
moutarde (F)	Senf *m*	mustard	—	senape *f*	mostaza *f*
mouth[1] (E)	Maul *n*	—	gueule *f*	muso *m*	hocico *m*
mouth[2] (E)	Mündung *f*	—	embouchure *f*	sbocco *m*	desembocadura *f*
mouth[3] (E)	Mund *m*	—	bouche *f*	bocca *f*	boca *f*
mouton (F)	Schaf *n*	sheep	—	pecora *f*	oveja *f*
mouvement (F)	Bewegung *f*	movement	—	movimento *m*	movimiento *m*
move[1] (E)	bewegen	—	bouger	muovere	mover
move[2] (E)	rücken	—	déplacer	muovere	mover
move[3] (E)	übersiedeln	—	émigrer	trasferirsi	transladarse
move[4] (E)	umziehen	—	déménager	cambiare casa	cambiar
move[5] (E)	Umzug *m*	—	déménagement *m*	trasloco *m*	mudanza *f*
move in (E)	einziehen	—	emménager	prendere alloggio	instalarse
movement (E)	Bewegung *f*	—	mouvement *m*	movimento *m*	movimiento *m*
move out (E)	ausziehen	—	déménager	sloggiare	mudarse
mover[1] (Es)	bewegen	move	bouger	muovere	—
mover[2] (Es)	rücken	move	déplacer	muovere	—
movimento (I)	Bewegung *f*	movement	mouvement *m*	—	movimiento *m*
movimiento (Es)	Bewegung *f*	movement	mouvement *m*	movimento *m*	—
mow (E)	mähen	—	faucher	falciare	cortar
Möwe (D)	—	seagull	mouette *f*	gabbiano *m*	gaviota *f*
moyen[1] (F)	Mittel *n*	means	—	mezzo *m*	medio *m*
moyen[2] (F)	durchschnittlich	average	—	medio(a)	medio(a)
mozo[1] (Es)	Bursche *m*	fellow	garçon *m*	ragazzo *m*	—
mozo[2] (Es)	Träger *m*	carrier	porteur *m*	facchino *m*	—
mucca (I)	Kuh *f*	cow	vache *f*	—	vaca *f*
mucchio (I)	Haufen *m*	heap	tas *m*	—	montón *m*
muchedumbre (Es)	Menschenmenge *f*	crowd	foule *f*	folla *f*	—
mucho[1] (Es)	sehr	very	très	molto(a)	—
mucho[2] (Es)	viel	a lot of	beaucoup de	molto(a)	—

	D	E	F	I	Es
muchos¹ (Es)	mehrere	several	plusieurs	parecchi	—
muchos² (Es)	viele	many/a lot of	beaucoup de	molti(e)	—
mucho tiempo (Es)	lange	long time	longtemps	molto tempo	—
Mücke (D)	—	mosquito	moustique *m*	zanzara *f*	mosquito *m*
mud (E)	Schlamm *m*	—	boue *f*	fango *m*	barro *m*
mudanza (Es)	Umzug *m*	move	déménagement *m*	trasloco *m*	—
mudarse (Es)	ausziehen	move out	déménager	sloggiare	—
müde (D)	—	tired	fatigué(e)	stanco(a)	cansado(a)
mudo (Es)	stumm	dumb	muet(te)	muto(a)	—
mueble (Es)	Möbel *n*	furniture	meuble *m*	mobile *m*	—
muerte (Es)	Tod *m*	death	mort *f*	morte *f*	—
muerto (Es)	tot	dead	mort(e)	morto(a)	—
muet (F)	stumm	dumb	—	muto(a)	mudo(a)
Mühe (D)	—	effort	peine *f*	fatica *f*	esfuerzo *m*
mujer¹ (Es)	Ehefrau *f*	wife	épouse *f*	moglie *f*	—
mujer² (Es)	Frau *f*	woman	femme *f*	donna *f*	—
mujer de la limpieza (Es)	Putzfrau *f*	charwoman	femme de ménage *f*	donna delle pulizie *f*	—
Mülleimer (D)	—	dustbin	poubelle *f*	secchio dei rifiuti *m*	cubo de la basura *m*
Mund (D)	—	mouth	bouche *f*	bocca *f*	boca *f*
mündlich (D)	—	oral	oral(e)	orale	oral
mundo (Es)	Welt *f*	world	monde *m*	mondo *m*	—
Mündung (D)	—	mouth	embouchure *f*	sbocco *m*	desembocadura *f*
muñeca (Es)	Puppe *f*	doll	poupée *f*	bambola *f*	—
municipio (I)	Rathaus *n*	town hall	mairie *f*	—	ayuntamiento *m*
munter (D)	—	lively	éveillé(e)	vivace	alegre
Münze (D)	—	coin	pièce de monnaie *f*	moneta *f*	moneda *f*
muovere¹ (I)	bewegen	move	bouger	—	mover
muovere² (I)	rücken	move	déplacer	—	mover
mur¹ (F)	Mauer *f*	wall	—	muro *m*	muro *m*
mur² (F)	Wand *f*	wall	—	parete *f*	pared *f*
mûr (F)	reif	ripe	—	maturo(a)	maduro(a)
murder (E)	Mord *m*	—	meurtre *m*	assassinio *m*	asesinato *m*
mûre (F)	Brombeere *f*	blackberry	—	mora *f*	zarzamora *f*
muro (Es)	Mauer *f*	wall	mur *m*	muro *m*	—
muro (I)	Mauer *f*	wall	mur *m*	—	muro *m*
Muschel (D)	—	mussel	moule *f*	cozza *f*	mejillón *m*
muscle (E)	Muskel *m*	—	muscle *m*	muscolo *m*	músculo *m*
muscle (F)	Muskel *m*	muscle	—	muscolo *m*	músculo *m*
muscolo (I)	Muskel *m*	muscle	muscle *m*	—	músculo *m*
músculo (Es)	Muskel *m*	muscle	muscle *m*	muscolo *m*	—
musée (F)	Museum *n*	museum	—	museo *m*	museo *m*
museo (Es)	Museum *n*	museum	musée *m*	museo *m*	—
museo (I)	Museum *n*	museum	musée *m*	—	museo *m*

	D	E	F	I	Es
Museum (D)	—	museum	musée *m*	museo *m*	museo *m*
museum (E)	Museum *n*	—	musée *m*	museo *m*	museo *m*
mushroom (E)	Pilz *m*	—	champignon *m*	fungo *m*	hongo *m*
music (E)	Musik *f*	—	musique *f*	musica *f*	música *f*
música (Es)	Musik *f*	music	musique *f*	musica *f*	—
musica (I)	Musik *f*	music	musique *f*	—	música *f*
Musik (D)	—	music	musique *f*	musica *f*	música *f*
musique (F)	Musik *f*	music	—	musica *f*	música *f*
Muskel (D)	—	muscle	muscle *m*	muscolo *m*	músculo *m*
muso (I)	Maul *n*	mouth	gueule *f*	—	hocico *m*
mussel (E)	Muschel *f*	—	moule *f*	conchiglia *f*	concha *f*
müssen (D)	—	have to	devoir	dovere	deber
mustard (E)	Senf *m*	—	moutarde *f*	senape *f*	mostaza *f*
Muster (D)	—	sample	modèle *m*	campione *m*	modelo *m*
Mut (D)	—	courage	courage *m*	coraggio *m*	coraje *m*
mutande (I)	Unterhose *f*	underpants	slip *m*	—	calzoncillos *m pl*/ bragas *f pl*
mutare (I)	verändern	change	transformer	—	cambiar
muto (I)	stumm	dumb	muet(te)	—	mudo(a)
Mutter (D)	—	mother	mère *f*	madre *f*	madre *f*
Muttersprache (D)	—	native language	langue maternelle *f*	lingua madre *f*	lengua materna *f*
Mütze (D)	—	cap	casquette *f*	berretto *m*	gorra *f*
Nabel (D)	—	navel	nombril *m*	ombelico *m*	ombligo *m*
nach (D)	—	after/to	après/selon	a/in/verso/dopo	a/hacia/después
nachahmen (D)	—	imitate	imiter	imitare	imitar
Nachbar (D)	—	neighbour	voisin *m*	vicino *m*	vecino *m*
nachdem (D)	—	after	après que	dopo	después que
nachdenken (D)	—	think	réfléchir	riflettere	reflexionar
Nachfrage (D)	—	demand	demande *f*	domanda *f*	demanda *f*
nachgeben (D)	—	yield	céder	cedere	ceder
nach Hause (D)	—	home	à la maison	a casa	a casa
nachher (D)	—	afterwards	ensuite	dopo	después
nachlassen (D)	—	slacken	apaiser, se	allentare	aflojar
Nachmittag (D)	—	afternoon	après-midi *m*	pomeriggio *m*	tarde *f*
nachmittags (D)	—	in the afternoon	l'aprés-midi	di pomeriggio	por la tarde
Nachnahme (D)	—	cash on delivery	remboursement *m*	contro assegno *m*	reembolso *m*
Nachname (D)	—	surname	nom de famille *m*	cognome *m*	apellido *m*
nachprüfen (D)	—	check	contrôler	controllare	comprobar
Nachricht (D)	—	message	nouvelle *f*	notizia *f*	noticia *f*
Nachrichten (D)	—	news	informations *f pl*	giornale radio *m*	noticiario *m*
nachsehen (D)	—	check	vérifier	controllare	examinar
nachsenden (D)	—	send on	faire suivre	inoltrare	enviar a la nueva dirección
nächste (D)	—	next	suivant(e)	prossimo(a)	siguiente

	D	E	F	I	Es
Nacht (D)	—	night	nuit f	notte f	noche m
Nachteil (D)	—	disadvantage	désavantage m	svantaggio m	desventaja f
Nachtisch (D)	—	dessert	dessert m	desert m	postre m
Nachtlokal (D)	—	club	boîte de nuit f	night m	local nocturno m
nachts (D)	—	at nighttime	de nuit	di notte	por la noche
Nachtwächter (D)	—	night-watchman	veilleur dc nuit m	guardia notturna f	sereno m
nacido (Es)	geboren	born	né(e)	nato(a)	—
nacimiento (Es)	Geburt f	birth	naissance f	nascita f	—
nacional (Es)	national	national	national(e)	nazionale	—
nacionalidad[1] (Es)	Nationalität f	nationality	nationalité f	nazionalità f	—
nacionalidad[2] (Es)	Staatsan- gehörigkeit f	nationality	nationalité f	cittadinanza f	—
nackt (D)	—	naked	nu(e)	nudo(a)	desnudo(a)
nada (Es)	nichts	nothing	rien	niente	—
nadar (Es)	schwimmen	swim	nager	nuotare	—
Nadel (D)	—	needle	aiguille f	ago m	aguja f
Nadelbaum (D)	—	conifer	conifère m	conifero m	conífera f
nadie (Es)	niemand	nobody	personne	nessuno(a)	—
Nagel[1] (D)	—	nail	clou m	chiodo m	clavo m
Nagel[2] (D)	—	nail	ongle m	unghia f	uña f
nager (F)	schwimmen	swim	—	nuotare	nadar
nahe (D)	—	near	près de	vicino(a)	contiguo(a)
Nähe (D)	—	proximity	environs m pl	vicinanza f	proximidad f
nähen (D)	—	sew	coudre	cucire	coser
nähern, sich (D)	—	approach	approcher, se	avvicinarsi	acercarse
Nahrung (D)	—	food	nourriture f	alimentazione f	nutrición f
nail[1] (E)	Nagel m	—	ongle m	unghia m	uña f
nail[2] (E)	Nagel m	—	clou m	chiodo m	clavo m
naissance (F)	Geburt f	birth	—	nascita f	nacimiento m
naître (F)	entstehen	arise	—	nascere	surgir
naked (E)	nackt	—	nu(e)	nudo(a)	desnudo(a)
Name (D)	—	name	nom m	nome m	nombre m
name (E)	Name m	—	nom m	nome m	nombre m
namely (E)	nämlich	—	à savoir	cioè	a saber
nämlich (D)	—	namely	à savoir	cioè	a saber
nappy (E)	Windel f	—	lange m	pannolino m	pañal m
naranja[1] (Es)	Apfelsine f	orange	orange f	arancia f	—
naranja[2] (Es)	Orange f	orange	orange f	arancia f	—
Narbe (D)	—	scar	cicatrice f	cicatrice f	cicatriz f
nariz (Es)	Nase f	nose	nez m	naso m	—
Narr (D)	—	fool	fou m	pazzo m	loco m
narrow (E)	eng	—	étroit(e)	stretto(a)	estrecho(a)
nascere (I)	entstehen	arise	naître	—	surgir
nascita (I)	Geburt f	birth	naissance f	—	nacimiento m

nascondere

	D	E	F	I	Es
nascondere[1] (I)	verstecken	hide	cacher	—	ocultar
nascondere[2] (I)	verbergen	hide	dissimuler	—	esconder
Nase (D)	—	nose	nez m	naso m	nariz f
naso (I)	Nase f	nose	nez m	—	nariz f
naß (D)	—	wet	mouillé(e)	bagnato(a)	húmedo(a)
nastro (I)	Band n	ribbon	bandeau m	—	cinta f
nastro magnetico (I)	Tonband n	tape	bande magnétique f	—	cinta magnetofónica f
nata (Es)	Sahne f	cream	crème f	panna f	—
Natale (I)	Weihnachten n	Christmas	Noël m	—	Navidad(es) f (pl)
national (D)	—	national	national(e)	nazionale	nacional
national (E)	national	—	national(e)	nazionale	nacional
national (F)	national	national	—	nazionale	nacional
Nationalität (D)	—	nationality	nationalité f	nazionalità f	nacionalidad f
nationalité[1] (F)	Nationalität f	nationality	—	nazionalità f	nacionalidad f
nationalité[2] (F)	Staatsangehörigkeit f	nationality	—	cittadinanza f	nacionalidad f
nationality[1] (E)	Nationalität f	—	nationalité f	nazionalità f	nacionalidad f
nationality[2] (E)	Staatsangehörigkeit f	—	nationalité f	cittadinanza f	nacionalidad f
native (E)	einheimisch	—	indigène	indigeno(a)	nativo(a)
native language (E)	Muttersprache f	—	langue maternelle f	lingua madre f	lengua materna f
nativo (Es)	einheimisch	native	indigène	indigeno(a)	—
nato (I)	geboren	born	né(e)	—	nacido(a)
natte[1] (F)	Matte f	mat	—	stuoia f	colchoneta f
natte[2] (F)	Zopf m	plait	—	treccia f	trenza f
Natur (D)	—	nature	nature f	natura f	naturaleza f
natura (I)	Natur f	nature	nature f	—	naturaleza f
natural (E)	natürlich	—	naturel(le)	naturale	natural
natural (Es)	natürlich	natural	naturel(le)	naturale	—
naturale (I)	natürlich	natural	naturel(le)	—	natural
naturaleza (Es)	Natur f	nature	nature f	natura f	—
naturalmente (I)	selbstverständlich	of course	évidemment	—	por su puesto
nature (E)	Natur f	—	nature f	natura f	naturaleza f
nature (F)	Natur f	nature	—	natura f	naturaleza f
naturel (F)	natürlich	natural	—	naturale	natural
natürlich (D)	—	natural	naturel(le)	naturale	natural
nausea (E)	Übelkeit f	—	nausée f	nausea f	náuseas f pl
nausea (I)	Übelkeit f	nausea	nausée f	—	náuseas f pl
náuseas (Es)	Übelkeit f	nausea	nausée f	nausea f	—
nausée (F)	Übelkeit f	nausea	—	nausea f	náuseas f pl
nave (I)	Schiff n	ship	navire m	—	barco m
navegar a vela (Es)	segeln	sail	faire de la voile	andare a vela	—
navel (E)	Nabel m	—	nombril m	ombelico m	ombligo m
Navidad(es) (Es)	Weihnachten n	Christmas	Noël m	Natale m	—
navire (F)	Schiff n	ship	—	nave f	barco m
nazionale (I)	national	national	national(e)	—	nacional
nazionalità (I)	Nationalität f	nationality	nationalité f	—	nacionalidad f
né (F)	geboren	born	—	nato(a)	nacido(a)

	D	E	F	I	Es
near (E)	nahe	—	près de	vicino(a)	contiguo(a)
nearly[1] (E)	beinahe	—	presque	circa/quasi	casi
nearly[2] (E)	fast	—	presque	quasi	casi
nebbia (I)	Nebel m	fog	brouillard m	—	niebla f
Nebel (D)	—	fog	brouillard m	nebbia f	niebla f
neben (D)	—	beside	près de	accanto a	al lado de
necesario[1] (Es)	erforderlich	necessary	nécessaire	necessario(a)	—
necesario[2] (Es)	notwendig	necessary	nécessaire	necessario(a)	—
necesario[3] (Es)	nötig	necessary	nécessaire	necessario(a)	—
necesidad[1] (Es)	Bedürfnis n	need	besoin m	bisogno m	—
necesidad[2] (Es)	Notwendigkeit f	necessity	nécessité f	necessità f	—
necesidad[3] (Es)	Not f	trouble	détresse f	miseria f	—
necesitar[1] (Es)	benötigen/ brauchen	need	avoir besoin de	aver bisogno di	—
necesitar[2] (Es)	bedürfen	need	nécessiter	aver bisogno di	—
nécessaire[1] (F)	erforderlich	necessary	—	necessario(a)	necesario(a)
nécessaire[2] (F)	notwendig	necessary	—	necessario(a)	necesario(a)
nécessaire[3] (F)	nötig	necessary	—	necessario(a)	necesario(a)
necessario[1] (I)	erforderlich	necessary	nécessaire	—	necesario(a)
necessario[2] (I)	notwendig	necessary	nécessaire	—	necesario(a)
necessario[3] (I)	nötig	necessary	nécessaire	—	necesario(a)
necessary[1] (E)	erforderlich	—	nécessaire	necessario(a)	necesario(a)
necessary[2] (E)	nötig	—	nécessaire	necessario(a)	necesario(a)
necessary[3] (E)	notwendig	—	nécessaire	necessario(a)	necesario(a)
necessità (I)	Notwendigkeit f	necessity	nécessité f	—	necesidad f
nécessité (F)	Notwendigkeit f	necessity	—	necessità f	necesidad f
nécessiter (F)	bedürfen	need	—	aver bisogno di	necesitar
nécessiteux (F)	dürftig	needy	—	misero(a)	escaso(a)
necessity (E)	Notwendigkeit f	—	nécessité f	necessità f	necesidad f
neck (E)	Hals m	—	cou m	collo m	cuello m
need[1] (E)	bedürfen	—	nécessiter	aver bisogno di	necesitar
need[2] (E)	benötigen/ brauchen	—	avoir besoin de	aver bisogno di	necesitar
need[3] (E)	Bedürfnis n	—	besoin m	bisogno m	necesidad f
needle (E)	Nadel f	—	aiguille f	ago m	aguja f
needy (E)	dürftig	—	nécessiteux	misero(a)	escaso(a)
Neffe (D)	—	nephew	neveu m	nipote m	sobrino m
negar[1] (Es)	leugnen	deny	nier	negare	—
negar[2] (Es)	verweigern	refuse	refuser	rifiutare	—
negare (I)	leugnen	deny	nier	—	negar
negativa (Es)	Absage f	refusal	refus m	risposta negativa f	—
neglect (E)	vernachlässigen	—	négliger	trascurare	descuidar
négliger (F)	vernachlässigen	neglect	—	trascurare	descuidar
negozio[1] (I)	Geschäft n	shop	magasin m	—	tienda f
negozio[2] (I)	Laden m	shop	magasin m	—	tienda f
negozio di alimentari (I)	Lebensmittel- geschäft n	grocer's	magasin d'alimentation m	—	tienda de comestibles f
negozio di prodotti dietetici (I)	Reformhaus n	health food shop	magasin diététique m	—	tienda de productos dietéticos f

	D	E	F	I	Es
negozio di scarpe (I)	Schuhgeschäft n	shoeshop	magasin de chaussures m	—	zapatería f
negro (Es)	schwarz	black	noir(e)	nero(a)	—
nehmen (D)	—	take	prendre	prendere	tomar
Neid (D)	—	envy	jalousie f	invidia f	envidia f
neidisch (D)	—	envious	envieux(-euse)	invidioso(a)	envidioso(a)
neige (F)	Schnee m	snow	—	neve f	nieve f
neiger (F)	schneien	snow	—	nevicare	nevar
neighbour (E)	Nachbar m	—	voisin m	vicino m	vecino m
neighbouring (E)	benachbart	—	avoisinant(e)	vicino(a)	vecino(a)
nei giorni feriali[1] (I)	wochentags	during the week	en semaine	—	entre semana
nei giorni feriali[2] (I)	werktags	on working days	les jours ouvrables	—	los días laborables
nein (D)	—	no	non	no	no
neither (E)	weder	—	ni	né…né	ni
ne…jamais (F)	niemals	never	—	mai	jamás
nel frattempo (I)	indessen	meanwhile	cependant	—	en eso
Nelke (D)	—	carnation	œillet m	garofano m	clavel m
nella maggior parte di (I)	meist	most	la plupart de	—	la mayor parte de
nemico (I)	Feind m	enemy	ennemi m	—	enemigo m
né…né (I)	weder	neither	ni	—	ni
nennen (D)	—	call	appeler	chiamare	nombrar
ne…pas (F)	nicht	not	—	non	no
ne personne (F)	niemand	nobody	—	nessuno(a)	nadie
nephew (E)	Neffe m	—	neveu m	nipote m	sobrino m
nero (I)	schwarz	black	noir(e)	—	negro(a)
nerveux (F)	nervös	nervous	—	nervoso(a)	nervioso(a)
nervioso (Es)	nervös	nervous	nerveux(-euse)	nervoso(a)	—
nervös (D)	—	nervous	nerveux(-euse)	nervoso(a)	nervioso(a)
nervoso[1] (I)	hektisch	hectic	fébrile	—	inquieto(a)
nervoso[2] (I)	nervös	nervous	nerveux(-euse)	—	nervioso(a)
nervous (E)	nervös	—	nerveux(-euse)	nervoso(a)	nervioso(a)
nessuno[1] (I)	niemand	nobody	personne	—	nadie
nessuno[2] (I)	keine(r,s)	none	aucun(e)	—	ninguno(a)
Nest (D)	—	nest	nid m	nido m	nido m
nest (E)	Nest n	—	nid m	nido m	nido m
net (E)	Netz n	—	filet m	rete f	red f
Netherlands (E)	Niederlande f	—	Pays-Bas m pl	Paesi Bassi m pl	los Países Bajos m pl
nett (D)	—	nice	joli(e)	carino(a)	agradable
nettoyage (F)	Reinigung f	cleaning	—	pulitura f	limpieza f
nettoyer[1] (F)	putzen	clean	—	pulire	limpiar
nettoyer[2] (F)	reinigen	clean	—	pulire	limpiar
Netz (D)	—	net	filet m	rete f	red f
neu (D)	—	new	nouveau, nouvel, nouvelle	nuovo(a)	nuevo(a)
neuf (F)	neun	nine	—	nove	nueve
neugierig (D)	—	curious	curieux(-euse)	curioso(a)	curioso(a)
Neuheit (D)	—	novelty	nouveauté f	novità f	originalidad f
Neuigkeit (D)	—	news	nouvelle f	novità f	novedad f

	D	E	F	I	Es
Neujahr (D)	—	New Year	nouvel an m	Capodanno m	Año Nuevo m
neulich (D)	—	recently	l'autre jour	recentemente	recientemente
neumático (Es)	Reifen m	tyre	pneu m	pneumatico m	—
neun (D)	—	nine	neuf	nove	nueve
neunzehn (D)	—	nineteen	dix-neuf	diciannove	diecinueve
neunzig (D)	—	ninety	quatre-vingt-dix	novanta	noventa
neutral (D)	—	neutral	neutre	neutro(a)	neutral
neutral (E)	neutral	—	neutre	neutro(a)	neutral
neutral (Es)	neutral	neutral	neutre	neutro(a)	—
neutre (F)	neutral	neutral	—	neutro(a)	neutral
neutro (I)	neutral	neutral	neutre	—	neutral
nevar (Es)	schneien	snow	neiger	nevicare	—
neve (I)	Schnee m	snow	neige f	—	nieve f
never (E)	niemals	—	ne…jamais	mai	jamás
nevera (Es)	Kühlschrank m	fridge	réfrigérateur m	frigorifero m	—
nevertheless[1] (E)	dennoch	—	cependant	tuttavia	sin embargo
nevertheless[2] (E)	trotzdem	—	malgré tout	tuttavia	no obstante
neveu (F)	Neffe m	nephew	—	nipote m	sobrino m
nevicare (I)	schneien	snow	neiger	—	nevar
new (E)	neu	—	nouveau, nouvel, nouvelle	nuovo(a)	nuevo(a)
news[1] (E)	Neuigkeit f	—	nouvelle f	novità f	novedad f
news[2] (E)	Nachrichten pl	—	informations f pl	giornale radio m	noticiario m
newspaper (E)	Zeitung f	—	journal m	giornale m	periódico m
New Year (E)	Neujahr n	—	nouvel an m	Capodanno m	Año Nuevo m
New Year's Eve (E)	Silvester n	—	Saint Sylvestre m	San Silvestro m	Noche Vieja f
next (E)	nächste(r,s)	—	suivant(e)	prossimo(a)	siguiente
nez (F)	Nase f	nose	—	naso m	nariz f
ni (Es)	weder	neither	ni	né…né	—
ni (F)	weder	neither	ni	né…né	ni
nice (E)	nett	—	joli(e)	carino(a)	agradable
nicht (D)	—	not	ne…pas	non	no
Nichte (D)	—	niece	nièce f	nipote f	sobrina f
nichts (D)	—	nothing	rien	niente	nada
nicken (D)	—	nod	faire un signe de tête	annuire	inclinar la cabeza
nid (F)	Nest n	nest	—	nido m	nido m
nido (Es)	Nest n	nest	nid m	nido m	—
nido (I)	Nest n	nest	nid m	—	nido m
niebla (Es)	Nebel m	fog	brouillard m	nebbia f	—
niece (E)	Nichte f	—	nièce f	nipote f	sobrina f
nièce (F)	Nichte f	niece	—	nipote f	sobrina f
nieder (D)	—	inferior	bas(se)	in basso	abajo
Niederlage (D)	—	defeat	défaite f	sconfitta f	derrota f
Niederlande (D)	—	Netherlands	Pays-Bas m pl	Paesi Bassi m pl	los Países Bajos m pl
niederlassen (D)	—	settle down	s'installer	stabilirsi	instalarse
niedlich (D)	—	sweet	mignon(ne)	carino(a)	gracioso(a)
niedrig (D)	—	low	bas(se)	basso(a)	bajo

	D	E	F	I	Es
niemals (D)	—	never	ne...jamais	mai	jamás
niemand (D)	—	nobody	personne	nessuno(a)	nadie
niente (I)	nichts	nothing	rien	—	nada
nier (F)	leugnen	deny	—	negare	negar
Niere (D)	—	kidney	rein *m*	rene *m*	riñón *m*
niesen (D)	—	sneeze	éternuer	starnutire	estornudar
nieta (Es)	Enkelin *f*	granddaughter	petite-fille *f*	nipote *f*	—
Niete (D)	—	blank	mauvais numéro *m*	biglietto non vincente *m*	número sin premio *m*
nieto[1] (Es)	Enkel *m*	grandson	petit-fils *m*	nipote *m*	—
nieto[2] (Es)	Enkelkind *n*	grandchild	petit-enfant *m*	nipote *m/f*	—
nieve (Es)	Schnee *m*	snow	neige *f*	neve *f*	—
night (E)	Nacht *f*	—	nuit *f*	notte *f*	noche *m*
night (I)	Nachtlokal *n*	(night) club	boîte de nuit *f*	—	local nocturno *m*
night club (E)	Nachtlokal *n*	—	boîte de nuit *f*	night *m*	local nocturno *m*
night-watchman (E)	Nachtwächter *m*	—	veilleur de nuit *m*	guardia notturna *f*	sereno *m*
n'importe comment (F)	irgendwie	somehow	—	in qualche modo	de alguna manera
n'importe où (F)	irgendwo	somewhere	—	in qualche posto	en alguna parte
n'importe quel (F)	beliebig	any	—	qualsiasi	a voluntad
n'importe qui (F)	irgend jemand	somebody	—	qualcuno	alguno(a)
n'importe quoi (F)	irgend etwas	something	—	qualsiasi cosa	algo
nine (E)	neun	—	neuf	nove	nueve
nineteen (E)	neunzehn	—	dix-neuf	diciannove	diecinueve
ninety (E)	neunzig	—	quatre-vingt-dix	novanta	noventa
niñez (Es)	Kindheit *f*	childhood	enfance *f*	infanzia *f*	—
ninguno (Es)	keine(r,s)	none	aucun(e)	nessuno(a)	—
niño (Es)	Kind *n*	child	enfant *m*	bambino *m*	—
nipote[1] (I)	Enkelin *f*	granddaughter	petite-fille *f*	—	nieta *f*
nipote[2] (I)	Enkel *m*	grandson	petit-fils *m*	—	nieto *m*
nipote[3] (I)	Nichte *f*	niece	nièce *f*	—	sobrina *f*
nipote[4] (I)	Neffe *m*	nephew	neveu *m*	—	sobrino *m*
nipote[5] (I)	Enkelkind *n*	grandchild	petit-enfant *m*	—	nieto *m*
nirgends (D)	—	nowhere	nulle part	da nessuna parte	en ninguna parte
niveau de la mer (F)	Meeresspiegel *m*	sea level	—	livello del mare *m*	nivel del mar *m*
nivel del mar (Es)	Meeresspiegel *m*	sea level	niveau de la mer *m*	livello del mare *m*	—
no (E)	nein	—	non	no	no
no[1] (Es)	nein	no	non	no	—
no[2] (Es)	nicht	not	ne...pas	non	—
no (I)	nein	no	non	—	no
no autorizado (Es)	unbefugt	unauthorized	non autorisé(e)	non autorizzato(a)	—
nobody (E)	niemand	—	personne	nessuno(a)	nadie
nocciolo (I)	Kern *m*	pip	noyau *m*	—	hueso *m*
noce (I)	Nuß *f*	nut	noix *f*	—	nuez *f*
noch (D)	—	still	encore	ancora	aún/todavía
noche[1] (Es)	Nacht *f*	night	nuit *f*	notte *f*	—
noche[2] (Es)	Abend *m*	evening	soir *m*	sera *f*	—
Nochebuena (Es)	Heiligabend *m*	Christmas Eve	nuit de Noël *f*	vigilia di Natale *f*	—

	D	E	F	I	Es
Noche Vieja (Es)	Silvester *n*	New Year's Eve	Saint Sylvestre *m*	San Silvestro *m*	—
nochmals (D)	—	again	encore une fois	di nuovo	otra vez
nocivo (I)	schädlich	harmful	nuisible	—	nocivo(a)
nocivo (Es)	schädlich	harmful	nuisible	nocivo(a)	—
nod (E)	nicken	—	faire un signe de la tête	annuire	inclinar la cabeza
nodo (I)	Knoten *m*	knot	nœud *m*	—	nudo *m*
Noël (F)	Weihnachten *n*	Christmas	—	Natale *m*	Navidad(es) *f (pl)*
nœud (F)	Knoten *m*	knot	—	nodo *m*	nudo *m*
noi (I)	wir	we	nous	—	nosotros(as)
noioso (I)	langweilig	boring	ennuyeux(-euse)	—	aburrido(a)
noir (F)	schwarz	black	—	nero(a)	negro(a)
noise[1] (E)	Krach *m*	—	bruit *m*	chiasso *m*	ruido *m*
noise[2] (E)	Lärm *m*	—	bruit *m*	rumore *m*	ruido *m*
noix (F)	Nuß *f*	nut	—	noce *f*	nuez *f*
nom (F)	Name *m*	name	—	nome *m*	nombre *m*
nombrar (Es)	nennen	call	appeler	chiamare	—
nombre (Es)	Name *m*	name	nom *m*	nome *m*	—
nombre (F)	Anzahl *f*	number	—	numero *m*	número *m*
nombre de pila (Es)	Vorname *m*	Christian name	prénom *m*	nome di battesimo *m*	—
nombreux (F)	zahlreich	numerous	—	numeroso(a)	numeroso(a)
nombril (F)	Nabel *m*	navel	—	ombelico *m*	ombligo *m*
nom de famille (F)	Nachname *m*	surname	—	cognome *m*	apellido *m*
nome (I)	Name *m*	name	nom *m*	—	nombre *m*
nome di battesimo (I)	Vorname *m*	Christian name	prénom *m*	—	nombre de pila *m*
non (F)	nein	no	—	no	no
non (I)	nicht	not	ne…pas	—	no
non affatto (I)	keineswegs	not at all	pas du tout	—	en modo alguno
non autorisé (F)	unbefugt	unauthorized	—	non autorizzato(a)	no autorizado(a)
non autorizzato (I)	unbefugt	unauthorized	non autorisé(e)	—	no autorizado(a)
none (E)	keine(r,s)	—	aucun(e)	nessuno(a)	ninguno(a)
non fidarsi (I)	mißtrauen	mistrust	méfier, se	—	desconfiar
non impegnativo (I)	unverbindlich	not binding	sans engagement	—	sin compromiso
non importante (I)	unwichtig	unimportant	sans importance	—	sin importancia
non marié (F)	unverheiratet	unmarried	—	celibe *m*/nubile *f*	soltero(a)
nonna (I)	Großmutter *f*	grandmother	grand-mère *f*	—	abuela *f*
Nonne (D)	—	nun	religieuse *f*	suora *f*	monja *f*
nonni (I)	Großeltern *pl*	grandparents	grands-parents *m pl*	—	abuelos *m pl*
nonno (I)	Großvater *m*	grandfather	grand-père *m*	—	abuelo *m*
nonostante (I)	trotz	despite	malgré	—	a pesar de
nonsense (E)	Unsinn *m*	—	bêtises *f pl*	nonsenso *m*	absurdo *m*
nonsensical (E)	unsinnig	—	insensé(e)	insensato(a)	absurdo(a)
nonsenso (I)	Unsinn *m*	nonsense	bêtises *f pl*		absurdo *m*
non valable (F)	ungültig	invalid	—	non valido(a)	caducado(a)
non valido (I)	ungültig	invalid	non valable	—	caducado(a)
non vedere (I)	übersehen	ignore	ignorer	—	no ver
no obstante (Es)	trotzdem	nevertheless	malgré tout	tuttavia	—

	D	E	F	I	Es
noodles (E)	Nudeln *pl*	—	nouilles *f pl*	pasta *f*	pastas *f pl*
no parking (E)	Parkverbot *n*	—	défense de stationner *f*	divieto di parcheggio *m*	estacionamiento prohibido *m*
nord (F)	Norden *m*	north	—	nord *m*	norte *m*
nord (I)	Norden *m*	north	nord *m*	—	norte *m*
Nordamerika (D)	—	North America	Amérique du Nord *f*	America del Nord *f*	América del Norte *f*
Norden (D)	—	north	nord *m*	nord *m*	norte *m*
nördlich (D)	—	northern	du nord	a nord	del norte
Nordsee (D)	—	North Sea	mer du Nord *f*	Mare del Nord *m*	mar del norte *m*
norma (I)	Vorschrift *f*	regulation	règle *f*	—	reglamento *m*
normal (D)	—	normal	normal(e)	normale	normal
normal (E)	normal	—	normal(e)	normale	normal
normal (Es)	normal	normal	normal(e)	normale	—
normal (F)	normal	normal	—	normale	normal
normale (I)	normal	normal	normal(e)	—	normal
normalement (F)	normalerweise	normally	—	normalmente	normalmente
normalerweise (D)	—	normally	normalement	normalmente	normalmente
normally (E)	normalerweise	—	normalement	normalmente	normalmente
normalmente (Es)	normalerweise	normally	normalement	normalmente	—
normalmente (I)	normalerweise	normally	normalement	—	normalmente
norte (Es)	Norden *m*	north	nord *m*	nord *m*	—
north (E)	Norden *m*	—	nord *m*	nord *m*	norte *m*
North America (E)	Nordamerika *n*	—	Amérique du Nord *f*	America del Nord *f*	América del Norte *f*
northern (E)	nördlich	—	du nord	a nord	del norte
North Sea (E)	Nordsee *f*	—	mer du Nord *f*	Mare del Nord *m*	mar del norte *m*
Noruega (Es)	Norwegen *n*	Norway	Norvège *f*	Norvegia *f*	—
Norvège (F)	Norwegen *n*	Norway	—	Norvegia *f*	Noruega *f*
Norvegia (I)	Norwegen *n*	Norway	Norvège *f*	—	Noruega *f*
Norway (E)	Norwegen *n*	—	Norvège *f*	Norvegia *f*	Noruega *f*
Norwegen (D)	—	Norway	Norvège *f*	Norvegia *f*	Noruega *f*
nose (E)	Nase *f*	—	nez *m*	naso *m*	nariz *f*
nosotros (Es)	wir	we	nous	noi	—
nostalgia (Es)	Heimweh *n*	homesickness	mal du pays *m*	nostalgia *f*	—
nostalgia (I)	Heimweh *n*	homesickness	mal du pays *m*	—	nostalgia *f*
Not (D)	—	trouble	détresse *f*	miseria *f*	necesidad *f*
not (E)	nicht	—	ne...pas	non	no
nota (Es)	Note *f*	note	note *f*	nota *f*	—
nota (I)	Note *f*	note	note *f*	—	nota *f*
notable (Es)	beträchtlich	considerable	considérable	considerevole	—
notaio (I)	Notar *m*	notary	notaire *m*	—	notario *m*
notaire (F)	Notar *m*	notary	—	notaio *m*	notario *m*
Notar (D)	—	notary	notaire *m*	notaio *m*	notario *m*
notar (Es)	merken	notice	remarquer	accorgersi di	—
notare (I)	bemerken	notice	remarquer	—	darse cuenta
notario (Es)	Notar *m*	notary	notaire *m*	notaio *m*	—
notary (E)	Notar *m*	—	notaire *m*	notaio *m*	notario *m*
not at all (E)	keineswegs	—	pas du tout	non affatto	en modo alguno

	D	E	F	I	Es
Notausgang (D)	—	emergency exit	sortie de secours *f*	uscita di sicurezza *f*	salida de emergencia *f*
not binding (E)	unverbindlich	—	sans engagement	non impegnativo(a)	sin compromiso
Note[1] (D)	—	mark	note *f*	voto *m*	calificación *f*
Note[2] (D)	—	note	note *f*	nota *f*	nota *f*
note[1] (E)	Note *f*	—	note *f*	nota *f*	nota *f*
note[2] (E)	Schein *m*	—	billet *m*	banconota *f*	billete *m*
note[1] (F)	Note *f*	note	—	nota *f*	nota *f*
note[2] (F)	Note *f*	mark	—	voto *m*	calificación *f*
note down (E)	notieren	—	noter	annotare	anotar
noter (F)	notieren	note down	—	annotare	anotar
Notfall (D)	—	emergency	cas d'urgence *m*	caso di emergenza *m*	caso de urgencia *m*
nothing (E)	nichts	—	rien	niente	nada
notice[1] (E)	bemerken	—	remarquer	notare	darse cuenta
notice[2] (E)	merken	—	remarquer	accorgersi di	notar
noticia (Es)	Nachricht *f*	message	nouvelle *f*	notizia *f*	—
noticiario (Es)	Nachrichten *pl*	news	informations *f pl*	giornale radio *m*	—
notieren (D)	—	note down	noter	annotare	anotar
notificar (Es)	mahnen	warn	exhorter	ammonire	—
nötig (D)	—	necessary	nécessaire	necessario(a)	necesario(a)
notizia (I)	Nachricht *f*	message	nouvelle *f*	—	noticia *f*
notte (I)	Nacht *f*	night	nuit *f*	—	noche *m*
notwendig (D)	—	necessary	nécessaire	necessario(a)	necesario(a)
Notwendigkeit (D)	—	necessity	nécessité *f*	necessità *f*	necesidad *f*
nouilles (F)	Nudeln *pl*	noodles	—	pasta *f*	pastas *f pl*
nourishment (E)	Ernährung *f*	—	nourriture *f*	alimentazione *f*	alimentación *f*
nourrir (F)	ernähren	feed	—	nutrire	alimentar
nourriture[1] (F)	Ernährung *f*	nourishment	—	alimentazione *f*	alimentación *f*
nourriture[2] (F)	Kost *f*	food	—	cibo *m*	alimento *m*
nourriture[3] (F)	Nahrung *f*	food	—	alimentazione *f*	nutrición *f*
nourriture[4] (F)	Verpflegung *f*	catering	—	vitto *m*	alimentación *f*
nous (F)	wir	we	—	noi	nosotros(as)
nouveau (F)	neu	new	—	nuovo(a)	nuevo(a)
nouveauté (F)	Neuheit *f*	novelty	—	novità *f*	originalidad *f*
nouvel an (F)	Neujahr *n*	New Year	—	Capodanno *m*	Año Nuevo *m*
nouvelle[1] (F)	Neuigkeit *f*	news	—	novità *f*	novedad *f*
nouvelle[2] (F)	Nachricht *f*	message	—	notizia *f*	noticia *f*
novanta (I)	neunzig	ninety	quatre-vingt-dix	—	noventa
nove (I)	neun	nine	neuf	—	nueve
novedad (Es)	Neuigkeit *f*	news	nouvelle *f*	novità *f*	—
novel (E)	Roman *m*	—	roman *m*	romanzo *m*	novela *f*
novela (Es)	Roman *m*	novel	roman *m*	romanzo *m*	—
novelty (E)	Neuheit *f*	—	nouveauté *f*	novità *f*	originalidad *f*
November (D)	—	November	novembre *m*	novembre *m*	noviembre *m*
November (E)	November *m*	—	novembre *m*	novembre *m*	noviembre *m*
novembre (F)	November *m*	November	—	novembre *m*	noviembre *m*
novembre (I)	November *m*	November	novembre *m*	—	noviembre *m*

	D	E	F	I	Es
noventa (Es)	neunzig	ninety	quatre-vingt-dix	novanta	—
no ver (Es)	übersehen	ignore	ignorer	non vedere	—
novia (Es)	Braut f	bride	mariée f	sposa f	—
noviembre (Es)	November m	November	novembre m	novembre m	—
novità[1] (I)	Neuigkeit f	news	nouvelle f	—	novedad f
novità[2] (I)	Neuheit f	novelty	nouveauté f	—	originalidad f
now[1] (E)	jetzt	—	maintenant	adesso	ahora
now[2] (E)	nun	—	maintenant	adesso	actualmente
nowadays (E)	heutzutage	—	de nos jours	oggigiorno	hoy en día
nowhere (E)	nirgends	—	nulle part	da nessuna parte	en ninguna parte
noyau (F)	Kern m	pip	—	nocciolo m	hueso m
noyer, se (F)	ertrinken	drown	—	annegare	ahogarse
nozze (I)	Hochzeit f	wedding	mariage m	—	boda f
nu (F)	nackt	naked	—	nudo(a)	desnudo(a)
nuage (F)	Wolke f	cloud	—	nuvola f	nube f
nube (Es)	Wolke f	cloud	nuage m	nuvola f	—
nublado (Es)	bewölkt	cloudy	couvert(e)	nuvoloso(a)	—
nüchtern (D)	—	sober	sobre	sobrio(a)	sobrio(a)
Nudeln (D)	—	noodles	nouilles f pl	pasta f	pastas f pl
nudo (Es)	Knoten m	knot	nœud m	nodo m	—
nudo (I)	nackt	naked	nu(e)	—	desnudo(a)
nueve (Es)	neun	nine	neuf	nove	—
nuevo (Es)	neu	new	nouveau, nouvel, nouvelle	nuovo(a)	—
nuez (Es)	Nuß f	nut	noix f	noce f	—
nuire (F)	schaden	damage	—	nuocere	dañar
nuisible (F)	schädlich	harmful	—	nocivo(a)	nocivo(a)
nuit (F)	Nacht f	night	—	notte f	noche m
nuit de Noël (F)	Heiligabend m	Christmas Eve	—	vigilia di Natale f	Nochebuena f
Null (D)	—	zero	zéro	zero	cero
nulle part (F)	nirgends	nowhere	—	da nessuna parte	en ninguna parte
number[1] (E)	Anzahl f	—	nombre m	numero m	número m
number[2] (E)	numerieren	—	numéroter	numerare	numerar
number[3] (E)	Nummer f	—	numéro	numero m	número m
number[4] (E)	Zahl f	—	chiffre m	numero m	número m
number plate (E)	Nummernschild n	—	plaque d'immatriculation f	targa f	matrícula f
numerar (Es)	numerieren	number	numéroter	numerare	—
numerare (I)	numerieren	number	numéroter	—	numerar
numerieren (D)	—	number	numéroter	numerare	numerar
número[1] (Es)	Anzahl f	number	nombre m	numero m	—
número[2] (Es)	Nummer f	number	numéro	numero m	—
número[3] (Es)	Zahl f	number	chiffre m	numero m	—
numéro (F)	Nummer f	number	—	numero m	número m
numero[1] (I)	Anzahl f	number	nombre m	—	número m

	D	E	F	I	Es
numero² (I)	Nummer f	number	numéro	—	número m
numero³ (I)	Zahl f	number	chiffre m	—	número m
número de teléfono (Es)	Telefonnummer f	phone number	numéro de téléphone m	numero telefonico m	—
numéro de téléphone (F)	Telefonnummer f	phone number	—	numero telefonico m	número de teléfono m
numeroso (Es)	zahlreich	numerous	nombreux(-euse)	numeroso(a)	—
numeroso (I)	zahlreich	numerous	nombreux(-euse)	—	numeroso(a)
numero telefonico (I)	Telefonnummer f	phone number	numéro de téléphone m	—	número de teléfono m
numéroter (F)	numerieren	number	—	numerare	numerar
numerous (E)	zahlreich	—	nombreux(-euse)	numeroso(a)	numeroso(a)
Nummer (D)	—	number	numéro	numero m	número m
Nummernschild (D)	—	number plate	plaque d'immatriculation f	targa f	matrícula f
nun (D)	—	now	maintenant	adesso	actualmente
nun (E)	Nonne f	—	religieuse f	suora f	monja f
nuocere (I)	schaden	damage	nuire	—	dañar
nuotare (I)	schwimmen	swim	nager	—	nadar
nuovo (I)	neu	new	nouveau, nouvel, nouvelle	—	nuevo(a)
nur (D)	—	only	seulement	solo	sólo
nurse (E)	Kranken-schwester f	—	infirmière f	infermiera f	enfermera f
nursery school (E)	Kindergarten m	—	jardin d'enfants m	asilo (infantile) m	jardín de infancia m
nursing orderly (E)	Kranken-pfleger m	—	infirmier m	infermiere m	enfermero m
Nuß (D)	—	nut	noix f	noce f	nuez f
nut (E)	Nuß f	—	noix f	noce f	nuez f
nutrición (Es)	Nahrung f	food	nourriture f	alimentazione f	—
nutrire (I)	ernähren	feed	nourrir	—	alimentar
nützlich (D)	—	useful	utile	utile	útil
nutzlos (D)	—	useless	inutile	inutile	inútil
nuvola (I)	Wolke f	cloud	nuage m	—	nube f
nuvoloso (I)	bewölkt	cloudy	couvert(e)	—	nublado(a)
o (Es)	oder	or	ou	o	—
o (I)	oder	or	ou	—	o
o...o (Es)	entweder...oder	either...or	ou...ou	o...o	—
o...o (I)	entweder...oder	either...or	ou...ou	—	o...o
oar (E)	Ruder n	—	rame f	remo m	remo m
Oase (D)	—	oasis	oasis f	oasi f	oasis m
oasi (I)	Oase f	oasis	oasis f	—	oasis m
oasis (E)	Oase f	—	oasis f	oasi f	oasis m
oasis (Es)	Oase f	oasis	oasis f	oasi f	—
oasis (F)	Oase f	oasis	—	oasi f	oasis m
ob (D)	—	if/whether	si	se	si
obbligare (I)	verpflichten	oblige	obliger	—	obligar

	D	E	F	I	Es
obbligo (I)	Verpflichtung *f*	obligation	obligation *f*	—	obligación *f*
obedecer (Es)	gehorchen	obey	obéir	ubbidire	—
obedient (E)	gehorsam	—	obéissant(e)	ubbidiente	obediente
obediente (Es)	gehorsam	obedient	obéissant(e)	ubbidiente	—
obéir (F)	gehorchen	obey	—	ubbidire	obedecer
obéissant (F)	gehorsam	obedient	—	ubbidiente	obediente
oben (D)	—	above	en haut	sopra	arriba
Ober (D)	—	waiter	garçon *m*	cameriere *m*	camarero *m*
Oberfläche (D)	—	surface	surface *f*	superficie *f*	superficie *f*
oberflächlich (D)	—	superficial	superficiel(le)	superficiale	superficial
obey (E)	gehorchen	—	obéir	ubbidire	obedecer
obgleich (D)	—	although	bien que	benché	aunque
object (E)	Gegenstand *m*	—	objet *m*	oggetto *m*	objeto *m*
objet (F)	Gegenstand *m*	object	—	oggetto *m*	objeto *m*
objeto (Es)	Gegenstand *m*	object	objet *m*	oggetto *m*	—
oblicuo (Es)	schief	sloped	oblique	obliquo(a)	—
obligación[1] (Es)	Pflicht *f*	duty	devoir *m*	dovere *m*	—
obligación[2] (Es)	Verpflichtung *f*	obligation	obligation *f*	obbligo *m*	—
obligar[1] (Es)	verpflichten	oblige	obliger	obbligare	—
obligar[2] (Es)	zwingen	force	forcer	costringere	—
obligation (E)	Verpflichtung *f*	—	obligation *f*	obbligo *m*	obligación *f*
obligation (F)	Verpflichtung *f*	obligation	—	obbligo *m*	obligación *f*
oblige (E)	verpflichten	—	obliger	obbligare	obligar
obligeance (F)	Gefälligkeit *f*	favour	—	favore *m*	complacencia *f*
obliger (F)	verpflichten	oblige	—	obbligare	obligar
obliging (E)	zuvorkommend	—	prévenant(e)	premuroso(a)	cortés
oblique (F)	schief	sloped	—	obliquo(a)	torcido(a)
obliquo (I)	schief	sloped	oblique	—	torcido(a)
obra (Es)	Werk *n*	work	œuvre *f*	opera *f*	—
obrar (Es)	handeln	act	agir	agire	—
obscurité (F)	Finsternis *f*	darkness	—	buio *m*	oscuridad *f*
observar (Es)	beobachten	observe	observer	osservare	—
observe (E)	beobachten	—	observer	osservare	observar
observer[1] (F)	beobachten	observe	—	osservare	observar
observer[2] (F)	beachten	take notice of	—	osservare	prestar atención a
Obst (D)	—	fruit	fruits *m pl*	frutta *f*	fruta *f*
obtain by force (E)	erzwingen	—	forcer	ottenere con la forza	forzar
obtener (Es)	erhalten	receive	recevoir	ricevere	—
obvious (E)	offensichtlich	—	manifeste	evidente	evidente
obwohl (D)	—	although	bien que	benché	aunque
oca (I)	Gans *f*	goose	oie *f*	—	ganso *m*
ocasional (Es)	gelegentlich	occasional	occasionnel(le)	occasionale	—
ocasionar (Es)	verursachen	cause	causer	causare	—
occasion (E)	Gelegenheit *f*	—	occasion *f*	occasione *f*	oportunidad *f*

	D	E	F	I	Es
occasion[1] (F)	Anlaß *m*	occasion	—	occasione *f*	causa *f*
occasion[2] (F)	Gelegenheit *f*	occasion	—	occasione *f*	oportunidad *f*
occasional (E)	gelegentlich	—	occasionnel(le)	occasionale	ocasional
occasionale (I)	gelegentlich	occasional	occasionnel(le)	—	ocasional
occasione[1] (I)	Anlaß *m*	cause	occasion *f*	—	ocasión *f*
occasione[2] (I)	Chance *f*	chance	possibilité *f*	—	oportunidad *f*
occasione[3] (I)	Gelegenheit *f*	cause	occasion *f*	—	oportunidad *f*
occasionnel (F)	gelegentlich	occasional	—	occasionale	ocasional
occhiali (I)	Brille *f*	glasses	lunettes *f pl*	—	gafas *f pl*
occhiali da sole (I)	Sonnenbrille *f*	sunglasses	lunettes de soleil *f pl*	—	gafas de sol *f pl*
occhio (I)	Auge *n*	eye	œil *m* (yeux *pl*)	—	ojo *m*
occidental (Es)	westlich	western	de l'ouest	ad ovest	—
occupare (I)	beschäftigen	occupy/employ	occuper	—	ocupar
occupato[1] (I)	besetzt	engaged	occupé(e)	—	ocupado(a)
occupato[2] (I)	beschäftigt	busy	occupé(e)	—	ocupado(a)
occupé[1] (F)	beschäftigt	busy	—	occupato(a)	ocupado(a)
occupé[2] (F)	besetzt	engaged	—	occupato(a)	ocupado(a)
occuper (F)	beschäftigen	occupy/employ	—	occupare	ocupar
occuper de, se[1] (F)	kümmern, sich	look after	—	interessarsi di	ocuparse de
occuper de, se[2] (F)	sorgen	worry about	—	prendersi cura di	atender
occupy (E)	beschäftigen	—	occuper	occupare	ocupar
occur (E)	vorkommen	—	exister	accadere	suceder
ocean (E)	Ozean *m*	—	océan *m*	oceano *m*	océano *m*
océan (F)	Ozean *m*	ocean	—	oceano *m*	océano *m*
océano (Es)	Ozean *m*	ocean	océan *m*	oceano *m*	—
oceano (I)	Ozean *m*	ocean	océan *m*	—	océano *m*
ochenta (Es)	achtzig	eighty	quatre-vingts	ottanta	—
ocho (Es)	acht	eight	huit	otto	—
Ochse (D)	—	ox	bœuf *m*	bue *m*	buey *m*
October (E)	Oktober *m*	—	octobre *m*	ottobre *m*	octubre *m*
octobre (F)	Oktober *m*	October	—	ottobre *m*	octubre *m*
octubre (Es)	Oktober *m*	October	octobre *m*	ottobre *m*	—
oculista (Es)	Augenarzt *m*	eye specialist	oculiste *m*	oculista *m*	—
oculista (I)	Augenarzt *m*	eye specialist	oculiste *m*	—	oculista *m*
oculiste (F)	Augenarzt *m*	eye specialist	—	oculista *m*	oculista *m*
ocultar (Es)	verstecken	hide	cacher	nascondere	—
oculto (Es)	heimlich	secret	secret(-ète)	segreto(a)	—
ocupado[1] (Es)	beschäftigt	busy	occupé(e)	occupato(a)	—
ocupado[2] (Es)	besetzt	engaged	occupé(e)	occupato(a)	—
ocupar (Es)	beschäftigen	occupy/employ	occuper	occupare	—
ocuparse de (Es)	kümmern, sich	look after	occuper de, se	interessarsi di	—
ocurrir (Es)	geschehen	happen	arriver	accadere	—
öde (D)	—	waste	désert(e)	deserto(a)	desierto(a)
oder (D)	—	or	ou	o	o

	D	E	F	I	Es
odeur¹ (F)	Duft *m*	scent	—	profumo *m*	aroma *m*
odeur² (F)	Geruch *m*	smell	—	odore *m*	olor *m*
odiar (Es)	hassen	hate	détester	odiare	—
odiare (I)	hassen	hate	détester	—	odear
odio (Es)	Haß *m*	hate	haine *f*	odio *m*	—
odio (I)	Haß *m*	hate	haine *f*	—	odio *m*
odore (I)	Geruch *m*	smell	odeur *f*	—	olor *m*
œil (F)	Auge *n*	eye	—	occhio *m*	ojo *m*
œillet (F)	Nelke *f*	carnation	—	garofano *m*	clavel *m*
oeste (Es)	Westen *m*	west	ouest *m*	ovest *m*	—
œuf (F)	Ei *n*	egg	—	uovo *m*	huevo *m*
œuvre (F)	Werk *n*	work	—	opera *f*	obra *f*
of age (E)	volljährig	—	majeur(e)	maggiorenne	mayor de edad
of course (E)	selbstverständlich	—	évidemment	naturalmente	por supuesto
Ofen (D)	—	oven	poêle *m*	stufa *f*	estufa *f*
ofender (Es)	beleidigen	insult	offenser	offendere	—
ofensa (Es)	Beleidigung *f*	insult	offense *f*	offesa *f*	—
oferta (Es)	Angebot *n*	offer	offre *f*	offerta *f*	—
oferta especial (Es)	Sonderangebot *n*	special offer	offre spéciale *f*	offerta speciale *f*	—
off¹ (E)	ab	—	à partir de/dès	da	a partir de/de
off² (E)	aus	—	de/par/hors de	da/di	de/por
off! (E)	los!	—	allons-y!	avanti!	¡adelante!
offen (D)	—	open	ouvert(e)	aperto(a)	abierto(a)
offendere (I)	beleidigen	insult	offenser	—	ofender
offense (F)	Beleidigung *f*	insult	—	offesa *f*	ofensa *f*
offenser (F)	beleidigen	insult	—	offendere	ofender
offensichtlich (D)	—	obvious	manifeste	evidente	evidente
öffentlich (D)	—	public	public(-ique)	pubblico(a)	público(a)
Öffentlichkeit (D)	—	public	public *m*	pubblico *m*	público *m*
offer¹ (E)	anbieten	—	offrir	offrire	ofrecer
offer² (E)	Angebot *n*	—	offre *f*	offerta *f*	oferta *f*
offer³ (E)	bieten	—	présenter	offrire	ofrecer
offerta (I)	Angebot *n*	offer	offre *f*	—	oferta *f*
offerta speciale (I)	Sonderangebot *n*	special offer	offre spéciale *f*	—	oferta especial *f*
offesa (I)	Beleidigung *f*	insult	offense *f*	—	ofensa *f*
office¹ (E)	Amt *n*	—	bureau *m*	ufficio *m*	oficio *m*
office² (E)	Büro *n*	—	bureau *m*	ufficio *m*	oficina *f*
office divin (F)	Gottesdienst *m*	service	—	messa *f*	servicio religioso *m*
official¹ (E)	amtlich	—	officiel(le)	ufficiale	oficial
official² (E)	offiziell	—	officiel(le)	ufficiale	oficial
officiel¹ (F)	amtlich	official	—	ufficiale	oficial
officiel² (F)	offiziell	official	—	ufficiale	oficial
officina (I)	Werkstatt *f*	workshop	atelier *m*	—	taller *m*
offiziell (D)	—	official	officiel(le)	ufficiale	oficial

	D	E	F	I	Es
öffnen (D)	—	open	ouvrir	aprire	abrir
Öffnungzeiten (D)	—	business hours	heures d'ouverture *f pl*	orario d'ufficio *m*	horario de oficina *m*
offre (F)	Angebot *n*	offer	—	offerta *f*	oferta *f*
offre spéciale (F)	Sonderangebot *n*	special offer	—	offerta speciale *f*	oferta especial *f*
offrir¹ (F)	anbieten	offer	—	offrire	ofrecer
offrir² (F)	schenken	give	—	regalare	regalar
offrire¹ (I)	anbieten	offer	offrir	—	ofrecer
offrire² (I)	bieten	offer	présenter	—	ofrecer
oficial¹ (Es)	amtlich	official	officiel(le)	ufficiale	—
oficial² (Es)	offiziell	official	officiel(le)	ufficiale	—
oficina (Es)	Büro *n*	office	bureau *m*	ufficio *m*	—
oficina de correos (Es)	Postamt *n*	post office	bureau de poste *m*	ufficio postale *m*	—
oficina de objetos perdidos (Es)	Fundbüro *n*	lost property office	bureau des objets trouvés *m*	ufficio oggetti smarriti *m*	—
oficina de turismo (Es)	Verkehrsbüro *n*	travel agency	bureau touristique *m*	ufficio turistico *m*	—
oficina de viajes (Es)	Reisebüro *f*	travel agency	agence de voyages *f*	agenzia turistica *f*	—
oficio (Es)	Amt *n*	office	bureau *m*	ufficio *m*	—
of it (E)	davon	—	en/de cela	di la/ne	de ello
ofrecer¹ (Es)	anbieten	offer	offrir	offrire	—
ofrecer² (Es)	bieten	offer	présenter	offrire	—
oft (D)	—	often	souvent	spesso	a menudo
often (E)	oft	—	souvent	spesso	a menudo
oggetti antichi (I)	Antiquitäten *pl*	antiques	antiquités *f pl*	—	antigüedades *f pl*
oggetto (I)	Gegenstand *m*	object	objet *m*	—	objeto *m*
oggi (I)	heute	today	aujourd'hui	—	hoy
oggigiorno (I)	heutzutage	nowadays	de nos jours	—	hoy en día
ogni, ognuno (I)	jede(r,s)	each/every	chaque	—	cada
ogni ora (I)	stündlich	hourly	toutes les heures	—	cada hora
ogni volta (I)	jedesmal	each time	chaque fois	—	cada vez
ohne (D)	—	without	sans	senza	sin
Ohnmacht (D)	—	faint	évanouissement *m*	svenimento *m*	desmayo *m*
Ohr (D)	—	ear	oreille *f*	orecchio *m*	oreja *f*
Ohrenarzt (D)	—	ear specialist	spécialiste de l'oreille *m*	otoiatra *m*	médico del oído *m*
Ohrenschmerzen (D)	—	earache	mal d'oreilles *m*	mal d'orecchi *m*	dolor de oídos *m*
oie (F)	Gans *f*	goose	—	oca *f*	ganso *m*
oignon (F)	Zwiebel *f*	onion	—	cipolla *f*	cebolla *f*
oil¹ (E)	Erdöl *n*	—	pétrole *m*	petrolio *m*	petróleo *m*
oil² (E)	Öl *n*	—	huile *f*	olio *m*	aceite *m*
ointment (E)	Salbe *f*	—	onguent *m*	pomata *f*	pomada *f*
oír (Es)	hören	hear	entendre	sentire	—
oiseau (F)	Vogel *m*	bird	—	uccello *m*	pájaro *m*

	D	E	F	I	Es
ojo (Es)	Auge n	eye	œil m (yeux pl)	occhio m	—
ojo de la cerradura (Es)	Schlüsselloch n	keyhole	trou de la serrure m	buco della chiave m	—
Oktober (D)	—	October	octobre m	ottobre m	octubre m
Öl (D)	—	oil	huile f	olio m	aceite m
ola (Es)	Welle f	wave	vague f	onda f	—
old (E)	alt	—	vieux, vieil, vieille	vecchio(a)	viejo(a)
old-fashioned (E)	altmodisch	—	démodé(e)	fuori moda	pasado(a) de moda
oler (Es)	riechen	smell	sentir	sentire	—
Olimpiadi (I)	Olympische Spiele pl	Olympic Games	jeux olympiques m pl	—	Juegos Olímpicos m pl
olio (I)	Öl n	oil	huile f	—	aceite m
olio combustibile (I)	Heizöl n	fuel	mazout m	—	combustible para la calefacción m
oliva (I)	Olive f	olive	olive f	—	aceituna f
Olive (D)	—	olive	olive f	oliva f	aceituna f
olive (E)	Olive f	—	olive f	oliva f	aceituna f
olive (F)	Olive f	olive	—	oliva f	aceituna f
olla¹ (Es)	Kochtopf m	saucepan	casserole f	pentola f	—
olla² (Es)	Topf m	pot	casserole f	pentola f	—
olor (Es)	Geruch m	smell	odeur f	odore m	—
olvidar (Es)	vergessen	forget	oublier	dimenticare	—
Olympic Games (E)	Olympische Spiele pl	—	jeux olympiques m pl	Olimpiadi f pl	Juegos Olímpicos m pl
Olympische Spiele (D)	—	Olympic Games	jeux olympiques m pl	Olimpiadi f pl	Juegos Olímpicos m pl
ombelico (I)	Nabel m	navel	nombril m	—	ombligo m
ombligo (Es)	Nabel m	navel	nombril m	ombelico m	—
ombra (I)	Schatten m	shadow	ombre f	—	sombra f
ombragé (F)	schattig	shady	—	ombroso(a)	a la sombra
ombre (F)	Schatten m	shadow	—	ombra f	sombra f
ombrello¹ (I)	Regenschirm m	umbrella	parapluie m	—	paraguas m
ombrello² (I)	Schirm m	umbrella	parapluie m	—	paraguas m
ombrellone (I)	Sonnenschirm m	parasol	parasol m	—	sombrilla f
ombroso (I)	schattig	shady	ombragé(e)	—	a la sombra
Omelett (D)	—	omelette	omelette f	frittata f	tortilla f
omelette (E)	Omelett n	—	omelette f	frittata f	tortilla f
omelette (F)	Omelett n	omelette	—	frittata f	tortilla f
Omnibus (D)	—	omnibus	autobus m	autobus m	autobús m
omnibus (E)	Omnibus m	—	autobus m	autobus m	autobús m
on (E)	auf	—	sur	su/sopra	sobre/en/hacia
on business (E)	geschäftlich	—	d'affaires	per affari	comercial
once (E)	einmal	—	une fois	una volta	una vez
once (Es)	elf	eleven	onze	undici	—
oncle (F)	Onkel m	uncle	—	zio m	tío m
onda (I)	Welle f	wave	vague f	—	ola f

	D	E	F	I	Es
one[1] (E)	eins	—	un	uno	uno(a)
one[2] (E)	eine(r,s)	—	un(e)	un(a)	una/un/uno
one after the other (E)	hintereinander	—	l'un derrière l'autre	uno dopo l'altro	uno detrás de otro
one and a half (E)	anderthalb	—	un(e) et demi(e)	uno e mezzo	uno(a) y medio(a)
one before last (E)	vorletzte(r,s)	—	avant-dernier (-ère)	penultimo(a)	penúltima(o)
one hundred (E)	einhundert	—	cent	cento	cien
one-sided (E)	einseitig	—	partial(e)	unilaterale	unilateral
onesto[1] (I)	ehrlich	honest	honnête	—	honesto(a)
onesto[2] (I)	aufrichtig	honest	sincère	—	sincero(a)
one upon the other (E)	übereinander	—	l'un(e) sur l'autre	uno sopra l'altro	uno sobre otro
one-way street (E)	Einbahnstraße *f*	—	rue à sens unique *f*	senso unico *m*	calle de dirección única *f*
ongle (F)	Nagel *m*	nail	—	unghia *f*	uña *f*
onguent (F)	Salbe *f*	ointment	—	pomata *f*	pomada *f*
onion (E)	Zwiebel *f*	—	oignon *m*	cipolla *f*	cebolla *f*
Onkel (D)	—	uncle	oncle *m*	zio *m*	tío *m*
only[1] (E)	bloß	—	seulement	soltanto	sólo
only[2] (E)	einzig	—	seul(e)	unico(a)	único(a)
only[3] (E)	nur	—	seulement	solo	sólo
on one hand (E)	einerseits	—	d'une part	da un lato	por un lado
onore (I)	Ehre *f*	honour	honneur *m*	—	honor *m*
on the other hand (E)	andererseits	—	d'autre part	d'altra parte	por otra parte
on the way (E)	unterwegs	—	en route	per strada	de camino
on working days (E)	werktags	—	les jours ouvrables	nei giorni feriali	los días laborables
onze (F)	elf	eleven	—	undici	once
opción (Es)	Wahl *f*	choice	choix *m*	scelta *f*	—
open[1] (E)	geöffnet	—	ouvert(e)	aperto(a)	abierto(a)
open[2] (E)	öffnen	—	ouvrir	aprire	abrir
open[3] (E)	offen	—	ouvert(e)	aperto(a)	abierto(a)
open-air swimming pool (E)	Freibad *n*	—	piscine en plein air *f*	piscina all'aperto *f*	piscina al aire libre *f*
opening (E)	Eröffnung *f*	—	ouverture *f*	apertura *f*	abertura *f*
Oper (D)	—	opera	opéra *m*	opera *f*	ópera *f*
opera (E)	Oper *f*	—	opéra *m*	opera *f*	ópera *f*
ópera (Es)	Oper *f*	opera	opéra *m*	opera *f*	—
opéra (F)	Oper *f*	opera	—	opera *f*	ópera *f*
opera[1] (I)	Oper *f*	opera	opéra *m*	—	ópera *f*
opera[2] (I)	Werk *n*	work	œuvre *f*	—	obra *f*
operación (Es)	Operation *f*	operation	opération *f*	operazione *f*	—
operaio (I)	Arbeiter *m*	worker	ouvrier *m*	—	trabajador *m*
opera teatrale (I)	Theaterstück *n*	play	pièce de théâtre *f*	—	pieza de teatro *f*
Operation (D)	—	operation	opération *f*	operazione *f*	operación *f*
operation (E)	Operation *f*	—	opération *f*	operazione *f*	operación *f*

	D	E	F	I	Es
opération (F)	Operation f	operation	—	operazione f	operación f
operazione (I)	Operation f	operation	opération f	—	operación f
Opfer¹ (D)	—	sacrifice	sacrifice m	sacrificio m	sacrificio m
Opfer² (D)	—	victim	victime f	vittima f	víctima f
opinar (Es)	meinen	think	penser	credere	—
opinion¹ (E)	Ansicht f	—	avis m	opinione f	opinión f
opinion² (E)	Meinung f	—	opinion f	opinione f	opinión f
opinión¹ (Es)	Ansicht f	opinion	avis m	opinione f	—
opinión² (Es)	Meinung f	opinion	opinion f	opinione f	—
opinion (F)	Meinung f	opinion	—	opinione f	opinión f
opinione¹ (I)	Ansicht f	opinion	avis m	—	opinión f
opinione² (I)	Meinung f	opinion	opinion f	—	opinión f
oportunidad¹ (Es)	Chance f	chance	possibilité f	occasione f	—
oportunidad² (Es)	Gelegenheit f	occasion	occasion f	occasione f	—
opponent (E)	Gegner m	—	adversaire m	avversario m	adversario m
opposé (F)	entgegengesetzt	opposite	—	opposto(a)	opuesto(a)
opposite¹ (E)	entgegengesetzt	—	opposé(e)	opposto(a)	opuesto(a)
opposite² (E)	gegenüber	—	en face de	di fronte(a)	en frente
opposite³ (E)	Gegenteil n	—	contraire m	contrario m	opuesto m
opposto (I)	entgegengesetzt	opposite	opposé(e)	—	opuesto(a)
oppress (E)	unterdrücken	—	opprimer	sopprimere	oprimir
opprimer (F)	unterdrücken	oppress	—	sopprimere	oprimir
oprimir (Es)	unterdrücken	oppress	opprimer	sopprimere	—
optician (E)	Optiker m	—	opticien m	ottico m	óptico m
opticien (F)	Optiker m	optician	—	ottico m	óptico m
óptico (Es)	Optiker m	optician	opticien m	ottico m	—
Optiker (D)	—	optician	opticien m	ottico m	óptico m
óptimo (Es)	beste(r,s)	best	meilleur(e)	migliore	—
opuesto¹ (Es)	Gegenteil n	opposite	contraire m	contrario m	—
opuesto² (Es)	entgegengesetzt	opposite	opposé(e)	opposto(a)	—
or (E)	oder	—	ou	o	o
or (F)	Gold n	gold	—	oro m	oro m
ora (I)	Stunde f	hour	heure f	—	hora f
oración (Es)	Satz m	sentence	phrase f	frase f	—
ora di ricevimento (I)	Sprechstunde f	consultation hour	heures de consultation f pl	—	hora de consulta f
orage (F)	Gewitter n	thunderstorm	—	temporale m	tormenta f
oral (E)	mündlich	—	oral(e)	orale	oral
oral (Es)	mündlich	oral	oral(e)	orale	—
oral (F)	mündlich	oral	—	orale	oral
orale (I)	mündlich	oral	oral(e)	—	oral
ora legale (I)	Sommerzeit f	summertime	heure d'été f	—	temporada de verano f
Orange (D)	—	orange	orange f	arancia f	naranja f
orange¹ (E)	Apfelsine f	—	orange f	arancia f	naranja f

	D	E	F	I	Es
orange² (E)	Orange *f*	—	orange *f*	arancia *f*	naranja *f*
orange¹ (F)	Apfelsine *f*	orange	—	arancia *f*	naranja *f*
orange³ (F)	Orange *f*	orange	—	arancia *f*	naranja *f*
orario (I)	Fahrplan *m*	timetable	horaire *m*	—	horario *m*
orario di apertura (I)	Öffnungszeiten *pl*	business hours	heures d'ouverture *f pl*	—	horario de abertura *m*
Orchester (D)	—	orchestra	orchestre *m*	orchestra *f*	orquesta *f*
orchestra (E)	Orchester *n*	—	orchestre *m*	orchestra *f*	orquesta *f*
orchestra (I)	Orchester *n*	orchestra	orchestre *m*	—	orquesta *f*
orchestre¹ (F)	Kapelle *f*	band	—	banda *f*	banda *f*
orchestre² (F)	Orchester *n*	orchestra	—	orchestra *f*	orquesta *f*
Orden¹ (D)	—	order	ordre *m*	ordine *m*	orden *m*
Orden² (D)	—	decoration	décoration *f*	decorazione *f*	condecoración *f*
orden¹ (Es)	Ordnung *f*	order	ordre *m*	ordine *m*	—
orden² (Es)	Orden *m*	order	ordre *m*	ordine *m*	—
ordenado (Es)	ordentlich	tidy	rangé(e)	ordinato(a)	—
ordenar (Es)	ordnen	put in order	ordonner	ordinare	—
ordentlich (D)	—	tidy	rangé(e)	ordinato(a)	ordenado(a)
order¹ (E)	bestellen	—	commander	ordinare	pedir
order² (E)	verfügen	—	disposer de	disporre	disponer
order³ (E)	Befehl *m*	—	ordre *m*	ordine *m*	mando *m*
order⁴ (E)	Ordnung *f*	—	ordre *m*	ordine *m*	orden *m*
order⁵ (E)	Orden *m*	—	ordre *m*	ordine *m*	orden *m*
ordinare¹ (I)	bestellen	order	commander	—	pedir
ordinare² (I)	ordnen	put in order	ordonner	—	ordenar
ordinato (I)	ordentlich	tidy	rangé(e)	—	ordenado(a)
ordine¹ (I)	Befehl *m*	order	ordre *m*	—	mando *m*
ordine² (I)	Ordnung *f*	order	ordre *m*	—	orden *m*
ordine³ (I)	Orden *m*	order	ordre *m*	—	orden *m*
ordnen (D)	—	put in order	ordonner	ordinare	ordenar
Ordnung (D)	—	order	ordre *m*	ordine *m*	orden *m*
ordonnance (F)	Rezept *n*	prescription	—	prescrizione *f*	prescripción médica *f*
ordonner (F)	ordnen	put in order	—	ordinare	ordenar
ordre¹ (F)	Befehl *m*	order	—	ordine *m*	mando *m*
ordre² (F)	Ordnung *f*	order	—	ordine *m*	orden *m*
ordre³ (F)	Orden *m*	order	—	ordine *m*	orden *m*
orecchio (I)	Ohr *n*	ear	oreille *f*	—	oreja *f*
oreille (F)	Ohr *n*	ear	—	orecchio *m*	oreja *f*
oreiller (F)	Kopfkissen *n*	pillow	—	guanciale *m*	almohada *f*
oreja¹ (Es)	Gehör *n*	hearing	ouïe *f*	udito *m*	—
oreja² (Es)	Ohr *n*	ear	oreille *f*	orecchio *m*	—
orfano (I)	Waise *f*	orphan	orphelin *m*	—	huérfano *m*
organiser¹ (F)	organisieren	organize	—	organizzare	organizar
organiser² (F)	veranstalten	organize	—	organizzare	organizar

	D	E	F	I	Es
organisieren (D)	—	organize	organiser	organizzare	organizar
organizar[1] (Es)	arrangieren	arrange	arranger	arrangiare	—
organizar[2] (Es)	organisieren	organize	organiser	organizzare	—
organizar[3] (Es)	veranstalten	organize	organiser	organizzare	—
organize[1] (E)	organisieren	—	organiser	organizzare	organizar
organize[2] (E)	veranstalten	—	organiser	organizzare	organizar
organizzare[1] (I)	organisieren	organize	organiser	—	organizar
organizzare[2] (I)	veranstalten	organize	organiser	—	organizar
orgoglioso (I)	stolz	proud	fier(-ère)	—	orgulloso(a)
orgulloso (Es)	stolz	proud	fier(-ère)	orgoglioso(a)	—
Orient (D)	—	Orient	Orient m	Oriente m	oriente m
Orient (E)	Orient m	—	Orient m	Oriente m	oriente m
Orient (F)	Orient m	Orient	—	Oriente m	oriente m
orientarse (Es)	zurechtfinden, sich	find one's way	retrouver, se	orientarsi	—
orientarsi (I)	zurechtfinden, sich	find one's way	retrouver, se	—	orientarse
oriente (Es)	Orient m	Orient	Orient m	Oriente m	—
Oriente (I)	Orient m	Orient	Orient m	—	oriente m
original[1] (E)	originell	—	original(e)	originale	original
original[2] (E)	ursprünglich	—	originel(le)	originario(a)	primitivo(a)
original (Es)	originell	original	original(e)	originale	—
original (F)	originell	original	—	originale	original
originale (I)	originell	original	original(e)	—	original
originalidad (Es)	Neuheit f	novelty	nouveauté f	novità f	—
originario (I)	ursprünglich	original	originel(le)	—	primitivo(a)
originel (F)	ursprünglich	original	—	originario(a)	primitivo(a)
originell (D)	—	original	original(e)	originale	original
orilla (Es)	Ufer n	shore	bord m	riva f	—
orina (Es)	Harn m	urine	urine f	urina f	—
orizzontale (I)	waagrecht	horizontal	horizontal(e)	—	horizontal
oro (Es)	Gold n	gold	or m	oro m	—
oro (I)	Gold n	gold	or m	—	oro m
orologio (I)	Uhr f	watch	montre f	—	reloj m
orphan (E)	Waise f	—	orphelin m	orfano m	huérfano m
orphelin (F)	Waise f	orphan	—	orfano m	huérfano m
orquesta (Es)	Orchester n	orchestra	orchestre m	orchestra f	—
orso (I)	Bär m	bear	ours m	—	oso m
Ort (D)	—	place	endroit m	luogo m	lugar m
örtlich (D)	—	local	local(e)	locale	local
os (F)	Knochen m	bone	—	osso m	hueso m
osare (I)	wagen	dare	oser	—	atreverse
oscuridad (Es)	Finsternis f	darkness	obscurité f	buio m	—
oscuro[1] (Es)	dunkel	dark	sombre	scuro(a)	—
oscuro[2] (Es)	finster	dark	sombre	buio(a)	—

	D	E	F	I	Es
oser (F)	wagen	dare	—	osare	atreverse
oso (Es)	Bär *m*	bear	ours *m*	orso *m*	—
ospedale (I)	Krankenhaus *n*	hospital	hôpital *m*	—	hospital *m*
ospitale (I)	gastfreundlich	hospitable	hospitalier(-ière)	—	hospitalario(a)
ospitalità (I)	Gastfreundschaft *f*	hospitality	hospitalité *f*	—	hospitalidad *f*
ospite¹ (I)	Gastgeber *m*	host	hôte *m*	—	anfitrión *m*
ospite² (I)	Gast *m*	guest	hôte *m*	—	invitado *m*
osservare¹ (I)	beachten	take notice of	observer	—	prestar atención
osservare² (I)	beobachten	observe	observer	—	observar
osso (I)	Knochen *m*	bone	os *m*	—	hueso *m*
oste (I)	Wirt *m*	landlord	patron *m*	—	dueño *m*
Osten (D)	—	east	est *m*	est *m*	este *m*
osteria¹ (I)	Gasthaus *n*	inn	auberge *f*	—	posada *f*
osteria² (I)	Kneipe *f*	pub	bistro *m*	—	tasca *f*
osteria³ (I)	Wirtshaus *n*	inn	auberge *f*	—	restaurante *m*
Ostern (D)	—	Easter	Pâques *f pl*	Pasqua *f*	Pascua *f*
Österreich (D)	—	Austria	Autriche *f*	Austria *f*	Austria *f*
Österreicher (D)	—	Austrian	Autrichien *m*	austriaco *m*	austríaco *m*
österreichisch (D)	—	Austrian	autrichien(ne)	austriaco(a)	austríaco(a)
Osterwoche (D)	—	Holy week	semaine sainte *f*	settimana santa *f*	Semana Santa *f*
östlich (D)	—	eastern	d'est	ad est	al este
ostra (Es)	Auster *f*	oyster	huître *f*	ostrica *f*	—
ostrica (I)	Auster *f*	oyster	huître *f*	—	ostra *f*
other (E)	andere(r,s)	—	autre	altro(a)	otro(a)
otherwise (E)	sonst	—	autrement	altrimenti	por lo demás
otoiatra (I)	Ohrenarzt *m*	ear specialist	spécialiste de l'oreille *m*	—	médico del oído *m*
otoño (Es)	Herbst *m*	autumn	automne *m*	autunno *m*	—
otra vez (Es)	nochmals	again	encore une fois	di nuovo	—
otro (Es)	andere(r,s)	other	autre	altro(a)	—
ottanta (I)	achtzig	eighty	quatre-vingts	—	ochenta
ottenere con la forza (I)	erzwingen	obtain by force	forcer	—	forzar
ottico (I)	Optiker *m*	optician	opticien *m*	—	óptico *m*
otto (I)	acht	eight	huit	—	ocho
ottobre (I)	Oktober *m*	October	octobre *m*	—	octubre *m*
ou (F)	oder	or	—	o	o
où¹ (F)	wohin	where to	—	dove	a dónde
où² (F)	wo	where	—	dove	dónde
ouate (F)	Watte *f*	cotton wool	—	ovatta *f*	algodón *m*
oublier (F)	vergessen	forget	—	dimenticare	olvidar
ouest (F)	Westen *m*	west	—	ovest *m*	oeste *m*
oui (F)	ja	yes	—	sì	sí
ouïe (F)	Gehör *n*	hearing	—	udito *m*	oreja *f*
ou...ou (F)	entweder...oder	either...or	—	o...o	o...o

	D	E	F	I	Es
ours (F)	Bär m	bear	—	orso m	oso m
out[1] (E)	hinaus	—	dehors	fuori	hacia afuera
out[2] (E)	heraus	—	dehors	fuori	hacia afuera
outil (F)	Werkzeug n	tool	—	utensile m	herramienta f
outing (E)	Ausflug m	—	excursion f	gita f	excursión f
outline (E)	Entwurf m	—	esquisse f	abbozzo m	proyecto m
out of (E)	außerhalb	—	hors de	fuori di	fuera de
outside[1] (E)	außen	—	au dehors	fuori	afuera
outside[2] (E)	draußen	—	dehors	fuori	afuera
outwards (E)	auswärts	—	à l'extérieur	fuori	fuera
ouvert[1] (F)	geöffnet	open	—	aperto(a)	abierto(a)
ouvert[2] (F)	offen	open	—	aperto(a)	abierto(a)
ouverture (F)	Eröffnung f	opening	—	apertura f	abertura f
ouvre-bouteilles (F)	Flaschenöffner m	bottle opener	—	apribottiglie m	abridor de botellas m
ouvrier (F)	Arbeiter m	worker	—	operaio m	trabajador m
ouvrir (F)	öffnen	open	—	aprire	abrir
ovatta (I)	Watte f	cotton wool	ouate f	—	algodón m
oveja (Es)	Schaf n	sheep	mouton m	pecora f	—
oven (E)	Ofen m	—	poêle m	stufa f	estufa f
over[1] (E)	herüber	—	par ici	da questa parte	a este lado
over[2] (E)	über	—	sur	su/sopra/per	por/sobre
overestimate (E)	überschätzen	—	surestimer	sopravvalutare	sobrevalorar
over here (E)	hierher	—	par ici	qua	para acá
overnight stay (E)	Übernachtung f	—	logement pour une nuit m	pernottamento m	pernoctación f
overtake (E)	überholen	—	doubler	sorpassare	adelantar
over there (E)	drüben	—	de l'autre côté	dall'altra parte	al otro lado
ovest (I)	Westen m	west	ouest m	—	oeste m
owe (E)	schulden	—	devoir qch à qn	dovere	deber
own (E)	eigen	—	propre	proprio(a)	propio(a)
owner[1] (E)	Besitzer m	—	propriétaire m	proprietario m	propietario m
owner[2] (E)	Eigentümer m	—	propriétaire m	proprietario m	propietario m
owner[3] (E)	Inhaber m	—	propriétaire m	proprietario m	propietario m
ox (E)	Ochse m	—	bœuf m	bue m	buey m
oxidado (Es)	rostig	rusty	rouillé(e)	arrugginito(a)	—
oxidarse (Es)	rosten	rust	rouiller	arrugginire	—
oyente (Es)	Hörer m	listener	auditeur m	ascoltatore m	—
oyster (E)	Auster f	—	huître f	ostrica f	ostra f
Ozean (D)	—	ocean	océan m	oceano m	océano m
Paar (D)	—	pair	paire f	paio m	par m
pacchetto (I)	Päckchen n	small package	petit paquet m	—	paquetito m
pacco (I)	Paket n	parcel	paquet m	—	paquete m
pace (I)	Friede m	peace	paix f	—	paz f
paciencia (Es)	Geduld f	patience	patience f	pazienza f	—

	D	E	F	I	Es
paciente (Es)	Patient *m*	patient	patient *m*	paziente *m*	—
Pacific (E)	Pazifik *m*	—	Pacifique *m*	Pacifico *m*	pacífico *m*
pacífico (Es)	friedlich	peaceful	paisible	pacifico(a)	—
Pacífico (Es)	Pazifik *m*	Pacific	Pacifique *m*	Pacifico *m*	—
pacifico (I)	friedlich	peaceful	paisible	—	pacífico(a)
Pacifico (I)	Pazifik *m*	Pacific	Pacifique *m*	—	pacífico *m*
Pacifique (F)	Pazifik *m*	Pacific	—	Pacifico *m*	pacífico *m*
pack¹ (E)	packen	—	faire les malles	impacchettare	hacer la maleta
pack² (E)	verpacken	—	emballer	impacchettare	empaquetar
Päckchen (D)	—	small package	petit paquet *m*	pacchetto *m*	paquetito *m*
packen (D)	—	pack	faire les malles	impacchettare	hacer la maleta
Paddelboot (D)	—	canoe	canoë *m*	canoa *f*	piragua *f*
padella (I)	Pfanne *f*	pan	poêle *f*	—	sartén *f*
padre (Es)	Vater *m*	father	père *m*	padre *m*	—
padre (I)	Vater *m*	father	père *m*	—	padre *m*
padres (Es)	Eltern *pl*	parents	parents *m pl*	genitori *m pl*	—
padrino (Es)	Pate *m*	godfather	parrain *m*	padrino *m*	—
padrino (I)	Pate *m*	godfather	parrain *m*	—	padrino *m*
paesaggio (I)	Landschaft *f*	landscape	paysage *m*	—	paisaje *m*
paese¹ (I)	Dorf *n*	village	village *m*	—	pueblo *m*
paese² (I)	Land *n*	land	pays *m*	—	país *m*
Paesi Bassi (I)	Niederlande *f*	Netherlands	Pays-Bas *m pl*	—	los Paìses Bajos *m pl*
pagamento¹ (I)	Bezahlung *f*	payment	paiement *m*	—	pago *m*
pagamento² (I)	Zahlung *f*	payment	paiement *m*	—	pago *m*
pagamento contro assegno (I)	Nachnahme *f*	cash on delivery	remboursement *m*	—	entrega contra reembolso *f*
pagar¹ (Es)	bezahlen	pay	payer	pagare	—
pagar² (Es)	zahlen	pay	payer	pagare	—
pagare¹ (I)	bezahlen	pay	payer	—	pagar
pagare² (I)	zahlen	pay	payer	—	pagar
page (E)	Seite *f*	—	page *f*	pagina *f*	página *f*
page (F)	Seite *f*	page	—	pagina *f*	página *f*
pagella (I)	Zeugnis *n*	report	bulletin *m*	—	informe *m*
página (Es)	Seite *f*	page	page *f*	pagina *f*	—
pagina (I)	Seite *f*	page	page *f*	—	página *f*
paglia (I)	Stroh *n*	straw	paille *f*	—	paja *f*
pago¹ (Es)	Bezahlung *f*	payment	paiement *m*	pagamento *m*	—
pago² (Es)	Zahlung *f*	payment	paiement *m*	pagamento *m*	—
paiement¹ (F)	Bezahlung *f*	payment	—	pagamento *m*	pago *m*
paiement² (F)	Zahlung *f*	payment	—	pagamento *m*	pago *m*
paille (F)	Stroh *n*	straw	—	paglia *f*	paja *f*
pain (E)	Schmerz *m*	—	douleur *f*	dolore *m*	dolor *m*
pain (F)	Brot *n*	bread	—	pane *m*	pan *m*
painful (E)	schmerzhaft	—	douloureux(-euse)	doloroso(a)	doloroso(a)

	D	E	F	I	Es
paint¹ (E)	malen	—	peindre	dipingere	pintar
paint² (E)	streichen	—	peindre	verniciare	pintar
painter (E)	Maler *m*	—	peintre *m*	pittore *m*	pintor *m*
painting¹ (E)	Gemälde *n*	—	tableau *m*	quadro *m*	cuadro *m*
painting² (E)	Malerei *f*	—	peinture *f*	pittura *f*	pintura *f*
paio (I)	Paar *n*	pair	paire *f*	—	par *m*
pair (E)	Paar *n*	—	paire *f*	paio *m*	par *m*
pair (F)	gerade	even	—	pari	par
paire (F)	Paar *n*	pair	—	paio *m*	par *m*
pair of scissors (E)	Schere *f*	—	ciseaux *m pl*	forbici *f pl*	tijeras *f pl*
país (Es)	Land *n*	land	pays *m*	paese *m*	—
paisaje (Es)	Landschaft *f*	landscape	paysage *m*	paesaggio *m*	—
paisible (F)	friedlich	peaceful	—	pacifico(a)	pacífico(a)
paix (F)	Friede *m*	peace	—	pace *f*	paz *f*
paja (Es)	Stroh *n*	straw	paille *f*	paglia *f*	—
pájaro (Es)	Vogel *m*	bird	oiseau *m*	uccello *m*	—
Paket (D)	—	parcel	paquet *m*	pacco *m*	paquete *m*
pala (Es)	Schaufel *f*	shovel	pelle *f*	pala *f*	—
pala (I)	Schaufel *f*	shovel	pelle *f*	—	pala *f*
palabra (Es)	Wort *n*	word	mot *m*	parola *f*	—
palace (E)	Palast *m*	—	palais	palazzo *m*	palacio *m*
palacio (Es)	Palast *m*	palace	palais	palazzo *m*	—
palais (F)	Palast *m*	palace	—	palazzo *m*	palacio *m*
Palast (D)	—	palace	palais	palazzo *m*	palacio *m*
palazzo (I)	Palast *m*	palace	palais	—	palacio *m*
palco (Es)	Loge *f*	box	loge *f*	palco *m*	—
palco (I)	Loge *f*	box	loge *f*	—	palco *m*
palcoscenico (I)	Bühne *f*	stage	scène *f*	—	escenario *m*
pale (E)	blaß	—	pâle	pallido(a)	pálido(a)
pâle (F)	blaß	pale	—	pallido(a)	pálido(a)
pálido (Es)	blaß	pale	pâle	pallido(a)	—
palla (I)	Ball *m*	ball	balle *f*	—	pelota *f*
pallido (I)	blaß	pale	pâle	—	pálido(a)
pallone (I)	Fußball *m*	football	football *m*	—	fútbol *m*
palma (I)	Palme *f*	palmtree	palmier *m*	—	palmera *f*
Palme (D)	—	palmtree	palmier *m*	palma *f*	palmera *f*
palmera (Es)	Palme *f*	palmtree	palmier *m*	palma *f*	—
palmier (F)	Palme *f*	palmtree	—	palma *f*	palmera *f*
palmtree (E)	Palme *f*	—	palmier *m*	palma *f*	palmera *f*
Pampelmuse (D)	—	grapefruit	pamplemousse *m*	pompelmo *m*	pomelo *m*
pamplemousse (F)	Pampelmuse *f*	grapefruit	—	pompelmo *m*	pomelo *m*
pan (E)	Pfanne *f*	—	poêle *f*	padella *f*	sartén *f*
pan (Es)	Brot *n*	bread	pain *m*	pane *m*	—
panadería (Es)	Bäckerei *f*	bakery	boulangerie *f*	panetteria *f*	—
pañal (Es)	Windel *f*	nappy	lange *m*	pannolino *m*	—
pancia (I)	Bauch *m*	stomach	ventre *m*	—	vientre *m*
pane (E)	Scheibe *f*	—	carreau *m*	vetro *m*	cristal *m*
pane (I)	Brot *n*	bread	pain *m*	—	pan *m*

	D	E	F	I	Es
panecillo (Es)	Brötchen n	roll	petit pain m	panino m	—
panetteria (I)	Bäckerei f	bakery	boulangerie f	—	panadería f
panfilo (I)	Jacht f	yacht	yacht m	—	yate m
panic (E)	Panik f	—	panique f	panico m	pánico m
pánico (Es)	Panik f	panic	panique f	panico m	—
panico (I)	Panik f	panic	panique f	—	pánico m
panier (F)	Korb m	basket	—	cesto m	cesta f
Panik (D)	—	panic	panique f	panico m	pánico m
panino (I)	Brötchen n	roll	petit pain m	—	panecillo m
panique (F)	Panik f	panic	—	panico m	pánico m
panna (I)	Sahne f	cream	crème f	—	nata f
Panne (D)	—	breakdown	panne f	panna f	avería f
panne (F)	Panne f	breakdown	—	panna f	avería f
panne (I)	Panne f	breakdown	panne f	—	avería f
panno (I)	Tuch n	cloth	étoffe f	—	paño m
pannolino (I)	Windel f	nappy	lange m	—	pañal m
paño (Es)	Tuch n	cloth	étoffe f	panno m	—
Panorama (D)	—	panorama	panorama m	panorama m	panorama m
panorama (E)	Panorama n	—	panorama m	panorama m	panorama m
panorama (Es)	Panorama n	panorama	panorama m	panorama m	—
panorama (F)	Panorama n	panorama	—	panorama m	panorama m
panorama (I)	Panorama n	panorama	panorama m	—	panorama m
pantalón (Es)	Hose f	trousers	pantalon m	pantaloni m pl	—
pantalon (F)	Hose f	trousers	—	pantaloni m pl	pantalón m
pantaloni (I)	Hose f	trousers	pantalon m	—	pantalón m
Pantoffel (D)	—	slipper	pantoufle f	pantofola f	zapatilla f
pantofola (I)	Pantoffel f	slipper	pantoufle f	—	zapatilla f
pantoufle (F)	Pantoffel f	slipper	—	pantofola f	zapatilla f
pañuelo[1] (Es)	Handtuch n	towel	serviette f	asciugamano m	—
pañuelo[2] (Es)	Taschentuch n	handkerchief	mouchoir m	fazzoletto m	—
pañuelo para el cuello (Es)	Halstuch n	scarf	écharpe f	sciarpa f	—
papagayo (Es)	Papagei m	parrot	perroquet m	pappagallo m	—
Papagei (D)	—	parrot	perroquet m	pappagallo m	papagayo m
papavero (I)	Mohn m	poppy	coquelicot m	—	amapola f
papel (Es)	Papier n	paper	papier m	carta f	—
papelería (Es)	Schreibwaren-handlung f	stationery shop	papeterie f	cartoleria f	—
paper (E)	Papier n	—	papier m	carta f	papel m
papeterie (F)	Schreibwaren-handlung f	stationery shop	—	cartoleria f	papelería f
Papier (D)	—	paper	papier m	carta f	papel m
papier (F)	Papier n	paper	—	carta f	papel m
papillon (F)	Schmetter-ling m	butterfly	—	farfalla f	mariposa f
pappagallo (I)	Papagei m	parrot	perroquet m	—	papagayo m
Pappe (D)	—	cardboard	carton m	cartone m	cartón m
paprica (I)	Paprika f	paprika	paprika m	—	pimentón m
Paprika (D)	—	paprika	paprika m	paprica f	pimentón m
paprika (E)	Paprika f	—	paprika m	paprica f	pimentón m

	D	E	F	I	Es
paprika (F)	Paprika f	paprika	—	paprica f	pimentón m
Pâques (F)	Ostern n	Easter	—	Pasqua f	Pascua f
paquet (F)	Paket n	parcel	—	pacco m	paquete m
paquete (Es)	Paket n	parcel	paquet m	pacco m	—
paquetito (Es)	Päckchen n	small package	petit paquet m	pacchetto m	—
par[1] (Es)	gerade	even	pair(e)	pari	—
par[2] (Es)	Paar n	pair	paire f	paio m	—
par (F)	durch	through	—	per	por
para (Es)	zu	to	de/à	da/di/a	—
para acá (Es)	hierher	over here	par ici	qua	—
parada (Es)	Haltestelle f	stop	arrêt m	fermata f	—
Paradies (D)	—	paradise	paradis m	paradiso m	paraíso m
paradis (F)	Paradies n	paradise	—	paradiso m	paraíso m
paradise (E)	Paradies n	—	paradis m	paradiso m	paraíso m
paradiso (I)	Paradies n	paradise	paradis m	—	paraíso m
para ello (Es)	dafür	for it	pour cela	per questo	—
paragonare (I)	vergleichen	compare	comparer	—	comparar
paragone (I)	Vergleich m	comparison	comparaison f	—	comparación f
paraguas[1] (Es)	Regenschirm m	umbrella	parapluie m	ombrello m	—
paraguas[2] (Es)	Schirm m	umbrella	parapluie m	ombrello m	—
paraíso (Es)	Paradies n	paradise	paradis m	paradiso m	—
paralelo (Es)	parallel	parallel	parallèle	parallelo(a)	—
paralítico (Es)	gelähmt	paralysed	paralysé(e)	paralizzato(a)	—
paralizzato (I)	gelähmt	paralysed	paralysé(e)	—	paralítico
parallel (D)	—	parallel	parallèle	parallelo(a)	paralelo(a)
parallel (E)	parallel	—	parallèle	parallelo(a)	paralelo(a)
parallèle (F)	parallel	parallel	—	parallelo(a)	paralelo(a)
parallelo (I)	parallel	parallel	parallèle	—	paralelo(a)
paralysé (F)	gelähmt	paralysed	—	paralizzato(a)	paralítico
paralysed (E)	gelähmt	—	paralysé(e)	paralizzato(a)	paralítico
parapluie[1] (F)	Regenschirm m	umbrella	—	ombrello m	paraguas m
parapluie[2] (F)	Schirm m	umbrella	—	ombrello m	paraguas m
¿para qué?[1] (Es)	wozu	what for	pourquoi	perché	—
¿para qué?[2] (Es)	wofür	what for	pourquoi	per cui	—
parar (Es)	anhalten	stop	arrêter	fermare	—
parasol (E)	Sonnenschirm m	—	parasol m	ombrellone m	sombrilla f
parasol (F)	Sonnenschirm m	parasol	—	ombrellone m	sombrilla f
parc (F)	Park m	park	—	parco m	parque m
parcel (E)	Paket n	—	paquet m	pacco m	paquete m
parce que (F)	weil	because	—	perché	porque
parcheggiare (I)	parken	park	garer	—	aparcar
parcheggio (I)	Parkplatz m	parking place	parking m	—	plaza de aparcamiento f
parco (I)	Park m	park	parc m	—	parque m
par cœur (F)	auswendig	by heart	—	a memoria	de memoria
pardon (F)	Verzeihung f	forgiveness	—	perdono m	perdón m
pardonner (F)	verzeihen	forgive	—	perdonare	perdonar
parecchi (I)	mehrere	several	plusieurs	—	muchos(as)

	D	E	F	I	Es
parecer (Es)	aussehen	look	avoir l'air	avere l'aspetto	—
parecerse (Es)	ähneln	resemble	ressembler	assomígliare	—
parecido (Es)	ähnlich	similar	semblable	simile	—
pared (Es)	Wand f	wall	mur m	parete f	—
parent[1] (F)	Verwandter m	relative	—	parente m	pariente m
parent[2] (F)	verwandt	related	—	imparentato(a)	emparentado(a)
parente (I)	Verwandter m	relative	parent m	—	pariente m
parents (E)	Eltern pl	—	parents m pl	genitori m pl	padres m pl
parents (F)	Eltern pl	parents	—	genitori m pl	padres m pl
parents-in-law (E)	Schwiegereltern pl	—	beaux-parents m pl	suoceri m pl	suegros m pl
paresseux (F)	faul	lazy	—	pigro(a)	perezoso(a)
parete (I)	Wand f	wall	mur m	—	pared f
parfait (F)	vollkommen	perfect	—	perfetto(a)	perfecto(a)
Parfüm (D)	—	perfume	parfum m	profumo m	perfume m
parfum (F)	Parfüm n	perfume	—	profumo m	perfume m
par hasard (F)	zufällig	by chance	—	per caso	por casualidad
pari (F)	Wette f	bet	—	scommessa f	apuesta f
pari (I)	gerade	even	pair(e)	—	par
par ici[1] (F)	herüber	over	—	da questa parte	a este lado
par ici[2] (F)	hierher	over here	—	qua	para acá
pariente (Es)	Verwandter m	relative	parent m	parente m	—
parier (F)	wetten	bet	—	scommettere	apostar
parir (Es)	gebären	give birth to	mettre au monde	partorire	—
Park (D)	—	park	parc m	parco m	parque m
park[1] (E)	parken	—	garer	parcheggiare	aparcar
park[2] (E)	Park m	—	parc m	parco m	parque m
parken (D)	—	park	garer	parcheggiare	aparcar
Parkett (D)	—	stalls	parquet m	parquet m	entarimado m
parking (F)	Parkplatz m	parking place	—	parcheggio m	plaza de aparcamiento f
parking place (E)	Parkplatz m	—	parking m	parcheggio m	plaza de aparcamiento f
Parkplatz (D)	—	parking place	parking m	parcheggio m	plaza de aparcamiento f
Parkverbot (D)	—	no parking	défense de stationner f	divieto di parcheggio m	estacionamiento prohibido m
parlare[1] (I)	reden	talk	parler	—	hablar
parlare[2] (I)	sprechen	speak	parler	—	hablar
parler[1] (F)	reden	talk	—	parlare	hablar
parler[2] (F)	sprechen	speak	—	parlare	hablar
parola (I)	Wort n	word	mot m	—	palabra f
par principe (F)	grundsätzlich	fundamental	—	basilare	en principio
parque (Es)	Park m	park	parc m	parco m	—
parquet (F)	Parkett n	stalls	—	parquet m	entarimado m
parquet (I)	Parkett n	stalls	parquet m	—	entarimado m
parrain (F)	Pate m	godfather	—	padrino m	padrino m
párroco (Es)	Pfarrer m	priest	curé m	parroco m	—
parroco (I)	Pfarrer m	priest	curé m	—	párroco m
parrot (E)	Papagei m	—	perroquet m	pappagallo m	papagayo m

	D	E	F	I	Es
parruchiere (I)	Friseur *m*	hairdresser	coiffeur *m*	—	peluquero *m*
parsimonioso (I)	sparsam	economical	économe	—	económico(a)
par suite de (F)	infolge	as a result of	—	in seguito a	por
part¹ (E)	scheiden	—	séparer	separare	separar
part² (E)	Teil *m*	—	partie *f*	parte *f*	parte *f*
partager (F)	teilen	share	—	dividere	partir
partager en deux (F)	halbieren	halve	—	dimezzare	dividir por la mitad
parte¹ (Es)	Stück *n*	piece	morceau *m*	pezzo *m*	—
parte² (Es)	Teil *m*	part	partie *f*	parte *f*	—
parte (I)	Teil *m*	part	partie *f*	—	parte *f*
partecipare (I)	teilnehmen	take part	participer	—	participar
Partei (D)	—	party	parti *m*	partito *m*	partido *m*
partenza¹ (I)	Abfahrt *f*	departure	départ *m*	—	salida *f*
partenza² (I)	Abreise *f*	departure	départ *m*	—	salida *f*
partenza³ (I)	Start *m*	start	départ *m*	—	partida *f*
Parterre (D)	—	ground floor	rez-de chaussée *m*	pianterreno *m*	planta baja *f*
parti¹ (F)	fort	away	—	via	lejos
parti² (F)	Partei *f*	party	—	partito *m*	partido *m*
partial (F)	einseitig	one-sided	—	unilaterale	unilateral
participar (Es)	teilnehmen	take part	participer	partecipare	—
participer (F)	teilnehmen	take part	—	partecipare	participar
particolarmente (I)	besonders	especially	surtout	—	sobre todo
partida (Es)	Start *m*	start	départ *m*	partenza *f*	—
partido (Es)	Partei *f*	party	parti *m*	partito *m*	—
partie (F)	Teil *m*	part	—	parte *f*	parte *f*
parting (E)	Abschied *m*	—	adieux *m pl*	addio *m*	despedida *f*
partir¹ (Es)	starten	start	démarrer	partire	—
partir² (Es)	teilen	share	partager	dividere	—
partir (F)	abreisen	leave	—	partire	salir
partir (de) (F)	abfahren	depart	—	partire	salir
partire¹ (I)	abfahren	depart	partir (de)	—	salir
partire² (I)	abreisen	leave	partir	—	salir
partire³ (I)	starten	start	démarrer	—	partir
partire in viaggio (I)	verreisen	go away	partir en voyage	—	irse de viaje
partir en voyage (F)	verreisen	go away	—	partire in viaggio	irse de viaje
partito (I)	Partei *f*	party	parti *m*	—	partido *m*
partly (E)	teilweise	—	en partie	in parte	en parte
partorire (I)	gebären	give birth to	mettre au monde	—	parir
partout (F)	überall	everywhere	—	dappertutto	por todas partes
Party (D)	—	party	fête *f*	festa *f*	fiesta *f*
party¹ (E)	Fest *n*	—	fête *f*	festa *f*	fiesta *f*
party² (E)	Party *f*	—	fête *f*	festa *f*	fiesta *f*
party³ (E)	Partei *f*	—	parti *m*	partito *m*	partido *m*
pas (F)	Schritt *m*	step	—	passo *m*	paso *m*
pasada (Es)	vergangene(r,s)	past	dernier(-ère)	passato(a)	—
pasado¹ (Es)	Vergangenheit *f*	past	passé *m*	passato *m*	—
pasado² (Es)	vorüber	past	passé(e)	passato(a)	—
pasado³ (Es)	vergangen	past	passé(e)	passato(a)	—

	D	E	F	I	Es
pasado⁴ (Es)	vorbei	past	passé(e)	passato(a)	—
pasado de moda (Es)	altmodisch	old-fashioned	démodé(e)	fuori moda	—
pasado mañana (Es)	übermorgen	day after tomorrow	après-demain	dopodomani	—
pasajero¹ (Es)	Fahrgast *m*	passenger	passager *m*	passeggero *m*	—
pasajero² (Es)	Passagier *m*	passenger	passager *m*	passeggero *m*	—
pasajero³ (Es)	vorübergehend	temporary	temporaire	temporaneo	—
pasaporte¹ (Es)	Paß *m*	passport	passeport *m*	passaporto *m*	—
pasaporte² (Es)	Reisepaß *m*	passport	passeport *m*	passaporto *m*	—
pasar¹ (Es)	durchgehen	go through	passer à travers	passare	—
pasar² (Es)	passieren	happen	arriver	succedere	—
pasar³ (Es)	vorbeigehen	pass	passer	passare	—
pasar⁴ (Es)	vergehen	pass by	passer	passare	—
pasar⁵ (Es)	verbringen	spend	passer	passare	—
pasar adelante (Es)	vorangehen	go ahead	marcher devant	andare avanti	—
pasar de mano en mano (Es)	herumreichen	pass around	faire passer	far circolare	—
pasarse sin (Es)	entbehren	do without	passer de, se	fare a meno di	—
Pascua (Es)	Ostern *n*	Easter	Pâques *f pl*	Pasqua *f*	—
Pascua de Pentecostés (Es)	Pfingsten *n*	Whitsun	Pentecôte *f*	Pentecoste *f*	—
pas du tout (F)	keineswegs	not at all	—	non affatto	en modo alguno
paseo (Es)	Spaziergang *m*	walk	promenade *f*	passeggiata *f*	—
pasillo (Es)	Korridor *m*	corridor	corridor *m*	corridoio *m*	—
pasión (Es)	Leidenschaft *f*	passion	passion *f*	passione *f*	—
pas là (F)	weg	away	—	via	fuera
paso¹ (Es)	Durchgang *m*	passage	passage *m*	passaggio *m*	—
paso² (Es)	Durchreise *f*	passing through	passage *m*	transito *m*	—
paso³ (Es)	Durchfahrt *f*	transit	passage *m*	passaggio *m*	—
paso⁴ (Es)	Paß *m*	pass	col *m*	passo *m*	—
paso⁵ (Es)	Schritt *m*	step	pas *m*	passo *m*	—
paso⁶ (Es)	Übergang *m*	crossing	passage *m*	passaggio *m*	—
paso inferior (Es)	Unterführung *f*	subway	passage souterrain *m*	sottopassaggio *m*	—
Pasqua (I)	Ostern *n*	Easter	Pâques *f pl*	—	Pascua *f*
Paß¹ (D)	—	passport	passeport *m*	passaporto *m*	pasaporte *m*
Paß² (D)	—	pass	col *m*	passo *m*	paso *m*
pass¹ (E)	Paß *m*	—	col *m*	passo *m*	paso *m*
pass² (E)	reichen	—	passer	passare	alcanzar
pass³ (E)	vorbeigehen	—	passer	passare	pasar
passage (E)	Durchgang *m*	—	passage *m*	passaggio *m*	paso *m*
passage¹ (F)	Durchfahrt *f*	transit	—	passaggio *m*	paso *m*
passage² (F)	Durchreise *f*	passing through	—	transito *m*	paso *m*
passage³ (F)	Durchgang *m*	passage	—	passaggio *m*	paso *m*
passage⁴ (F)	Übergang *m*	crossing	—	passaggio *m*	paso *m*
passager¹ (F)	Fahrgast *m*	passenger	—	passeggero *m*	pasajero *m*
passager² (F)	Passagier *m*	passenger	—	passeggero *m*	pasajero *m*
passage souterrain (F)	Unterführung *f*	subway	—	sottopassaggio *m*	paso inferior *m*

	D	E	F	I	Es
passaggio¹ (I)	Durchgang *m*	passage	passage *m*	—	paso *m*
passaggio² (I)	Durchfahrt *f*	transit	passage *m*	—	paso *m*
passaggio³ (I)	Übergang *m*	crossing	passage *m*	—	paso *m*
Passagier (D)	—	passenger	passager *m*	passeggero *m*	pasajero *m*
passaporto¹ (I)	Paß *m*	passport	passeport *m*	—	pasaporte *m*
passaporto² (I)	Reisepaß *m*	passport	passeport *m*	—	pasaporte *m*
passare¹ (I)	durchgehen	go through	passer à travers	—	pasar
passare² (I)	reichen	pass	passer	—	alcanzar
passare³ (I)	vorbeigehen	pass	passer	—	pasar
passare⁴ (I)	verbringen	spend	passer	—	pasar
passare⁵ (I)	vergehen	pass by	passer	—	pasar
pass around (E)	herumreichen	—	faire passer	far circolare	pasar de mano en mano
passato¹ (I)	vorüber	past	passé(e)	—	pasado(a)
passato² (I)	vergangen	past	passé(e)	—	pasado(a)
passato³ (I)	vorbei	past	passé(e)	—	pasado(a)
passato⁴ (I)	Vergangenheit *f*	past	passé *m*	—	pasado *m*
passato⁵ (I)	vergangene(r,s)	past	dernier(-ère)	—	pasada(o)
pass by (E)	vergehen	—	passer	passare	pasar
passé¹ (F)	Vergangenheit *f*	past	—	passato *m*	pasado *m*
passé² (F)	vorbei	past	—	passato(a)	pasado(a)
passé³ (F)	vergangen	past	—	passato(a)	pasado(a)
passé⁴ (F)	vorüber	past	—	passato(a)	pasado(a)
passeggero¹ (I)	Fahrgast *m*	passenger	passager *m*	—	pasajero *m*
passeggero² (I)	Passagier *m*	passenger	passager *m*	—	pasajero *m*
passeggiare (I)	spazierengehen	go for a walk	promener, se	—	ir de paseo
passeggiata (I)	Spaziergang *m*	walk	promenade *f*	—	paseo *m*
passen (D)	—	suit	aller bien	stare bene	venir bien
passend (D)	—	suitable	assorti(e)	adatto(a)	apropiado(a)
passenger¹ (E)	Beifahrer *m*	—	passager *m*	passeggero *m*	pasajero *m*
passenger² (E)	Fahrgast *m*	—	passager *m*	passeggero *m*	pasajero *m*
passenger³ (E)	Passagier *m*	—	passager *m*	passeggero *m*	pasajero *m*
passeport¹ (F)	Paß *m*	passport	—	passaporto *m*	pasaporte *m*
passeport² (F)	Reisepaß *m*	passport	—	passaporto *m*	pasaporte *m*
passer¹ (F)	reichen	pass	—	passare	alcanzar
passer² (F)	verbringen	spend	—	passare	pasar
passer³ (F)	vergehen	pass by	—	passare	pasar
passer⁴ (F)	vorbeigehen	pass	—	passare	pasar
passer à travers (F)	durchgehen	go through	—	passare	pasar
passer de, se (F)	entbehren	do without	—	fare a meno di	pasarse sin
passer la nuit (F)	übernachten	stay the night	—	pernottare	pernoctar
passieren (D)	—	happen	arriver	succedere	pasar
passing through (E)	Durchreise *f*	—	passage *m*	transito *m*	paso *m*
passion (E)	Leidenschaft *f*	—	passion *f*	passione *f*	pasión *f*
passion (F)	Leidenschaft *f*	passion	—	passione *f*	pasión *f*
passione (I)	Leidenschaft *f*	passion	passion *f*	—	pasión *f*
passo¹ (I)	Paß *m*	pass	col *m*	—	paso *m*
passo² (I)	Schritt *m*	step	pas *m*	—	paso *m*

	D	E	F	I	Es
pass on a message (E)	ausrichten	—	transmettre	riferire	comunicar
passport¹ (E)	Ausweis *m*	—	pièce d'identité *f*	documento d'identità *m*	documento de identidad *m*
passport² (E)	Paß *m*	—	passeport *m*	passaporto *m*	pasaporte *m*
passport³ (E)	Reisepaß *m*	—	passeport *m*	passaporto *m*	pasaporte *m*
past¹ (E)	vergangen	—	passé(e)	passato(a)	pasado(a)
past² (E)	vergangene(r,s)	—	dernier(-ère)	passato(a)	pasada(o)
past³ (E)	vorbei	—	passé(e)	passato(a)	pasado(a)
past⁴ (E)	vorüber	—	passé(e)	passato(a)	pasado(a)
past⁵ (E)	Vergangenheit *f*	—	passé *m*	passato *m*	pasado *m*
pasta (E)	Teigwaren *pl*	—	pâtes *f pl*	pasta *f*	pastas *f pl*
pasta¹ (I)	Nudeln *pl*	noodles	nouilles *f pl*	—	pastas *f pl*
pasta² (I)	Teig *m*	dough	pâte *f*	—	masa *f*
pasta³ (I)	Teigwaren *pl*	pasta	pâtes *f pl*	—	pastas *f pl*
pasta dentífrica (Es)	Zahnpasta *f*	toothpaste	dentifrice *m*	dentifricio *m*	—
pastas¹ (Es)	Gebäck *n*	pastry	pâtisserie *f*	biscotti *m pl*	—
pastas² (Es)	Nudeln *pl*	noodles	nouilles *f pl*	pasta *f*	—
pastas³ (Es)	Teigwaren *pl*	pasta	pâtes *f pl*	pasta *f*	—
pastel (Es)	Kuchen *m*	cake	gâteau *m*	dolce *m*	—
pastelería (Es)	Konditorei *f*	cake shop	pâtisserie *f*	pasticceria *f*	—
Pastete (D)	—	pie	pâté *m*	vol-au-vent *m*	empanada *f*
pasticceria (I)	Konditorei *f*	cake shop	pâtisserie *f*	—	pastelería *f*
pastilla (Es)	Tablette *f*	tablet	comprimé *m*	compressa *f*	—
pasto (I)	Mahlzeit *f*	meal	repas *m*	—	comida *f*
pastry (E)	Gebäck *n*	—	pâtisserie *f*	biscotti *m pl*	pastas *f pl*
patata (Es)	Kartoffel *f*	potato	pomme de terre *f*	patata *f*	—
patata (I)	Kartoffel *f*	potato	pomme de terre *f*	—	patata *f*
patatas fritas (Es)	Pommes frites *pl*	French fries	frites *f pl*	patate fritte *f pl*	—
patate fritte (I)	Pommes frites *pl*	French fries	frites *f pl*	—	patatas fritas *f pl*
Pate (D)	—	godfather	parrain *m*	padrino *m*	padrino *m*
pâté (F)	Pastete *f*	pie	—	vol-au-vent *m*	empanada *f*
pâte (F)	Teig *m*	dough	—	pasta *f*	masa *f*
patente (I)	Führerschein *m*	driving licence	permis de conduire *m*	—	permiso de conducir *m*
pâtes (F)	Teigwaren *pl*	pasta	—	pasta *f*	pastas *f pl*
patience (E)	Geduld *f*	—	patience *f*	pazienza *f*	paciencia *f*
patience (F)	Geduld *f*	patience	—	pazienza *f*	paciencia *f*
Patient (D)	—	patient	patient *m*	paziente *m*	paciente *m*
patient¹ (E)	geduldig	—	patient(e)	paziente	con paciencia
patient² (E)	Patient *m*	—	patient *m*	paziente *m*	paciente *m*
patient¹ (F)	geduldig	patient	—	paziente	con paciencia
patient² (F)	Patient *m*	patient	—	paziente *m*	paciente *m*
Patin (D)	—	godmother	marraine *f*	madrina *f*	madrina *f*
patio (Es)	Hof *m*	yard	cour *f*	cortile *m*	—
pâtisserie¹ (F)	Gebäck *n*	pastry	—	biscotti *m pl*	pastas *f pl*
pâtisserie² (F)	Konditorei *f*	cake shop	—	pasticceria *f*	pastelería *f*
pato (Es)	Ente *f*	duck	canard *m*	anatra *f*	—
patria (Es)	Heimat *f*	home	patrie *f*	patria *f*	—

	D	E	F	I	Es
patria (I)	Heimat f	home	patrie f	—	patria f
patrie (F)	Heimat f	home	—	patria f	patria f
patron[1] (F)	Chef m	boss	—	capo m	jefe m
patron[2] (F)	Wirt m	landlord	—	oste m	dueño m
pattumiera (I)	Abfalleimer m	bin	poubelle f	—	cubo de la basura m
paura (I)	Angst f	fear	peur f	—	miedo m
pauroso (I)	ängstlich	fearful	peureux(-euse)	—	miedoso(a)
pausa (Es)	Pause f	break	pause f	pausa f	—
pausa (I)	Pause f	break	pause f	—	pausa f
Pause (D)	—	break	pause f	pausa f	pausa f
pause (F)	Pause f	break	—	pausa f	pausa f
pauvre (F)	arm	poor	—	povero(a)	pobre
pavé (F)	Pflaster n	pavement	—	lastricato m	adoquinado m
pavement[1] (E)	Gehweg m	—	trottoir m	marciapiede m	acera f
pavement[2] (E)	Pflaster n	—	pavé m	lastricato m	adoquinado m
pavillon (F)	Flagge f	flag	—	bandiera f	bandera f
pavimento (I)	Fußboden m	floor	sol m	—	suelo m
pavo (Es)	Truthahn m	turkey	dindon m	tacchino m	—
pay[1] (E)	bezahlen	—	payer	pagare	pagar
pay[2] (E)	zahlen	—	payer	pagare	pagar
pay attention (E)	aufpassen	—	faire attention	fare attenzione	prestar atención
pay back (E)	zurückzahlen	—	rembourser	rimborsare	devolver
payer[1] (F)	bezahlen	pay	—	pagare	pagar
payer[2] (F)	zahlen	pay	—	pagare	pagar
payment[1] (E)	Bezahlung f	—	paiement m	pagamento m	pago m
payment[2] (E)	Zahlung f	—	paiement m	pagamento m	pago m
pay off (E)	abbezahlen	—	finir de payer	pagare a rate	pagar a plazos
pays (F)	Land n	land	—	paese m	país m
paysage (F)	Landschaft f	landscape	—	paesaggio m	paisaje m
paysan (F)	Bauer m	farmer	—	contadino m	campesino m
Pays-Bas (F)	Niederlande f	Netherlands	—	Paesi Bassi m pl	los Paìses Bajos m pl
paz (Es)	Friede m	peace	paix f	pace f	—
paziente[1] (I)	geduldig	patient	patient(e)	—	con paciencia
paziente[2] (I)	Patient m	patient	patient m	—	paciente m
pazienza (I)	Geduld f	patience	patience f	—	paciencia f
Pazifik (D)	—	Pacific	Pacifique m	Pacifico m	pacífico m
pazzo[1] (I)	Narr m	fool	fou m	—	loco m
pazzo[2] (I)	verrückt	mad	fou (folle)	—	loco(a)
pea (E)	Erbse f	—	pois m	pisello m	guisante m
peace (E)	Friede m	—	paix f	pace f	paz f
peaceful (E)	friedlich	—	paisible	pacifico	pacífico
peach (E)	Pfirsich m	—	pêche f	pesca f	melocotón m
peak (E)	Gipfel m	—	sommet m	cima f	cumbre f
pear (E)	Birne f	—	poire f	pera f	pera f
pearl (E)	Perle f	—	perle f	perla f	perla f
peatón (Es)	Fußgänger m	pedestrian	piéton m	pedone m	—
peau[1] (F)	Haut f	skin	—	pelle f	piel f

	D	E	F	I	Es
peau² (F)	Schale f	peel	—	buccia f	piel f
pecado (Es)	Sünde f	sin	péché m	peccato m	—
peccato (I)	Sünde f	sin	péché m	—	pecado m
Pech (D)	—	bad luck	malchance f	sfortuna f	mala suerte f
pêche (F)	Pfirsich m	peach	—	pesca f	melocotón m
péché (F)	Sünde f	sin	—	peccato m	pecado m
pêcher¹ (F)	angeln	fish	—	pescare	pescar con caña
pêcher² (F)	fischen	fish	—	pescare	pescar
pêcheur (F)	Fischer m	fisher	—	pescatore m	pescador m
pecho (Es)	Brust f	breast	poitrine f	petto m	—
pecora (I)	Schaf n	sheep	mouton m	—	oveja f
pedazo (Es)	Scherbe f	broken piece	tesson m	coccio m	—
pedestrian (E)	Fußgänger m	—	piéton m	pedone m	peatón m
pedir¹ (Es)	anfordern	request	demander	esigere	—
pedir² (Es)	bestellen	order	commander	ordinare	—
pedone (I)	Fußgänger m	pedestrian	piéton m	—	peatón m
peel¹ (E)	schälen	—	éplucher	sbucciare	pelar
peel² (E)	Schale f	—	peau f	buccia f	piel f
pegar (Es)	kleben	stick	coller	incollare	—
pegno (I)	Pfand n	pledge	gage m	—	prenda f
peigne (F)	Kamm m	comb	—	pettine m	peine m
peigner (F)	kämmen	comb	—	pettinare	peinar
peinado (Es)	Frisur f	hairstyle	coiffure f	pettinatura f	—
peinar (Es)	kämmen	comb	peigner	pettinare	—
peindre¹ (F)	malen	paint	—	dipingere	pintar
peindre² (F)	streichen	paint	—	verniciare	pintar
peine (Es)	Kamm m	comb	peigne m	pettine m	—
peine (F)	Mühe f	effort	—	fatica f	esfuerzo m
peinlich (D)	—	embarrassing	gênant(e)	imbarazzante	desagradable
peintre (F)	Maler m	painter	—	pittore m	pintor m
peinture (F)	Malerei f	painting	—	pittura f	pintura f
pelar (Es)	schälen	peel	éplucher	sbucciare	—
pêle-mêle (F)	durcheinander	in a muddle	—	sottosopra	en desorden
película (Es)	Film m	film	film m	film m	—
peligro (Es)	Gefahr f	danger	danger m	pericolo m	—
peligroso (Es)	gefährlich	dangerous	dangereux(-euse)	pericoloso(a)	—
pelle (F)	Schaufel f	shovel	—	pala f	pala f
pelle (I)	Haut f	skin	peau f	—	piel f
pelliccia (I)	Pelz m	fur	fourrure f	—	piel f
pelo (Es)	Haar n	hair	cheveu m	capello m	—
pelota (Es)	Ball m	ball	balle f	palla f	—
pelouse (F)	Rasen m	lawn	—	prato m	césped m
peluquero (Es)	Friseur m	hairdresser	coiffeur m	parrucchiere m	—
Pelz (D)	—	fur	fourrure f	pelliccia f	piel f
pencil¹ (E)	Bleistift m	—	crayon m	matita f	lápiz m
pencil² (E)	Stift m	—	crayon m	penna f	lápiz m
pendant (F)	während	during	—	durante	durante
pendere (I)	hängen	hang	pendre	—	colgar

	D	E	F	I	Es
pendiente (Es)	Hang *m*	slope	versant *m*	pendio *m*	—
pendio (I)	Hang *m*	slope	versant *m*	—	pendiente *m*
pendre (F)	hängen	hang	—	pendere	colgar
peninsula (E)	Halbinsel *f*	—	presqu'île *f*	penisola *f*	península *f*
península (Es)	Halbinsel *f*	peninsula	presqu'île *f*	penisola *f*	—
penisola (I)	Halbinsel *f*	peninsula	presqu'île *f*	—	península *f*
penna[1] (I)	Feder *f*	pen nib	plume *f*	—	pluma *f*
penna[2] (I)	Stift *m*	pencil	crayon *m*	—	lápiz *m*
penna stilografica (I)	Füller *m*	fountain pen	stylo *m*	—	pluma *f*
pennello (I)	Pinsel *m*	brush	pinceau *m*	—	pincel *m*
pen nib (E)	Feder *f*	—	plume *f*	penna *f*	pluma *f*
penniless (E)	pleite	—	fauché(e)	fallito(a)	sin dinero
pensamiento (Es)	Gedanke *m*	thought	pensée *f*	pensiero *m*	—
pensar[1] (Es)	denken	think	penser	pensare	—
pensar[2] (Es)	überlegen	consider	réfléchir à	riflettere	—
pensare (I)	denken	think	penser	—	pensar
pensée (F)	Gedanke *m*	thought	—	pensiero *m*	pensamiento *m*
penser[1] (F)	denken	think	—	pensare	pensar
penser[2] (F)	meinen	think	—	credere	opinar
pensiero (I)	Gedanke *m*	thought	pensée *f*	—	pensamiento *m*
Pension (D)	—	boarding house	pension *f*	pensione *f*	pensión *f*
pension (E)	Rente *f*	—	retraite *f*	pensione *f*	pensión *f*
pensión[1] (Es)	Pension *f*	boarding house	pension *f*	pensione *f*	—
pensión[2] (Es)	Rente *f*	pension	retraite *f*	pensione *f*	—
pension (F)	Pension *f*	boarding house	—	pensione *f*	pensión *f*
pensionato (I)	Rentner *m*	pensioner	retraité *m*	—	pensionista *m*
pensión completa (Es)	Vollpension *f*	full board	pension complète *f*	pensione completa *f*	—
pension complète (F)	Vollpension *f*	full board	—	pensione completa *f*	pensión completa *f*
pensione[1] (I)	Pension *f*	boarding house	pension *f*	—	pensión *f*
pensione[2] (I)	Ruhestand *m*	retirement	retraite *f*	—	retiro *m*
pensione[3] (I)	Rente *f*	pension	retraite *f*	—	pensión *f*
pensione completa (I)	Vollpension *f*	full board	pension complète *f*	—	pensión completa *f*
pensioner (E)	Rentner *m*	—	retraité *m*	pensionato *m*	pensionista *m*
pensionista (Es)	Rentner *m*	pensioner	retraité *m*	pensionato *m*	—
Pentecoste (I)	Pfingsten *n*	Whitsun	Pentecôte *f*	—	Pascua de Pentecostés *f*
Pentecôte (F)	Pfingsten *n*	Whitsun	—	Pentecoste *f*	Pascua de Pentecostés *f*
pentirsi (I)	bereuen	regret	regretter	—	arrepentirse
pentola[1] (I)	Kochtopf *m*	saucepan	casserole *f*	—	olla *f*
pentola[2] (I)	Topf *m*	pot	casserole *f*	—	olla *f*
penúltimo (Es)	vorletzte(r,s)	one before last	avant-dernier(-ère)	penultimo(a)	—
penultimo (I)	vorletzte(r,s)	one before last	avant-dernier(-ère)	—	penúltima(o)
people[1] (E)	Leute *pl*	—	gens *m pl*	gente *f*	gente *f*
people[2] (E)	Volk *n*	—	peuple *m*	popolo *m*	pueblo *m*
pepe (I)	Pfeffer *m*	pepper	poivre *m*	—	pimienta *f*

	D	E	F	I	Es
pepino (Es)	Gurke f	cucumber	concombre m	cetriolo m	—
pepper (E)	Pfeffer m	—	poivre m	pepe m	pimienta f
pequeño[1] (Es)	gering	slight	minime	poco(a)	—
pequeño[2] (Es)	klein	small/little	petit(e)	piccolo(a)	—
pequeño burgués (Es)	spießig	bourgeois	bourgeois(e)	da piccolo(a) borghese m	—
per[1] (I)	durch	through	par	—	por
per[2] (I)	für	for	pour	—	por/para
pera (Es)	Birne f	pear	poire f	pera f	—
pera (I)	Birne f	pear	poire f	—	pera f
per affari (I)	geschäftlich	on business	d'affaires	—	comercial
per caso (I)	zufällig	by chance	par hasard	—	por casualidad
percent (E)	Prozent n	—	pour cent	percentuale f	por ciento m
percentuale (I)	Prozent n	percent	pour cent	—	por ciento m
perché[1] (I)	denn	for/than	car	—	pues/porque
perché[2] (I)	weil	because	parce que	—	porque
perché[3] (I)	weshalb	why	pourquoi	—	por qué
perché[4] (I)	warum	why	pourquoi	—	por qué
perché[5] (I)	wozu	what for	pourquoi	—	para qué
perció (I)	deshalb	therefore	c'est pourquoi	—	por eso
per cui (I)	wofür	what for	pourquoi	—	para qué
perder[1] (Es)	einbüßen	lose	perdre	perdere	—
perder[2] (Es)	versäumen	miss	manquer	perdere	—
perder[3] (Es)	verlieren	lose	perdre	perdere	—
perdere[1] (I)	einbüßen	lose	perdre	—	perder
perdere[2] (I)	versäumen	miss	manquer	—	perder
perdere[3] (I)	verlegen	mislay	égarer	—	extraviar
perdere[4] (I)	verlieren	lose	perdre	—	perder
perderse (Es)	verlaufen, sich	get lost	perdre, se	perdersi	—
perdersi (I)	verlaufen, sich	get lost	perdre, se	—	perderse
pérdida (Es)	Verlust m	loss	perte f	perdita f	—
perdita (I)	Verlust m	loss	perte f		pérdida f
perdón (Es)	Verzeihung f	forgiveness	pardon m	perdono m	—
perdonar (Es)	verzeihen	forgive	pardonner	perdonare	—
perdonare (I)	verzeihen	forgive	pardonner	—	perdonar
perdono (I)	Verzeihung f	forgiveness	pardon m	—	perdón m
perdre[1] (F)	einbüßen	lose	—	perdere	perder
perdre[2] (F)	verlieren	lose	—	perdere	perder
perdre, se (F)	verlaufen, sich	get lost	—	perdersi	perderse
père (F)	Vater m	father	—	padre m	padre m
perezoso (Es)	faul	lazy	paresseux(-euse)	pigro(a)	—
perfect (E)	vollkommen	—	parfait(e)	perfetto(a)	perfecto(a)
perfecto (Es)	vollkommen	perfect	parfait(e)	perfetto(a)	—
perferire (I)	bevorzugen	prefer	préférer	—	preferir
perfetto (I)	vollkommen	perfect	parfait(e)	—	perfecto(a)
perfino (I)	sogar	even	même	—	incluso
performance[1] (E)	Aufführung f	—	représentation f	recita f	representación f
performance[2] (E)	Vorstellung f	—	représentation f	rappresentazione f	representación f

	D	E	F	I	Es
perfume (E)	Parfüm *n*	—	parfum *m*	profumo *m*	perfume *m*
perfume (Es)	Parfüm *n*	perfume	parfum *m*	profumo *m*	—
pericolo (I)	Gefahr *f*	danger	danger *m*	—	peligro *m*
pericoloso (I)	gefährlich	dangerous	dangereux(-euse)	—	peligroso(a)
periódico (Es)	Zeitung *f*	newspaper	journal *m*	giornale *m*	—
periodista (Es)	Journalist *m*	journalist	journaliste *m*	giornalista *m*	—
perjudicar (Es)	benachteiligen	disadvantage	désavantager	svantaggiare	—
perla (Es)	Perle *f*	pearl	perle *f*	perla *f*	—
perla (I)	Perle *f*	pearl	perle *f*	—	perla *f*
Perle (D)	—	pearl	perle *f*	perla *f*	perla *f*
perle (F)	Perle *f*	pearl	—	perla *f*	perla *f*
per lo meno (I)	zumindest	at least	au moins	—	por lo menos
permanent (F)	ständig	permanent	—	fisso(a)	permanente
permanent (E)	ständig	—	permanent(e)	fisso(a)	permanente
permanente (Es)	ständig	permanent	permanent(e)	fisso(a)	—
permesso[1] (I)	Erlaubnis *f*	permission	permission *f*	—	permiso *m*
permesso[2] (I)	Genehmigung *f*	authorization	autorisation *f*	—	permiso *m*
permesso[3] (I)	zulässig	permissable	permis(e)	—	permitido(a)
permettere[1] (I)	erlauben	allow	permettre	—	permitir
permettere[2] (I)	gestatten	allow	permettre	—	permitir
permettere[3] (I)	zulassen	permit	admettre	—	permitir
permettre[1] (F)	erlauben	allow	—	permettere	permitir
permettre[2] (F)	gestatten	allow	—	permettere	permitir
permis (F)	zulässig	permissable	—	permesso	permitido(a)
permis de conduire (F)	Führerschein *m*	driving licence	—	patente *f*	permiso de conducir *m*
permiso[1] (Es)	Erlaubnis *f*	permission	permission *f*	permesso *m*	—
permiso[2] (Es)	Genehmigung *f*	authorization	autorisation *f*	permesso *m*	—
permiso de conducir (Es)	Führerschein *m*	driving licence	permis de conduire *m*	patente *f*	—
permissable (E)	zulässig	—	permis(e)	permesso(a)	permitido(a)
permission (E)	Erlaubnis *f*	—	permission *f*	permesso *m*	permiso *m*
permission (F)	Erlaubnis *f*	permission	—	permesso *m*	permiso *m*
permit (E)	zulassen	—	admettre	permettere	permitir
permitido (Es)	zulässig	permissable	permis(e)	permesso(a)	—
permitir[1] (Es)	erlauben	allow	permettre	permettere	—
permitir[2] (Es)	gestatten	allow	permettre	permettere	—
permitir[3] (Es)	genehmigen	approve	autoriser	approvare	—
permitir[4] (Es)	zulassen	permit	admettre	permettere	—
per niente (I)	umsonst	for nothing	en vain	—	en vano
pernoctación (Es)	Übernachtung *f*	overnight stay	logement pour une nuit *m*	pernottamento *m*	—
pernoctar (Es)	übernachten	stay the night	passer la nuit	pernottare	—
pernottamento (I)	Übernachtung *f*	overnight stay	logement pour une nuit *m*	—	pernoctación *f*
pernottare (I)	übernachten	stay the night	passer la nuit	—	pernoctar
pero (Es)	aber	but	mais	ma	—
per questo (I)	dafür	for it	pour cela	—	para ello
perro (Es)	Hund *m*	dog	chien *m*	cane *m*	—
perroquet (F)	Papagei *m*	parrot	—	pappagallo *m*	papagayo *m*

	D	E	F	I	Es
perseguir (Es)	verfolgen	pursue	poursuivre	inseguire	—
Person (D)	—	person	personne f	persona f	persona f
person (E)	Person f	—	personne f	persona f	persona f
persona¹ (Es)	Mensch m	human being	homme m	essere umano m	—
persona² (Es)	Person f	person	personne f	persona f	—
persona (I)	Person f	person	personne f	—	persona f
Personal (D)	—	personnel	personnel m	personale m	personal m
personal (E)	persönlich	—	personnel(le)	personale	en persona
personal (Es)	Personal n	personnel	personnel m	personale m	—
Personalausweis (D)	—	identity card	carte d'identité f	carta d'identitá f	documento de identidad m
personale¹ (I)	persönlich	personal	personnel(le)	—	en persona
personale² (I)	Personal n	personnel	personnel m	—	personal m
persönlich (D)	—	personal	personnel(le)	personale	en persona
personne (F)	Person f	person	—	persona f	persona f
personnel (E)	Personal n	—	personnel m	personale m	personal m
personnel¹ (F)	Personal n	personnel	—	personale m	personal m
personnel² (F)	persönlich	personal	—	personale	en persona
per strada (I)	unterwegs	on the way	en route	—	de camino
persuader (F)	überreden	convince	—	persuadere	persuadir
persuadere (I)	überreden	convince	persuader	—	persuadir
persuadir (Es)	überreden	convince	persuader	persuadere	—
perte (F)	Verlust m	loss	—	perdita f	pérdida f
per te (I)	deinetwegen	for your sake	pour toi	—	por ti
pertenecer (Es)	gehören	belong	appartenir	appartenere	—
pesado (Es)	schwer	heavy	lourd(e)	pesante	—
pésame (Es)	Beileid n	condolence	condoléances f pl	condoglianza f	—
pesante (I)	schwer	heavy	lourd(e)	—	pesado(a)
pesar¹ (Es)	Kummer m	grief	chagrin m	dolore m	—
pesar² (Es)	wiegen	weigh	peser	pesare	—
pesare (I)	wiegen	weigh	peser	—	pesar
pesca (I)	Pfirsich m	peach	pêche f	—	melocotón m
pescador (Es)	Fischer m	fisher	pêcheur m	pescatore m	—
pescar (Es)	fischen	fish	pêcher	pescare	—
pescar con caña (Es)	angeln	fish	pêcher	pescare	—
pescare¹ (I)	angeln	fish	pêcher	—	pescar con caña
pescare² (I)	fischen	fish	pêcher	—	pescar
pescatore (I)	Fischer m	fisher	pêcheur m	—	pescador m
pesce (I)	Fisch m	fish	poisson m	—	pez m
pescecane (I)	Hai m	shark	requin m	—	tiburón m
peser (F)	wiegen	weigh	—	pesare	pesar
peso¹ (Es)	Gewicht n	weight	poids m	peso m	—
peso² (Es)	Last f	load	charge f	carico m	—
peso (I)	Gewicht n	weight	poids m	—	peso m
pestaña (Es)	Wimper f	eyelash	cil m	ciglia f	—
pestare (I)	treten	step	mettre le pied sur	—	pisar
petit (F)	klein	small/little	—	piccolo	pequeño(a)
petit-déjeuner (F)	Frühstück n	breakfast	—	colazione f	desayuno m

	D	E	F	I	Es
petite-fille (F)	Enkelin *f*	granddaughter	—	nipote *f*	nieta *f*
petit-enfant (F)	Enkelkind *n*	grandchild	—	nipote *m/f*	nieto *m*
petit-fils (F)	Enkel *m*	grandson	—	nipote *m*	nieto *m*
petit pain (F)	Brötchen *n*	roll	—	panino *m*	panecillo *m*
petit paquet (F)	Päckchen *n*	small package	—	pacchetto *m*	paquetito *m*
petrol (E)	Benzin *n*	—	essence *f*	benzina	gasolina *f*
pétrole (F)	Erdöl *n*	oil	—	petrolio *m*	petróleo *m*
petróleo (Es)	Erdöl *n*	oil	pétrole *m*	petrolio *m*	—
petrolio (I)	Erdöl *n*	oil	pétrole *m*	—	petróleo *m*
pettinare (I)	kämmen	comb	peigner	—	peinar
pettinatura (I)	Frisur *f*	hairstyle	coiffure *f*	—	peinado *m*
pettine (I)	Kamm *m*	comb	peigne *m*	—	peine *m*
petto (I)	Brust *f*	breast	poitrine *f*	—	pecho *m*
peu (F)	wenige	few	—	pochi	pocos(as)
peu aimable (F)	unfreundlich	unfriendly	—	sgarbato(a)	descortés
peu de (F)	wenig	little	—	poco(a)	poco(a)
peuple (F)	Volk *n*	people	—	popolo *m*	pueblo *m*
peur (F)	Angst *f*	fear	—	paura *f*	miedo *m*
peureux (F)	ängstlich	fearful	—	pauroso(a)	miedoso(a)
peut-être (F)	vielleicht	maybe	—	forse	tal vez
pez (Es)	Fisch *m*	fish	poisson *m*	pesce *m*	—
pezzo (I)	Stück *n*	piece	morceau *m*	—	parte *f*
Pfand (D)	—	pledge	gage *m*	pegno *m*	prenda *f*
Pfanne (D)	—	pan	poêle *f*	padella *f*	sartén *f*
Pfarrer (D)	—	priest	curé *m*	parroco *m*	párroco *m*
Pfeffer (D)	—	pepper	poivre *m*	pepe *m*	pimienta *f*
Pfeife[1] (D)	—	whistle	sifflet *m*	fischietto *m*	silbato *m*
Pfeife[2] (D)	—	pipe	pipe *f*	pipa *f*	pipa *f*
Pfeil (D)	—	arrow	flèche *f*	freccia *f*	flecha *f*
Pferd (D)	—	horse	cheval *m*	cavallo *m*	caballo *m*
Pfingsten (D)	—	Whitsun	Pentecôte *f*	Pentecoste *f*	Pascua de Pentecostés *f*
Pfirsich (D)	—	peach	pêche *f*	pesca *f*	melocotón *m*
Pflanze (D)	—	plant	plante *f*	pianta *f*	planta *f*
pflanzen (D)	—	plant	planter	piantare	plantar
Pflaster[1] (D)	—	plaster	emplâtre *m*	cerotto *m*	esparadrapo *m*
Pflaster[2] (D)	—	pavement	pavé *m*	lastricato *m*	adoquinado *m*
Pflaume (D)	—	plum	prune *f*	prugna *f*	ciruela *f*
Pflege (D)	—	care	soins *m pl*	cura *f*	aseo *m*
pflegen (D)	—	look after	soigner	curare	cuidar
Pflicht (D)	—	duty	devoir *m*	dovere *m*	obligación *f*
pflücken (D)	—	pick	cueillir	cogliere	coger
Pförtner (D)	—	porter	concierge *m*	portiere *m*	portero *m*
Pfund (D)	—	pound	livre *f*	mezzo chilo *m*	libra *f*
Pfütze (D)	—	puddle	flaque *f*	pozzanghera *f*	charco *m*
pharmacie (F)	Apotheke *f*	chemist's	—	farmacia *f*	farmacia *f*
phone book (E)	Telefonbuch *n*	—	annuaire du téléphone *m*	elenco telefonico *m*	guía telefónica *f*

	D	E	F	I	Es
phone box (E)	Telefonzelle f	—	cabine téléphonique f	cabina telefonica f	cabina de teléfono f
phone call[1] (E)	Telefongespräch n	—	communication téléphonique f	conversazione telefonica f	conversación telefónica f
phone call[2] (E)	Telefonanruf m	—	coup de téléphone m	telefonata f	llamada telefónica f
phone number (E)	Telefonnummer f	—	numéro de téléphone m	numero telefonico m	número de teléfono m
phoque (F)	Robbe f	seal	—	foca f	foca f
photo (E)	Foto n	—	photo f	foto f	foto f
photo (F)	Foto n	photo	—	foto f	foto f
photocopie (F)	Fotokopie f	photocopy	—	fotocopia f	fotocopia f
photocopy (E)	Fotokopie f	—	photocopie f	fotocopia f	fotocopia f
photograph (E)	aufnehmen	—	photographier	fotografare	fotografiar
photographie (F)	Aufnahme f	photograph	—	fotografia f	fotografía f
photographier[1] (F)	aufnehmen	photograph	—	fotografare	fotografiar
photographier[2] (F)	fotografieren	take pictures	—	fotografare	fotografiar
photographier[3] (F)	knipsen	take a snap	—	scattare una foto	hacer una foto
phrase (F)	Satz m	sentence	—	frase f	oración f
piacere[1] (I)	Belieben n	will	plaisir m	—	placer m
piacere[2] (I)	gefallen	please	plaire	—	gustar
piacere[3] (I)	Genuß m	pleasure	plaisir m	—	deleite m
piacere[4] (I)	Lust f	delight	plaisir m	—	ganas f pl
piacere[5] (I)	mögen	like	aimer	—	querer
piacere[6] (I)	schmecken	taste	sentir	—	gustar
pianeta (I)	Planet m	planet	planète f	—	planeta m
piangere (I)	weinen	cry	pleurer	—	llorar
piano (E)	Klavier n	—	piano m	pianoforte m	piano m
piano (Es)	Klavier n	piano	piano m	pianoforte m	—
piano (F)	Klavier n	piano	—	pianoforte m	piano m
piano[1] (I)	eben	even	plan(e)	—	plano
piano[2] (I)	Etage f	floor	étage m	—	piso m
pianoforte (I)	Klavier n	piano	piano m	—	piano m
pianta (I)	Pflanze f	plant	plante f	—	planta f
piantare (I)	pflanzen	plant	planter	—	plantar
pianterreno[1] (I)	Erdgeschoß n	ground floor	rez-de-chaussée m	—	piso bajo m
pianterreno[2] (I)	Parterre n	ground floor	rez-de chaussée m	—	planta baja f
pianura (I)	Ebene f	plain	plaine f	—	llanura f
piattino (I)	Untertasse f	saucer	soucoupe f	—	platillo m
piatto[1] (I)	flach	flat	plat(e)	—	llano(a)
piatto[2] (I)	Gericht n	dish	plat m	—	comida f
piatto[3] (I)	Teller m	plate	assiette f	—	plato m
piazza (I)	Platz m	place	place f	—	plaza f
picante (Es)	scharf	hot	épicé(e)	piccante	—
picar[1] (Es)	jucken	itch	démanger	prudere	—
picar[2] (Es)	stechen	prick	piquer	pungere	—
piccante (I)	scharf	hot	épicé(e)	—	picante
piccolo (I)	klein	small/little	petit(e)	—	pequeño(a)
pick (E)	pflücken	—	cueillir	cogliere	coger
Picknick (D)	—	picnic	pique-nique m	picnic m	picnic m

	D	E	F	I	Es
pick up (E)	abholen	—	aller chercher	andare a prendere	recoger
picnic (E)	Picknick *n*	—	pique-nique *m*	picnic *m*	picnic *m*
picnic (Es)	Picknick *n*	picnic	pique-nique *m*	picnic *m*	—
picnic (I)	Picknick *n*	picnic	pique-nique *m*	—	picnic *m*
picture (E)	Bild *n*	—	image *f*	immagine *f*	cuadro *m*
picture magazine (E)	Illustrierte *f*	—	illustré *m*	rivista *f*	revista
picturesque (E)	malerisch	—	pittoresque	pittoresco(a)	pintoresco(a)
pie (E)	Pastete *f*	—	pâté *m*	vol-au-vent *m*	empanada *f*
pie (Es)	Fuß *m*	foot	pied *m*	piede *m*	—
piece (E)	Stück *n*	—	morceau *m*	pezzo *m*	parte *f*
pièce (F)	Raum *m*	room	—	stanza *f*	habitación *f*
pièce de monnaie (F)	Münze *f*	coin	—	moneta *f*	moneda *f*
pièce de théâtre (F)	Theaterstück *n*	play	—	opera teatrale *f*	pieza de teatro *f*
pièce d'identité (F)	Ausweis *m*	passport	—	documento d'identità *m*	documento de identidad *m*
pied (F)	Fuß *m*	foot	—	piede *m*	pie *m*
piede (I)	Fuß *m*	foot	pied *m*	—	pie *m*
piedra (Es)	Stein *m*	stone	pierre *f*	sasso *m*	—
piegare (I)	biegen	bend	plier	—	doblar
piel[1] (Es)	Haut *f*	skin	peau *f*	pelle *f*	—
piel[2] (Es)	Pelz *m*	fur	fourrure *f*	pelliccia *f*	—
pieno (I)	voll	full	plein(e)	—	lleno(a)
pieno di successi (I)	erfolgreich	successful	avec succès	—	afortunado(a)
pieno zeppo (I)	überfüllt	crowded	bondé	—	abarrotado(a)
pierna (Es)	Bein *n*	leg	jambe *f*	gamba *f*	—
pierre (F)	Stein *m*	stone	—	sasso *m*	piedra *f*
piéton (F)	Fußgänger *m*	pedestrian	—	pedone *m*	peatón *m*
pieux (F)	fromm	pious	—	devoto(a)	religioso(a)
pieza de teatro (Es)	Theaterstück *n*	play	pièce de théâtre *f*	opera teatrale *f*	—
pig (E)	Schwein *n*	—	cochon *m*	maiale *m*	cerdo *m*
pigro (I)	faul	lazy	paresseux(-euse)	—	perezoso(a)
píldora (Es)	Pille *f*	pill	pilule *f*	pillola *f*	—
pill (E)	Pille *f*	—	pilule *f*	pillola *f*	píldora *f*
pillar (E)	Säule *f*	—	colonne *f*	colonna *f*	columna *f*
Pille (D)	—	pill	pilule *f*	pillola *f*	píldora *f*
piller (F)	plündern	loot	—	saccheggiare	desvalijar
pillola (I)	Pille *f*	pill	pilule *f*	—	píldora *f*
pillow (E)	Kopfkissen *n*	—	oreiller *m*	guanciale *m*	almohada *f*
pilule (F)	Pille *f*	pill	—	pillola *f*	píldora *f*
Pilz (D)	—	mushroom	champignon *m*	fungo *m*	hongo *m*
pimentón (Es)	Paprika *f*	paprika	paprika *m*	paprica *f*	—
pimienta (Es)	Pfeffer *m*	pepper	poivre *m*	pepe *m*	—
piña (Es)	Ananas *f*	pineapple	ananas *m*	ananas *m*	—
pinceau (F)	Pinsel *m*	brush	—	pennello *m*	pincel *m*
pincel (Es)	Pinsel *m*	brush	pinceau *m*	pennello *m*	—
pineapple (E)	Ananas *f*	—	ananas *m*	ananas *m*	piña *f*
ping-pong (F)	Tischtennis *n*	tabletennis	—	tennis da tavolo *m*	tenis de mesa *m*

	D	E	F	I	Es
pink (E)	rosa	—	rose	rosa	de color rosa
Pinsel (D)	—	brush	pinceau *m*	pennello *m*	pincel *m*
pintar¹ (Es)	malen	paint	peindre	dipingere	—
pintar² (Es)	streichen	paint	peindre	verniciare	—
pintor (Es)	Maler *m*	painter	peintre *m*	pittore *m*	—
pintoresco (Es)	malerisch	picturesque	pittoresque	pittoresco(a)	—
pintura (Es)	Malerei *f*	painting	peinture *f*	pittura *f*	—
pioggia (I)	Regen *m*	rain	pluie *f*	—	lluvia *f*
pious (E)	fromm	—	pieux(-euse)	devoto(a)	religioso(a)
piovere (I)	regnen	rain	pleuvoir	—	llover
pip (E)	Kern *m*	—	noyau *m*	nocciolo	hueso *m*
pipa (Es)	Pfeife *f*	pipe	pipe *f*	pipa *f*	—
pipa (I)	Pfeife *f*	pipe	pipe *f*	—	pipa *f*
pipe¹ (E)	Leitung *f*	—	tuyau *m*	conduttura *f*	tubería *f*
pipe² (E)	Pfeife *f*	—	pipe *f*	pipa *f*	pipa *f*
pipe (F)	Pfeife *f*	pipe	—	pipa *f*	pipa *f*
pique-nique (F)	Picknick *n*	picnic	—	picnic *m*	picnic *m*
piquer (F)	stechen	prick	—	pungere	picar
piqûre (F)	Spritze *f*	injection	—	iniezione *f*	inyección *f*
piragua (Es)	Paddelboot *n*	canoe	canoë *m*	canoa *f*	—
pirogue (F)	Paddelboot *n*	canoe	—	canoa *f*	piragua *f*
pisar (Es)	treten	step	mettre le pied sur	pestare	—
piscina (Es)	Schwimmbad *n*	swimming pool	piscine *f*	piscina *f*	—
piscina (I)	Schwimmbad *n*	swimming pool	piscine *f*	—	piscina *f*
piscina al aire libre (Es)	Freibad *n*	open-air swimming pool	piscine en plein air *f*	piscina all'aperto *f*	—
piscina all'aperto (I)	Freibad *n*	open-air swimming pool	piscine en plein air *f*	—	piscina al aire libre *f*
piscina coperta (I)	Hallenbad *n*	indoor swimming pool	piscine *f*	—	piscina cubierta *f*
piscina cubierta (Es)	Hallenbad *n*	indoor swimming pool	piscine *f*	piscina coperta *f*	—
piscine¹ (F)	Hallenbad *n*	indoor swimming pool	—	piscina coperta *f*	piscina cubierta *f*
piscine² (F)	Schwimmbad *n*	swimming pool	—	piscina *f*	piscina *f*
piscine en plein air (F)	Freibad *n*	open-air swimming pool	—	piscina all'aperto *f*	piscina al aire libre *f*
pisello (I)	Erbse *f*	pea	pois *m*	—	guisante *m*
piso¹ (Es)	Etage *f*	floor	étage *m*	piano *m*	—
piso² (Es)	Wohnung *f*	flat	appartement *m*	appartamento *m*	—
piso bajo (Es)	Erdgeschoß *n*	ground floor	rez-de-chaussée *m*	pianterreno *m*	—
pistol (E)	Pistole *f*	—	pistolet *m*	pistola *f*	pistola *f*
pistola (Es)	Pistole *f*	pistol	pistolet *m*	pistola *f*	—
pistola (I)	Pistole *f*	pistol	pistolet *m*	—	pistola *f*
Pistole (D)	—	pistol	pistolet *m*	pistola *f*	pistola *f*
pistolet (F)	Pistole *f*	pistol	—	pistola *f*	pistola *f*
pittore (I)	Maler *m*	painter	peintre *m*	—	pintor *m*
pittoresco (I)	malerisch	picturesque	pittoresque	—	pintoresco(a)
pittoresque (F)	malerisch	picturesque	—	pittoresco(a)	pintoresco(a)
pittura (I)	Malerei *f*	painting	peinture *f*	—	pintura *f*
pity¹ (E)	bemitleiden	—	plaindre	compatire	compadecerse de

	D	E	F	I	Es
pity² (E)	Mitleid *n*	—	compassion *f*	compassione *f*	compasión *f*
più¹ (I)	mehr	more	plus	—	más
più² (I)	plus	plus	plus	—	más
più ampio (I)	weiter	further	plus éloigné(e)	—	adelante
piuma (I)	Feder *f*	feather	plume *f*	—	pluma *f*
piú tardi (I)	später	later	plus tard	—	más tarde
piuttosto (I)	lieber	rather	mieux	—	más bien
più vecchio (I)	ältere(r,s)	elder	aîné(e)	—	mayor
place¹ (E)	Ort *m*	—	endroit *m*	luogo *m*	lugar *m*
place² (E)	Platz *m*	—	place *f*	piazza *f*	plaza *f*
place³ (E)	Stelle *f*	—	place *f*	posto *m*	puesto *m*
place⁴ (E)	stellen	—	mettre	mettere	colocar
place¹ (F)	Platz *m*	place	—	piazza *f*	plaza *f*
place² (F)	Stelle *f*	place	—	posto *m*	puesto *m*
place assise (F)	Sitzplatz *m*	seat	—	posto a sedere *m*	asiento *m*
placer¹ (Es)	Belieben *n*	will	plaisir *m*	piacere *m*	—
placer² (Es)	Vergnügen *n*	pleasure	plaisir *m*	divertimento *m*	—
plage (F)	Strand *m*	beach	—	spiaggia *f*	playa *f*
plain (E)	Ebene *f*	—	plaine *f*	pianura *f*	llanura *f*
plaindre (F)	bemitleiden	pity	—	compatire	compadecerse de
plaindre de, se¹ (F)	beklagen	deplore	—	lamentare	quejarse
plaindre de, se² (F)	reklamieren	complain	—	reclamare	reclamar
plaindre, se (F)	beschweren, sich	complain	—	lamentarsi	quejarse
plaine (F)	Ebene *f*	plain	—	pianura *f*	llanura *f*
plainte¹ (F)	Beschwerde *f*	complaint	—	reclamo *m*	reclamación *f*
plainte² (F)	Klage *f*	complaint	—	lamento *m*	lamento *m*
plaire (F)	gefallen	please	—	piacere	gustar
plaisanter (F)	spaßen	joke	—	scherzare	bromear
plaisanterie¹ (F)	Scherz *m*	joke	—	scherzo *m*	broma *f*
plaisanterie² (F)	Witz *m*	joke	—	barzelletta *f*	chiste *m*
plaisir¹ (F)	Belieben *n*	will	—	piacere *m*	placer *m*
plaisir² (F)	Genuß *m*	pleasure	—	piacere *m*	deleite *m*
plaisir³ (F)	Lust *f*	delight	—	piacere *m*	ganas *f pl*
plaisir⁴ (F)	Spaß *m*	fun	—	scherzo *m*	broma *f*
plaisir⁵ (F)	Vergnügen *n*	pleasure	—	divertimento *m*	placer *m*
plait (E)	Zopf *m*	—	natte *f*	treccia *f*	trenza *f*
Plakat (D)	—	poster	affiche *f*	affisso *m*	cartel *m*
Plan (D)	—	plan	plan *m*	progetto *m*	plan *m*
plan¹ (E)	planen	—	projeter	progettare	planear
plan² (E)	Plan *m*	—	plan *m*	progetto *m*	plan *m*
plan (Es)	Plan *m*	plan	plan *m*	progetto *m*	—
plan¹ (F)	eben	even	—	piano(a)	plano(a)
plan² (F)	Plan *m*	plan	—	progetto *m*	plan *m*
plancha (Es)	Bügeleisen *n*	iron	fer à repasser *m*	ferro da stiro *m*	—
planchar (Es)	bügeln	iron	repasser	stirare	—
planear (Es)	planen	plan	projeter	progettare	—
planen (D)	—	plan	projeter	progettare	planear
Planet (D)	—	planet	planète *f*	pianeta *m*	planeta *m*

	D	E	F	I	Es
planet (E)	Planet *m*	—	planète *f*	pianeta *m*	planeta *m*
planeta (Es)	Planet *m*	planet	planète *f*	pianeta *m*	—
planète (F)	Planet *m*	planet	—	pianeta *m*	planeta *m*
plano (Es)	eben	even	plan(e)	piano(a)	—
plant¹ (E)	Anlage *f*	—	construction *f*	impianto *m*	establecimiento *m*
plant² (E)	Pflanze *f*	—	plante *f*	pianta *f*	planta *f*
plant³ (E)	pflanzen	—	planter	piantare	plantar
planta (Es)	Pflanze *f*	plant	plante *f*	pianta *f*	—
planta baja (Es)	Parterre *n*	ground floor	rez-de chaussée *m*	pianterreno *m*	—
plantar (Es)	pflanzen	plant	planter	piantare	—
plante (F)	Pflanze *f*	plant	—	pianta *f*	planta *f*
planter (F)	pflanzen	plant	—	piantare	plantar
plaque d'immatriculation (F)	Nummernschild *n*	number plate	—	targa *f*	matrícula *f*
plaster (E)	Pflaster *n*	—	emplâtre *m*	cerotto *m*	esparadrapo *m*
plastic (E)	Plastik *n*	—	plastique *m*	plastica *f*	plástico *m*
plastica (I)	Plastik *n*	plastic	plastique *m*	—	plástico *m*
plástico (Es)	Plastik *n*	plastic	plastique *m*	plastica *f*	—
Plastik (D)	—	plastic	plastique *m*	plastica *f*	plástico *m*
plastique (F)	Plastik *n*	plastic	—	plastica *f*	plástico *m*
plat¹ (F)	Gericht *n*	dish	—	piatto *m*	comida *f*
plat² (F)	Gang *m*	course	—	portata *f*	plato *m*
plat³ (F)	flach	flat	—	piatto(a)	llano(a)
plata (Es)	Silber *n*	silver	argent *m*	d'argento	—
plátano (Es)	Banane *f*	banana	banane *f*	banana *f*	—
plate (E)	Teller *m*	—	assiette *f*	piatto *m*	plato *m*
plateado (Es)	silbern	silver	d'argent	argenteo	—
plateau (F)	Tablett *n*	tray	—	vassoio *m*	bandeja *f*
platillo (Es)	Untertasse *f*	saucer	soucoupe *f*	piattino *m*	—
plato¹ (Es)	Gang *m*	course	plat *m*	portata *f*	—
plato² (Es)	Gericht *n*	dish	plat *m*	piatto *m*	—
plato³ (Es)	Teller *m*	plate	assiette *f*	piatto *m*	—
Platte (D)	—	record	disque *m*	disco *m*	disco *m*
Plattenspieler (D)	—	record player	tourne-disque *m*	giradischi *m*	tocadiscos *m*
Platz (D)	—	place	place *f*	piazza *f*	plaza *f*
platzen (D)	—	burst	éclater	scoppiare	reventar
plaudern (D)	—	chat	causer	chiacchierare	conversar
play¹ (E)	spielen	—	jour	giocare	jugar
play² (E)	Schauspiel *n*	—	spectacle *m*	spettacolo *m*	espectáculo *m*
play³ (E)	Theaterstück *n*	—	pièce de théâtre *f*	opera teatrale *f*	pieza de teatro *f*
playa (Es)	Strand *m*	beach	plage *f*	spiaggia *f*	—
player (E)	Spieler *m*	—	joueur *m*	giocatore *m*	jugador *m*
playground (E)	Spielplatz *m*	—	terrain de jeu *m*	campo dei giochi *m*	campo de juego *m*
plaza (Es)	Platz *m*	place	place *f*	piazza *f*	—
plaza de aparcamiento (Es)	Parkplatz *m*	parking place	parking *m*	parcheggio *m*	—
plazo (Es)	Rate *f*	instalment	quote-part *f*	rata *f*	—
pleasant (E)	angenehm	—	agréable	gradevole	agradable

please

	D	E	F	I	Es
please[1] (E)	bitte	—	s'il vous plaît	prego	por favor
please[2] (E)	gefallen	—	plaire	piacere	gustar
pleasure[1] (E)	Genuß m	—	plaisir m	piacere m	deleite m
pleasure[2] (E)	Vergnügen n	—	plaisir m	divertimento m	placer m
pledge (E)	Pfand n	—	gage m	pegno m	prenda f
plein (F)	voll	full	—	pieno(a)	lleno(a)
pleine saison (F)	Hochsaison f	high season	—	alta stagione f	temporada alta f
pleite (D)	—	penniless	fauché(e)	fallito(a)	sin dinero
pleurer (F)	weinen	cry	—	piangere	llorar
pleuvoir (F)	regnen	rain	—	piovere	llover
plier (F)	biegen	bend	—	piegare	doblar
plonger (F)	tauchen	dive	—	immergere	bucear
plötzlich (D)	—	suddenly	tout à coup	di colpo	de repente
pluie (F)	Regen m	rain	—	pioggia f	lluvia f
plum (E)	Pflaume f	—	prune f	prugna f	ciruela f
pluma[1] (Es)	Feder f	pen nib	plume f	penna f	—
pluma[2] (Es)	Feder f	feather	plume f	piuma f	—
pluma[3] (Es)	Füller m	fountain pen	stylo m	penna stilografica f	—
plume[1] (F)	Feder f	pen nib	—	penna f	pluma f
plume[2] (F)	Feder f	feather	—	piuma f	pluma f
plündern (D)	—	loot	piller	saccheggiare	desvalijar
plural (E)	Mehrzahl f	—	pluriel m	plurale m	plural m
plural (Es)	Mehrzahl f	plural	pluriel m	plurale m	—
plurale (I)	Mehrzahl f .	plural	pluriel m	—	plural m
pluriel (F)	Mehrzahl f	plural	—	plurale m	plural m
plus (D)	—	plus	plus	più	más
plus (E)	plus	—	plus	più	más
plus[1] (F)	mehr	more	—	più	más
plus[2] (F)	plus	plus	—	più	más
plus éloigné (F)	weiter	further	—	più ampio(a)	adelante
plusieurs (F)	mehrere	several	—	parecchi	muchos(as)
plus tard (F)	später	later	—	piú tardi	más tarde
plus tôt (F)	eher	sooner	—	prima	antes
pneu (F)	Reifen m	tyre	—	pneumatico m	neumático m
pneumatico (I)	Reifen m	tyre	pneu m	—	neumático m
población (Es)	Bevölkerung f	population	population f	popolazione f	—
pobre (Es)	arm	poor	pauvre	povero(a)	—
pochen (D)	—	knock	frapper	battere	golpear
pochi (I)	wenige	few	peu	—	pocos(as)
pocket money (E)	Taschengeld n	—	argent de poche f	denaro per le piccole spese m	dinero de bolsillo m
poco (Es)	wenig	little	peu de	poco(a)	—
poco[1] (I)	gering	slight	minime	—	pequeño(a)
poco[2] (I)	wenig	little	peu de	—	poco(a)
poco accogliente (I)	ungemütlich	uncomfortable	désagréable	—	incómodo(a)
poco fa (I)	soeben	just now	à l'instant même	—	ahora mismo
pocos (Es)	wenige	few	peu	pochi	—
poder[1] (Es)	dürfen	be allowed	avoir le droit	potere	—

politeness

	D	E	F	I	Es
poder² (Es)	Gewalt f	force	force f	forza f	—
poder³ (Es)	Macht f	power	pouvoir m	potere m	—
poder⁴ (Es)	Vollmacht f	authority	procuration f	delega f	—
podere (I)	Anwesen n	premises	domaine m	—	posesión f
poêle¹ (F)	Ofen m	oven	—	stufa f	estufa f
poêle² (F)	Pfanne f	pan	—	padella f	sartén f
poem (E)	Gedicht n	—	poème m	poesia f	poema m
poema (Es)	Gedicht n	poem	poème m	poesia f	—
poème (F)	Gedicht n	poem	—	poesia f	poema m
poesia (I)	Gedicht n	poem	poème m	—	poema m
poet (E)	Dichter m	—	poète m	poeta m	poeta m
poeta (Es)	Dichter m	poet	poète m	poeta m	—
poeta (I)	Dichter m	poet	poète m	—	poeta m
poète (F)	Dichter m	poet	—	poeta m	poeta m
poi (I)	danach	afterwards	après	—	después
poids (F)	Gewicht n	weight	—	peso m	peso m
poignée (F)	Griff m	handle	—	maniglia f	asidero m
poindre (F)	dämmern	dawn	—	spuntare	amanecer
poing (F)	Faust f	fist	—	pugno m	puño m
point¹ (E)	Punkt m	—	point m	punto m	punto m
point² (E)	Spitze f	—	pointe f	punta f	punta f
point (F)	Punkt m	point	—	punto m	punto m
point de vue (F)	Standpunkt m	standpoint	—	punto di vista m	punto de vista m
pointe (F)	Spitze f	point	—	punta f	punta f
pointed (E)	spitz	—	pointu(e)	appuntito(a)	puntiagudo(a)
pointless (E)	zwecklos	—	inutile	inutile	inútil
pointu (F)	spitz	pointed	—	appuntito(a)	puntiagudo(a)
poire (F)	Birne f	pear	—	pera f	pera f
pois (F)	Erbse f	pea	—	pisello m	guisante m
poison (E)	Gift n	—	poison m	veleno m	veneno m
poison (F)	Gift n	poison	—	veleno m	veneno m
poisonous (E)	giftig	—	toxique	velenoso	venenoso(a)
poisson (F)	Fisch m	fish	—	pesce m	pez m
poitrine (F)	Brust f	breast	—	petto m	pecho m
poivre (F)	Pfeffer m	pepper	—	pepe m	pimienta f
Poland (E)	Polen	—	Pologne f	Polonia f	Polonia f
pole (E)	Stange f	—	barre f	asta f	vara f
Polen (D)	—	Poland	Pologne f	Polonia f	Polonia f
poli (F)	höflich	polite	—	cortese	cortés
police (E)	Polizei f	—	police f	polizia f	policía f
police (F)	Polizei f	police	—	polizia f	policía f
policeman (E)	Polizist m	—	agent de police m	poliziotto m	policía m
policía¹ (Es)	Polizei f	police	police f	polizia f	—
policía² (Es)	Polizist m	policeman	agent de police m	poliziotto m	—
polieren (D)	—	polish	astiquer	lucidare	pulir
polish (E)	polieren	—	astiquer	lucidare	pulir
polite (E)	höflich	—	poli(e)	cortese	cortés
politeness (E)	Höflichkeit f	—	politesse f	cortesia f	cortesía f

	D	E	F	I	Es
politesse (F)	Höflichkeit f	politeness	—	cortesia f	cortesía f
política (Es)	Politik f	politics	politique f	politica f	—
politica (I)	Politik f	politics	politique f	—	política f
politician (E)	Politiker m	—	politicien m	politico m	político m
politicien (F)	Politiker m	politician	—	politicò m	político m
político (Es)	Politiker m	politician	politicien m	politico m	—
politico (I)	Politiker m	politician	politicien m	—	político m
politics (E)	Politik f	—	politique f	politica f	política f
Politik (D)	—	politics	politique f	politica f	política f
Politiker (D)	—	politician	politicien m	politico m	político m
politique (F)	Politik f	politics	—	politica f	política f
Polizei (D)	—	police	police f	polizia f	policía f
polizia (I)	Polizei f	police	police f	—	policía f
poliziotto (I)	Polizist m	policeman	agent de police m	—	policía m
Polizist (D)	—	policeman	agent de police m	poliziotto m	policía m
poll (E)	Umfrage f	—	enquête f	inchiesta f	encuesta f
pollame (I)	Geflügel n	poultry	volaille f	—	aves f pl
pollice (I)	Daumen m	thumb	pouce m	—	pulgar m
pollo (I)	Huhn n	chicken	poule f	—	gallina f
polmone (I)	Lunge f	lung	poumon m	—	pulmón m
Pologne (F)	Polen	Poland	—	Polonia f	Polonia f
Polonia (Es)	Polen	Poland	Pologne f	Polonia f	—
Polonia (I)	Polen	Poland	Pologne f	—	Polonia f
polso (I)	Puls m	pulse	pouls m	—	pulso m
poltrona (I)	Sessel m	armchair	fauteuil m	—	sillón m
polvere[1] (I)	Pulver n	powder	poudre f	—	pólvora f
polvere[2] (I)	Staub m	dust	poussière f	—	polvo m
polveroso (I)	staubig	dusty	poussiéreux (-euse)	—	polvoriento(a)
polvo (Es)	Staub m	dust	poussière f	polvere f	—
pólvora (Es)	Pulver n	powder	poudre f	polvere f	—
polvoriento (Es)	staubig	dusty	poussiéreux (-euse)	polveroso(a)	—
polvos (Es)	Puder n	powder	poudre f	cipria f	—
pomada (Es)	Salbe f	ointment	onguent m	pomata f	—
pomata (I)	Salbe f	ointment	onguent m	—	pomada f
pomelo (Es)	Pampelmuse f	grapefruit	pamplemousse m	pompelmo m	—
pomeriggio (I)	Nachmittag m	afternoon	après-midi m	—	tarde f
pomme (F)	Apfel m	apple	—	mela f	manzana f
pomme de terre (F)	Kartoffel f	potato	—	patata f	patata f
Pommes frites (D)	—	French fries	frites f pl	patate fritte f pl	patatas fritas f pl
pomodoro (I)	Tomate f	tomato	tomate f	—	tomate m
pompa (I)	Pumpe f	pump	pompe f	—	bomba f
pompe (F)	Pumpe f	pump	—	pompa f	bomba f
pompelmo (I)	Pampelmuse f	grapefruit	pamplemousse m	—	pomelo m
ponctuel (F)	pünktlich	punctual	—	puntuale	puntual
pond (E)	Teich m	—	étang m	stagno m	estanque m
poner[1] (Es)	anstellen	turn on	mettre en marche	accendere	—
poner[2] (Es)	hinlegen	put down	poser	posare	—

	D	E	F	I	Es
poner³ (Es)	setzen	put	mettre	mettere	—
poner en cuenta (Es)	anrechnen	charge	compter	mettere in conto	—
poner en libertad (Es)	freilassen	release	libérer	mettere in libertà	—
poner las señas en (Es)	adressieren	address	adresser	indirizzare	—
ponerse (Es)	anziehen	dress	mettre	indossare	—
ponerse de acuerdo (Es)	einigen, sich	agree	mettre d'accord, se	accordarsi	—
pont¹ (F)	Brücke f	bridge	—	ponte m	puente m
pont² (F)	Deck n	deck	—	ponte m	cubierta f
ponte¹ (I)	Brücke f	bridge	pont m	—	puente m
ponte² (I)	Deck n	deck	pont m	—	cubierta f
poor (E)	arm	—	pauvre	povero(a)	pobre
popolare (I)	beliebt	popular	populaire	—	estimado(a)
popolazione (I)	Bevölkerung f	population	population f	—	población f
popolo (I)	Volk n	people	peuple m	—	pueblo m
poppy (E)	Mohn m	—	coquelicot m	papavero m	amapola f
populaire (F)	beliebt	popular	—	popolare	estimado(a)
popular (E)	beliebt	—	populaire	popolare	estimado(a)
population (E)	Bevölkerung f	—	population f	popolazione f	población f
population (F)	Bevölkerung f	population	—	popolazione f	población f
por¹ (Es)	durch	through	par	per	—
por² (Es)	für	for	pour	per	—
por³ (Es)	infolge	as a result of	par suite de	in seguito a	—
por⁴ (Es)	über	over/about	sur	su/sopra/per	—
por casualidad (Es)	zufällig	by chance	par hasard	per caso	—
porcelain (E)	Porzellan n	—	porcelaine f	porcellana f	porcelana f
porcelaine (F)	Porzellan n	porcelain	—	porcellana f	porcelana f
porcelana (Es)	Porzellan n	porcelain	porcelaine f	porcellana f	—
porcellana (I)	Porzellan n	porcelain	porcelaine f	—	porcelana f
por ciento (Es)	Prozent n	percent	pour cent	percentuale f	—
por debajo (Es)	darunter	underneath	en dessous	sotto	—
por encima (Es)	darüber	above	au dessus	sopra	—
por escrito (Es)	schriftlich	written	écrit(e)	scritto(a)	—
por eso (Es)	deshalb	therefore	c'est pourquoi	perció	—
¡por favor! (Es)	bitte!	please!	s'il vous plaît!	prego!	—
pork (E)	Schweinefleisch n	—	viande de porc f	carne di maiale f	carne de cerdo f
por la mañana (Es)	vormittags	in the morning	le matin	di mattina	—
por la noche (Es)	nachts	at nighttime	la nuit	di notte	—
por la tarde¹ (Es)	abends	in the evening	le soir m	di sera	—
por la tarde² (Es)	nachmittags	in the afternoon	l'après-midi	di pomeriggio	—
por lo común (Es)	meistens	generally	généralement	di solito	—
por lo demás¹ (Es)	sonst	otherwise	autrement	altrimenti	—
por lo demás² (Es)	übrigens	by the way	d'ailleurs	del resto	—
por lo menos¹ (Es)	mindestens	at least	au moins	almeno	—
por lo menos² (Es)	wenigstens	at least	au moins	almeno	—
por lo menos³ (Es)	zumindest	at least	au moins	per lo meno	—
por medio (Es)	durchschnittlich	average	moyen(ne)	medio(a)	—

	D	E	F	I	Es
por otra parte (Es)	andererseits	on the other hand	d'autre part	d'altra parte	—
porque (Es)	weil	because	parce que	perché	—
¿por qué?[1] (Es)	warum	why	pourquoi	perché	—
¿por qué?[2] (Es)	weshalb	why	pourquoi	perché	—
¿por qué?[3] (Es)	wieso	why	pourquoi	come mai	—
por supuesto (Es)	selbstverständlich	of course	évidemment	naturalmente	—
port (E)	Hafen *m*	—	port *m*	porto *m*	puerto *m*
port[1] (F)	Hafen *m*	port	—	porto *m*	puerto *m*
port[2] (F)	Porto *n*	postage	—	affrancatura *f*	franqueo *m*
porta[1] (I)	Tür *f*	door	porte *f*	—	puerta *f*
porta[2] (I)	Tor *n*	gate	porte *f*	—	puerta *f*
portabagagli (I)	Kofferraum *m*	boot	coffre *m*	—	maletero *m*
portacenere (I)	Aschenbecher *m*	ashtray	cendrier *m*	—	cenicero *m*
portare[1] (I)	bringen	fetch	porter	—	llevar
portare[2] (I)	tragen	carry	porter	—	llevar
portare[3] (I)	überbringen	deliver	remettre	—	transmitir
portare con sé (I)	mitbringen	bring (along)	apporter	—	traer
portata (I)	Gang *m*	course	plat *m*	—	plato *m*
porte[1] (F)	Tür *f*	door	—	porta *f*	puerta *f*
porte[2] (F)	Tor *n*	gate	—	porta *f*	puerta *f*
porte-documents (F)	Aktenmappe *f*	file	—	cartella *f*	cartera *f*
porter[1] (E)	Portier *m*	—	portier *m*	portiere *m*	portero *m*
porter[2] (E)	Pförtner *m*	—	concierge *m*	portiere *m*	portero *m*
porter[1] (F)	anhaben	have on	—	indossare	llevar
porter[2] (F)	bringen	fetch	—	portare	llevar
porter[3] (F)	tragen	carry	—	portare	llevar
portero[1] (Es)	Hausmeister *m*	caretaker	concierge *m*	portinaio *m*	—
portero[2] (Es)	Portier *m*	porter	portier *m*	portiere *m*	—
portero[3] (Es)	Pförtner *m*	porter	concierge *m*	portiere *m*	—
porteur (F)	Träger *m*	carrier	—	facchino *m*	mozo *m*
por ti (Es)	deinetwegen	for your sake	pour toi	per te	—
Portier (D)	—	porter	portier *m*	portiere *m*	portero *m*
portier (F)	Portier *m*	porter	—	portiere *m*	portero *m*
portiere[1] (I)	Portier *m*	porter	portier *m*	—	portero *m*
portiere[2] (I)	Pförtner *m*	porter	concierge *m*	—	portero *m*
portinaio (I)	Hausmeister *m*	caretaker	concierge *m*	—	portero *m*
Porto (D)	—	postage	port *m*	affrancatura *f*	franqueo *m*
porto (I)	Hafen *m*	port	port *m*	—	puerto *m*
por todas partes (Es)	überall	everywhere	partout	dappertutto	—
Portogallo (I)	Portugal	Portugal	Portugal *m*	—	Portugal *m*
Portugal (D)	—	Portugal	Portugal *m*	Portogallo *m*	Portugal *m*
Portugal (E)	Portugal	—	Portugal *m*	Portogallo *m*	Portugal *m*
Portugal (Es)	Portugal	Portugal	Portugal *m*	Portogallo *m*	—
Portugal (F)	Portugal	Portugal	—	Portogallo *m*	Portugal *m*
por último (Es)	zuletzt	finally	finalement	infine	—
por un lado (Es)	einerseits	on one hand	d'une part	da un lato	—
Porzellan (D)	—	porcelain	porcelaine *f*	porcellana *f*	porcelana *f*
posada (Es)	Gasthaus *n*	hotel	auberge *f*	osteria *f*	—

	D	E	F	I	Es
posare (I)	hinlegen	put down	poser	—	poner
poseer (Es)	besitzen	possess	posséder	possedere	—
poser (F)	hinlegen	put down	—	posare	poner
poser sa candidature (F)	bewerben, sich	apply	—	concorrere	presentarse
posesión[1] (Es)	Anwesen *n*	premises	domaine *m*	podere *m*	—
posesión[2] (Es)	Besitz *m*	possession	propriété *f*	proprietà *f*	—
posibilidad (Es)	Möglichkeit *f*	possibility	possibilité *f*	possibilità *f*	—
posible (Es)	möglich	possible	possible	possibile	—
posición (Es)	Stellung *f*	position	position *f*	posizione *f*	—
positif (F)	positiv	positive	—	positivo(a)	positivo(a)
position[1] (E)	Posten *m*	—	poste *m*	posto *m*	puesto *m*
position[2] (E)	Stellung *f*	—	position *f*	posizione *f*	posición *f*
position[3] (E)	Stand *m*	—	état *m*	stato *m*	estado *m*
position (F)	Stellung *f*	position	—	posizione *f*	posición *f*
positiv (D)	—	positive	positif(-ive)	positivo(a)	positivo(a)
positive (E)	positiv	—	positif(-ive)	positivo(a)	positivo(a)
positivo (Es)	positiv	positive	positif(-ive)	positivo(a)	—
positivo (I)	positiv	positive	positif(-ive)	—	positivo(a)
posizione (I)	Stellung *f*	position	position *f*	—	posición *f*
posséder (F)	besitzen	possess	—	possedere	poseer
possedere (I)	besitzen	possess	posséder	—	poseer
possess (E)	besitzen	—	posséder	possedere	poseer
possession (E)	Besitz *m*	—	propriété *f*	proprietà *f*	posesión *f*
possibile (I)	möglich	possible	possible	—	posible
possibilità (I)	Möglichkeit *f*	possibility	possibilité *f*	—	posibilidad *f*
possibilité[1] (F)	Chance *f*	chance	—	occasione *f*	oportunidad *f*
possibilité[2] (F)	Möglichkeit *f*	possibility	—	possibilità *f*	posibilidad *f*
possibility (E)	Möglichkeit *f*	—	possibilité *f*	possibilità *f*	posibilidad *f*
possible[1] (E)	eventuell	—	éventuel(le)	eventuale	eventual
possible[2] (E)	möglich	—	possible	possibile	posible
possible (F)	möglich	possible	—	possibile	posible
Post (D)	—	post	poste *f*	posta *f*	correo *m*
post[1] (E)	einwerfen	—	poster	imbucare	echar
post[2] (E)	Post *f*	—	poste *f*	posta *f*	correo *m*
posta (I)	Post *f*	post	poste *f*	—	correo *m*
posta aerea (I)	Luftpost *f*	air mail	poste aérienne *f*	—	correo aéreo *m*
postage (E)	Porto *n*	—	port *m*	affrancatura *f*	franqueo *m*
postal[1] (Es)	Karte *f*	card	carte *f*	cartolina *f*	—
postal[2] (Es)	Postkarte *f*	postcard	carte postale *f*	cartolina *f*	—
Postamt (D)	—	post office	bureau de poste *m*	ufficio postale *m*	oficina de correos *f*
Postbote (D)	—	postman	facteur *m*	postino *m*	cartero *m*
postcard[1] (E)	Ansichtskarte *f*	—	carte postale *f*	cartolina *f*	tarjeta postal *f*
postcard[2] (E)	Postkarte *f*	—	carte postale *f*	cartolina *f*	postal *f*
poste[1] (F)	Posten *m*	position	—	posto *m*	puesto *m*
poste[2] (F)	Post *f*	post	—	posta *f*	correo *m*
poste aérienne (F)	Luftpost *f*	air mail	—	posta aerea *f*	correo aéreo *m*
poste de télévision (F)	Fernseher *m*	television set	—	televisore *m*	televisor *m*

	D	E	F	I	Es
Posten (D)	—	position	poste *m*	posto *m*	puesto *m*
poster (E)	Plakat *n*	—	affiche *f*	affisso *m*	cartel *m*
poster (F)	einwerfen	post	—	imbucare	echar
postino (I)	Postbote *m*	postman	facteur *m*	—	cartero *m*
Postkarte (D)	—	postcard	carte postale *f*	cartolina *f*	postal *f*
postman (E)	Postbote *m*	—	facteur *m*	postino *m*	cartero *m*
posto[1] (I)	Posten *m*	position	poste *m*	—	puesto *m*
posto[2] (I)	Stelle *f*	place	place *f*	—	puesto *m*
posto a sedere (I)	Sitzplatz *m*	seat	place assise *f*	—	asiento *m*
post office (E)	Postamt *n*	—	bureau de poste *m*	ufficio postale *m*	oficina de correos *f*
postpone (E)	verschieben	—	remettre	rimandare	aplazar
postre (Es)	Nachtisch *m*	dessert	dessert *m*	desert *m*	—
pot (E)	Topf *m*	—	casserole *f*	pentola *f*	olla *f*
potabile (I)	trinkbar	drinkable	potable	—	potable
potable (Es)	trinkbar	drinkable	potable	potabile	—
potable (F)	trinkbar	drinkable	—	potabile	potable
potato (E)	Kartoffel *f*	—	pomme de terre *f*	patata *f*	patata *f*
potere[1] (I)	dürfen	be allowed	avoir le droit	—	poder
potere[2] (I)	Macht *f*	power	pouvoir *m*	—	poder *m*
poubelle[1] (F)	Abfalleimer *m*	bin	—	pattumiera *f*	cubo de la basura *m*
poubelle[2] (F)	Mülleimer *m*	dustbin	—	secchio dei rifiuti *m*	cubo de la basura *m*
pouce (F)	Daumen *m*	thumb	—	pollice *m*	pulgar *m*
poudre[1] (F)	Pulver *n*	powder	—	polvere *f*	pólvora *f*
poudre[2] (F)	Puder *n*	powder	—	cipria *f*	polvos *m pl*
poule[1] (F)	Huhn *n*	chicken	—	pollo *m*	gallina *f*
poule[2] (F)	Henne *f*	hen	—	gallina *f*	gallina *f*
pouls (F)	Puls *m*	pulse	—	polso *m*	pulso *m*
poultry (E)	Geflügel *n*	—	volaille *f*	pollame *m*	aves *f pl*
poumon (F)	Lunge *f*	lung	—	polmone *m*	pulmón *m*
pound (E)	Pfund *n*	—	livre *f*	mezzo chilo *m*	libra *f*
poupée (F)	Puppe *f*	doll	—	bambola *f*	muñeca *f*
pour[1] (E)	eingießen	—	verser	versare	echar
pour[2] (E)	schütten	—	verser	versare	verter
pour (F)	für	for	—	per	por/para
pourboire (F)	Trinkgeld *n*	tip	—	mancia *f*	propina *f*
pour cela (F)	dafür	for it	—	per questo	para ello
pour cent (F)	Prozent *n*	percent	—	percentuale *f*	por ciento *m*
pour l'instant (F)	zunächst	first of all	—	dapprima	en primer lugar
pourquoi[1] (F)	wofür	what for	—	per cui	para qué
pourquoi[2] (F)	warum	why	—	perché	por qué
pourquoi[3] (F)	wieso	why	—	come mai	por qué
pourquoi[4] (F)	weshalb	why	—	perché	por qué
pourquoi[5] (F)	wozu	what for	—	perché	para qué
poursuivre (F)	verfolgen	pursue	—	inseguire	perseguir
pousser[1] (F)	stoßen	push	—	spingere	empujar
pousser[2] (F)	schieben	push	—	spingere	empujar

	D	E	F	I	Es
pousser des cris de joie (F)	jubeln	rejoice	—	giubilare	dar gritos de alegría
poussière (F)	Staub *m*	dust	—	polvere *f*	polvo *m*
poussiéreux (F)	staubig	dusty	—	polveroso(a)	polvoriento(a)
pouvoir¹ (F)	können	can	—	sapere	saber
pouvoir² (F)	Macht *f*	power	—	potere *m*	poder *m*
povero (I)	arm	poor	pauvre	—	pobre
powder¹ (E)	Pulver *n*	—	poudre *f*	polvere *f*	pólvora *f*
powder² (E)	Puder *n*	—	poudre *f*	cipria *f*	polvos *m pl*
power (E)	Macht *f*	—	pouvoir *m*	potere *m*	poder *m*
pozzanghera (I)	Pfütze *f*	puddle	flaque *f*	—	charco *m*
prächtig (D)	—	splendid	magnifique	meraviglioso(a)	magnífico(a)
práctica (Es)	Praxis *f*	practice	pratique *f*	pratica *f*	—
practical (E)	praktisch	—	pratique	pratico(a)	práctico(a)
practical training (E)	Praktikum *n*	—	stage *m*	tirocinio *m*	prácticas *f pl*
practicar (Es)	üben	practise	étudier	esercitarsi	—
prácticas (Es)	Praktikum *n*	practical training	stage *m*	tirocinio *m*	—
practice (E)	Praxis *f*	—	pratique *f*	pratica *f*	práctica *f*
práctico (Es)	praktisch	practical	pratique	pratico(a)	—
practise¹ (E)	ausüben	—	exercer	esercitare	ejercer
practise² (E)	üben	—	étudier	esercitarsi	practicar
practise magic (E)	zaubern	—	faire de la magie	esercitare la magia	hacer magia
prado (Es)	Wiese *f*	meadow	pré *m*	prato *m*	—
praise (E)	loben	—	louer	lodare	elogiar
Praktikum (D)	—	practical training	stage *m*	tirocinio *m*	prácticas *f pl*
praktisch (D)	—	practical	pratique	pratico(a)	práctico(a)
pranzo (I)	Mittagessen *n*	lunch	déjeuner *m*	—	comida *f*
Präsident (D)	—	president	président *m*	presidente *m*	presidente *m*
pratica (I)	Praxis *f*	practice	pratique *f*	—	práctica *f*
pratico (I)	praktisch	practical	pratique	—	práctico(a)
pratique¹ (F)	praktisch	practical	—	pratico(a)	práctico(a)
pratique² (F)	Praxis *f*	practice	—	pratica *f*	práctica *f*
prato¹ (I)	Rasen *m*	lawn	pelouse *f*	—	césped *m*
prato² (I)	Wiese *f*	meadow	pré *m*	—	prado *m*
Praxis (D)	—	practice	pratique *f*	pratica *f*	práctica *f*
pray (E)	beten	—	prier	pregare	rezar
prayer (E)	Gebet *n*	—	prière *f*	preghiera *f*	horación *f*
pré (F)	Wiese *f*	meadow	—	prato *m*	prado *m*
précédent¹ (F)	vorhergehend	preceding	—	precedente	anterior(a)
précédent² (F)	vorig	previous	—	precedente	precedente
precedente (Es)	vorig	previous	précédent(e)	precedente	—
precedente¹ (I)	vorig	previous	précédent(e)	—	precedente
precedente² (I)	vorhergehend	preceding	antécédent	—	anterior
precedenza (I)	Vorfahrt *f*	right of way	priorité *f*	—	preferencia *f*
preceding (E)	vorhergehend	—	antécédent	precedente	anterior
précieux¹ (F)	wertvoll	valuable	—	prezioso(a)	valioso(a)
précieux² (F)	kostbar	precious	—	prezioso(a)	valioso(a)
precio (Es)	Preis *m*	price	prix *m*	prezzo *m*	—

	D	E	F	I	Es
precio máximo (Es)	Höchstpreis *m*	maximum price	prix plafond *m*	prezzo massimo *m*	—
precious (E)	kostbar	—	précieux(-euse)	prezioso(a)	valioso(a)
precipitare (I)	abstürzen	crash	faire une chute	—	caer a tierra
precisione (I)	Genauigkeit *f*	accuracy	exactitude *f*	—	exactitud *f*
preciso (I)	genau	exact	exact(e)	—	exacto(a)
predict (E)	vorhersagen	—	prédire	prognosticare	pronosticar
prédire (F)	vorhersagen	predict	—	prognosticare	pronosticar
preface (E)	Vorwort *n*	—	préface *f*	prefazione *f*	prólogo *m*
préface (F)	Vorwort *n*	preface	—	prefazione *f*	prólogo *m*
prefazione (I)	Vorwort *n*	preface	préface *f*	—	prólogo *m*
prefer[1] (E)	bevorzugen	—	préférer	perferire	preferir
prefer[2] (E)	vorziehen	—	préférer	preferire	preferir
preference (E)	Vorzug *m*	—	préférence *f*	preferenza *f*	preferencia *f*
préférence (F)	Vorzug *m*	preference	—	preferenza *f*	preferencia *f*
preferencia[1] (Es)	Vorfahrt *f*	right of way	priorité *f*	precedenza *f*	—
preferencia[2] (Es)	Vorzug *m*	preference	préférence *f*	preferenza *f*	—
preferenza (I)	Vorzug *m*	preference	préférence *f*	—	preferencia *f*
préférer[1] (F)	bevorzugen	prefer	—	perferire	preferir
préférer[2] (F)	vorziehen	prefer	—	preferire	preferir
preferir[1] (Es)	bevorzugen	prefer	préférer	perferire	—
preferir[2] (Es)	vorziehen	prefer	préférer	preferire	—
preferire (I)	vorziehen	prefer	préférer	—	preferir
prefijo (Es)	Vorwahl *f*	dialling code	indicatif téléphonique *m*	prefisso *m*	—
prefisso (I)	Vorwahl *f*	dialling code	indicatif téléphonique *m*	—	prefijo *m*
pregare[1] (I)	beten	pray	prier	—	rezar
pregare[2] (I)	bitten	request	demander	—	rogar
preghiera (I)	Gebet *n*	prayer	prière *f*	—	oración *f*
pregnant (E)	schwanger	—	enceinte	incinta	embarazada
prego! (I)	bitte!	please!	s'il vous plaît!	—	¡por favor!
pregunta (Es)	Frage *f*	question	question *f*	domanda *f*	—
preguntar (Es)	fragen	ask	demander	domandare	—
Preis (D)	—	price	prix *m*	prezzo *m*	precio *m*
preiswert (D)	—	inexpensive	bon marché	conveniente	económico
premere (I)	drücken	press	presser	—	apretar
premiare (I)	belohnen	reward	récompenser	—	recompensar
premier (F)	erste(r,s)	first	—	primo(a)	primera(o)
Premierminister (D)	—	prime minister	président du Conseil *m*	primo ministro *m*	primer ministro *m*
premises (E)	Anwesen *n*	—	domaine *m*	podere *m*	posesión *f*
premuroso (I)	zuvorkommend	obliging	prévenant(e)	—	cortés
prenda (Es)	Pfand *n*	pledge	gage *m*	pegno *m*	—
prendere[1] (I)	fassen	grasp	saisir	—	coger
prendere[2] (I)	nehmen	take	prendre	—	tomar
prendere alloggio (I)	einziehen	move in	emménager	—	instalarse
prendere con sè (I)	mitnehmen	take along	emmener	—	llevar consigo
prendere indietro (I)	zurücknehmen	take back	retirer	—	retirar
prendere nota di (I)	vormerken	book	prendre note de	—	tomar nota

315 **presente**

	D	E	F	I	Es
prendersi cura di (I)	sorgen	worry about	occuper de, se	—	atender
prendre (F)	nehmen	take	—	prendere	tomar
prendre congé de (F)	verabschieden	say goodbye to	—	congedare	despedir
prendre de l'essence (F)	tanken	fill up with petrol	—	fare benzina	llenar de gasolina
prendre note de (F)	vormerken	book	—	prendere nota di	tomar nota
prénom (F)	Vorname *m*	Christian name	—	nome di battesimo *m*	nombre de pila *m*
prenotare¹ (I)	buchen	book	retenir	—	reservar
prenotare² (I)	vorbestellen	book	réserver	—	hacer reservar
prensa (Es)	Presse *f*	press	presse *f*	stampa *f*	—
preoccupare (I)	beunruhigen	disturb	inquiéter	—	inquietar
preoccupazione (I)	Sorge *f*	concern	souci *m*	—	preocupación *f*
preocupación (Es)	Sorge *f*	concern	souci *m*	preoccupazione *f*	—
preparar¹ (Es)	vorbereiten	prepare	préparer	preparare	—
preparar² (Es)	zubereiten	prepare	préparer	preparare	—
preparare¹ (I)	vorbereiten	prepare	préparer	—	preparar
preparare² (I)	zubereiten	prepare	préparer	—	preparar
prepare¹ (E)	vorbereiten	—	préparer	preparare	preparar
prepare² (E)	zubereiten	—	préparer	preparare	preparar
préparer¹ (F)	vorbereiten	prepare	—	preparare	preparar
préparer² (F)	zubereiten	prepare	—	preparare	preparar
presa (I)	Steckdose *f*	socket	prise électrique *f*	—	enchufe *m*
prescribe (E)	verschreiben	—	prescrire	prescrivere	prescribir
prescribir (Es)	verschreiben	prescribe	prescrire	prescrivere	—
prescripción médica (Es)	Rezept *n*	prescription	ordonnance *f*	prescrizione *f*	—
prescription (E)	Rezept *n*	—	ordonnance *f*	prescrizione *f*	prescripción médica *f*
prescrire (F)	verschreiben	prescribe	—	prescrivere	prescribir
prescrivere (I)	verschreiben	prescribe	prescrire	—	prescribir
prescrizione (I)	Rezept *n*	prescription	ordonnance *f*	—	prescripción médica *f*
près de¹ (F)	neben	beside	—	accanto a	al lado de
près de² (F)	nahe	near by	—	vicino(a)	contiguo(a)
present¹ (E)	anwesend	—	présent(e)	presente	presente
present² (E)	Geschenk *n*	—	cadeau *m*	regalo *m*	regalo *m*
present³ (E)	Gegenwart *f*	—	présent *m*	presente *m*	presente *m*
présent¹ (F)	Gegenwart *f*	present	—	presente *m*	presente *m*
présent² (F)	anwesend	present	—	presente	presente
présent³ (F)	vorhanden	available	—	disponibile	presente
presentar¹ (Es)	darstellen	represent	représenter	rappresentare	—
presentar² (Es)	vorstellen	introduce	présenter	presentare	—
presentar³ (Es)	vorzeigen	show	monter	esibire	—
presentare (I)	vorstellen	introduce	présenter	—	presentar
presentarse (Es)	bewerben, sich	apply	poser sa candidature	concorrere	—
presente¹ (Es)	anwesend	present	présent(e)	presente	—
presente² (Es)	Gegenwart *f*	present	présent *m*	presente *m*	—
presente³ (Es)	vorhanden	available	présent(e)	disponibile	—
presente¹ (I)	anwesend	present	présent(e)	—	presente

	D	E	F	I	Es
presente² (I)	Gegenwart f	present	présent m	—	presente m
présenter¹ (F)	bieten	offer	—	offrire	ofrecer
présenter² (F)	überreichen	hand over	—	consegnare	entregar
présenter³ (F)	vorstellen	introduce	—	presentare	presentar
presentiment (E)	Ahnung f	—	pressentiment m	presentimento m	presentimiento m
presentimento (I)	Ahnung f	presentiment	pressentiment m	—	presentimiento m
presentimiento (Es)	Ahnung f	presentiment	pressentiment m	presentimento m	—
president (E)	Präsident m	—	président m	presidente m	presidente m
président (F)	Präsident m	president	—	presidente m	presidente m
président du Conseil (F)	Premier-minister m	prime minister	—	primo ministro m	primer ministro m
presidente (Es)	Präsident m	president	président m	presidente m	—
presidente (I)	Präsident m	president	président m	—	presidente m
presión (Es)	Zwang m	compulsion	contrainte f	costrizione f	—
presque¹ (F)	beinahe	nearly	—	circa/quasi	casi
presque² (F)	fast	nearly	—	quasi	casi
presqu'île (F)	Halbinsel f	peninsula	—	penisola f	península f
press¹ (E)	drücken	—	presser	premere	apretar
press² (E)	Presse f	—	presse f	stampa f	prensa f
pressappoco¹ (I)	etwa	about	environ	—	unos
pressappoco² (I)	ungefähr	about	environ	—	aproximadamente
Presse (D)	—	press	presse f	stampa f	prensa f
presse (F)	Presse f	press	—	stampa f	prensa f
pressé (F)	eilig	hurried	—	frettoloso(a)	rápido(a)
pressentiment (F)	Ahnung f	presentiment	—	presentimento m	presentimiento m
presser (F)	drücken	press	—	premere	apretar
prestar¹ (Es)	ausleihen	lend	prêter	dare in prestito	—
prestar² (Es)	borgen	lend	prêter	prestare	—
prestar³ (Es)	leihen	lend	prêter	prestare	—
prestar⁴ (Es)	verleihen	lend	prêter	prestare	—
prestar atención¹ (Es)	aufpassen	pay attention	faire attention	fare attenzione	—
prestar atención² (Es)	beachten	take notice	observer	osservare	—
prestare¹ (I)	borgen	lend	prêter	—	prestar
prestare² (I)	leihen	lend	prêter	—	prestar
prestare³ (I)	verleihen	lend	prêter	—	prestar
presto¹ (I)	bald	soon	bientôt	—	pronto
presto² (I)	demnächst	shortly	prochainement	—	próximamente
presto³ (I)	früh	early	tôt	—	temprano(a)
presumendo (I)	vorausgesetzt	provided	à condition que	—	supuesto
presunto (I)	angeblich	pretended	prétendu(e)	—	supuesto(a)
presupporre (I)	voraussetzen	assume	supposer	—	suponer
prêt¹ (F)	bereit	ready	—	pronto(a)	dispuesto(a)
prêt² (F)	fertig	ready	—	pronto(a)	listo(a)
prete (I)	Priester m	priest	prêtre m	—	sacerdote m
pretemporada (Es)	Vorsaison f	low season	basse saison f	bassa stagione f	—
pretended (E)	angeblich	—	prétendu(e)	presunto(a)	supuesto(a)
pretendere (I)	zumuten	expect	exiger	—	exigir

	D	E	F	I	Es
prétendu (F)	angeblich	pretended	—	presunto(a)	supuesto(a)
prêter¹ (F)	ausleihen	lend	—	dare in prestito	prestar
prêter² (F)	borgen	lend	—	prestare	prestar
prêter³ (F)	leihen	lend	—	prestare	prestar
prêter⁴ (F)	verleihen	lend	—	prestare	prestar
pretesto (I)	Vorwand m	pretext	prétexte m	—	pretexto m
pretext (E)	Vorwand m	—	prétexte m	pretesto m	pretexto m
prétexte (F)	Vorwand m	pretext	—	pretesto m	pretexto m
pretexto (Es)	Vorwand m	pretext	prétexte m	pretesto m	—
prêtre (F)	Priester m	priest	—	prete m	sacerdote m
pretty (E)	hübsch	—	joli(e)	carino(a)	bonito(a)
preuve (F)	Beweis m	proof	—	prova f	prueba f
prévenant (F)	zuvorkommend	obliging	—	premuroso(a)	cortés
prévenir (F)	verständigen	inform	—	informare	informar
prévenir de (F)	warnen	warn	—	ammonire	advertir
prevent (E)	verhindern	—	empêcher	impedire	evitar
previous (E)	vorig	—	précédent(e)	precedente	precedente
previsioni del tempo (I)	Wetter-vorhersage f	weather forecast	prévisions météorologiques f pl	—	pronóstico del tiempo m
prévisions météorologiques (F)	Wetter-vorhersage f	weather forecast	—	previsioni del tempo f pl	pronóstico del tiempo m
prezioso¹ (I)	kostbar	precious	précieux(-euse)	—	valioso(a)
prezioso² (I)	wertvoll	valuable	précieux(euse)	—	valioso(a)
prezzo (I)	Preis m	price	prix m	—	precio m
prezzo massimo (I)	Höchstpreis m	maximum price	prix plafond m	—	precio máximo m
price (E)	Preis m	—	prix m	prezzo m	precio m
prick (E)	stechen	—	piquer	pungere	picar
prier (F)	beten	pray	—	pregare	rezar
prière (F)	Gebet n	prayer	—	preghiera f	oración f
priest¹ (E)	Priester m	—	prêtre m	prete m	sacerdote m
priest² (E)	Pfarrer m	—	curé	parroco m	párroco m
Priester (D)	—	priest	prêtre m	prete m	sacerdote m
prigione (I)	Gefängnis n	prison	prison f	—	cárcel f
prima (Es)	Cousine f	cousin	cousine f	cugina f	—
prima¹ (I)	eher	sooner	plus tôt	—	antes
prima² (I)	früher	earlier	autrefois	—	antes
prima³ (I)	vorher	before	avant	—	antes
prima⁴ (I)	zuvor	before	auparavant	—	antes
prima che¹ (I)	bevor	before	avant que	—	antes que
prima che² (I)	ehe	before	avant que	—	antes que
primavera (Es)	Frühjahr n	spring	printemps m	primavera f	—
primavera (I)	Frühjahr n	spring	printemps m	—	primavera f
prime minister (E)	Premier-minister m	—	président du Conseil m	primo ministro m	primer ministro m
primer ministro (Es)	Premier-minister m	prime minister	président du Conseil m	primo ministro m	—
primero¹ (Es)	erst	first	d'abord	dapprima	—
primero² (Es)	zuerst	at first	d'abord	dapprima	—
primero³ (Es)	erste(r,s)	first	premier(-ière)	primo(a)	—

	D	E	F	I	Es
primer pago (Es)	Anzahlung *f*	deposit	acompte *m*	acconto *m*	—
primer plato (Es)	Vorspeise *f*	appetizer	hors-d'œuvre *m*	antipasto *m*	—
primitivo (Es)	ursprünglich	original	originel(le)	originario(a)	—
primo (Es)	Vetter *m*	cousin	cousin *m*	cugino *m*	—
primo (I)	erste(r,s)	first	premier(-ière)	—	primera(o)
primo ministro (I)	Premier-minister *m*	prime minister	président du Conseil *m*	—	primer ministro *m*
prince[1] (E)	Fürst *m*	—	prince *m*	principe *m*	príncipe *m*
prince[2] (E)	Prinz *m*	—	prince *m*	principe *m*	príncipe *m*
prince[1] (F)	Fürst *m*	prince	—	principe *m*	príncipe *m*
prince[2] (F)	Prinz *m*	prince	—	principe *m*	príncipe *m*
principalmente (Es)	hauptsächlich	mainly	surtout	principalmente	—
principalmente (I)	hauptsächlich	mainly	surtout	—	principalmente
principante (Es)	Anfänger *m*	beginner	débutant(e)	principiante *m*	—
príncipe[1] (Es)	Fürst *m*	prince	prince *m*	principe *m*	—
príncipe[2] (Es)	Prinz *m*	prince	prince *m*	principe *m*	—
principe[1] (I)	Fürst *m*	prince	prince *m*	—	príncipe *m*
principe[2] (I)	Prinz *m*	prince	prince *m*	—	príncipe *m*
principiante (I)	Anfänger *m*	beginner	débutant(e)	—	principante *m*
principio (Es)	Beginn *m*	beginning	commencement *m*	inizio *m*	—
printemps (F)	Frühjahr *n*	spring	—	primavera *f*	primavera *f*
Prinz (D)	—	prince	prince *m*	principe *m*	príncipe *m*
priorité (F)	Vorfahrt *f*	right of way	—	precedenza *f*	preferencia *f*
prisa (Es)	Eile *f*	haste	hâte *f*	fretta *f*	—
prise électrique (F)	Steckdose *f*	socket	—	presa *f*	enchufe *m*
prison (E)	Gefängnis *n*	—	prison *f*	prigione *f*	cárcel *f*
prison (F)	Gefängnis *n*	prison	—	prigione *f*	cárcel *f*
privado (Es)	privat	private	privé(e)	privato(a)	—
privat (D)	—	private	privé(e)	privato(a)	privado(a)
private (E)	privat	—	privé(e)	privato(a)	privado(a)
privato (I)	privat	private	privé(e)	—	privado(a)
privé (F)	privat	private	—	privato(a)	privado(a)
prix (F)	Preis *m*	price	—	prezzo *m*	precio *m*
prix plafond (F)	Höchstpreis *m*	maximum price	—	prezzo massimo *m*	precio máximo *m*
probabilmente (I)	wahrscheinlich	probably	probablement	—	probablemente
probablement (F)	wahrscheinlich	probably	—	probabilmente	probablemente
probablemente (Es)	wahrscheinlich	probably	probablement	probabilmente	—
probably (E)	wahrscheinlich	—	probablement	probabilmente	probablemente
probar[1] (Es)	anprobieren	try on	essayer	provare	—
probar[2] (Es)	beweisen	prove	prouver	provare	—
probar[3] (Es)	probieren	try	essayer	assaggiare	—
probar[4] (Es)	testen	test	tester	collaudare	—
probar[5] (Es)	versuchen	try	essayer	assagiare	—
Probe (D)	—	test	essai *m*	prova *f*	prueba *f*
probieren (D)	—	try	essayer	assaggiare	probar
Problem (D)	—	problem	problème *m*	problema *m*	problema *m*
problem (E)	Problem *n*	—	problème *m*	problema *m*	problema *m*
problema (Es)	Problem *n*	problem	problème *m*	problema *m*	—

	D	E	F	I	Es
problema (I)	Problem *n*	problem	problème *m*	—	problema *m*
problème (F)	Problem *n*	problem	—	problema *m*	problema *m*
proceder¹ (Es)	verfahren	act	procéder	procedere	—
proceder² (Es)	vorgehen	proceed	avancer	procedere	—
procéder (F)	verfahren	act	—	procedere	proceder
procedere¹ (I)	verfahren	act	procéder	—	proceder
procedere² (I)	vorgehen	proceed	avancer	—	proceder
proceed (E)	vorgehen	—	avancer	andare avanti	proceder
procès (F)	Prozeß *m*	trial	—	processo *m*	proceso *m*
proceso¹ (Es)	Fortschritt *m*	progress	progrès *m*	progresso *m*	—
proceso² (Es)	Prozeß *m*	trial	procès *m*	processo *m*	—
processo (I)	Prozeß *m*	trial	procès *m*	—	proceso *m*
prochainement (F)	demnächst	shortly	—	presto	próximamente
procurare¹ (I)	beschaffen	get	procurer	—	proporcionar
procurare² (I)	besorgen	acquire	procurer	—	conseguir
procurare³ (I)	verschaffen	procure	procurer	—	procurarse algo
procurarse algo (Es)	verschaffen	procure	procurer	procurare	—
procuration (F)	Vollmacht *f*	authority	—	delega *f*	poder *m*
procure (E)	verschaffen	—	procurer	procurare	procurarse algo
procurer¹ (F)	beschaffen	get	—	procurare	proporcionar
procurer² (F)	besorgen	acquire	—	procurare	conseguir
procurer³ (F)	verschaffen	procure	—	procurare	procurarse algo
prodotto¹ (I)	Erzeugnis *n*	product	produit *m*	—	producto *m*
prodotto² (I)	Produkt *n*	product	produit *m*	—	producto *m*
produce¹ (E)	erzeugen	—	produire	fabbricare	producir
produce² (E)	produzieren	—	produire	produrre	producir
producir¹ (Es)	erzeugen	produce	produire	fabbricare	—
producir² (Es)	herstellen	manufacture	produire	fabbricare	—
producir³ (Es)	produzieren	produce	produire	produrre	—
product¹ (E)	Erzeugnis *n*	—	produit *m*	prodotto *m*	producto *m*
product² (E)	Produkt *n*	—	produit *m*	prodotto *m*	producto *m*
producteur (F)	Hersteller *m*	manufacturer	—	produttore *m*	productor *m*
producto¹ (Es)	Erzeugnis *n*	product	produit *m*	prodotto *m*	—
producto² (Es)	Produkt *n*	product	produit *m*	prodotto *m*	—
productor (Es)	Hersteller *m*	manufacturer	producteur *m*	produttore *m*	—
produire¹ (F)	erzeugen	produce	—	fabbricare	producir
produire² (F)	herstellen	manufacture	—	fabbricare	producir
produire³ (F)	produzieren	produce	—	produrre	producir
produit¹ (F)	Erzeugnis *n*	product	—	prodotto *m*	producto *m*
produit² (F)	Produkt *n*	product	—	prodotto *m*	producto *m*
produits alimentaires (F)	Eßwaren *pl*	victuals	—	alimentari *m pl*	comestibles *m pl*
Produkt (D)	—	product	produit *m*	prodotto *m*	producto *m*
produrre (I)	produzieren	produce	produire	—	producir
produttore (I)	Hersteller *m*	manufacturer	producteur *m*	—	productor *m*
produzieren (D)	—	produce	produire	produrre	producir
profesión (Es)	Beruf *m*	profession	profession *f*	professione *f*	—
profesor (Es)	Lehrer *m*	teacher	professeur *m*	maestro *m*	—

	D	E	F	I	Es
professeur (F)	Lehrer *m*	teacher	—	maestro *m*	profesor *m*
profession (E)	Beruf *m*	—	profession *f*	professione *f*	profesión *f*
profession (F)	Beruf *m*	profession	—	professione *f*	profesión *f*
professione (I)	Beruf *m*	profession	profession *f*	—	profesión *f*
profit (E)	Gewinn *m*	—	gain *m*	guadagno *m*	ganancia *f*
profond (F)	tief	deep	—	profondo(a)	profundo(a)
profondeur (F)	Tiefe *f*	depth	—	profondità *f*	profundidad *f*
profondità (I)	Tiefe *f*	depth	profondeur *f*	—	profundidad *f*
profondo (I)	tief	deep	profond(e)	—	profundo(a)
profumo[1] (I)	Duft *m*	scent	odeur *f*	—	aroma *m*
profumo[2] (I)	Parfüm *n*	perfume	parfum *m*	—	perfume *m*
profundidad (Es)	Tiefe *f*	depth	profondeur *f*	profondità *f*	—
profundo (Es)	tief	deep	profond(e)	profondo(a)	—
progettare (I)	planen	plan	projeter	—	planear
progetto (I)	Plan *m*	plan	plan *m*	—	plan *m*
prognosticare (I)	vorhersagen	predict	prédire	—	pronosticar
programa (Es)	Programm *n*	programme	programme *m*	programma *m*	—
Programm (D)	—	programme	programme *m*	programma *m*	programa *m*
programma (I)	Programm *n*	programme	programme *m*	—	programa *m*
programme (E)	Programm *n*	—	programme *m*	programma *m*	programa *m*
programme (F)	Programm *n*	programme	—	programma *m*	programa *m*
progrès (F)	Fortschritt *m*	progress	—	progresso *m*	progreso *m*
progress (E)	Fortschritt *m*	—	progrès *m*	progresso *m*	progreso *m*
progresso (I)	Fortschritt *m*	progress	progrès *m*	—	progreso *m*
prohibición (Es)	Verbot *n*	prohibition	défense *f*	divieto *m*	—
prohibido (Es)	verboten	forbidden	interdit(e)	vietato(a)	—
prohibir[1] (Es)	untersagen	forbid	interdire qch à qn	proibire	—
prohibir[2] (Es)	verbieten	forbid	défendre	proibire	—
prohibition (E)	Verbot *n*	—	défense *f*	divieto *m*	prohibición *f*
proibire[1] (I)	untersagen	forbid	interdire qch à qn	—	prohibir
proibire[2] (I)	verbieten	forbid	défendre	—	prohibir
projeter (F)	planen	plan	—	progettare	planear
prólogo (Es)	Vorwort *n*	preface	préface *f*	prefazione *f*	—
prolonger (F)	verlängern	extend	—	allungare	alargar
promenade (F)	Spaziergang *m*	walk	—	passeggiata *f*	paseo *m*
promener, se (F)	spazierengehen	go for a walk	—	passeggiare	ir de paseo
promesa (Es)	Versprechen *n*	promise	promesse *f*	promessa *f*	—
promessa (I)	Versprechen *n*	promise	promesse *f*	—	promesa *f*
promesse (F)	Versprechen *n*	promise	—	promessa *f*	promesa *f*
prometer[1] (Es)	versprechen	promise	promettre	promettere	—
prometer[2] (Es)	zusagen	promise	promettre	promettere	—
prometerse (Es)	verloben	get engaged	fiancer, se	fidanzarsi	—
prometido (Es)	Verlobter *m*	fiancé	fiancé *m*	fidanzato *m*	—
promettere[1] (I)	versprechen	promise	promettre	—	prometer
promettere[2] (I)	zusagen	promise	promettre	—	prometer
promettre[1] (F)	versprechen	promise	—	promettere	prometer
promettre[2] (F)	zusagen	promise	—	promettere	prometer
promise[1] (E)	versprechen	—	promettre	promettere	prometer

	D	E	F	I	Es
promise² (E)	Versprechen *n*	—	promesse *f*	promessa *f*	promesa *f*
promise³ (E)	zusagen	—	promettre	promettere	prometer
prononcer (F)	aussprechen	pronounce	—	pronunciare	pronunciar
prononciation (F)	Aussprache *f*	pronunciation	—	pronuncia *f*	pronunciación *f*
pronosticar (Es)	vorhersagen	predict	prédire	prognosticare	—
pronóstico del tiempo (Es)	Wetter- vorhersage *f*	weather forecast	prévisions météorologiques *f pl*	previsioni del tempo *f pl*	—
pronounce (E)	aussprechen	—	prononcer	pronunciare	pronunciar
pronto (Es)	bald	soon	bientôt	presto	—
pronto¹ (I)	bereit	ready	prêt(e)	—	dispuesto(a)
pronto² (I)	fertig	ready	prêt(e)	—	listo(a)
pronto! (I)	hallo!	hello!	allô!	—	¡diga!
pronuncia (I)	Aussprache *f*	pronunciation	prononciation *f*	—	pronunciación *f*
pronunciación (Es)	Aussprache *f*	pronunciation	prononciation *f*	pronuncia *f*	—
pronunciar (Es)	aussprechen	pronounce	prononcer	pronunciare	—
pronunciare (I)	aussprechen	pronounce	prononcer	—	pronunciar
pronunciation (E)	Aussprache *f*	—	prononciation *f*	pronuncia *f*	pronunciación *f*
proof (E)	Beweis *m*	—	preuve *f*	prova *f*	prueba *f*
propager (F)	verbreiten	spread	—	diffondere	difundir
propietario¹ (Es)	Eigentümer *m*	owner	propriétaire *m*	proprietario *m*	—
propietario² (Es)	Inhaber *m*	owner	propriétaire *m*	proprietario *m*	—
propietario³ (Es)	Besitzer *m*	owner	propriétaire *m*	proprietario *m*	—
propina (Es)	Trinkgeld *n*	tip	pourboire *m*	mancia *f*	—
propio (Es)	eigen	own	propre	proprio(a)	—
proponer (Es)	vorschlagen	propose	proposer	proporre	—
proporcionar (Es)	beschaffen	get	procurer	procurare	—
proporre (I)	vorschlagen	propose	proposer	—	proponer
proposal (E)	Vorschlag *m*	—	proposition *f*	proposta *f*	proposición *f*
propose (E)	vorschlagen	—	proposer	proporre	proponer
proposer (F)	vorschlagen	propose	—	proporre	proponer
proposición (Es)	Vorschlag *m*	proposal	proposition *f*	proposta *f*	—
proposition (F)	Vorschlag *m*	proposal	—	proposta *f*	proposición *f*
proposta (I)	Vorschlag *m*	proposal	proposition *f*	—	proposición *f*
propre¹ (F)	eigen	own	—	proprio(a)	propio(a)
propre² (F)	sauber	clean	—	pulito(a)	limpio(a)
proprietà (I)	Besitz *m*	possession	propriété *f*	—	posesión *f*
propriétaire¹ (F)	Besitzer *m*	owner	—	proprietario *m*	propietario *m*
propriétaire² (F)	Eigentümer *m*	owner	—	proprietario *m*	propietario *m*
propriétaire³ (F)	Inhaber *m*	owner	—	proprietario *m*	propietario *m*
proprietario¹ (I)	Besitzer *m*	owner	propriétaire *m*	—	propietario *m*
proprietario² (I)	Eigentümer *m*	owner	propriétaire *m*	—	propietario *m*
proprietario³ (I)	Inhaber *m*	owner	propriétaire *m*	—	propietario *m*
propriété (F)	Besitz *m*	possession	—	proprietà *f*	posesión *f*
proprio (I)	eigen	own	propre	—	propio(a)
prosciutto (I)	Schinken *m*	ham	jambon *m*	—	jamón *m*
proseguir¹ (Es)	fortsetzen	continue	continuer	continuare	—
proseguir² (Es)	weitergehen	go on	aller plus loin	proseguire	—
proseguire (I)	weitergehen	go on	aller plus loin	—	proseguir

	D	E	F	I	Es
prospecto (Es)	Prospekt *m*	brochure	prospectus *m*	dépliant *m*	—
prospectus (F)	Prospekt *m*	brochure	—	dépliant *m*	prospecto *m*
Prospekt (D)	—	brochure	prospectus *m*	dépliant *m*	prospecto *m*
prossimo (I)	nächste(r,s)	next	suivant(e)	—	siguiente
prost! (D)	—	cheers!	santé!	salute!	¡salud!
protección (Es)	Schutz *m*	protection	protection *f*	protezione *f*	—
protect[1] (E)	beschützen	—	protéger	proteggere	proteger
protect[2] (E)	schützen	—	protéger	proteggere	proteger
protection (E)	Schutz *m*	—	protection *f*	protezione *f*	protección *f*
protection (F)	Schutz *m*	protection	—	protezione *f*	protección *f*
proteger[1] (Es)	beschützen	protect	protéger	proteggere	—
proteger[2] (Es)	schützen	protect	protéger	proteggere	—
protéger[1] (F)	beschützen	protect	—	proteggere	proteger
protéger[2] (F)	schützen	protect	—	proteggere	proteger
proteggere[1] (I)	beschützen	protect	protéger	—	proteger
proteggere[2] (I)	schützen	protect	protéger	—	proteger
Protestant (E)	evangelisch	—	protestant(e)	protestante	protestante
protestant (F)	evangelisch	Protestant	—	protestante	protestante
protestante (Es)	evangelisch	Protestant	protestant(e)	protestante	—
protestante (I)	evangelisch	Protestant	protestant(e)	—	protestante
protezione (I)	Schutz *m*	protection	protection *f*	—	protección *f*
proud (E)	stolz	—	fier(-ère)	orgoglioso(a)	orgulloso(a)
prouver (F)	beweisen	prove	—	provare	probar
prova[1] (I)	Beweis *m*	proof	preuve *f*	—	prueba *f*
prova[2] (I)	Probe *f*	test	essai *m*	—	prueba *f*
provare[1] (I)	anprobieren	try on	essayer	—	probar
provare[2] (I)	beweisen	prove	prouver	—	probar
provare[3] (I)	probieren	try	essayer	—	probar
prove (E)	beweisen	—	prouver	provare	probar
proveer (Es)	versorgen	provide	fournir	approvvigionare	—
proverb (E)	Sprichwort *n*	—	proverbe *m*	proverbio *m*	proverbio *m*
proverbe (F)	Sprichwort *n*	proverb	—	proverbio *m*	proverbio *m*
proverbio (Es)	Sprichwort *n*	proverb	proverbe *m*	proverbio *m*	—
proverbio (I)	Sprichwort *n*	proverb	proverbe *m*	—	proverbio *m*
provide (E)	versorgen	—	fournir	approvvigionare	proveer
provided (E)	vorausgesetzt	—	à condition que	presumendo	supuesto
Provision (D)	—	commission	commission *f*	provvigione *f*	comisión *f*
provisión (Es)	Vorrat *m*	stock	réserves *f pl*	scorte *f pl*	—
provisional (Es)	vorläufig	temporary	provisoire	provvisorio(a)	—
provisoire (F)	vorläufig	temporary	—	provvisorio(a)	provisional
provvigione (I)	Provision *f*	commission	commission *f*	—	comisión *f*
provvisorio (I)	vorläufig	temporary	provisoire	—	provisional
proximamente (Es)	demnächst	shortly	prochainement	presto	—
próximidad (Es)	Nähe *f*	proximity	environs *m pl*	vicinanza *f*	—
proximity (E)	Nähe *f*	—	environs *m pl*	vicinanza *f*	próximidad *f*
proyectar (Es)	beabsichtigen	intend	avoir l'intention de	avere (l')intenzione di	—
proyecto (Es)	Entwurf *m*	outline	esquisse *f*	abbozzo *m*	—

	D	E	F	I	Es
Prozent (D)	—	percent	pour cent	percentuale f	por ciento m
Prozeß (D)	—	trial	procès m	processo m	proceso m
prudence (F)	Vorsicht f	caution	—	prudenza f	cuidado m
prudent (F)	vorsichtig	careful	—	prudente	cauto(a)
prudente (I)	vorsichtig	careful	prudent(e)	—	cauto(a)
prudenza (I)	Vorsicht f	caution	prudence f	—	cuidado m
prudere (I)	jucken	itch	démanger	—	picar
prueba[1] (Es)	Beweis m	proof	preuve f	prova f	—
prueba[2] (Es)	Probe f	test	essai m	prova f	—
prüfen (D)	—	test	tester	esaminare	examinar
Prüfung (D)	—	examination	examen m	esame m	examen m
prugna (I)	Pflaume f	plum	prune f	—	ciruela f
prune (F)	Pflaume f	plum	—	prugna f	ciruela f
pub[1] (E)	Kneipe f	—	bistro m	osteria f	tasca f
pub[2] (E)	Lokal n	—	restaurant m	locale m	local m
pubblicare[1] (I)	herausgeben	publish	éditer	—	editar
pubblicare[2] (I)	veröffentlichen	publish	publier	—	publicar
pubblicità (I)	Werbung f	advertising	publicité f	—	publicidad f
pubblico[1] (I)	öffentlich	public	public(-ique)	—	público(a)
pubblico[2] (I)	Öffentlichkeit f	public	public m	—	público m
pubblico[3] (I)	Publikum n	audience	spectateurs m pl	—	público m
public[1] (E)	öffentlich	—	public(-ique)	pubblico(a)	público(a)
public[2] (E)	Öffentlichkeit f	—	public m	pubblico m	público m
public[1] (F)	Öffentlichkeit f	public	—	pubblico m	público m
public[2] (F)	öffentlich	public	—	pubblico(a)	público(a)
publicar (Es)	veröffentlichen	publish	publier	pubblicare	—
publicidad (Es)	Werbung f	advertising	publicité f	pubblicità f	—
publicité[1] (F)	Reklame f	advertisement	—	réclame f	anuncio m
publicité[2] (F)	Werbung f	advertising	—	pubblicità f	publicidad f
público[1] (Es)	Öffentlichkeit f	public	public m	pubblico m	—
público[2] (Es)	Publikum n	audience	spectateurs m pl	pubblico m	—
público[3] (Es)	öffentlich	public	public(-ique)	pubblico(a)	—
publier (F)	veröffentlichen	publish	—	pubblicare	publicar
Publikum (D)	—	audience	spectateurs m pl	pubblico m	público m
publish[1] (E)	herausgeben	—	éditer	pubblicare	editar
publish[2] (E)	veröffentlichen	—	publier	pubblicare	publicar
puce (F)	Floh m	flea	—	pulce f	pulga f
Pudding (D)	—	pudding	flan m	budino m	flan m
pudding (E)	Pudding m	—	flan m	budino m	flan m
puddle (E)	Pfütze f	—	flaque f	pozzanghera f	charco m
Puder (D)	—	powder	poudre f	cipria f	polvos m pl
pueblo[1] (Es)	Dorf n	village	village m	paese m	—
pueblo[2] (Es)	Volk n	people	peuple m	popolo m	—
puente (Es)	Brücke f	bridge	pont m	ponte m	—
puer (F)	stinken	stink	—	puzzare	apestar
puerta[1] (Es)	Tür f	door	porte f	porta f	—
puerta[2] (Es)	Tor n	gate	porte f	porta f	—
puerto (Es)	Hafen m	port	port m	porto m	—

	D	E	F	I	Es
pues (Es)	denn	for/than	car	perchè	—
puesta del sol (Es)	Sonnenuntergang *m*	sunset	coucher du soleil *m*	tramonto del sole *m*	—
puesto[1] (Es)	Posten *m*	position	poste *m*	posto *m*	—
puesto[2] (Es)	Stelle *f*	place	place *f*	posto *m*	—
pugno (I)	Faust *f*	fist	poing *m*	—	puño *m*
puissance (F)	Stärke *f*	strength	—	forza *f*	fuerza *f*
pulce (I)	Floh *m*	flea	puce *f*	—	pulga *f*
pulga (Es)	Floh *m*	flea	puce *f*	pulce *f*	—
pulgar (Es)	Daumen *m*	thumb	pouce *m*	pollice *m*	—
pulir (Es)	polieren	polish	astiquer	lucidare	—
pulire[1] (I)	putzen	clean	nettoyer	—	limpiar
pulire[2] (I)	reinigen	clean	nettoyer	—	limpiar
pulire[3] (I)	wischen	wipe	essuyer	—	fregar
pulito (I)	sauber	clean	propre	—	limpio(a)
pulitura (I)	Reinigung *f*	cleaning	nettoyage *m*	—	limpieza *f*
pull (E)	ziehen	—	tirer	tirare	tirar
Pullover (D)	—	pullover	pull-over *m*	pullover *m*	jersey *m*
pullover (E)	Pullover *m*	—	pull-over *m*	pullover *m*	jersey *m*
pull-over (F)	Pullover *m*	pullover	—	pullover *m*	jersey *m*
pullover (I)	Pullover *m*	pullover	pull-over *m*	—	jersey *m*
pulmón (Es)	Lunge *f*	lung	poumon *m*	polmone *m*	—
Puls (D)	—	pulse	pouls *m*	polso *m*	pulso *m*
pulse (E)	Puls *m*	—	pouls *m*	polso *m*	pulso *m*
pulsera (Es)	Armband *n*	bracelet	bracelet *m*	bracciale *m*	—
pulso (Es)	Puls *m*	pulse	pouls *m*	polso *m*	—
Pulver (D)	—	powder	poudre *f*	polvere *f*	pólvora *f*
pump (E)	Pumpe *f*	—	pompe *f*	pompa *f*	bomba *f*
Pumpe (D)	—	pump	pompe *f*	pompa *f*	bomba *f*
punctual (E)	pünktlich	—	ponctuel(le)	puntuale	puntual
pungere (I)	stechen	prick	piquer	—	picar
punir (F)	strafen	punish	—	punire	castigar
punire (I)	strafen	punish	punir	—	castigar
punish (E)	strafen	—	punir	punire	castigar
punishment (E)	Strafe *f*	—	punition *f*	punizione *f*	castigo *m*
punition (F)	Strafe *f*	punishment	—	punizione *f*	castigo *m*
punizione (I)	Strafe *f*	punishment	punition *f*	—	castigo *m*
Punkt (D)	—	point	point *m*	punto *m*	punto *m*
pünktlich (D)	—	punctual	ponctuel(le)	puntuale	puntual
puño (Es)	Faust *f*	fist	poing *m*	pugno *m*	—
punta (Es)	Spitze *f*	point	pointe *f*	punta *f*	—
punta (I)	Spitze *f*	point	pointe *f*	—	punta *f*
puntiagudo (Es)	spitz	pointed	pointu(e)	appuntito(a)	—
punto (Es)	Punkt *m*	point	point *m*	punto *m*	—
punto (I)	Punkt *m*	point	point *m*	—	punto *m*

	D	E	F	I	Es
punto de vista (Es)	Standpunkt *m*	standpoint	point de vue *m*	punto di vista *m*	—
punto di vista (I)	Standpunkt *m*	standpoint	point de vue *m*	—	punto de vista *m*
puntual (Es)	pünktlich	punctual	ponctuel(le)	puntuale	—
puntuale (I)	pünktlich	punctual	ponctuel(le)	—	puntual
pupil (E)	Schüler *m*	—	élève *m*	scolaro *m*	alumno *m*
Puppe (D)	—	doll	poupée *f*	bambola *f*	muñeca *f*
pur (D)	—	pure	pur(e)	puro(a)	puro
pur¹ (F)	pur	pure	—	puro(a)	puro
pur² (F)	rein	pure	—	puro(a)	puro(a)
purchase (E)	Kauf *m*	—	achat *m*	acquisto *m*	compra *f*
pure¹ (E)	pur	—	pur(e)	puro(a)	puro
pure² (E)	rein	—	pur(e)	puro(a)	puro(a)
puro¹ (I)	pur	pure	pur(e)	—	puro
puro² (I)	rein	pure	pur(e)	—	puro(a)
puro (Es)	rein	pure	pur(e)	puro(a)	—
purple (E)	lila	—	mauve	lilla	de color lila
purpose (E)	Zweck *m*	—	but *m*	scopo *m*	finalidad *f*
pursue (E)	verfolgen	—	poursuivre	inseguire	perseguir
purtroppo (I)	leider	unfortunately	malheureusement	—	desgraciadamente
push¹ (E)	stoßen	—	pousser	spingere	empujar
push² (E)	schieben	—	pousser	spingere	empujar
put (E)	setzen	—	mettre	mettere	poner
put down (E)	hinlegen	—	poser	posare	poner
put in order (E)	ordnen	—	ordonner	ordinare	ordenar
put on¹ (E)	anmachen	—	allumer	accendere	encender
put on² (E)	anziehen	—	mettre	indossare	ponerse
putzen (D)	—	clean	nettoyer	pulire	limpiar
Putzfrau (D)	—	charwoman	femme de ménage *f*	donna delle pulizie *f*	mujer de la limpicza *f*
puzzare (I)	stinken	stink	puer	—	apestar
qua¹ (I)	hierher	over here	par ici	—	para acá
qua² (I)	her	here/ago	ici	—	aquí
quaderno (I)	Heft *n*	exercise book	cahier *m*	—	cuaderno *m*
Quadrat (D)	—	square	carré *m*	quadrato *m*	cuadrado *m*
quadratisch (D)	—	square	carré(e)	quadrato(a)	cuadrado(a)
Quadratmeter (D)	—	square metre	mètre carré *m*	metro quadrato *m*	metro cuadrado *m*
quadrato¹ (I)	quadratisch	square	carré(e)	—	cuadrado(a)
quadrato² (I)	Quadrat *f*	square	carré *m*	—	cuadrado *m*
quadrato³ (I)	viereckig	square	carré(e)		cuadrangular
quadro (I)	Gemälde *n*	painting	tableau *m*	—	cuadro *m*
qualcosa (I)	etwas	something	quelque chose	—	algo
qualcuno¹ (I)	irgend jemand	somebody	n'importe qui	—	alguno(a)
qualcuno² (I)	jemand	somebody	quelqu'un	—	alguien
qualcuno³ (I)	irgendein(e)	some/any	quelconque	—	cualquiera

	D	E	F	I	Es
quälen (D)	—	torture	torturer	tormentare	atormentar
qualità[1] (I)	Eigenschaft f	quality	qualité f	—	atributo m
qualità[2] (I)	Qualität f	quality	qualité f	—	cualidad f
Qualität (D)	—	quality	qualité f	qualità f	cualidad f
qualité[1] (F)	Eigenschaft f	quality	—	qualità f	atributo m
qualité[2] (F)	Qualität f	quality	—	qualità f	cualidad f
quality[1] (E)	Eigenschaft f	—	qualité f	qualità f	atributo m
quality[2] (E)	Qualität f	—	qualité f	qualità f	cualidad f
qualora (I)	falls	in case	au cas où	—	en caso de que
qualsiasi (I)	beliebig	any	n'importe quel	—	a voluntad
qualsiasi cosa (I)	irgend etwas	something	n'importe quoi	—	algo
quand[1] (F)	als	when	—	quando	cuando
quand[2] (F)	wann	when	—	quando	cuando
quando[1] (I)	als	when	quand	—	cuando
quando[2] (I)	wann	when	quand	—	cuando
quanti (I)	wieviele	how many	combien	—	¿cuántos(as)?
quantità[1] (I)	Menge f	quantity	quantité f	—	cantidad f
quantità[2] (I)	Quantität f	quantity	quantité f	—	cantidad f
Quantität (D)	—	quantity	quantité f	quantità f	cantidad f
quantité[1] (F)	Menge f	quantity	—	quantità f	cantidad f
quantité[2] (F)	Quantität f	quantity	—	quantità f	cantidad f
quantity[1] (E)	Menge f	—	quantité f	quantità f	cantidad f
quantity[2] (E)	Quantität f	—	quantité f	quantità f	cantidad f
quanto[1] (I)	wieviel	how much	combien	—	¿cuánto?
quanto[2] (I)	soviel	so much	tant	—	tanto
quaranta (I)	vierzig	forty	quarante	—	cuarenta
quarante (F)	vierzig	forty	—	quaranta	cuarenta
Quark (D)	—	curd cheese	fromage blanc m	ricotta f	requesón m
quarrel (E)	streiten	—	disputer, se	litigare	discutir
quart (F)	Viertel n	a quarter	—	quarto m	barrio m
Quartett (D)	—	quartet	quatuor m	quartetto m	cuarteto m
quartet (E)	Quartett n	—	quatuor m	quartetto m	cuarteto m
quartetto (I)	Quartett n	quartet	quatuor m	—	cuarteto m
quarto (I)	Viertel n	a quarter	quart m	—	barrio m
quasi (I)	fast	nearly	presque	—	casi
quatorze (F)	vierzehn	fourteen	—	quattordici	catorce
quatre (F)	vier	four	—	quattro	cuatro
quatre-vingt-dix (F)	neunzig	ninety	—	novanta	noventa
quatre-vingts (F)	achtzig	eighty	—	ottanta	ochenta
quattordici (I)	vierzehn	fourteen	quatorze	—	catorce
quattro (I)	vier	four	quatre	—	cuatro
quatuor (F)	Quartett n	quartet	—	quartetto m	cuarteto m
que (Es)	daß	that	que	che	—
que (F)	daß	that	—	che	que

	D	E	F	I	Es
¿qué?[1] (Es)	was	what	quoi/ qu'est-ce que	che/cosa	—
¿qué?[2] (Es)	welch	what a	quel(le)	che	—
Quecksilber (D)	—	mercury	mercure *m*	mercurio *m*	mercurio *m*
quedar (Es)	übrigbleiben	be left	rester	avanzare	—
quedarse (Es)	blciben	stay	rester	rimanere	—
quedarse aquí (Es)	hierbleiben	stay here	rester	restare qui	—
queen (E)	Königin *f*	—	reine *f*	regina *f*	reina *f*
quejarse[1] (Es)	beschweren, sich	complain	plaindre, se	lamentarsi	—
quejarse[2] (Es)	beklagen	deplore	plaindre de, se	lamentare	—
quel (F)	welch	what a	—	che	¿qué?
quelconque (F)	irgendein(e)	some/any	—	qualcuno(a)	cualquiera
Quelle (D)	—	spring	source *f*	sorgente *f*	fuente *f*
quello (I)	jene(r,s)	that, those *pl*	ce, cette, ces *pl*	—	aquella, aquel, aquello
quelque chose (F)	etwas	something	—	qualcosa	algo
quelquefois (F)	manchmal	sometimes	—	talvolta	a veces
quelques[1] (F)	etliche	several	—	alcuni(e)	algunos(as)
quelques[2] (F)	einige	some	—	alcuni(e)	algunos(as)
quelqu'un (F)	jemand	somebody	—	qualcuno	alguien
quemadura solar (Es)	Sonnenbrand *m*	sunburn	coup de soleil *m*	scottatura solare *f*	—
quemar (Es)	verbrennen	burn	brûler	bruciare	—
que puede adquirirse (Es)	erhältlich	available	en vente	acquistabile	—
quer (D)	—	across	en travers	di trasverso	al través
querer[1] (Es)	mögen	like	aimer	piacere	—
querer[2] (Es)	wollen	want	vouloir	volere	—
querido[1] (Es)	Liebling *m*	darling	chéri *m*	tesoro *m*	—
querido[2] (Es)	wert	worth	cher(ère)	che vale	—
Querstraße (D)	—	intersecting road	rue transversale *f*	traversa *f*	travesía *f*
queso (Es)	Käse *m*	cheese	fromage *m*	formaggio *m*	—
question (E)	Frage *f*	—	question *f*	domanda *f*	pregunta *f*
question (F)	Frage *f*	question	—	domanda *f*	pregunta *f*
questo (I)	diese(r,s)	this	ce, cette	—	esta, e
queue (F)	Schwanz *m*	tail	—	coda *f*	rabo *m*
qui[1] (F)	wer	who	—	chi	¿quién?
qui[2] (F)	welche(r,s)	which	—	il(la) quale	¿cuál?
qui[1] (I)	hier	here	ici	—	aquí
qui[2] (I)	da	there	là/ici	—	allí
quick (E)	rasch	—	rapide	rapido(a)	impulsivo(a)
¿quién? (Es)	wer	who	qui	chi	—
quiet[1] (E)	ruhig	—	tranquille	calmo(a)	quieto(a)
quiet[2] (E)	still	—	calme	calmo(a)	tranquilo(a)
quietly (E)	leise	—	à voix basse	a bassa voce	sin ruido
quieto (Es)	ruhig	quiet	tranquille	calmo(a)	—

	D	E	F	I	Es
quietud (Es)	Ruhe f	calm	calme m	silenzio m	—
químico (Es)	chemisch	chemical	chimique	chimico(a)	—
quince (Es)	fünfzehn	fifteen	quinze	quindici	—
quindici (I)	fünfzehn	fifteen	quinze	—	quince
quinze (F)	fünfzehn	fifteen	—	quindici	quince
quitar¹ (Es)	entfernen	remove	éloigner	allontanare	—
quitar² (Es)	wegnehmen	take away	enlever	togliere	—
quitarse (Es)	ausziehen	take off	enlever	levare	—
quite (E)	ziemlich	—	assez	abbastanza	bastante
quittance (F)	Quittung f	receipt	—	ricevuta f	recibo m
Quittung (D)	—	receipt	quittance f	ricevuta f	recibo m
quoi (F)	was	what	—	che/cosa	¿qué?
quote-part (F)	Rate f	instalment	—	rata f	plazo m
quotidiano (I)	täglich	daily	quotidien(ne)	—	cotidiano(a)
quotidien (F)	täglich	daily	—	quotidiano(a)	cotidiano(a)
rabais (F)	Rabatt m	discount	—	sconto m	rebaja f
Rabatt (D)	—	discount	rabais m	sconto m	rebaja f
rabbia (I)	Wut f	anger	colère f	—	rabia f
Rabe (D)	—	raven	corbeau m	corvo m	cuervo m
rabia (Es)	Wut f	anger	colère f	rabbia f	—
rabo (Es)	Schwanz m	tail	queue f	coda f	—
raccogliere (I)	sammeln	collect	collecter	—	recolectar
raccoglitore (I)	Mappe f	folder	serviette f	—	carpeta f
raccolta (I)	Sammlung f	collection	collection f	—	colección f
raccolto (I)	Ernte f	harvest	moisson f	—	cosecha f
raccomandare (I)	empfehlen	recommend	recommander	—	recomendar
raccomandazione (I)	Empfehlung f	recommendation	recommandation f	—	recomendación f
raccontare (I)	erzählen	tell	raconter	—	contar
Rache (D)	—	revenge	vengeance f	vendetta f	venganza f
Rachen (D)	—	throat	gorge f	faringe m	garganta f
racine (F)	Wurzel f	root	—	radice f	raíz f
raconter (F)	erzählen	tell	—	raccontare	contar
Rad (D)	—	wheel	roue f	ruota f	rueda f
Radarkontrolle (D)	—	speed trap	contrôle radar m	controllo radar m	control de radar m
radice (I)	Wurzel f	root	racine f	—	raíz f
Radio (D)	—	radio	radio f	radio f	radio f
radio (E)	Radio n	—	radio f	radio f	radio f
radio (Es)	Radio n	radio	radio f	radio f	—
radio¹ (F)	Radio n	radio	—	radio f	radio f
radio² (F)	Rundfunk m	broadcasting	—	radio f	radiodifusión f
radio¹ (I)	Rundfunk m	broadcasting	radio f	—	radiodifusión f
radio² (I)	Radio n	radio	radio f	—	radio f
radiodifusión (Es)	Rundfunk m	broadcasting	radio f	radio f	—
radiografiar (Es)	röntgen	X-ray	radiographier	fare una radiografia	—

	D	E	F	I	Es
radiographier (F)	röntgen	X-ray	—	fare una radiografia	radiografiar
raffreddore[1] (I)	Erkältung *f*	cold	refroidissement *m*	—	catarro *m*
raffreddore[2] (I)	Schnupfen *m*	cold	rhume *m*	—	resfriado *m*
rafraîchissement (F)	Erfrischung *f*	refreshment	—	rinfresco *m*	refresco *m*
ragazza (I)	Mädchen *n*	girl	jeune fille *f*	—	chica *f*
ragazzo[1] (I)	Bursche *m*	fellow	garçon *m*	—	chico *m*
ragazzo[2] (I)	Junge *m*	boy	garçon *m*	—	chico *m*
raggio (I)	Strahl *m*	ray	rayon *m*	—	rayo *m*
raggiungere (I)	erreichen	reach	atteindre	—	alcanzar
ragionevole (I)	vernünftig	sensible	raisonnable	—	razonable
ragno (I)	Spinne *f*	spider	araignée *f*	—	araña *f*
Rahmen (D)	—	frame	cadre *m*	cornice *f*	marco *m*
raid[1] (E)	überfallen	—	attaquer	assalire	asaltar
raid[2] (E)	Überfall *m*	—	attaque *f*	aggressione *f*	asalto *m*
raide (F)	steil	steep	—	ripido(a)	inclinado(a)
railway (E)	Eisenbahn *f*	—	chemin de fer *m*	ferrovia *f*	ferrocarril *m*
rain[1] (E)	regnen	—	pleuvoir	piovere	llover
rain[2] (E)	Regen *m*	—	pluie *f*	pioggia *f*	lluvia *f*
raincoat (E)	Regenmantel *m*	—	imperméable *m*	impermeabile *m*	impermeable *m*
raise[1] (E)	erhöhen	—	augmenter	innalzare	elevar
raise[2] (E)	erheben	—	lever	alzare	elevar
raison (F)	Grund *m*	reason	—	causa *f*	causa *f*
raisonnable (F)	vernünftig	sensible	—	ragionevole	razonable
raíz (Es)	Wurzel *f*	root	racine *f*	radice *f*	—
rallegrarsi (I)	freuen, sich	be glad	être heureux(-euse)	—	alegrarse
rama[1] (Es)	Ast *m*	branch	branche *f*	ramo *m*	—
rama[2] (Es)	Zweig *m*	branch	branche *f*	ramo *m*	—
rame (F)	Ruder *n*	oar	—	remo *m*	remo *m*
ramer (F)	rudern	row	—	remare	remar
ramo (Es)	Strauß *m*	bunch	bouquet *m*	mazzo *m*	—
ramo[1] (I)	Ast *m*	branch	branche *f*	—	rama *f*
ramo[2] (I)	Zweig *m*	branch	branche *f*	—	rama *f*
rana (Es)	Frosch *m*	frog	grenouille *f*	rana *f*	—
rana (I)	Frosch *m*	frog	grenouille *f*	—	rana *f*
Rand (D)	—	brim	bord *m*	margine *m*	borde *m*
Rang (D)	—	rank	rang *m*	ceto *m*	clase *f*
rang (F)	Rang *m*	rank	—	ceto *m*	clase *f*
rangé (F)	ordentlich	tidy	—	ordinato(a)	ordenado(a)
rangée (F)	Reihe *f*	row	—	fila *f*	fila *f*
ranger[1] (F)	aufräumen	clear away	—	mettere in ordine	arreglar
ranger[2] (F)	unterbringen	stow	—	sistemare	colocar
rango (I)	Grad *m*	rank	grade *m*	—	titulo *m*
rank[1] (E)	Grad *m*	—	grade *m*	rango *m*	título *m*
rank[2] (E)	Rang *m*	—	rang *m*	ceto *m*	clase *f*
rape (E)	vergewaltigen	—	violer	violentare	violar
rapide[1] (F)	rasch	quick	—	rapido(a)	impulsivo(a)
rapide[2] (F)	schnell	fast	—	veloce	rápido(a)

	D	E	F	I	Es
rapide³ (F)	Schnellzug *m*	express train	—	treno direttissimo *m*	tren expreso *m*
rapidez (Es)	Schnelligkeit *f*	speed	rapidité *f*	velocità *f*	—
rapidité (F)	Schnelligkeit *f*	speed	—	velocità *f*	rapidez *f*
rapido (I)	rasch	quick	rapide	—	impulsivo(a)
rápido¹ (Es)	eilig	hurried	pressé(e)	frettoloso(a)	—
rápido² (Es)	schnell	fast	rapide	veloce	—
rapinare (I)	rauben	rob	voler	—	robar
rapport¹ (F)	Beziehung *f*	relation	—	relazione *f*	relación *f*
rapport² (F)	Bericht *m*	report	—	relazione *f*	relación *f*
rapporter (F)	zurückbringen	bring back	—	riportare	devolver
rapporto (I)	Beziehung *f*	relationship	relation *f*	—	relaciones *f pl*
rappresentante (I)	Vertreter *m*	representative	représentant *m*	—	representante
rappresentare¹ (I)	darstellen	represent	représenter	—	presentar
rappresentare² (I)	vertreten	represent	représenter	—	representar
rappresentazione (I)	Vorstellung *f*	performance	représentation *f*	—	representación *f*
rare (E)	selten	—	rare	raro(a)	raro(a)
rare (F)	selten	rare	—	raro(a)	raro(a)
rareté (F)	Seltenheit *f*	rarity	—	rarità *f*	rareza *f*
rareza (Es)	Seltenheit *f*	rarity	rareté *f*	rarità *f*	—
rarità (I)	Seltenheit *f*	rarity	rareté *f*	—	rareza *f*
rarity (E)	Seltenheit *f*	—	rareté *f*	rarità *f*	rareza *f*
raro (Es)	selten	rare	rare	raro(a)	—
raro (I)	selten	rare	rare	—	raro(a)
rasch (D)	—	quick	rapide	rapido(a)	impulsivo(a)
Rasen (D)	—	lawn	pelouse *f*	prato *m*	césped *m*
raser (F)	rasieren	shave	—	fare la barba	afeitar
rasgo (Es)	Merkmal *n*	characteristic	signe *m*	caratteristica *f*	—
Rasierapparat (D)	—	shaver	rasoir *m*	rasoio *m*	máquina de afeitar *f*
rasieren (D)	—	shave	raser	fare la barba	afeitar
rasoio (I)	Rasierapparat *m*	shaver	rasoir *m*	—	máquina de afeitar *f*
rasoir (F)	Rasierapparat *m*	shaver	—	rasoio *m*	máquina de afeitar *f*
raspberry (E)	Himbeere *f*	—	framboise *f*	lampone *m*	frambuesa *f*
rassasié (F)	satt	full	—	sazio(a)	satisfecho(a)
rastro (Es)	Flohmarkt *m*	fleamarket	marché aux puces *m*	mercato delle pulci *m*	—
Rat (D)	—	advice	conseil *m*	consiglio *m*	consejo *m*
rat (E)	Ratte *f*	—	rat *m*	ratto *m*	rata *f*
rat (F)	Ratte *f*	rat	—	ratto *m*	rata *f*
rata (Es)	Ratte *f*	rat	rat *m*	ratto *m*	—
rata (I)	Rate *f*	instalment	quote-part *f*	—	plazo *m*
Rate (D)	—	instalment	quote-part *f*	rata *f*	plazo *m*
rate (E)	Kurs *m*	—	cours *m*	corso *m*	curso *m*
raten¹ (D)	—	guess	deviner	indovinare	adivinar
raten² (D)	—	advise	conseiller	consigliare	aconsejar
Rathaus (D)	—	town hall	mairie *f*	municipio *m*	ayuntamiento *m*
rather (E)	lieber	—	mieux	piuttosto	más bien

	D	E	F	I	Es
rato (Es)	Weile *f*	while	moment *m*	momento *m*	—
ratón (Es)	Maus *f*	mouse	souris *f*	topo *m*	—
Rätsel (D)	—	riddle	devinette	enigma *m*	adivinanza *f*
Ratte (D)	—	rat	rat *m*	ratto *m*	rata *f*
ratto (I)	Ratte *f*	rat	rat *m*	—	rata *f*
rauben (D)	—	rob	voler	rapinare	robar
Rauch (D)	—	smoke	fumée *f*	fumo *m*	humo *m*
rauchen (D)	—	smoke	fumer	fumare	fumar
Raucher (D)	—	smoker	fumeur *m*	fumatore *m*	fumador *m*
rauh (D)	—	rough	rêche	ruvido(a)	rudo(a)
Raum (D)	—	room	pièce *f*	stanza *f*	habitación *f*
rauschen (D)	—	rush	bruire	mormorare	susurrar
raven (E)	Rabe *m*	—	corbeau *m*	corvo *m*	cuervo *m*
ravi (F)	entzückt	delighted	—	affascinato(a)	encantado(a)
ravissant (F)	entzückend	delightful	—	affascinante	encantador(a)
raw (E)	roh	—	cru(e)	crudo(a)	crudo(a)
ray (E)	Strahl *m*	—	rayon *m*	raggio *m*	rayo *m*
rayo[1] (Es)	Blitz *m*	lightning	éclair *m*	lampo *m*	—
rayo[2] (Es)	Strahl *m*	ray	rayon *m*	raggio *m*	—
rayon (F)	Strahl *m*	ray	—	raggio *m*	rayo *m*
razón (Es)	Verstand *m*	intelligence	intelligence *f*	intelligenza *f*	—
razonable (Es)	vernünftig	sensible	raisonnable	ragionevole	—
re (I)	König *m*	king	roi *m*	—	rey *m*
reacción (Es)	Reaktion *f*	reaction	réaction *f*	reazione *f*	—
reach (E)	erreichen	—	atteindre	raggiungere	alcanzar
reaction (E)	Reaktion *f*	—	réaction *f*	reazione *f*	reacción *f*
réaction (F)	Reaktion *f*	reaction	—	reazione *f*	reacción *f*
read (E)	lesen	—	lire	leggere	leer
ready[1] (E)	bereit	—	prêt(e)	pronto(a)	dispuesto(a)
ready[2] (E)	fertig	—	prêt(e)	pronto(a)	listo(a)
Reaktion (D)	—	reaction	réaction *f*	reazione *f*	reacción *f*
real (E)	wirklich	—	réel(le)	reale	real
real (Es)	wirklich	real	réel(le)	reale	—
reale (I)	wirklich	real	réel(le)	—	real
realidad (Es)	Wirklichkeit *f*	reality	réalité *f*	realtà *f*	—
réalisateur (F)	Regisseur *m*	director	—	regista *m*	director *m*
réaliser (F)	verwirklichen	realize	—	realizzare	llevar a cabo
réalité (F)	Wirklichkeit *f*	reality	—	realtà *f*	realidad *f*
reality (E)	Wirklichkeit *f*	—	réalité *f*	realtà *f*	realidad *f*
realize (E)	verwirklichen	—	réaliser	realizzare	llevar a cabo
realizzare (I)	verwirklichen	realize	réaliser	—	llevar a cabo
really (E)	tatsächlich	—	vraiment	realmente	realmente
realmente (Es)	tatsächlich	really	vraiment	realmente	—
realmente (I)	tatsächlich	really	vraiment	—	realmente
realtà (I)	Wirklichkeit *f*	reality	réalité *f*	—	realidad *f*
reason (E)	Grund *m*	—	raison *f*	causa *f*	causa *f*
reazione (I)	Reaktion *f*	reaction	réaction *f*	—	reacción *f*
rebaja[1] (Es)	Ermäßigung *f*	reduction	réduction *f*	riduzione *f*	—

	D	E	F	I	Es
rebaja² (Es)	Rabatt *m*	discount	rabais *m*	sconto *m*	—
rebajar (Es)	herabsetzen	lower	baisser	diminuire	—
rebellion (E)	Aufstand *m*	—	soulèvement *m*	insurrezione *f*	revuelta *f*
receipt (E)	Quittung *f*	—	quittance *f*	ricevuta *f*	recibo *m*
receive¹ (E)	aufnehmen	—	accueillir	accogliere	recibir
receive² (E)	empfangen	—	recevoir	ricevere	recibir
receive³ (E)	erhalten	—	recevoir	ricevere	obtener
receiver¹ (E)	Empfänger *m*	—	destinataire *f*	destinatario *m*	destinatario *m*
receiver² (E)	Hörer *m*	—	récepteur *m*	ricevitore *m*	auricular *m*
récemment (F)	kürzlich	lately	—	recente	reciente
recente (I)	kürzlich	lately	récemment	—	reciente
recentemente (I)	neulich	recently	l'autre jour	—	recientemente
recently (E)	neulich	—	l'autre jour	recentemente	recientemente
recepción (Es)	Empfang *m*	reception	réception *f*	ricerzionc *f*	—
recepción de equipajes (Es)	Gepäckannahme *f*	luggage desk	enregistrement des bagages *m*	accettazione bagagli *f*	—
récepteur (F)	Hörer *m*	receiver	—	ricevitore *m*	auricular *m*
reception¹ (E)	Aufnahme *f*	—	accueil *m*	accoglienza *f*	acogida *f*
reception² (E)	Empfang *m*	—	réception *f*	ricezione *f*	recepción *f*
réception¹ (F)	Annahme *f*	acceptance	—	accettazione *f*	aceptación *f*
réception³ (F)	Empfang *m*	reception	—	ricezione *f*	recepción *f*
receta (Es)	Rezept *n*	recipe	recette *f*	ricetta *f*	—
recette (F)	Rezept *n*	recipe	—	ricetta *f*	receta *f*
recevoir¹ (F)	bekommen	get	—	ricevere	recibir
recevoir² (F)	erhalten	receive	—	ricevere	obtener
recevoir³ (F)	empfangen	receive	—	ricevere	recibir
rêche (F)	rauh	rough	—	ruvido(a)	rudo(a)
rechercher (F)	forschen	research	—	ricercare	investigar
rechnen (D)	—	calculate	calculer	fare i conti	calcular
Rechnung (D)	—	bill	facture *f*	fattura *f*	factura *f*
Recht (D)	—	right	droit *m*	diritto *m*	derecho *m*
rechts (D)	—	right	à droite	a destra	a la derecha
Rechtsanwalt (D)	—	lawyer	avocat *m*	avvocato *m*	abogado *m*
rechtzeitig (D)	—	in time	à temps	in tempo	a tiempo
recibir¹ (Es)	aufnehmen	receive	accueillir	accogliere	—
recibir² (Es)	bekommen	get	recevoir	ricevere	—
recibir³ (Es)	empfangen	receive	recevoir	ricevere	—
recibo (Es)	Quittung *f*	receipt	quittance *f*	ricevuta *f*	—
reciente (Es)	kürzlich	lately	récemment	recente	—
recientemente (Es)	neulich	recently	l'autre jour	recentemente	—
recinto (I)	Zaun *m*	fence	clôture *f*	—	valla *f*
recipe (E)	Rezept *n*	—	recette *f*	ricetta *f*	receta *f*
récipient¹ (F)	Behälter *m*	container	—	recipiente *m*	recipiente *m*
récipient² (F)	Gefäß *n*	container	—	recipiente *m*	recipiente *m*
recipiente¹ (Es)	Behälter *m*	container	récipient *m*	recipiente *m*	—
recipiente² (Es)	Gefäß *n*	container	récipient *m*	recipiente *m*	—
recipiente¹ (I)	Behälter *m*	container	récipient *m*	—	recipiente *m*
recipiente² (I)	Gefäß *n*	container	récipient *m*	—	recipiente *m*

	D	E	F	I	Es
recita (I)	Aufführung *f*	performance	représentation *f*	—	representación *f*
réclam (I)	Reklame *f*	advertisement	publicité *f*	—	anuncio *m*
reclamación[1] (Es)	Beschwerde *f*	complaint	plainte *f*	reclamo *m*	—
reclamación[2] (Es)	Reklamation *f*	complaint	réclamation *f*	reclamo *m*	—
reclamar (Es)	reklamieren	complain	plaindre de, se	reclamare	—
reclamare (I)	reklamieren	complain	plaindre de, se	—	reclamar
réclamation (F)	Reklamation *f*	complaint	—	reclamo *m*	reclamación *f*
reclamo[1] (I)	Beschwerde *f*	complaint	plainte *f*	—	reclamación *f*
reclamo[2] (I)	Reklamation *f*	complaint	réclamation *f*	—	reclamación *f*
recoger (Es)	abholen	pick up	aller chercher	andare a prendere	—
recognize (E)	erkennen	—	reconnaître	riconoscere	reconocer
recolectar (Es)	sammeln	collect	collecter	raccogliere	—
recomendación (Es)	Empfehlung *f*	recommendation	recommandation *f*	raccomandazione *f*	—
recomendar (Es)	empfehlen	recommend	recommander	raccomandare	—
recommandation (F)	Empfehlung *f*	recommendation	—	raccomandazione *f*	recomendación *f*
recommander (F)	empfehlen	recommend	—	raccomandare	recomendar
recommend (E)	empfehlen	—	recommander	raccomandare	recomendar
recommendation (E)	Empfehlung *f*	—	recommandation *f*	raccomandazione *f*	recomendación *f*
recompensa (Es)	Belohnung *f*	reward	récompense *f*	ricompensa *f*	—
recompensar (Es)	belohnen	reward	récompenser	premiare	—
récompense (F)	Belohnung *f*	reward	—	ricompensa *f*	recompensa *f*
récompenser (F)	belohnen	reward	—	premiare	recompensar
reconnaissant (F)	dankbar	grateful	—	grato(a)	agradecido(a)
reconnaître (F)	erkennen	recognize	—	riconoscere	reconocer
reconocer (Es)	erkennen	recognize	reconnaître	riconoscere	—
record[1] (E)	Platte *f*	—	disque *m*	disco *m*	disco *m*
record[2] (E)	Rekord *m*	—	record *m*	record *m*	record *m*
record[3] (E)	Schallplatte *f*	—	disque *m*	disco *m*	disco *m*
record (Es)	Rekord *m*	record	record *m*	record *m*	—
record (F)	Rekord *m*	record	—	record *m*	record *m*
record (I)	Rekord *m*	record	record *m*	—	record *m*
recordar (Es)	erinnern	remember	souvenir	ricordare	—
recorded delivery letter (E)	Einschreibebrief *m*	—	lettre recommandée *f*	lettera raccomandata *f*	carta certificada *f*
record player (E)	Plattenspieler *m*	—	tourne-disque *m*	giradischi *m*	tocadiscos *m*
recouvrer (F)	einkassieren	call in	—	incassare	cobrar
recouvrir (F)	beziehen	cover	—	ricoprire	tapizar
recover (E)	erholen, sich	—	reposer, se	rimettersi	aliviarse
recovery (E)	Erholung *f*	—	repos *m*	riposo *m*	descanso *m*
recruter (F)	einstellen	employ	—	assumere	emplear
red (E)	rot	—	rouge	rosso(a)	rojo(a)
red (Es)	Netz *n*	net	filet *m*	rete *f*	—
Rede (D)	—	speech	discours *m*	discorso *m*	discurso *m*
reden (D)	—	talk	parler	parlare	hablar
Red Indian (E)	Indianer *m*	—	Indien *m*	indiano *m*	indio *m*
redondo (Es)	rund	round	rond(e)	rotondo(a)	—
reduce (E)	verringern	—	diminuer	diminuire	disminuir
reducir (Es)	verkleinern	make smaller	réduire	ridurre	—

	D	E	F	I	Es
reduction (E)	Ermäßigung f	—	réduction f	riduzione f	rebaja f
réduction (F)	Ermäßigung f	reduction	—	riduzione f	rebaja f
réduire (F)	verkleinern	make smaller	—	ridurre	reducir
reel (E)	taumeln	—	tituber	barcollare	vacilar
réel (F)	wirklich	real	—	reale	real
reembolso (Es)	Nachnahme f	cash on delivery	remboursement m	contro assegno	—
referee (E)	Schiedsrichter m	—	arbitre m	arbitro m	árbitro m
réfléchi (F)	besonnen	sensible	—	avveduto(a)	sensato(a)
réfléchir (F)	nachdenken	think	—	riflettere	reflexionar
réfléchir à (F)	überlegen	consider	—	riflettere	pensar
reflexionar (Es)	nachdenken	think	réfléchir	riflettere	—
Reformhaus (D)	—	health food shop	magasin diététique m	negozio di prodotti dietetici m	tienda de productos dietéticos f
refresco (Es)	Erfrischung f	refreshment	rafraîchissement m	rinfresco m	—
refreshment (E)	Erfrischung f	—	rafraîchissement m	rinfresco m	refresco m
refrigerador (Es)	Eisschrank m	freezer	réfrigérateur m	frigorifero m	—
réfrigérateur[1] (F)	Eisschrank m	freezer	—	frigorifero m	refrigerador m
réfrigérateur[2] (F)	Kühlschrank m	fridge	—	frigorifero m	nevera f
refrigerio (Es)	Imbiß m	snack	casse-croûte m	spuntino m	—
refroidissement (F)	Erkältung f	cold	—	raffreddore m	catarro m
refus (F)	Absage f	refusal	—	risposta negativa f	negativa f
refusal (E)	Absage f	—	refus m	risposta negativa f	negativa f
refuse[1] (E)	verweigern	—	refuser	rifiutare	negar
refuse[2] (E)	weigern	—	refuser	rifiutare	resistirse
refuser[1] (F)	ablehnen	reject	—	rifiutare	rehusar
refuser[2] (F)	verweigern	refuse	—	rifiutare	negar
refuser[3] (F)	weigern	refuse	—	rifiutare	resistirse
Regal (D)	—	shelves	étagère f	scaffale m	estantería f
regalar (Es)	schenken	give	offrir	regalare	—
regalare (I)	schenken	give	offrir	—	regalar
regalo (Es)	Geschenk n	present	cadeau m	regalo m	—
regalo (I)	Geschenk n	present	cadeau m	—	regalo m
regar (Es)	gießen	water	arroser	annaffiare	—
regard (F)	Blick m	look	—	sguardo m	vista f
regarder[1] (F)	anschauen	look at	—	guardare	mirar
regarder[2] (F)	ansehen	look at	—	guardare	mirar
regarder[3] (F)	blicken	look	—	guardare	mirar
regarder[4] (F)	schauen	look	—	guardare	mirar
regarder[5] (F)	zusehen	watch	—	stare a guardare	mirar
regarder[6] (F)	zuschauen	watch	—	stare a guardare	mirar
regarder la télévision (F)	fernsehen	watch television	—	guardare la TV	ver la televisión
regelmäßig (D)	—	regular	régulier(-ière)	regolare	regular
regeln (D)	—	regulate	régler	regolare	dirigir
Regen (D)	—	rain	pluie f	pioggia f	lluvia f
Regenmantel (D)	—	raincoat	imperméable m	impermeabile m	impermeable m
Regenschirm (D)	—	umbrella	parapluie m	ombrello m	paraguas m
Regierung (D)	—	government	gouvernement m	governo m	gobierno m

	D	E	F	I	Es
regina (I)	Königin *f*	queen	reine *f*	—	reina *f*
region¹ (E)	Gebiet *n*	—	région *f*	regione *f*	zona *f*
region² (E)	Gegend *f*	—	région *f*	regione *f*	región *f*
región (Es)	Gegend *f*	region	région *f*	regione *f*	—
région¹ (F)	Gegend *f*	region	—	regione *f*	región *f*
région² (F)	Gebiet *n*	region	—	regione *f*	zona *f*
regione¹ (I)	Gegend *f*	region	région *f*	—	región *f*
regione² (I)	Gebiet *n*	region	région *f*	—	zona *f*
Regisseur (D)	—	director	réalisateur *m*	regista *m*	director *m*
regista (I)	Regisseur *m*	director	réalisateur *m*	—	director *m*
registrare (I)	verzeichnen	list	enregistrer	—	hacer una hista
registre (F)	Verzeichnis *n*	list	—	elenco *m*	lista *f*
regla (Es)	Lineal *n*	ruler	règle *f*	riga *f*	—
reglamento (Es)	Vorschrift *f*	regulation	règle *f*	norma *f*	—
règle¹ (F)	Lineal *n*	ruler	—	riga *f*	regla *f*
règle² (F)	Vorschrift *f*	regulation	—	norma *f*	reglamento *m*
régler¹ (F)	erledigen	take care of	—	sbrigare	acabar
régler² (F)	einstellen	adjust	—	regolare	ajustar
régler³ (F)	regeln	regulate	—	regolare	dirigir
regnen (D)	—	rain	pleuvoir	piovere	llover
régner (F)	herrschen	rule	—	dominare	mandar
regolare¹ (I)	einstellen	adjust	régler	—	ajustar
regolare² (I)	regeln	regulate	régler	—	dirigir
regolare³ (I)	regelmäßig	regular	régulier(-ière)	—	regular
regresar¹ (Es)	umkehren	turn back	retourner	ritornare	—
regresar² (Es)	zurückkommen	come back	revenir	ritornare	—
regreso (Es)	Rückkehr *f*	return	retour *m*	ritorno *m*	—
regret¹ (E)	bedauern	—	regretter	deplorare	lamentar
regret² (E)	bereuen	—	regretter	pentirsi	arrepentirse
regret³ (E)	Bedauern *n*	—	regret *m*	dispiacere *m*	compasión *f*
regret (F)	Bedauern *n*	regret	—	dispiacere *m*	compasión *f*
regretter¹ (F)	bedauern	regret	—	deplorare	lamentar
regretter² (F)	bereuen	regret	—	pentirsi	arrepentirse
regular¹ (E)	regelmäßig	—	régulier(-ière)	regolare	regular
regular² (E)	Stammgast *m*	—	habitué *m*	cliente abituale *m*	cliente habitual *m*
regular (Es)	regelmäßig	regular	régulier(-ière)	regolare	—
regulate (E)	regeln	—	régler	regolare	dirigir
regulation (E)	Vorschrift *f*	—	règle	norma *f*	reglamento *m*
régulier (F)	regelmäßig	regular	—	regolare	regular
Reh (D)	—	deer	chevreuil *m*	capriolo *m*	corzo *m*
rehusar (Es)	ablehnen	reject	refuser	rifiutare	—
reiben (D)	—	rub	frotter	sfregare	frotar
reich (D)	—	rich	riche	ricco(a)	rico(a)
reichen (D)	—	pass	passer	passare	alcanzar
reif (D)	—	ripe	mûr(e)	maturo(a)	maduro(a)
Reifen (D)	—	tyre	pneu *m*	pneumatico *m*	neumático *m*
Reihe (D)	—	row	rangée *f*	fila *f*	fila *f*
rein (D)	—	pure	pur(e)	puro(a)	puro(a)

	D	E	F	I	Es
rein (F)	Niere *f*	kidney	—	rene *m*	riñón *m*
reina (Es)	Königin *f*	queen	reine *f*	regina *f*	—
reine (F)	Königin *f*	queen	—	regina *f*	reina *f*
reinigen (D)	—	clean	nettoyer	pulire	limpiar
Reinigung (D)	—	cleaning	nettoyage *m*	pulitura *f*	limpieza *f*
reír (Es)	lachen	laugh	rire	ridere	—
reírse de (Es)	auslachen	laugh at	rire de qn	deridere	—
Reis (D)	—	rice	riz *m*	riso *m*	arroz *m*
Reise (D)	—	journey	voyage *m*	viaggio *m*	viaje *m*
Reisebüro (D)	—	travel agency	agence de voyages *f*	agenzia turistica *f*	oficina de viajes *f*
Reiseführer (D)	—	guide	guide *m*	guida *f*	guía *m*
reisen (D)	—	travel	voyager	viaggiare	viajar
Reisender (D)	—	traveller	voyageur *m*	viaggiatore *m*	viajero *m*
Reisepaß (D)	—	passport	passeport *m*	passaporto *m*	pasaporte *m*
Reiseroute (D)	—	route	itinéraire *m*	itinerario *m*	itinerario *m*
Reisescheck (D)	—	traveller's cheque	chèque de voyage *m*	assegno turistico *m*	cheque de viaje *m*
reißen (D)	—	tear	déchirer, se	strappare	desgarrarse
Reißverschluß (D)	—	zip	fermeture éclair *f*	chiusura lampo *f*	cremallera *f*
reiten (D)	—	ride	monter	cavalcare	cabalgar
reject (E)	ablehnen	—	refuser	rifiutare	rehusar
rejoice (E)	jubeln	—	pousser des cris de joie	giubilare	dar gritos de alegría
réjoui (F)	erfreut	delighted	—	lieto(a)	contento(a)
Reklamation (D)	—	complaint	réclamation *f*	reclamo *m*	reclamación *f*
Reklame (D)	—	advertisement	publicité *f*	réclame *f*	anuncio *m*
reklamieren (D)	—	complain	plaindre de, se	reclamare	reclamar
Rekord (D)	—	record	record *m*	record *m*	record *m*
relación[1] (Es)	Beziehung *f*	relation	rapport *m*	relazione *f*	—
relación[2] (Es)	Bericht *m*	report	rapport *m*	relazione *f*	—
relación[3] (Es)	Verbindung *f*	connection	relation *f*	relazione *f*	—
relaciones (Es)	Beziehung *f*	relationship	relation *f*	rapporto *m*	—
related (E)	verwandt	—	parent(e)	imparentato(a)	emparentado(a)
relation (E)	Beziehung *f*	—	rapport *m*	relazione *f*	relación *f*
relation[1] (F)	Beziehung *f*	relationship	—	rapporto *m*	relaciones *f pl*
relation[2] (F)	Verbindung *f*	connection	—	relazione *f*	relación *f*
relationship (E)	Beziehung *f*	—	relation *f*	rapporto *m*	relaciones *f pl*
relative (E)	Verwandter *m*	—	parent *m*	parente *m*	pariente *m*
relazione[1] (I)	Bericht *m*	report	rapport *m*	—	relación *f*
relazione[2] (I)	Beziehung *f*	relation	rapport *m*	—	relación *f*
relazione[3] (I)	Verbindung *f*	connection	relation *f*	—	relación *f*
release[1] (E)	entlassen	—	renvoyer	lizenziare	despedir
release[2] (E)	freilassen	—	libérer	mettere in libertà	poner en libertad
reliable (E)	zuverlässig	—	sûr(e)	affidabile	de confianza
relier (F)	verbinden	connect	—	unire	unir
religieuse (F)	Nonne *f*	nun	—	suora *f*	monja *f*
religieux (F)	religiös	religious	—	religioso(a)	religioso(a)
Religion (D)	—	religion	religion *f*	religione *f*	religión *f*

rendre visite à

	D	E	F	I	Es
religion (E)	Religion f	—	religion f	religione f	religión f
religión (Es)	Religion f	religion	religion f	religione f	—
religion (F)	Religion f	religion	—	religione f	religión f
religione (I)	Religion f	religion	religion f	—	religión f
religiös (D)	—	religious	religieux(-euse)	religioso(a)	religioso(a)
religioso (I)	religiös	religious	religieux(-euse)	—	religioso(a)
religioso¹ (Es)	fromm	pious	pieux(-euse)	devoto(a)	—
religioso² (Es)	religiös	religious	religieux(-euse)	religioso(a)	—
religious (E)	religiös	—	religieux(-euse)	religioso(a)	religioso(a)
reloj (Es)	Uhr f	watch	montre f	orologio m	—
reluctantly (E)	ungern	—	de mauvaise grâce	malvolentieri	de mala gana
remar (Es)	rudern	row	ramer	remare	—
remare (I)	rudern	row	ramer	—	remar
remarquer¹ (F)	bemerken	notice	—	notare	darse cuenta
remarquer² (F)	merken	notice	—	accorgersi di	notar
remboursement (F)	Nachnahme f	cash on delivery	—	pagamento contro assegno	entrega contra reembolso f
rembourser (F)	zurückzahlen	pay back	—	rimborsare	devolver
remember¹ (E)	erinnern	—	souvenir	ricordare	recordar
remember² (E)	gedenken	—	souvenir de, se	ricordare	conmemorar
remerciement (F)	Dank m	thanks	—	ringraziamento m	agradecimiento m
remercier¹ (F)	bedanken	say thank you	—	ringraziare	agradecer algo
remercier² (F)	danken	thank	—	ringraziare	agradecer
remettre¹ (F)	übergeben	hand over	—	consegnare	transmitir
remettre² (F)	überbringen	deliver	—	portare	transmitir
remettre³ (F)	verschieben	postpone	—	rimandare	aplazar
remitente (Es)	Absender m	sender	expéditeur m	mittente m	—
remo (Es)	Ruder n	oar	rame f	remo m	—
remo (I)	Ruder n	oar	rame f	—	remo m
remolcar (Es)	abschleppen	take in tow	remorquer	rimorchiare	—
remonte-pente (F)	Skilift m	skilift	—	sciovia f	telesilla f
remorquer (F)	abschleppen	take in tow	—	rimorchiare	remolcar
remove (E)	entfernen	—	éloigner	allontanare	quitar
remplacement (F)	Ersatz m	substitute	—	sostituzione f	sustitución f
remplacer (F)	ersetzen	replace	—	sostituire	sustituir
remplir¹ (F)	ausfüllen	fill in	—	riempire	llenar
remplir² (F)	erfüllen	fulfil	—	esaudire	conceder
remplir³ (F)	füllen	fill	—	riempire	llenar
renard (F)	Fuchs m	fox	—	volpe f	zorro m
rencontre (F)	Treffen n	meeting	—	incontro m	encuentro m
rencontrer¹ (F)	begegnen	meet	—	incontrare	encontrar
rencontrer² (F)	treffen	meet	—	incontrare	encontrar
rendere possibile (I)	ermöglichen	make possible	rendre possible	—	facilitar
rendez-vous (F)	Verabredung f	date	—	appuntamento m	cita f
rendre¹ (F)	wiedergeben	return	—	restituire	devolver
rendre² (F)	zurückgeben	give back	—	restituire	devolver
rendre possible (F)	ermöglichen	make possible	—	rendere possibile	facilitar
rendre visite à (F)	besuchen	visit	—	andare a trovare	visitar

	D	E	F	I	Es
rene (I)	Niere *f*	kidney	rein *m*	—	riñón *m*
renew (E)	erneuern	—	rénover	rinnovare	renovar
renfermer (F)	einschließen	lock up	—	rinchiudere	encerrar
rennen (D)	—	run	courir	correre	correr
renoncer (F)	verzichten	forgo	—	rinunciare	renunciar
renovar¹ (Es)	erneuern	renew	rénover	rinnovare	—
renovar² (Es)	renovieren	renovate	rénover	rinnovare	—
renovate (E)	renovieren	—	rénover	rinnovare	renovar
rénover¹ (F)	erneuern	renew	—	rinnovare	renovar
rénover² (F)	renovieren	renovate	—	rinnovare	renovar
renovieren (D)	—	renovate	rénover	rinnovare	renovar
renseignement (F)	Auskunft *f*	information	—	informazione *f*	información *f*
renseigner, se (F)	erkundigen, sich	inquire	—	informarsi	informarse
rent¹ (E)	mieten	—	louer	affittare	alquilar
rent² (E)	Miete *f*	—	loyer *m*	affitto *m*	alquiler *m*
rent³ (E)	vermieten	—	louer	affittare	alquilar
Rente (D)	—	pension	retraite *f*	pensione *f*	pensión *f*
Rentner (D)	—	pensioner	retraité *m*	pensionato *m*	pensionista *m*
renunciar¹ (Es)	aufgeben	give up	abandonner	rinunciare	—
renunciar² (Es)	verzichten	forgo	renoncer	rinunciare	—
renverser (F)	umschmeißen	throw over	—	rovesciare	derribar
renvoi (F)	Hinweis *m*	hint	—	indicazione *f*	indicación *f*
renvoyer (F)	entlassen	release	—	licenziare	despedir
repair¹ (E)	reparieren	—	réparer	riparare	reparar
repair² (E)	Reparatur *f*	—	réparation *f*	riparazione *f*	reparación *f*
repair shop (E)	Autowerkstatt *f*	—	atelier de réparation d'autos *m*	autofficina *f* reparaciones *m*	taller de
reparación (Es)	Reparatur *f*	repair	réparation *f*	riparazione *f*	—
reparar (Es)	reparieren	repair	réparer	riparare	—
réparation (F)	Reparatur *f*	repair	—	riparazione *f*	reparación *f*
Reparatur (D)	—	repair	réparation *f*	riparazione *f*	reparación *f*
réparer¹ (F)	reparieren	repair	—	riparare	reparar
réparer² (F)	wiedergutmachen	make up for	—	riparare	subsanar
reparieren (D)	—	repair	réparer	riparare	reparar
repartir (Es)	verteilen	distribute	distribuer	distribuire	—
reparto (I)	Abteilung *f*	department	section *f*	—	departamento *m*
repas¹ (F)	Essen *n*	food	—	alimentazione *f*	comida *f*
repas² (F)	Mahlzeit *f*	meal	—	pasto *m*	comida *f*
repasser (F)	bügeln	iron	—	stirare	planchar
repeat (E)	wiederholen	—	répéter	ripetere	repetir
répéter (F)	wiederholen	repeat	—	ripetere	repetir
repetir (Es)	wiederholen	repeat	répéter	ripetere	—
replace (E)	ersetzen	—	remplacer	sostituire	sustituir
répondre (F)	antworten	answer	—	rispondere	responder
répondre à (F)	beantworten	answer	—	rispondere a	responder a
répondre par l'affirmative à (F)	bejahen	agree with	—	approvare	afirmar
réponse (F)	Antwort *f*	answer	—	risposta *f*	respuesta *f*
report¹ (E)	berichten	—	faire un rapport	riferire	informar

	D	E	F	I	Es
report[2] (E)	Bericht *m*	—	rapport *m*	relazione *f*	relación *f*
report[3] (E)	melden	—	annoncer	annunciare	declarar
report[4] (E)	Meldung *f*	—	annonce *f*	annuncio *m*	aviso *m*
report[5] (E)	Zeugnis *n*	—	bulletin *m*	pagella *f*	diploma *m*
repos (F)	Erholung *f*	recovery	—	riposo *m*	descanso *m*
reposer, se[1] (F)	ausruhen	rest	—	riposare	descansar
reposer, se[2] (F)	erholen, sich	recover	—	rimettersi	recuperarse
reposer, se[3] (F)	ruhen	rest	—	riposare	descansar
repoussant (F)	widerlich	disgusting	—	ripugnante	repugnante
reprendre (F)	übernehmen	take over	—	accettare	tomar posesión de
represent (E)	vertreten	—	représenter	rappresentare	representar
representación[1] (Es)	Aufführung *f*	performance	représentation *f*	recita *f*	—
representación[2] (Es)	Veranstaltung *f*	event	manifestation *f*	manifestazione *f*	—
representación[3] (Es)	Vorstellung *f*	performance	représentation *f*	rappresentazione *f*	—
représentant (F)	Vertreter *m*	representative	—	rappresentante *m*	representante
representante (Es)	Vertreter *m*	representative	représentant *m*	rappresentante *m*	—
representar (Es)	vertreten	represent	représenter	rappresentare	—
représentation[1] (F)	Aufführung *f*	performance	—	recita *f*	representación *f*
représentation[2] (F)	Vorstellung *f*	performance	—	rappresentazione *f*	representación *f*
representative (E)	Vertreter *m*	—	représentant *m*	rappresentante *m*	representante
représenter (F)	darstellen	represent	—	rappresentare	representar
reprocher (F)	vorwerfen	blame	—	rimproverare	echar en cara
repugnante (Es)	widerlich	disgusting	repoussant(e)	ripugnante	—
requesón (Es)	Quark *m*	curd cheese	fromage blanc *m*	ricotta *f*	—
request[1] (E)	anfordern	—	demander	esigere	pedir
request[2] (E)	bitten	—	demander	pregare	rogar
request[3] (E)	Bitte *f*	—	demande *f*	domanda *f*	ruego *m*
requin (F)	Hai *m*	shark	—	pescecane *m*	tiburón *m*
resbalar (Es)	rutschen	slide	glisser	scivolare	—
research (E)	forschen	—	rechercher	ricercare	investigar
resemble (E)	ähneln	—	ressembler	assomigliare	parecer
reserva (Es)	Vorbehalt *m*	reservation	réserve *f*	riserva *f*	—
reservar[1] (Es)	buchen	book	retenir	prenotare	—
reservar[2] (Es)	reservieren	reserve	réserver	riservare	—
reservation (E)	Vorbehalt *m*	—	réserve *f*	riserva *f*	reserva *f*
reserve (E)	reservieren	—	réserver	riservare	reservar
réserve (F)	Vorbehalt *m*	reservation	—	riserva *f*	reserva *f*
réserver[1] (F)	reservieren	reserve	—	riservare	reservar
réserver[2] (F)	vorbestellen	book	—	prenotare	hacer reservar
réserves (F)	Vorrat *m*	stock	—	scorte *f pl*	provisión *f*
reservieren (D)	—	reserve	réserver	riservare	reservar
resfriado (Es)	Schnupfen *m*	cold	rhume *m*	raffreddore *m*	—
residencia (Es)	Wohnort *m*	domicile	domicile *m*	residenza *f*	—
residenza (I)	Wohnort *m*	domicile	domicile *m*	—	residencia *f*
résilier (F)	kündigen	sack	—	licenziare	despedir
resistance (E)	Widerstand *m*	—	résistance *f*	resistenza *f*	resistencia *f*
résistance (F)	Widerstand *m*	resistance	—	resistenza *f*	resistencia *f*
résistant (F)	haltbar	durable	—	durevole	duradero

	D	E	F	I	Es
resistencia (Es)	Widerstand *m*	resistance	résistance *f*	resistenza *f*	—
resistenza (I)	Widerstand *m*	resistance	résistance *f*	—	resistencia *f*
resistirse (Es)	weigern	refuse	refuser	rifiutare	—
résoudre (F)	lösen	solve	—	sciogliere	desatar
respirar (Es)	atmen	breathe	respirer	respirare	—
respirare (I)	atmen	breathe	respirer	—	respirar
respiration (F)	Atem *m*	breath	—	fiato *m*	respiro *m*
respirer (F)	atmen	breathe	—	respirare	respirar
respiro (Es)	Atem *m*	breath	respiration *f*	fiato *m*	—
responder (Es)	antworten	answer	répondre	rispondere	—
responder a (Es)	beantworten	answer	répondre à	rispondere a	—
responsabile (I)	verantwortlich	responsible	responsable	—	responsable
responsable (Es)	verantwortlich	responsible	responsable	responsabile	—
responsable (F)	verantwortlich	responsible	—	responsabile	responsable
responsible (E)	verantwortlich	—	responsable	responsabile	responsable
respuesta (Es)	Antwort *f*	answer	réponse *f*	risposta *f*	—
ressembler (F)	ähneln	resemble	—	assomigliare	parecer
Rest (D)	—	rest	reste *m*	resto *m*	resto *m*
rest¹ (E)	ausruhen	—	reposer, se	riposare	descansar
rest² (E)	ruhen	—	reposer, se	riposare	descansar
rest³ (E)	Rest *m*	—	reste *m*	resto *m*	resto *m*
restablecimiento (Es)	Besserung *f*	improvement	amélioration *f*	miglioramento *m*	—
restant (F)	übrig	left	—	restante	restante
restante (Es)	übrig	left	restant(e)	restante	—
restante (I)	übrig	left	restant(e)	—	restante
restar (Es)	abziehen	subtract	retirer	sottrarre	—
restare qui (I)	hierbleiben	stay here	rester	—	quedarse aquí
Restaurant (D)	—	restaurant	restaurant *m*	ristorante *m*	restaurante *m*
restaurant (E)	Restaurant *n*	—	restaurant *m*	ristorante *m*	restaurante *m*
restaurant¹ (F)	Lokal *n*	pub	—	locale *m*	local *m*
restaurant² (F)	Restaurant *n*	restaurant	—	ristorante *m*	restaurante *m*
restaurante¹ (Es)	Restaurant *n*	restaurant	restaurant *m*	ristorante *m*	—
restaurante² (Es)	Wirtshaus *n*	inn	auberge *f*	osteria *f*	—
reste (F)	Rest *m*	rest	—	resto *m*	resto *m*
rester¹ (F)	bleiben	stay	—	rimanere	quedarse
rester² (F)	hierbleiben	stay here	—	restare qui	quedarse aquí
rester³ (F)	übrigbleiben	be left	—	avanzare	quedar
restituire (I)	zurückgeben	give back	rendre	—	devolver
restless (E)	unruhig	—	inquiet(-ète)	inquieto(a)	intranquilo(a)
restlos (D)	—	completely	complètement	interamente	totalmente
resto (Es)	Rest *m*	rest	reste *m*	resto *m*	—
resto (I)	Rest *m*	rest	reste *m*	—	resto *m*
result (E)	Ergebnis *n*	—	résultat *m*	risultato *m*	resultado *m*
resultado (Es)	Ergebnis *n*	result	résultat *m*	risultato *m*	—
résultat (F)	Ergebnis *n*	result	—	risultato *m*	resultado *m*
retard (F)	Verspätung *f*	delay	—	ritardo *m*	retraso *m*
rete (I)	Netz *n*	net	filet *m*	—	red *f*

	D	E	F	I	Es
retener¹ (Es)	behalten	keep	garder	tenere	—
retener² (Es)	einbehalten	keep	retenir	trattenere	—
retenir¹ (F)	buchen	book	—	prenotare	reservar
retenir² (F)	einbehalten	keep	—	trattenere	retener
retirar¹ (Es)	zurücknehmen	take back	retirer	prendere indietro	—
retirar² (Es)	zurückziehen	withdraw	retirer	ritirare	—
retire (E)	zurücktreten	—	démissionner	dare le dimissioni	dimitir
retirement (E)	Ruhestand m	—	retraite f	pensione f	descanso m
retirer¹ (F)	abziehen	subtract	—	sottrarre	restar
retirer² (F)	zurückziehen	withdraw	—	ritirare	retirar
retirer³ (F)	zurücknehmen	take back	—	prendere indietro	retirar
retour (F)	Rückkehr f	return	—	ritorno m	regreso m
retourner¹ (F)	umkehren	turn back	—	ritornare	regresar
retourner² (F)	zurückfahren	drive back	—	tornare indietro	retroceder
retract (E)	widerrufen	—	démentir	revocare	revocación f
retraite¹ (F)	Rente f	pension	—	pensione f	pensión f
retraite² (F)	Ruhestand m	retirement	—	pensione f	descanso m
retraité (F)	Rentner m	pensioner	—	pensionato m	pensionista m
retraso (Es)	Verspätung f	delay	retard m	ritardo m	—
retrete (Es)	Klosett n	lavatory	cabinets m pl	gabinetto m	—
retroceder (Es)	zurückfahren	drive back	retourner	tornare indietro	—
retrouver, se (F)	zurechtfinden, sich	find one's way	—	orientarsi	orientarse
retten (D)	—	save	sauver	salvare	salvar
Rettungsring (D)	—	lifebelt	bouée de sauvetage f	salvagente m	salvavidas m
return¹ (E)	Rückkehr f	—	retour m	ritorno m	regreso m
return² (E)	wiedergeben	—	rendre	restituire	devolver
return³ (E)	zurückkehren	—	revenir	ritornare	volver
reunión (Es)	Sitzung f	meeting	séance f	seduta f	—
réussir (F)	gelingen	succeed	—	riuscire	acertar
réussir à faire (F)	schaffen	create	—	creare	crear
rêve (F)	Traum m	dream	—	sogno m	sueño m
réveil (F)	Wecker m	alarm clock	—	sveglia f	despertador m
réveillé (F)	wach	awake	—	sveglio(a)	despierto(a)
réveiller¹ (F)	aufwecken	wake up	—	svegliare	despertar
réveiller² (F)	wecken	wake (up)	—	svegliare	despertar
réveiller, se¹ (F)	aufwachen	wake up	—	svegliarsi	despertarse
réveiller, se² (F)	erwachen	wake up	—	svegliarsi	despertar
revenge (E)	Rache f	—	vengeance f	vendetta f	venganza f
revenir¹ (F)	wiederkommen	come back	—	ritornare	venir de nuevo
revenir² (F)	zurückkommen	come back	—	ritornare	regresar
revenir³ (F)	zurückkehren	return	—	ritornare	volver
reventar (Es)	platzen	burst	éclater	scoppiare	—
revenu (F)	Einkommen n	income	—	entrate f pl	ingresos m pl
revenus (F)	Verdienst n	income	—	guadagno m	ganancia f
rêver (F)	träumen	dream	—	sognare	soñar
réverbère (F)	Laterne f	street light	—	lampione m	farola f
Revier (D)	—	district	district m	distretto m	distrito m

	D	E	F	I	Es
revisor (Es)	Schaffner *m*	conductor	contrôleur *m*	bigliettaio *m*	—
revista¹ (Es)	Illustrierte *f*	illustrated magazine	illustré *m*	rivista *f*	—
revista² (Es)	Zeitschrift *f*	magazine	revue *f*	rivista *f*	—
revocación (Es)	widerrufen	retract	démentir	revocare	—
revocare (I)	widerrufen	retract	démentir	—	revocación *f*
revoir (F)	wiedersehen	see again	—	rivedere	volver a ver
révolté (F)	empört	indignant	—	indignato(a)	indignado(a)
revolución (Es)	Revolution *f*	revolution	révolution *f*	rivoluzione *f*	—
Revolution (D)	—	revolution	révolution *f*	rivoluzione *f*	revolución *f*
revolution (E)	Revolution *f*	—	révolution *f*	rivoluzione *f*	revolución *f*
révolution (F)	Revolution *f*	revolution	—	rivoluzione *f*	revolución *f*
revolver (Es)	wühlen	scrabble	fouiller	rovistare	—
revue (F)	Zeitschrift *f*	magazine	—	rivista *f*	revista *f*
revuelta (Es)	Aufstand *m*	rebellion	soulèvement *m*	insurrezione *f*	—
reward¹ (E)	belohnen	—	récompenser	premiare	recompensar
reward² (E)	Belohnung *f*	—	récompense *f*	ricompensa *f*	recompensa *f*
rey (Es)	König *m*	king	roi *m*	re *m*	—
rezar (Es)	beten	pray	prier	pregare	—
rez-de-chaussée¹ (F)	Parterre *n*	ground floor	—	pianterreno *m*	planta baja *f*
rez-de-chaussée² (F)	Erdgeschoß *n*	ground floor	—	pianterreno *m*	piso bajo *m*
Rezept¹ (D)	—	recipe	recette *f*	ricetta *f*	receta *f*
Rezept² (D)	—	prescription	ordonnance *f*	prescrizione *f*	prescripción médica *f*
rhume (F)	Schnupfen *m*	cold	—	raffreddore *m*	resfriado *m*
rib (E)	Rippe *f*	—	côte *f*	costola *f*	costilla *f*
ribbon (E)	Band *n*	—	bandeau *m*	nastro *m*	cinta *f*
ribes (I)	Johannisbeere *f*	currant	groseille *f*	—	grosella *f*
ricatto (I)	Erpressung *f*	blackmail	chantage *m*	—	chantaje *m*
riccio (I)	Locke *f*	curl	boucle *f*	—	rizo *m*
ricco (I)	reich	rich	riche	—	rico(a)
rice (E)	Reis *m*	—	riz	riso *m*	arroz *m*
ricercare (I)	forschen	research	rechercher	—	investigar
ricetta (I)	Rezept *n*	recipe	recette *f*	—	receta *f*
ricevere¹ (I)	bekommen	get	recevoir	—	recibir
ricevere² (I)	empfangen	receive	recevoir	—	recibir
ricevere³ (I)	erhalten	receive	recevoir	—	obtener
ricevitore (I)	Hörer *m*	receiver	récepteur *m*	—	auricular *m*
ricevuta (I)	Quittung *f*	receipt	quittance *f*	—	recibo *m*
ricezione (I)	Empfang *m*	reception	réception *f*	—	recepción *f*
rich (E)	reich	—	riche	ricco(a)	rico(a)
riche (F)	reich	rich	—	ricco(a)	rico(a)
richiedere (I)	verlangen	demand	demander	—	exigir
richten (D)	—	direct to	diriger	dirigere	dirigir
Richter (D)	—	judge	juge *m*	giudice *m*	juez *m*
richtig (D)	—	correct	juste	giusto(a)	correcto(a)
Richtung (D)	—	direction	direction *f*	direzione *f*	dirección *f*
rico (Es)	reich	rich	riche	ricco(a)	—
ricompensa (I)	Belohnung *f*	reward	récompense *f*	—	recompensa *f*

	D	E	F	I	Es
riconoscere (I)	erkennen	recognize	reconnaître	—	reconocer
ricoprire (I)	beziehen	cover	recouvrir	—	tapizar
ricordare[1] (I)	erinnern	remember	souvenir	—	recordar
ricordare[2] (I)	gedenken	remember	souvenir de, se	—	conmemorar
ricordo[1] (I)	Andenken n	souvenir	souvenir m	—	recuerdo m
ricordo[2] (I)	Erinnerung f	memory	souvenir m	—	memoria f
ricotta (I)	Quark m	curd cheese	fromage blanc m	—	requesón m
ridare (I)	wiedergeben	return	rendre	—	devolver
riddle (E)	Rätsel n	—	devinette	enigma m	adivinanza f
ride (E)	reiten	—	monter	cavalcare	cabalgar
rideau[1] (F)	Gardine f	curtain	—	tenda f	cortina f
rideau[2] (F)	Vorhang m	curtain	—	tenda f	cortina f
ridere (I)	lachen	laugh	rire	—	reír
ridicolo (I)	lächerlich	ridiculous	ridicule	—	ridículo(a)
ridicule (F)	lächerlich	ridiculous	—	ridicolo(a)	ridículo(a)
ridículo (Es)	lächerlich	ridiculous	ridicule	ridicolo(a)	—
ridiculous (E)	lächerlich	—	ridicule	ridicolo(a)	ridículo(a)
ridurre (I)	verkleinern	make smaller	réduire	—	reducir
riduzione (I)	Ermäßigung f	reduction	réduction f	—	rebaja f
riechen (D)	—	smell	sentir	sentire	oler
Riegel (D)	—	bar	verrou m	catenaccio m	cerrojo m
Riemen (D)	—	strap	courroie f	cinghia f	correa f
riempire[1] (I)	ausfüllen	fill in	remplir	—	llenar
riempire[2] (I)	füllen	fill	remplir	—	llenar
rien (F)	nichts	nothing	—	niente	nada
riesgo (Es)	Risiko n	risk	risque m	rischio m	—
riesig (D)	—	huge	énorme	enorme	enorme
riferire[1] (I)	ausrichten	pass on a message	transmettre	—	comunicar
riferire[2] (I)	berichten	report	faire un rapport	—	informar
rifiutare[1] (I)	ablehnen	reject	refuser	—	rehusar
rifiutare[2] (I)	verweigern	refuse	refuser	—	negar
rifiutare[3] (I)	weigern	refuse	refuser	—	resistirse
riflettere[1] (I)	nachdenken	think	réfléchir	—	reflexionar
riflettere[2] (I)	überlegen	consider	réfléchir à	—	pensar
riga[1] (I)	Lineal n	ruler	règle f	—	regla f
riga[2] (I)	Zeile f	line	ligne f	—	línea f
right[1] (E)	rechts	—	à droite	a destra	a la derecha
right[2] (E)	Recht n	—	droit m	diritto m	derecho m
right of way (E)	Vorfahrt f	—	priorité f	precedenza f	preferencia f
rigid (E)	starr	—	rigide	rigido(a)	fijo(a)
rigide[1] (F)	starr	rigid	—	rigido(a)	fijo(a)
rigide[2] (F)	steif	stiff	—	rigido(a)	rígido(a)
rigido[1] (I)	starr	rigid	rigide	—	fijo(a)
rigido[2] (I)	steif	stiff	rigide	—	rígido(a)
rígido (Es)	steif	stiff	rigide	rigido(a)	—
riguardare (I)	betreffen	concern	concerner	—	concernir
riguroso (Es)	streng	strict	sévère	severo(a)	—

	D	E	F	I	Es
rilevante (I)	erheblich	considerable	considérable	—	considerable
rimandare (I)	verschieben	postpone	remettre	—	aplazar
rimanere (I)	bleiben	stay	rester	—	quedarse
rimborsare (I)	zurückzahlen	pay back	rembourser	—	devolver
rimettersi (I)	erholen, sich	recover	reposer, se	—	aliviarse
rimorchiare (I)	abschleppen	take in tow	remorquer	—	remolcar
rimproverare (I)	vorwerfen	blame	reprocher	—	echar en cara
rinchiudere (I)	einschließen	lock up	renfermer	—	encerrar
rincón (Es)	Winkel m	corner	coin m	cantuccio m	—
Rind (D)	—	cow	bœuf m	manzo m	buey m
Rindfleisch (D)	—	beef	viande de bœuf f	carne di manzo f	carne de vaca f
rinfresco (I)	Erfrischung f	refreshment	rafraîchissement m	—	refresco m
Ring (D)	—	ring	bague f	anello m	sortija f
ring[1] (E)	läuten	—	sonner	suonare	tocar
ring[2] (E)	Ring m	—	bague f	anello m	sortija f
ringraziare[1] (I)	bedanken	say thank you	remercier	—	agradecer algo
ringraziare[3] (I)	danken	thank	remercier	—	agradecer
ring the bell (E)	klingeln	—	sonner	suonare	tocar el timbre
ring up (E)	anrufen	—	téléphoner	telefonare	llamar por teléfono
rinnovare[1] (I)	erneuern	renew	rénover	—	renovar
rinnovare[2] (I)	renovieren	renovate	rénover	—	renovar
riñón (Es)	Niere f	kidney	rein m	rene m	—
rinse (E)	spülen	—	rincer	sciacquare	lavar
rinunciare[1] (I)	aufgeben	give up	abandonner	—	renunciar
rinunciare[2] (I)	verzichten	forgo	renoncer	—	renunciar
río (Es)	Fluß m	river	fleuve m	fiume m	—
rip (E)	zerreißen	—	déchirer	strappare	romper
riparare[1] (I)	reparieren	repair	réparer	—	reparar
riparare[2] (I)	wiedergutmachen	make up for	réparer	—	subsanar
riparazione (I)	Reparatur f	repair	réparation f	—	reparación f
ripe (E)	reif	—	mûr(e)	maturo(a)	maduro(a)
ripetere (I)	wiederholen	repeat	répéter	—	repetir
ripido (I)	steil	steep	raide	—	inclinado(a)
riportare (I)	zurückbringen	bring back	rapporter	—	devolver
riporto (I)	Umbuchung f	alteration	transfert m	—	cambio m
riposare[1] (I)	ausruhen	rest	reposer, se	—	descansar
riposare[2] (I)	ruhen	rest	reposer, se	—	descansar
riposo (I)	Erholung f	recovery	repos m	—	descanso m
Rippe (D)	—	rib	côte f	costola f	costilla f
ripugnante (I)	widerlich	disgusting	repoussant(e)	—	repugnante
rire[1] (F)	lachen	laugh	—	ridere	reír
rire[2] (F)	Lachen n	laughter	—	riso m	risa f
rire de qn (F)	auslachen	laugh at	—	deridere	reírse de
rires (F)	Gelächter n	laughter	—	risata f	risa f

	D	E	F	I	Es
risa¹ (Es)	Gelächter n	laughter	rires m pl	risata f	—
risa² (Es)	Lachen n	laughter	rire m	riso m	—
risata (I)	Gelächter n	laughter	rires m pl	—	risa f
riscaldamento (I)	Heizung f	heating	chauffage m	—	calefacción f
riscaldamento centrale (I)	Zentralheizung f	central heating	chauffage central m	—	calefacción central f
riscaldare¹ (I)	heizen	heat	chauffer	—	calentar
riscaldare² (I)	wärmen	warm	chauffer	—	calentar
rischiare (I)	riskieren	risk	risquer	—	arriesgar
rischio (I)	Risiko n	risk	risque m	—	riesgo m
riserva (I)	Vorbehalt m	reservation	réserve f	—	reserva f
riservare (I)	reservieren	reserve	réserver	—	reservar
Risiko (D)	—	risk	risque m	rischio m	riesgo m
risk¹ (E)	riskieren	—	risquer	rischiare	arriesgar
risk² (E)	Risiko n	—	risque m	rischio m	riesgo m
riskieren (D)	—	risk	risquer	rischiare	arriesgar
riso¹ (I)	Lachen n	laughter	rire m	—	risa f
riso² (I)	Reis m	rice	riz m	—	arroz m
risparmiare (I)	sparen	save	économiser	—	ahorrar
rispondere (I)	antworten	answer	répondre	—	responder
rispondere a (I)	beantworten	answer	répondre à	—	responder a
risposta (I)	Antwort f	answer	réponse f	—	respuesta f
risposta negativa (I)	Absage f	refusal	refus m	—	negativa f
risque (F)	Risiko n	risk	—	rischio m	riesgo m
risquer (F)	riskieren	risk	—	rischiare	arriesgar
ristorante (I)	Restaurant n	restaurant	restaurant m	—	restaurante m
risultato (I)	Ergebnis n	result	résultat m	—	resultado m
ritardare (I)	verspäten	be late	être en retard	—	llevar retraso
ritardo (I)	Verspätung f	delay	retard m	—	retraso m
ritirare (I)	zurückziehen	withdraw	retirer	—	retirar
ritornare¹ (I)	umkehren	turn back	retourner	—	regresar
ritornare² (I)	wiederkommen	come back	revenir	—	venir de nuevo
ritornare³ (I)	zurückkommen	come back	revenir	—	regresar
ritornare⁴ (I)	zurückkehren	return	revenir	—	volver
ritorno (I)	Rückkehr f	return	retour m	—	regreso m
riuscire (I)	gelingen	succeed	réussir	—	acertar
riva (I)	Ufer n	shore	bord m	—	orilla f
rivedere (I)	wiedersehen	see again	revoir	—	volver a ver
river (E)	Fluß m	—	fleuve m	fiume m	río m
rivista¹ (I)	Illustrierte f	picture magazine	illustré m	—	revista
rivista² (I)	Zeitschrift f	magazine	revue f	—	revista f
rivoluzione (I)	Revolution f	revolution	révolution f	—	revolución f
riz (F)	Reis m	rice	—	riso m	arroz m
rizo (Es)	Locke f	curl	boucle f	riccio m	—

	D	E	F	I	Es
roadway (E)	Fahrbahn f	—	chaussée f	carreggiata f	calzada f
roast¹ (E)	braten	—	rôtir	arrostire	asar
roast² (E)	Braten m	—	rôti m	arrosto m	asado m
roast³ (E)	rösten	—	griller	abbrustolire	tostar
rob (E)	rauben	—	voler	rapinare	robar
robar¹ (Es)	einbrechen	break in	cambrioler	rubare	—
robar² (Es)	rauben	rob	voler	rapinare	—
robar³ (Es)	stehlen	steal	voler	rubare	—
Robbe (D)	—	seal	phoque m	foca f	foca f
robe (F)	Kleid n	dress	—	vestito m	vestido m
rocca (I)	Burg f	castle	château m	—	fortaleza f
Rock (D)	—	skirt	jupe f	gonna f	falda f
rodar (Es)	rollen	roll	rouler	ruotare	—
rodear (Es)	umgeben	surround	entourer	circondare	—
rodeo (Es)	Umweg m	detour	détour m	deviazione f	—
rodilla (Es)	Knie n	knee	genou m	ginocchio m	—
rogar (Es)	bitten	request	demander	pregare	—
roh (D)	—	raw	cru(e)	crudo(a)	crudo(a)
Rohr (D)	—	tube	tube m	tubo m	tubo m
roi (F)	König m	king	—	re m	rey m
rojo (Es)	rot	red	rouge	rosso(a)	—
roll¹ (E)	Brötchen n	—	petit pain m	panino m	panecillo m
roll² (E)	rollen	—	rouler	ruotare	rodar
rollen (D)	—	roll	rouler	ruotare	rodar
Rolltreppe (D)	—	escalator	escalier roulant m	scala mobile f	escalera mecánica f
Roman (D)	—	novel	roman m	romanzo m	novela f
roman (F)	Roman m	novel	—	romanzo m	novela f
romanzo (I)	Roman m	novel	roman m	—	novela f
romper¹ (Es)	brechen	break	casser	rompere	—
romper² (Es)	einschlagen	smash	casser	rompere	—
romper³ (Es)	zerbrechen	break	casser	rompere	—
romper⁴ (Es)	zerreißen	rip	déchirer	strappare	—
rompere¹ (I)	brechen	break	casser	—	romper
rompere² (I)	einschlagen	smash	casser	—	romper
rompere³ (I)	zerbrechen	break	casser	—	romper
roncar (Es)	schnarchen	snore	ronfler	russare	—
rond (F)	rund	round	—	rotondo(a)	redondo(a)
ronfler (F)	schnarchen	snore	—	russare	roncar
röntgen (D)	—	X-ray	radiographier	fare una radiografia	radiografiar
roof (E)	Dach n	—	toit m	tetto m	techo m
room¹ (E)	Raum m	—	pièce f	stanza f	habitación f
room² (E)	Zimmer n	—	chambre f	camera f	habitación f
root (E)	Wurzel f	—	racine f	radice f	raíz f

	D	E	F	I	Es
ropa (Es)	Wäsche f	washing	linge m	biancheria f	—
ropa interior (Es)	Unterwäsche f	underwear	sous-vêtements m pl	biancheria intima f	—
rope[1] (E)	Strick m	—	corde f	corda f	cuerda f
rope[2] (E)	Seil n	—	corde f	fune f	soga f
rosa (D)	—	pink	rose	rosa	de color rosa
rosa (Es)	Rose f	rose	rose f	rosa f	—
rosa[1] (I)	rosa	pink	rose	—	de color rosa
rosa[2] (I)	Rose f	rose	rose f	—	rosa f
Rose (D)	—	rose	rose f	rosa f	rosa f
rose (E)	Rose f	—	rose f	rosa f	rosa f
rose[1] (F)	rosa	pink	—	rosa	de color rosa
rose[2] (F)	Rose f	rose	—	rosa f	rosa f
rosso (I)	rot	red	rouge	—	rojo(a)
rosten (D)	—	rust	rouiller	arrugginire	oxidarse
rösten (D)	—	roast	griller	abbrustolire	tostar
rostig (D)	—	rusty	rouillé(e)	arrugginito(a)	oxidado(a)
rot (D)	—	red	rouge	rosso	rojo(a)
rôti[1] (F)	Braten m	roast	—	arrosto m	asado m
rôti[2] (F)	gebraten	fried	—	arrosto(a)	asado(a)
rôtir (F)	braten	roast	—	arrostire	asar
roto (Es)	kaputt	broken	cassé(e)	rotto(a)	—
rotondo (I)	rund	round	rond(e)	—	redondo(a)
rotto (I)	kaputt	broken	cassé(e)	—	roto(a)
roue (F)	Rad n	wheel	—	ruota f	rueda f
rouge (F)	rot	red	—	rosso(a)	rojo(a)
rougeole (F)	Masern pl	measles	—	morbillo m	sarampión m
rough (E)	rauh	—	rêche	ruvido(a)	rudo(a)
rouillé (F)	rostig	rusty	—	arrugginito(a)	oxidado(a)
rouiller (F)	rosten	rust	—	arrugginire	oxidarse
rouler (F)	rollen	roll	—	ruotare	rodar
roulotte (I)	Wohnwagen m	caravan	caravane f	—	rulota f
round (E)	rund	—	rond(e)	rotondo(a)	redondo(a)
roundabout (E)	Karussell n	—	manège m	giostra f	tiovivo m
round trip (E)	Rundfahrt f	—	circuit m	giro m	gira f
route (E)	Reiseroute f	—	itinéraire m	itinerario m	itinerario m
route (F)	Landstraße f	country road	—	strada provinciale f	carretera nacional f
route nationale (F)	Bundesstraße f	Federal Highway/main road	—	strada statale f	carretera nacional f
routier (F)	Fernfahrer m	long-distance driver	—	camionista m	camionero m
rovesciare (I)	umschmeißen	throw over	renverser	—	derribar
rovina (I)	Ruine f	ruin	ruine f	—	ruina f
rovinare (I)	verderben	ruin	détruire	—	arrruinar
rovistare (I)	wühlen	scrabble	fouiller	—	revolver

	D	E	F	I	Es
row[1] (E)	rudern	—	ramer	remare	remar
row[2] (E)	Reihe f	—	rangée f	fila f	fila f
rozzo (I)	grob	coarse	grossier(-ière)	—	tosco(a)
rub (E)	reiben	—	frotter	sfregare	frotar
rubare[1] (I)	einbrechen	break in	cambrioler	—	robar
rubare[2] (I)	stehlen	steal	voler	—	robar
rubber (E)	Gummi m	—	gomme f	gomma f	goma f
(rubber) dinghy (E)	Schlauchboot n	—	canot pneumatique m	canotto pneumatico m	bote neumático m
rubbish (E)	Abfall m	—	déchets m pl	immondizia f	basura f
rubio (Es)	blond	blond	blond(e)	biondo(a)	—
rücken (D)	—	move	déplacer	muovere	mover
Rücken (D)	—	back	dos m	schiena f	espalda m
Rückkehr (D)	—	return	retour m	ritorno m	regreso m
Rucksack (D)	—	rucksack	sac à dos m	zaino m	mochila f
rucksack (E)	Rucksack m	—	sac à dos m	zaino m	mochila f
rückwärts (D)	—	backwards	en arrière	in dietro	marcha atrás
Ruder (D)	—	oar	rame f	remo m	remo m
rudern (D)	—	row	ramer	remare	remar
rudo (Es)	rauh	rough	rêche	ruvido(a)	—
rue (F)	Straße f	street	—	strada f	calle f
rue à sens unique (F)	Einbahnstraße f	one-way street	—	senso unico m	calle de dirección única f
rueda (Es)	Rad n	wheel	roue f	ruota f	—
ruego (Es)	Bitte f	request	demande f	domanda f	—
ruelle (F)	Gasse f	lane	—	vicolo m	callejón m
rue transversale (F)	Querstraße f	intersecting road	—	traversa f	travesía f
rufen (D)	—	shout	appeler	chiamare	llamar
Ruhe (D)	—	calm	calme m	silenzio m	quietud f
ruhen (D)	—	rest	reposer, se	riposare	descansar
Ruhestand (D)	—	retirement	retraite f	pensione f	retiro m
Ruhetag (D)	—	closing day	jour de repos m	giorno di riposo m	día de descanso m
ruhig (D)	—	quiet	tranquille	calmo(a)	quieto(a)
ruido[1] (Es)	Geräusch n	sound	bruit m	rumore m	—
ruido[2] (Es)	Krach m	noise	bruit m	chiasso m	—
ruido[3] (Es)	Lärm m	noise	bruit m	rumore m	—
ruin[1] (E)	Ruine f	—	ruine f	rovina f	ruina f
ruin[2] (E)	verderben	—	détruire	rovinare	arrruinar
ruina (Es)	Ruine f	ruin	ruine f	rovina f	—
Ruine (D)	—	ruin	ruine f	rovina f	ruina f
ruine (F)	Ruine f	ruin	—	rovina f	ruina f
ruins (E)	Trümmer pl	—	décombres m pl	macerie f pl	escombros m pl
rule (E)	herrschen	—	régner	dominare	mandar
ruler (E)	Lineal n	—	règle f	riga f	regla f
rulota (Es)	Wohnwagen m	caravan	caravane f	roulotte f	—

	D	E	F	I	Es
rumeur (F)	Gerücht *n*	rumour	—	voce *f*	rumor *m*
rumor (Es)	Gerücht *n*	rumour	rumeur *f*	voce *f*	—
rumore[1] (I)	Geräusch *n*	sound	bruit *m*	—	ruido *m*
rumore[2] (I)	Lärm *m*	noise	bruit *m*	—	ruido *m*
rumoroso (I)	laut	loud	fort(e)	—	fuerte
rumour (E)	Gerücht *n*	—	rumeur *f*	voce *f*	rumor *m*
run[1] (E)	laufen	—	courir	correre	correr
run[2] (E)	rennen	—	courir	correre	correr
rund (D)	—	round	rond(e)	rotondo(a)	redondo(a)
Rundfahrt (D)	—	round trip	circuit *m*	giro *m*	gira *f*
Rundfunk (D)	—	broadcasting	radio *f*	radio *f*	radiodifusión *f*
run over (E)	überfahren	—	écraser	investire	atropellar
ruota (I)	Rad *n*	wheel	roue *f*	—	rueda *f*
ruotare (I)	rollen	roll	rouler	—	rodar
rush (E)	rauschen	—	bruire	mormorare	susurrar
Rusia (Es)	Rußland	Russia	Russie *f*	Russia *f*	—
rusk (E)	Zwieback *m*	—	biscotte *f*	fette biscottate *f pl*	bizcocho *m*
russare (I)	schnarchen	snore	ronfler	—	roncar
Russia (E)	Rußland	—	Russie *f*	Russia *f*	Rusia *f*
Russia (I)	Rußland	Russia	Russie *f*	—	Rusia *f*
Russie (F)	Rußland	Russia	—	Russia *f*	Rusia *f*
Rußland (D)	—	Russia	Russie *f*	Russia *f*	Rusia *f*
rust (E)	rosten	—	rouiller	arrugginire	oxidarse
rusty (E)	rostig	—	rouillé(e)	arrugginito(a)	oxidado(a)
rutschen (D)	—	slide	glisser	scivolare	resbalar
ruvido (I)	rauh	rough	rêche	—	rudo(a)
Saal (D)	—	hall	salle *f*	sala *f*	sala *f*
sábado[1] (Es)	Sonnabend *m*	Saturday	samedi *m*	sabato *m*	—
sábado[2] (Es)	Samstag *m*	Saturday	samedi *m*	sabato *m*	—
sábana (Es)	Laken *n*	sheet	drap *m*	lenzuolo *m*	—
sabato[1] (I)	Sonnabend *m*	Saturday	samedi *m*	—	sábado *m*
sabato[2] (I)	Samstag *m*	Saturday	samedi *m*	—	sábado *m*
sabbia (I)	Sand *m*	sand	sable *m*	—	arena *f*
saber[1] (Es)	können	can	pouvoir	sapere	—
saber[2] (Es)	wissen	know	savoir	sapere	—
saber[3] (Es)	Wissen *n*	knowledge	savoir *m*	sapere *m*	—
sabio (Es)	weise	wise	sage	saggio(a)	—
sable (F)	Sand *m*	sand	—	sabbia *f*	arena *f*
sabor (Es)	Geschmack *m*	taste	goût *m*	gusto *m*	—
sac[1] (F)	Sack *m*	sack	—	sacco *m*	saco *m*
sac[2] (F)	Tasche *f*	handbag	—	borsa *f*	bolso *m*
sac[3] (F)	Tüte *f*	bag	—	sacchetto *m*	bolsa *f*
sacacorchos (Es)	Korkenzieher *m*	corkscrew	tire-bouchon *m*	cavatappi *m*	—
sac à dos (F)	Rucksack *m*	rucksack	—	zaino *m*	mochila *f*

	D	E	F	I	Es
sac à main (F)	Handtasche f	handbag	—	borsetta f	bolso m
sac à provision (F)	Einkaufstasche f	shopping bag	—	borsa della spesa f	bolsa de compra f
saccheggiare (I)	plündern	loot	piller	—	desvalijar
sacchetto (I)	Tüte f	bag	sac m	—	bolsa f
sacco (I)	Sack m	sack	sac m	—	saco m
sacerdote (Es)	Priester m	priest	prêtre m	prete m	—
Sache (D)	—	thing	chose f	cosa f	cosa f
Sack (D)	—	sack	sac m	sacco m	saco m
sack (E)	Sack m	—	sac m	sacco m	saco m
saco (Es)	Sack m	sack	sac m	sacco m	—
sacrifice (E)	Opfer n	—	sacrifice m	sacrificio m	sacrificio m
sacrifice (F)	Opfer n	sacrifice	—	sacrificio m	sacrificio m
sacrificio (Es)	Opfer n	sacrifice	sacrifice m	sacrificio m	—
sacrificio (I)	Opfer n	sacrifice	sacrifice m	—	sacrificio m
sad (E)	traurig	—	triste	triste	triste
safety (E)	Sicherheit f	—	sécurité f	sicurezza f	seguridad f
Saft (D)	—	juice	jus m	succo m	zumo m
Säge (D)	—	saw	scie f	sega f	sierra f
sage (F)	weise	wise	—	saggio	sabio(a)
sagen (D)	—	say	dire	dire	decir
saggio (I)	weise	wise	sage	—	sabio(a)
Sahne (D)	—	cream	crème f	panna f	nata f
saigner (F)	bluten	bleed	—	sanguinare	sangrar
sail (E)	segeln	—	faire de la voile	andare a vela	navegar a vela
sailor (E)	Matrose m	—	matelot m	marinaio m	marinero m
sain (F)	gesund	healthy	—	sano(a)	sano(a)
saint (F)	heilig	holy	—	santo(a)	santo(a)
Saint-Sylvestre (F)	Silvester n	New Year's Eve	—	San Silvestro m	Noche Vieja f
saisir¹ (F)	ergreifen	seize	—	afferrare	coger
saisir² (F)	fassen	grasp	—	prendere	coger
saisir³ (F)	greifen	seize	—	afferrare	coger
Saison (D)	—	season	saison f	stagione f	temporada f
saison¹ (F)	Jahreszeit f	time of year	—	stagione f	estación del año f
saison² (F)	Saison f	season	—	stagione f	temporada f
sal (Es)	Salz n	salt	sel m	sale m	—
sala (Es)	Saal m	hall	salle f	sala f	—
sala (I)	Saal m	hall	salle f	—	sala f
salad (E)	Salat m	—	salade f	insalata f	ensalada f
sala da pranzo (I)	Eßzimmer n	dining room	salle à manger f	—	comedor m
sala d'attesa (I)	Wartesaal m	waiting room	salle d'attente f	—	sala de espera f
salade (F)	Salat m	salad	—	insalata f	ensalada f
sala de espera (Es)	Wartesaal m	waiting room	salle d'attente f	sala d'attesa f	—
sala de estar (Es)	Wohnzimmer n	living room	salle de séjour f	salotto m	—
salaire¹ (F)	Gehalt n	salary	—	stipendio m	sueldo m
salaire² (F)	Lohn m	wages	—	salario m	salario m
salario (Es)	Lohn m	wages	salaire m	salario m	—
salario (I)	Lohn m	wages	salaire m	—	salario m
salary (E)	Gehalt n	—	salaire m	stipendio m	sueldo m

	D	E	F	I	Es
Salat (D)	—	salad	salade *f*	insalata *f*	ensalada *f*
Salbe (D)	—	ointment	onguent *m*	pomata *f*	pomada *f*
saldar (Es)	abbezahlen	pay off	finir de payer	saldare	—
saldare (I)	abbezahlen	pay off	finir de payer	—	saldar
saldi (I)	Ausverkauf *m*	sale	soldes *m pl*	—	liquidación *f*
sale[1] (E)	Ausverkauf *m*	—	soldes *m pl*	saldi *m*	liquidación *f*
sale[2] (E)	Verkauf *m*	—	vente *f*	vendita *f*	venta *f*
sale[1] (F)	dreckig	dirty	—	sporco(a)	sucio(a)
sale[2] (F)	schmutzig	dirty	—	sporco(a)	sucio(a)
sale (I)	Salz *n*	salt	sel *m*	—	sal *f*
salesman (E)	Verkäufer *m*	—	vendeur *m*	venditore *m*	vendedor *m*
saleté (F)	Schmutz *m*	dirt	—	sporcizia *f*	suciedad *f*
salida[1] (Es)	Ausgang *m*	exit	sortie *f*	uscita *f*	—
salida[2] (Es)	Ausreise *f*	departure	départ *m*	partenza *f*	—
salida[3] (Es)	Abfahrt *f*	departure	départ *m*	partenza *f*	—
salida[4] (Es)	Abreise *f*	departure	départ *m*	partenza *f*	—
salida de emergencia (Es)	Notausgang *m*	emergency exit	sortie de secours *f*	uscita di sicurezza *f*	—
salida del sol (Es)	Sonnen-aufgang *m*	sunrise	lever du soleil *m*	sorgere del sole *m*	—
salir[1] (Es)	abfahren	depart	partir (de)	partire	—
salir[2] (Es)	abreisen	leave	partir	partire	—
salir[3] (Es)	ausgehen	go out	sortir	uscire	—
salir[4] (Es)	heraustreten	step out	sortir	uscire fuori	—
salir afuera (Es)	hinausgehen	go out	sortir	uscire	—
salire[1] (I)	aufsteigen	ascend	monter	—	subir
salire[2] (I)	einsteigen	get in	monter	—	subir a
salire[3] (I)	hinaufsteigen	climb	monter	—	subir
salire[4] (I)	steigen	go up	monter	—	subir
salita d'ingresso (I)	Auffahrt *f*	drive	allée *f*	—	entrada *f*
salle (F)	Saal *m*	hall	—	sala *f*	sala *f*
salle à manger (F)	Eßzimmer *n*	dining room	—	sala da pranzo *f*	comedor *m*
salle d'attente (F)	Wartesaal *m*	waiting room	—	sala d'attesa *f*	sala de espera *f*
salle de bains (F)	Badezimmer *n*	bathroom	—	stanza da bagno *f*	cuarto de baño *m*
salle de séjour (F)	Wohnzimmer *n*	living room	—	salotto *m*	sala de estar *f*
salmon (E)	Lachs *m*	—	saumon *m*	salmone *m*	salmón *m*
salmón (Es)	Lachs *m*	salmon	saumon *m*	salmone *m*	—
salmone (I)	Lachs *m*	salmon	saumon *m*	—	salmón *m*
salotto (I)	Wohnzimmer *n*	living room	salle de séjour *f*	—	sala de estar *f*
salpicar (Es)	spritzen	squirt	asperger	spruzzare	—
salsa (Es)	Soße *f*	sauce	sauce *f*	salsa *f*	—
salsa (I)	Soße *f*	sauce	sauce *f*	—	salsa *f*
salsiccia (I)	Wurst *f*	sausage	saucisse *f*	—	salchicha *f*
salt (E)	Salz *n*	—	sel *m*	sale *m*	sal *f*
saltar[1] (Es)	hüpfen	jump	sautiller	saltellare	—
saltar[2] (Es)	springen	jump	sauter	saltare	—
saltare (I)	springen	jump	sauter	—	saltar
saltellare (I)	hüpfen	jump	sautiller	—	saltar
salto (Es)	Sprung *m*	jump	saut *m*	salto *m*	—

	D	E	F	I	Es
salto (I)	Sprung *m*	jump	saut *m*	—	salto *m*
salud (Es)	Gesundheit *f*	health	santé *f*	salute *f*	—
¡salud! (Es)	prost!	cheers!	santé!	salute!	—
saludar¹ (Es)	begrüßen	greet	saluer	salutare	—
saludar² (Es)	grüßen	greet	saluer	salutare	—
saludo (Es)	Gruß *m*	greeting	salut *m*	saluto *m*	—
saluer¹ (F)	begrüßen	greet	—	salutare	saludar
saluer² (F)	grüßen	greet	—	salutare	saludar
salut (F)	Gruß *m*	greeting	—	saluto *m*	saludo *m*
salu! (F)	tschüs!	bye!	—	ciao!	¡hasta luego!
salutare¹ (I)	begrüßen	greet	saluer	—	saludar
salutare² (I)	grüßen	greet	saluer	—	saludar
salute (I)	Gesundheit *f*	health	santé *f*	—	salud *f*
salute! (I)	prost!	cheers!	santé!	—	¡salud!
saluto (I)	Gruß *m*	greeting	salut *m*	—	saludo *m*
salvagente (I)	Rettungsring *m*	lifebelt	bouée de sauvetage *f*	—	salvavidas *m*
salvaje (Es)	wild	wild	sauvage	selvatico(a)	—
salvar (Es)	retten	save	sauver	salvare	—
salvare (I)	retten	save	sauver	—	salvar
salvavidas (Es)	Rettungsring *m*	lifebelt	bouée de sauvetage *f*	salvagente *m*	—
salvo (Es)	außer	except	hors de	eccetto	—
Salz (D)	—	salt	sel *m*	sale *m*	sal *f*
same (E)	gleich	—	égal(e)	identico(a)	idéntico(a)
samedi¹ (F)	Sonnabend *m*	Saturday	—	sabato *m*	sábado *m*
samedi² (F)	Samstag *m*	Saturday	—	sabato *m*	sábado *m*
sammeln (D)	—	collect	collecter	raccogliere	recolectar
Sammlung (D)	—	collection	collection *f*	raccolta *f*	colección *f*
sample (E)	Muster *n*	—	modèle *m*	campione *m*	modelo *m*
Samstag (D)	—	Saturday	samedi *m*	sabato *m*	sábado *m*
Sand (D)	—	sand	sable *m*	sabbia *f*	arena *f*
sand (E)	Sand *m*	—	sable *m*	sabbia *f*	arena *f*
sandal (E)	Sandale *f*	—	sandale *f*	sandalo *m*	sandalia *f*
Sandale (D)	—	sandal	sandale *f*	sandalo *m*	sandalia *f*
sandale (F)	Sandale *f*	sandal	—	sandalo *m*	sandalia *f*
sandalia (Es)	Sandale *f*	sandal	sandale *f*	sandalo *m*	—
sandalo (I)	Sandale *f*	sandal	sandale *f*	—	sandalia *f*
sanft (D)	—	gentle	doux(douce)	dolce	dulce
sang (F)	Blut *n*	blood	—	sangue *m*	sangre *f*
Sänger (D)	—	singer	chanteur *m*	cantante *m*	cantante *m*
sangrar (Es)	bluten	bleed	saigner	sanguinare	—
sangre (Es)	Blut *n*	blood	sang *m*	sangue *m*	—
sangue (I)	Blut *n*	blood	sang *m*	—	sangre *f*
sangue misto (I)	Mischling *m*	halfcaste	métis *m*	—	mestizo *m*
sanguinare (I)	bluten	bleed	saigner	—	sangrar
sano (Es)	gesund	healthy	sain(e)	sano(a)	—
sano (I)	gesund	healthy	sain(e)	—	sano(a)
sans (F)	ohne	without	—	senza	sin

save

	D	E	F	I	Es
sans doute (F)	zweifellos	doubtless	—	senza dubbio	sin duda
sans engagement (F)	unverbindlich	not binding	—	non impegnativo(a)	sin compromiso
San Silvestro (I)	Silvester n	New Year's Eve	Saint-Sylvestre m	—	noche vieja f
sans importance (F)	unwichtig	unimportant	—	non importante	sin importancia
sans valeur (F)	wertlos	worthless	—	senza valore	sin valor
santé (F)	Gesundheit f	health	—	salute f	salud f
santé! (F)	prost!	cheers!	—	salute!	¡salud!
santo (Es)	heilig	holy	saint(e)	santo(a)	—
santo (I)	heilig	holy	saint(e)	—	santo(a)
sapere¹ (I)	können	can	pouvoir	—	saber
sapere² (I)	wissen	know	savoir	—	saber
sapere³ (I)	Wissen n	knowledge	savoir m	—	saber m
sapeurs-pompiers (F)	Feuerwehr f	fire brigade	—	vigili del fuoco	cuerpo de bomberos m
sapone (I)	Seife f	soap	savon m	—	jabón m
Sarg (D)	—	coffin	cercueil m	bara f	ataúd m
sartén (Es)	Pfanne f	pan	poêle f	padella f	—
sarto (I)	Schneider m	tailor	tailleur m	—	sastre m
sasso (I)	Stein m	stone	pierre f	—	piedra f
sastre (Es)	Schneider m	tailor	tailleur m	sarto m	—
satisfacer (Es)	befriedigen	satisfy	satisfaire	soddisfare	—
satisfaire (F)	befriedigen	satisfy	—	soddisfare	satisfacer
satisfecho¹ (Es)	satt	full	rassasié(e)	sazio(a)	—
satisfecho² (Es)	zufrieden	satisfied	content(e)	contento(a)	—
satisfied (E)	zufrieden	—	content(e)	contento(a)	satisfecho(a)
satisfy (E)	befriedigen	—	satisfaire	soddisfare	satisfacer
satt (D)	—	full	rassasié(e)	sazio(a)	satisfecho(a)
Saturday¹ (E)	Sonnabend m	—	samedi m	sabato m	sábado m
Saturday² (E)	Samstag m	—	samedi m	sabato m	sábado m
Satz (D)	—	sentence	phrase f	frase f	oración f
sauber (D)	—	clean	propre	pulito(a)	limpio(a)
sauce (E)	Soße f	—	sauce f	salsa f	salsa f
sauce (F)	Soße f	sauce	—	salsa f	salsa f
saucepan (E)	Kochtopf m	—	casserole f	pentola f	olla f
saucer (E)	Untertasse f	—	soucoupe f	piattino m	platillo m
saucisse (F)	Wurst f	sausage	—	salsiccia f	salchicha f
sauer (D)	—	sour	aigre	acido(a)	agrio(a)
Säule (D)	—	pillar	colonne f	colonna f	columna f
saumon (F)	Lachs m	salmon	—	salmone m	salmón m
Säure (D)	—	acid	acide m	acido m	ácido m
sausage (E)	Wurst f	—	saucisse f	salsiccia f	salchicha f
saut (F)	Sprung m	jump	—	salto m	salto m
sauter (F)	springen	jump	—	saltare	saltar
sautiller (F)	hüpfen	jump	—	saltellare	saltar
sauvage (F)	wild	wild	—	selvatico(a)	salvaje
sauver (F)	retten	save	—	salvare	salvar
save¹ (E)	retten	—	sauver	salvare	salvar
save² (E)	sparen	—	économiser	risparmiare	ahorrar

	D	E	F	I	Es
savings bank (E)	Sparkasse f	—	caisse d'épargne f	cassa di risparmio f	caja de ahorros f
savings book (E)	Sparbuch n	—	livret de caisse d'épargne m	libretto di risparmio m	libreta de ahorro f
savoir¹ (F)	wissen	know	—	sapere	saber
savoir² (F)	Wissen n	knowledge	—	sapere m	saber m
savon (F)	Seife f	soap	—	sapone m	jabón m
savoureux (F)	köstlich	delicious	—	squisito(a)	exquisito(a)
saw (E)	Säge f	—	scie f	sega f	sierra f
say (E)	sagen	—	dire	dire	decir
say goodbye to (E)	verabschieden	—	prendre congé de	congedare	despedir
say thank you (E)	bedanken	—	remercier	ringraziare	agradecer algo
sazio (I)	satt	full	rassasié(e)	—	satisfecho(a)
sbagliare (I)	irren	be mistaken	tromper, se	—	equivocarse
sbagliato (I)	verkehrt	wrong	faux(fausse)	—	equivocado(a)
sbaglio (I)	Fehler m	mistake	faute f	—	falta f
sbarra (I)	Schranke f	barrier	barrière f	—	barrera f
sbocco (I)	Mündung f	mouth	embouchure f	—	desembocadura f
sbrigare (I)	erledigen	take care of	régler	—	acabar
sbucciare (I)	schälen	peel	éplucher	—	pelar
scaffale (I)	Regal n	shelves	étagère f	—	estantería f
scala¹ (I)	Aufgang m	staircase	montée f	—	subida f
scala² (I)	Leiter f	ladder	échelle f	—	escalera f
scala³ (I)	Treppe f	stairs	escalier m	—	escalera f
scala mobile (I)	Rolltreppe f	escalator	escalier roulant m	—	escalera mecánica f
scales (E)	Waage f	—	balance f	bilancia f	balanza f
scalo intermedio (I)	Zwischen- landung f	intermediate landing	escale f	—	escala f
scambiare¹ (I)	austauschen	exchange	échanger	—	cambiar
scambiare² (I)	tauschen	swap	échanger	—	cambiar
scambiare³ (I)	verwechseln	confuse	confondre	—	confundir
scambiare⁴ (I)	vertauschen	exchange	échanger	—	cambiar
scambio (I)	Austausch m	exchange	échange m	—	cambio m
scandal (E)	Skandal m	—	scandale m	scandalo m	escándalo m
scandale (F)	Skandal m	scandal	—	scandalo m	escándalo m
scandalo (I)	Skandal m	scandal	scandale m	—	escándalo m
Scandinavia (E)	Skandinavien	—	Scandinavie f	Scandinavia f	Escandinavia f
Scandinavia (I)	Skandinavien	Scandinavia	Scandinavie f	—	Escandinavia f
Scandinavie (F)	Skandinavien	Scandinavia	—	Scandinavia f	Escandinavia f
scapolo (I)	Junggeselle m	bachelor	célibataire m	—	soltero m
scappare¹ (I)	entkommen	escape	échapper	—	escapar
scappare² (I)	entfliehen	escape	échapper, se	—	huir
scar (E)	Narbe f	—	cicatrice f	cicatrice f	cicatriz f
scarf¹ (E)	Halstuch n	—	écharpe f	sciarpa f	pañuelo para el cuello m
scarf² (E)	Schal m	—	écharpe f	sciarpa f	chal m
scaricare¹ (I)	ausladen	unload	décharger	—	descargar
scaricare² (I)	abladen	unload	décharger	—	descargar
scarpa (I)	Schuh m	shoe	chaussure f	—	zapato m

	D	E	F	I	Es
scarso (I)	knapp	tight	étroit(e)	—	estrecho(a)
scatola¹ (I)	Dose f	tin	boîte f	—	lata f
scatola² (I)	Schachtel f	box	boîte f	—	caja f
scattare una foto (I)	knipsen	take a snap	photographier	—	hacer una foto
scattered (E)	zerstreut	—	dispersé(e)	disperso(a)	disperso(a)
scavare (I)	graben	dig	creuser	—	cavar
scegliere¹ (I)	aussuchen	select	choisir	—	escoger
scegliere² (I)	auswählen	choose	choisir	—	eligir
scelta¹ (I)	Auswahl f	choice	choix m	—	elección f
scelta² (I)	Wahl f	choice	choix m	—	opción f
scemo (I)	doof	daft	bête	—	estúpido(a)
scendere¹ (I)	aussteigen	get off	descendre	—	bajar
scendere² (I)	absteigen	dismount	descendre	—	descender
scendere³ (I)	hinuntergehen	descend	descendre	—	bajar
scène (F)	Bühne f	stage	—	palcoscenico m	escenario m
scent (E)	Duft m	—	odeur f	profumo m	aroma m
Schachtel (D)	—	box	boîte f	scatola f	caja f
Schädel (D)	—	skull	crâne m	cranio m	cráneo m
schaden (D)	—	damage	nuire	nuocere	dañar
Schaden (D)	—	damage	dommage m	danno m	daño m
schädlich (D)	—	harmful	nuisible	nocivo(a)	nocivo(a)
Schaf (D)	—	sheep	mouton m	pecora f	oveja f
schaffen (D)	—	create	réussir à faire	creare	crear
Schaffner (D)	—	conductor	contrôleur m	bigliettaio m	revisor m
Schal (D)	—	scarf	écharpe f	sciarpa f	chal m
Schale (D)	—	peel	peau f	buccia f	piel m
schälen (D)	—	peel	éplucher	sbucciare	pelar
Schallplatte (D)	—	record	disque m	disco m	disco m
schalten (D)	—	switch	connecter	commutare	conectar
Schalter (D)	—	counter	guichet m	sportello m	ventanilla f
schämen (D)	—	be ashamed	avoir honte	vergognarsi	tener vergüenza
Schande (D)	—	disgrace	honte f	vergogna f	deshonra f
Schar (D)	—	band	bande f	schiera f	grupo m
scharf¹ (D)	—	sharp	tranchant(e)	tagliente	cortante
scharf² (D)	—	hot	épicé(e)	piccante	picante
schärfen (D)	—	sharpen	aiguiser	affilare	afilar
Schatten (D)	—	shadow	ombre f	ombra f	sombra f
schattig (D)	—	shady	ombragé(e)	ombroso(a)	a la sombra
Schatz (D)	—	treasure	trésor m	tesoro m	tesoro m
schätzen (D)	—	estimate	estimer	stimare	estimar
schauderhaft (D)	—	horrible	horrible	spaventoso(a)	espantoso(a)
schauen (D)	—	look	regarder	guardare	mirar
Schaufel (D)	—	shovel	pelle f	pala f	pala f
Schaufenster (D)	—	shop window	vitrine f	vetrina f	escaparate m
schaukeln (D)	—	swing	balancer, se	dondolare	columpiarse
Schaum (D)	—	foam	écume f	schiuma f	espuma f
Schauspiel (D)	—	play	spectacle m	spettacolo m	espectáculo m

	D	E	F	I	Es
Schauspieler (D)	—	actor	acteur *m*	attore *m*	actor *m*
Scheck (D)	—	cheque	chèque *m*	assegno *m*	cheque *m*
Scheckbuch (D)	—	cheque book	carnet de chèques *m*	libretto degli assegni *m*	talonario de cheques *m*
Scheibe¹ (D)	—	disc	disque *m*	disco *m*	disco *m*
Scheibe² (D)	—	pane	carreau *m*	vetro *m*	cristal *m*
scheiden (D)	—	part	séparer	separare	separar
Schein¹ (D)	—	light	lumière *f*	luce *f*	luz *f*
Schein² (D)	—	note	billet *m*	banconota *f*	billete *m*
schenken (D)	—	give	offrir	regalare	regalar
Scherbe (D)	—	broken piece	tesson *m*	coccio *m*	pedazo *m*
Schere (D)	—	pair of scissors	ciseaux *m pl*	forbici *f pl*	tijeras *f pl*
Scherz (D)	—	joke	plaisanterie *f*	scherzo *m*	broma *f*
scherzare (I)	spaßen	joke	plaisanter	—	bromear
scherzo¹ (I)	Scherz *m*	joke	plaisanterie *f*	—	broma *f*
scherzo² (I)	Spaß *m*	fun	plaisir *m*	—	broma *f*
scheu (D)	—	shy	timide	timido(a)	tímido(a)
schiavo (I)	Sklave *m*	slave	esclave *m*	—	esclavo *m*
schick (D)	—	stylish	chic	elegante	elegante
schicken (D)	—	send	envoyer	inviare	mandar
Schicksal (D)	—	fate	destin *m*	destino *m*	destino *m*
schieben (D)	—	push	pousser	spingere	empujar
Schiedsrichter (D)	—	referee	arbitre *m*	arbitro *m*	árbitro *m*
schief (D)	—	sloped	oblique	obliquo(a)	torcido(a)
schiena (I)	Rücken *m*	back	dos *m*	—	espalda *m*
schiera (I)	Schar *f*	band	bande *f*	—	grupo *m*
schießen (D)	—	shoot	tirer	sparare	disparar
Schiff (D)	—	ship	navire *m*	nave *f*	barco *m*
Schild (D)	—	shield	bouclier *m*	scudo *m*	escudo *m*
schimpfen (D)	—	scold	gronder	imprecare	insultar
Schinken (D)	—	ham	jambon *m*	prosciutto *m*	jamón *m*
Schirm (D)	—	umbrella	parapluie *m*	ombrello *m*	paraguas *m*
schiuma (I)	Schaum *m*	foam	écume *f*	—	espuma *f*
schizzo (I)	Skizze *f*	sketch	esquisse *f*	—	boceto *m*
Schlaf (D)	—	sleep	sommeil *m*	sonno *m*	sueño *m*
schlafen (D)	—	sleep	dormir	dormire	dormir
Schlafzimmer (D)	—	bedroom	chambre à coucher *f*	camera da letto *f*	dormitorio *m*
Schlag (D)	—	blow	coup *m*	colpo *m*	golpe *m*
schlagen (D)	—	hit	battre	battere	golpear
Schlagzeile (D)	—	headline	manchette *f*	titolo *m*	título *m*
Schlamm (D)	—	mud	boue *f*	fango *m*	barro *m*
Schlange (D)	—	snake	serpent *m*	serpente *m*	serpiente *f*
schlank (D)	—	slim	mince	snello(a)	delgado(a)
schlau (D)	—	clever	astucieux(-euse)	astuto(a)	astuto(a)
Schlauchboot (D)	—	(rubber) dinghy	canot pneumatique *m*	canotto pneumatico *m*	bote neumático *m*
schlecht (D)	—	bad	mauvais(e)	cattivo	malo(a)
schließen (D)	—	close	fermer	chiudere	cerrar

D	E	F	I	Es
schließlich (D)	—	finally	finalement	finalmente	finalmente
Schloß[1] (D)	—	lock	serrure *f*	serratura *f*	cerradura *f*
Schloß[2] (D)	—	castle	château *m*	castello *m*	castillo *m*
schlucken (D)	—	swallow	avaler	inghiottire	tragar
Schluß (D)	—	end	fin *f*	fine *f*	conclusión *f*
Schlüssel (D)	—	key	clé *f*	chiave *f*	llave *f*
Schlüsselloch (D)	—	keyhole	trou de la serrure *m*	buco della chiave *m*	ojo de la cerradura *m*
schmecken (D)	—	taste	sentir	piacere	gustar
Schmerz (D)	—	pain	douleur *f*	dolore *m*	dolor *m*
schmerzhaft (D)	—	painful	douloureux(-euse)	doloroso(a)	doloroso(a)
Schmetterling (D)	—	butterfly	papillon *m*	farfalla *f*	mariposa *f*
Schminke (D)	—	make-up	maquillage *m*	trucco *m*	maquillaje *m*
Schmuck (D)	—	jewellery	bijoux *m pl*	gioielli *m pl*	joyas *f pl*
Schmutz (D)	—	dirt	saleté *f*	sporcizia *f*	suciedad *f*
schmutzig (D)	—	dirty	sale	sporco(a)	sucio(a)
Schnaps (D)	—	spirits	eau-de-vie *f*	acquavite *f*	aguardiente *m*
schnarchen (D)	—	snore	ronfler	russare	roncar
Schnee (D)	—	snow	neige *f*	neve *f*	nieve *f*
schneiden (D)	—	cut	couper	tagliare	cortar
Schneider (D)	—	tailor	tailleur *m*	sarto *m*	sastre *m*
schneien (D)	—	snow	neiger	nevicare	nevar
schnell (D)	—	fast	rapide	veloce	rápido(a)
Schnelligkeit (D)	—	speed	rapidité *f*	velocità *f*	rapidez *f*
Schnellstraße (D)	—	expressway	voie rapide *f*	superstrada *f*	carretera de circulación rápida *f*
Schnellzug (D)	—	express train	rapide *m*	treno direttissimo *m*	tren expreso *m*
Schnitt (D)	—	cut	coupe *f*	taglio *m*	corte *m*
Schnupfen (D)	—	cold	rhume *m*	raffreddore *m*	resfriado *m*
Schnur (D)	—	string	ficelle *f*	corda *f*	cordel *m*
Schnurrbart (D)	—	moustache	moustache *f*	baffi *m pl*	bigote *m*
Schokolade (D)	—	chocolate	chocolat *m*	cioccolato *m*	chocolate *m*
schon (D)	—	already	déjà	già	ya
schön (D)	—	beautiful	beau, bel, belle	bello(a)	hermoso(a)
Schönheit (D)	—	beauty	beauté *f*	bellezza *f*	belleza *f*
school (E)	Schule *f*	—	école *f*	scuola *f*	escuela *f*
Schrank (D)	—	cupboard	armoire *f*	armadio *m*	armario *m*
Schranke (D)	—	barrier	barrière *f*	sbarra *f*	barrera *f*
Schraube (D)	—	screw	vis *f*	vite *f*	tornillo *m*
Schraubenzieher (D)	—	screwdriver	tournevis *m*	cacciavite *m*	destornillador *m*
schrecklich (D)	—	terrible	terrible	spaventoso(a)	horrible
Schrei (D)	—	scream	cri *m*	grido *m*	grito *m*
schreiben (D)	—	write	écrire	scrivere	escribir
Schreibmaschine (D)	—	typewriter	machine à écrire *f*	macchina da scrivere *f*	máquina de escribir *f*
Schreibwarenhandlung (D)	—	stationery shop	papeterie *f*	cartoleria *f*	papelería *f*
schreien (D)	—	scream	crier	gridare	gritar
Schrift (D)	—	writing	écriture *f*	scrittura *f*	escritura *f*

	D	E	F	I	Es
schriftlich (D)	—	written	écrit(e)	scritto	por escrito
Schriftsteller (D)	—	writer	écrivain *m*	scrittore *m*	escritor *m*
Schritt (D)	—	step	pas *m*	passo *m*	paso *m*
Schublade (D)	—	drawer	tiroir *m*	cassetto *m*	cajón *m*
schüchtern (D)	—	shy	timide	timido(a)	tímido(a)
Schuh (D)	—	shoe	chaussure *f*	scarpa *f*	zapato *m*
Schuhcreme (D)	—	shoe polish	cirage *m*	lucido per scarpe *m*	betún *m*
Schuhgeschäft (D)	—	shoeshop	magasin de chaussures *m*	negozio di scarpe *m*	zapatería *f*
Schuld (D)	—	fault	culpabilité *f*	colpa *f*	culpa *f*
schulden (D)	—	owe	devoir qch à qn	dovere	deber
Schulden (D)	—	debt	dette *f*	debiti *m pl*	deudas *f pl*
schuldig (D)	—	guilty	coupable	colpevole	culpable
Schule (D)	—	school	école *f*	scuola *f*	escuela *f*
Schüler (D)	—	pupil	élève *m*	scolaro *m*	alumno *m*
schulfrei (D)	—	holiday	de congé	vacanza	sin colegio
Schulter (D)	—	shoulder	épaule *f*	spalla *f*	hombro *m*
Schuß (D)	—	shot	coup *m*	sparo *m*	disparo *m*
Schüssel (D)	—	bowl	jatte *f*	scodella *f*	fuente *f*
Schuster (D)	—	shoemaker	cordonnier *m*	calzolaio *m*	zapatero *m*
schütteln (D)	—	shake	secouer	agitare	agitar
schütten (D)	—	pour	verser	versare	verter
Schutz (D)	—	protection	protection *f*	protezione *f*	protección *f*
schützen (D)	—	protect	protéger	proteggere	proteger
schwach (D)	—	weak	faible	debole	débil
Schwäche (D)	—	weakness	faiblesse *f*	debolezza *f*	debilidad *f*
Schwager (D)	—	brother-in-law	beau-frère *m*	cognato *m*	cuñado *m*
Schwägerin (D)	—	sister-in-law	belle-sœur *f*	cognata *f*	cuñada *f*
Schwamm (D)	—	sponge	éponge *f*	spugna *f*	esponja *f*
schwanger (D)	—	pregnant	enceinte	incinta	embarazada
Schwanz (D)	—	tail	queue *f*	coda *f*	rabo *m*
schwarz (D)	—	black	noir(e)	nero(a)	negro(a)
schwatzen (D)	—	chatter	bavarder	chiacchierare	charlar
Schweden (D)	—	Sweden	Suède *f*	Svezia *f*	Suecia *f*
schweigen (D)	—	be silent	taire, se	tacere	callar
Schwein (D)	—	pig	cochon *m*	maiale *m*	cerdo *m*
Schweine-fleisch (D)	—	pork	viande de porc *f*	carne di maiale *f*	carne de cerdo *f*
Schweiz (D)	—	Switzerland	Suisse *f*	Svizzera *f*	Suiza *f*
Schweizer (D)	—	Swiss	Suisse *m*	svizzero	suizo *m*
schwer (D)	—	heavy	lourd(e)	pesante	pesado(a)
Schwester (D)	—	sister	sœur *f*	sorella *f*	hermana *f*
Schwiegereltern (D)	—	parents-in-law	beaux-parents *m pl*	suoceri *m pl*	suegros *m pl*
Schwiegermutter (D)	—	mother-in-law	belle-mère *f*	suocera *f*	suegra *f*
schwierig (D)	—	difficult	difficile	difficile	difícil
Schwierigkeit (D)	—	difficulty	difficulté *f*	difficoltà *f*	dificultad *f*
Schwimmbad (D)	—	swimming pool	piscine *f*	piscina *f*	piscina *f*
schwimmen (D)	—	swim	nager	nuotare	nadar

	D	E	F	I	Es
Schwimmweste (D)	—	life jacket	gilet de sauvetage *m*	giubbotto di salvataggio *m*	chaleco salvavidas *m*
schwitzen (D)	—	sweat	transpirer	sudare	sudar
schwören (D)	—	swear	jurer	giurare	jurar
schwül (D)	—	sultry	lourd(e)	afoso(a)	sofocante
sci (I)	Ski *m*	ski	ski *m*	—	esquí *m*
sciacquare (I)	abspülen	wash up	faire la vaisselle	—	lavar
sciarpa[1] (I)	Halstuch *n*	scarf	écharpe *f*	—	pañuelo para el cuello *m*
sciarpa[2] (I)	Schal *m*	scarf	écharpe *f*	—	chal *m*
scie (F)	Säge *f*	saw	—	sega *f*	sierra *f*
science (E)	Wissenschaft *f*	—	science *f*	scienza *f*	ciencia *f*
science (F)	Wissenschaft *f*	science	—	scienza *f*	ciencia *f*
scientifique (F)	Wissenschaftler *m*	scientist	—	scienziato *m*	científico *m*
scientist (E)	Wissenschaftler *m*	—	scientifique *m*	scienziato *m*	científico *m*
scienza (I)	Wissenschaft *f*	science	science *f*	—	ciencia *f*
scienziato (I)	Wissenschaftler *m*	scientist	scientifique *m*	—	científico *m*
scimmia (I)	Affe *m*	ape	singe *m*	—	mono *m*
sciocco (I)	albern	foolish	sot(te)	—	tonto
sciogliere[1] (I)	auflösen	dissolve	dénouer	—	deshacer
sciogliere[2] (I)	lösen	solve	résoudre	—	desatar
sciogliere[3] (I)	losbinden	free	délier	—	desatar
sciogliersi (I)	tauen	thaw	fondre	—	deshelar
scioperare (I)	streiken	be on strike	faire grève	—	hacer huelga
sciopero (I)	Streik *m*	strike	grève *f*	—	huelga *f*
sciovia (I)	Skilift *m*	skilift	remonte-pente *m*	—	telesilla *f*
scivolare (I)	rutschen	slide	glisser	—	resbalar
scodella (I)	Schüssel *f*	bowl	jatte *f*	—	fuente *f*
scolaro (I)	Schüler *m*	pupil	élève *m*	—	alumno *m*
scold (E)	schimpfen	—	gronder	imprecare	insultar
scommessa (I)	Wette *f*	bet	pari *m*	—	apuesta *f*
scommettere (I)	wetten	bet	parier	—	apostar
scomodo (I)	unbequem	uncomfortable	inconfortable	—	incómodo(a)
scompartimento (I)	Abteil *n*	compartment	compartiment *m*	—	compartimiento *m*
scomparto (I)	Fach *n*	compartment	compartiment *m*	—	compartimiento *m*
sconfitta (I)	Niederlage *f*	defeat	défaite *f*	—	derrota *f*
sconosciuto (I)	unbekannt	unknown	inconnu(e)	—	desconocido(a)
sconsigliare (I)	abraten	warn	déconseiller	—	desaconsejar
scontento (I)	unzufrieden	dissatisfied	mécontent(e)	—	descontento(a)
sconto (I)	Rabatt *m*	discount	rabais *m*	—	rebaja *f*
sconveniente (I)	unpassend	inappropriate	mal à prospos	—	inadecuado(a)
scopa (I)	Besen *m*	broom	balai *m*	—	escoba *f*
scopare[1] (I)	fegen	sweep	balayer	—	barrer
scopare[2] (I)	kehren	sweep	balayer	—	barrer
scopo (I)	Zweck *m*	purpose	but *m*	—	finalidad *f*
scoppiare (I)	platzen	burst	éclater	—	reventar
scoprire (I)	entdecken	discover	découvrir	—	descubrir
scorpion (E)	Skorpion *m*	—	scorpion *m*	scorpione *m*	escorpión *m*
scorpion (F)	Skorpion *m*	scorpion	—	scorpione *m*	escorpión *m*

	D	E	F	I	Es
scorpione (I)	Skorpion *m*	scorpion	scorpion *m*	—	escorpión *m*
scorrere (I)	fließen	flow	couler	—	correr
scorte (I)	Vorrat *m*	stock	réserves *f pl*	—	provisión *f*
scortese (I)	unhöflich	impolite	impoli(e)	—	descortés
scottatura solare (I)	Sonnenbrand *m*	sunburn	coup de soleil *m*	—	quemadura solar *f*
scrabble (E)	wühlen	—	fouiller	rovistare	revolver
scream¹ (E)	schreien	—	crier	gridare	gritar
scream² (E)	Schrei *m*	—	cri *m*	grido *m*	grito *m*
screw (E)	Schraube *f*	—	vis *f*	vite *f*	tornillo *m*
screwdriver (E)	Schraubenzieher *m*	—	tournevis *m*	cacciavite *m*	destornillador *m*
scritto (I)	schriftlich	written	écrit(e)	—	por escrito
scrittore (I)	Schriftsteller *m*	writer	écrivain *m*	—	escritor *m*
scrittura (I)	Schrift *f*	writing	écriture *f*	—	escritura *f*
scrivere (I)	schreiben	write	écrire	—	escribir
scudo (I)	Schild *n*	shield	bouclier *m*	—	escudo *m*
sculpteur (F)	Bildhauer *m*	sculptor	—	scultore *m*	escultor(a) *m(f)*
sculptor (E)	Bildhauer *m*	—	sculpteur *m*	scultore *m*	escultor(a) *m(f)*
sculpture (E)	Skulptur *f*	—	sculpture *f*	scultura *f*	escultura *f*
sculpture (F)	Skulptur *f*	sculpture	—	scultura *f*	escultura *f*
scultore (I)	Bildhauer *m*	sculptor	sculpteur *m*	—	escultor(a) *m(f)*
scultura (I)	Skulptur *f*	sculpture	sculpture *f*	—	escultura *f*
scuola (I)	Schule *f*	school	école *f*	—	escuela *f*
scuro (I)	dunkel	dark	sombre	—	oscuro(a)
scusa (I)	Entschuldigung *f*	apology	excuse *f*	—	disculpa *f*
scusarsi (I)	entschuldigen, sich	apologize	excuser, se	—	disculparse
sdoganare (I)	verzollen	declare	dédouaner	—	declarar en la aduana
se¹ (I)	ob	if/whether	si	—	si
se² (I)	wenn	when/if	si/quand	—	cuando
sea (E)	Meer *n*	—	mer *f*	mare *m*	mar *m*
seagull (E)	Möwe *f*	—	mouette *f*	gabbiano *m*	gaviota *f*
seal (E)	Robbe *f*	—	phoque *m*	foca *f*	foca *f*
sea level (E)	Meeresspiegel *m*	—	niveau de la mer *m*	livello del mare *m*	nivel del mar *m*
séance (F)	Sitzung *f*	meeting	—	seduta *f*	reunión *f*
season¹ (E)	Saison *f*	—	saison *f*	stagione *f*	temporada *f*
season² (E)	würzen	—	épicer	condire	condimentar
seat¹ (E)	Sitz *m*	—	siège *m*	sede *f*	asiento *m*
seat² (E)	Sitzplatz *m*	—	place assise *f*	posto a sedere *m*	asiento *m*
seau (F)	Eimer *m*	bucket	—	secchio *m*	cubo *m*
sec (F)	trocken	dry	—	asciutto(a)	seco(a)
secar (Es)	trocknen	dry	sécher	asciugare	—
secchio (I)	Eimer *m*	bucket	seau *m*	—	cubo *m*
secchio dei rifiuti (I)	Mülleimer *m*	dustbin	poubelle *f*	—	cubo de la basura *m*
secco (I)	dürr	skinny	maigre	—	árido(a)
sécher (F)	trocknen	dry	—	asciugare	secar
sechs (D)	—	six	six	sei	seis
sechzehn (D)	—	sixteen	seize	sedici	dieciséis

segretaria

	D	E	F	I	Es
sechzig (D)	—	sixty	soixante	sessanta	sesenta
seco (Es)	trocken	dry	sec(sèche)	asciutto(a)	—
secolo (I)	Jahrhundert *n*	century	siècle *m*	—	siglo *m*
second[1] (E)	Sekunde *f*	—	seconde *f*	secondo *m*	segundo *m*
second[2] (E)	zweite(r,s)	—	second(e)	secondo(a)	segunda(o)
second (F)	zweite(r,s)	second	—	secondo(a)	segunda(o)
seconde (F)	Sekunde *f*	second	—	secondo *m*	segundo *m*
secondo[1] (I)	Sekunde *f*	second	seconde *f*	—	segundo *m*
secondo[2] (I)	zweite(r,s)	second	second(e)	—	segunda(o)
secouer (F)	schütteln	shake	—	agitare	agitar
secret[1] (E)	geheim	—	secret(-ète)	segreto(a)	secreto(a)
secret[2] (E)	Geheimnis *n*	—	secret *m*	segreto *m*	secreto *m*
secret[3] (E)	heimlich	—	secret(-ète)	segreto(a)	oculto(a)
secret[1] (F)	Geheimnis *n*	secret	—	segreto *m*	secreto *m*
secret[2] (F)	geheim	secret	—	segreto(a)	secreto(a)
secret[3] (F)	heimlich	secret	—	segreto(a)	oculto(a)
secrétaire (F)	Sekretärin *f*	secretary	—	segretaria *f*	secretaria *f*
secretaria[1] (Es)	Sekretärin *f*	secretary	secrétaire *f*	segretaria *f*	—
secretaría[2] (Es)	Sekretariat *n*	secretariat	secrétariat *m*	segretariato *m*	—
secretariat (E)	Sekretariat *n*	—	secrétariat *m*	segretariato *m*	secretaría *f*
secrétariat (F)	Sekretariat *n*	secretariat	—	segretariato *m*	secretaría *f*
secretary (E)	Sekretärin *f*	—	secrétaire *f*	segretaria *f*	secretaria *f*
secreto[1] (Es)	Geheimnis *n*	secret	secret *m*	segreto *m*	—
secreto[2] (Es)	geheim	secret	secret(-ète)	segreto(a)	—
section (F)	Abteilung *f*	department	—	reparto *m*	departamento *m*
sécurité (F)	Sicherheit *f*	safety	—	sicurezza *f*	seguridad *f*
sed (Es)	Durst *m*	thirst	soif *f*	sete *f*	—
seda (Es)	Seide *f*	silk	soie *f*	seta *f*	—
sede (I)	Sitz *m*	seat	siège *m*	—	asiento *m*
sedersi (I)	hinsetzen	sit down	asseoir, s'	—	sentarse
sedia (I)	Stuhl *m*	chair	chaise *f*	—	silla *f*
sedia a sdraio (I)	Liegestuhl *m*	deck chair	chaise longue *f*	—	tumbona *f*
sedici (I)	sechzehn	sixteen	seize	—	dieciséis
sediento (Es)	durstig	thirsty	assoiffé(e)	assetato(a)	—
seduce (E)	verführen	—	séduire	sedurre	seducir
séduire (F)	verführen	seduce	—	sedurre	seducir
sedurre (I)	verführen	seduce	séduire	—	seducir
seduta (I)	Sitzung *f*	meeting	séance *f*	—	reunión *f*
See (D)	—	lake	lac *m*	lago *m*	lago *m*
see (E)	sehen	—	voir	vedere	ver
see again (E)	wiedersehen	—	revoir	rivedere	volver a ver
seemingly (E)	anscheinend	—	apparemment	apparentemente	aparentemente
Seezunge (D)	—	sole	sole *f*	sogliola *f*	lenguado *m*
sega (I)	Säge *f*	saw	scie *f*	—	sierra *f*
segeln (D)	—	sail	faire de la voile	andare a vela	navegar a vela
segnale (I)	Zeichen *n*	sign	signe *m*	—	signo *m*
segno (I)	Mal *n*	mark	marque *f*	—	marca *f*
segretaria (I)	Sekretärin *f*	secretary	secrétaire *f*	—	secretaria *f*

	D	E	F	I	Es
segretariato (I)	Sekretariat n	secretariat	secrétariat m	—	secretaría f
segreto¹ (I)	geheim	secret	secret(-ète)	—	secreto(a)
segreto² (I)	Geheimnis n	secret	secret m	—	secreto m
segreto³ (I)	heimlich	secret	secret(-ète)	—	oculto(a)
seguente (I)	folgend	following	suivant(e)	—	siguiente
seguir (Es)	folgen	follow	suivre	seguire	—
seguir durmiendo (Es)	weiterschlafen	sleep on	continuer à dormir	continuare a dormire	—
seguire (I)	folgen	follow	suivre	—	seguir
segunda (Es)	zweite(r,s)	second	second(e)	secondo(a)	—
segundo (Es)	Sekunde f	second	seconde f	secondo m	—
seguridad (Es)	Sicherheit f	safety	sécurité f	sicurezza f	—
seguro¹ (Es)	sicher	sure	sûr(e)	sicuro(a)	—
seguro² (Es)	Versicherung f	insurance	assurance f	assicurazione f	—
seguro de sí mismo (Es)	selbstsicher	self-assured	sûr(e) de soi	sicuro di sé	—
sehen (D)	—	see	voir	vedere	ver
Sehenswürdigkeit (D)	—	sight	curiosité f	curiosità f	lugares de interés m pl
sehr (D)	—	very	très	molto	mucho/muy
sei (I)	sechs	six	six	—	seis
seiche (F)	Tintenfisch m	cuttlefish	—	seppia f	calamar m
Seide (D)	—	silk	soie f	seta f	seda f
Seife (D)	—	soap	savon m	sapone m	jabón m
Seil (D)	—	rope	corde f	fune f	soga f
sein (D)	—	be	être	essere	ser/estar
seis (Es)	sechs	six	six	sei	—
seit (D)	—	since/for	depuis	da	de/desde
Seite (D)	—	page	page f	pagina f	página f
seize¹ (E)	ergreifen	—	saisir	afferrare	coger
seize² (E)	festhalten	—	tenir ferme	tener fermo	sujetar
seize³ (E)	greifen	—	saisir	afferrare	coger
seize (F)	sechzehn	sixteen	—	sedici	dieciséis
séjour (F)	Aufenthalt m	stay	—	soggiorno m	estancia f
Sekretariat (D)	—	secretariat	secrétariat m	segretariato m	secretaría f
Sekretärin (D)	—	secretary	secrétaire f	segretaria f	secretaria f
Sekt (D)	—	champagne	champagne m	spumante m	champán m
Sekunde (D)	—	second	seconde f	secondo m	segundo m
sel (F)	Salz n	salt	—	sale m	sal f
selbständig (D)	—	independent	indépendant(e)	indipendente	independiente
Selbstbedienung (D)	—	self service	libre-service m	self-service m	autoservicio m
Selbstmord (D)	—	suicide	suicide m	suicidio m	suicidio m
selbstsicher (D)	—	self-assured	sûr(e) de soi	sicuro di sé	seguro de sí mismo
Selbstsucht (D)	—	selfishness	égoïsme m	egoismo m	egoísmo m
selbstverständlich (D)	—	of course	évidemment	naturalmente	por supuesto
select (E)	aussuchen	—	choisir	scegliere	escoger
self-assured (E)	selbstsicher	—	sûr(e) de soi	sicuro di sé	seguro de sí mismo
selfishness (E)	Selbstsucht f	—	égoïsme m	egoismo m	egoísmo m

	D	E	F	I	Es
self service (E)	Selbstbedienung *f*	—	libre-service *m*	self-service *m*	autoservicio *m*
self-service (I)	Selbstbedienung *f*	self service	libre-service *m*	—	autoservicio *m*
sell (E)	verkaufen	—	vendre	vendere	vender
sello[1] (Es)	Briefmarke *f*	stamp	timbre *m*	francobollo *m*	—
sello[2] (Es)	Stempel *m*	stamp	timbre *m*	timbro *m*	—
selten (D)	—	rare	rare	raro(a)	raro(a)
Seltenheit (D)	—	rarity	rareté *f*	rarità *f*	rareza *f*
seltsam (D)	—	strange	bizarre	strano(a)	extraño(a)
selvaggina (I)	Wild *n*	game	gibier *m*	—	caza *f*
selvatico (I)	wild	wild	sauvage	—	salvaje
semáforo (Es)	Ampel *f*	traffic lights	feux *m pl*	semaforo *m*	—
semaforo (I)	Ampel *f*	traffic lights	feux *m pl*	—	semáforo *m*
semaine (F)	Woche *f*	week	—	settimana *f*	semana *f*
semaine sainte (F)	Osterwoche *f*	Holy week	—	settimana santa *f*	Semana Santa *f*
semana (Es)	Woche *f*	week	semaine *f*	settimana *f*	—
semanal (Es)	wöchentlich	weekly	hebdomadaire	settimanale	—
Semana Santa (Es)	Osterwoche *f*	Holy week	semaine sainte *f*	settimana santa *f*	—
semblable (F)	ähnlich	similar	—	simile	parecido(a)
semelle (F)	Sohle *f*	sole	—	suola *f*	suela *f*
semilla (Es)	Korn *n*	corn	grain *m*	grano *m*	—
semplice[1] (I)	einfach	simple	simple	—	sencillo(a)
semplice[2] (I)	leicht	easy	facile	—	ligero(a)
sempre[1] (I)	immer	always	toujours	—	siempre
sempre[2] (I)	stets	always	toujours	—	siempre
senape (I)	Senf *m*	mustard	moutarde *f*	—	mostaza *f*
sencillo[1] (Es)	einfach	simple	simple	semplice	—
sencillo[2] (Es)	leicht	light	léger(-ère)	leggero(a)	—
send[1] (E)	schicken	—	envoyer	inviare	mandar
send[2] (E)	übersenden	—	envoyer	spedire	enviar
senden (D)	—	broadcast	transmettre	trasmettere	transmitir
Sender (D)	—	station	émetteur *m*	trasmettitore *m*	emisora *f*
sender (E)	Absender *m*	—	expéditeur *m*	mittente *m*	remitente *m*
send on (E)	nachsenden	—	faire suivre	inoltrare	enviar a la nueva dirección
Sendung (D)	—	transmission	diffusion *f*	trasmissione *f*	emisión *f*
Senf (D)	—	mustard	moutarde *f*	senape *f*	mostaza *f*
senken (D)	—	lower	baisser	abbassare	bajar
senkrecht (D)	—	vertical	vertical(e)	verticale	vertical
señor (Es)	Herr *m*	gentleman	monsieur *m*	signore *m*	—
señora (Es)	Dame *f*	lady	dame *f*	signora *f*	—
señorita (Es)	Fräulein *n*	Miss	mademoiselle	signorina *f*	—
sens (F)	Sinn *m*	sense	—	senso *m*	sentido *m*
sensato (Es)	besonnen	sensible	réfléchi(e)	avveduto(a)	—
sensazione (I)	Gefühl *n*	feeling	sentiment *m*	—	sentimiento *m*
sense (E)	Sinn *m*	—	sens *m*	senso *m*	sentido *m*
senseless (E)	sinnlos	—	insensé(e)	assurdo(a)	inútil
sensibile (I)	empfindlich	sensitive	sensible	—	sensible
sensible[1] (E)	besonnen	—	réfléchi	avveduto	sensato(a)

	D	E	F	I	Es
sensible² (E)	vernünftig	—	raisonnable	ragionevole	razonable
sensible (Es)	empfindlich	sensitive	sensible	sensibile	—
sensible (F)	empfindlich	sensitive	—	sensibile	sensible
sensitive (E)	empfindlich	—	sensible	sensibile	sensible
senso (I)	Sinn m	sense	sens m	—	sentido m
senso unico (I)	Einbahnstraße f	one-way street	rue à sens unique f	—	calle de dirección única f
sentarse (Es)	hinsetzen	sit down	asseoir, se	sedersi	—
sentence (E)	Satz m	—	phrase f	frase f	oración f
sentenciar (Es)	verurteilen	condemn	condamner	condannare	—
sentido (Es)	Sinn m	sense	sens m	senso m	—
sentiment (F)	Gefühl n	feeling	—	sensazione f	sentimiento m
sentimiento (Es)	Gefühl n	feeling	sentiment m	sensazione f	—
sentir (Es)	fühlen	feel	sentir	sentire	—
sentir¹ (F)	fühlen	feel	—	sentire	sentir
sentir² (F)	riechen	smell	—	sentire	oler
sentir³ (F)	schmecken	taste	—	piacere	gustar
sentire¹ (I)	fühlen	feel	sentir	—	sentir
sentire² (I)	hören	hear	entendre	—	oír
sentire³ (I)	riechen	smell	sentir	—	oler
sentire la mancanza (I)	vermissen	miss	manquer	—	echar de menos
senza (I)	ohne	without	sans	—	sin
senza dubbio (I)	zweifellos	doubtless	sans doute	—	sin duda
senza valore (I)	wertlos	worthless	sans valeur	—	sin valor
separación (Es)	Trennung f	separation	séparation f	separazione f	—
separado¹ (Es)	extra	extra	à part	a parte	—
separado² (Es)	getrennt	separate	séparé(e)	separato(a)	—
separar¹ (Es)	scheiden	part	séparer	separare	—
separar² (Es)	trennen	separate	séparer	separare	—
separare¹ (I)	scheiden	part	séparer	—	separar
separare² (I)	trennen	separate	séparer	—	separar
separate¹ (E)	trennen	—	séparer	separare	separar
separate² (E)	getrennt	—	séparé(e)	separato(a)	separado(a)
separation (E)	Trennung f	—	séparation f	separazione f	separación f
séparation (F)	Trennung f	separation	—	separazione f	separación f
separato¹ (I)	auseinander	apart	séparé(e)	—	lejos/distante
separato² (I)	getrennt	separate	séparé(e)	—	separado(a)
separazione (I)	Trennung f	separation	séparation f	—	separación f
séparé¹ (F)	getrennt	separate	—	separato(a)	separado(a)
séparé² (F)	auseinander	apart	—	separato(a)	lejos/distante
séparer¹ (F)	scheiden	part	—	separare	separar
séparer² (F)	trennen	separate	—	separare	separar
seppia (I)	Tintenfisch m	cuttlefish	seiche f	—	calamar m
sept (F)	sieben	seven	—	sette	siete
September (D)	—	September	septembre m	settembre m	septiembre m
September (E)	September m	—	septembre m	settembre m	septiembre m
septembre (F)	September m	September	—	settembre m	septiembre m
septiembre (Es)	September m	September	septembre m	settembre m	—

	D	E	F	I	Es
ser¹ (Es)	Wesen *n*	being	être *m*	essere *m*	—
ser² (Es)	sein	be	être	essere	—
sera (I)	Abend *m*	evening	soir *m*	—	noche *f*
sereno (Es)	Nachtwächter *m*	night-watchman	veilleur de nuit *m*	guardia notturna *f*	—
sereno (I)	sonnig	sunny	ensoleillé(e)	—	soleado(a)
serie (Es)	Folge *f*	consequence	suite *f*	conseguenza *f*	—
seriedad (Es)	Ernst *m*	seriousness	sérieux *m*	serietà *f*	—
serietà (I)	Ernst *m*	seriousness	sérieux *m*	—	seriedad *f*
sérieux¹ (F)	Ernst *m*	seriousness	—	serietà *f*	seriedad *f*
sérieux² (F)	ernst	serious	—	serio(a)	serio(a)
serio (I)	ernst	serious	sérieux(-ieuse)	—	serio(a)
serio (Es)	ernst	serious	sérieux(-ieuse)	serio(a)	—
serious (E)	ernst	—	sérieux(-ieuse)	serio(a)	serio(a)
seriousness (E)	Ernst *m*	—	sérieux *m*	serietà *f*	seriedad *f*
serpent (F)	Schlange *f*	snake	—	serpente *m*	serpiente *f*
serpente (I)	Schlange *f*	snake	serpent *m*	—	serpiente *f*
serpiente (Es)	Schlange *f*	snake	serpent *m*	serpente *m*	—
serratura (I)	Schloß *n*	lock	serrure *f*	—	cerradura *f*
serrure (F)	Schloß *n*	lock	—	serratura *f*	cerradura *f*
serve¹ (E)	bedienen	—	servir	servire	servir
serve² (E)	dienen	—	servir	servire	servir
serve³ (E)	servieren	—	servir	servire	servir
service¹ (E)	Bedienung *f*	—	service *m*	servizio *m*	servicio *m*
service² (E)	Dienst *m*	—	service *m*	servizio *m*	servicio *m*
service³ (E)	Gottesdienst *m*	—	office divin *m*	messa *f*	servicio religioso *m*
service¹ (F)	Bedienung *f*	service	—	servizio *m*	servicio *m*
service² (F)	Dienst *m*	service	—	servizio *m*	servicio *m*
service³ (F)	Gefallen *m*	favour	—	favore *m*	favor *m*
servicio¹ (Es)	Bedienung *f*	service	service *m*	servizio *m*	—
servicio² (Es)	Dienst *m*	service	service *m*	servizio *m*	—
servicio religioso (Es)	Gottesdienst *m*	service	office divin *m*	messa *f*	—
servieren (D)	—	serve	servir	servire	servir
Serviette (D)	—	serviette	serviette *f*	tovagliolo *m*	servilleta *f*
serviette (E)	Serviette *f*	—	serviette *f*	tovagliolo *m*	servilleta *f*
serviette¹ (F)	Handtuch *n*	towel	—	asciugamano *m*	pañuelo *m*
serviette² (F)	Mappe *f*	folder	—	raccoglitore *m*	carpeta *f*
serviette² (F)	Serviette *f*	serviette	—	tovagliolo *m*	servilleta *f*
servilleta (Es)	Serviette *f*	serviette	serviette *f*	tovagliolo *m*	—
servir¹ (Es)	bedienen	serve	servir	servire	servir
servir² (Es)	dienen	serve	servir	servire	—
servir³ (Es)	servieren	serve	servir	servire	—
servir¹ (F)	bedienen	serve	—	servire	servir
servir² (F)	dienen	serve	—	servire	servir
servir³ (F)	servieren	serve	—	servire	servir
servire¹ (I)	bedienen	serve	servir	—	servir
servire² (I)	dienen	serve	servir	—	servir
servire³ (I)	servieren	serve	servir	—	servir

servizio

	D	E	F	I	Es
servizio¹ (I)	Bedienung f	service	service m	—	servicio m
servizio² (I)	Dienst m	service	service m	—	servicio m
sesenta (Es)	sechzig	sixty	soixante	sessanta	—
sessanta (I)	sechzig	sixty	soixante	—	sesenta
Sessel (D)	—	armchair	fauteuil m	poltrona f	sillón m
sesso (I)	Geschlecht n	sex	sexe m	—	sexo m
seta (I)	Seide f	silk	soie f	—	seda f
setaccio (I)	Sieb n	sieve	tamis m	—	colador m
sete (I)	Durst m	thirst	soif f	—	sed f
setenta (Es)	siebzig	seventy	soixante-dix	settanta	—
settanta (I)	siebzig	seventy	soixante-dix	—	setenta
sette (I)	sieben	seven	sept	—	siete
settembre (I)	September m	September	septembre m	—	septiembre m
settimana (I)	Woche f	week	semaine f	—	semana f
settimanale (I)	wöchentlich	weekly	hebdomadaire	—	semanal
settimana santa (I)	Osterwoche f	Holy week	semaine sainte f	—	Semana Santa f
settle down¹ (E)	einleben, sich	—	acclimater, se	ambientarsi	familiarizarse
settle down² (E)	niederlassen	—	s'installer	stabilirsi	instalarse
settlement (E)	Siedlung f	—	cité f	agglomerato m	colonia f
setzen (D)	—	put	mettre	mettere	poner
seul¹ (F)	allein	alone	—	solo(a)	solo(a)
seul² (F)	einzeln	single	—	singolo(a)	singular
seul³ (F)	einzig	only	—	unico(a)	único(a)
seulement¹ (F)	bloß	only	—	soltanto	sólo
seulement² (F)	nur	only	—	solo	sólo
seven (E)	sieben	—	sept	sette	siete
seventeen (E)	siebzehn	—	dix-sept	diciassette	diecisiete
seventy (E)	siebzig	—	soixante-dix	settanta	setenta
several¹ (E)	etliche	—	quelques	alcuni(e)	algunos(as)
several² (E)	mehrere	—	plusieurs	parecchi	muchos(as)
sévère (F)	streng	strict	—	severo(a)	riguroso(a)
severo (I)	streng	strict	sévère	—	riguroso(a)
sew (E)	nähen	—	coudre	cucire	coser
sex (E)	Geschlecht n	—	sexe m	sesso m	sexo m
sexe (F)	Geschlecht n	sex	—	sesso m	sexo m
sexo (Es)	Geschlecht n	sex	sexe m	sesso m	—
sfacciato (I)	frech	cheeky	insolent(e)	—	atrevido(a)
sfiducia (I)	Mißtrauen n	distrust	méfiance f	—	desconfianza f
sfortuna (I)	Pech n	bad luck	malchance f	—	mala suerte f
sfortunato (I)	unglücklich	unhappy	malheureux(-euse)	—	desgraciado(a)
sforzarsi (I)	bemühen, sich	make an effort	efforcer, se	—	esforzarse
sforzo (I)	Bemühung f	effort	effort m	—	esfuerzo m
sfregare (I)	reiben	rub	frotter	—	frotar
sgarbato (I)	unfreundlich	unfriendly	peu aimable	—	descortés
sgualcire (I)	zerdrücken	squash	écraser	—	aplastar
sguardo (I)	Blick m	look	regard m	—	vista f
shadow (E)	Schatten m	—	ombre f	ombra f	sombra f
shady (E)	schattig	—	ombragé(e)	ombroso(a)	a la sombra

	D	E	F	I	Es
shake (E)	schütteln	—	secouer	agitare	agitar
share (E)	teilen	—	partager	dividere	partir
shark (E)	Hai m	—	requin m	pescecane m	tiburón m
sharp (E)	scharf	—	tranchant(e)	tagliente	cortante
sharpen (E)	schärfen	—	aiguiser	affilare	afilar
shave (E)	rasieren	—	raser	fare la barba	afeitar
shaver (E)	Rasierapparat m	—	rasoir m	rasoio m	máquina de afeitar f
she (E)	sie	—	elle	lei	ella
sheep (E)	Schaf n	—	mouton m	pecora f	oveja f
sheet (E)	Laken n	—	drap m	lenzuolo m	sábana f
sheet metal (E)	Blech n	—	tôle f	latta f	chapa f
shelves (E)	Regal n	—	étagère f	scaffale m	estantería f
shield (E)	Schild n	—	bouclier m	scudo m	escudo m
shine (E)	glänzen, scheinen	—	briller	splendere	brillar
ship (E)	Schiff n	—	navire m	nave f	barco m
shirt (E)	Hemd n	—	chemise f	camicia f	camisa f
shoe (E)	Schuh m	—	chaussure f	scarpa f	zapato m
shoemaker (E)	Schuster m	—	cordonnier m	calzolaio m	zapatero m
shoe polish (E)	Schuhcreme f	—	cirage m	lucido per scarpe m	betún m
shoeshop (E)	Schuhgeschäft n	—	magasin de chaussures m	negozio di scarpe m	zapatería f
shoot (E)	schießen	—	tirer	sparare	disparar
shop¹ (E)	Geschäft n	—	magasin m	negozio m	tienda f
shop² (E)	Laden m	—	magasin m	negozio m	tienda f
shopping (E)	Einkauf m	—	achat m	spesa f	compra f
shopping bag (E)	Einkaufstasche f	—	sac à provision m	borsa della spesa f	bolsa de compra f
shop-window (E)	Schaufenster n	—	vitrine f	vetrina f	escaparate m
shore (E)	Ufer n	—	bord m	riva f	orilla f
short (E)	kurz	—	court(e)	corto(a)	corto(a)
shortly (E)	demnächst	—	prochainement	presto	próximamente
shot¹ (E)	Foto n	—	photo f	foto f	foto f
shot² (E)	Schuß m	—	coup m	sparo m	disparo m
shoulder (E)	Schulter f	—	épaule f	spalla f	hombro m
shout (E)	rufen	—	appeler	chiamare	llamar
shovel (E)	Schaufel f	—	pelle f	pala f	pala f
show¹ (E)	vorzeigen	—	monter	esibire	presentar
show² (E)	zeigen	—	montrer	mostrare	indicar
shower (E)	Dusche f	—	douche f	doccia f	ducha f
shut (E)	zumachen	—	fermer	chiudere	cerrar
shy¹ (E)	scheu	—	timide	timido(a)	tímido(a)
shy² (E)	schüchtern	—	timide	timido(a)	tímido(a)
sí (Es)	ja	yes	oui	sì	—
si (Es)	ob	if/whether	si	se	—
si¹ (F)	doch	still	—	si!	sin embargo
si² (F)	ob	if/whether	—	se	si
si³ (F)	wenn	when/if	—	se/quando	cuando
sì (I)	ja	yes	oui	—	sí

si! 368

	D	E	F	I	Es
si! (I)	doch	still	si	—	sin embargo
sicher (D)	—	sure	sûr(e)	sicuro(a)	seguro(a)
Sicherheit (D)	—	safety	sécurité f	sicurezza f	seguridad f
Sicht (D)	—	view	vue f	vista f	vista f
sichtbar (D)	—	visible	visible	visibile	visible
sicurezza (I)	Sicherheit f	safety	sécurité f	—	seguridad f
sicuro (I)	sicher	sure	sûr(e)	—	seguro(a)
sicuro di sé (I)	selbstsicher	self-assured	sûr(e) de soi	—	seguro de sí mismo
sie (D)	—	she	elle	lei	ella
sie (D)	—	they	ils/elles	loro	ellos, ellas
Sieb (D)	—	sieve	tamis m	setaccio m	colador m
sieben (D)	—	seven	sept	sette	siete
siebzehn (D)	—	seventeen	dix-sept	diciassette	diecisiete
siebzig (D)	—	seventy	soixante-dix	settanta	setenta
siècle (F)	Jahrhundert n	century	—	secolo m	siglo m
Siedlung (D)	—	settlement	cité f	agglomerato m	colonia f
Sieg (D)	—	victory	victoire f	vittoria f	victoria f
siège (F)	Sitz m	seat	—	sede f	asiento m
siegen (D)	—	win	gagner	vincere	vencer
siempre[1] (Es)	immer	always	toujours	sempre	—
siempre[2] (Es)	stets	always	toujours	sempre	—
sierra (Es)	Säge f	saw	scie f	sega f	—
siete (Es)	sieben	seven	sept	sette	—
sieve (E)	Sieb n	—	tamis m	setaccio m	colador m
sifflet (F)	Pfeife f	whistle	—	fischietto m	silbato m
sigaretta (I)	Zigarette f	cigarette	cigarette f	—	cigarrillo m
sigaro (I)	Zigarre f	cigar	cigare m	—	cigarro m
sight (E)	Sehenswürdig- keit f	—	curiosité f	curiosità f	lugares de interés m pl
siglo (Es)	Jahrhundert n	century	siècle m	secolo m	—
sign[1] (E)	unterschreiben	—	signer	firmare	firmar
sign[2] (E)	Zeichen n	—	signe m	segnale m	signo m
signature (E)	Unterschrift f	—	signature f	firma f	firma f
signature (F)	Unterschrift f	signature	—	firma f	firma f
signe[1] (F)	Merkmal n	characteristic	—	caratteristica f	rasgo m
signe[2] (F)	Zeichen n	sign	—	segnale m	signo m
signer (F)	unterschreiben	sign	—	firmare	firmar
significado (Es)	Bedeutung f	meaning	signification f	significato m	—
significant (E)	bedeutend	—	important(e)	importante	importante
significar (Es)	bedeuten	mean	signifier	significare	—
significare (I)	bedeuten	mean	signifier	—	significar
signification (F)	Bedeutung f	meaning	—	significato m	significado m
significato (I)	Bedeutung f	meaning	signification f	—	significado m
signifier (F)	bedeuten	mean	—	significare	significar
signo (Es)	Zeichen n	sign	signe m	segnale m	—
signora (I)	Dame f	lady	dame f	—	señora f
signore (I)	Herr m	gentleman	monsieur m	—	señor m
signorina (I)	Fräulein n	Miss	mademoiselle	—	señorita f

	D	E	F	I	Es
siguiente[1] (Es)	folgend	following	suivant(e)	seguente	—
siguiente[2] (Es)	nächste(r,s)	next	suivant(e)	prossimo(a)	—
silbato (Es)	Pfeife *f*	whistle	sifflet *m*	fischietto *m*	—
Silber (D)	—	silver	argent *m*	argento *m*	plata *f*
silbern (D)	—	silver	d'argent	d'argento	plateado(a)
silenzio (I)	Ruhe *f*	calm	calme *m*	—	quietud *f*
silk (E)	Seide *f*	—	soie *f*	seta *f*	seda *f*
silla (Es)	Stuhl *m*	chair	chaise *f*	sedia *f*	—
sillabare (I)	buchstabieren	spell	épeler	—	deletrear
sillón (Es)	Sessel *m*	armchair	fauteuil *m*	poltrona *f*	—
silver[1] (E)	silbern	—	d'argent	d'argento	plateado(a)
silver[2] (E)	Silber *n*	—	argent *m*	argento *m*	plata *f*
Silvester (D)	—	New Year's Eve	Saint-Sylvestre *m*	San Silvestro *m*	Noche Vieja *f*
s'il vous plaît (F)	bitte	please	—	prego	por favor
similar (E)	ähnlich	—	semblable	simile	parecido(a)
simile (I)	ähnlich	similar	semblable	—	parecido(a)
simpatico (I)	sympathisch	likeable	sympathique	—	simpático(a)
simpático (Es)	sympathisch	likeable	sympathique	simpatico(a)	—
simple (E)	einfach	—	simple	semplice	sencillo(a)
simple (F)	einfach	simple	—	semplice	sencillo(a)
simultaneous (E)	gleichzeitig	—	en même temps	contemporaneo(a)	a la vez
sin (E)	Sünde *f*	—	péché *m*	peccato *m*	pecado *m*
sin (Es)	ohne	without	sans	senza	—
since (E)	seit	—	depuis	da	de/desde
sincère (F)	aufrichtig	honest	—	onesto(a)	sincero(a)
sincero (Es)	aufrichtig	honest	sincère	onesto(a)	—
sin colegio (Es)	schulfrei	holiday	de congé	vacanza	—
sin compromiso (Es)	unverbindlich	not binding	sans engagement	non impegnativo(a)	—
sindacato (I)	Gewerkschaft *f*	trade union	syndicat *m*	—	sindicato *m*
sindaco (I)	Bürgermeister *m*	mayor	maire *m*	—	alcalde *m*
sindicato (Es)	Gewerkschaft *f*	trade union	syndicat *m*	sindacato *m*	—
sin dinero (Es)	pleite	penniless	fauché(e)	fallito(a)	—
sin duda (Es)	zweifellos	doubtless	sans doute	senza dubbio	—
sin embargo[1] (Es)	doch	still	si	si!	—
sin embargo[2] (Es)	dennoch	nevertheless	cependant	tuttavia	—
sin embargo[3] (Es)	jedoch	however	cependant	tutta via	—
sing (E)	singen	—	chanter	cantare	cantar
singe (F)	Affe *m*	ape	—	scimmia *f*	mono *m*
singen (D)	—	sing	chanter	cantare	cantar
singer (E)	Sänger *m*	—	chanteur *m*	cantante *m*	cantante *m*
singing (E)	Gesang *m*	—	chant *m*	canto *m*	canto *m*
single[1] (E)	einzeln	—	seul(e)	singolo(a)	singular
single[2] (E)	ledig	—	célibataire	celibe *m*/nubile *f*	soltero(a)
singolo (I)	einzeln	single	seul(e)	—	singular
singular (Es)	einzeln	single	seul(e)	singolo(a)	—
singulier (F)	eigenartig	strange	—	strano(a)	extraño(a)
sin importancia (Es)	unwichtig	unimportant	sans importance	non importante	—

	D	E	F	I	Es
sink¹ (E)	sinken	—	couler	affondare	hundirse
sink² (E)	versinken	—	enfoncer, se	affondare	hundirse
sinken (D)	—	sink	couler	affondare	hundirse
Sinn (D)	—	sense	sens *m*	senso *m*	sentido *m*
sinnlos (D)	—	senseless	insensé(e)	assurdo(a)	inútil
sino (Es)	sondern	but	mais	ma/bensì	—
sin ruido (Es)	leise	quietly	à voix basse	a bassa voce	—
sin valor (Es)	wertlos	worthless	sans valeur	senza valore	—
sistema (Es)	System *n*	system	système *m*	sistema *m*	—
sistema (I)	System *n*	system	système *m*	—	sistema *m*
sistemare (I)	unterbringen	stow	ranger	—	colocar
sister (E)	Schwester *f*	—	sœur *f*	sorella *f*	hermana *f*
sister-in-law (E)	Schwägerin *f*	—	belle-sœur *f*	cognata *f*	cuñada *f*
sit (E)	sitzen	—	être assis(e)	stare seduto(a)	estar sentado(a)
sit down (E)	hinsetzen	—	asseoir, se	sedersi	sentarse
Sitte (D)	—	custom	coutume *f*	usanza *f*	costumbre *f*
sittlich (D)	—	moral	moral(e)	morale	moral
situación¹ (Es)	Lage *f*	situation	situation *f*	situazione *f*	—
situación² (Es)	Situation *f*	situation	situation *f*	situazione *f*	—
Situation (D)	—	situation	situation *f*	situazione *f*	situación *f*
situation¹ (E)	Lage *f*	—	situation *f*	situazione *f*	situación *f*
situation² (E)	Situation *f*	—	situation *f*	situazione *f*	situación *f*
situation¹ (F)	Lage *f*	situation	—	situazione *f*	situación *f*
situation² (F)	Situation *f*	situation	—	situazione *f*	situación *f*
situazione¹ (I)	Lage *f*	situation	situation *f*	—	situación *f*
situazione² (I)	Situation *f*	situation	situation *f*	—	situación *f*
Sitz (D)	—	seat	siège *m*	sede *f*	asiento *m*
sitzen (D)	—	sit	être assis(e)	stare seduto(a)	estar sentado(a)
Sitzplatz (D)	—	seat	place assise *f*	posto a sedere *m*	asiento *m*
Sitzung (D)	—	meeting	séance *f*	seduta *f*	reunión *f*
six (E)	sechs	—	six	sei	seis
six (F)	sechs	six	—	sei	seis
sixteen (E)	sechzehn	—	seize	sedici	dieciseis
sixty (E)	sechzig	—	soixante	sessanta	sesenta
size (E)	Größe *f*	—	taille *f*	taglia *f*	talla *f*
Skandal (D)	—	scandal	scandale *m*	scandalo *m*	escándalo *m*
Skandinavien (D)	—	Scandinavia	Scandinavie *f*	Scandinavia *f*	Escandinavia *f*
sketch (E)	Skizze *f*	—	esquisse *f*	schizzo *m*	boceto *m*
Ski (D)	—	ski	ski *m*	sci *m*	esquí *m*
ski (E)	Ski *m*	—	ski *m*	sci *m*	esquí *m*
ski (F)	Ski *m*	ski	—	sci *m*	esquí *m*
Skilift (D)	—	skilift	remonte-pente *m*	sciovia *f*	telesilla *f*
skilift (E)	Skilift *m*	—	remonte-pente *m*	sciovia *f*	telesilla *f*
skillful (E)	geschickt	—	habile	abile	mañoso(a)
skin (E)	Haut *f*	—	peau *f*	pelle *f*	piel *f*
skinny¹ (E)	dürr	—	maigre	secco(a)	árido(a)
skinny² (E)	mager	—	maigre	magro(a)	delgado(a)
skirt (E)	Rock *m*	—	jupe *f*	gonna *f*	falda *f*

	D	E	F	I	Es
Skizze (D)	—	sketch	esquisse *f*	schizzo *m*	boceto *m*
Sklave (D)	—	slave	esclave *m*	schiavo *m*	esclavo *m*
Skorpion (D)	—	scorpion	scorpion *m*	scorpione *m*	escorpión *m*
skull (E)	Schädel *m*	—	crâne *m*	cranio *m*	cráneo *m*
Skulptur (D)	—	sculpture	sculpture *f*	scultura *f*	escultura *f*
sky (E)	Himmel *m*	—	ciel *m*	cielo *m*	cielo *m*
slacken (E)	nachlassen	—	apaiser, se	allentare	aflojar
slave (E)	Sklave *m*	—	esclave *m*	schiavo *m*	esclavo *m*
sleep[1] (E)	schlafen	—	dormir	dormire	dormir
sleep[2] (E)	Schlaf *m*	—	sommeil *m*	sonno *m*	sueño *m*
sleep on (E)	weiterschlafen	—	continuer à dormir	continuare a dormire	seguir durmiendo
sleeve (E)	Ärmel *m*	—	manche *f*	manica *f*	manga *f*
slide[1] (E)	Dia *n*	—	diapositive *f*	diapositiva *f*	diapositiva *f*
slide[2] (E)	rutschen	—	glisser	scivolare	resbalar
slight (E)	gering	—	minime	poco(a)	pequeño(a)
slim (E)	schlank	—	mince	snello(a)	delgado(a)
slip (E)	Unterrock *m*	—	jupon *m*	sottoveste *f*	combinación *f*
slip (F)	Unterhose *f*	underpants	—	mutande *f pl*	calzoncillos *m pl*
slip de bain (F)	Badehose *f*	swimming trunks	—	costume da bagno *m*	bañador *m*
slipper (E)	Pantoffel *f*	—	pantoufle *f*	pantofola *f*	zapatilla *f*
slip road (E)	Auffahrt *f*	—	bretelle d'accès *f*	entrata *f*	vía de acceso *f*
sloggiare (I)	ausziehen	move out	déménager	—	mudarse
slope (E)	Hang *m*	—	versant *m*	pendio *m*	pendiente *m*
sloped (E)	schief	—	en pente	obliquo(a)	torcido(a)
slow (E)	langsam	—	lent(e)	lento(a)	despacio(a)
small (E)	klein	—	petit(e)	piccolo(a)	pequeño(a)
small change (E)	Kleingeld *n*	—	monnaie *f*	spiccioli *m pl*	cambio *m*
small package (E)	Päckchen *n*	—	petit paquet *m*	pacchetto *m*	paquetito *m*
Smaragd (D)	—	emerald	émeraude *f*	smeraldo *m*	esmeralda *f*
smash (E)	einschlagen	—	casser	rompere	romper
smell[1] (E)	Geruch *m*	—	odeur *f*	odore *m*	olor *m*
smell[2] (E)	riechen	—	sentir	sentire	oler
smeraldo (I)	Smaragd *m*	emerald	émeraude *f*	—	esmeralda *f*
smile[1] (E)	lächeln	—	sourire	sorridere	sonreír
smile[2] (E)	Lächeln *n*	—	sourire *m*	sorriso *m*	sonrisa *f*
smoke[1] (E)	rauchen	—	fumer	fumare	fumar
smoke[2] (E)	Rauch *m*	—	fumée *f*	fumo *m*	humo *m*
smoker (E)	Raucher *m*	—	fumeur *m*	fumatore *m*	fumador *m*
smooth (E)	glatt	—	lisse	liscio(a)	liso(a)
snack (E)	Imbiß *m*	—	casse-croûte *m*	spuntino *m*	refrigerio *m*
snake (E)	Schlange *f*	—	serpent *m*	serpente *m*	serpiente *f*
sneeze (E)	niesen	—	éternuer	starnutire	estornudar
snello (I)	schlank	slim	mince	—	delgado(a)
snore (E)	schnarchen	—	ronfler	russare	roncar
snow[1] (E)	schneien	—	neiger	nevicare	nevar
snow[2] (E)	Schnee *m*	—	neige *f*	neve *f*	nieve *f*
so (D)	—	like this	ainsi	così	así

	D	E	F	I	Es
soap (E)	Seife f	—	savon m	sapone m	jabón m
sobald (D)	—	as soon as	dès que	appena	tan pronto como
sobborgo (I)	Vorort m	suburb	faubourg m	—	suburbio m
sober (E)	nüchtern	—	sobre	sobrio(a)	sobrio(a)
sobre[1] (Es)	Umschlag m	envelope	enveloppe f	busta f	—
sobre[2] (Es)	auf	on/on top/onto	sur	su/sopra	—
sobre (F)	nüchtern	sober	—	sobrio(a)	sobrio(a)
sobre todo (Es)	besonders	especially	surtout	particolarmente	—
sobrevalorar (Es)	überschätzen	overestimate	surestimer	sopravvalutare	—
sobrevivir (Es)	überleben	survive	survivre	sopravvivere	—
sobrina (Es)	Nichte f	niece	nièce f	nipote f	—
sobrino (Es)	Neffe m	nephew	neveu m	nipote m	—
sobrio (Es)	nüchtern	sober	sobre	sobrio(a)	—
sobrio (I)	nüchtern	sober	sobre	—	sobrio(a)
soccombere (I)	unterliegen	be defeated	être vaincu(e) par qn	—	sucumbir
sociedad (Es)	Gesellschaft f	society	société f	società f	—
società (I)	Gesellschaft f	society	société f	—	sociedad f
société (F)	Gesellschaft f	society	—	società f	sociedad f
society (E)	Gesellschaft f	—	société f	società f	sociedad f
sock (E)	Socke f	—	chausette f	calzino m	calcetín m
Socke (D)	—	sock	chausette f	calzino m	calcetín m
socket (E)	Steckdose f	—	prise électrique f	presa f	enchufe m
soddisfare (I)	befriedigen	satisfy	satisfaire	—	satisfacer
soeben (D)	—	just now	à l'instant même	poco fa	ahora mismo
sœur (F)	Schwester f	sister	—	sorella f	hermana f
Sofa (D)	—	sofa	canapé m	sofà m	sofá m
sofa (E)	Sofa n	—	canapé m	sofà m	sofá m
sofá (Es)	Sofa n	sofa	canapé m	sofà m	—
sofà (I)	Sofa n	sofa	canapé m	—	sofá m
so far (E)	bisher	—	jusqu'à présent	finora	hasta ahora
soffiare (I)	blasen	blow	souffler	—	soplar
soffrire (I)	leiden	suffer	souffrir	—	sufrir
sofocante (Es)	schwül	sultry	lourd(e)	afoso(a)	—
sofort (D)	—	immediately	immédiatement	subito	en seguida
soft[1] (E)	weich	—	doux(douce)	morbido(a)	tierno(a)
soft[2] (E)	zart	—	doux (douce)	tenero(a)	suave
soga (Es)	Seil n	rope	corde f	fune f	—
sogar (D)	—	even	même	perfino	incluso
soggiorno (I)	Aufenthalt m	stay	séjour m	—	estancia f
sogliola (I)	Seezunge f	sole	sole f	—	lenguado m
sognare (I)	träumen	dream	rêver	—	soñar
sogno (I)	Traum m	dream	rêve m	—	sueño m
Sohle (D)	—	sole	semelle f	suola f	suela f
Sohn (D)	—	son	fils m	figlio m	hijo m
soie (F)	Seide f	silk	—	seta f	seda f
soif (F)	Durst m	thirst	—	sete f	sed f
soigné (F)	gepflegt	looked-after	—	curato(a)	cuidado(a)

	D	E	F	I	Es
soigner (F)	pflegen	look after	—	curare	cuidar
soigneux (F)	sorgfältig	careful(ly)	—	accurato(a)	cuidadoso(a)
soins (F)	Pflege f	care	—	cura f	aseo m
soir (F)	Abend m	evening	—	sera f	noche f
soixante (F)	sechzig	sixty	—	sessanta	sesenta
soixante-dix (F)	siebzig	seventy	—	settanta	setenta
sol (Es)	Sonne f	sun	soleil m	sole m	—
sol (F)	Fußboden m	floor	—	pavimento m	suelo m
solange (D)	—	as long	tant que	finché	en tanto que
solche (D)	—	such	tel(le)	tale(i)	un(a) tal
soldado (Es)	Soldat m	soldier	soldat m	soldato m	—
Soldat (D)	—	soldier	soldat m	soldato m	soldado m
soldat (F)	Soldat m	soldier	—	soldato m	soldado m
soldato (I)	Soldat m	soldier	soldat m	—	soldado m
soldes (F)	Ausverkauf m	sale	—	saldi m	liquidación f
soldier (E)	Soldat m	—	soldat m	soldato m	soldado m
sold out (E)	ausverkauft	—	épuisé(e)	esaurito(a)	vendido(a)
sole¹ (E)	Sohle f	—	semelle f	suola f	suela f
sole² (E)	Seezunge f	—	sole f	sogliola f	lenguado m
sole (F)	Seezunge f	sole	—	sogliola f	lenguado m
sole (I)	Sonne f	sun	soleil m	—	sol m
soleado (Es)	sonnig	sunny	ensoleillé(e)	sereno(a)	—
soleil (F)	Sonne f	sun	—	sole m	sol m
solicitud (Es)	Antrag m	application	demande f	domanda f	—
solid (E)	fest	—	solide	solido(a)	firme
solide (F)	fest	solid	—	solido(a)	firme
solido (I)	fest	solid	solide	—	firme
solitaire (F)	einsam	lonely	—	solitario(a)	solitario(a)
solitario (Es)	einsam	lonely	solitaire	solitario(a)	—
solitario (I)	einsam	lonely	solitaire	—	solitario(a)
solito (I)	üblich	usual	habituel(le)	—	usual
sollen (D)	—	have to	devoir	dovere	deber
solo¹ (Es)	allein	alone	seul	solo(a)	—
sólo² (Es)	bloß	only	seulement	soltanto	—
sólo³ (Es)	nur	only	seulement	solo	—
solo¹ (I)	allein	alone	seul	—	solo(a)
solo² (I)	nur	only	seulement	—	sólo
soltanto (I)	bloß	only	seulement	—	sólo
soltero¹ (Es)	Junggeselle m	bachelor	célibataire m	scapolo m	—
soltero² (Es)	ledig	single	célibataire	celibe m/nubile f	—
soltero³ (Es)	unverheiratet	unmarried	non marié(e)	celibe m/nubile f	—
solución (Es)	Lösung f	solution	solution f	soluzione f	—
solution (E)	Lösung f	—	solution f	soluzione f	solución f
solution (F)	Lösung f	solution	—	soluzione f	solución f
soluzione (I)	Lösung f	solution	solution f	—	solución f
solve (E)	lösen	—	résoudre	sciogliere	desatar
sombra (Es)	Schatten m	shadow	ombre f	ombra f	—
sombre¹ (F)	dunkel	dark	—	scuro(a)	oscuro(a)

	D	E	F	I	Es
sombre² (F)	finster	dark	—	buio(a)	oscuro(a)
sombrero (Es)	Hut m	hat	chapeau m	cappello m	—
sombrilla (Es)	Sonnenschirm m	parasol	parasol m	ombrellone m	—
some¹ (E)	einige	—	quelques	alcuni(e)	algunos(as)
some² (E)	irgendein(e)	—	quelconque	qualcuno(a)	cualquiera
somebody¹ (E)	irgend jemand	—	n'importe qui	qualcuno(a)	alguno(a)
somebody² (E)	jemand	—	quelqu'un	qualcuno(a)	alguien
somehow (E)	irgendwie	—	n'importe comment	in qualche modo	de alguna manera
someter (Es)	unterwerfen	subject	soumettre	sottomettere	—
something¹ (E)	etwas	—	quelque chose	qualcosa	algo
something² (E)	irgend etwas	—	n'importe quoi	qualsiasi cosa	algo
sometimes (E)	manchmal	—	quelquefois	talvolta	a veces
somewhere (E)	irgendwo	—	n'importe où	in qualche posto	en alguna parte
somma¹ (I)	Betrag m	amount	montant m	—	importe m
somma² (I)	Summe f	sum	somme f	—	suma f
sommare (I)	addieren	add up	additionner	—	sumar
somme (F)	Summe f	sum	—	somma f	suma f
sommeil (F)	Schlaf m	sleep	—	sonno m	sueño m
Sommer (D)	—	summer	été m	estate f	verano m
Sommerzeit (D)	—	summertime	heure d'été f	ora legale f	temporada de verano f
sommet (F)	Gipfel m	peak	—	cima f	cumbre f
so much (E)	soviel	—	tant	quanto/tanto	tanto
son (E)	Sohn m	—	fils m	figlio m	hijo m
son¹ (F)	Klang m	sound	—	suono m	sonido m
son² (F)	Ton m	sound	—	suono m	sonido m
soñar (Es)	träumen	dream	rêver	sognare	—
Sonderangebot (D)	—	special offer	offre spéciale f	offerta speciale f	oferta especial f
sondern (D)	—	but	mais	ma/bensì	sino
song (E)	Lied n	—	chanson f	canzone f	canción f
sonido¹ (Es)	Klang m	sound	son m	suono m	—
sonido² (Es)	Ton m	sound	son m	suono m	—
Sonnabend (D)	—	Saturday	samedi m	sabato m	sábado m
Sonne (D)	—	sun	soleil m	sole m	sol m
Sonnenaufgang (D)	—	sunrise	lever du soleil m	sorgere del sole m	salida del sol f
Sonnenbrand (D)	—	sunburn	coup de soleil m	scottatura solare f	quemadura solar f
Sonnenbrille (D)	—	sunglasses	lunettes de soleil f pl	occhiali da sole m pl	gafas de sol f pl
Sonnenschirm (D)	—	parasol	parasol m	ombrellone m	sombrilla f
Sonnen-untergang (D)	—	sunset	coucher du soleil m	tramonto del sole m	puesta del sol f
sonner¹ (F)	klingeln	ring the bell	—	suonare	tocar el timbre
sonner² (F)	läuten	ring	—	suonare	tocar
sonnette (F)	Klingel f	bell	—	campanello m	timbre m
sonnig (D)	—	sunny	ensoleillé(e)	sereno(a)	soleado(a)
sonno (I)	Schlaf m	sleep	sommeil m	—	sueño m
Sonntag (D)	—	Sunday	dimanche m	domenica f	domingo m
sonreír (Es)	lächeln	smile	sourire	sorridere	—
sonrisa (Es)	Lächeln n	smile	sourire m	sorriso m	—

	D	E	F	I	Es
sonst (D)	—	otherwise	autrement	altrimenti	por lo demás
soon (E)	bald	—	bientôt	presto	pronto
sooner (E)	eher	—	plus tôt	prima	antes
sopa (Es)	Suppe *f*	soup	soupe *f*	zuppa *f*	—
soplar (Es)	blasen	blow	souffler	soffiare	—
soportar (Es)	ertragen	bear	supporter	sopportare	—
sopportare[1] (I)	aushalten	bear	supporter	—	aguantar
sopportare[2] (I)	ertragen	bear	supporter	—	soportar
sopprimere (I)	unterdrücken	oppress	opprimer	—	oprimir
sopra[1] (I)	darüber	above	au dessus	—	por encima
sopra[2] (I)	oben	above	en haut	—	arriba
sopravvalutare (I)	überschätzen	overestimate	surestimer	—	sobrevalorar
sopravvivere (I)	überleben	survive	survivre	—	sobrevivir
sorcière (F)	Hexe *f*	witch	—	strega *f*	bruja *f*
sordo (Es)	taub	deaf	sourd(e)	sordo(a)	—
sordo (I)	taub	deaf	sourd(e)	—	sordo(a)
sorella (I)	Schwester *f*	sister	sœur *f*	—	hermana *f*
sore throat (E)	Halsschmerzen *pl*	—	mal de gorge *m*	mal di gola *m*	dolor de garganta *m*
Sorge (D)	—	concern	souci *m*	preoccupazione *f*	preocupación *f*
sorgen (D)	—	worry about	occuper de, se	prendersi cura di	atender
sorgente (I)	Quelle *f*	spring	source *f*	—	fuente *f*
sorgere del sole (I)	Sonnenaufgang *m*	sunrise	lever du soleil *m*	—	salida del sol *f*
sorgfältig (D)	—	careful(ly)	soigneux(-euse)	accurato(a)	cuidadoso(a)
sorpassare (I)	überholen	overtake	doubler	—	adelantar
sorprender (Es)	überraschen	surprise	surprendre	sorprendere	—
sorprendere (I)	überraschen	surprise	surprendre	—	sorprender
sorprendido (Es)	überrascht	surprised	surpris(e)	sorpreso(a)	—
sorpresa (Es)	Überraschung *f*	surprise	surprise *f*	sorpresa *f*	—
sorpresa (I)	Überraschung *f*	surprise	surprise *f*	—	sorpresa *f*
sorpreso (I)	überrascht	surprised	surpris(e)	—	sorprendido(a)
sorridere (I)	lächeln	smile	sourire	—	sonreír
sorriso (I)	Lächeln *n*	smile	sourire *m*	—	sonrisa *f*
sort[1] (E)	sortieren	—	trier	assortire	clasificar
sort[2] (E)	Sorte *f*	—	sorte *f*	specie *f*	clase *f*
Sorte (D)	—	sort	sorte *f*	specie *f*	clase *f*
sorte (F)	Sorte *f*	sort	—	specie *f*	clase *f*
sortie (F)	Ausgang *m*	exit	—	uscita *f*	salida *f*
sortie de secours (F)	Notausgang *m*	emergency exit	—	uscita di sicurezza *f*	salida de emergencia *f*
sortieren (D)	—	sort	trier	assortire	clasificar
sortija (Es)	Ring *m*	ring	bague *f*	anello *m*	—
sortir[1] (F)	ausgehen	go out	—	uscire	salir
sortir[2] (F)	hinausgehen	go out	—	uscire	salir afuera
sortir[3] (F)	heraustreten	step out	—	uscire fuori	salir
sorvegliare[1] (I)	bewachen	guard	garder	—	vigilar
sorvegliare[2] (I)	überwachen	supervise	surveiller	—	vigilar
soso (Es)	fade	dull	fade	insipido(a)	—
sospechoso (Es)	verdächtig	suspicious	suspect(e)	sospetto(a)	—

	D	E	F	I	Es
sospetto (I)	verdächtig	suspicious	suspect(e)	—	sospechoso(a)
Soße (D)	—	sauce	sauce *f*	salsa *f*	salsa *f*
sostegno (I)	Unterstützung *f*	support ·	soutien *m*	—	apoyo *m*
sostituire (I)	ersetzen	replace	remplacer	—	sustituir
sostituzione (I)	Ersatz *m*	substitute	remplacement *m*	—	sustitución *f*
sot (F)	albern	foolish	—	sciocco(a)	tonto(a)
sótano (Es)	Keller *m*	cellar	cave *f*	cantina *f*	—
sottile (I)	fein	fine	fin(e)	—	fino(a)
sotto[1] (I)	darunter	underneath	en dessous	—	por debajo
sotto[2] (I)	unten	downstairs	dessous	—	abajo
sottolineare (I)	unterstreichen	underline	souligner	—	subrayar
sottomettere (I)	unterwerfen	subject	soumettre	—	someter
sottopassaggio (I)	Unterführung *f*	subway	passage souterrain *m*	—	paso inferior *m*
sottosopra (I)	durcheinander	in a muddle	pêle-mêle	—	en desorden
sottoveste (I)	Unterrock *m*	slip	jupon *m*	—	combinación *f*
sottrarre[1] (I)	abziehen	subtract	retirer	—	restar
sottrarre[2] (I)	unterschlagen	embezzle	soustraire	—	sustraer
souci (F)	Sorge *f*	concern	—	preoccupazione *f*	preocupación *f*
soucoupe (F)	Untertasse *f*	saucer	—	piattino *m*	platillo *m*
souffler[1] (F)	abblasen	call off	—	disdire	anular
souffler[2] (F)	blasen	blow	—	soffiare	soplar
souffrir (F)	leiden	suffer	—	soffrire	sufrir
souhait (F)	Wunsch *m*	wish	—	desiderio *m*	deseo *m*
souhaiter (F)	wünschen	wish	—	desiderare	desear
soûl (F)	betrunken	drunk	—	ubriaco	borracho(a)
soulèvement (F)	Aufstand *m*	rebellion	—	insurrezione *f*	revuelta *f*
soulever (F)	heben	lift	—	alzare	levantar
souligner (F)	unterstreichen	underline	—	sottolineare	subrayar
soumettre (F)	unterwerfen	subject	—	sottomettere	someter
sound[1] (E)	Geräusch *n*	—	bruit *m*	rumore *m*	ruido *m*
sound[2] (E)	Klang *m*	—	son *m*	suono *m*	sonido *m*
sound[3] (E)	Ton *m*	—	son *m*	suono *m*	sonido *m*
soup (E)	Suppe *f*	—	soupe *f*	zuppa *f*	sopa *f*
soupe (F)	Suppe *f*	soup	—	zuppa *f*	sopa *f*
sour (E)	sauer	—	aigre	acido(a)	agrio(a)
source (F)	Quelle *f*	spring	—	sorgente *f*	fuente *f*
sourd (F)	taub	deaf	—	sordo(a)	sordo(a)
sourire[1] (F)	lächeln	smile	—	sorridere	sonreír
sourire[2] (F)	Lächeln *n*	smile	—	sorriso *m*	sonrisa *f*
souris (F)	Maus *f*	mouse	—	topo *m*	ratón *m*
sous (F)	unter	under	—	al di sotto di	debajo de
sous-louer (F)	untervermieten	sublet	—	subaffittare	realquilar
soustraire (F)	unterschlagen	embezzle	—	sottrarre	sustraer
sous-vêtements (F)	Unterwäsche *f*	underwear	—	biancheria intima *f*	ropa interior *f*
soutenir (F)	unterstützen	support	—	assistere	apoyar
South (E)	Süden *m*	—	sud *m*	sud	sur *m*
southern (E)	südlich	—	du sud	a sud	al sur

	D	E	F	I	Es
soutien (F)	Unterstützung f	support	—	sostegno m	apoyo m
souvenir (E)	Andenken n	—	souvenir m	ricordo m	recuerdo m
souvenir[1] (F)	Andenken n	souvenir	—	ricordo m	recuerdo m
souvenir[2] (F)	erinnern	remember	—	ricordare	recordar
souvenir[3] (F)	Erinnerung f	memory	—	ricordo m	memoria f
souvenir de, se (F)	gedenken	remember	—	ricordare	conmemorar
souvent (F)	oft	often	—	spesso	a menudo
soviel (D)	—	so much	tant	quanto/tanto	tanto
soweit (D)	—	as far as	autant que	fin dove	hasta tanto
sowohl (D)	—	as well as	aussi bien	tanto...quanto	tanto...
space (E)	Zwischenraum m	—	espace m	spazio m	espacio intermedio m
spacieux (F)	geräumig	spacious	—	spazioso(a)	espacioso(a)
spacious (E)	geräumig	—	spacieux(-euse)	spazioso(a)	espacioso(a)
Spagna (I)	Spanien n	Spain	Espagne f	—	España f
spagnolo[1] (I)	spanisch	Spanish	espagnol(e)	—	español(a)
spagnolo[2] (I)	Spanier m	Spaniard	Espagnol m	—	español m
Spain (E)	Spanien n	—	Espagne f	Spagna f	España f
spalla (I)	Schulter f	shoulder	épaule f	—	hombro m
Spaniard (E)	Spanier m	—	Espagnol m	spagnolo m	español m
Spanien (D)	—	Spain	Espagne f	Spagna f	España f
Spanier (D)	—	Spaniard	Espagnol m	spagnolo m	español m
spanisch (D)	—	Spanish	espagnol(e)	spagnolo(a)	español(a)
Spanish (E)	spanisch	—	espagnol(e)	spagnolo(a)	español(a)
sparare (I)	schießen	shoot	tirer	—	disparar
Sparbuch (D)	—	savings book	livret de caisse d'épargne m	libretto di risparmio m	libreta de ahorro f
sparen (D)	—	save	économiser	risparmiare	ahorrar
sparire (I)	verschwinden	disappear	disparaître	—	desaparecer
Sparkasse (D)	—	savings bank	caisse d'épargne f	cassa di risparmio f	caja de ahorros f
sparo (I)	Schuß m	shot	coup m	—	disparo m
sparsam (D)	—	economical	économe	parsimonioso(a)	económico(a)
Spaß (D)	—	fun	plaisir m	scherzo m	broma f
spaßen (D)	—	joke	plaisanter	scherzare	bromear
spät (D)	—	late	tard	tardi	tarde
später (D)	—	later	plus tard	piú tardi	más tarde
spaventare (I)	erschrecken	frighten	effrayer	—	asustar
spaventoso[1] (I)	schrecklich	terrible	terrible	—	horrible
spaventoso[2] (I)	schauderhaft	horrible	horrible	—	espantoso(a)
spazierengehen (D)	—	go for a walk	promener, se	passeggiare	ir de paseo
Spaziergang (D)	—	walk	promenade f	passeggiata f	paseo m
spazio (I)	Zwischenraum m	space	espace m	—	espacio intermedio m
spazioso (I)	geräumig	spacious	spacieux(-euse)	—	espacioso(a)
spazzola (I)	Bürste f	brush	brosse f	—	cepillo m
spazzolino da denti (I)	Zahnbürste f	toothbrush	brosse à dents f	—	cepillo de dientes m
speak (E)	sprechen	—	parler	parlare	hablar
specchio (I)	Spiegel m	mirror	miroir m	—	espejo m
special[1] (E)	besondere(r,s)	—	spécial(e)	straordinario(a)	extraordinario(a)

	D	E	F	I	Es
special² (E)	speziell	—	spécial(e)	speciale	especial
spécial¹ (F)	besondere(r,s)	special	—	straordinario(a)	extraordinario(a)
spécial² (F)	speziell	special	—	speciale	especial
speciale (I)	speziell	special	spécial(e)	—	especial
spécialiste de l'oreille (F)	Ohrenarzt m	ear specialist	—	otoiatra m	médico del oído m
special offer (E)	Sonderangebot n	—	offre spéciale f	offerta speciale f	oferta especial f
specie¹ (I)	Art f	species	espèce f	—	especie f
specie² (I)	Sorte f	sort	sorte f	—	clase f
species (E)	Art f	—	espèce f	specie f	especie f
Speck (D)	—	bacon	lard m	lardo m	tocino m
spectacle (F)	Schauspiel n	play	—	spettacolo m	espectáculo m
spectateur (F)	Zuschauer m	spectator	—	spettatore m	espectador m
spectateurs (F)	Publikum n	audience	—	pubblico m	público m
spectator (E)	Zuschauer m	—	spectateur m	spettatore m	espectador m
spedire (I)	übersenden	send	envoyer	—	enviar
speech (E)	Rede f	—	discours m	discorso m	discurso m
speed¹ (E)	Geschwindigkeit f	—	vitesse f	velocità f	velocidad f
speed² (E)	Schnelligkeit f	—	rapidité f	velocità f	rapidez f
speed³ (E)	Tempo n	—	vitesse f	velocità f	velocidad f
speed trap (E)	Radarkontrolle f	—	contrôle radar m	controllo radar m	control de radar m
spegnere¹ (I)	ausmachen	switch off	éteindre	—	apagar
spegnere² (I)	ausschalten	switch off	arrêter	—	desconectar
spegnere³ (I)	abschalten	switch off	éteindre	—	desconectar
spegnere⁴ (I)	abstellen	turn off	arrêter	—	desconectar
spegnere⁵ (I)	löschen	extinguish	éteindre	—	apagar
Speise (D)	—	food	aliment m	cibo m	comida f
Speisekarte (D)	—	menu	menu m	menu m	lista de platos f
speisen (D)	—	dine	manger	mangiare	comer
Speisewagen (D)	—	dining car	wagon-restaurant m	vagone ristorante m	vagón restaurante m
spell (E)	buchstabieren	—	épeler	sillabare	deletrear
spend (E)	verbringen	—	passer	passare	pasar
Spende (D)	—	donation	don m	donazione f	donativo m
spensierato (I)	leichtsinnig	careless	étourdi(e)	—	imprudente
sperare (I)	hoffen	hope	espérer	—	esperar
speriamo che (I)	hoffentlich	hopefully	espérons	—	espero que
spesa (I)	Einkauf m	shopping	achat m	—	compra f
spese¹ (I)	Kosten pl	expenses	coûts m pl	—	costas m pl
spese² (I)	Spesen pl	expenses	frais m pl	—	gastos m pl
spese³ (I)	Unkosten pl	expenses	frais m pl	—	gastos m pl
Spesen (D)	—	expenses	frais m pl	spese f pl	gastos m pl
spesso (I)	oft	often	souvent	—	a menudo
spettacolo (I)	Schauspiel n	play	spectacle m	—	espectáculo m
spettatore (I)	Zuschauer m	spectator	spectateur m	—	espectador m
spezia (I)	Gewürz n	spice	épice f	—	especia f
speziell (D)	—	special	spécial(e)	speciale	especial
spiacevole (I)	unangenehm	unpleasant	désagréable	—	desagradable
spiaggia (I)	Strand m	beach	plage f	—	playa f

	D	E	F	I	Es
spiccioli (I)	Kleingeld n	small change	monnaie f	—	cambio m
spice (E)	Gewürz n	—	épice f	spezia f	especia f
spicy (E)	würzig	—	épicé(e)	aromatico(a)	aromático(a)
spider (E)	Spinne f	—	araignée f	ragno m	araña f
spiegare (I)	erklären	explain	expliquer	—	explicar
Spiegel (D)	—	mirror	miroir m	specchio m	espejo m
Spiel (D)	—	game	jeu m	gioco m	juego m
spielen (D)	—	play	jouer	giocare	jugar
Spieler (D)	—	player	joueur m	giocatore m	jugador m
Spielplatz (D)	—	playground	terrain de jeu m	campo dei giochi m	campo de juego m
spießig (D)	—	bourgeois	bourgeois(e)	da piccolo(a) borghese m	pequeño(a) burgués(-esa)
spinach (E)	Spinat m	—	épinard m	spinaci m pl	espinacas f pl
spinaci (I)	Spinat m	spinach	épinard m	—	espinacas f pl
Spinat (D)	—	spinach	épinard m	spinaci m pl	espinacas f pl
spine (E)	Wirbelsäule f	—	colonne vertébrale f	colonna vertebrale f	columna vertebral f
spingere[1] (I)	stoßen	push	pousser	—	empujar
spingere[2] (I)	schieben	push	pousser	—	empujar
spingere[3] (I)	treiben	drive	mener	—	estimular
Spinne (D)	—	spider	araignée f	ragno m	araña f
spinta (I)	Stoß m	blow	coup m	—	empujón m
spirit (E)	Geist m	—	esprit m	spirito m	espíritu m
spirito (I)	Geist m	spirit	esprit m	—	espíritu m
spirits (E)	Schnaps m	—	eau-de-vie f	acquavite f	aguardiente m
spit (E)	spucken	—	cracher	sputare	escupir
spitz (D)	—	pointed	pointu(e)	appuntito(a)	puntiagudo(a)
Spitze (D)	—	point	pointe f	punta f	punta f
splendere (I)	glänzen	shine	briller	—	brillar
splendid (E)	prächtig	—	magnifique	meraviglioso(a)	magnífico(a)
spoil (E)	verwöhnen	—	gâter	viziare	mimar
sponge (E)	Schwamm m	—	éponge f	spugna f	esponja f
spoon (E)	Löffel m	—	cuiller f	cucchiaio m	cuchara f
sporcizia (I)	Schmutz m	dirt	saleté f	—	suciedad f
sporco[1] (I)	dreckig	dirty	sale	—	sucio(a)
sporco[2] (I)	schmutzig	dirty	sale	—	sucio(a)
Sport (D)	—	sport	sport m	sport m	deporte m
sport (E)	Sport m	—	sport m	sport m	deporte m
sport (F)	Sport m	sport	—	sport m	deporte m
sport (I)	Sport m	sport	sport m	—	deporte m
sportello (I)	Schalter m	counter	guichet m	—	ventanilla f
sposa (I)	Braut f	bride	mariée f	—	novia f
sposarsi (I)	heiraten	marry	marier, se	—	casarse
sposato (I)	verheiratet	married	marié(e)	—	casado(a)
Sprache (D)	—	language	langage m	lingua f	lengua f
spread (E)	verbreiten	—	propager	diffondere	difundir
sprecare (I)	verschwenden	waste	gaspiller	—	desperdiciar
sprechen (D)	—	speak	parler	parlare	hablar

	D	E	F	I	Es
Sprechstunde (D)	—	consultation hour	heures de consultation *f pl*	ora di ricevimento *f*	hora de consulta *f*
Sprichwort (D)	—	proverb	proverbe *m*	proverbio *m*	proverbio *m*
spring[1] (E)	Frühjahr *n*	—	printemps *m*	primavera *f*	primavera *f*
spring[2] (E)	Quelle *f*	—	source *f*	sorgente *f*	fuente *f*
springen (D)	—	jump	sauter	saltare	saltar
Spritze (D)	—	injection	piqûre *f*	iniezione *f*	inyección *f*
spritzen (D)	—	squirt	asperger	spruzzare	salpicar
Sprung (D)	—	jump	saut *m*	salto *m*	salto *m*
spruzzare (I)	spritzen	squirt	asperger	—	salpicar
spucken (D)	—	spit	cracher	sputare	escupir
spugna (I)	Schwamm *m*	sponge	éponge *f*	—	esponja *f*
spülen (D)	—	rinse	rincer	sciacquare	lavar
spumante (I)	Sekt *m*	champagne	champagne *m*	—	champán *m*
spuntare (I)	dämmern	dawn	poindre	—	amanecer
spuntino (I)	Imbiß *m*	snack	casse-croûte *m*	—	refrigerio *m*
sputare (I)	spucken	spit	cracher	—	escupir
squadra (I)	Mannschaft *f*	team	équipe *f*	—	equipo *m*
square[1] (E)	quadratisch	—	carré(e)	quadrato(a)	cuadrado(a)
square[2] (E)	Quadrat *n*	—	carré *m*	quadrato *m*	cuadrado *m*
square[3] (E)	viereckig	—	carré(e)	quadrato(a)	cuadrangular
square metre (E)	Quadratmeter *m*	—	mètre carré *m*	metro quadrato *m*	metro cuadrado *m*
squash (E)	zerdrücken	—	écraser	sgualcire	aplastar
squirt (E)	spritzen	—	asperger	spruzzare	salpicar
squisito (I)	köstlich	delicious	savoureux(-euse)	—	exquisito(a)
Staat (D)	—	state	état *m*	stato *m*	estado *m*
Staatsangehörigkeit (D)	—	nationality	nationalité *f*	cittadinanza *f*	nacionalidad *f*
stabilire[1] (I)	ausmachen	agree	convenir	—	convenir
stabilire[2] (I)	festsetzen	fix	fixer	—	fijar
stabilirsi (I)	niederlassen	settle down	s'installer	—	instalarse
staccare (I)	abnehmen	take away	décrocher	—	descolgar
Stadt (D)	—	town	ville *f*	città *f*	ciudad *f*
stage[1] (E)	Bühne *f*	—	scène *f*	palcoscenico *m*	escenario *m*
stage[2] (E)	inszenieren	—	mettre en scène	mettere in scena	escenificar
stage (F)	Praktikum *n*	practical training	—	tirocinio *m*	prácticas *f pl*
stagger (E)	wanken	—	chanceller	barcollare	vacilar
stagione[1] (I)	Jahreszeit *f*	time of year	saison *f*	—	estación del año *f*
stagione[2] (I)	Saison *f*	season	saison *f*	—	temporada *f*
stagno (I)	Teich *m*	pond	étang *m*	—	estanque *m*
Stahl (D)	—	steel	acier *m*	acciaio *m*	acero *m*
stain (E)	Fleck *m*	—	tache *f*	macchia *f*	mancha *f*
staircase (E)	Aufgang *m*	—	montée *f*	scala *f*	subida *f*
stairs (E)	Treppe *f*	—	escalier *m*	scala *f*	escalera *f*
stalls (E)	Parkett *n*	—	parquet *m*	parquet *m*	entarimado *m*
Stammgast (D)	—	regular	habitué *m*	cliente abituale *m*	cliente habitual *m*
stamp[1] (E)	Briefmarke *f*	—	timbre *m*	francobollo *m*	sello *m*
stamp[2] (E)	frankieren	—	affranchir	affrancare	franquear
stamp[3] (E)	Stempel *m*	—	timbre *m*	timbro *m*	sello *m*

	D	E	F	I	Es
stampa (I)	Presse *f*	press	presse *f*	—	prensa *f*
stancarsi (I)	ermüden	tire	fatiguer	—	cansar
stanco (I)	müde	tired	fatigué(e)	—	cansado(a)
Stand (D)	—	position	état *m*	stato *m*	estado *m*
stand (E)	stehen	—	être debout	stare in piedi	estar en pie
stand by s.b. (E)	beistehen	—	assister	assistere	asistir a
ständig (D)	—	permanent	permanent(e)	fisso(a)	permanente
standpoint (E)	Standpunkt *m*	—	point de vue *m*	punto di vista *m*	punto de vista *m*
Standpunkt (D)	—	standpoint	point de vue *m*	punto di vista *m*	punto de vista *m*
Stange (D)	—	pole	barre *f*	asta *f*	vara *f*
stanza (I)	Raum *m*	room	pièce *f*	—	habitación *f*
stanza da bagno (I)	Badezimmer *n*	bathroom	salle de bains *f*	—	cuarto de baño *m*
star (E)	Stern *m*	—	étoile *f*	stella *f*	estrella *f*
stare a guardare[1] (I)	zusehen	watch	regarder	—	mirar
stare a guardare[2] (I)	zuschauen	watch	regarder	—	mirar
stare bene (I)	passen	suit	aller bien	—	venir bien
stare in piedi (I)	stehen	stand	être debout	—	estar en pie
stare seduto (I)	sitzen	sit	être assis(e)	—	estar sentado(a)
stark (D)	—	strong	fort(e)	forte	fuerte
Stärke (D)	—	strength	puissance *f*	forza *f*	fuerza *f*
starnutire (I)	niesen	sneeze	éternuer	—	estornudar
starr (D)	—	rigid	rigide	rigido(a)	fijo(a)
Start (D)	—	start	départ *m*	partenza *f*	partida *f*
start[1] (E)	anfangen	—	commencer	cominciare	empezar
start[2] (E)	starten	—	démarrer	partire	partir
start[3] (E)	Start *m*	—	départ *m*	partenza *f*	partida *f*
starten (D)	—	start	démarrer	partire	partir
starve (E)	verhungern	—	mourir de faim	morire di fame	morir de hambre
state (E)	Staat *m*	—	état *m*	stato *m*	estado *m*
statement (E)	Aussage *f*	—	déclaration *f*	dichiarazione *f*	afirmación *f*
Station (D)	—	station	station *f*	stazione *f*	estación *f*
station[1] (E)	Bahnhof *m*	—	gare *f*	stazione *f*	estación *f*
station[2] (E)	Station *f*	—	station *f*	stazione *f*	estación *f*
station[3] (E)	Sender *m*	—	émetteur *m*	trasmettitore *m*	emisora *f*
station (F)	Station *f*	station	—	stazione *f*	estación *f*
stationery shop (E)	Schreibwaren-handlung *f*	—	papeterie *f*	cartoleria *f*	papelería *f*
station-service (F)	Tankstelle *f*	filling station	—	distributore di benzina *m*	gasolinera *f*
Stati Uniti (I)	Vereinigte Staaten *pl*	United States	Etats-Unis *m pl*	—	Estados Unidos *m pl*
stato[1] (I)	Staat *m*	state	état *m*	—	estado *m*
stato[2] (I)	Stand *m*	position	état *m*	—	estado *m*
stato[3] (I)	Zustand *m*	condition	état *m*	—	estado *m*
statt (D)	—	instead	au lieu de	invece di	en vez de
stattfinden (D)	—	take place	avoir lieu	avere luogo	tener lugar
Stau (D)	—	traffic jam	embouteillage *m*	ingorgo *m*	embotellamiento *m*
Staub (D)	—	dust	poussière *f*	polvere *f*	polvo *m*
staubig (D)	—	dusty	poussiéreux(-euse)	polveroso(a)	polvoriento(a)

	D	E	F	I	Es
Staubsauger (D)	—	vacuum-cleaner	aspirateur *m*	aspirapolvere *m*	aspirador *m*
staunen (D)	—	be astonished	étonner, s'	stupirsi	asombrarse
stay[1] (E)	Aufenthalt *m*	—	séjour *m*	soggiorno *m*	estancia *f*
stay[2] (E)	bleiben	—	rester	rimanere	quedarse
stay here (E)	hierbleiben	—	rester	restare qui	quedarse aquí
stay the night (E)	übernachten	—	passer la nuit	pernottare	pernoctar
stazione[1] (I)	Bahnhof *m*	station	gare *f*	—	estación *f*
stazione[2] (I)	Station *f*	station	station *f*	—	estación *f*
stazione centrale (I)	Hauptbahnhof *m*	central station	gare centrale *f*	—	estación central *f*
steal (E)	stehlen	—	voler	rubare	robar
steam (E)	Dampf *m*	—	vapeur *f*	vapore *m*	vapor *m*
stechen (D)	—	prick	piquer	pungere	picar
Steckdose (D)	—	socket	prise électrique *f*	presa *f*	enchufe *m*
stecken (D)	—	insert	enfoncer	inserire	introducir
steel (E)	Stahl *m*	—	acier *m*	acciaio *m*	acero *m*
steep (E)	steil	—	raide	ripido(a)	inclinado(a)
steer (E)	lenken	—	conduire	guidare	encauzar
steering wheel (E)	Lenkrad *n*	—	volant *m*	volante *m*	volante *m*
stehen (D)	—	stand	être debout	stare in piedi	estar en pie
stehlen (D)	—	steal	voler	rubare	robar
steif (D)	—	stiff	rigide	rigido(a)	rígido(a)
steigen (D)	—	go up	monter	salire	subir
steil (D)	—	steep	raide	ripido(a)	inclinado(a)
Stein (D)	—	stone	pierre *f*	sasso *m*	piedra *f*
stella (I)	Stern *m*	star	étoile *f*	—	estrella *f*
Stelle (D)	—	place	place *f*	posto *m*	puesto *m*
stellen (D)	—	place	mettre	mettere	colocar
Stellung (D)	—	position	position *f*	posizione *f*	posición *f*
Stempei (D)	—	stamp	timbre *m*	timbro *m*	sello *m*
stendere (I)	strecken	stretch	allonger	—	alargar
step[1] (E)	Stufe *f*	—	marche *f*	gradino *m*	escalón *m*
step[2] (E)	Schritt *m*	—	pas *m*	passo *m*	paso *m*
step[3] (E)	treten	—	mettre le pied sur	pestare	pisar
step out (E)	heraustreten	—	sortir	uscire fuori	salir
sterben (D)	—	die	mourir	morire	morir
Stern (D)	—	star	étoile *f*	stella *f*	estrella *f*
stets (D)	—	always	toujours	sempre	siempre
Steuern (D)	—	tax	impôt *m*	imposte *f pl*	impuesto *m*
Stewardeß (D)	—	stewardess	hôtesse de l'air *f*	hostess *f*	azafata *f*
stewardess (E)	Stewardeß *f*	—	hôtesse de l'air *f*	hostess *f*	azafata *f*
stick[1] (E)	kleben	—	coller	incollare	pegar
stick[2] (E)	Stock *m*	—	bâton *m*	bastone *m*	bastón *m*
Stiefel (D)	—	boot	botte *f*	stivale *m*	bota *f*
Stier (D)	—	bull	taureau *m*	toro *m*	toro *m*
stiff (E)	steif	—	rigide	rigido(a)	rígido(a)
Stift (D)	—	pencil	crayon *m*	penna *f*	lápiz *m*
still (D)	—	quiet	calme	calmo(a)	tranquilo(a)
still[1] (E)	doch	—	si	si	sin embargo

	D	E	F	I	Es
still² (E)	noch	—	encore	ancora	aún/todavía
stimare (I)	schätzen	estimate	estimer	—	estimar
Stimme (D)	—	voice	voix *f*	voce *f*	voz *f*
stink (E)	stinken	—	puer	puzzare	apestar
stinken (D)	—	stink	puer	puzzare	apestar
stipendio (I)	Gehalt *n*	salary	salaire *m*	—	sueldo *m*
stirare (I)	bügeln	iron	repasser	—	planchar
Stirn (D)	—	forehead	front *m*	fronte *f*	frente *f*
stivale (I)	Stiefel *m*	boot	botte *f*	—	bota *f*
Stock (D)	—	stick	bâton *m*	bastone *m*	bastón *m*
stock (E)	Vorrat *m*	—	réserves *f pl*	scorte *f pl*	provisión *f*
stocking (E)	Strumpf *m*	—	bas *m*	calza *f*	media *f*
Stoff (D)	—	cloth	tissu *m*	stoffa *f*	tela *f*
stoffa (I)	Stoff *m*	cloth	tissu *m*	—	tela *f*
stolpern (D)	—	stumble	trébucher	inciampare	tropezar
stolz (D)	—	proud	fier(-ère)	orgoglioso(a)	orgulloso(a)
stomach¹ (E)	Bauch *m*	—	ventre *m*	pancia *f*	vientre *m*
stomach² (E)	Magen *m*	—	estomac *m*	stomaco *m*	estómago *m*
stomach-ache (E)	Magen-schmerzen *pl*	—	mal d'estomac *m*	mal di stomaco *m*	dolor de estómago *m*
stomaco (I)	Magen *m*	stomach	estomac *m*	—	estómago *m*
stone (E)	Stein *m*	—	pierre *f*	sasso *m*	piedra *f*
stop¹ (E)	aufhören	—	arrêter	cessare	terminar
stop² (E)	anhalten	—	arrêter	fermare	parar
stop² (E)	beenden	—	terminer	terminare	terminar
stop⁴ (E)	Haltestelle *f*	—	arrêt *m*	fermata *f*	parada *f*
stop! (E)	halt!	—	stop!	alt!	¡alto!
stop! (F)	halt!	stop!	—	alt!	¡alto!
store (E)	Lager *n*	—	magasin *m*	magazzino *m*	almacén *m*
stören (D)	—	disturb	déranger	disturbare	molestar
storia (I)	Geschichte *f*	history	histoire *f*	—	historia *f*
storm (E)	Sturm *m*	—	tempête *f*	tempesta *f*	tempestad *f*
storto (I)	krumm	crooked	tordu(e)	—	torcido(a)
Störung (D)	—	interference	trouble *m*	disturbo *m*	molestia *f*
Stoß (D)	—	blow	coup *m*	spinta *f*	empujón *m*
stoßen (D)	—	push	pousser	spingere	empujar
stottern (D)	—	stutter	bégayer	balbettare	tartamudear
stoviglie (I)	Geschirr *n*	crockery	vaiselle *f*	—	vajilla *f*
stow (E)	unterbringen	—	ranger	sistemare	colocar
strada (I)	Straße *f*	street	rue *f*	—	calle *f*
strada principale (I)	Hauptstraße *f*	main street	grand-rue *f*	—	calle central *f*
strada provinciale (I)	Landstraße *f*	country road	route *f*	—	carretera nacional *f*
strada statale (I)	Bundesstraße *f*	Federal Highway/ main road	route nationale *f*	—	carretera nacional *f*
Strafe (D)	—	punishment	punition *f*	punizione *f*	castigo *m*
strafen (D)	—	punish	punir	punire	castigar
Strahl (D)	—	ray	rayon *m*	raggio *m*	rayo *m*
straight (E)	gerade	—	droit(e)	diritto(a)	derecho(a)

	D	E	F	I	Es
straight ahead (E)	geradeaus	—	tout droit	dritto	todo derecho
strain (E)	Anstrengung *f*	—	effort *m*	fatica *f*	esfuerzo *m*
Strand (D)	—	beach	plage *f*	spiaggia *f*	playa *f*
strange[1] (E)	eigenartig	—	singulier(-ière)	strano(a)	extraño(a)
strange[2] (E)	merkwürdig	—	curieux(-euse)	curioso(a)	curioso(a)
strange[3] (E)	seltsam	—	bizarre	strano(a)	extraño(a)
straniero[1] (I)	ausländisch	foreign	étranger(-ère)	—	extranjero(a)
straniero[2] (I)	Ausländer *m*	foreigner	étranger *m*	—	extranjero *m*
straniero[3] (I)	Fremder *m*	foreigner	étranger *m*	—	extranjero *m*
strano[1] (I)	eigenartig	strange	singulier(-ière)	—	extraño(a)
strano[2] (I)	seltsam	strange	bizarre	—	extraño(a)
straordinario[1] (I)	außerordentlich	extraordinary	exeptionnel(le)	—	extraordinario(a)
straordinario[2] (I)	außergewöhnlich	exceptional	extraordinaire	—	excepcional
straordinario[3] (I)	besondere(r,s)	special	exeptionnel(le)	—	extraordinario(a)
strap (E)	Riemen *m*	—	courroie *f*	cinghia *f*	correa *f*
strappare[1] (I)	zerreißen	rip	déchirer	—	romper
strappare[2] (I)	reißen	tear	déchirer, se	—	desgarrarse
Straße (D)	—	street	rue *f*	strada *f*	calle *f*
Straßenbahn (D)	—	tram	tramway *m*	tram *m*	tranvía *m*
Strauch (D)	—	bush	buisson *m*	cespuglio *m*	arbusto *m*
Strauß (D)	—	bunch	bouquet *m*	mazzo *m*	ramo *m*
straw (E)	Stroh *n*	—	paille *f*	paglia *f*	paja *f*
strawberry (E)	Erdbeere *f*	—	fraise *f*	fragola *f*	fresa *f*
Strecke (D)	—	stretch	trajet *m*	tratto *m*	trayecto *m*
strecken (D)	—	stretch	allonger	stendere	alargar
street (E)	Straße *f*	—	rue *f*	strada *f*	calle *f*
street light (E)	Laterne *f*	—	réverbère *m*	lampione *m*	farola *f*
strega (I)	Hexe *f*	witch	sorcière *f*	—	bruja *f*
streichen (D)	—	paint	peindre	verniciare	pintar
Streichholz (D)	—	match	allumette *f*	fiammifero *m*	cerilla *f*
Streik (D)	—	strike	grève *f*	sciopero *m*	huelga *f*
streiken (D)	—	be on strike	faire grève	scioperare	hacer huelga
Streit (D)	—	argument	dispute *f*	lite *f*	disputa *f*
streiten (D)	—	quarrel	disputer, se	litigare	discutir
streng (D)	—	strict	sévère	severo(a)	riguroso(a)
strength[1] (E)	Kraft *f*	—	force *f*	forza *f*	fuerza *f*
strength[2] (E)	Stärke *f*	—	puissance *f*	forza *f*	fuerza *f*
stretch[1] (E)	strecken	—	allonger	stendere	alargar
stretch[2] (E)	Strecke *f*	—	trajet *m*	tratto *m*	trayecto *m*
stretcher (E)	Bahre *f*	—	brancard *m*	barella *f*	camilla *f*
stretto (I)	eng	narrow	étroit(e)	—	estrecho(a)
Strich (D)	—	line	trait *m*	linea *f*	línea *f*
Strick (D)	—	rope	corde *f*	corda *f*	cuerda *f*
stricken (D)	—	knit	tricoter	lavorare a maglia	hacer punto
Strickjacke (D)	—	cardigan	veste en tricot *f*	giacca di maglia	chaqueta de punto *f*
strict (E)	streng	—	sévère	severo	riguroso(a)
strike (E)	Streik *m*	—	grève *f*	sciopero *m*	huelga *f*

	D	E	F	I	Es
string (E)	Schnur f	—	ficelle f	corda f	cordel m
Stroh (D)	—	straw	paille f	paglia f	paja f
stroll (E)	bummeln	—	flâner	girellare	callejear
Strom (D)	—	current	courant m	corrente f	corriente f
strong¹ (E)	kräftig	—	fort(e)	forte	fuerte
strong² (E)	stark	—	fort(e)	forte	fuerte
strumento (I)	Instrument n	instrument	instrument m	—	instrumento m
Strumpf (D)	—	stocking	bas m	calza f	media f
Strumpfhose (D)	—	tights	collants m pl	calzamaglia f	leotardos m pl
Stück (D)	—	piece	morceau m	pezzo m	parte f
Student (D)	—	student	étudiant m	studente m	estudiante m
student (E)	Student m	—	étudiant m	studente m	estudiante m
studente (I)	Student m	student	étudiant m	—	estudiante m
studi (I)	Studium n	studies	études f pl	—	estudio m
studiare (I)	studieren	study	étudier	—	estudiar
studieren (D)	—	study	étudier	studiare	estudiar
studies (E)	Studium n	—	études f pl	studi m pl	estudio m
Studium (D)	—	studies	études f pl	studi m pl	estudio m
study (E)	studieren	—	étudier	studiare	estudiar
stufa (I)	Ofen m	oven	poêle m	—	estufa f
Stufe (D)	—	step	marche f	gradino m	escalón m
stuff (E)	Zeug n	—	truc m	cose f pl	cosa f
Stuhl (D)	—	chair	chaise f	sedia f	silla f
stumble (E)	stolpern	—	trébucher	inciampare	tropezar
stumm (D)	—	dumb	muet(te)	muto(a)	mudo(a)
Stunde (D)	—	hour	heure f	ora f	hora f
stündlich (D)	—	hourly	toutes les heures	ogni ora	cada hora
stuoia (I)	Matte f	mat	natte f	—	colchoneta f
stupendo (I)	herrlich	marvellous	magnifique	—	maravilloso(a)
stupid (E)	dumm	—	bête	stupido(a)	tonto(a)
stupido (I)	dumm	stupid	bête	—	tonto(a)
stupire (I)	wundern	wonder	étonner	—	asombrar
stupirsi (I)	staunen	be astonished	étonner, se	—	asombrarse
Sturm (D)	—	storm	tempête f	tempesta f	tempestad f
Sturz (D)	—	fall	chute f	caduta f	caída f
stürzen (D)	—	fall	tomber	cadere	caer
stutter (E)	stottern	—	bégayer	balbettare	tartamudear
stylish (E)	schick	—	chic	elegante	elegante
stylo (F)	Füller m	fountain pen	—	penna stilografica f	pluma f
stylo à bille (F)	Kugelschreiber m	biro	—	biro f	bolígrafo m
su¹ (I)	auf	on/on top/onto	sur	—	sobre/en/hacia
su² (I)	herauf	up	vers le haut	—	hacia arriba
su³ (I)	hinauf	up	vers le haut	—	hacia arriba
su⁴ (I)	über	over/about	sur	—	por/sobre
suave (Es)	zart	soft	doux (douce)	tenero(a)	—
subaffittare (I)	untervermieten	sublet	sous-louer	—	subarrendar
subarrendar (Es)	untervermieten	sublet	sous-louer	subaffittare	—

	D	E	F	I	Es
subida¹ (Es)	Auffahrt f	drive	allée f	salita d'ingresso f	—
subida² (Es)	Aufgang m	staircase	montée f	scala f	—
subir¹ (Es)	aufsteigen	ascend	monter	salire	—
subir² (Es)	hinaufsteigen	climb	monter	salire	—
subir³ (Es)	steigen	go up	monter	salire	—
subir a (Es)	einsteigen	get in	monter	salire	—
subit (F)	abrupt	abrupt	—	improvviso(a)	súbito(a)
súbito (Es)	abrupt	abrupt	subit(e)	improvviso(a)	—
subito (I)	sofort	immediately	immédiatement	—	en seguida
subject¹ (E)	Fach n	—	matière f	materia f	materia f
subject² (E)	unterwerfen	—	soumettre	sottomettere	someter
sublet (E)	untervermieten	—	sous-louer	subaffittare	realquilar
subrayar (Es)	unterstreichen	underline	souligner	sottolineare	—
subsanar (Es)	wiedergut-machen	make up for	réparer	riparare	—
substitute (E)	Ersatz m	—	remplacement m	sostituzione f	sustitución f
subtract (E)	abziehen	—	retirer	sottrarre	restar
suburb (E)	Vorort m	—	faubourg m	sobborgo m	suburbio m
suburbio (Es)	Vorort m	suburb	faubourg m	sobborgo m	—
subway (E)	Unterführung f	—	passage souterrain m	sottopassaggio m	paso inferior m
succedere (I)	passieren	happen	arriver	—	pasar
succeed (E)	gelingen	—	réussir	riuscire	acertar
succès (F)	Erfolg m	success	—	successo m	éxito m
success (E)	Erfolg m	—	succès m	successo m	éxito m
successful (E)	erfolgreich	—	avec succès	pieno(a) di successi	afortunado(a)
successo (I)	Erfolg m	success	succès m	—	éxito m
succhiare (I)	lutschen	suck	sucer	—	chupar
succo (I)	Saft m	juice	jus m	—	zumo m
succursale (F)	Filiale f	branch	—	filiale f	sucursal f
suceder (Es)	vorkommen	occur	exister	accadere	—
sucer (F)	lutschen	suck	—	succhiare	chupar
suceso¹ (Es)	Ereignis n	event	événement m	avvenimento m	—
suceso² (Es)	Vorfall m	incident	cas m	caso m	—
such (E)	solche(r,s)	—	tel(le)	tale(i)	un(a) tal
suchen (D)	—	look for	chercher	cercare	buscar
suciedad (Es)	Schmutz m	dirt	saleté f	sporcizia f	—
sucio¹ (Es)	dreckig	dirty	sale	sporco(a)	—
sucio² (Es)	schmutzig	dirty	sale	sporco(a)	—
suck (E)	lutschen	—	sucer	succhiare	chupar
sucre (F)	Zucker m	sugar	—	zucchero m	azúcar m
sucré (F)	süß	sweet	—	dolce	dulce
sucumbir (Es)	unterliegen	be defeated	être vaincu(e) par qn	soccombere	—
sucursal (Es)	Filiale f	branch	succursale f	filiale f	—
sud (F)	Süden m	South	—	sud	sur m
sud (I)	Süden m	South	sud m	—	sur m
sudar (Es)	schwitzen	sweat	transpirer	sudare	—
sudare (I)	schwitzen	sweat	transpirer	—	sudar

	D	E	F	I	Es
suddenly (E)	plötzlich	—	tout à coup	di colpo	de repente
Süden (D)	—	South	sud m	sud	sur m
südlich (D)	—	southern	du sud	a sud	al sur
Suecia (Es)	Schweden	Sweden	Suède f	Svezia f	—
Suède (F)	Schweden	Sweden	—	Svezia f	Suecia f
suegra (Es)	Schwieger-mutter f	mother-in-law	belle-mère f	suocera f	—
suegros (Es)	Schwieger-eltern pl	parents-in-law	beaux-parents m pl	suoceri m pl	—
suela (Es)	Sohle f	sole	semelle f	suola f	—
sueldo (Es)	Gehalt n	salary	salaire m	stipendio m	—
suelo[1] (Es)	Boden m	floor	terre f	terra f	—
suelo[2] (Es)	Fußboden m	floor	sol m	pavimento m	—
sueño[1] (Es)	Schlaf m	sleep	sommeil m	sonno m	—
sueño[2] (Es)	Traum m	dream	rêve m	sogno m	—
suerte (Es)	Glück n	luck	chance f	fortuna f	—
suffer (E)	leiden	—	souffrir	soffrire	sufrir
suffice (E)	genügen	—	suffire	bastare	bastar
suffire (F)	genügen	suffice	—	bastare	bastar
sufrir (Es)	leiden	suffer	souffrir	soffrire	—
sugar (E)	Zucker m	—	sucre m	zucchero m	azúcar m
suicide (E)	Selbstmord m	—	suicide m	suicidio m	suicidio m
suicide (F)	Selbstmord m	suicide	—	suicidio m	suicidio m
suicidio (Es)	Selbstmord m	suicide	suicide m	suicidio m	—
suicidio (I)	Selbstmord m	suicide	suicide m	—	suicidio m
Suisse[1] (F)	Schweizer m	Swiss	—	svizzero m	suizo m
Suisse[2] (F)	Schweiz f	Switzerland	—	Svizzera f	Suiza f
suit[1] (E)	Anzug m	—	costume m	vestito m	traje m
suit[2] (E)	passen	—	aller bien	stare bene	venir bien
suitable[1] (E)	geeignet	—	approprié(e)	adatto(a)	indicado(a)
suitable[2] (E)	passend	—	assorti(e)	adatto(a)	apropiado(a)
suitable[3] (E)	zweckmäßig	—	approprié(e)	adatto(a)	adecuado(a)
suitcase (E)	Koffer m	—	valise f	valigia f	maleta f
suite (F)	Folge f	consequence	—	conseguenza f	serie f
suivant[1] (F)	folgend	following	—	seguente	siguiente
suivant[2] (F)	nächste(r,s)	next	—	prossimo(a)	siguiente
suivre (F)	folgen	follow	—	seguire	seguir
Suiza (Es)	Schweiz f	Switzerland	Suisse f	Svizzera f	—
suizo (Es)	Schweizer m	Swiss	Suisse m	svizzero m	—
sujet (F)	Thema n	topic	—	tema m	tema m
sujetar[1] (Es)	befestigen	fasten	fixer	fissare	—
sujetar[2] (Es)	festhalten	seize	tenir ferme	tener fermo	—
sujetar[3] (Es)	halten	hold	tenir	tenere	—
sultry (E)	schwül	—	lourd(e)	afoso(a)	sofocante
sum (E)	Summe f	—	somme f	somma f	suma f
suma (Es)	Summe f	sum	somme f	somma f	—
sumar (Es)	addieren	add up	additionner	sommare	—
suministrar (Es)	liefern	deliver	livrer	fornire	—
suministro (Es)	Lieferung f	delivery	livraison f	fornitura f	—

	D	E	F	I	Es
Summe (D)	—	sum	somme f	somma f	suma f
summer (E)	Sommer m	—	été m	estate f	verano m
summertime (E)	Sommerzeit f	—	heure d'été f	ora legale f	temporada de verano f
summon (E)	vorladen	—	assigner	citare in giudizio	citar
sun (E)	Sonne f	—	soleil m	sole m	sol m
sunburn (E)	Sonnenbrand m	—	coup de soleil m	scottatura solare f	quemadura solar f
Sunday (E)	Sonntag m	—	dimanche m	domenica f	domingo m
Sünde (D)	—	sin	péché m	peccato m	pecado m
sunglasses (E)	Sonnenbrille f	—	lunettes de soleil f pl	occhiali da sole m pl	gafas de sol f pl
sunny (E)	sonnig	—	ensoleillé(e)	sereno(a)	soleado(a)
sunrise (E)	Sonnenaufgang m	—	lever du soleil m	sorgere del sole m	salida del sol f
sunset (E)	Sonnen-untergang m	—	coucher du soleil m	tramonto del sole m	puesta del sol f
suocera (I)	Schwiegermutter f	mother-in-law	belle-mère f	—	suegra f
suoceri (I)	Schwiegereltern pl	parents-in-law	beaux-parents m pl	—	suegros m pl
suola (I)	Sohle f	sole	semelle f	—	suela f
suonare[1] (I)	klingeln	ring the bell	sonner	—	tocar el timbre
suonare[2] (I)	läuten	ring	sonner	—	tocar
suono[1] (I)	Klang m	sound	son m	—	sonido m
suono[2] (I)	Ton m	sound	son m	—	sonido m
suora (I)	Nonne f	nun	religieuse f	—	monja f
superficial (E)	oberflächlich	—	superficiel(le)	superficiale	superficial
superficial[1] (Es)	äußerlich	external	externe	esterno(a)	—
superficial[2] (Es)	oberflächlich	superficial	superficiel(le)	superficiale	—
superficiale (I)	oberflächlich	superficial	superficiel(le)	—	superficial
superficie (Es)	Oberfläche f	surface	surface f	superficie f	—
superficie (I)	Oberfläche f	surface	surface f	—	superficie f
superficiel (F)	oberflächlich	superficial	—	superficiale	superficial
superflu (F)	überflüssig	superfluous	—	superfluo(a)	superfluo(a)
superfluo (I)	überflüssig	superfluous	superflu(e)	—	superfluo(a)
superfluo (Es)	überflüssig	superfluous	superflu(e)	superfluo(a)	—
superfluous (E)	überflüssig	—	superflu(e)	superfluo(a)	superfluo(a)
supermarché (F)	Supermarkt m	supermarket	—	supermercato m	supermercado m
supermarket (E)	Supermarkt m	—	supermarché m	supermercato m	supermercado m
Supermarkt (D)	—	supermarket	supermarché m	supermercato m	supermercado m
supermercado (Es)	Supermarkt m	supermarket	supermarché m	supermercato m	—
supermercato (I)	Supermarkt m	supermarket	supermarché m	—	supermercado m
supersticioso (Es)	abergläubisch	superstitious	superstitieux (-euse)	superstizioso(a)	—
superstitieux (F)	abergläubisch	superstitious	—	superstizioso(a)	supersticioso(a)
superstitious (E)	abergläubisch	—	superstitieux (-euse)	superstizioso(a)	supersticioso(a)
superstizioso (I)	abergläubisch	superstitious	superstitieux (-euse)	—	supersticioso(a)
superstrada (I)	Schnellstraße f	expressway	voie rapide f	—	carretera de circulación rápida f
supervise (E)	überwachen	—	surveiller	sorvegliare	vigilar
suplemento[1] (Es)	Beilage f	supplement	supplément m	supplemento m	—

	D	E	F	I	Es
suplemento² (Es)	Zuschlag *m*	extra charge	supplément *m*	supplemento *m*	—
suponer¹ (Es)	annehmen	suppose	supposer	supporre	—
suponer² (Es)	ahnen	suspect	douter, se	supporre	—
suponer³ (Es)	voraussetzen	assume	supposer	presupporre	—
suponer⁴ (Es)	vermuten	suppose	supposer	supporre	—
suposición¹ (Es)	Annahme *f*	assumption	supposition *f*	supposizione *f*	—
suposición² (Es)	Vermutung *f*	supposition	supposition *f*	supposizione *f*	—
Suppe (D)	—	soup	soupe *f*	zuppa *f*	sopa *f*
supper (E)	Abendessen *n*	—	dîner *m*	cena *f*	cena *f*
supplement (E)	Beilage *f*	—	supplément *m*	supplemento *m*	suplemento *m*
supplément¹ (F)	Beilage *f*	supplement	—	supplemento *m*	suplemento *m*
supplément² (F)	Zuschlag *m*	extra charge	—	supplemento *m*	suplemento *m*
supplémentaire (F)	zusätzlich	in addition	—	supplementare	adicional
supplementare (I)	zusätzlich	in addition	supplémentaire	—	adicional
supplemento¹ (I)	Beilage *f*	supplement	supplément *m*	—	suplemento *m*
supplemento² (I)	Zuschlag *m*	extra charge	supplément *m*	—	suplemento *m*
supporre¹ (I)	ahnen	suspect	douter, se	—	suponer
supporre² (I)	annehmen	suppose	supposer	—	suponer
supporre³ (I)	vermuten	suppose	supposer	—	suponer
support¹ (E)	unterstützen	—	soutenir	assistere	apoyar
support² (E)	Unterstützung *f*	—	soutien *m*	sostegno *m*	apoyo *m*
supporter¹ (F)	aushalten	bear	—	sopportare	aguantar
supporter² (F)	ertragen	bear	—	sopportare	soportar
suppose¹ (E)	annehmen	—	supposer	supporre	suponer
suppose² (E)	vermuten	—	supposer	supporre	suponer
supposer¹ (F)	annehmen	suppose	—	supporre	suponer
supposer² (F)	vermuten	suppose	—	supporre	suponer
supposer³ (F)	voraussetzen	assume	—	presupporre	suponer
supposition (E)	Vermutung *f*	—	supposition *f*	supposizione *f*	suposición *f*
supposition¹ (F)	Annahme *f*	assumption	—	supposizione *f*	suposición *f*
supposition² (F)	Vermutung *f*	supposition	—	supposizione *f*	suposición *f*
supposizione¹ (I)	Annahme *f*	assumption	supposition *f*	—	suposición *f*
supposizione² (I)	Vermutung *f*	supposition	supposition *f*	—	suposición *f*
supuesto¹ (Es)	vorausgesetzt	provided	à condition que	presumendo	—
supuesto² (Es)	angeblich	pretended	prétendu(e)	presunto(a)	—
sur (Es)	Süden *m*	South	sud *m*	sud	—
sur¹ (F)	auf	on/on top/onto	—	su/sopra	sobre/en/hacia
sur² (F)	über	over/about	—	su/sopra/per	por/sobre
sûr¹ (F)	sicher	sure	—	sicuro(a)	seguro(a)
sûr² (F)	zuverlässig	reliable	—	affidabile	de confianza
sûr de soi (F)	selbstsicher	self-assured	—	sicuro di sé	seguro de sí mismo
sure (E)	sicher	—	sûr(e)	sicuro(a)	seguro(a)
surestimer (F)	überschätzen	overestimate	—	sopravvalutare	sobrevalorar
surface (E)	Oberfläche *f*	—	surface *f*	superficie *f*	superficie *f*
surface¹ (F)	Fläche *f*	area	—	area *f*	áera *f*
surface² (F)	Oberfläche *f*	surface	—	superficie *f*	superficie *f*
surgeon (E)	Chirurg *m*	—	chirurgien *m*	chirurgo *m*	cirujano *m*
surgir (Es)	entstehen	arise	naître	nascere	—

	D	E	F	I	Es
surname (E)	Nachname *m*	—	nom de famille *m*	cognome *m*	apellido *m*
surprendre (F)	überraschen	surprise	—	sorprendere	sorprender
surpris (F)	überrascht	surprised	—	sorpreso(a)	sorprendido(a)
surprise¹ (E)	überraschen	—	surprendre	sorprendere	sorprender
surprise² (E)	Überraschung *f*	—	surprise *f*	sorpresa *f*	sorpresa *f*
surprise (F)	Überraschung *f*	surprise	—	sorpresa *f*	sorpresa *f*
surprised (E)	überrascht	—	surpris(e)	sorpreso(a)	sorprendido(a)
surround (E)	umgeben	—	entourer	circondare	rodear
surroundings (E)	Umgebung *f*	—	environs *m pl*	dintorni *m pl*	alrededores *m pl*
surtout¹ (F)	besonders	especially	—	particolarmente	sobre todo
surtout² (F)	hauptsächlich	mainly	—	principalmente	principalmente
surveiller (F)	überwachen	supervise	—	sorvegliare	vigilar
survive (E)	überleben	—	survivre	sopravvivere	sobrevivir
survivre (F)	überleben	survive	—	sopravvivere	sobrevivir
suspect (E)	ahnen	—	douter, se	supporre	suponer
suspect (F)	verdächtig	suspicious	—	sospetto(a)	sospechoso(a)
suspicious (E)	verdächtig	—	suspect(e)	sospetto(a)	sospechoso(a)
süß (D)	—	sweet	sucré(e)	dolce	dulce
sustitución (Es)	Ersatz *m*	substitute	remplacement *m*	sostituzione *f*	—
sustituir (Es)	ersetzen	replace	remplacer	sostituire	—
sustraer (Es)	unterschlagen	embezzle	soustraire	sottrarre	—
susurrar (Es)	rauschen	rush	bruire	mormorare	—
svantaggiare (I)	benachteiligen	disadvantage	désavantager	—	perjudicar
svantaggio (I)	Nachteil *m*	disadvantage	désavantage *m*	—	desventaja *f*
sveglia (I)	Wecker *m*	alarm clock	réveil *m*	—	despertador *m*
svegliare¹ (I)	aufwecken	wake up	réveiller	—	despertar
svegliare² (I)	wecken	wake (up)	réveiller	—	despertar
svegliarsi¹ (I)	aufwachen	wake up	réveiller, se	—	despertarse
svegliarsi² (I)	erwachen	wake up	réveiller, se	—	despertar
sveglio (I)	wach	awake	réveillé(e)	—	despierto(a)
svenimento (I)	Ohnmacht *f*	faint	évanouissement *m*	—	desmayo *m*
Svezia (I)	Schweden	Sweden	Suède *f*	—	Suecia *f*
sviluppare (I)	entwickeln	develop	développer	—	desarrollar
sviluppo (I)	Entwicklung *f*	development	développement *m*	—	desarrollo *m*
Svizzera (I)	Schweiz *f*	Switzerland	Suisse *f*	—	Suiza *f*
svizzero (I)	Schweizer *m*	Swiss	Suisse *m*	—	suizo *m*
svoltare¹ (I)	abbiegen	turn off	tourner	—	torcer
svoltare² (I)	einbiegen	turn	tourner	—	doblar
swallow (E)	schlucken	—	avaler	inghiottire	tragar
swap (E)	tauschen	—	échanger	scambiare	cambiar
swear (E)	schwören	—	jurer	giurare	jurar
sweat (E)	schwitzen	—	transpirer	sudare	sudar
Sweden (E)	Schweden	—	Suède *f*	Svezia *f*	Suecia *f*
sweep¹ (E)	fegen	—	balayer	scopare	barrer

	D	E	F	I	Es
sweep² (E)	kehren	—	balayer	scopare	barrer
sweet¹ (E)	Bonbon n	—	bonbon m	caramella f	caramelo m
sweet² (E)	lieb	—	gentil(le)	caro(a)	amable
sweet³ (E)	niedlich	—	mignon(ne)	carino(a)	gracioso(a)
sweet⁴ (E)	süß	—	sucré(e)	dolce	dulce
swim (E)	schwimmen	—	nager	nuotare	nadar
swimming pool (E)	Schwimmbad n	—	piscine f	piscina f	piscina f
swimming trunks (E)	Badehose f	—	slip de bain m	costume da bagno m	bañador m
swimsuit (E)	Badeanzug m	—	maillot de bain m	costume da bagno m	traje de baño m
swing (E)	schaukeln	—	balancer, se	dondolare	columpiarse
Swiss (E)	Schweizer m	—	Suisse m	svizzero	suizo m
switch (E)	schalten	—	connecter	commutare	conectar
switch off¹ (E)	ausschalten	—	arrêter	spegnere	desconectar
switch off² (E)	abschalten	—	éteindre	spegnere	desconectar
switch off⁴ (E)	ausmachen	—	éteindre	spegnere	apagar
switch on (E)	einschalten	—	allumer	accendere	conectar
Switzerland (E)	Schweiz f	—	Suisse f	Svizzera f	Suiza f
swollen (E)	geschwollen	—	enflé(e)	gonfio(a)	hinchado(a)
sympathique (F)	sympathisch	likeable	—	simpatico(a)	simpático(a)
sympathisch (D)	—	likeable	sympathique	simpatico(a)	simpático(a)
syndicat (F)	Gewerkschaft f	trade union	—	sindacato m	sindicato m
syndicat d'initiative (F)	Verkehrsbüro n	travel agency	—	ufficio turistico m	oficina de turismo f
System (D)	—	system	système m	sistema m	sistema m
system (E)	System n	—	système m	sistema m	sistema m
système (F)	System n	system	—	sistema m	sistema m
tabac (F)	Tabak m	tabacco	—	tabacco m	tabaco m
tabacco (E)	Tabak m	—	tabac m	tabacco m	tabaco m
tabacco (I)	Tabak m	tabacco	tabac m	—	tabaco m
tabaco (Es)	Tabak m	tabacco	tabac m	tabacco m	—
Tabak (D)	—	tabacco	tabac m	tabacco m	tabaco m
table (E)	Tisch m	—	table f	tavolo m	mesa f
table (F)	Tisch m	table	—	tavolo m	mesa f
tableau (F)	Gemälde n	painting	—	quadro m	cuadro m
table des matières (F)	Inhalts-verzeichnis n	table of contents	—	indice m	índice m
table of contents (E)	Inhalts-verzeichnis n	—	table des matières f	indice m	índice m
tablespoon (E)	Eßlöffel m	—	cuiller f	cucchiaio m	cuchara f
tablet (E)	Tablette f	—	comprimé m	compressa f	pastilla f
tabletennis (E)	Tischtennis n	—	ping-pong m	tennis da tavolo m	tenis de mesa m
Tablett (D)	—	tray	plateau m	vassoio m	bandeja f
Tablette (D)	—	tablet	comprimé m	compressa f	pastilla f
tacchino (I)	Truthahn m	turkey	dindon m	—	pavo m
tacere (I)	schweigen	be silent	taire, se	—	callar

	D	E	F	I	Es
tache (F)	Fleck *m*	stain	—	macchia *f*	mancha *f*
tâche (F)	Aufgabe *f*	task	—	incarico *m*	tarea *f*
Tag (D)	—	day	jour *m*	giorno *m*	día *m*
taglia (I)	Größe *f*	size	taille *f*	—	talla *f*
tagliare (I)	schneiden	cut	couper	—	cortar
täglich (D)	—	daily	quotidien(ne)	quotidiano(a)	cotidiano(a)
tagliente (I)	scharf	sharp	tranchant(e)	—	cortante
taglio (I)	Schnitt *m*	cut	coupe *f*	—	corte *m*
tail (E)	Schwanz *m*	—	queue *f*	coda *f*	rabo *m*
taille (F)	Größe *f*	size	—	taglia	talla *f*
tailleur (F)	Schneider *m*	tailor	—	sarto *m*	sastre *m*
tailleur (I)	Kostüm *n*	costume	costume *m*	—	vestido *m*
tailor (E)	Schneider *m*	—	tailleur *m*	sarto *m*	sastre *m*
taire, se (F)	schweigen	be silent	—	tacere	callar
take¹ (E)	kassieren	—	encaisser	incassare	cobrar
take² (E)	nehmen	—	prendre	prendere	tomar
take along (E)	mitnehmen	—	emmener	prendere con sè	llevar consigo
take a snap (E)	knipsen	—	photographier	scattare	hacer una foto
take away¹ (E)	abnehmen	—	décrocher	staccare	descolgar
take away² (E)	wegnehmen	—	enlever	togliere	quitar
take back (E)	zurücknehmen	—	retirer	prendere indietro	retirar
take care (E)	achtgeben	—	faire attention	badare	atender
take care of (E)	erledigen	—	régler	sbrigare	acabar
take in tow (E)	abschleppen	—	remorquer	rimorchiare	remolcar
take notice of (E)	beachten	—	observer	osservare	prestar atención a
take off (E)	ausziehen	—	enlever	levare	quitarse
take-off (E)	Abflug *m*	—	décollage *m*	partenza *f*	despegue *m*
take over (E)	übernehmen	—	reprendre	accettare	aceptar
take part (E)	teilnehmen	—	participer	partecipare	participar
take pictures (E)	fotografieren	—	photographier	fotografare	fotografiar
take place (E)	stattfinden	—	avoir lieu	avere luogo	tener lugar
take turns (E)	abwechseln	—	alterner	alternarsi	alternar
Tal (D)	—	valley	vallée *f*	valle *f*	valle *m*
tale (I)	solche(r,s)	such	tel(le)	—	un(a) tal
talk¹ (E)	reden	—	parler	parlare	hablar
talk² (E)	unterhalten, sich	—	entretenir, se	conversare	conversar
talk³ (E)	Unterredung *f*	—	entrevue *f*	colloquio *m*	entrevista *f*
talla (Es)	Größe *f*	size	taille *f*	taglia *f*	—
taller (Es)	Werkstatt *f*	workshop	atelier *m*	officina *f*	—
taller de reparaciones (Es)	Autowerkstatt *f*	repair shop	atelier de réparation d'autos *m*	autofficina *f*	—
talonario de cheques (Es)	Scheckbuch *n*	cheque book	carnet de chèques *m*	libretto degli assegni *m*	—
tal vez (Es)	vielleicht	maybe	peut-être	forse	—
talvolta (I)	manchmal	sometimes	quelquefois	—	a veces
también¹ (Es)	auch	also/too	aussi	anche/pure	—
también² (Es)	ebenfalls	likewise	aussi	altrettanto	—
tamis (F)	Sieb *n*	sieve	—	setaccio *m*	colador *m*

taste

	D	E	F	I	Es
tanken (D)	—	fill up with petrol	prendre de l'essence	fare benzina	llenar de gasolina
Tankstelle (D)	—	filling station	station-service *f*	distributore di benzina *m*	gasolinera *f*
tan pronto... como (Es)	sobald	as soon as	dès que	appena	—
tant (F)	soviel	so much	—	quanto/tanto	tanto
Tante (D)	—	aunt(ie)	tante *f*	zia *f*	tía *f*
tante (F)	Tante *f*	aunt(ie)	—	zia *f*	tía *f*
tanto (Es)	soviel	so much	tant	quanto/tanto	—
tanto... (Es)	sowohl	as well as	aussi bien	tanto...quanto	—
tanto...quanto (I)	sowohl	as well as	aussi bien	—	tanto...
tant que (F)	solange	as long	—	finché	en tanto que
Tanz (D)	—	dance	danse *f*	ballo *m*	baile *f*
tanzen (D)	—	dance	danser	ballare	bailar
tapa (Es)	Deckel *m*	lid	couvercle *m*	coperchio *m*	—
tapar (Es)	zudecken	cover (up)	couvrir	coprire	—
tape (E)	Tonband *n*	—	bande magnétique *f*	nastro magnetico *m*	cinta magnetofónica *f*
taper (à la machine) (F)	tippen	type	—	battere a macchina	escribir a máquina
tapfer (D)	—	brave	courageux(-euse)	coraggioso(a)	valiente
tapis (F)	Teppich *m*	carpet	—	tappeto *m*	alfombra *f*
tapizar (Es)	beziehen	cover	recouvrir	ricoprire	—
tappeto (I)	Teppich *m*	carpet	tapis *m*	—	alfombra *f*
tard (F)	spät	late	—	tardi	tarde
tarde¹ (Es)	Nachmittag *m*	afternoon	après-midi *m*	pomeriggio *m*	—
tarde² (Es)	spät	late	tard	tardi	—
tardi (I)	spät	late	tard	—	tarde
tarea (Es)	Aufgabe *f*	task	tâche *f*	incarico *m*	—
targa (I)	Nummernschild *n*	number plate	plaque d'immatriculation *f*	—	matrícula *f*
tarifa (Es)	Gebühr *f*	fee	droit *m*	tassa *f*	—
tarjeta postal (Es)	Ansichtskarte *f*	postcard	carte postale *f*	cartolina *f*	—
tarta (Es)	Torte *f*	cake	gâteau *m*	torta *f*	—
tartamudear (Es)	stottern	stutter	bégayer	balbettare	—
tas (F)	Haufen *m*	heap	—	mucchio *m*	montón *m*
tasca (Es)	Kneipe *f*	pub	bistro *m*	osteria *f*	—
Tasche (D)	—	handbag	sac *m*	borsa *f*	bolso *m*
Taschengeld (D)	—	pocket money	argent de poche *f*	denaro per le piccole spese *m*	dinero de bolsillo *m*
Taschenlampe (D)	—	torch	lampe de poche *f*	lampadina tascabile *f*	linterna *f*
Taschentuch (D)	—	handkerchief	mouchoir *m*	fazzoletto *m*	pañuelo *m*
task (E)	Aufgabe *f*	—	tâche *f*	incarico *m*	tarea *f*
tassa (I)	Gebühr *f*	fee	droit *m*	—	tarifa *f*
Tasse (D)	—	cup	tasse *f*	tazza *f*	taza *f*
tasse (F)	Tasse *f*	cup	—	tazza *f*	taza *f*
tassì (I)	Taxi *n*	taxi	taxi *m*	—	taxi *m*
taste¹ (E)	Geschmack *m*	—	goût *m*	gusto *m*	sabor *m*
taste² (E)	schmecken	—	sentir	piacere	gustar

Tat

	D	E	F	I	Es
Tat (D)	—	deed	action f	azione f	acción f
tätig (D)	—	active	actif(-ive)	attivo(a)	activo(a)
Tätigkeit (D)	—	activity	activité f	attività f	actividad f
Tatsache (D)	—	fact	fait m	fatto m	hecho m
tatsächlich (D)	—	really	vraiment	realmente	realmente
taub (D)	—	deaf	sourd(e)	sordo(a)	sordo(a)
tauchen (D)	—	dive	plonger	immergere	bucear
tauen (D)	—	thaw	fondre	sciogliersi	deshelar
Taufe (D)	—	baptism	baptême m	battesimo m	bautizo m
taugen (D)	—	be of use	convenir pour	essere portato(a)	valer
taumeln (D)	—	reel	tituber	barcollare	vacilar
taureau (F)	Stier m	bull	—	toro m	toro m
tauschen (D)	—	swap	échanger	scambiare	cambiar
täuschen (D)	—	deceive	tromper	ingannare	engañar
tausend (D)	—	thousand	mille	mille	mil
tavolo (I)	Tisch m	table	table f	—	mesa f
tax (E)	Steuern pl	—	impôt m	imposte f pl	impuesto m
taxe sur la valeur ajoutée (F)	Mehrwertsteuer f	value added tax	—	imposta sul'valore aggiunto f	impuesto sobre el valor añadido m
Taxi (D)	—	taxi	taxi m	tassì m	taxi m
taxi (E)	Taxi n	—	taxi m	tassì m	taxi m
taxi (Es)	Taxi n	taxi	taxi m	tassì m	—
taxi (F)	Taxi n	taxi	—	tassì m	taxi m
taza (Es)	Tasse f	cup	tasse f	tazza f	—
tazza (I)	Tasse f	cup	tasse f	—	taza f
Tchécoslovaquie (F)	Tschechoslowakei f	Czechoslovakia	—	Cecoslovacchia f	Checoslovaquia f
té (Es)	Tee m	tea	thé m	tè m	—
tè (I)	Tee m	tea	thé m	—	té m
tea (E)	Tee m	—	thé m	tè m	té m
teach (E)	lehren	—	enseigner	insegnare	enseñar
teacher (E)	Lehrer m	—	professeur m	maestro m	profesor m
team (E)	Mannschaft f	—	équipe f	squadra f	equipo m
teapot (E)	Teekanne f	—	théière f	teiera f	tetera f
tear[1] (E)	reißen	—	déchirer, se	strappare	desgarrarse
tear[2] (E)	Träne f	—	larme f	lacrima f	lágrima f
teaspoon (E)	Teelöffel m	—	cuiller à thé f	cucchiaino da tè m	cucharilla f
teatro (Es)	Theater n	theatre	théâtre m	teatro m	
teatro (I)	Theater n	theatre	théâtre m	—	teatro m
Technik (D)	—	technology	technique f	tecnica f	técnica f
technique (F)	Technik f	technology	—	tecnica f	técnica f
technology (E)	Technik f	—	technique f	tecnica f	técnica f
techo[1] (Es)	Dach n	roof	toit m	tetto m	—
techo[2] (Es)	Decke f	blanket	couverture f	coperta f	—
técnica (Es)	Technik f	technology	technique f	tecnica f	—
tecnica (I)	Technik f	technology	technique f	—	técnica f
tedesco[1] (I)	Deutscher m	German	Allemand m	—	alemán m
tedesco[2] (I)	deutsch	German	allemand(e)	—	alemán(a)
Tee (D)	—	tea	thé m	tè m	té m

	D	E	F	I	Es
Teekanne (D)	—	teapot	théière f	teiera f	tetera f
Teelöffel (D)	—	teaspoon	cuiller à thé f	cucchiaino da tè m	cucharilla f
teeth (E)	Gebiß n	—	dents f pl	denti m pl	dentadura f
Teich (D)	—	pond	étang m	stagno m	estanque m
teiera (I)	Teekanne f	teapot	théière f	—	tetera f
Teig (D)	—	dough	pâte f	pasta f	masa f
Teigwaren (D)	—	pasta	pâtes f pl	pasta f	pastas f pl
Teil (D)	—	part	partie f	parte f	parte f
teilen (D)	—	share	partager	dividere	partir
teilnehmen (D)	—	take part	participer	partecipare	participar
teilweise (D)	—	partly	en partie	in parte	en parte
tel (F)	solche(r,s)	such	—	tale(i)	un(a) tal
tela¹ (Es)	Gewebe n	fabric	tissu m	tessuto m	—
tela² (Es)	Stoff m	cloth	tissu m	stoffa f	—
Telefon (D)	—	telephone	téléphone m	telefono m	teléfono m
Telefonanruf (D)	—	phone call	coup de téléphone m	telefonata f	llamada telefónica f
telefonare¹ (I)	anrufen	ring up	téléphoner	—	llamar por teléfono
telefonare² (I)	telefonieren	telephone	téléphoner	—	llamar por teléfono
telefonata (I)	Telefonanruf m	phone call	coup de téléphone m	—	llamada telefónica f
telefonata interurbana (I)	Ferngespräch n	long-distance call	communication interurbaine f	—	llamada interurbana f
Telefonbuch (D)	—	phone book	annuaire du téléphone m	elenco telefonico m	guía telefónica f
Telefongespräch (D)	—	phone call	communication téléphonique f	conversazione telefonica f	conversación telefónica f
telefonieren (D)	—	telephone	téléphoner	telefonare	llamar por teléfono
Telefonnummer (D)	—	phone number	numéro de téléphone m	numero telefonico m	número de teléfono m
teléfono (Es)	Telefon n	telephone	téléphone m	telefono m	—
telefono (I)	Telefon n	telephone	téléphone m	—	teléfono m
Telefonzelle (D)	—	phone box	cabine téléphonique f	cabina telefonica f	cabina de teléfono f
telegram (E)	Telegramm n	—	télégramme m	telegramma f	telegrama f
telegrama (Es)	Telegramm n	telegram	télégramme m	telegramma f	—
Telegramm (D)	—	telegram	télégramme m	telegramma f	telegrama f
telegramma (I)	Telegramm n	telegram	télégramme m	—	telegrama f
télégramme (F)	Telegramm n	telegram	—	telegramma f	telegrama f
telephone¹ (E)	telefonieren	—	téléphoner	telefonare	llamar por teléfono
telephone² (E)	Telefon n	—	téléphone m	telefono m	teléfono m
téléphone (F)	Telefon n	telephone	—	telefono m	teléfono m
téléphoner¹ (F)	anrufen	ring up	—	telefonare	llamar por teléfono
téléphoner² (F)	telefonieren	telephone	—	telefonare	llamar por teléfono
telesilla (Es)	Skilift m	skilift	remonte-pente m	sciovia f	—
television (E)	Fernsehen n	—	télévision f	televisione f	televisión f
televisión (Es)	Fernsehen n	television	télévision f	televisione f	—
télévision (F)	Fernsehen n	television	—	televisione f	televisión f
televisione (I)	Fernsehen n	television	télévision f	—	televisión f
television set (E)	Fernseher m	—	poste de télévision m	televisore m	televisor m

	D	E	F	I	Es
televisor (Es)	Fernseher *m*	television set	poste de télévision *m*	televisore *m*	—
televisore (I)	Fernseher *m*	television set	poste de télévision *m*	—	televisor *m*
tell (E)	erzählen	—	raconter	raccontare	contar
Teller (D)	—	plate	assiette *f*	piatto *m*	plato *m*
tema (Es)	Thema *n*	topic	sujet *m*	tema *m*	—
tema (I)	Thema *n*	topic	sujet *m*	—	tema *m*
temer[1] (Es)	befürchten	fear	craindre	temere	—
temer[2] (Es)	fürchten	fear	craindre	temere	—
temere[1] (I)	befürchten	fear	craindre	—	temer
temere[2] (I)	fürchten	fear	craindre	—	temer
témoin (F)	Zeuge *m*	witness	—	testimone *m*	testigo *m*
Temperatur (D)	—	temperature	température *f*	temperatura *f*	temperatura *f*
temperatura (Es)	Temperatur *f*	temperature	température *f*	temperatura *f*	—
temperatura (I)	Temperatur *f*	temperature	température *f*	—	temperatura *f*
temperature (E)	Temperatur *f*	—	température *f*	temperatura *f*	temperatura *f*
température (F)	Temperatur *f*	temperature	—	temperatura *f*	temperatura *f*
tempesta (I)	Sturm *m*	storm	tempête *f*	—	tempestad *f*
tempestad (Es)	Sturm *m*	storm	tempête *f*	tempesta *f*	—
tempête[1] (F)	Sturm *m*	storm	—	tempesta *f*	tempestad *f*
tempête[2] (F)	Unwetter *n*	thunderstorm	—	maltempo *m*	tormenta *f*
templado (Es)	lauwarm	lukewarm	tiède	tiepido(a)	—
Tempo (D)	—	speed	vitesse *f*	velocità *f*	velocidad *f*
tempo[1] (I)	Wetter *n*	weather	temps *m*	—	tiempo *m*
tempo[2] (I)	Zeit *f*	time	temps *m*	—	tiempo *m*
tempo libero (I)	Freizeit *f*	free time	loisirs *m pl*	—	tiempo libre *m*
temporada (Es)	Saison *f*	season	saison *f*	stagione *f*	—
temporada alta (Es)	Hochsaison *f*	high season	pleine saison *f*	alta stagione *f*	—
temporada de verano (Es)	Sommerzeit *f*	summertime	heure d'été *f*	ora legale *f*	—
temporaire (F)	vorübergehend	temporar	—	temporaneo(a)	pasajero(a)
temporale (I)	Gewitter *n*	thunderstorm	orage *m*	—	tormenta *f*
temporaneo (I)	vorübergehend	temporary	temporaire	—	pasajero(a)
temporary[1] (E)	vorläufig	—	provisoire	temporaneo(a)	pasajero(a)
temporary[2] (E)	vorübergehend	—	temporaire	provvisorio(a)	provisional
temprano (Es)	früh	early	tôt	presto	—
temps[1] (F)	Wetter *n*	weather	—	tempo *m*	tiempo *m*
temps[2] (F)	Zeit *f*	time	—	tempo *m*	tiempo *m*
ten (E)	zehn	—	dix	dieci	diez
tenant (E)	Mieter *m*	—	locataire *m*	inquilino *m*	inquilino *m*
tenda[1] (I)	Gardine *f*	curtain	rideau *m*	—	cortina *f*
tenda[2] (I)	Vorhang *m*	curtain	rideau *m*	—	cortina *f*
tenda[3] (I)	Zelt *n*	tent	tente *f*	—	tienda *f*
tenderness (E)	Zärtlichkeit *f*	—	tendresse *f*	tenerezza *f*	cariño *m*
tendresse (F)	Zärtlichkeit *f*	tenderness	—	tenerezza *f*	cariño *m*
tendu (F)	gespannt	tense	—	teso(a)	tenso(a)
tenedor (Es)	Gabel *f*	fork	fourchette *f*	forchetta *f*	—
tener (Es)	haben	have	avoir	avere	—

terrain

	D	E	F	I	Es
tenere[1] (I)	behalten	keep	garder	—	retener
tenere[2] (I)	halten	hold	tenir	—	sujetar
tenerezza (I)	Zärtlichkeit *f*	tenderness	tendresse *f*	—	cariño *m*
tener fermo (I)	festhalten	seize	tenir ferme	—	sujetar
tener frío (Es)	frieren	be cold	avoir froid	avere freddo	—
tener la intención de (Es)	vorhaben	intend	avoir l'intention de	avere intenzione	—
tener lugar (Es)	stattfinden	take place	avoir lieu	avere luogo	—
tenero (I)	zart	soft	doux (douce)	—	suave
tener vergüenza (Es)	schämen	be ashamed	avoir honte	vergognarsi	—
tenir (F)	halten	hold	—	tenere	sujetar
tenir ferme (F)	festhalten	seize	—	tener fermo	sujetar
tenis (Es)	Tennis *n*	tennis	tennis *m*	tennis *m*	—
tenis de mesa (Es)	Tischtennis *n*	tabletennis	ping-pong *m*	tennis da tavolo *m*	—
Tennis (D)	—	tennis	tennis *m*	tennis *m*	tenis *m*
tennis (E)	Tennis *n*	—	tennis *m*	tennis *m*	tenis *m*
tennis (F)	Tennis *n*	tennis	—	tennis *m*	tenis *m*
tennis (I)	Tennis *n*	tennis	tennis *m*	—	tenis *m*
tennis da tavolo (I)	Tischtennis *n*	tabletennis	ping-pong *m*	—	tenis de mesa *m*
tense (E)	gespannt	—	tendu(e)	teso(a)	tenso(a)
tenso (Es)	gespannt	tense	tendu(e)	teso(a)	—
tent (E)	Zelt *n*	—	tente *f*	tenda *f*	tienda *f*
tentativo (I)	Versuch *m*	try	essai *m*	—	intento *m*
tente (F)	Zelt *n*	tent	—	tenda *f*	tienda *f*
Teppich (D)	—	carpet	tapis *m*	tappeto *m*	alfombra *f*
tercera (Es)	dritte(r,s)	third	troisième	terzo(a)	—
tercio (Es)	Drittel *n*	a third	tiers *m*	terzo *m*	—
terme (F)	Termin *m*	date	—	termine *m*	fecha *f*
Termin (D)	—	date	terme *m*	termine *m*	fecha *f*
terminar[1] (Es)	aufhören	stop	arrêter	cessare	—
terminar[2] (Es)	beenden	stop	terminer	terminare	—
terminare (I)	beenden	stop	terminer	—	terminar
termine (I)	Termin *m*	date	terme *m*	—	fecha *f*
terminer (F)	beenden	stop	—	terminare	terminar
término (Es)	Ausdruck *m*	expression	expression *f*	espressione *f*	—
terminus (E)	Endstation *f*	—	terminus *m*	capolinea *m*	estación terminal *f*
terminus (F)	Endstation *f*	terminus	—	capolinea *m*	estación terminal *f*
termo (Es)	Thermosflasche *f*	thermos flask	thermos *m*	thermos *m*	—
termómetro (Es)	Thermometer *n*	thermometer	thermomètre *m*	termometro *m*	—
termometro (I)	Thermometer *n*	thermometer	thermomètre *m*	—	termómetro *m*
ternera (Es)	Kalb *n*	calf	veau *m*	vitello *m*	—
terra[1] (I)	Boden *m*	floor	terre *f*	—	suelo *m*
terra[2] (I)	Erde *f*	earth	terre *f*	—	tierra *f*
terrace (E)	Terrasse *f*	—	terrasse *f*	terrazza *f*	terraza *f*
terraferma (I)	Festland *n*	mainland	continent *m*	—	tierra firme *f*
terrain (E)	Gelände *n*	—	terrain *m*	terreno *m*	terreno *m*
terrain (F)	Gelände *n*	terrain	—	terreno *m*	terreno *m*

	D	E	F	I	Es
terrain de camping (F)	Campingplatz m	campsite	—	campeggio m	camping m
terrain de jeu (F)	Spielplatz m	playground	—	campo dei giochi m	campo de juego m
Terrasse (D)	—	terrace	terrasse f	terrazza f	terraza f
terrasse (F)	Terrasse f	terrace	—	terrazza f	terraza f
terraza (Es)	Terrasse f	terrace	terrasse f	terrazza f	—
terrazza (I)	Terrasse f	terrace	terrasse f	—	terraza f
terre[1] (F)	Boden m	floor	—	terra f	suelo m
terre[2] (F)	Erde f	earth	—	terra f	tierra f
terremoto (Es)	Erdbeben n	earthquake	tremblement de terre m	terremoto m	—
terremoto (I)	Erdbeben n	earthquake	tremblement de terre m	—	terremoto m
terreno (Es)	Gelände n	terrain	terrain m	terreno m	—
terreno (I))	Gelände n	terrain	terrain m	—	terreno m
terribile (I)	fürchterlich	terrible	terrible	—	terrible
terrible[1] (E)	fürchterlich	—	terrible	terribile	terrible
terrible[2] (E)	schrecklich	—	terrible	spaventoso(a)	horrible
terrible (Es)	fürchterlich	terrible	terrible	terribile	—
terrible[1] (F)	fürchterlich	terrible	—	terribile	terrible
terrible[2] (F)	schrecklich	terrible	—	spaventoso(a)	horrible
territorio nacional (Es)	Inland n	inland	intérieur m	territorio nazionale m	—
territorio nazionale (I)	Inland n	inland	intérieur m	—	territorio nacional m
terzo[1] (I)	Drittel n	a third	tiers m	—	tercio m
terzo[2] (I)	dritte(r,s)	third	troisième	—	tercera(o)
teso (I)	gespannt	tense	tendu(e)	—	tenso(a)
tesoro (Es)	Schatz m	treasure	trésor m	tesoro m	—
tesoro[1] (I)	Liebling m	darling	chéri m	—	querido m
tesoro[2] (I)	Schatz m	treasure	trésor m	—	tesoro m
tesson (F)	Scherbe f	broken piece	—	coccio m	pedazo m
tessuto (I)	Gewebe n	fabric	tissu m	—	tela f
Test (D)	—	test	test m	test m	test m
test[1] (E)	prüfen	—	tester	esaminare	examinar
test[2] (E)	Probe f	—	essai m	prova f	prueba f
test[3] (E)	testen	—	tester	collaudare	probar
test[4] (E)	Test m	—	test m	test m	test m
test (Es)	Test m	test	test m	test m	—
test (F)	Test m	test	—	test m	test m
test (I)	Test m	test	test m	—	test m
testa (I)	Kopf m	head	tête f	—	cabeza f
Testament (D)	—	will	testament m	testamento m	testamento m
testament (F)	Testament n	will	—	testamento m	testamento m
testamento (Es)	Testament n	will	testament m	testamento m	—
testamento (I)	Testament n	will	testament m	—	testamento m
testen (D)	—	test	tester	collaudare	probar
tester[1] (F)	prüfen	test	—	esaminare	examinar
tester[2] (F)	testen	test	—	collaudare	probar
testigo (Es)	Zeuge m	witness	témoin m	testimone m	—

	D	E	F	I	Es
testimone (I)	Zeuge *m*	witness	témoin *m*	—	testigo *m*
tête (F)	Kopf *m*	head	—	testa *f*	cabeza *f*
tetera (Es)	Teekanne *f*	teapot	théière *f*	teiera *f*	—
tetto (I)	Dach *n*	roof	toit *m*	—	techo *m*
teuer (D)	—	expensive	cher, chère	caro(a)	caro(a)
Teufel (D)	—	devil	diable *m*	diavolo *m*	diablo *m*
thank (E)	danken	—	remercier	ringraziare	agradecer
thanks (E)	Dank *m*	—	remerciement *m*	ringraziamento *m*	agradecimiento *m*
thank you (E)	danke	—	merci	grazie	¡gracias!
that¹ (E)	daß	—	que	che	que
that² (E)	jene(r,s)	—	ce, cette	quello(a)	aquella, aquel, aquello
that³ (E)	das	—	le, la	il, la	lo
thaw (E)	tauen	—	fondre	sciogliersi	deshelar
the (E)	der, die, das	—	le, la	il, la	el, la, lo
thé (F)	Tee *m*	tea	—	tè *m*	té *m*
Theater (D)	—	theatre	théâtre *m*	teatro *m*	teatro *m*
Theaterstück (D)	—	play	pièce de théâtre *f*	opera teatrale *f*	pieza de teatro *f*
theatre (E)	Theater *n*	—	théâtre *m*	teatro *m*	teatro *m*
théâtre (F)	Theater *n*	theatre	—	teatro *m*	teatro *m*
théière (F)	Teekanne *f*	teapot	—	teiera *f*	tetera *f*
Thema (D)	—	topic	sujet *m*	tema *m*	tema *m*
then (E)	dann	—	ensuite	in seguito	luego
there¹ (E)	dort	—	là/y	là	allí
there² (E)	da	—	là/ici	qui/là	allí
there³ (E)	hin	—	jusqu'à/vers	là	hacia allá/hasta
therefore¹ (E)	also	—	donc	dunque/quindi	así
therefore² (E)	deshalb	—	c'est pourquoi	perció	por eso
Thermo-meter (D)	—	thermometer	thermomètre *m*	termometro *m*	termómetro *m*
thermometer (E)	Thermometer *n*	—	thermomètre *m*	termometro *m*	termómetro *m*
thermomètre (F)	Thermometer *n*	thermometer	—	termometro *m*	termómetro *m*
thermos (F)	Thermosflasche *f*	thermos flask	—	thermos *m*	termo *m*
thermos (I)	Thermosflasche *f*	thermos flask	thermos *m*	—	termo *m*
Thermosflasche (D)	—	thermos flask	thermos *m*	thermos *m*	termo *m*
thermos flask (E)	Thermosflasche *f*	—	thermos *m*	thermos *m*	termo *m*
the same¹ (E)	derselbe	—	le même	lo stesso	el mismo
the same² (E)	dasselbe	—	la même chose	lo stesso	lo mismo
they (E)	sie (pl)	—	ils/elles	loro	ellos, ellas
thief (E)	Dieb *m*	—	voleur *m*	ladro *m*	ladrón *m*
thin (E)	dünn	—	mince	magro(a)	delgado(a)
thing¹ (E)	Ding *n*	—	chose *f*	cosa *f*	cosa *f*
thing² (E)	Sache *f*	—	chose *f*	cosa *f*	cosa *f*
think¹ (E)	denken	—	penser	pensare	pensar
think² (E)	meinen	—	penser	credere	opinar
think³ (E)	nachdenken	—	réfléchir	riflettere	reflexionar
third (E)	dritte(r,s)	—	troisième	terzo(a)	tercera(o)
thirst (E)	Durst *m*	—	soif *f*	sete *f*	sed *f*
thirsty (E)	durstig	—	assoiffé(e)	assetato(a)	sediento(a)

	D	E	F	I	Es
thirteen (E)	dreizehn	—	treize	tredici	trece
thirty (E)	dreißig	—	trente	trenta	treinta
this (E)	diese(r,s)	—	ce, cette	questo(a)	esta, este, esto
thon (F)	Thunfisch *m*	tuna	—	tonno *m*	atún *m*
thorough (E)	gründlich	—	a fond	a fondo	a fondo
thought (E)	Gedanke *m*	—	pensée *f*	pensiero *m*	pensamiento *m*
thousand (E)	tausend	—	mille	mille	mil
thread (E)	Faden *m*	—	fil *m*	filo *m*	hilo *m*
threaten[1] (E)	bedrohen	—	menacer	minacciare	amenazar
threaten[2] (E)	drohen	—	menacer	minacciare	amenazar (a alguien)
threaten s.b. (E)	androhen	—	menacer	minacciare	amenazar
three (E)	drei	—	trois	tre	tres
throat (E)	Rachen *m*	—	gorge *f*	faringe *m*	garganta *f*
through[1] (E)	durch	—	par	per	por
through[2] (E)	hindurch	—	à travers	attraverso	a través de
through train (E)	D-Zug *m*	—	express *m*	direttissimo *m*	tren expreso *m*
throw (E)	werfen	—	lancer	lanciare	tirar
throw over (E)	umschmeißen	—	renverser	rovesciare	derribar
thumb (E)	Daumen *m*	—	pouce *m*	pollice *m*	pulgar *m*
thunder (E)	Donner *m*	—	tonnerre *m*	tuono *m*	trueno *m*
thunderstorm[1] (E)	Gewitter *n*	—	orage *m*	temporale *m*	tormenta *f*
thunderstorm[2] (E)	Unwetter *n*	—	tempête *f*	maltempo *m*	tormenta *f*
Thunfisch (D)	—	tuna	thon *m*	tonno *m*	atún *m*
Thursday (E)	Donnerstag *m*	—	jeudi *m*	giovedì *m*	jueves *m*
tía (Es)	Tante *f*	aunt(ie)	tante *f*	zia *f*	—
tiburón (Es)	Hai *m*	shark	requin *m*	pescecane *m*	—
ticket[1] (E)	Fahrschein *m*	—	ticket *m*	biglietto *m*	billete *m*
ticket[2] (E)	Fahrkarte *f*	—	billet *m*	biglietto *m*	billete *m*
ticket (F)	Fahrschein *m*	ticket	—	biglietto *m*	billete *m*
tidy (E)	ordentlich	—	rangé(e)	ordinato(a)	ordenado(a)
tie (E)	Krawatte *f*	—	cravate *f*	cravatta *f*	corbata *f*
tiède (F)	lauwarm	lukewarm	—	tiepido(a)	templado(a)
tief (D)	—	deep	profond(e)	profondo(a)	profundo(a)
Tiefe (D)	—	depth	profondeur *f*	profondità *f*	profundidad *f*
tiempo[1] (Es)	Wetter *n*	weather	temps *m*	tempo *m*	—
tiempo[2] (Es)	Zeit *f*	time	temps *m*	tempo *m*	—
tiempo libre (Es)	Freizeit *f*	free time	loisirs *m pl*	tempo libero *m*	—
tienda[1] (Es)	Geschäft *n*	shop	magasin *m*	negozio *m*	—
tienda[2] (Es)	Laden *m*	shop	magasin *m*	negozio *m*	—
tienda[3] (Es)	Zelt *n*	tent	tente *f*	tenda *f*	—
tienda de productos dietéticos (Es)	Reformhaus *n*	health food shop	magasin diététique *m*	negozio di prodotti dietetici *m*	—
tienda de ultramarinos (Es)	Lebensmittel-geschäft *n*	grocer's	magasin d'alimentation *m*	negozio di alimentari *m*	—
tiepido (I)	lauwarm	lukewarm	tiède	—	templado(a)
Tier (D)	—	animal	animal *m*	animale *m*	animal *m*
Tierarzt (D)	—	vet	vétérinaire *m*	veterinario *m*	veterinario *m*

	D	E	F	I	Es
tierno (Es)	weich	soft	doux(douce)	morbido(a)	—
tierra (Es)	Erde f	earth	terre f	terra f	—
tierra firme (Es)	Festland n	mainland	continent m	terraferma f	—
tiers (F)	Drittel n	a third	—	terzo m	tercio m
tight (E)	knapp	—	étroit(e)	scarso(a)	estrecho(a)
tights (E)	Strumpfhose f	—	collants m pl	calzamaglia f	leotardos m pl
tijeras (Es)	Schere f	pair of scissors	ciseaux m pl	forbici f pl	—
tilgen (D)	—	erase	effacer	estinguere	anular
till (E)	Kasse f	—	caisse f	cassa f	caja f
timbre (Es)	Klingel f	bell	sonnette f	campanello m	—
timbre[1] (F)	Briefmarke f	stamp	—	francobollo m	sello m
timbre[2] (F)	Stempel m	stamp	—	timbro m	sello m
timbro (I)	Stempel m	stamp	timbre m	—	sello m
time (E)	Zeit f	—	temps m	tempo m	tiempo m
time of year (E)	Jahreszeit f	—	saison f	stagione f	estación del año f
timetable (E)	Fahrplan m	—	horaire m	orario m	horario m
timide[1] (F)	schüchtern	shy	—	timido(a)	tímido(a)
timide[2] (F)	scheu	shy	—	timido(a)	tímido(a)
timido[1] (I)	scheu	shy	timide	—	tímido(a)
timido[2] (I)	schüchtern	shy	timide	—	tímido(a)
tímido[1] (Es)	schüchtern	shy	timide	timido(a)	—
tímido[2] (Es)	scheu	shy	timide	timido(a)	—
tin (E)	Dose f	—	boîte f	scatola f	lata f
tingere (I)	färben	dye	colorer	—	colorear
Tintenfisch (D)	—	cuttlefish	seiche f	seppia f	calamar m
tío (Es)	Onkel m	uncle	oncle m	zio m	—
tíovivo (Es)	Karussell n	roundabout	manège m	giostra f	—
tip (E)	Trinkgeld n	—	pourboire m	mancia f	propina f
tipico (I)	typisch	typical	typique	—	típico(a)
típico (Es)	typisch	typical	typique	tipico	—
tippen (D)	—	type	taper (à la machine)	battere a macchina	escribir a máquina
tirar[1] (Es)	werfen	throw	lancer	lanciare	—
tirar[2] (Es)	ziehen	pull	tirer	tirare	—
tirare (I)	ziehen	pull	tirer	—	tirar
tirare in avanti (I)	vorziehen	draw	tirer	—	correr
tire (E)	ermüden	—	fatiguer	stancarsi	cansar
tire-bouchon (F)	Korkenzieher m	corkscrew	—	cavatappi m	sacacorchos m
tired (E)	müde	—	fatigué(e)	stanco	cansado(a)
tirer[1] (F)	schießen	shoot	—	sparare	disparar
tirer[2] (F)	vorziehen	draw	—	tirare in avanti	correr
tirer[3] (F)	ziehen	pull	—	tirare	tirar
tiring (E)	anstrengend	—	fatigant(e)	faticoso(a)	fatigoso(a)
tiritar (Es)	zittern	tremble	trembler	tremare	—
tirocinio (I)	Praktikum n	practical training	stage m	—	prácticas f pl
tiroir (F)	Schublade f	drawer	—	cassetto m	cajón m
Tisch (D)	—	table	table f	tavolo m	mesa f
Tischler (D)	—	carpenter	menuisier m	falegname m	carpintero m

	D	E	F	I	Es
Tischtennis (D)	—	tabletennis	ping-pong *m*	tennis da tavolo *m*	tenis de mesa *m*
tissu[1] (F)	Gewebe *n*	fabric	—	tessuto *m*	tela *f*
tissu[2] (F)	Stoff *m*	cloth	—	stoffa *f*	tela *f*
Titel (D)	—	title	titre *m*	titolo *m*	título *m*
title (E)	Titel *m*	—	titre *m*	titolo *m*	título *m*
titolo[1] (I)	Schlagzeile *f*	headline	manchette *f*	—	título *m*
titolo[2] (I)	Titel *m*	title	titre *m*	—	título *m*
titolo[3] (I)	Überschrift *f*	heading	titre *m*	—	título *m*
titre[1] (F)	Titel *m*	title	—	titolo *m*	título *m*
titre[2] (F)	Überschrift *f*	heading	—	titolo *m*	título *m*
tituber (F)	taumeln	reel	—	barcollare	vacilar
título[1] (Es)	Grad *m*	rank	grade *m*	rango *m*	—
título[2] (Es)	Schlagzeile *f*	headline	manchette *f*	titolo *m*	—
título[3] (Es)	Titel *m*	title	titre *m*	titolo *m*	—
título[4] (Es)	Überschrift *f*	heading	titre *m*	titolo *m*	—
to (E)	zu	—	de/á	da/di/a	para
tobillo (Es)	Knöchel *m*	ankle	cheville *f*	caviglia *f*	—
tocadiscos (Es)	Plattenspieler *m*	record player	tourne-disque *m*	giradischi *m*	—
tocar[1] (Es)	berühren	touch	toucher	toccare	—
tocar[2] (Es)	läuten	ring	sonner	suonare	—
tocar el timbre (Es)	klingeln	ring the bell	sonner	suonare	—
toccare (I)	berühren	touch	toucher	—	tocar
Tochter (D)	—	daughter	fille *f*	figlia *f*	hija *f*
tocino (Es)	Speck *m*	bacon	lard *m*	lardo *m*	—
Tod (D)	—	death	mort *f*	morte *f*	muerte *f*
today (E)	heute	—	aujourd'hui	oggi	hoy
todo[1] (Es)	alles	everything	tout	tutto	—
todo[2] (Es)	Ganze(s) *n*	lot	le tout	insieme *m*	—
todo derecho (Es)	geradeaus	straight ahead	tout droit	dritto	—
todos (Es)	alle	all	tous(toutes)	tutti(e)	—
toe (E)	Zehe *f*	—	doigt du pied *m*	dito del piede *m*	dedo del pie *m*
together[1] (E)	gemeinsam	—	ensemble	comune	juntos(as)
together[2] (E)	miteinander	—	ensemble	insieme	juntos(as)
together[3] (E)	zusammen	—	ensemble	insieme	juntos(as)
togliere (I)	wegnehmen	take away	enlever	—	quitar
toilet (E)	Toilette *f*	—	toilette *f*	toilette *f*	lavabo *m*
Toilette (D)	—	toilet	toilette *f*	toilette *f*	lavabo *m*
toilette (F)	Toilette *f*	toilet	—	toilette *f*	lavabo *m*
toilette (I)	Toilette *f*	toilet	toilette *f*	—	lavabo *m*
toit (F)	Dach *n*	roof	—	tetto *m*	techo *m*
tôle (F)	Blech *n*	sheet metal	—	latta *f*	chapa *f*
tomar (Es)	nehmen	take	prendre	prendere	—
tomar nota (Es)	vormerken	book	prendre note de	prendere nota di	—
Tomate (D)	—	tomato	tomate *f*	pomodoro *m*	tomate *m*
tomate (Es)	Tomate *f*	tomato	tomate *f*	pomodoro *m*	—
tomate (F)	Tomate *f*	tomato	—	pomodoro *m*	tomate *m*
tomato (E)	Tomate *f*	—	tomate *f*	pomodoro *m*	tomate *m*
tomba (I)	Grab *n*	grave	tombe *f*	—	tumba *f*

	D	E	F	I	Es
tombe (F)	Grab n	grave	—	tomba f	tumba f
tomber[1] (F)	fallen	fall	—	cadere	caer
tomber[2] (F)	stürzen	fall	—	cadere	caer
tomber[3] (F)	umfallen	fall over	—	cadere	caerse
tomber amoureux (F)	verlieben	fall in love	—	innamorarsi	enamorarse
tomber malade (F)	erkranken	get ill	—	ammalarsi	enfermar
tomorrow (E)	morgen	—	demain	domani	mañana
Ton (D)	—	sound	son m	suono m	sonido m
ton (E)	Tonne f	—	tonne f	tonnellata f	tonelada f
Tonband (D)	—	tape	bande magnétique f	nastro magnetico m	cinta magnetofónica f
tonelada (Es)	Tonne f	ton	tonne f	tonnellata f	—
tongue (E)	Zunge f	—	langue f	lingua f	lengua f
Tonne[1] (D)	—	barrel	tonneau m	botte f	barril m
Tonne[2] (D)	—	ton	tonne f	tonnellata f	tonelada f
tonne (F)	Tonne f	ton	—	tonnellata f	tonelada f
tonneau (F)	Tonne f	barrel	—	botte f	barril m
tonnellata (I)	Tonne f	ton	tonne f	—	tonelada f
tonnerre (F)	Donner m	thunder	—	tuono m	trueno m
tonno (I)	Thunfisch m	tuna	thon m	—	atún m
tonto[1] (Es)	albern	foolish	sot(te)	sciocco(a)	—
tonto[2] (Es)	dumm	stupid	bête	stupido(a)	—
tool (E)	Werkzeug n	—	outil m	utensile m	herramienta f
too little (E)	zuwenig	—	trop peu	troppo poco	demasiado poco
too many (E)	zuviele	—	trop	troppi(e)	demasiados(as)
too much (E)	zuviel	—	trop	troppo	demasiado
tooth (E)	Zahn m	—	dent f	dente m	diente m
toothache (E)	Zahnschmerzen pl	—	mal de dents m	mal di denti m	dolor de muelas m
toothbrush (E)	Zahnbürste f	—	brosse à dents f	spazzolino da denti m	cepillo de dientes m
toothpaste (E)	Zahnpasta f	—	dentifrice m	dentifricio m	pasta dentífrica f
Topf (D)	—	pot	casserole f	pentola f	olla f
topic (E)	Thema n	—	sujet m	tema m	tema m
topo (I)	Maus f	mouse	souris f	—	ratón m
Tor (D)	—	gate	porte f	porta f	puerta f
torbido (I)	trüb	dull	trouble	—	turbio(a)
torcer (Es)	abbiegen	turn off	tourner	svoltare	—
torch (E)	Taschenlampe f	—	lampe de poche f	lampadina tascabile f	linterna f
torcido (Es)	krumm	crooked	tordu(e)	storto(a)	—
tordu (F)	krumm	crooked	—	storto(a)	torcido(a)
tormenta[1] (Es)	Gewitter n	thunderstorm	orage m	temporale m	—
tormenta[2] (Es)	Unwetter n	thunderstorm	tempête f	maltempo m	—
tormentare (I)	quälen	torture	torturer	—	atormentar
tornare indietro (I)	zurückfahren	drive back	retourner	—	retroceder
tornillo (Es)	Schraube f	screw	vis f	vite f	—
toro (Es)	Stier m	bull	taureau m	toro m	—
toro (I)	Stier m	bull	taureau m	—	toro m

	D	E	F	I	Es
torpe (Es)	ungeschickt	clumsy	maladroit(e)	impacciato(a)	—
torre (Es)	Turm *m*	tower	tour *f*	torre *f*	—
torre (I)	Turm *m*	tower	tour *f*	—	torre *f*
torta (I)	Torte *f*	cake	gâteau *m*	—	tarta *f*
Torte (D)	—	cake	gâteau *m*	torta *f*	tarta *f*
tortilla (Es)	Omelett *n*	omelette	omelette *f*	frittata *f*	—
torto (I)	Unrecht *n*	wrong	injustice *f*	—	injusticia *f*
torture (E)	quälen	—	torturer	tormentare	atormentar
torturer (F)	quälen	torture	—	tormentare	atormentar
tos (Es)	Husten *m*	cough	toux *m*	tosse *f*	—
tosco (Es)	grob	coarse	grossier(-ière)	rozzo(a)	—
toser (Es)	husten	cough	tousser	tossire	—
tosse (I)	Husten *m*	cough	toux *m*	—	tos *f*
tossire (I)	husten	cough	tousser	—	toser
tostar (Es)	rösten	roast	griller	abbrustolire	—
tot (D)	—	dead	mort(e)	morto(a)	muerto(a)
tôt (F)	früh	early	—	presto	temprano
totale (I)	gesamt	entire	tout(e)	—	entero(a)
totalmente (Es)	restlos	completely	complètement	interamente	—
töten (D)	—	kill	tuer	uccidere	matar
touch (E)	berühren	—	toucher	toccare	tocar
toucher[1] (F)	berühren	touch	—	toccare	tocar
toucher[2] (F)	treffen	hit	—	colpire	alcanzar
tough (E)	zäh	—	coriace	duro(a)	duro(a)
toujours[1] (F)	immer	always	—	sempre	siempre
toujours[2] (F)	stets	always	—	sempre	siempre
Tour (D)	—	tour	excursion *f*	giro *m*	excursión *f*
tour (E)	Tour *f*	—	excursion *f*	giro *m*	excursión *f*
tour (F)	Turm *m*	tower	—	torre *f*	torre *f*
Tourist (D)	—	tourist	touriste *m*	turista *m*	turista *m*
tourist (E)	Tourist *m*	—	touriste *m*	turista *m*	turista *m*
touriste (F)	Tourist *m*	tourist	—	turista *m*	turista *m*
tourne-disque (F)	Plattenspieler *m*	record player	—	giradischi *m*	tocadiscos *m*
tourner[1] (F)	abbiegen	turn off	—	svoltare	torcer
tourner[2] (F)	drehen	turn	—	girare	girar
tourner[3] (F)	einbiegen	turn	—	svoltare	doblar
tourner[4] (F)	herumdrehen	turn around	—	girare	dar vuelta
tourner[5] (F)	umdrehen	turn around	—	girare	volver
tourner[6] (F)	wenden	turn	—	voltare	volver
tourner la page (F)	umblättern	turn over	—	voltare pagina	volver la hoja
tournevis (F)	Schrauben-zieher *m*	screwdriver	—	cacciavite *m*	destornillador *m*
tous (F)	alle	all!	—	tutti(e)	todos(as)
tous les deux (F)	beide	both	—	entrambi(e)	ambos(as)
tousser (F)	husten	cough	—	tossire	tocer
tout[1] (F)	ganz	whole	—	intero(a)	entero(a)
tout[2] (F)	gesamt	entire	—	totale	entero(a)
tout[3] (F)	alles	everything	—	tutto	todo

	D	E	F	I	Es
tout à coup (F)	plötzlich	suddenly	—	di colpo	de repente
tout au plus (F)	höchstens	at the most	—	al massimo	a lo sumo
tout droit (F)	geradeaus	straight ahead	—	dritto	todo derecho
toutes les heures (F)	stündlich	hourly	—	ogni ora	cada hora
toux (F)	Husten *m*	cough	—	tosse *f*	tos *f*
tovagliolo (I)	Serviette *f*	serviette	serviette *f*	—	servilleta *f*
towel (E)	Handtuch *n*	—	serviette *f*	asciugamano *m*	pañuelo *m*
tower (E)	Turm *m*	—	tour *f*	torre *f*	torre *f*
town (E)	Stadt *f*	—	ville *f*	città *f*	ciudad *f*
town centre (E)	Innenstadt *f*	—	centre ville *m*	centro città *m*	centro de ciudad *m*
town hall (E)	Rathaus *n*	—	mairie *f*	municipio *m*	ayuntamiento *m*
toxique (F)	giftig	poisonous	—	velenoso(a)	venenoso(a)
tra (I)	zwischen	between	entre	—	entre
trabajador (Es)	Arbeiter *m*	worker	ouvrier *m*	operaio *m*	—
trabajar (Es)	arbeiten	work	travailler	lavorare	—
trabajo (Es)	Arbeit *f*	work	travail *m*	lavoro *m*	—
track (E)	Gleis *n*	—	voie *f*	binario *m*	vía *f*
trade union (E)	Gewerkschaft *f*	—	syndicat *m*	sindacato *m*	sindicato *m*
tradire (I)	verraten	betray	trahir	—	traicionar
traducción (Es)	Übersetzung *f*	translation	traduction *f*	traduzione *f*	—
traducir (Es)	übersetzen	translate	traduire	tradurre	—
traduction (F)	Übersetzung *f*	translation	—	traduzione *f*	traducción *f*
traduire (F)	übersetzen	translate	—	tradurre	traducir
tradurre (I)	übersetzen	translate	traduire	—	traducir
traduzione (I)	Übersetzung *f*	translation	traduction *f*	—	traducción *f*
traer¹ (Es)	holen	fetch	aller chercher	andare a prendere	—
traer² (Es)	mitbringen	bring (along)	apporter	portare con sé	—
traffic (E)	Verkehr *m*	—	circulation *f*	traffico *m*	tráfico *m*
traffic jam (E)	Stau *m*	—	embouteillage *m*	ingorgo *m*	embotellamiento *m*
traffic lights (E)	Ampel *f*	—	feux *m pl*	semaforo *m*	semáforo *m*
traffico (I)	Verkehr *m*	traffic	circulation *f*	—	tráfico *m*
tráfico (Es)	Verkehr *m*	traffic	circulation *f*	traffico *m*	—
tragar (Es)	schlucken	swallow	avaler	inghiottire	—
tragedia (Es)	Tragödie *f*	tragedy	tragédie *f*	tragedia *f*	—
tragedia (I)	Tragödie *f*	tragedy	tragédie *f*	—	tragedia *f*
tragédie (F)	Tragödie *f*	tragedy	—	tragedia *f*	tragedia *f*
tragedy (E)	Tragödie *f*	—	tragédie *f*	tragedia *f*	tragedia *f*
tragen (D)	—	carry	porter	portare	llevar
Träger (D)	—	carrier	porteur *m*	facchino *m*	mozo *m*
traghetto (I)	Fähre *f*	ferry	bac *m*	—	transbordador *m*
Tragödie (D)	—	tragedy	tragédie *f*	tragedia *f*	tragedia *f*
trahir (F)	verraten	betray	—	tradire	traicionar
traicionar (Es)	verraten	betray	trahir	tradire	—
train (E)	Zug *m*	—	train *m*	treno *m*	tren *m*
train (F)	Zug *m*	train	—	treno *m*	tren *m*
trait (F)	Strich *m*	line	—	linea *f*	línea *f*
traitement (F)	Behandlung *f*	treatment	—	trattamento *m*	tratamiento *m*

	D	E	F	I	Es
traiter (F)	behandeln	treat	—	trattare	tratar
traje (Es)	Anzug *m*	suit	costume *m*	vestito *m*	—
traje de baño (Es)	Badeanzug *m*	swimsuit	maillot de bain *m*	costume da bagno *m*	—
trajet (F)	Strecke *f*	stretch	—	tratto *m*	trayecto *m*
tram (E)	Straßenbahn *f*	—	tramway *m*	tram *m*	tranvía *m*
tram (I)	Straßenbahn *f*	tram	tramway *m*	—	tranvía *m*
tramonto del sole (I)	Sonnen-untergang *m*	sunset	coucher du soleil *m*	—	puesta del sol *f*
tramway (F)	Straßenbahn *f*	tram	—	tram *m*	tranvía *m*
tranchant (F)	scharf	sharp	—	tagliente	cortante
Träne (D)	—	tear	larme *f*	lacrima *f*	lágrima *f*
tranquille (F)	ruhig	quiet	—	calmo(a)	quieto(a)
tranquilo (Es)	still	quiet	calme	calmo(a)	—
transbordador (Es)	Fähre *f*	ferry	bac *m*	traghetto *m*	—
transbordar[1] (Es)	umsteigen	change	changer (de train)	cambiare	—
transbordar[2] (Es)	umladen	transfer	transborder	trasbordare	—
transborder (F)	umladen	transfer	—	trasbordare	transbordar
transfer[1] (E)	überweisen	—	virer	trasferire	transferir
transfer[2] (E)	umladen	—	transborder	trasbordare	transbordar
transfer[3] (E)	Überweisung *f*	—	virement *m*	trasferimento *m*	transferencia *f*
transferencia (Es)	Überweisung *f*	transfer	virement *m*.	trasferimento *m*	—
transferir[1] (Es)	überschreiben	make over	céder	cedere	—
transferir[2] (Es)	überweisen	transfer	virer	trasferire	—
transfert (F)	Umbuchung *f*	alteration	—	riporto *m*	cambio *m*
transformer (F)	verändern	change	—	mutare	cambiar
Transit (D)	—	transit	transit *m*	transito *m*	tránsito *m*
transit[1] (E)	Durchfahrt *f*	—	passage *m*	passaggio *m*	paso *m*
transit[2] (E)	Transit *m*	—	transit *m*	transito *m*	tránsito *m*
transit (F)	Transit *m*	transit	—	transito *m*	tránsito *m*
tránsito (Es)	Transit *m*	transit	transit *m*	transito *m*	—
transito[1] (I)	Durchreise *f*	passing through	passage *m*	—	paso *m*
transito[2] (I)	Transit *m*	transit	transit *m*	—	tránsito *m*
translate (E)	übersetzen	—	traduire	tradurre	traducir
translation (E)	Übersetzung *f*	—	traduction *f*	traduzione *f*	traducción *f*
transmettre[1] (F)	ausrichten	pass on a message	—	riferire	comunicar
transmettre[2] (F)	senden	broadcast	—	trasmettere	transmitir
transmettre[3] (F)	übermitteln	convey	—	trasmettere	transmitir
transmission (E)	Sendung *f*	—	diffusion *f*	trasmissione *f*	emisión *f*
transmitir[1] (Es)	senden	broadcast	transmettre	trasmettere	—
transmitir[2] (Es)	überbringen	deliver	remettre	portare	—
transmitir[3] (Es)	übermitteln	convey	transmettre	trasmettere	—
transmitir[4] (Es)	übergeben	hand over	remettre	consegnare	—
transmitir hereditariamente (Es)	vererben	bequeath	léguer	lasciare in eredità	—
transpirer (F)	schwitzen	sweat	—	sudare	sudar
Transport (D)	—	transport	transport *m*	trasporto *m*	transporte *m*
transport[1] (E)	transportieren	—	transporter	trasportare	transportar
transport[2] (E)	Transport *m*	—	transport *m*	trasporto *m*	transporte *m*

	D	E	F	I	Es
transport (F)	Transport *m*	transport	—	trasporto *m*	transporte *m*
transportar (Es)	transportieren	transport	transporter	trasportare	—
transporte (Es)	Transport *m*	transport	transport *m*	trasporto *m*	—
transporter (F)	transportieren	transport	—	trasportare	transportar
transportieren (D)	—	transport	transporter	trasportare	transportar
tranvía (Es)	Straßenbahn *f*	tram	tramway *m*	tram *m*	—
trasbordare (I)	umladen	transfer	transborder	—	transbordar
trascurare (I)	vernachlässigen	neglect	négliger	—	descuidar
trasferimento (I)	Überweisung *f*	transfer	virement *m*	—	tranferencia *f*
trasferire (I)	überweisen	transfer	virer	—	transferir
trasferirsi (I)	übersiedeln	move	émigrer	—	trasladarse
trasladarse (Es)	übersiedeln	move	émigrer	trasferirsi	—
trasloco (I)	Umzug *m*	move	déménagement *m*	—	mudanza *f*
trasmettere[1] (I)	senden	broadcast	transmettre	—	transmitir
trasmettere[2] (I)	übermitteln	convey	transmettre	—	transmitir
trasmettitore (I)	Sender *m*	station	émetteur *m*	—	emisora *f*
trasmissione (I)	Sendung *f*	transmission	diffusion *f*	—	emisión *f*
trasportare (I)	transportieren	transport	transporter	—	transportar
trasporto (I)	Transport *m*	transport	transport *m*	—	transporte *m*
tratamiento (Es)	Behandlung *f*	treatment	traitement *m*	trattamento *m*	—
tratar (Es)	behandeln	treat	traiter	trattare	—
trattamento (I)	Behandlung *f*	treatment	traitement *m*	—	tratamiento *m*
trattare (I)	behandeln	treat	traiter	—	tratar
trattenere (I)	einbehalten	keep	retenir	—	retener
tratto (I)	Strecke *f*	stretch	trajet *m*	—	trayecto *m*
Traube (D)	—	grape	grappe *f*	uva *f*	uva *f*
Traum (D)	—	dream	rêve *m*	sogno *m*	sueño *m*
träumen (D)	—	dream	rêver	sognare	soñar
traurig (D)	—	sad	triste	triste	triste
travail (F)	Arbeit *f*	work	—	lavoro *m*	trabajo *m*
travailler (F)	arbeiten	work	—	lavorare	trabajar
travailleur (F)	fleißig	diligent	—	diligente	activo(a)
travel (E)	reisen	—	voyager	viaggiare	viajar
travel agency[1] (E)	Reisebüro *n*	—	agence de voyages *f*	agenzia turistica *f*	oficina de viajes *f*
travel agency[2] (E)	Verkehrsbüro *n*	—	bureau touristique *m*	ufficio turistico *m*	oficina de turismo *f*
traveller (E)	Reisender *m*	—	voyageur *m*	viaggiatore *m*	viajero *m*
traveller's cheque (E)	Reisescheck *m*	—	chèque de voyage *m*	assegno turistico *m*	cheque de viaje *m*
traversa (I)	Querstraße *f*	intersecting road	rue transversale *f*	—	travesía *f*
traversata (I)	Überfahrt *f*	crossing	traversée *f*	—	travesía *f*
traversée (F)	Überfahrt *f*	crossing	—	traversata *f*	travesía *f*
traverser (F)	überqueren	cross	—	attraversare	atraveasar
travesía[1] (Es)	Querstraße *f*	intersecting road	rue transversale *f*	traversa *f*	—
travesía[2] (Es)	Überfahrt *f*	crossing	traversée *f*	traversata *f*	—
tray (E)	Tablett *n*	—	plateau *m*	vassoio *m*	bandeja *f*
trayecto (Es)	Strecke *f*	stretch	trajet *m*	tratto *m*	—
tre (I)	drei	three	trois	—	tres

	D	E	F	I	Es
treasure (E)	Schatz *m*	—	trésor *m*	tesoro *m*	tesoro *m*
treat (E)	behandeln	—	traiter	trattare	tratar
treatment[1] (E)	Behandlung *f*	—	traitement *m*	trattamento *m*	tratamiento *m*
treatment[2] (E)	Kur *f*	—	cure *f*	cura *f*	cura *f*
trébucher (F)	stolpern	stumble	—	inciampare	tropezar
treccia (I)	Zopf *m*	plait	natte *f*	—	trenza *f*
trece (Es)	dreizehn	thirteen	treize	tredici	—
tredici (I)	dreizehn	thirteen	treize	—	trece
tree (E)	Baum *m*	—	arbre *m*	albero *m*	árbol *m*
treffen[1] (D)	—	hit	toucher	colpire	alcanzar
treffen[2] (D)	—	meet	rencontrer	incontrare	encontrar
Treffen (D)	—	meeting	rencontre *f*	incontro *m*	encuentro *m*
treiben (D)	—	drive	mener	spingere	estimular
treinta (Es)	dreißig	thirty	trente	trenta	—
treize (F)	dreizehn	thirteen	—	tredici	trece
tremare (I)	zittern	tremble	trembler	—	tiritar
tremble (E)	zittern	—	trembler	tremare	tiritar
tremblement de terre (F)	Erdbeben *n*	earthquake	—	terremoto *m*	terremoto *m*
trembler (F)	zittern	tremble	—	tremare	tiritar
tremendous (E)	gewaltig	—	énorme	enorme	formidable
tren (Es)	Zug *m*	train	train *m*	treno *m*	—
tren expreso[1] (Es)	D-Zug *m*	through train	express *m*	direttissimo *m*	—
tren expreso[2] (Es)	Eilzug *m*	limited stop train	express *m*	treno diretto *m*	—
tren expreso[3] (Es)	Schnellzug *m*	express train	rapide *m*	treno direttissimo *m*	—
trennen (D)	—	separate	séparer	separare	separar
Trennung (D)	—	separation	séparation *f*	separazione *f*	separación *f*
treno (I)	Zug *m*	train	train *m*	—	tren *m*
treno direttissimo (I)	Schnellzug *m*	express train	rapide *m*	—	tren expreso *m*
treno diretto (I)	Eilzug *m*	limited stop train	express *m*	—	tren expreso *m*
trenta (I)	dreißig	thirty	trente	—	treinta
trente (F)	dreißig	thirty	—	trenta	treinta
trenza (Es)	Zopf *m*	plait	natte *f*	treccia *f*	—
Treppe (D)	—	stairs	escalier *m*	scala *f*	escalera *f*
tres (Es)	drei	three	trois	tre	—
très (F)	sehr	very	—	molto	mucho/muy
trésor (F)	Schatz *m*	treasure	—	tesoro *m*	tesoro *m*
treten (D)	—	kick	mettre le pied sur	pestare	pisar
treu (D)	—	faithful	fidèle	fedele	fiel
trial (E)	Prozeß *m*	—	procès *m*	processo *m*	proceso *m*
tribunal (Es)	Gericht *n*	court	tribunal *m*	tribunale *m*	—
tribunal (F)	Gericht *n*	court	—	tribunale *m*	tribunal *m*
tribunale (I)	Gericht *n*	court	tribunal *m*	—	tribunal *m*
tricot (F)	Unterhemd *n*	vest	—	canottiera *f*	camiseta *f*

	D	E	F	I	Es
tricoter (F)	stricken	knit	—	lavorare a maglia	hacer punto
trier (F)	sortieren	sort	—	assortire	clasificar
trigo (Es)	Weizen *m*	wheat	blé *m*	frumento *m*	—
trinkbar (D)	—	drinkable	potable	potabile	potable
trinken (D)	—	drink	boire	bere	beber
Trinkgeld (D)	—	tip	pourboire *m*	mancia *f*	propina *f*
Trinkwasser (D)	—	drinking water	eau potable *f*	acqua potabile *f*	agua potable *f*
triste (Es)	traurig	sad	triste	triste	—
triste (F)	traurig	sad	—	triste	triste
triste (I)	traurig	sad	triste	—	triste
trocken (D)	—	dry	sec(sèche)	asciutto(a)	seco(a)
trocknen (D)	—	dry	sécher	asciugare	secar
trois (F)	drei	three	—	tre	tres
troisième (F)	dritte(r,s)	third	—	terzo(a)	tercera(o)
tromper[1] (F)	betrügen	cheat	—	ingannare	engañar
tromper[2] (F)	täuschen	deceive	—	ingannare	engañar
tromper, se (F)	irren	be mistaken	—	sbagliare	equivocarse
tromperie (F)	Betrug *m*	fraud	—	inganno *m*	engaño *m*
trop[1] (F)	zuviel	too much	—	troppo	demasiado
trop[2] (F)	zuviele	too many	—	troppi(e)	demasiados(as)
tropezar (Es)	stolpern	stumble	trébucher	inciampare	—
tropfen (D)	—	drip	dégoutter	gocciolare	gotear
Tropfen (D)	—	drop	goutte *f*	goccia *f*	gota *f*
tropical (E)	tropisch	—	tropical(e)	tropicale	tropical
tropical (Es)	tropisch	tropical	tropical(e)	tropicale	—
tropical (F)	tropisch	tropical	—	tropicale	tropical
tropicale (I)	tropisch	tropical	tropical(e)	—	tropical
tropisch (D)	—	tropical	tropical(e)	tropicale	tropical
trop peu (F)	zuwenig	too little	—	troppo poco	demasiado poco
troppi (I)	zuviele	too many	trop	—	demasiados(as)
troppo (I)	zuviel	too much	trop	—	demasiado
troppo poco (I)	zuwenig	too little	trop peu	—	demasiado poco
Trost (D)	—	consolation	consolation *f*	consolazione *f*	consuelo *m*
trösten (D)	—	comfort	consoler	consolare	consolar
trota (I)	Forelle *f*	trout	truite *f*	—	trucha *f*
trottoir (F)	Gehweg *m*	pavement	—	marciapiede *m*	acera *f*
trotz (D)	—	despite	malgré	nonostante	a pesar de
trotzdem (D)	—	nevertheless	malgré tout	tuttavia	no obstante
trou (F)	Loch *n*	hole	—	buco *m*	agujero *m*
trouble (E)	Not *f*	—	détresse *f*	miseria *f*	necesidad *f*
trouble[1] (F)	Störung *f*	interference	—	disturbo *m*	molestia *f*
trouble[2] (F)	trüb	dull	—	torbido(a)	turbio(a)
troublesome (E)	lästig	—	importun(e)	molesto(a)	desagradable
trou de la serrure (F)	Schlüsselloch *n*	keyhole	—	buco della chiave *m*	ojo de la cerradura *m*

	D	E	F	I	Es
trousers (E)	Hose f	—	pantalon m	pantaloni m pl	pantalón m
trout (E)	Forelle f	—	truite f	trota f	trucha f
trouver (F)	finden	find	—	trovare	encontrar
trouver, se[1] (F)	befinden, sich	feel	—	trovarsi	encontrarse
trouver, se[2] (F)	liegen	lie	—	giacere	estar tumbado(a)
trovare (I)	finden	find	trouver	—	encontrar
trovarsi (I)	befinden, sich	feel	trouver, se	—	encontrarse
trüb (D)	—	dull	trouble	torbido(a)	turbio(a)
truc (F)	Zeug n	stuff	—	cose f pl	cosa f
trucco (I)	Schminke f	make-up	maquillage m	—	maquillaje m
trucha (Es)	Forelle f	trout	truite f	trota f	—
true (E)	wahr	—	vrai(e)	vero	verdadero(a)
trueno (Es)	Donner m	thunder	tonnerre m	tuono m	—
truite (F)	Forelle f	trout	—	trota f	trucha f
Trümmer (D)	—	ruins	décombres m pl	macerie f pl	escombros m pl
trust (E)	vertrauen	—	avoir confiance	fidarsi	confiar
truth (E)	Wahrheit f	—	vérité f	verità f	verdad f
Truthahn (D)	—	turkey	dindon m	tacchino m	pavo m
try[1] (E)	probieren	—	essayer	assaggiare	probar
try[2] (E)	Versuch m	—	essai m	tentativo m	intento m
try[3] (E)	versuchen	—	essayer	provare	probar
try on (E)	anprobieren	—	essayer	provare	probar
Tschecho-slowakei (D)	—	Czechoslovakia	Tchécoslovaquie f	Cecoslovacchia f	Checoslovaquia f
tschüs! (D)	—	bye!	salut!	ciao!	¡hasta luego!
tú (Es)	du	you	tu/toi	tu	—
tu (I)	du	you	tu/toi	—	tú
tu (F)	du	you	—	tu	tú
tube (E)	Rohr n	—	tube m	tubo m	tubo m
tube (F)	Rohr n	tube	—	tubo m	tubo m
tubería (Es)	Leitung f	pipe	tuyau m	conduttura f	—
tubo (Es)	Rohr n	tube	tube m	tubo m	—
tubo (I)	Rohr n	tube	tube m	—	tubo m
Tuch (D)	—	cloth	étoffe f	panno m	paño m
tuer[1] (F)	töten	kill	—	uccidere	matar
tuer[2] (F)	umbringen	kill	—	uccidere	matar
Tuesday (E)	Dienstag m	—	mardi m	martedì m	martes m
tulip (E)	Tulpe f	—	tulipe f	tulipano m	tulipán m
tulipán (Es)	Tulpe f	tulip	tulipe f	tulipano m	—
tulipano (I)	Tulpe f	tulip	tulipe f	—	tulipán m
tulipe (F)	Tulpe f	tulip	—	tulipano m	tulipán m
Tulpe (D)	—	tulip	tulipe f	tulipano m	tulipán m
tumba (Es)	Grab n	grave	tombe f	tomba f	—
tumbona (Es)	Liegestuhl m	deck chair	chaise longue f	sedia a sdraio f	—
tun (D)	—	do	faire	fare	hacer

	D	E	F	I	Es
tuna (E)	Thunfisch *m*	—	thon *m*	tonno *m*	atún *m*
túnel (Es)	Tunnel *m*	tunnel	tunnel *m*	galleria *f*	—
Tunnel (D)	—	tunnel	tunnel *m*	galleria *f*	túnel *m*
tunnel (E)	Tunnel *m*	—	tunnel *m*	galleria *f*	túnel *m*
tunnel (F)	Tunnel *m*	tunnel	—	galleria *f*	túnel *m*
tuono (I)	Donner *m*	thunder	tonnerre *m*	—	trueno *m*
Tür (D)	—	door	porte *f*	porta *f*	puerta *f*
turbio (Es)	trüb	dull	trouble	torbido(a)	—
Turchia (I)	Türkei *f*	Turkey	Turquie *f*	—	Turquía *f*
turista (Es)	Tourist *m*	tourist	touriste *m*	turista *m*	—
turista (I)	Tourist *m*	tourist	touriste *m*	—	turista *m*
Türkei (D)	—	Turkey	Turquie *f*	Turchia *f*	Turquía *f*
turkey (E)	Truthahn *m*	—	dindon *m*	tacchino *m*	pavo *m*
Turkey (E)	Türkei *f*	—	Turquie *f*	Turchia *f*	Turquía *f*
Turm (D)	—	tower	tour *f*	torre *f*	torre *f*
turn[1] (E)	drehen	—	tourner	girare	girar
turn[2] (E)	einbiegen	—	tourner	svoltare	doblar
turn[3] (E)	wenden	—	tourner	voltare	volver
turn around[1] (E)	herumdrehen	—	tourner	girare	dar vuelta
turn around[2] (E)	umdrehen	—	tourner	girare	volver
turn back (E)	umkehren	—	retourner	ritornare	regresar
turnen (D)	—	do gymnastic exercises	faire de la gymnastique	fare ginnastica	hacer gimnasia
turn off[1] (E)	abstellen	—	arrêter	spegnere	desconectar
turn off[2] (E)	abbiegen	—	tourner	svoltare	torcer
turn off[3] (E)	zudrehen	—	fermer	chiudere	cerrar
turn on (E)	anstellen	—	mettre en marche	accendere	poner
turn over (E)	umblättern	—	tourner la page	voltare pagina	volver la hoja
Turquía (Es)	Türkei *f*	Turkey	Turquie *f*	Turchia *f*	—
Turquie (F)	Türkei *f*	Turkey	—	Turchia *f*	Turquía *f*
Tüte (D)	—	bag	sac *m*	sacchetto *m*	bolsa *f*
tutear (Es)	duzen	use the familiar form	tutoyer	dare del tu	—
tutoyer (F)	duzen	use the familiar form	—	dare del tu	tutear
tuttavia[1] (I)	jedoch	however	cependant	—	sin embargo
tuttavia[2] (I)	dennoch	nevertheless	cependant	—	sin embargo
tuttavia[3] (I)	trotzdem	nevertheless	malgré tout	—	no obstante
tutti (I)	alle	all	tous(toutes)	—	todos(as)
tutto (I)	alles	everything	tout	—	todo
tuyau (F)	Leitung *f*	pipe	—	conduttura *f*	tubería *f*
twelve (E)	zwölf	—	douze	dodici	doce
twenty (E)	zwanzig	—	vingt	venti	veinte
twice (E)	zweimal	—	deux fois	due volte	dos veces
twins (E)	Zwillinge *pl*	—	jumeaux *m pl*	gemelli *m pl*	gemelos *m pl*

	D	E	F	I	Es
two (E)	zwei	—	deux	due	dos
type (E)	tippen	—	taper (à la machine)	battere a macchina	escribir a máquina
typewriter (E)	Schreibmaschine f	—	machine à écrire f	macchina da scrivere f	máquina de escribir f
typical (E)	typisch	—	typique	tipico(a)	típico(a)
typique (F)	typisch	typical	—	tipico(a)	típico(a)
typisch (D)	—	typical	typique	tipico(a)	típico(a)
tyre (E)	Reifen m	—	pneu m	pneumatico m	neumático m
U-Bahn (D)	—	underground	métro m	metropolitana f	metro m
ubbidiente (I)	gehorsam	obedient	obéissant(e)	—	obediente
ubbidire (I)	gehorchen	obey	obéir	—	obedecer
übel (D)	—	bad	mauvais(e)	cattivo(a)	malo(a)
Übelkeit (D)	—	nausea	nausée f	nausea f	náuseas f pl
üben (D)	—	practise	étudier	esercitarsi	practicar
über (D)	—	over/about	sur	su/sopra/per	por/sobre
überall (D)	—	everywhere	partout	dappertutto	por todas partes
überbringen (D)	—	deliver	remettre	portare	transmitir
übereinander (D)	—	one upon the other	l'un(e) sur l'autre	uno sopra l'altro	uno sobre otro
übereinstimmen (D)	—	agree	être d'accord	concordare	estar de acuerdo
überfahren (D)	—	run over	écraser	investire	atropellar
Überfahrt (D)	—	crossing	traversée f	traversata f	travesía f
Überfall (D)	—	raid	attaque f	aggressione f	asalto m
überfallen (D)	—	raid	attaquer	assalire	asaltar
überflüssig (D)	—	superfluous	superflu(e)	superfluo(a)	superfluo(a)
überfüllt (D)	—	crowded	bondé(e)	pieno(a) zeppo(a)	abarrotado(a)
Übergang (D)	—	crossing	passage m	passaggio m	paso m
übergeben (D)	—	hand over	remettre	consegnare	transmitir
überhaupt (D)	—	at all	en général	in genere	en general
überholen (D)	—	overtake	doubler	sorpassare	adelantar
überleben (D)	—	survive	survivre	sopravvivere	sobrevivir
überlegen (D)	—	consider	réfléchir à	riflettere	pensar
übermitteln (D)	—	convey	transmettre	trasmettere	transmitir
übermorgen (D)	—	day after tomorrow	après-demain	dopodomani	pasado mañana
übernachten (D)	—	stay the night	passer la nuit	pernottare	pernoctar
Übernachtung (D)	—	spending the night	logement pour une nuit m	pernottamento m	pernoctación f
übernehmen (D)	—	take over	reprendre	accettare	aceptar
überprüfen (D)	—	check	contrôler	esaminare	examinar
überqueren (D)	—	cross	traverser	attraversare	atraveasar
überraschen (D)	—	surprise	surprendre	sorprendere	sorprender
überrascht (D)	—	surprised	surpris(e)	sorpreso(a)	sorprendido(a)
Überraschung (D)	—	surprise	surprise f	sorpresa f	sorpresa f
überreden (D)	—	convince	persuader	persuadere	persuadir
überreichen (D)	—	hand over	présenter	consegnare	entregar
überschätzen (D)	—	overestimate	surestimer	sopravvalutare	sobrevalorar
überschreiben (D)	—	make over	céder	cedere	transferir
Überschrift (D)	—	heading	titre m	titolo m	título m

	D	E	F	I	Es
Überschwemmung (D)	—	flood	inondation f	inondazione f	inundación f
übersehen (D)	—	ignore	ignorer	non vedere	no ver
übersenden (D)	—	send	envoyer	spedire	envíar
übersetzen (D)	—	translate	traduire	tradurre	traducir
Übersetzung (D)	—	translation	traduction f	traduzione f	traducción f
übersiedeln (D)	—	move	émigrer	trasferirsi	transladarse
übertreiben (D)	—	exaggerate	exagérer	esagerare	exagerar
Übertreibung (D)	—	exaggeration	exagération f	esagerazione f	exageración f
übertrieben (D)	—	exaggerated	exagéré(e)	esagerato(a)	exagerado(a)
überwachen (D)	—	supervise	surveiller	sorvegliare	vigilar
überweisen (D)	—	transfer	virer	trasferire	transferir
Überweisung (D)	—	transfer	virement m	versamento m	transferencia f
überzeugen (D)	—	convince	convaincre	convincere	convencer
üblich (D)	—	usual	habituel(le)	solito(a)	usual
ubriacarsi (I)	betrinken, sich	get drunk	enivrer, se	—	emborracharse
ubriaco (I)	betrunken	drunk	soûl(e)	—	borracho(a)
übrig (D)	—	left	restant(e)	restante	restante
übrigbleiben (D)	—	be left	rester	avanzare	quedar
übrigens (D)	—	by the way	d'ailleurs	del resto	por lo demás
übriglassen (D)	—	leave	laisser	lasciare	dejar
Übung (D)	—	exercise	exercice m	esercizio f	ejercicio m
uccello (I)	Vogel m	bird	oiseau m	—	pájaro m
uccidere[1] (I)	töten	kill	tuer	—	matar
uccidere[2] (I)	umbringen	kill	tuer	—	matar
udito (I)	Gehör n	hearing	ouïe f	—	oreja f
Ufer (D)	—	shore	bord m	riva f	orilla f
ufficiale[1] (I)	amtlich	official	officiel(le)	—	oficial
ufficiale[2] (I)	offiziell	official	officiel(le)	—	oficial
ufficio[1] (I)	Amt n	office	bureau m	—	oficio m
ufficio[2] (I)	Büro n	office	bureau m	—	oficina f
ufficio di cambio (I)	Wechselstube f	bureau de change	bureau de change m		casa de cambio f
ufficio oggetti smarriti (I)	Fundbüro n	lost property office	bureau des objets trouvés m	—	oficina de objetos perdidos f
ufficio postale (I)	Postamt n	post office	bureau de poste m	—	oficina de correos f
ufficio turistico (I)	Verkehrsbüro n	travel agency	bureau touristique m	—	oficina de turismo f
ugly (E)	häßlich	—	laid(e)	brutto(a)	feo(a)
uguale (I)	egal	all the same	égal(e)	—	igual
Uhr (D)	—	watch	montre f	orologio m	reloj m
última (Es)	letzte(r,s)	last	dernier(-ière)	ultimo(a)	—
ultimo (I)	letzte(r,s)	last	dernier(-ière)	—	última(o)
um (D)	—	at/around	autour de/à	intorno a/a	alrededor de/a las
umano (I)	menschlich	human	humain(e)	—	humano(a)
umarmen (D)	—	embrace	embrasser	abbracciare	abrazar
umblättern (D)	—	turn over	tourner la page	voltare pagina	volver la hoja
umbrella[1] (E)	Regenschirm m	—	parapluie m	ombrello m	paraguas m
umbrella[2] (E)	Schirm m	—	parapluie m	ombrello m	paraguas m
umbringen (D)	—	kill	tuer	uccidere	matar

	D	E	F	I	Es
Umbuchung (D)	—	alteration	transfert m	riporto m	cambio m
umdrehen (D)	—	turn around	tourner	girare	volver
umfallen (D)	—	fall over	tomber	cadere	caerse
Umfrage (D)	—	poll	enquête f	inchiesta f	encuesta f
Umgangssprache (D)	—	colloquial language	langue familière f	linguaggio corrente m	lenguaje coloquial m
umgeben (D)	—	surround	entourer	circondare	rodear
Umgebung (D)	—	surroundings	environs m pl	dintorni m pl	alrededores m pl
umgekehrt (D)	—	vice versa	vice versa	inverso(a)	contrario(a)
umido (I)	feucht	damp	humide	—	húmedo(a)
umkehren (D)	—	turn back	retourner	ritornare	regresar
umkleiden (D)	—	change	changer de vêtements	cambiarsi	cambiarse de ropa
umladen (D)	—	transfer	transborder	trasbordare	transbordar
Umleitung (D)	—	diversion	déviation f	deviazione f	desviación f
umore (I)	Laune f	mood	humeur f	—	humor m
umrechnen (D)	—	convert	convertir	convertire	convertir
Umschlag (D)	—	envelope	enveloppe f	busta f	sobre m
umschmeißen (D)	—	throw over	renverser	rovesciare	derribar
umsonst (D)	—	for nothing	en vain	per niente	en vano
Umstände (D)	—	circumstances	circonstances f pl	circostanze f pl	circunstancias f pl
umständlich (D)	—	complicated	compliqué(e)	complicato(a)	complicado(a)
umsteigen (D)	—	change	changer (de train)	cambiare	transbordar
umtauschen (D)	—	exchange	échanger	cambiare	cambiar
umwechseln (D)	—	change	changer	cambiare	cambiar
Umweg (D)	—	detour	détour m	deviazione f	rodeo m
Umwelt (D)	—	environment	environnement m	ambiente m	medio ambiente m
umziehen¹ (D)	—	change	changer, se	cambiarsi	cambiarse
umziehen² (D)	—	move	déménager	cambiare casa	cambiar
Umzug (D)	—	move	déménagement m	trasloco m	mudanza f
un¹ (F)	eins	one	—	uno(a)	uno(a)
un² (F)	eine(r,s)	one	—	un(a)	una/un/uno
un (I)	eine(r,s)	one	un(e)	—	una/un/uno
una (Es)	eine(r,s)	one	un(e)	un(a)	—
uña (Es)	Nagel m	nail	ongle m	unghia f	—
unabhängig (D)	—	independent	indépendant(e)	indipendente	independiente
unable to make it (E)	verhindert	—	empêché(e)	impedito(a)	impedido(a)
unangenehm (D)	—	unpleasant	désagréable	spiacevole	desagradable
unanständig (D)	—	indecent	indécent(e)	indecente	inmoral
unauthorized (E)	unbefugt	—	non autorisé(e)	non autorizzato(a)	no autorizado(a)
una vez (Es)	einmal	once	une fois	una volta	—
una volta (I)	einmal	once	une fois	—	una vez
unbearable (E)	unerträglich	—	insupportable	insopportabile	inaguantable
unbedingt (D)	—	absolutely	absolument	assolutamente	absolutamente
unbefugt (D)	—	unauthorized	non autorisé(e)	non autorizzato(a)	no autorizado(a)
unbegrenzt (D)	—	unlimited	illimité(e)	illimitato(a)	ilimitado(a)
unbekannt (D)	—	unknown	inconnu(e)	sconosciuto(a)	desconocido(a)

	D	E	F	I	Es
unbequem (D)	—	uncomfortable	inconfortable	scomodo(a)	incómodo(a)
unbesetzt (D)	—	unoccupied	vacant(e)	libero(a)	desocupado(a)
unbestimmt (D)	—	uncertain	indéfini(e)	incerto(a)	indeterminado(a)
uncertain[1] (E)	unsicher	—	incertain(e)	incerto(a)	inseguro(a)
uncertain[2] (E)	unbestimmt	—	indéfini(e)	incerto(a)	indeterminado(a)
uncertain[3] (E)	ungewiß	—	incertain(e)	incerto(a)	incierto(a)
uncle (E)	Onkel m	—	oncle m	zio m	tío m
uncomfortable[1] (E)	ungemütlich	—	désagréable	poco accogliente	incómodo(a)
uncomfortabie[2] (E)	unbequem	—	inconfortable	scomodo(a)	incómodo(a)
und (D)	—	and	et	e	y
undankbar (D)	—	ungrateful	ingrat(e)	ingrato(a)	desagradecido(a)
undecided (E)	unentschlossen	—	irrésolu(e)	indeciso(a)	irresoluto(a)
under (E)	unter	—	sous	al di sotto di	debajo de
underground (E)	U-Bahn f	—	métro m	metropolitana f	metro m
underline (E)	unterstreichen	—	souligner	sottolineare	subrayar
underneath (E)	darunter	—	en dessous	sotto	por debajo
underpants (E)	Unterhose f	—	slip m	mutande f pl	calzoncillos m pl
understand (E)	verstehen	—	comprendre	capire	entender
understanding (E)	Verständnis n	—	compréhension f	comprensione f	comprensión f
undertake (E)	unternehmen	—	entreprendre	intraprendere	emprender
underwear (E)	Unterwäsche f	—	sous-vêtements m pl	biancheria intima f	ropa interior f
undici (I)	elf	eleven	onze	—	once
unecht (D)	—	fake	imité(e)	falso(a)	falso(a)
une fois (F)	einmal	once	—	una volta	una vez
unemployed (E)	arbeitslos	—	en chômage	disoccupato(a)	desempleado(a)
unemployment (E)	Arbeitslosigkeit f	—	chômage m	disoccupazione f	desempleo m
unentbehrlich (D)	—	indispensable	indispensable	indispensabile	indispensable
unentschlossen (D)	—	undecided	irrésolu(e)	indeciso(a)	irresoluto(a)
unequivocal (E)	eindeutig	—	incontestable	univoco(a)	evidente
unerfahren (D)	—	inexperienced	inexpérimenté(e)	inesperto(a)	inexperto(a)
unerträglich (D)	—	unbearable	insupportable	insopportabile	inaguantable
unerwartet (D)	—	unexpected	inattendu(e)	inatteso(a)	inesperado(a)
unerwünscht (D)	—	unwelcome	inopportun(e)	indesiderato(a)	indeseado(a)
un et demi (F)	anderthalb	one and a half	—	uno(a) e mezzo	uno(a) y medio(a)
uneven (E)	ungerade	—	impair(e)	dispari	impar
unexpected (E)	unerwartet	—	inattendu(e)	inatteso(a)	inesperado(a)
unfähig (D)	—	incapable	incapable	incapace	incapaz
Unfali (D)	—	accident	accident m	incidente m	accidente m
unfit (E)	untauglich	—	incapable	incapace	inútil
unfortunately (E)	leider	—	malheureusement	purtroppo	desgraciadamente
unfreundlich (D)	—	unfriendly	peu aimable	sgarbato(a)	descortés
unfriendly (E)	unfreundlich	—	peu aimable	sgarbato(a)	descortés
ungeduldig (D)	—	impatient	impatient(e)	impaziente	inpaciente
ungefähr (D)	—	about	environ	pressappoco	aproximadamente
ungemütlich (D)	—	uncomfortable	désagréable	poco accogliente	incómodo(a)
ungenaa (D)	—	inaccurate	inexact(e)	impreciso(a)	inexacto(a)
ungenügend (D)	—	insufficient	insuffisant(e)	insufficiente	insuficiente

D	E	F	I	Es
ungerade (D)	—	uneven	impair(e)	dispari	impar
ungerecht (D)	—	unjust	injuste	ingiusto(a)	injusto(a)
Ungerechtigkeit (D)	—	injustice	injustice f	ingiustizia f	injusticia f
ungern (D)	—	reluctantly	de mauvaise grâce	malvolentieri	de mala gana
ungeschickt (D)	—	clumsy	maladroit(e)	impacciato(a)	torpe
ungesund (D)	—	unhealthy	malsain(e)	malsano(a)	enfermizo(a)
ungewiß (D)	—	uncertain	incertain(e)	incerto(a)	incierto(a)
ungewöhnlich (D)	—	unusual	exceptionnel(le)	insolito(a)	desacostumbrado(a)
unghia (I)	Nagel m	nail	ongle m	—	uña f
unglaublich (D)	—	incredible	incroyable	incredibile	increíble
Unglück (D)	—	misfortune	malheur m	disgrazia f	desgracia f
unglücklich (D)	—	unhappy	malheureux (-euse)	sfortunato(a)	desgraciado(a)
ungrateful (E)	undankbar	—	ingrat(e)	ingrato(a)	desagradecido(a)
ungültig (D)	—	invalid	non valable	non valido(a)	caducado(a)
unhappy (E)	unglücklich	—	malheureux (-euse)	sfortunato(a)	desgraciado(a)
unhealthy (E)	ungesund	—	malsain(e)	malsano(a)	enfermizo(a)
unhöflich (D)	—	impolite	impoli(e)	scortese	descortés
uni (F)	einfarbig	all one colour	—	monocolore	de un solo color
unico (I)	einzig	only	seul(e)	—	único(a)
único (Es)	einzig	only	seul(e)	unico(a)	—
Uniform (D)	—	uniform	uniforme m	divisa f	uniforme m
uniform (E)	Uniform f	—	uniforme m	divisa f	uniforme m
uniforme (F)	Uniform f	uniform	—	divisa f	uniforme m
uniforme (Es)	Uniform f	uniform	uniforme m	divisa f	—
unilateral (Es)	einseitig	one-sided	partial(e)	unilaterale	—
unilaterale (I)	einseitig	one-sided	partial(e)	—	unilateral
unimportant (E)	unwichtig	—	sans importance	non importante	sin importancia
unir[1] (Es)	vereinigen	unite	unir	unire	—
unir[2] (Es)	verbinden	connect	relier	unire	—
unir (F)	vereinigen	unite	—	unire	unir
unire[1] (I)	verbinden	connect	relier	—	unir
unire[2] (I)	vereinigen	unite	unir	—	unir
unite (E)	vereinigen	—	unir	unire	unir
United States (E)	Vereinigte Staaten pl	—	Etats-Unis m pl	Stati Uniti m pl	Estados Unidos m pl
univers (F)	Weltall n	universe	—	universo m	universo m
universe (E)	Weltall n	—	univers m	universo m	universo m
universidad (Es)	Universität f	university	université f	università f	—
università (I)	Universität f	university	université f	—	universidad f
Universität (D)	—	university	université f	università f	universidad f
université[1] (F)	Hochschule f	university	—	istituto superiore m	escuela superior f
université[2] (F)	Universität f	university	—	università f	universidad f
university[1] (E)	Hochschule f	—	université f	istituto superiore m	escuela superior f
university[2] (E)	Universität f	—	université f	università f	universidad f
universo (Es)	Weltall n	universe	univers m	universo m	—
universo (I)	Weltall n	universe	univers m	—	universo m

	D	E	F	I	Es
univoco (I)	eindeutig	unequivocal	incontestable	—	evidente
unjust (E)	ungerecht	—	injuste	ingiusto(a)	injusto(a)
unknown (E)	unbekannt	—	inconnu(e)	sconosciuto(a)	desconocido(a)
Unkosten (D)	—	expenses	frais *m pl*	spese *f pl*	gastos *m pl*
unlawful (E)	unrechtmäßig	—	illégitime	illegale	ilegítimo(a)
unlikely (E)	unwahrscheinlich	—	invraisemblable	improbabile	improbable
unlimited (E)	unbegrenzt	—	illimité(e)	illimitato(a)	ilimitado(a)
unload[1] (E)	abladen	—	décharger	scaricare	descargar
unload[2] (E)	ausladen	—	décharger	scaricare	descargar
unmarried (E)	unverheiratet	—	non marié(e)	celibe *m*/nubile *f*	soltero(a)
unmittelbar (D)	—	immediate	immédiat(e)	immediato(a)	directo(a)
unmöglich (D)	—	impossible	impossible	impossibile	imposible
unnecessary (E)	unnötig	—	inutile	inutile	inútil
unnötig (D)	—	unnecessary	inutile	inutile	inútil
uno (Es)	eins	one	un	uno	—
uno (I)	eins	one	un	—	uno(a)
unoccupied (E)	unbesetzt	—	vacant(e)	libero(a)	desocupado(a)
uno detras de otro (Es)	hintereinander	one after the other	l'un derrière l'autre	uno dopo l'altro	—
uno dopo l'altro (I)	hintereinander	one after the other	l'un derrière l'autre	—	uno detras de otro
uno e mezzo (I)	anderthalb	one and a half	un(e) et demi(e)	—	uno(a) y medio(a)
uno en otro (Es)	ineinander	into one another	l'un dans l'autre	l'uno nell'altro	—
unordentlich (D)	—	untidy	désordonné(e)	disordinato(a)	desordenado(a)
Unordnung (D)	—	mess	désordre *m*	disordine *m*	desorden *m*
unos (Es)	etwa	about	environ	pressappoco	—
uno sobre otro (Es)	übereinander	one upon the other	l'un(e) sur l'autre	uno sopra l'altro	—
uno sopra l'altro (I)	übereinander	one upon the other	l'un(e) sur l'autre	—	uno sobre otro
uno y medio (Es)	anderthalb	one and a half	un(e) et demi(e)	uno(a) e mezzo	—
unpack (E)	auspacken		défaire	disfare	deshacer
unpassend (D)	—	inappropriate	mal à propos	sconveniente	inadecuado(a)
un peu (F)	bißchen	a little	—	un po'	un poquito
unpleasant (E)	unangenehm	—	désagréable	spiacevole	desagradable
un po (I)	bißchen	a little	un peu	—	un poquito
un poquito (Es)	bißchen	a little	un peu	un po'	—
Unrecht (D)	—	wrong	injustice *f*	torto *m*	injusticia *f*
unrechtmäßig (D)	—	unlawful	illégitime	illegale	ilegítimo(a)
unregelmäßig (D)	—	irregular	irrégulier(ère)	irregolare	irregular
unruhig (D)	—	restless	inquiet(-iète)	inquieto(a)	intranquilo(a)
unschuldig (D)	—	innocent	innocent(e)	innocente	inocente/puro(a)
unsicher (D)	—	uncertain	incertain(e)	incerto(a)	inseguro(a)
Unsinn (D)	—	nonsense	bêtises *f pl*	nonsenso *m*	absurdo *m*
unsinnig (D)	—	nonsensical	insensé(e)	insensato(a)	absurdo(a)
un tal (Es)	solche(r,s)	such	tel(le)	tale(i)	—
Untat (D)	—	crime	méfait *m*	misfatto *m*	crimen *m*
untauglich (D)	—	unfit	incapable	incapace	inútil
unten (D)	—	downstairs	dessous	sotto/giù	abajo
unter (D)	—	under	sous	al di sotto di	debajo de

	D	E	F	I	Es
unterbrechen (D)	—	interrupt	interrompre	interrompere	interrumpir
Unterbrechung (D)	—	interruption	interruption *f*	interruzione *f*	interrupción *f*
unterbringen (D)	—	stow	ranger	sistemare	colocar
unterdrücken (D)	—	oppress	opprimer	sopprimere	oprimir
Unterführung (D)	—	subway	passage souterrain *m*	sottopassaggio *m*	paso inferior *m*
unterhalten (D)	—	entertain	entretenir	divertire	entretener
unterhalten, sich (D)	—	talk	entretenir, se	conversare	conversar
Unterhaltung (D)	—	conversation	entretien *m*	conversazione *f*	conversación *f*
Unterhemd (D)	—	vest	tricot *m*	canottiere *f*	camiseta *f*
Unterhose (D)	—	underpants	slip *m*	mutande *f pl*	calzoncillos *m pl*
Unterkunft (D)	—	accommodation	logement *m*	alloggio *m*	hospedaje *m*
unterliegen (D)	—	be defeated	être vaincu(e) par qn	soccombere	sucumbir
unternehmen (D)	—	undertake	entreprendre	intraprendere	emprender
Unternehmen (D)	—	company	entreprise *f*	impresa *f*	empresa *f*
Unterredung (D)	—	talk	entrevue *f*	colloquio *m*	entrevista *f*
Unterricht (D)	—	lessons	cours	lezione *f*	enseñanza *f*
unterrichten (D)	—	teach	enseigner	insegnare	enseñar
Unterrichts-stunde (D)	—	lesson	leçon *f*	lezione *f*	clase *f*
Unterrock (D)	—	slip	jupon *m*	sottoveste *f*	combinación *f*
untersagen (D)	—	forbid	interdire qch à qn	proibire	prohibir
unterscheiden (D)	—	distinguish	distinguer	distinguere	distinguir
Unterschied (D)	—	difference	différence *f*	differenza *f*	diferencia *f*
unterschiedlich (D)	—	different	différent(e)	diverso(a)	distinto(a)
unterschlagen (D)	—	embezzle	soustraire	sottrarre	sustraer
unterschreiben (D)	—	sign	signer	firmare	firmar
Unterschrift (D)	—	signature	signature *f*	firma *f*	firma *f*
unterste (D)	—	lowest	inférieur(e)	inferiore	inferior
unterstreichen (D)	—	underline	souligner	sottolineare	subrayar
unterstützen (D)	—	support	soutenir	assistere	apoyar
Unterstützung (D)	—	support	soutien *m*	sostegno *m*	apoyo *m*
untersuchen (D)	—	examine	examiner	esaminare	examinar
Untertasse (D)	—	saucer	soucoupe *f*	piattino *m*	platillo *m*
untervermieten (D)	—	sublet	sous-louer	subaffittare	realquilar
Unterwäsche (D)	—	underwear	sous-vêtements *m pl*	biancheria intima *f*	ropa interior *f*
unterwegs (D)	—	on the way	en route	per strada	de camino
unterwerfen (D)	—	subject	soumettre	sottomettere	someter
untidy (E)	unordentlich	—	désordonné(e)	disordinato(a)	desordenado(a)
until (E)	bis	—	jusqu'à	fino a	hasta
unusual (E)	ungewöhnlich	—	exceptionnel(le)	insolito(a)	desacostum-brado(a)
unverbindlich (D)	—	not binding	sans engagement	non impegnativo(a)	sin compromiso
unverheiratet (D)	—	unmarried	non marié(e)	celibe *m*/nubile *f*	soltero(a)
unvermeidlich (D)	—	inevitable	inévitable	inevitabile	inevitable
unvollständig (D)	—	incomplete	incomplet(-ète)	incompleto(a)	incompleto(a)
unvorsichtig (D)	—	careless	imprudent(e)	imprudente	descuidado(a)

	D	E	F	I	Es
unwahr-scheinlich (D)	—	unlikely	invraisemblable	improbabile	improbable
unwelcome (E)	unerwünscht	—	inopportun(e)	indesiderato(a)	indeseado(a)
unwell (E)	unwohl	—	indisposé(e)	indisposto(a)	indispuesto(a)
Unwetter (D)	—	thunderstorm	tempête f	maltempo m	tormenta f
unwichtig (D)	—	unimportant	sans importance	non importante	sin importancia
unwohl (D)	—	unwell	indisposé(e)	indisposto(a)	indispuesto(a)
unzufrieden (D)	—	dissatisfied	mécontent(e)	scontento(a)	descontento(a)
uomo (I)	Mann m	man	homme m	—	hombre m
uovo (I)	Ei n	egg	œuf m	—	huevo m
up¹ (E)	hinauf	—	vers le haut	su	hacia arriba
up² (E)	herauf	—	vers le haut	su	hacia arriba
up³ (E)	hoch	—	haut(e)	alto(a)	alto(a)
uphill (E)	bergauf	—	en montant	in salita	cuesta arriba
upright (E)	aufrecht	—	droit(e)	diritto(a)	derecho(a)
upwards (E)	aufwärts	—	vers le haut	in su	hacia arriba
urbe (Es)	Großstadt f	large town	grande ville f	grande città f	—
urgent (E)	dringend	—	urgent(e)	urgente	urgente
urgent (F)	dringend	urgent	—	urgente	urgente
urgente (Es)	dringend	urgent	urgent(e)	urgente	—
urgente (I)	dringend	urgent	urgent(e)	—	urgente
Urgroßeltern (D)	—	great-grandparents	arrière-grands-parents m pl	bisnonni m pl	bisabuelos m pl
urina (I)	Harn m	urine	urine f	—	orina f
urine (E)	Harn m	—	urine f	urina f	orina f
urine (F)	Harn m	urine	—	urina f	orina f
Urkunde (D)	—	document	document m	documento m	documento m
Urlaub (D)	—	vacation	vacances f pl	vacanze f pl	vacaciones f pl
urn (E)	Urne f	—	urne f	urna f	urna f
urna (Es)	Urne f	urn	urne f	urna f	—
urna (I)	Urne f	urn	urne f	—	urna f
Urne (D)	—	urn	urne f	urna f	urna f
urne (F)	Urne f	urn	—	urna f	urna f
Ursache (D)	—	cause	cause f	causa f	causa f
ursprünglich (D)	—	original	originel(le)	originario(a)	primitivo(a)
urtare (I)	anstoßen	bump	heurter	—	empujar
Urteil (D)	—	judgement	jugement m	giudizio m	juicio m
urteilen (D)	—	judge	juger	giudicare	juzgar
usado (Es)	gebraucht	used	d'occasion	usato(a)	—
usage (F)	Gebrauch m	custom	—	uso m	uso m
usanza (I)	Sitte f	custom	coutume f	—	costumbre f
usar¹ (Es)	anwenden	apply	employer	impiegare	—
usar² (Es)	benutzen	use	utiliser	usare	—
usar³ (Es)	gebrauchen	use	utiliser	usare	—
usare¹ (I)	benutzen	use	utiliser	—	usar
usare² (I)	gebrauchen	use	utiliser	—	usar
usare³ (I)	verwenden	use	employer	—	utilizar
usato (I)	gebraucht	used	d'occasion	—	usado(a)
uscire¹ (I)	ausgehen	go out	sortir	—	salir

	D	E	F	I	Es
uscire² (I)	hinausgehen	go out	sortir	—	salir afuera
uscire fuori (I)	heraustreten	step out	sortir	—	salir
uscita (I)	Ausgang *m*	exit	sortie *f*	—	salida *f*
uscita di sicurezza (I)	Notausgang *m*	emergency exit	sortie de secours *f*	—	salida de emergencia *f*
use¹ (E)	benutzen	—	utiliser	usare	usar
use² (E)	gebrauchen	—	utiliser	usare	usar
use³ (E)	verwenden	—	employer	usare	utilizar
use⁴ (E)	Verwendung *f*	—	emploi *m*	uso *m*	utilización *f*
used (E)	gebraucht	—	d'occasion	usato(a)	usado(a)
useful (E)	nützlich	—	utile	utile	útil
useless (E)	nutzlos	—	inutile	inutile	inútil
user (F)	abnutzen	wear out	—	consumare	desgastar
use the familiar form (E)	duzen	—	tutoyer	dare del tu	tutear
usine (F)	Fabrik *f*	factory	—	fabbrica *f*	fábrica *f*
uso (Es)	Gebrauch *m*	custom	usage *m*	uso *m*	—
uso¹ (I)	Gebrauch *m*	custom	usage *m*	—	uso *m*
uso² (I)	Verwendung *f*	use	emploi *m*	—	utilización *f*
usual¹ (E)	gewöhnlich	—	habituel(le)	abituale	habitual
usual² (E)	üblich	—	habituel(le)	solito(a)	usual
usual (Es)	üblich	usual	habituel(le)	solito(a)	—
utensile (I)	Werkzeug *n*	tool	outil *m*	—	herramienta *f*
utensilio (Es)	Gerät *n*	appliance	appareil *m*	apparecchio *m*	—
útil (Es)	nützlich	useful	utile	utile	—
utile (F)	nützlich	useful	—	utile	útil
utile (I)	nützlich	useful	utile	—	útil
utiliser¹ (F)	benutzen	use	—	usare	usar
utiliser² (F)	gebrauchen	use	—	usare	usar
utilización (Es)	Verwendung *f*	use	emploi *m*	uso *m*	—
utilizar (Es)	verwenden	use	employer	usare	—
uva (Es)	Traube *f*	grape	grappe *f*	uva *f*	—
uva (I)	Traube *f*	grape	grappe *f*	—	uva *f*
vaca (Es)	Kuh *f*	cow	vache *f*	mucca *f*	—
vacaciones¹ (Es)	Ferien *f*	holidays	vacances *f pl*	vacanze *f pl*	—
vacaciones² (Es)	Urlaub *m*	vacation	vacances *f pl*	vacanze *f pl*	—
vacances¹ (F)	Ferien *f*	holidays	—	vacanze *f pl*	vacaciones *f pl*
vacances² (F)	Urlaub *m*	vacation	—	vacanze *f pl*	vacaciones *f pl*
vacant (F)	unbesetzt	unoccupied	—	libero(a)	desocupado(a)
vacanza (I)	schulfrei	holiday	de congé	—	sin colegio
vacanze¹ (I)	Ferien *f*	holidays	vacances *f pl*	—	vacaciones *f pl*
vacanze² (I)	Urlaub *m*	vacation	vacances *f pl*	—	vacaciones *f pl*
vacation (E)	Urlaub *m*	—	vacances *f pl*	vacanze *f pl*	vacaciones *f pl*
vaccinare (I)	impfen	vaccinate	vacciner	—	vacunar
vaccinate (E)	impfen	—	vacciner	vaccinare	vacunar
vaccination (E)	Impfung *f*	—	vaccination *f*	vaccinazione *f*	vacunación *f*
vaccination (F)	Impfung *f*	vaccination	—	vaccinazione *f*	vacunación *f*
vaccinazione (I)	Impfung *f*	vaccination	vaccination *f*	—	vacunación *f*
vacciner (F)	impfen	vaccinate	—	vaccinare	vacunar

	D	E	F	I	Es
vache (F)	Kuh *f*	cow	—	mucca *f*	vaca *f*
vacilar[1] (Es)	taumeln	reel	tituber	barcollare	—
vacilar[2] (Es)	wanken	stagger	chanceller	barcollare	—
vacilar[3] (Es)	zögern	hesitate	hésiter	esitare	—
vacío (Es)	leer	empty	vide	vuoto(a)	—
vacunación (Es)	Impfung *f*	vaccination	vaccination *f*	vaccinazione *f*	—
vacunar (Es)	impfen	vaccinate	vacciner	vaccinare	—
vacuum-cleaner (E)	Staubsauger *m*	—	aspirateur *m*	aspirapolvere *m*	aspirador *m*
vagón (Es)	Waggon *m*	carriage	wagon *m*	vagone *m*	—
vagone (I)	Waggon *m*	carriage	wagon *m*	—	vagón *m*
vagone ristorante (I)	Speisewagen *m*	dining car	wagon-restaurant *m*	—	vagón restaurante *m*
vagón restaurante (Es)	Speisewagen *m*	dining car	wagon-restaurant *m*	vagone ristorante *m*	—
vague (F)	Welle *f*	wave	—	onda *f*	ola *f*
vain (E)	eitel	—	vaniteux(-euse)	vanitoso(a)	vanidoso(a)
vaisselle (F)	Geschirr *n*	crockery	—	stoviglie *f pl*	vajilla *f*
vajilla (Es)	Geschirr *n*	crockery	vaisselle *f*	stoviglie *f pl*	—
valable (F)	gültig	valid	—	valido(a)	válido(a)
vale (Es)	Gutschein *m*	voucher	bon *m*	buono *m*	—
valer[1] (Es)	gelten	be worth	valoir	valere	—
valer[2] (Es)	taugen	be of use	convenir pour	essere portato(a)	—
valere (I)	gelten	be worth	valoir	—	valer
valere la pena (I)	lohnen	be worth while	en valoir la peine	—	valer la pena
valer la pena (Es)	lohnen	be worth while	en valoir la peine	valere la pena	—
valeur (F)	Wert *m*	value	—	valore *m*	valor *m*
valid (E)	gültig	—	valable	valido(a)	válido(a)
validez (Es)	Gültigkeit *f*	validity	validité *f*	validità *f*	—
validità (I)	Gültigkeit *f*	validity	validité *f*	—	validez *f*
validité (F)	Gültigkeit *f*	validity	—	validità *f*	validez *f*
validity (E)	Gültigkeit *f*	—	validité *f*	validità *f*	validez *f*
valido (I)	gültig	valid	valable	—	válido(a)
válido (Es)	gültig	valid	valable	valido(a)	—
valiente (Es)	tapfer	brave	courageux(-euse)	coraggioso(a)	—
valigia (I)	Koffer *m*	suitcase	valise *f*	—	maleta *f*
valioso[1] (Es)	kostbar	precious	précieux(-euse)	prezioso(a)	—
valioso[2] (Es)	wertvoll	valuable	précieux(-euse)	prezioso(a)	—
valise (F)	Koffer *m*	suitcase	—	valigia *f*	maleta *f*
valla (Es)	Zaun *m*	fence	clôture *f*	recinto *m*	—
valle (Es)	Tal *n*	valley	vallée *f*	valle *f*	—
valle (I)	Tal *n*	valley	vallée *f*	—	valle *m*
vallée (F)	Tal *n*	valley	—	valle *f*	valle *m*
valley (E)	Tal *n*	—	vallée *f*	valle *f*	valle *m*
valoir (F)	gelten	be worth	—	valere	valer
valor (Es)	Wert *m*	value	valeur *f*	valore *m*	—
valore (I)	Wert *m*	value	valeur *f*	—	valor *m*
valuable (E)	wertvoll	—	précieux(-euse)	prezioso(a)	valioso(a)
value (E)	Wert *m*	—	valeur *f*	valore *m*	valor *m*

	D	E	F	I	Es
value added tax (E)	Mehrwertsteuer f	—	taxe sur la valeur ajoutée f	imposta sul'valore aggiunto f	impuesto sobre el valor añadido m
valuta (I)	Währung f	currency	monnaie f	—	moneda f
vanidoso (Es)	eitel	vain	vaniteux(-euse)	vanitoso(a)	—
vaniteux (F)	eitel	vain	—	vanitoso(a)	vanidoso(a)
vanitoso (I)	eitel	vain	vaniteux(-euse)	—	vanidoso(a)
vantaggio (I)	Vorteil m	advantage	avantage m	—	ventaja f
vapeur (F)	Dampf m	steam	—	vapore m	vapor m
vapor (Es)	Dampf m	steam	vapeur f	vapore m	—
vapore (I)	Dampf m	steam	vapeur f	—	vapor m
vara (Es)	Stange f	pole	barre f	asta f	—
variabile (I)	veränderlich	changeable	variable	—	variable
variable (Es)	veränderlich	changeable	variable	variabile	—
variable (F)	veränderlich	changeable	—	variabile	variable
variopinto (I)	bunt	coloured	coloré(e)	—	de colores
vasca da bagno (I)	Badewanne f	bath tub	baignoire f	—	bañera f
Vase (D)	—	vase	vase m	vaso m	florero m
vase (E)	Vase f	—	vase m	vaso m	florero m
vase (F)	Vase f	vase	—	vaso m	florero m
vaso (Es)	Glas n	glass	verre m	bicchiere m	—
vaso (I)	Vase f	vase	vase m	—	florero m
vassoio (I)	Tablett n	tray	plateau m	—	bandeja f
Vater (D)	—	father	père m	padre m	padre m
veau (F)	Kalb n	calf	—	vitello m	ternera f
vecchio (I)	alt	old	vieux , vieil, vieille	—	viejo(a)
vecino[1] (Es)	Nachbar m	neighbour	voisin m	vicino m	—
vecino[2] (Es)	benachbart	neighbouring	avoisinant(e)	vicino(a)	—
vedere (I)	sehen	see	voir	—	ver
vedova (I)	Witwe f	widow	veuve f	—	viuda f
vedovo (I)	Witwer m	widower	veuf m	—	viudo m
vegetables (E)	Gemüse n	—	légumes m pl	verdura f	legumbres f pl
vegetarian (E)	Vegetarier m	—	végétarien m	vegetariano m	vegetariano m
vegetariano (Es)	Vegetarier m	vegetarian	végétarien m	vegetariano m	—
vegetariano (I)	Vegetarier m	vegetarian	végétarien m	—	vegetariano m
végétarien (F)	Vegetarier m	vegetarian	—	vegetariano m	vegetariano m
Vegetarier (D)	—	vegetarian	végétarien m	vegetariano m	vegetariano m
vehicle (E)	Fahrzeug n	—	véhicule m	veicolo m	vehículo m
véhicule (F)	Fahrzeug n	vehicle	—	veicolo m	vehículo m
vehículo (Es)	Fahrzeug n	vehicle	véhicule m	veicolo m	—
veicolo (I)	Fahrzeug n	vehicle	véhicule m	—	vehículo m
veille (F)	Vorabend m	evening before	—	vigilia f	víspera f
veilleur de nuit (F)	Nachtwächter m	night-watchman	—	guardia notturna f	sereno m
vein (E)	Ader f	—	veine f	vena f	vena f
veine (F)	Ader f	vein	—	vena f	vena f
veinte (Es)	zwanzig	twenty	vingt	venti	—
vejiga (Es)	Blase f	bladder	vessie f	vescica f	—
vela (Es)	Kerze f	candle	bougie f	candela f	—
veleno (I)	Gift n	poison	poison m	—	veneno m

	D	E	F	I	Es
velenoso (I)	giftig	poisonous	toxique	—	venenoso(a)
veloce (I)	schnell	fast	rapide	—	rápido(a)
velocidad[1] (Es)	Geschwindigkeit f	speed	vitesse f	velocità f	—
velocidad[2] (Es)	Tempo n	speed	vitesse f	velocità f	—
velocidad máxima (Es)	Höchst-geschwindigkeit f	maximum speed	vitesse maximum f	velocità massima f	—
velocità[1] (I)	Geschwindigkeit f	speed	vitesse f	—	velocidad f
velocità[2] (I)	Schnelligkeit f	speed	rapidité f	—	rapidez f
velocità[3] (I)	Tempo n	speed	vitesse f	—	velocidad f
velocità massima (I)	Höchst-geschwindigkeit f	maximum speed	vitesse maximum f	—	velocidad máxima f
vena (Es)	Ader f	vein	veine f	vena f	—
vena (I)	Ader f	vein	veine f	—	vena f
vencer (Es)	siegen	win	gagner	vincere	—
vendedor (Es)	Verkäufer m	salesman	vendeur m	venditore m	—
vender (Es)	verkaufen	sell	vendre	vendere	—
vendere (I)	verkaufen	sell	vendre	—	vender
vendetta (I)	Rache f	revenge	vengeance f	—	venganza f
vendeur (F)	Verkäufer m	salesman	—	venditore m	vendedor m
vendido (Es)	ausverkauft	sold out	épuisé(e)	esaurito(a)	—
vending machine (E)	Automat m	—	distributeur automatique m	distributore automatico m	distribuidor automático m
vendita (I)	Verkauf m	sale	vente f	—	venta f
vendita anticipata (I)	Vorverkauf m	advance booking	location f	—	venta anticipada f
venditore (I)	Verkäufer m	salesman	vendeur m	—	vendedor m
vendre (F)	verkaufen	sell	—	vendere	vender
vendredi (F)	Freitag m	Friday	—	venerdì m	viernes m
veneno (Es)	Gift n	poison	poison m	veleno m	—
venenoso (Es)	giftig	poisonous	toxique	velenoso(a)	—
venerdì (I)	Freitag m	Friday	vendredi	—	viernes m
venganza (Es)	Rache f	revenge	vengeance f	vendetta f	—
vengeance (F)	Rache f	revenge	—	vendetta f	venganza f
venir (Es)	kommen	come	venir	venire	—
venir (F)	kommen	come	—	venire	venir
venir à la rencontre (F)	entgegenkommen	approach	—	venire incontro	venir al encuentro
venir al encuentro (Es)	entgegenkommen	approach	venir à la rencontre	venire incontro	—
venir bien (Es)	passen	suit	aller bien	stare bene	—
venir de nuevo (Es)	wiederkommen	come back	revenir	ritornare	—
venire (I)	kommen	come	venir	—	venir
venire a sapere (I)	erfahren	learn	apprendre	—	enterarse
venire incontro (I)	entgegenkommen	approach	venir à la rencontre	—	venir al encuentro
vent (F)	Wind m	wind	—	vento m	viento m
venta (Es)	Verkauf m	sale	vente f	vendita f	—
venta anticipada (Es)	Vorverkauf m	advance booking	location f	vendita anticipata f	—
ventaja (Es)	Vorteil m	advantage	avantage m	vantaggio m	—
ventana (Es)	Fenster n	window	fenêtre f	finestra f	—
ventanilla (Es)	Schalter m	counter	guichet m	sportello m	—

	D	E	F	I	Es
vente (F)	Verkauf *m*	sale	—	vendita *f*	venta *f*
venti (I)	zwanzig	twenty	vingt	—	veinte
ventilar (Es)	lüften	air	aérer	arrieggiare	—
vento (I)	Wind *m*	wind	vent *m*	—	viento *m*
ventoso (I)	windig	windy	éventé(e)	—	ventoso
ventoso (Es)	windig	windy	éventé(e)	ventoso(a)	—
ventre (F)	Bauch *m*	stomach	—	pancia *f*	vientre *m*
ver (Es)	sehen	see	voir	vedere	—
verabreden (D)	—	arrange to meet	prendre rendez-vous	darsi appuntamento	concertar una cita
Verabredung (D)	—	date	rendez-vous *m*	appuntamento *m*	cita *f*
verabschieden (D)	—	say goodbye to	prendre congé de	congedare	despedir
veränderlich (D)	—	changeable	variable	variabile	variable
verändern (D)	—	change	transformer	mutare	cambiar
Veränderung (D)	—	change	changement *m*	cambiamento *m*	cambio *m*
verano (Es)	Sommer *m*	summer	été *m*	estate *f*	—
veranstalten (D)	—	organize	organiser	organizzare	organizar
Veranstaltung (D)	—	event	manifestation *f*	manifestazione *f*	representación *f*
verantwortlich (D)	—	responsible	responsable	responsabile	responsable
verbergen (D)	—	hide	dissimuler	nascondere	esconder
verbessern (D)	—	improve	améliorer	migliorare	mejorar
verbieten (D)	—	forbid	défendre	proibire	prohibir
verbinden (D)	—	connect	relier	unire	unir
Verbindung (D)	—	connection	relation *f*	relazione *f*	relación *f*
Verbot (D)	—	prohibition	défense *f*	divieto *m*	prohibición *f*
verboten (D)	—	forbidden	interdit(e)	vietato(a)	prohibido(a)
Verbrauch (D)	—	consumption	consommation *f*	consumo *m*	consumo *m*
verbrauchen (D)	—	consume	consommer	consumare	consumir
Verbrechen (D)	—	crime	crime *m*	delitto *m*	crimen *m*
verbreiten (D)	—	spread	propager	diffondere	difundir
verbrennen (D)	—	burn	brûler	bruciare	quemar
verbringen (D)	—	spend	passer	passare	pasar
verdächtig (D)	—	suspicious	suspect(e)	sospetto(a)	sospechoso(a)
verdad (Es)	Wahrheit *f*	truth	vérité *f*	verità *f*	—
verdadero[1] (Es)	echt	genuine	vrai(e)	vero(a)	—
verdadero[2] (Es)	wahr	true	vrai(e)	vero(a)	—
verdauen (D)	—	digest	digérer	digerire	digerir
verde (Es)	grün	green	vert(e)	verde	—
verde (I)	grün	green	vert(e)	—	verde
verderben (D)	—	ruin	détruire	rovinare	arrruinar
verdienen (D)	—	earn	gagner	guadagnare	ganar
Verdienst[1] (D)	—	merit	mérite *m*	merito *m*	mérito *m*
Verdienst[2] (D)	—	income	revenus *m pl*	guadagno *m*	ganancia *f*
verdura (I)	Gemüse *n*	vegetables	légumes *m pl*	—	legumbres *f pl*
Verein (D)	—	club	association *f*	associazione *f*	asociación *f*
vereinbaren (D)	—	agree upon	convenir de	fissare	convenir
vereinigen (D)	—	unite	unir	unire	unir
Vereinigte Staaten (D)	—	United States	Etats-Unis *m pl*	Stati Uniti *m pl*	Estados Unidos *m pl*

D	E	F	I	Es
vererben (D)	—	bequeath	léguer	lasciare in eredità	transmitir hereditariamente
verfahren (D)	—	act	procéder	procedere	proceder
Verfassung[1] (D)	—	constitution	état *m*	condizioni *f pl*	estado *m*
Verfassung[2] (D)	—	constitution	constitution *f*	costituzione *f*	constitución *f*
verfolgen (D)	—	pursue	poursuivre	inseguire	perseguir
verfügen (D)	—	order	disposer de	disporre	disponer
verführen (D)	—	seduce	séduire	sedurre	seducir
vergangen (D)	—	past	passé(e)	passato(a)	pasado(a)
vergangene (D)	—	past	dernier(-ère)	passato(a)	pasada(o)
Vergangenheit (D)	—	past	passé *m*	passato *m*	pasado *m*
vergehen (D)	—	pass by	passer	passare	pasar
vergessen (D)	—	forget	oublier	dimenticare	olvidar
vergewaltigen (D)	—	rape	violer	violentare	violar
vergine (I)	Jungfrau *f*	virgin	vierge *f*	—	virgen *f*
Vergleich (D)	—	comparison	comparaison *f*	paragone *m*	comparación *f*
vergleichen (D)	—	compare	comparer	paragonare	comparar
Vergnügen (D)	—	pleasure	plaisir *m*	divertimento *m*	placer *m*
vergogna (I)	Schande *f*	disgrace	honte *f*	—	deshonra *f*
vergognarsi (I)	schämen	be ashamed	avoir honte	—	tener vergüenza
vergrößern (D)	—	enlarge	agrandir	ingrandire	agrandar
verhaften (D)	—	arrest	arrêter	arrestare	detener
verheiratet (D)	—	married	marié(e)	sposato(a)	casado(a)
verhindern (D)	—	prevent	empêcher	impedire	evitar
verhindert (D)	—	unable to make it	empêché(e)	impedito(a)	impedido(a)
verhungern (D)	—	starve	mourir de faim	morire di fame	morir de hambre
vérifier (F)	nachsehen	check	—	controllare	examinar
verità (I)	Wahrheit *f*	truth	vérité *f*	—	verdad *f*
vérité (F)	Wahrheit *f*	truth	—	verità *f*	verdad *f*
Verkauf (D)	—	sale	vente *f*	vendita *f*	venta *f*
verkaufen (D)	—	sell	vendre	vendere	vender
Verkäufer (D)	—	salesman	vendeur *m*	venditore *m*	vendedor *m*
Verkehr (D)	—	traffic	circulation *f*	traffico *m*	tráfico *m*
Verkehrsbüro (D)	—	travel agency	bureau touristique *m*	ufficio turistico *m*	oficina de turismo *f*
verkehrt (D)	—	wrong	faux (fausse)	sbagliato(a)	equivocado(a)
verkleinern (D)	—	make smaller	réduire	ridurre	reducir
verladen (D)	—	load	charger	caricare	cargar
verlangen (D)	—	demand	demander	richiedere	exigir
verlängern (D)	—	extend	prolonger	allungare	alargar
verlassen (D)	—	leave	abandonner	lasciare	dejar
ver la televisión (Es)	fernsehen	watch television	regarder la télévision	guardare la TV	—
verlaufen (D)	—	get lost	perdre, se	perdersi	perderse
verlegen (D)	—	mislay	égarer	perdere	extraviar
Verlegenheit (D)	—	embarrassment	gêne *f*	imbarazzo *m*	contratiempo *m*
verleihen (D)	—	lend	prêter	prestare	prestar
verletzen (D)	—	injure	blesser	ferire	herir
Verletzung (D)	—	injury	blessure *f*	ferita *f*	herida *f*

	D	E	F	I	Es
verlieben (D)	—	fall in love	tomber amoureux(-euse)	innamorarsi	enamorarse
verliebt (D)	—	in love	amoureux(-euse)	innamorato	enamorado(a)
verlieren (D)	—	lose	perdre	perdere	perder
verloben (D)	—	get engaged	fiancer, se	fidanzarsi	prometerse
Verlobter (D)	—	fiancé	fiancé *m*	fidanzato *m*	prometido *m*
Verlust (D)	—	loss	perte *f*	perdita *f*	pérdida *f*
vermehren (D)	—	increase	augmenter	aumentare	aumentar
vermeiden (D)	—	avoid	éviter	evitare	evitar
vermieten (D)	—	rent	louer	affittare	alquilar
vermissen (D)	—	miss	manquer	sentire la mancanza	echar de menos
vermuten (D)	—	suppose	supposer	supporre	suponer
Vermutung (D)	—	supposition	supposition *f*	supposizione *f*	suposición *f*
vernachlässigen (D)	—	neglect	négliger	trascurare	descuidar
vernichten (D)	—	destroy	détruire	distruggere	destruir
verniciare (I)	streichen	paint	peindre	—	pintar
vernünftig (D)	—	sensible	raisonnable	ragionevole	razonable
vero[1] (I)	echt	genuine	vrai(e)	—	verdadero(a)
vero[2] (I)	wahr	true	vrai(e)	—	verdadero(a)
veröffentlichen (D)	—	publish	publier	pubblicare	publicar
verpachten (D)	—	lease out	affermer	affittare	arrendar
verpacken (D)	—	pack	emballer	impacchettare	empaquetar
Verpflegung (D)	—	catering	nourriture *f*	vitto *m*	alimentación *f*
verpflichten (D)	—	oblige	obliger	obbligare	obligar
Verpflichtung (D)	—	obligation	obligation *f*	obbligo *m*	obligación *f*
verraten (D)	—	betray	trahir	tradire	traicionar
verre (F)	Glas *n*	glass	—	bicchiere *m*	vaso *m*
verreisen (D)	—	go away	partir en voyage	partire in viaggio	irse de viaje
verringern (D)	—	reduce	diminuer	diminuire	disminuir
verrou (F)	Riegel *m*	bar	—	catenaccio *m*	cerrojo *m*
verrückt (D)	—	mad	fou (folle)	pazzo(a)	loco(a)
versant (F)	Hang *m*	slope	—	pendio *m*	pendiente *m*
versare[1] (I)	eingießen	pour	verser	—	echar
versare[2] (I)	schütten	pour	verser	—	verter
versäumen (D)	—	miss	manquer	perdere	perder
verschaffen (D)	—	procure	procurer	procurare	procurarse algo
verschieben (D)	—	postpone	remettre	rimandare	aplazar
verschieden (D)	—	different	différent(e)	diverso(a)	diferente
verschließen (D)	—	lock (up)	fermer à clé	chiudere	cerrar con llave
Verschluß (D)	—	lock	fermeture *f*	chiusura *f*	cierre *m*
verschreiben (D)	—	prescribe	prescrire	prescrivere	prescribir
verschwenden (D)	—	waste	gaspiller	sprecare	desperdiciar
verschwinden (D)	—	disappear	disparaître	sparire	desaparecer
verser[1] (F)	eingießen	pour	—	versare	echar
verser[2] (F)	schütten	pour	—	versare	verter
versichern (D)	—	assure	assurer	assicurare	asegurar
Versicherung (D)	—	insurance	assurance *f*	assicurazione *f*	seguro *m*
versinken (D)	—	sink	enfoncer, se	affondare	hundirse

	D	E	F	I	Es
vers le bas (F)	herab/hinab	down	—	giù	hacia abajo
vers le haut[1] (F)	aufwärts	upwards	—	in su	hacia arriba
vers le haut[2] (F)	herauf	up	—	su	hacia arriba
vers le haut[3] (F)	hinauf	up	—	su	hacia arriba
vers l'intérieur (F)	herein	in	—	dentro	adentro
versorgen (D)	—	provide	fournir	approvvigionare	proveer
verspäten (D)	—	be late	être en retard	ritardare	llevar retraso
Verspätung (D)	—	delay	retard *m*	ritardo *m*	retraso *m*
versprechen (D)	—	promise	promettre	promettere	prometer
Versprechen (D)	—	promise	promesse *f*	promessa *f*	promesa *f*
Verstand (D)	—	intelligence	intelligence *f*	intelligenza *f*	razón *f*
verständigen (D)	—	inform	prévenir	informare	informar
Verständigung (D)	—	agreement	accord *m*	accordo *m*	acuerdo *m*
Verständnis (D)	—	understanding	compréhension *f*	comprensione *f*	comprensión *f*
verstecken (D)	—	hide	cacher	nascondere	ocultar
verstehen (D)	—	understand	comprendre	capire	entender
Versuch (D)	—	try	essai *m*	tentativo *m*	intento *m*
versuchen (D)	—	try	essayer	assaggiare	probar
vert (F)	grün	green	—	verde	verde
vertauschen (D)	—	exchange	échanger	scambiare	cambiar
verteidigen (D)	—	defend	défendre	difendere	defender
Verteidigung (D)	—	defence	défense *f*	difesa *f*	defensa *f*
verteilen (D)	—	distribute	distribuer	distribuire	repartir
verter (Es)	schütten	pour	verser	versare	—
vertical (E)	senkrecht	—	vertical(e)	verticale	vertical
vertical (Es)	senkrecht	vertical	vertical(e)	verticale	—
vertical (F)	senkrecht	vertical	—	verticale	vertical
verticale (I)	senkrecht	vertical	vertical(e)	—	vertical
Vertrag (D)	—	contract	contrat *m*	contratto *m*	contrato *m*
vertrauen (D)	—	trust	avoir confiance	fidarsi	confiar
Vertrauen (D)	—	confidence	confiance *f*	fiducia *f*	confianza *f*
vertreten (D)	—	represent	représenter	rappresentare	representar
Vertreter (D)	—	representative	représentant *m*	rappresentante *m*	representante
verursachen (D)	—	cause	causer	causare	ocasionar
verurteilen (D)	—	condemn	condamner	condannare	sentenciar
Verwaltung (D)	—	administration	administration *f*	amministrazione *f*	administración *f*
verwandt (D)	—	related	parent(e)	imparentato(a)	emparentado(a)
Verwandter (D)	—	relative	parent *m*	parente *m*	pariente *m*
verwechseln (D)	—	confuse	confondre	scambiare	confundir
verweigern (D)	—	refuse	refuser	rifiutare	negar
verwenden (D)	—	use	employer	usare	utilizar
Verwendung (D)	—	use	emploi *m*	uso *m*	utilización *f*
verwirklichen (D)	—	realize	réaliser	realizzare	llevar a cabo
verwirrt (D)	—	confused	confus(e)	confuso(a)	confundido(a)
Verwirrung (D)	—	confusion	confusion *f*	confusione *f*	confusión *f*
verwöhnen (D)	—	spoil	gâter	viziare	mimar
verwunden (D)	—	wound	blesser	ferire	herir
very (E)	sehr	—	très	molto	mucho/muy

	D	E	F	I	Es
verzeichnen (D)	—	list	enregistrer	registrare	hacer una lista
Verzeichnis (D)	—	list	registre *m*	elenco *m*	lista *f*
verzeihen (D)	—	forgive	pardonner	perdonare	perdonar
Verzeihung (D)	—	forgiveness	pardon *m*	perdono *m*	perdón *m*
verzichten (D)	—	forgo	renoncer	rinunciare	renunciar
verzollen (D)	—	clear through customs	dédouaner	sdoganare	pagar la aduana
verzweifelt (D)	—	desperate	désespéré(e)	disperato(a)	desesperado(a)
vescica (I)	Blase *f*	bladder	vessie *f*	—	vejiga *f*
vespa (I)	Wespe *f*	wasp	guêpe *f*	—	avispa *f*
vessie (F)	Blase *f*	bladder	—	vescica *f*	vejiga *f*
vest (E)	Unterhemd *n*	—	tricot *m*	canottiera *f*	camiseta *f*
veste (F)	Jacke *f*	jacket	—	giacca *f*	chaqueta *f*
veste en tricot (F)	Strickjacke *f*	cardigan	—	giacca di maglia *f*	chaqueta de punto *f*
vestiaire (F)	Garderobe *f*	wardrobe	—	guardaroba *m*	guardaropa *m*
vestibule (F)	Diele *f*	hall	—	corridoio *m*	vestíbulo *m*
vestíbulo (Es)	Diele *f*	hall	vestibule *m*	corridoio *m*	—
vestido¹ (Es)	Kleid *n*	dress	robe *f*	vestito *m*	—
vestido² (Es)	Kostüm *n*	costume	costume *m*	tailleur *m*	—
vestir (Es)	kleiden	dress	habiller	vestire	—
vestire (I)	kleiden	dress	habiller	—	vestir
vestito¹ (I)	Anzug *m*	suit	costume *m*	—	traje *m*
vestito² (I)	Kleid *n*	dress	robe *f*	—	vestido *m*
vestuario (Es)	Kleidung *f*	clothing	habits *m pl*	abbigliamento *m*	—
vet (E)	Tierarzt *m*	—	vétérinaire *m*	veterinario *m*	veterinario *m*
veta (Es)	Masern *pl*	speckle	rougeole *f*	morbillo *m*	—
vétérinaire (F)	Tierarzt *m*	vet	—	veterinario *m*	veterinario *m*
veterinario (Es)	Tierarzt *m*	vet	vétérinaire *m*	veterinario *m*	—
veterinario (I)	Tierarzt *m*	vet	vétérinaire *m*	—	veterinario *m*
vetrina (I)	Schaufenster *n*	shop window	vitrine *f*	—	escaparate *m*
vetro (I)	Scheibe *f*	pane	carreau *m*	—	cristal *m*
Vetter (D)	—	cousin	cousin *m*	cugino *m*	primo *m*
vettura (I)	Wagen *m*	car	voiture *f*	—	coche *m*
veuf (F)	Witwer *m*	widower	—	vedovo *m*	viudo *m*
veuve (F)	Witwe *f*	widow	—	vedova *f*	viuda *f*
vía (Es)	Gleis *n*	track	voie *f*	binario *m*	—
via¹ (I)	fort	away	parti	—	lejos
via² (I)	weg	away	pas là	—	fuera
via³ (I)	Weg *m*	way	chemin *m*	—	camino *m*
vía de acceso (Es)	Auffahrt *f*	slip road	bretelle d'accès *f*	entrata *f*	—
viaggiare (I)	reisen	travel	voyager	—	viajar
viaggiatore (I)	Reisender *m*	traveller	voyageur *m*	—	viajero *m*
viaggio¹ (I)	Fahrt *f*	journey	voyage *f*	—	viaje *m*
viaggio² (I)	Reise *f*	journey	voyage *m*	—	viaje *m*
viajar (Es)	reisen	travel	voyager	viaggiare	viajar
viaje¹ (Es)	Fahrt *f*	journey	voyage *f*	viaggio *m*	—
viaje² (Es)	Reise *f*	journey	voyage *m*	viaggio *m*	—
viajero (Es)	Reisender *m*	traveller	voyageur *m*	viaggiatore *m*	—

	D	E	F	I	Es
viande (F)	Fleisch *n*	meat	—	carne *f*	carne *f*
viande de bœuf (F)	Rindfleisch *n*	beef	—	carne di manzo *f*	carne de vaca *f*
viande de porc (F)	Schweinefleisch *n*	pork	—	carne di maiale *f*	carne de cerdo *f*
viande hachée (F)	Hackfleisch *n*	minced meat	—	carne tritata *f*	carne picada *f*
vice versa (E)	umgekehrt	—	vice versa	inverso(a)	contrario(a)
vice versa (F)	umgekehrt	vice versa	—	inverso(a)	contrario(a)
vicinanza (I)	Nähe *f*	proximity	environs *m pl*	—	proximidad *f*
vicino[1] (I)	benachbart	neighbouring	avoisinant(e)	—	vecino(a)
vicino[2] (I)	nahe	near	près de	—	contiguo(a)
vicino[3] (I)	Nachbar *m*	neighbour	voisin *m*	—	vecino *m*
vicolo (I)	Gasse *f*	lane	ruelle *f*	—	callejón *m*
victim (E)	Opfer *n*	—	victime *f*	vittima *f*	víctima *f*
víctima (Es)	Opfer *n*	victim	victime *f*	vittima *f*	—
victime (F)	Opfer *n*	victim	—	vittima *f*	víctima *f*
victoire (F)	Sieg *m*	victory	—	vittoria *f*	victoria *f*
victoria (Es)	Sieg *m*	victory	victoire *f*	vittoria *f*	—
victory (E)	Sieg *m*	—	victoire *f*	vittoria *f*	victoria *f*
victuals (E)	Eßwaren *pl*	—	produits alimentaires *m pl*	alimentari *m pl*	comestibles *m pl*
vida (Es)	Leben *n*	life	vie *f*	vita *f*	—
vida cotidiana (Es)	Alltag *m*	everyday life	vie quotidienne *f*	vita quotidiana *f*	—
vide (F)	leer	empty	—	vuoto(a)	vacío(a)
vie (F)	Leben *n*	life	—	vita *f*	vida *f*
viejo (Es)	alt	old	vieux, vieil, vieille	vecchio(a)	—
viel (D)	—	a lot of	beaucoup de	molto(a)	mucho(a)
viele (D)	—	many/a lot of	beaucoup de	molti(e)	muchos(as)
vielleicht (D)	—	maybe	peut-être	forse	tal vez
viento (Es)	Wind *m*	wind	vent *m*	vento *m*	—
vientre (Es)	Bauch *m*	stomach	ventre *m*	pancia *f*	—
vie quotidienne (F)	Alltag *m*	everyday life	—	vita quotidiana *f*	vida cotidiana *f*
vier (D)	—	four	quatre	quattro	cuatro
viereckig (D)	—	square	carré(e)	quadrato(a)	cuadrangular
vierge (F)	Jungfrau *f*	virgin	—	vergine *f*	virgen *f*
viernes (Es)	Freitag *m*	Friday	vendredi	venerdì *m*	—
Viertel (D)	—	a quarter	quart *m*	quarto *m*	barrio *m*
vierzehn (D)	—	fourteen	quatorze	quattordici	catorce
vierzig (D)	—	forty	quarante	quaranta	cuarenta
vietato (I)	verboten	forbidden	interdit(e)	—	prohibido(a)
vieux (F)	alt	old	—	vecchio(a)	viejo(a)
view[1] (E)	Aussicht *f*	—	vue *f*	vista *f*	vista *f*
view[2] (E)	Sicht *f*	—	vue *f*	vista *f*	vista *f*
vif (F)	lebhaft	lively	—	vivace	vivaz
vigilante (Es)	Aufseher *m*	guard	gardien *m*	custode *m*	—
vigilar[1] (Es)	bewachen	guard	garder	sorvegliare	—
vigilar[2] (Es)	überwachen	supervise	surveiller	sorvegliare	—
vigilia (I)	Vorabend *m*	evening before	veille *f*	—	víspera *f*
vigilia di Natale (I)	Heiligabend *m*	Christmas Eve	nuit de Noël *f*	—	Nochebuena *f*

	D	E	F	I	Es
vigili del fuoco (I)	Feuerwehr *f*	fire brigade	sapeurs-pompiers *m pl*	—	cuerpo de bomberos *m*
vile (I)	feig	cowardly	lâche	—	cobarde
village (E)	Dorf *n*	—	village *m*	paese *m*	pueblo *m*
village (F)	Dorf *n*	village	—	paese *m*	pueblo *m*
ville (F)	Stadt *f*	town	—	città *f*	ciudad *f*
vin (F)	Wein *m*	wine	—	vino *m*	vino *m*
vinagre (Es)	Essig *m*	vinegar	vinaigre *m*	aceto *m*	—
vinaigre (F)	Essig *m*	vinegar	—	aceto *m*	vinagre *m*
vincere[1] (I)	gewinnen	win	gagner	—	ganar
vincere[2] (I)	siegen	win	gagner	—	vencer
vinegar (E)	Essig *m*	—	vinaigre *m*	aceto *m*	vinagre *m*
vingt (F)	zwanzig	twenty	—	venti	veinte
vino (Es)	Wein *m*	wine	vin *m*	vino *m*	—
vino (I)	Wein *m*	wine	vin *m*	—	vino *m*
violar (Es)	vergewaltigen	rape	violer	violentare	—
violent (F)	heftig	fierce	—	violento	fuerte
violentare (I)	vergewaltigen	rape	violer	—	violar
violento (I)	heftig	fierce	violent(e)	—	fuerte
violer (F)	vergewaltigen	rape	—	violentare	violar
violin (E)	Geige *f*	—	violon *m*	violino *m*	violín *m*
violín (Es)	Geige *f*	violin	violon *m*	violino *m*	—
violino (I)	Geige *f*	violin	violon *m*	—	violín *m*
violon (F)	Geige *f*	violin	—	violino *m*	violín *m*
virage (F)	Kurve *f*	bend	—	curva *f*	curva *f*
virement (F)	Überweisung *f*	transfer	—	trasferimento *m*	transferencia *f*
virer (F)	überweisen	transfer	—	trasferire	transferir
virgen (Es)	Jungfrau *f*	virgin	vierge *f*	vergine *f*	—
virgin (E)	Jungfrau *f*	—	vierge *f*	vergine *f*	virgen *f*
vis (F)	Schraube *f*	screw	—	vite *f*	tornillo *m*
visa (E)	Visum *n*	—	visa *m*	visto *m*	visado *m*
visa (F)	Visum *n*	visa	—	visto *m*	visado *m*
visado (Es)	Visum *n*	visa	visa *m*	visto *m*	—
visage (F)	Gesicht *n*	face	—	faccia *f*	cara *f*
visibile (I)	sichtbar	visible	visible	—	visible
visible (E)	sichtbar	—	visible	visibile	visible
visible (Es)	sichtbar	visible	visible	visibile	—
visible (F)	sichtbar	visible	—	visibile	visible
visit[1] (E)	besuchen	—	rendre visite à	andare a trovare	visitar
visit[2] (E)	Besuch *m*	—	visite *f*	visita *f*	visita *f*
visita (Es)	Besuch *m*	visit	visite *f*	visita *f*	—
visita (I)	Besuch *m*	visit	visite *f*	—	visita *f*
visita guidata (I)	Führung *f*	guided tour	visite guidée *f*	—	vista guiada *f*
visitante (Es)	Besucher *m*	visitor	visiteur *m*	visitatore *m*	—
visitar[1] (Es)	besuchen	visit	rendre visite à	andare a trovare	—
visitar[2] (Es)	besichtigen	have a look at	visiter	visitare	—
visitare (I)	besichtigen	have a look at	visiter	—	visitar
visitatore (I)	Besucher *m*	visitor	visiteur *m*	—	visitante *m*

	D	E	F	I	Es
visite (F)	Besuch *m*	visit	—	visita *f*	visita *f*
visite guidée (F)	Führung *f*	guided tour	—	visita guidata *f*	vista guiada *f*
visiter (F)	besichtigen	have a look at	—	visitare	visitar
visiteur (F)	Besucher *m*	visitor	—	visitatore *m*	visitante *m*
visitor (E)	Besucher *m*	—	visiteur *m*	visitatore *m*	visitante *m*
víspera (Es)	Vorabend *m*	evening before	veille *f*	vigilia *f*	—
vista¹ (Es)	Aussicht *f*	view	vue *f*	vista *f*	—
vista² (Es)	Blick *m*	look	regard *m*	sguardo *m*	—
vista³ (Es)	Sicht *f*	view	vue *f*	vista *f*	—
vista¹ (I)	Aussicht *f*	view	vue *f*	—	vista *f*
vista² (I)	Sicht *f*	view	vue *f*	—	vista *f*
visto (I)	Visum *n*	visa	visa *m*	—	visado *m*
Visum (D)	—	visa	visa *m*	visto *m*	visado *m*
vita (I)	Leben *n*	life	vie *f*	—	vida *f*
Vitamin (D)	—	vitamin	vitamine *f*	vitamina *f*	vitamina *f*
vitamin (E)	Vitamin *n*	—	vitamine *f*	vitamina *f*	vitamina *f*
vitamina (Es)	Vitamin *n*	vitamin	vitamine *f*	vitamina *f*	—
vitamina (I)	Vitamin *n*	vitamin	vitamine *f*	—	vitamina *f*
vitamine (F)	Vitamin *n*	vitamin	—	vitamina *f*	vitamina *f*
vita quotidiana (I)	Alltag *m*	everyday life	vie quotidienne *f*	—	vida cotidiana *f*
vite (I)	Schraube *f*	screw	vis *f*	—	tornillo *m*
vitello (I)	Kalb *n*	calf	veau *m*	—	ternera *f*
vitesse¹ (F)	Gang *m*	gear	—	marcia *f*	marcha *f*
vitesse² (F)	Geschwindigkeit *f*	speed	—	velocità *f*	velocidad *f*
vitesse³ (F)	Tempo *n*	speed	—	velocità *f*	velocidad *f*
vitesse maximum (F)	Höchst-geschwindigkeit *f*	maximum speed	—	velocità massima *f*	velocidad máxima *f*
vitrine (F)	Schaufenster *n*	shop window	—	vetrina *f*	escaparate *m*
vittima (I)	Opfer *n*	victim	victime *f*	—	víctima *f*
vitto (I)	Verpflegung *f*	catering	nourriture *f*	—	alimentación *f*
vittoria (I)	Sieg *m*	victory	victoire *f*	—	victoria *f*
viuda (Es)	Witwe *f*	widow	veuve *f*	vedova *f*	—
viudo (Es)	Witwer *m*	widower	veuf *m*	vedovo *m*	—
vivace¹ (I)	lebhaft	lively	vif(vivre)	—	vivaz
vivace² (I)	munter	lively	éveillé(e)	—	alegre
vivant (F)	lebendig	alive	—	vivo(a)	vivo(a)
vivaz (Es)	lebhaft	lively	vif(vivre)	vivace	—
vivere¹ (I)	erleben	experience	être témoin de	—	experimentar
vivere² (I)	leben	live	vivre	—	vivir
vivir¹ (Es)	leben	live	vivre	vivere	—
vivir² (Es)	wohnen	live	habiter	abitare	—
vivo (I)	lebendig	alive	vivant(e)	—	vivo(a)
vivre (F)	leben	live	—	vivere	vivir
viziare (I)	verwöhnen	spoil	gâter	—	mimar
voce¹ (I)	Gerücht *n*	rumour	rumeur *f*	—	rumor *m*
voce² (I)	Stimme *f*	voice	voix *f*	—	voz *f*
Vogel (D)	—	bird	oiseau *m*	uccello *m*	pájaro *m*
voi (I)	ihr	you	vous	—	vosotros

	D	E	F	I	Es
voice (E)	Stimme f	—	voix f	voce f	voz f
voie (F)	Gleis n	track	—	binario m	vía f
voie rapide (F)	Schnellstraße f	expressway	—	superstrada f	carretera de circulación rápida f
voir (F)	sehen	see	—	vedere	ver
voisin (F)	Nachbar m	neighbour	—	vicino m	vecino m
voiture[1] (F)	Auto n	car	—	automobile f / macchina f	coche m
voiture[2] (F)	Wagen m	car	—	vettura f	coche m
voix (F)	Stimme f	voice	—	voce f	voz f
vol (F)	Flug m	flight	—	volo m	vuelo m
volaille (F)	Geflügel n	poultry	—	pollame m	aves f pl
volant (F)	Lenkrad n	steering wheel	—	volante m	volante m
volante (Es)	Lenkrad n	steering wheel	volant m	volante m	—
volante (I)	Lenkrad n	steering wheel	volant m	—	volante m
volar (Es)	fliegen	fly	voler	volare	—
volare (I)	fliegen	fly	voler	—	volar
vol-au-vent (I)	Pastete f	pie	pâté m	—	empanada f
volentieri (I)	gern	willingly	avec plaisir	—	con gusto
voler[1] (F)	fliegen	fly	—	volare	volar
voler[2] (F)	rauben	rob	—	rapinare	robar
voler[3] (F)	stehlen	steal	—	rubare	robar
volere (I)	wollen	want	vouloir	—	querer
voleur (F)	Dieb m	thief	—	ladro m	ladrón m
volgare (I)	gemein	mean	méchant(e)	—	vulgar
Volk (D)	—	people	peuple m	popolo m	pueblo m
voll (D)	—	full	plein(e)	pieno(a)	lleno(a)
völlig (D)	—	completely	complètement	completamente	completamente
volljährig (D)	—	of age	majeur(e)	maggiorenne	mayor de edad
vollkommen (D)	—	perfect	parfait(e)	perfetto(a)	perfecto(a)
Vollmacht (D)	—	authority	procuration f	delega f	poder m
Vollpension (D)	—	full board	pension complète f	pensione completa f	pensión completa f
vollständig (D)	—	complete	complet(-ète)	completo(a)	completo(a)
volo (I)	Flug m	flight	vol m	—	vuelo m
volontaire (F)	freiwillig	voluntary	—	volontario(a)	voluntario(a)
volontario (I)	freiwillig	voluntary	volontaire	—	voluntario(a)
volpe (I)	Fuchs m	fox	renard m	—	zorro m
voltare (I)	wenden	turn	tourner	—	volver
voltare pagina (I)	umblättern	turn over	tourner la page	—	volver la hoja
voluntario (Es)	freiwillig	voluntary	volontaire	volontario(a)	—
voluntary (E)	freiwillig	—	volontaire	volontario(a)	voluntario(a)
volver[1] (Es)	umdrehen	turn around	tourner	girare	—
volver[2] (Es)	wenden	turn	tourner	voltare	—
volver[3] (Es)	zurückkehren	return	revenir	ritornare	—
volver a ver (Es)	wiedersehen	see again	revoir	rivedere	—
volver la hoja (Es)	umblättern	turn over	tourner la page	voltare pagina	—
von (D)	—	from/by	de	di/da	de
vor (D)	—	before/ in front of	devant/avant	davanti a	delante de

	D	E	F	I	Es
Vorabend (D)	—	evening before	veille f	vigilia f	víspera f
vorangehen (D)	—	go ahead	marcher devant	andare avanti	pasar adelante
voraus (D)	—	ahead	en avant	avanti	delante
vorausgesetzt (D)	—	provided	à condition que	presumendo	supuesto
voraussetzen (D)	—	assume	supposer	presupporre	suponer
Vorbehalt (D)	—	reservation	réserve f	riserva f	reserva f
vorbei (D)	—	past	passé(e)	passato(a)	pasado(a)
vorbeigehen (D)	—	pass	passer	passare	pasar
vorbereiten (D)	—	prepare	préparer	preparare	preparar
vorbestellen (D)	—	book	réserver	prenotare	hacer reservar
Vorbild (D)	—	ideal	modèle m	modello m	modelo m
Vorfahrt (D)	—	right of way	priorité f	precedenza f	preferencia f
Vorfall (D)	—	incident	cas m	caso m	suceso m
vorgehen (D)	—	proceed	avancer	procedere	proceder
vorgestern (D)	—	day before yesterday	avant-hier	l'altro ieri	anteayer
vorhaben (D)	—	intend	avoir l'intention de	avere intenzione	tener la intención de
vorhanden (D)	—	available	présent(e)	disponibile	presente
Vorhang (D)	—	curtain	rideau m	tenda f	cortina f
vorher (D)	—	before	avant	prima	antes
vorhergehend (D)	—	preceding	précédent(e)	precedente	anterior
vorhersagen (D)	—	predict	prédire	prognosticare	pronosticar
vorig (D)	—	previous	précédent(e)	precedente	precedente
vorkommen (D)	—	occur	exister	accadere	suceder
vorladen (D)	—	summon	assigner	citare in giudizio	citar
vorläufig (D)	—	temporary	provisoire	provvisorio(a)	provisional
Vorlesung (D)	—	lecture	cours magistral m	lezione f	clase f
vorletzter (D)	—	one before last	avant-dernier(-ère)	penultimo(a)	penúltima(o)
vormerken (D)	—	book	prendre note de	prendere nota di	tomar nota
Vormittag (D)	—	before noon	matinée f	mattina f	mañana f
vormittags (D)	—	in the morning	le matin	di mattina	por la mañana
vorn(e) (D)	—	at the front	devant	davanti	delante
Vorname (D)	—	Christian name	prénom m	nome di battesimo m	nombre m
vornehm (D)	—	distinguished	distingué(e)	distinto(a)	distinguido(a)
Vorort (D)	—	suburb	faubourg m	sobborgo m	suburbio m
Vorrat (D)	—	stock	réserves f pl	scorte f pl	provisión f
Vorsaison (D)	—	low season	basse saison f	bassa stagione f	pretemporada f
Vorschlag (D)	—	proposal	proposition f	proposta f	proposición f
vorschlagen (D)	—	propose	proposer	proporre	proponer
Vorschrift (D)	—	regulation	règle f	norma f	reglamento m
Vorsicht (D)	—	caution	prudence f	prudenza f	cuidado m
vorsichtig (D)	—	careful	prudent(e)	prudente	cauto(a)
Vorspeise (D)	—	appetizer	hors-d'œuvre m	antipasto m	primer plato m
vorstellen (D)	—	introduce	présenter	presentare	presentar
Vorstellung[1] (D)	—	idea	idée f	idea f	idea f
Vorstellung[2] (D)	—	performance	représentation f	rappresentazione f	representación f
Vorteil (D)	—	advantage	avantage m	vantaggio m	ventaja f
vorüber (D)	—	past	passé(e)	passato(a)	pasado(a)

	D	E	F	I	Es
vorübergehend (D)	—	temporary	temporaire	temporaneo(a)	pasajero(a)
Vorverkauf (D)	—	advance booking	location *f*	vendita anticipata *f*	venta anticipada *f*
Vorwahl (D)	—	dialling code	indicatif téléphonique *m*	prefisso *m*	prefijo *m*
Vorwand (D)	—	pretext	prétexte *m*	pretesto *m*	pretexto *m*
vorwärts (D)	—	forward(s)	en avant	avanti	adelante
vorwerfen (D)	—	blame	reprocher	rimproverare	echar en cara
Vorwort (D)	—	preface	préface *f*	prefazione *f*	prólogo *m*
vorzeigen (D)	—	show	monter	esibire	presentar
vorziehen[1] (D)	—	draw	tirer	tirare in avanti	correr
vorziehen[2] (D)	—	prefer	préférer	preferire	preferir
Vorzug (D)	—	preference	préférence *f*	preferenza *f*	preferencia *f*
vosotros (Es)	ihr	you	vous	voi	—
voto (I)	Note *f*	mark	note *f*	—	calificación *f*
voucher (E)	Gutschein *m*	—	bon *m*	buono *m*	vale *m*
vouloir (F)	wollen	want	—	volere	querer
vous (F)	ihr	you	—	voi	vosotros
voyage[1] (F)	Fahrt *f*	journey	—	viaggio *m*	viaje *m*
voyage[2] (F)	Reise *f*	journey	—	viaggio *m*	viaje *m*
voyager (F)	reisen	travel	—	viaggiare	viajar
voyageur (F)	Reisender *m*	traveller	—	viaggiatore *m*	viajero *m*
voz (Es)	Stimme *f*	voice	voix *f*	voce *f*	—
vrai[1] (F)	echt	genuine	—	vero(a)	verdadero(a)
vrai[2] (F)	wahr	true	—	vero(a)	verdadero(a)
vraiment (F)	tatsächlich	really	—	realmente	realmente
vue[1] (F)	Aussicht *f*	view	—	vista *f*	vista *f*
vue[2] (F)	Sicht *f*	view	—	vista *f*	vista *f*
vuelo (Es)	Flug *m*	flight	vol *m*	volo *m*	—
vulgar (Es)	gemein	mean	méchant(e)	volgare	—
vuoto (I)	leer	empty	vide	—	vacío(a)
Waage (D)	—	scales	balance *f*	bilancia *f*	balanza *f*
waagrecht (D)	—	horizontal	horizontal(e)	orizzontale	horizontal
wach (D)	—	awake	réveillé(e)	sveglio(a)	despierto(a)
wachsen (D)	—	grow	grandir	crescere	crecer
Waffe (D)	—	weapon	arme *f*	arma *f*	arma *m*
wagen (D)	—	dare	oser	osare	atreverse
Wagen (D)	—	car	voiture *f*	vettura *f*	coche *m*
wages (E)	Lohn *m*	—	salaire *m*	salario *m*	salario *m*
Waggon (D)	—	carriage	wagon *m*	vagone *m*	vagón *m*
wagon (F)	Waggon *m*	carriage	—	vagone *m*	vagón *m*
wagon-couchette (F)	Liegewagen *m*	couchette	—	cuccetta *f*	coche cama *m*
wagon-restaurant (F)	Speisewagen *m*	dining car	—	vagone ristorante *m*	vagón restaurante *m*
Wahl[1] (D)	—	choice	choix *m*	scelta *f*	opción *f*
Wahl[2] (D)	—	election	élection *f*	elezioni *f pl*	elección *f*
wählen (D)	—	elect	élire	eleggere	elegir
wahr (D)	—	true	vrai(e)	vero(a)	verdadero(a)
während (D)	—	during	pendant	durante	durante

	D	E	F	I	Es
Wahrheit (D)	—	truth	vérité f	verità f	verdad f
wahrscheinlich (D)	—	probably	probablement	probabile	probablemente
Währung (D)	—	currency	monnaie f	valuta f	moneda f
Waise (D)	—	orphan	orphelin m	orfano m	huérfano m
wait (E)	warten	—	attendre	aspettare	esperar
waiter (E)	Kellner m/ Ober m	—	garçon m	cameriere m	camarero m
waiting room (E)	Wartesaal m	—	salle d'attente f	sala d'attesa f	sala de espera f
wake (up) (E)	wecken	—	réveiller	svegliare	despertar
wake up[1] (E)	aufwachen	—	réveiller, se	svegliarsi	despertarse
wake up[2] (E)	aufwecken	—	réveiller	svegliare	despertar
wake up[3] (E)	erwachen	—	réveiller, se	svegliarsi	despertar
Wald (D)	—	forest	forêt f	bosco m	bosque m
walk (E)	Spaziergang m	—	promenade f	passeggiata f	paseo m
wall[1] (E)	Mauer f	—	mur m	muro m	muro m
wall[2] (E)	Wand f	—	mur m	parete f	pared f
Wand (D)	—	wall	mur m	parete f	pared f
wandern (D)	—	hike	marcher	fare escursioni a piedi	hacer excursiones
Wange (D)	—	cheek	joue f	guancia f	mejilla f
wanken (D)	—	stagger	chanceller	barcollare	vacilar
wann (D)	—	when	quand	quando	cuando
want (E)	wollen	—	vouloir	volere	querer
war (E)	Krieg m	—	guerre f	guerra f	guerra f
wardrobe[1] (E)	Garderobe f	—	vestiaire m	guardaroba m	guardaropa m
wardrobe[2] (E)	Kleiderschrank m	—	garde-robe f	armadio m	armario ropero m
Ware (D)	—	goods	marchandise f	merce f	mercancía f
warm (D)	—	warm	chaud(e)	caldo(a)	caliente
warm[1] (E)	wärmen	—	chauffer	riscaldare	calentar
warm[2] (E)	warm	—	chaud(e)	caldo(a)	caliente
Wärme (D)	—	warmth	chaleur f	calore m	calor m
wärmen (D)	—	warm	chauffer	riscaldare	calentar
warmth (E)	Wärme f	—	chaleur f	calore m	calor m
warn[1] (E)	abraten	—	déconseiller	sconsigliare	desaconsejar
warn[2] (E)	mahnen	—	exhorter	ammonire	notificar
warn[3] (E)	warnen	—	prévenir de	ammonire	advertir
warnen (D)	—	warn	prévenir de	ammonire	advertir
warten (D)	—	wait	attendre	aspettare	esperar
Wärter (D)	—	attendant	gardien m	custode m	guarda m
Wartesaal (D)	—	waiting room	salle d'attente f	sala d'attesa f	sala de espera f
warum (D)	—	why	pourquoi	perché	por qué
was (D)	—	what	quoi/qu'est-ce que	che/cosa	qué
waschbar (D)	—	washable	lavable	lavabile	lavable
Waschbecken (D)	—	wash-basin	lavabo m	lavandino m	lavabo m
Wäsche (D)	—	washing	linge m	biancheria f	ropa f
waschen (D)	—	wash	laver	lavare	lavar
Wäscherei (D)	—	laundry	blanchisserie f	lavanderia f	lavandería f
Waschmaschine (D)	—	washing machine	machine à laver f	lavatrice f	lavadora f
Waschmittel (D)	—	detergent	lessive f	detersivo m	detergente m

	D	E	F	I	Es
wash (E)	waschen	—	laver	lavare	lavar
wash up (E)	abspülen	—	faire la vaissèlle	sciacquare	lavar
washable (E)	waschbar	—	lavable	lavabile	lavable
wash-basin (E)	Waschbecken *n*	—	lavabo *m*	lavandino *m*	lavabo *m*
washing (E)	Wäsche *f*	—	linge *m*	biancheria *f*	ropa *f*
washing machine (E)	Waschmaschine *f*	—	machine à laver *f*	lavatrice *f*	lavadora *f*
wash off (E)	abwaschen	—	laver	lavar via	lavar
wasp (E)	Wespe *f*	—	guêpe *f*	vespa *f*	avispa *f*
Wasser (D)	—	water	eau *f*	acqua *f*	agua *f*
waste¹ (E)	öde	—	désert(e)	deserto(a)	desierto(a)
waste² (E)	verschwenden	—	gaspiller	sprecare	desperdiciar
watch¹ (E)	Uhr *f*	—	montre *f*	orologio *m*	reloj *m*
watch² (E)	zuschauen	—	regarder	stare a guardare	mirar
watch³ (E)	zusehen	—	regarder	stare a guardare	mirar
watch television (E)	fernsehen	—	regarder la télévision	guardare la TV	ver la televisión
water¹ (E)	gießen	—	arroser	annaffiare	regar
water² (E)	Wasser *n*	—	eau *f*	acqua *f*	agua *f*
waters (E)	Gewässer *n*	—	eaux *f pl*	acque *f pl*	aguas *f pl*
Watte (D)	—	cotton wool	ouate *f*	ovatta *f*	algodón *m*
wave¹ (E)	winken	—	faire signe	chiamare con cenni	llamar con gestos
wave² (E)	Welle *f*	—	vague *f*	onda *f*	ola *f*
way¹ (E)	Art *f*	—	manière *f*	modo *m*	manera *f*
way² (E)	Weise *f*	—	manière *f*	maniera *f*	manera *f*
way³ (E)	Weg *m*	—	chemin *m*	via *f*	camino *m*
we (E)	wir	—	nous	noi	nosotros(as)
weak (E)	schwach	—	faible	debole	débil
weakness (E)	Schwäche *f*	—	faiblesse *f*	debolezza *f*	debilidad *f*
weapon (E)	Waffe *f*	—	arme *f*	arma *f*	arma *m*
wear out (E)	abnutzen	—	user	consumare	desgastar
weather (E)	Wetter *n*	—	temps *m*	tempo *m*	tiempo *m*
weather forecast (E)	Wetter-vorhersage *f*	—	prévisions météorologiques *f pl*	previsioni del tempo *f pl*	pronóstico del tiempo *m*
weather report (E)	Wetterbericht *m*	—	bulletin météorologique *m*	bollettino metereologico *m*	informe metereológico *m*
Wechsel (D)	—	change	changement *m*	cambiamento *m*	cambio *m*
wechseln (D)	—	change	changer	cambiare	cambiar
Wechselstube (D)	—	bureau de change	bureau de change *m*	ufficio di cambio *m*	casa de cambio *f*
wecken (D)	—	wake (up)	réveiller	svegliare	despertar
Wecker (D)	—	alarm clock	réveil *m*	sveglia *f*	despertador *m*
wedding (E)	Hochzeit *f*	—	mariage *m*	nozze *f pl*	boda *f*
weder (D)	—	neither	ni	né...né	ni
Wednesday (E)	Mittwoch *m*	—	mercredi *m*	mercoledì *m*	miércoles *m*
week (E)	Woche *f*	—	semaine *f*	settimana *f*	semana *f*
weekend (E)	Wochenende *n*	—	week-end *m*	fine settimana *m*	fin de semana *m*
week-end (F)	Wochenende *n*	weekend	—	fine settimana *m*	fin de semana *m*
weekly (E)	wöchentlich	—	hebdomadaire	settimanale	semanal
weg (D)	—	away	pas là	via	fuera

	D	E	F	I	Es
Weg (D)	—	way	chemin *m*	via *f*	camino *m*
wegen (D)	—	because of	à cause de	a causa di	a causa de
weggehen (D)	—	go away	s'en aller	andare via	marcharse
wegnehmen (D)	—	take away	enlever	togliere	quitar
weh (D)	—	hurt	douloureux(-euse)	dolente	doloroso(a)
wehren, sich (D)	—	defend	défendre, se	difendersi	defenderse
weiblich (D)	—	feminine	féminin(e)	femminile	femenino
weich (D)	—	soft	doux (douce)	morbido(a)	tierno(a)
weigern (D)	—	refuse	refuser	rifiutare	resistirse
weigh (E)	wiegen	—	peser	pesare	pesar
weight (E)	Gewicht *n*	—	poids *m*	peso *m*	peso *m*
Weihnachten (D)	—	Christmas	Noël *m*	Natale *m*	Navidad(es) *f (pl)*
weil (D)	—	because	parce que	perché	porque
Weile (D)	—	while	moment *m*	momento *m*	rato *m*
Wein (D)	—	wine	vin *m*	vino *m*	vino *m*
weinen (D)	—	cry	pleurer	piangere	llorar
weise (D)	—	wise	sage	saggio(a)	sabio(a)
Weise (D)	—	way	manière *f*	maniera *f*	manera *f*
weiß (D)	—	white	blanc, blanche	bianco(a)	blanco(a)
weit (D)	—	far	éloigné(e)	largo(a)	ancho(a)
weiter (D)	—	further	plus éloigné(e)	più ampio(a)	adelante
weitergehen (D)	—	go on	aller plus loin	proseguire	proseguir
weitermachen (D)	—	carry on	continuer	continuare	continuar
weiterschlafen (D)	—	sleep on	continuer à dormir	continuare a dormire	seguir durmiendo
Weizen (D)	—	wheat	blé *m*	frumento *m*	trigo *m*
welch (D)	—	what a	quel(le)	che	¿qué?
welche (D)	—	which	qui/que	il(la) quale	¿cual?
welcome (E)	willkommen	—	bienvenu(e)	benvenuto(a)	bienvenido(a)
welfare (E)	Wohl *n*	—	bien *m*	benessere *m*	bienestar *m*
welken (D)	—	wither	faner, se	appassire	machitarse
well (E)	wohl	—	bien	bene/forse	bien
Welle (D)	—	wave	vague *f*	onda *f*	ola *f*
well known (E)	bekannt	—	connu(e)	conosciuto(a)	conocido(a)
Welt (D)	—	world	monde *m*	mondo *m*	mundo *m*
Weltall (D)	—	universe	univers *m*	universo *m*	universo *m*
Weltsprache (D)	—	world language	langue internationale *f*	lingua mondiale *f*	lengua universal *f*
wenden (D)	—	turn	tourner	voltare	volver
wenig (D)	—	little	peu de	poco	poco(a)
wenige (D)	—	few	peu	pochi	pocos(as)
weniger (D)	—	less	moins	di meno	menos
wenigstens (D)	—	at least	au moins	almeno	por lo menos
wenn (D)	—	when/if	si/quand	se/quando	cuando
wer (D)	—	who	qui	chi	quién
werben (D)	—	advertise	faire de la publicité	fare propaganda	hacer publicidad
Werbung (D)	—	advertising	publicité *f*	pubblicità *f*	publicidad *f*
werden (D)	—	become	devenir	diventare	llegar
werfen (D)	—	throw	lancer	lanciare	tirar

	D	E	F	I	Es
Werk (D)	—	work	œuvre f	opera f	obra f
Werkstatt (D)	—	workshop	atelier m	officina f	taller m
Werktag (D)	—	working day	jour ouvrable m	giorno feriale m	día laborable m
werktags (D)	—	on working days	les jours ouvrables	nei giorni feriali	los días laborables
Werkzeug (D)	—	tool	outils m pl	utensile m	herramienta f
wert (D)	—	worth	cher, chère	che vale	querido(a)
Wert (D)	—	value	valeur f	valore m	valor m
wertlos (D)	—	worthless	sans valeur	senza valore	sin valor
wertvoll (D)	—	valuable	précieux(-euse)	prezioso(a)	valioso(a)
Wesen (D)	—	being	être m	essere m	ser m
wesentlich (D)	—	essential	essentiel(-le)	essenziale	esencial
weshalb (D)	—	why	pourquoi	perché	por qué
Wespe (D)	—	wasp	guêpe f	vespa f	avispa f
wessen (D)	—	whose	de qui	di chi	de quién
west (E)	Westen m	—	ouest m	ovest m	oeste m
Westen (D)	—	west	ouest m	ovest m	oeste m
western (E)	westlich	—	de l'ouest	ad ovest	del oeste
westlich (D)	—	western	de l'ouest	ad ovest	del oeste
wet (E)	naß	—	mouillé(e)	bagnato	húmedo(a)
Wettbewerb (D)	—	competition	concours m	concorso m	concurso m
Wette (D)	—	bet	pari m	scommessa f	apuesta f
wetten (D)	—	bet	parier	scommettere	apostar
Wetter (D)	—	weather	temps m	tempo m	tiempo m
Wetterbericht (D)	—	weather report	bulletin météorologique m	bollettino metereologico m	informe metereológico m
Wetter-vorhersage (D)	—	weather forecast	prévisions météorologiques f pl	previsioni del tempo f pl	pronóstico del tiempo m
what (E)	was	—	quoi/qu'est-ce que	che/cosa	qué
what a (E)	welch	—	quel(le)	che	qué
what for[1] (E)	wofür	—	pourquoi	per cui	para qué
what for[2] (E)	wozu	—	pourquoi	perché	para qué
wheat (E)	Weizen m	—	blé m	frumento m	trigo m
wheel (E)	Rad n	—	roue f	ruota f	rueda f
when[1] (E)	als	—	quand	quando	cuando
when[2] (E)	wann	—	quand	quando	cuando
when[3] (E)	wenn	—	si/quand	se/quando	cuando
where (E)	wo	—	où	dove	dónde
where from (E)	woher	—	d'où	da dove	de dónde
where to (E)	wohin	—	où	dove	a dónde
which (E)	welche(r,s)	—	qui/que	il(la) quale	cual
while (E)	Weile f	—	moment m	momento m	rato m
whisper (E)	flüstern	—	chuchoter	bisbigliare	cuchichear
whistle (E)	Pfeife f	—	sifflet m	fischietto m	silbato m
white (E)	weiß	—	blanc(he)	bianco(a)	blanco(a)
Whitsun (E)	Pfingsten n	—	Pentecôte f	Pentecoste f	Pascua de Pentecostés f
who (E)	wer	—	qui	chi	quién
whole (E)	ganz	—	tout(e)	intero(a)	entero(a)
whose (E)	wessen	—	de qui	di chi	de quién

	D	E	F	I	Es
why[1] (E)	warum	—	pourquoi	perché	por qué
why[2] (E)	wieso	—	pourquoi	come mai	por qué
why[3] (E)	weshalb	—	pourquoi	perché	por qué
wichtig (D)	—	important	important(e)	importante	importante
wicked (E)	böse	—	méchant(e)	cattivo(a)	malo(a)
wickeln (D)	—	wind	enrouler	avvolgere	envolver
widerlich (D)	—	disgusting	repoussant(e)	ripugnante	repugnante
widerrufen (D)	—	retract	démentir	revocare	revocación f
widersprechen (D)	—	contradict	contredire	contraddire	contradecir
Widerstand (D)	—	resistance	résistance f	resistenza f	resistencia f
widmen (D)	—	dedicate	dédier	dedicare	dedicar
widow (E)	Witwe f	—	veuve f	vedova f	viuda f
widower (E)	Witwer m	—	veuf m	vedovo m	viudo m
width (E)	Breite f	—	largeur f	larghezza f	extensión f
wie (D)	—	how	comment	come	cómo
wieder (D)	—	again	de nouveau	di nuovo	de nuevo
wiedergeben (D)	—	return	rendre	restituire	devolver
wiedergut-machen (D)	—	make up for	réparer	riparare	subsanar
wiederholen (D)	—	repeat	répéter	ripetere	repetir
wiederhören! (D)	—	good-bye!	au revoir!	a risentirci!	¡adiós!
wieder-kommen (D)	—	come back	revenir	ritornare	venir de nuevo
wiedersehen (D)	—	see again	revoir	rivedere	volver a ver
wiedersehen! (D)	—	good-bye!	au revoir!	arrivederci!	¡adiós!
wiegen (D)	—	weigh	peser	pesare	pesar
Wiese (D)	—	meadow	pré m	prato m	prado m
wieso (D)	—	why	pourquoi	come mai	por qué
wieviel (D)	—	how much	combien	quanto	cuánto
wieviele (D)	—	how many	combien	quanti(e)	cuántos(as)
wife (E)	Ehefrau f	—	épouse f	moglie f	mujer f
wild (D)	—	wild	sauvage	selvatico(a)	salvaje
Wild (D)	—	game	gibier m	selvaggina f	caza f
wild (E)	wild	—	sauvage	selvatico(a)	salvaje
will[1] (E)	Belieben n	—	plaisir m	piacere m	placer m
will[2] (E)	Testament n	—	testament m	testamento m	testamento m
willingly (E)	gern	—	avec plaisir	volentieri	con gusto
willkommen (D)	—	welcome	bienvenu(e)	benvenuto(a)	bienvenido(a)
Wimper (D)	—	eyelash	cil m	ciglia f	pestaña f
win[1] (E)	gewinnen	—	gagner	vincere	ganar
win[2] (E)	siegen	—	gagner	vincere	vencer
Wind (D)	—	wind	vent m	vento m	viento m
wind[1] (E)	wickeln	—	enrouler	avvolgere	envolver
wind[2] (E)	Wind m	—	vent m	vento m	viento m
Windel (D)	—	nappy	lange m	pannolino m	pañal m
windig (D)	—	windy	éventé(e)	ventoso(a)	ventoso
window (E)	Fenster n	—	fenêtre f	finestra f	ventana f
windy (E)	windig	—	éventé(e)	ventoso	ventoso
wine (E)	Wein m	—	vin m	vino m	vino m

	D	E	F	I	Es
wing (E)	Flügel *m*	—	aile *f*	ala *f*	ala *f*
Winkel (D)	—	corner	coin *m*	cantuccio *m*	rincón *m*
winken (D)	—	wave	faire signe	chiamare con cenni	llamar con gestos
Winter (D)	—	winter	hiver *m*	inverno *m*	invierno *m*
winter (E)	Winter *m*	—	hiver *m*	inverno *m*	invierno *m*
wipe (E)	wischen	—	essuyer	pulire	fregar
wir (D)	—	we	nous	noi	nosotros(as)
Wirbelsäule (D)	—	spine	colonne vertébrale *f*	colonna vertebrale *f*	columna vertebral *f*
wire (E)	Draht *m*	—	fil de fer *m*	filo metallico *m*	alambre *m*
wirklich (D)	—	real	réel(le)	reale	real
Wirklichkeit (D)	—	reality	réalité *f*	realtà *f*	realidad *f*
wirksam (D)	—	effective	efficace	efficace	eficaz
Wirkung (D)	—	effect	effet *m*	effetto *m*	efecto *m*
Wirt (D)	—	landlord	patron *m*	oste *m*	dueño *m*
Wirtshaus (D)	—	inn	auberge *f*	osteria *f*	restaurante *m*
wischen (D)	—	wipe	essuyer	pulire	fregar
wise (E)	weise	—	sage	saggio(a)	sabio(a)
wish¹ (E)	wünschen	—	souhaiter	desiderare	desear
wish² (E)	Wunsch *m*	—	souhait *m*	desiderio *m*	deseo *m*
wissen (D)	—	know	savoir	sapere	saber
Wissen (D)	—	knowledge	savoir *m*	sapere *m*	saber *m*
Wissenschaft (D)	—	science	science *f*	scienza *f*	ciencia *f*
Wissenschaftler (D)	—	scientist	scientifique *m*	scienziato *m*	científico *m*
witch (E)	Hexe *f*	—	sorcière *f*	strega *f*	bruja *f*
with (E)	mit	—	avec	con	con
withdraw (E)	zurückziehen	—	retirer	ritirare	retirar
wither (E)	welken	—	faner, se	appassire	marchitarse
within (E)	innerhalb	—	à l'intérieur de	entro	dentro de
with it (E)	damit	—	avec cela	con questo	con ello
without (E)	ohne	—	sans	senza	sin
witness (E)	Zeuge *m*	—	témoin *m*	testimone *m*	testigo *m*
Witwe (D)	—	widow	veuve *f*	vedova *f*	viuda *f*
Witwer (D)	—	widower	veuf *m*	vedovo *m*	viudo *m*
Witz (D)	—	joke	plaisanterie *f*	barzelletta *f*	chiste *m*
wo (D)	—	where	où	dove	dónde
woanders (D)	—	elsewhere	ailleurs	altrove	en otra parte
Woche (D)	—	week	semaine *f*	settimana *f*	semana *f*
Wochenende (D)	—	weekend	week-end *m*	fine settimana *m*	fin de semana *m*
wochentags (D)	—	during the week	en semaine	nei giorni feriali	entre semana
wöchentlich (D)	—	weekly	hebdomadaire	settimanale	semanal
wofür (D)	—	what for	pourquoi	per cui	para qué
woher (D)	—	where from	d'où	da dove	de dónde
wohin (D)	—	where to	où	dove	a dónde
wohl (D)	—	well	bien	bene/forse	bien
Wohl (D)	—	welfare	bien *m*	benessere *m*	bienestar *m*
wohnen (D)	—	live	habiter	abitare	vivir
Wohnmobil (D)	—	camper	caravane *f*	camper *m*	caravana *f*

	D	E	F	I	Es
Wohnort (D)	—	domicile	domicile *m*	residenza *f*	residencia *f*
Wohnung (D)	—	flat	appartement *m*	appartamento *m*	piso *m*
Wohnwagen (D)	—	caravan	caravane *f*	roulotte *f*	rulota *f*
Wohnzimmer (D)	—	living room	salle de séjour *f*	salotto *m*	sala de estar *f*
Wolke (D)	—	cloud	nuage *m*	nuvola *f*	nube *f*
Wolle (D)	—	wool	laine *f*	lana *f*	lana *f*
wollen (D)	—	want	vouloir	volere	querer
woman (E)	Frau *f*	—	femme *f*	donna *f*	mujer *f*
wonder (E)	wundern	—	étonner	stupire	asombrar
wonderful (E)	wunderbar	—	miraculeux (-euse)	meraviglioso(a)	maravilloso(a)
wood (E)	Holz *n*	—	bois *m*	legno *m*	madera *f*
wool (E)	Wolle *f*	—	laine *f*	lana *f*	lana *f*
word (E)	Wort *n*	—	mot *m*	parola *f*	palabra *f*
work¹ (E)	arbeiten	—	travailler	lavorare	trabajar
work² (E)	Arbeit *f*	—	travail *m*	lavoro *m*	trabajo *m*
work³ (E)	funktionieren	—	fonctionner	funzionare	funcionar
work⁴ (E)	Werk *n*	—	œuvre *f*	opera *f*	obra *f*
worker (E)	Arbeiter *m*	—	ouvrier *m*	operaio *m*	trabajador *m*
working day (E)	Werktag *m*	—	jour ouvrable *m*	giorno feriale *m*	día laborable *m*
workshop (E)	Werkstatt *f*	—	atelier *m*	officina *f*	taller *m*
world (E)	Welt *f*	—	monde *m*	mondo *m*	mundo *m*
world language (E)	Weltsprache *f*	—	langue internationale *f*	lingua mondiale *f*	lengua universal *f*
worry about (E)	sorgen	—	occuper de, se	prendersi cura di	atender
worship (E)	anbeten	—	adorer	adorare	adorar
Wort (D)	—	word	mot *m*	parola *f*	palabra *f*
Wörterbuch (D)	—	dictionary	dictionnaire *m*	dizionario *m*	diccionario *m*
worth (E)	wert	—	cher, chère	che vale	querido(a)
worthless (E)	wertlos	—	sans valeur	senza valore	sin valor
wound¹ (E)	verwunden	—	blesser	ferire	herir
wound² (E)	Wunde *f*	—	blessure *f*	ferita *f*	herida *f*
wozu (D)	—	what for	pourquoi	perchè	¿para qué?
wrap up (E)	einwickeln	—	envelopper	avvolgere	envolver
write (E)	schreiben	—	écrire	scrivere	escribir
writer (E)	Schriftsteller *m*	—	écrivain *m*	scrittore *m*	escritor *m*
writing (E)	Schrift *f*	—	écriture *f*	scrittura *f*	escritura *f*
written (E)	schriftlich	—	écrit(e)	scritto(a)	por escrito
wrong¹ (E)	falsch	—	faux (fausse)	falso(a)	falso(a)
wrong² (E)	Unrecht *n*	—	injustice *f*	torto *m*	injusticia *f*
wrong³ (E)	verkehrt	—	faux (fausse)	sbagliato(a)	equivocado(a)
wühlen (D)	—	scrabble	fouiller	rovistare	revolver
Wunde (D)	—	wound	blessure *f*	ferita *f*	herida *f*
Wunder (D)	—	miracle	miracle *m*	miracolo *m*	milagro *m*
wunderbar (D)	—	wonderful	miraculeux(-euse)	meraviglioso(a)	maravilloso(a)
wundern (D)	—	wonder	étonner	stupire	asombrar
Wunsch (D)	—	wish	souhait *m*	desiderio *m*	deseo *m*
wünschen (D)	—	wish	souhaiter	desiderare	desear
Würfel (D)	—	dice	dé *m*	dado *m*	dado *m*

	D	E	F	I	Es
Wurst (D)	—	sausage	saucisse f	salsiccia f	salchichón m
Wurzel (D)	—	root	racine f	radice f	raíz f
würzen (D)	—	season	épicer	condire	condimentar
würzig (D)	—	spicy	épicé(e)	aromatico(a)	aromático(a)
Wüste (D)	—	desert	désert m	deserto m	desierto m
Wut (D)	—	anger	colère f	rabbia f	rabia f
wütend (D)	—	furious	furieux(-euse)	arrabbiato(a)	furioso(a)
X-ray (E)	röntgen	—	radiographier	fare una radiografia	radiografiar
y (Es)	und	and	et	e	—
ya (Es)	bereits/schon	already	déjà	già	—
yacht (E)	Jacht f	—	yacht m	panfilo m	yate m
yacht (F)	Jacht f	yacht	—	panfilo m	yate m
yaourt (F)	Joghurt m	yogurt	—	yoghurt m	yogur(t) m
yard (E)	Hof m	—	cour f	cortile m	patio m
yate (Es)	Jacht f	yacht	yacht m	panfilo m	—
y compris (F)	einschließlich	including	—	incluso(a)	incluído
year (E)	Jahr n	—	année f	anno m	año m
yellow (E)	gelb	—	jaune	giallo(a)	amarillo(a)
yema (Es)	Knospe f	bud	bourgeon m	bocciolo m	—
yes (E)	ja	—	oui	sì	sí
yesterday (E)	gestern	—	hier	ieri	ayer
yield (E)	nachgeben	—	céder	cedere	ceder
yo (Es)	ich	I	je/moi	io	—
yoghurt (I)	Joghurt m	yogurt	yaourt m	—	yogur(t) m
yogur(t) (Es)	Joghurt m	yogurt	yaourt m	yoghurt m	—
yogurt (E)	Joghurt m	—	yaourt m	yoghurt m	yogur(t) m
you[1] (E)	du	—	tu/toi	tu	tú
you[2] (E)	ihr	—	vous	voi	vosotros
young (E)	jung	—	jeune	giovane	joven
youth (E)	Jugend f	—	jeunesse f	gioventù f	juventud f
zäh (D)	—	tough	coriace	duro(a)	duro(a)
Zahl (D)	—	number	chiffre m	numero m	número m
zahlen (D)	—	pay	payer	pagare	pagar
zählen (D)	—	count	compter	contare	contar
zahlreich (D)	—	numerous	nombreux (-euse)	numeroso(a)	numeroso(a)
Zahlung (D)	—	payment	paiement m	pagamento m	pago m
Zahn (D)	—	tooth	dent f	dente m	diente m
Zahnarzt (D)	—	dentist	dentiste m	dentista m	dentista m
Zahnbürste (D)	—	toothbrush	brosse à dents f	spazzolino da denti m	cepillo de dientes m
Zahnpasta (D)	—	toothpaste	dentifrice m	dentifricio m	pasta dentífrica f
Zahnschmerzen (D)	—	toothache	mal de dents m	mal di denti m	dolor de muelas m
zaino (I)	Rucksack m	rucksack	sac à dos m	—	mochila f

	D	E	F	I	Es
zanahoria (Es)	Karotte f / Möhre f	carrot	carotte f	carota f	—
zanzara (I)	Mücke f	mosquito	moustique m	—	mosquito m
zapatería (Es)	Schuhgeschäft n	shoeshop	magasin de chaussures m	negozio di scarpe m	—
zapatero (Es)	Schuster m	shoemaker	cordonnier m	calzolaio m	—
zapatilla (Es)	Pantoffel f	slipper	pantoufle f	pantofola f	—
zapato (Es)	Schuh m	shoe	chaussure f	scarpa f	—
zart (D)	—	soft	doux(douce)	tenero(a)	suave
Zärtlichkeit (D)	—	tenderness	tendresse f	tenerezza f	cariño m
zarzamora (Es)	Brombeere f	blackberry	mûre f	mora f	—
Zauberer (D)	—	magician	magicien m	mago m	mago m
zaubern (D)	—	practise magic	faire de la magie	esercitare la magia	hacer magia
Zaun (D)	—	fence	clôture f	recinto m	valla f
Zehe (D)	—	toe	doigt de pied m	dito del piede m	dedo del pie m
zehn (D)	—	ten	dix	dieci	diez
Zeichen (D)	—	sign	signe m	segnale m	signo m
zeichnen (D)	—	draw	dessiner	disegnare	dibujar
Zeichnung (D)	—	drawing	dessin m	disegno m	dibujo m
zeigen (D)	—	show	montrer	mostrare	indicar
Zeile (D)	—	line	ligne f	riga f	línea f
Zeit (D)	—	time	temps m	tempo m	tiempo m
zeitgenössisch (D)	—	contemporary	contemporain(e)	contemporaneo(a)	contemporáneo(a)
Zeitschrift (D)	—	magazine	revue f	rivista f	revista f
Zeitung (D)	—	newspaper	journal m	giornale m	periódico m
zélé (F)	eifrig	keen	—	diligente	diligente
Zelt (D)	—	tent	tente f	tenda f	tienda f
zelten (D)	—	camp	camper	campeggiare	acampar
zentral (D)	—	central	central(e)	centrale	céntrico(a)
Zentralheizung (D)	—	central heating	chauffage central m	riscaldamento centrale m	calefacción central f
Zentrum (D)	—	centre	centre m	centro m	centro m
zerbrechen (D)	—	break	casser	rompere	romper
zerbrechlich (D)	—	fragile	fragile	fragile	frágil
zerdrücken (D)	—	squash	écraser	sgualcire	aplastar
zero (E)	Null f	—	zéro	zero	cero
zéro (F)	Null f	zero	—	zero	cero
zero (I)	Null f	zero	zéro	—	cero
zerreißen (D)	—	rip	déchirer	strappare	romper
zerstören (D)	—	destroy	détruire	distruggere	destruir
zerstreut (D)	—	scattered	dispersé(e)	disperso(a)	disperso(a)
Zeug (D)	—	stuff	truc m	cose f pl	cosa f
Zeuge (D)	—	witness	témoin m	testimone m	testigo m
Zeugnis (D)	—	report	bulletin m	pagella f	informe m
zia (I)	Tante f	aunt(ie)	tante f	—	tía f

	D	E	F	I	Es
Ziege (D)	—	goat	chèvre f	capra f	cabra f
Ziegel (D)	—	brick	brique f	mattone m	ladrillo m
ziehen (D)	—	pull	tirer	tirare	tirar
Ziel (D)	—	goal	but m	meta f	intención f
ziemlich (D)	—	quite	assez	abbastanza	bastante
Zigarette (D)	—	cigarette	cigarette f	sigaretta f	cigarrillo m
Zigarre (D)	—	cigar	cigare m	sigaro m	cigarro m
Zimmer (D)	—	room	chambre f	camera f	habitación f
zio (I)	Onkel m	uncle	oncle m	—	tío m
zip (E)	Reiß-verschluß m	—	fermeture f	chiusura lampo f	cremallera f
Zirkus (D)	—	circus	cirque m	circo m	circo m
Zitrone (D)	—	lemon	citron m	limone m	limón m
zittern (D)	—	tremble	trembler	tremare	tiritar
Zivilisation (D)	—	civilisation	civilisation f	civiltà f	civilización f
zögern (D)	—	hesitate	hésiter	esitare	vacilar
Zoll¹ (D)	—	customs	douane f	dogana f	aduana f
Zoll² (D)	—	duty	droits de douane m pl	dazio m	arbitrio m
zona (Es)	Gebiet n	region	région f	regione f	—
Zopf (D)	—	plait	natte f	treccia f	trenza f
zorro (Es)	Fuchs m	fox	renard m	volpe f	—
zu (D)	—	to	de/à	da/di/a	para
zubereiten (D)	—	prepare	préparer	preparare	preparar
zucchero (I)	Zucker m	sugar	sucre m	—	azúcar m
züchten (D)	—	breed	élever	allevare	críar
Zucker (D)	—	sugar	sucre m	zucchero m	azúcar m
zudecken (D)	—	cover (up)	couvrir	coprire	tapar
zudrehen (D)	—	turn off	fermer	chiudere	cerrar
zuerst (D)	—	at first	d'abord	dapprima	primero
Zufall (D)	—	chance	hasard m	caso m	casualidad f
zufällig (D)	—	by chance	par hasard	per caso	por casualidad
zufrieden (D)	—	satisfied	content(e)	contento(a)	satisfecho(a)
Zug (D)	—	train	train m	treno m	tren m
Zugang (D)	—	access	accès m	entrata f	entrada f
zuhören (D)	—	listen	écouter	ascoltare	escuchar
Zukunft (D)	—	future	avenir m	futuro m	futuro m
zukünftig (D)	—	future	futur(e)	futuro(a)	en el futuro
zulassen (D)	—	permit	admettre	permettere	permitir
zulässig (D)	—	permissable	permis(e)	permesso(a)	permítido(a)
zuletzt (D)	—	finally	finalement	infine	por último
zumachen (D)	—	shut	fermer	chiudere	cerrar
zumindest (D)	—	at least	au moins	per lo meno	por lo menos
zumo (Es)	Saft m	juice	jus m	succo m	—
zumuten (D)	—	expect	exiger	pretendere	exigir

	D	E	F	I	Es
zunächst (D)	—	first of all	pour l'instant	dapprima	en primer lugar
zünden (D)	—	ignite	allumer, se	accendersi	encender
zunehmen (D)	—	increase	augmenter	aumentare	aumentar
Zunge (D)	—	tongue	langue f	lingua f	lengua f
zuppa (I)	Suppe f	soup	soupe f	—	sopa f
zurechtfinden, sich (D)	—	find one's way	retrouver, se	orientarsi	orientarse
zurück (D)	—	back	de retour	indietro	atrás
zurückbringen (D)	—	bring back	rapporter	riportare	devolver
zurückfahren (D)	—	drive back	retourner	tornare indietro	retroceder
zurückgeben (D)	—	give back	rendre	restituire	devolver
zurückkehren (D)	—	return	revenir	ritornare	volver
zurückkommen (D)	—	come back	revenir	ritornare	regresar
zurücknehmen (D)	—	take back	retirer	prendere indietro	retirar
zurücktreten (D)	—	retire	démissionner	dare le dimissioni	dimitir
zurückzahlen (D)	—	pay back	rembourser	rimborsare	devolver
zurückziehen (D)	—	withdraw	retirer	ritirare	retirar
zusagen (D)	—	promise	promettre	promettere	prometer
zusammen (D)	—	together	ensemble	insieme	juntos
zusammen-brechen (D)	—	collapse	s'éffondrer	crollare	desmayarse
zusätzlich (D)	—	in addition	supplémentaire	supplementare	adicional
zuschauen (D)	—	watch	regarder	stare a guardare	mirar
Zuschauer (D)	—	spectator	spectateur m	spettatore m	espectador m
Zuschlag (D)	—	extra charge	supplément m	supplemento m	suplemento m
zuschließen (D)	—	lock (up)	fermer à clé	chiudere a chiave	cerrar con llave
zusehen (D)	—	watch	regarder	stare a guardare	mirar
Zustand (D)	—	condition	état m	stato m	estado m
zuständig (D)	—	competent	compétent(e)	competente	competente
zustimmen (D)	—	agree	être d'accord	acconsentire	consentir
Zutritt (D)	—	admission	accès m	accesso m	acceso m
zuverlässig (D)	—	reliable	sûr(e)	affidabile	de confianza
zuviel (D)	—	too much	trop	troppo	demasiado
zuviele (D)	—	too many	trop	troppi(e)	demasiados(as)
zuvor (D)	—	before	auparavant	prima	antes
zuvorkommend (D)	—	obliging	prévenant(e)	premuroso(a)	cortés
zuwenig (D)	—	too little	trop peu	troppo poco	demasiado poco
Zwang (D)	—	compulsion	contrainte f	costrizione f	presión f
zwanzig (D)	—	twenty	vingt	venti	veinte
Zweck (D)	—	purpose	but m	scopo m	finalidad f
zwecklos (D)	—	useless	inutile	inutile	inútil
zweckmäßig (D)	—	suitable	approprié(e)	adatto	adecuado(a)
zwei (D)	—	two	deux	due	dos
zweifach (D)	—	double	double	duplice	doble

	D	E	F	I	Es
Zweifel (D)	—	doubt	doute *m*	dubbio *m*	duda *f*
zweifelhaft (D)	—	doubtful	douteux(-euse)	dubbioso(a)	dudoso(a)
zweifellos (D)	—	doubtless	sans doute	senza dubbio	sin duda
zweifeln (D)	—	doubt	douter	dubitare	dudar
Zweig (D)	—	branch	branche *f*	ramo *m*	rama *f*
zweimal (D)	—	twice	deux fois	due volte	dos veces
zweisprachig (D)	—	bilingual	bilingue	bilingue	bilingüe
zweiter (D)	—	second	second(e)	secondo(a)	segunda(o)
Zwieback (D)	—	rusk	biscotte *f*	fette biscottate *f pl*	bizcocho *m*
Zwiebel (D)	—	onion	oignon *m*	cipolla *f*	cebolla *f*
Zwillinge (D)	—	twins	jumeaux *m pl*	gemelli *m pl*	gemelos *m pl*
zwingen (D)	—	force	forcer	costringere	obligar
zwischen (D)	—	between	entrer	tra/fra	entre
Zwischen-landung (D)	—	intermediate landing	escale *f*	scalo intermedio *m*	escala *f*
Zwischenraum (D)	—	space	espace *m*	spazio *m*	espacio intermedio *m*
zwölf (D)	—	twelve	douze	dodici	doce

	D	E	F	I	Es
	Grundzahlen	**cardinal numbers**	**nombres cardinaux**	**numeri cardinali**	**números cardinales**
1	eins	one	un, une	uno	uno
2	zwei	two	deux	due	dos
3	drei	three	trois	tre	tres
4	vier	four	quatre	quattro	cuatro
5	fünf	five	cinq	cinque	cinco
6	sechs	six	six	sei	seis
7	sieben	seven	sept	sette	siete
8	acht	eight	huit	otto	ocho
9	neun	nine	neuf	nove	nueve
10	zehn	ten	dix	diece	diez
11	elf	eleven	onze	undici	once
12	zwölf	twelf	douze	dodici	doce
13	dreizehn	thirteen	treize	tredici	trece
14	vierzehn	fourteen	quatorze	quattordici	catorce
15	fünfzehn	fifteen	quinze	quindici	quince
16	sechzehn	sixteen	seize	seidici	dieciséis
17	siebzehn	seventeen	dix-sept	diciasette	diecisiete
18	achtzehn	eighteen	dix-huit	dicio	dieciocho
19	neunzehn	nineteen	dix-neuf	dicinove	diecinueve
20	zwanzig	twenty	vingt	venti	veinte
21	einundzwanzig	twenty-one	vingt et un	ventuno	veintiuno
22	zweiundzwanzig	twenty-two	vingt-deux	ventidue	veintidos
30	dreißig	thirty	trente	trenta	treinta
40	vierzig	forty	quarante	quaranta	cuarenta
50	fünfzig	fifty	cinquante	cinquanta	cincuenta
60	sechzig	sixty	soixante	settanta	sesanta
70	siebzig	seventy	soixante-dix	settanta	setenta
80	achtzig	eighty	quatre-vingts	ottanta	ochenta
90	neunzig	ninety	quatre-vingt-dix	novanta	noventa
100	hundert	(one) hundred	cent	cento	cien(to)
200	zweihundert	two hundred	deux cents	duecento	descientos, -as
300	dreihundert	three hundred	trois cents	trecento	trescientos, -as
400	vierhundert	four hundred	quatre cents	quattrocento	cuatrocientos, -as
500	fünfhundert	five hundred	cinq cents	cinquacento	quinientos, -as
600	sechshundert	six hundred	six cents	seicento	seiscientos, -as
700	siebenhundert	seven hundred	sept cents	settecento	setecientos, -as
800	achthundert	eight hundred	huit cents	ottocento	ochocientos, -as
900	neunhundert	nine hundred	neuf cents	novecento	novecientos, -as
1000	tausend	(one) thousand	mille	mille	mil
5000	fünftausend	five thousand	cinq mille	cinquemilla	cinco mil
10.000	zehntausend	ten thousand	dix mille	diecemilla	diez mil
100.000	hunderttausend	hundred thousand	cent mille	centomilla	cien mil
200.000	zweihundert-tausend	two hundred thousand	deux cents mille	duecentamilla	descientos mil
500.000	fünfhundert-tausend	five hundred thousand	cinq cents mille	cinquacentamilla	quinientos mil
1.000.000	eine Million	(one) million	un million	un millione	un millón

D	E	F	I	Es
Wochentage	**weekdays**	**jours de la semaine**	**giorni della settimana**	**días de semana**
Montag	Monday	lundi	lunedì	lunes
Dienstag	Tuesday	mardi	martedì	martes
Mittwoch	Wednesday	mercredi	mercoledì	miércoles
Donnerstag	Thursday	jeudi	giovedì	jueves
Freitag	Friday	vendredi	venerdì	viernes
Samstag	Saturday	samedi	sabato	sábado
Sonntag	Sunday	dimanche	domenica	domingo

D	E	F	I	Es
Monate	**months**	**mois**	**mesi**	**meses**
Januar	January	janvier	gennoaio	enero
Februar	February	février	febbraio	febrero
März	March	mars	marzo	marzo
April	April	avril	aprile	abril
Mai	May	mai	maggio	mayo
Juni	June	juin	giugno	junio
Juli	July	juillet	luglio	julio
August	August	août	agosto	agosto
September	September	septembre	settembre	septiembre
Oktober	October	octobre	ottobre	octubre
November	November	novembre	novembre	noviembre
Dezember	December	décembre	dicembre	diciembre